Network Warrior

SECOND EDITION

Network Warrior

Gary A. Donahue

Beijing · Cambridge · Farnham · Köln · Sebastopol · Tokyo

Network Warrior, Second Edition

by Gary A. Donahue

Copyright © 2011 Gary Donahue. All rights reserved.

Published by O'Reilly Media, Inc., 1005 Gravenstein Highway North, Sebastopol, CA 95472.

O'Reilly books may be purchased for educational, business, or sales promotional use. Online editions are also available for most titles (*http://my.safaribooksonline.com*). For more information, contact our corporate/institutional sales department: (800) 998-9938 or *corporate@oreilly.com*.

Editor: Mike Loukides
Production Editor: Adam Zaremba
Copyeditor: Amy Thomson
Proofreader: Rachel Monaghan
Production Services: Molly Sharp

Indexer: Lucie Haskins
Cover Designer: Karen Montgomery
Interior Designer: David Futato
Illustrator: Robert Romano

Printing History:

June 2007:	First Edition.
May 2011:	Second Edition.

Nutshell Handbook, the Nutshell Handbook logo, and the O'Reilly logo are registered trademarks of O'Reilly Media, Inc. *Network Warrior*, the image of a German boarhound, and related trade dress are trademarks of O'Reilly Media, Inc.

Many of the designations used by manufacturers and sellers to distinguish their products are claimed as trademarks. Where those designations appear in this book, and O'Reilly Media, Inc. was aware of a trademark claim, the designations have been printed in caps or initial caps.

While every precaution has been taken in the preparation of this book, the publisher and author assume no responsibility for errors or omissions, or for damages resulting from the use of the information contained herein.

ISBN: 978-1-449-38786-0

[LSI]

1305135207

Table of Contents

Preface

The examples used in this book are taken from my own experiences, as well as from the experiences of those with or for whom I have had the pleasure of working. Of course, for obvious legal and honorable reasons, the exact details and any information that might reveal the identities of the other parties involved have been changed.

Cisco equipment is used for the examples within this book and, with very few exceptions, the examples are TCP/IP-based. You may argue that a book of this type should include examples using different protocols and equipment from a variety of vendors, and, to a degree, that argument is valid. However, a book that aims to cover the breadth of technologies contained herein, while also attempting to show examples of these technologies from the point of view of different vendors, would be quite an impractical size. The fact is that Cisco Systems (much to the chagrin of its competitors, I'm sure) is the premier player in the networking arena. Likewise, TCP/IP is the protocol of the Internet, and the protocol used by most networked devices. Is it the best protocol for the job? Perhaps not, but it is the protocol in use today, so it's what I've used in all my examples. Not long ago, the Cisco CCIE exam still included Token Ring Source Route Bridging, AppleTalk, and IPX. Those days are gone, however, indicating that even Cisco understands that TCP/IP is where everyone is heading. I have included a chapter on IPv6 in this edition, since it looks like we're heading that way eventually.

WAN technology can include everything from dial-up modems (which, thankfully, are becoming quite rare) to T1, DS3, SONET, MPLS, and so on. We will look at many of these topics, but we will not delve too deeply into them, for they are the subject of entire books unto themselves—some of which may already sit next to this one on your O'Reilly bookshelf.

Again, all the examples used in this book are drawn from real experiences, most of which I faced myself during my career as a networking engineer, consultant, manager, and director. I have run my own company and have had the pleasure of working with some of the best people in the industry. The solutions presented in these chapters are the ones my teams and I discovered or learned about in the process of resolving the issues we encountered.

I faced a very tough decision when writing the second edition of this book. Should I keep the CatOS commands or discard them in favor of newer Nexus NX-OS examples? This decision was tough not only because my inclusion of CatOS resulted in some praise from my readers, but also because as of this writing in early 2011, I'm still seeing CatOS switches running in large enterprise and ecommerce networks. As such, I decided to keep the CatOS examples and simply add NX-OS commands.

I have added many topics in this book based mostly on feedback from readers. New topics include Cisco Nexus, wireless, MPLS, IPv6, and Voice over IP (VoIP). Some of these topics are covered in depth, and others, such as MPLS, are purposely light for reasons outlined in the chapters. Topics such as Nexus and VoIP are vast and added significantly to the page count of an already large and expensive book. I have also removed the chapters on server load balancing, both because I was never really happy with those chapters and because I could not get my hands on an ACE module or appliance in order to update the examples.

On the subject of examples, I have updated them to reflect newer hardware in every applicable chapter. Where I used 3550 switches in the first edition, I now use 3750s. Where I used PIX firewalls, I now use ASA appliances. I have also included examples from Cisco Nexus switches in every chapter that I felt warranted them. Many chapters therefore have examples from Cat-OS, IOS, and NX-OS. Enjoy them, because I guarantee that CatOS will not survive into the third edition.

Who Should Read This Book

This book is intended for anyone with first-level certification knowledge of data networking. Anyone with a CCNA or equivalent (or greater) knowledge should benefit from this book. My goal in writing *Network Warrior* is to explain complex ideas in an easy-to-understand manner. While the book contains introductions to many topics, you can also consider it a reference for executing common tasks related to those topics. I am a teacher at heart, and this book allows me to teach more people than I'd ever thought possible. I hope you will find the discussions both informative and enjoyable.

I have noticed over the years that people in the computer, networking, and telecom industries are often misinformed about the basics of these disciplines. I believe that in many cases, this is the result of poor teaching or the use of reference material that does not convey complex concepts well. With this book, I hope to show people how easy some of these concepts are. Of course, as I like to say, "It's easy when you know how," so I have tried very hard to help anyone who picks up my book understand the ideas contained herein.

If you are reading this, my guess is that you would like to know more about networking. So would I! Learning should be a never-ending adventure, and I am honored that you have let me be a part of your journey. I have been studying and learning about computers, networking, and telecom for the last 29 years, and my journey will never end.

This book does not explain the OSI stack, but it does briefly explain the differences between hubs, switches, and routers. You will need to have a basic understanding of what Layer 2 means as it relates to the OSI stack. Beyond that, this book tries to cover it all, but not like most other books.

This book attempts to teach you what you need to know in the real world. When should you choose a Layer-3 switch over a Layer-2 switch? How can you tell if your network is performing as it should? How do you fix a broadcast storm? How do you know you're having one? How do you know you have a spanning tree loop, and how do you fix it? What is a T1, or a DS3 for that matter? How do they work? In this book, you'll find the answers to all of these questions and many, many more. I tried to fill this book with information that many network engineers seem to get wrong through no fault of their own. *Network Warrior* includes configuration examples from real-world events and designs, and is littered with anecdotes from my time in the field—I hope you enjoy them.

Conventions Used in This Book

The following typographical conventions are used in this book:

Italic
> Used for new terms where they are defined, for emphasis, and for URLs

`Constant width`
> Used for commands, output from devices as it is seen on the screen, and samples of Request for Comments (RFC) documents reproduced in the text

`Constant width italic`
> Used to indicate arguments within commands for which you should supply values

`Constant width bold`
> Used for commands to be entered by the user and to highlight sections of output from a device that have been referenced in the text or are significant in some way

> Indicates a tip, suggestion, or general note

> Indicates a warning or caution

Using Code Examples

This book is here to help you get your job done. In general, you may use the code in this book in your programs and documentation. You do not need to contact us for permission unless you're reproducing a significant portion of the code. For example, writing a program that uses several chunks of code from this book does not require permission. Selling or distributing a CD-ROM of examples from O'Reilly books does require permission. Answering a question by citing this book and quoting example code does not require permission. Incorporating a significant amount of example code from this book into your product's documentation does require permission.

We appreciate, but do not require, attribution. An attribution usually includes the title, author, publisher, and ISBN. For example: "*Network Warrior, Second Edition,* by Gary A. Donahue (O'Reilly). Copyright 2011 Gary Donahue, 978-1-449-38786-0."

If you feel your use of code examples falls outside fair use or the permission given above, feel free to contact us at *permissions@oreilly.com*.

We'd Like to Hear from You

Please address comments and questions concerning this book to the publisher:

O'Reilly Media, Inc.
1005 Gravenstein Highway North
Sebastopol, CA 95472
800-998-9938 (in the United States or Canada)
707-829-0515 (international or local)
707-829-0104 (fax)

We have a web page for this book, where we list errata, examples, and any additional information. You can access this page at:

http://www.oreilly.com/catalog/9781449387860

To comment or ask technical questions about this book, send email to:

bookquestions@oreilly.com

For more information about our books, courses, conferences, and news, see our website at *http://www.oreilly.com*.

Find us on Facebook: *http://facebook.com/oreilly*

Follow us on Twitter: *http://twitter.com/oreillymedia*

Watch us on YouTube: *http://www.youtube.com/oreillymedia*

Safari® Books Online

Safari Books Online is an on-demand digital library that lets you easily search over 7,500 technology and creative reference books and videos to find the answers you need quickly.

With a subscription, you can read any page and watch any video from our library online. Read books on your cell phone and mobile devices. Access new titles before they are available for print, and get exclusive access to manuscripts in development and post feedback for the authors. Copy and paste code samples, organize your favorites, download chapters, bookmark key sections, create notes, print out pages, and benefit from tons of other time-saving features.

O'Reilly Media has uploaded this book to the Safari Books Online service. To have full digital access to this book and others on similar topics from O'Reilly and other publishers, sign up for free at *http://my.safaribooksonline.com*.

Acknowledgments

Writing a book is hard work—far harder than I ever imagined. Though I spent countless hours alone in front of a keyboard, I could not have accomplished the task without the help of many others.

I would like to thank my lovely wife, Lauren, for being patient, loving, and supportive. Lauren, being my in-house proofreader, was also the first line of defense against grammatical snafus. Many of the chapters no doubt bored her to tears, but I know she enjoyed at least a few. Thank you for helping me achieve this goal in my life.

I would like to thank Meghan and Colleen for trying to understand that when I was writing, I couldn't play. I hope I've helped instill in you a sense of perseverance by completing this book. If not, you can be sure that I'll use it as an example for the rest of your lives. I love you both "bigger than the universe" bunches.

I would like to thank my mother—because she's my mom, and because she never gave up on me, always believed in me, and always helped me even when she shouldn't have (Hi, Mom!).

I would like to thank my father for being tough on me when he needed to be, for teaching me how to think logically, and for making me appreciate the beauty in the details. I have fond memories of the two of us sitting in front of my RadioShack Model III computer while we entered basic programs from a magazine. I am where I am today largely because of your influence, direction, and teachings. You made me the man I am today. Thank you, Papa. I miss you.

I would like to thank my Cozy, my faithful Newfoundland dog who was tragically put to sleep in my arms so she would no longer have to suffer the pains of cancer. Her body failed while I was writing the first edition of this book, and if not for her, I probably would not be published today. Her death caused me great grief, which I assuaged by writing. I miss you my Cozy—may you run pain free at the rainbow bridge until we meet again.

I would like to thank Matt Maslowski for letting me use the equipment in his lab that was lacking in mine, and for helping me with Cisco questions when I wasn't sure of myself. I can't think of anyone I would trust more to help me with networking topics. Thanks, buddy.

I would like to thank Jeff Fry, CCIE# 22061, for providing me temporary access to a pair of unconfigured Cisco Nexus 7000 switches. This was a very big deal, and the second edition is much more complete as a result.

I would like to thank Jeff Cartwright for giving me my first exciting job at an ISP and for teaching me damn-near everything I know about telecom. I still remember being taught about one's density while Jeff drove us down Interstate 80, scribbling waveforms on a pad on his knee while I tried not to be visibly frightened. Thanks also for proof-reading some of my telecom chapters. There is no one I would trust more to do so.

I would like to thank Mike Stevens for help with readability and for some of the more colorful memories that have been included in this book. His help with PIX firewalls was instrumental to the completion of the first edition. You should also be thankful that I haven't included any pictures. I have this one from the Secaucus data center…

I would like to thank Peter Martin for helping me with some subjects in the lab for which I had no previous experience. And I'd like to extend an extra thank you for your aid as one of the tech reviewers for *Network Warrior*—your comments were always spot-on and your efforts made this a better book.

I would like to thank another tech reviewer, Yves Eynard: you caught some mistakes that floored me, and I appreciate the time you spent reviewing. This is a better book for your efforts.

I would like to thank Sal Conde and Ed Hom for access to 6509E switches and modules.

I would like to thank Michael Heuberger, Helge Brummer, Andy Vassaturo, Kelly Huffman, Glenn Bradley, Bill Turner, and the rest of the team in North Carolina for allowing me the chance to work extensively on the Nexus 5000 platform and for listening to me constantly reference this book in daily conversation. I imagine there's nothing worse than living or working with a know-it-all writer.

I would like to thank Christopher Leong for his technical reviews on the telecom and VoIP chapters.

I would like to thank Robert Schaffer for helping me remember stuff we'd worked on that I'd long since forgotten.

I would like to thank Jennifer Frankie for her help getting me in touch with people and information that I otherwise could not find.

I would like to thank Mike Loukides, my editor, for not cutting me any slack, for not giving up on me, and for giving me my chance in the first place. You have helped me become a better writer, and I cannot thank you enough.

I would like to thank Rachel Head, the copyeditor who made the first edition a much more readable book.

I would like to thank all the wonderful people at O'Reilly. Writing this book was a great experience, due in large part to the people I worked with at O'Reilly.

I would like to thank my good friend, John Tocado, who once told me, "If you want to write, then write!" This book is proof that you can change someone's life with a single sentence. You'll argue that I changed my own life, and that's fine, but you'd be wrong. When I was overwhelmed with the amount of remaining work to be done, I seriously considered giving up. Your words are the reason I did not. Thank you.

I cannot begin to thank everyone else who has given me encouragement. Living and working with a writer must, at times, be maddening. Under the burden of deadlines, I've no doubt been cranky, annoying, and frustrating, for which I apologize.

My purpose for the last year has been the completion of this book. All other responsibilities, with the exception of health and family, took a back seat to my goal. Realizing this book's publication is a dream come true for me. You may have dreams yourself, for which I can offer only this one bit of advice: work toward your goals, and you will realize them. It really is that simple.

## CHAPTER 1

What Is a Network?

Before we get started, I would like to define some terms and set some ground rules. For the purposes of this book (and your professional life, I hope), a *computer network* can be defined as "two or more computers connected by some means through which they are capable of sharing information." Don't bother looking for that in an RFC because I just made it up, but it suits our needs just fine.

There are many types of networks: local area networks (LANs), wide area networks (WANs), metropolitan area networks (MANs), campus area networks (CANs), Ethernet networks, Token Ring networks, Fiber Distributed Data Interface (FDDI) networks, Asynchronous Transfer Mode (ATM) networks, Frame Relay networks, T1 networks, DS3 networks, bridged networks, routed networks, and point-to-point networks, to name a few. If you're old enough to remember the program Laplink, which allowed you to copy files from one computer to another over a special parallel port cable, you can consider that connection a network as well. It wasn't very scalable (only two computers) or very fast, but it was a means of sending data from one computer to another via a connection.

Connection is an important concept. It's what distinguishes a *sneaker net*, in which information is physically transferred from one computer to another via removable media, from a real network. When you slap a USB drive (does anyone still use floppy disks?) into a computer, there is no indication that the files came from another computer—there is no connection. A connection involves some sort of addressing or identification of the nodes on the network (even if it's just master/slave or primary/ secondary).

The machines on a network are often connected physically via cables. However, wireless networks, which are devoid of obvious physical connections, are connected through the use of radios. Each node on a wireless network has an address. Frames received on the wireless network have a specific source and destination, as with any network.

Networks are often distinguished by their reach. LANs, WANs, MANs, and CANs are all examples of network types defined by their areas of coverage. LANs are, as their name implies, local to something—usually a single building or floor. WANs cover broader areas, and are usually used to connect LANs. WANs can span the globe, and there's nothing that says they couldn't go farther. MANs are common in areas where technology like Metropolitan Area Ethernet is possible; they typically connect LANs within a given geographical region such as a city or town. A CAN is similar to a MAN, but is limited to a *campus* (a campus is usually defined as a group of buildings under the control of one entity, such as a college or a single company).

One could argue that the terms MAN and CAN can be interchanged and, in some cases, this is true (conversely, there are plenty of people out there who would argue that a CAN exists only in certain specific circumstances and that calling a CAN by any other name is madness). The difference is usually that in a campus environment, there will probably be conduits to allow direct physical connections between buildings, while running private fiber between buildings in a city is generally not possible. Usually, in a city, telecom providers are involved in delivering some sort of technology that allows connectivity through their networks.

MANs and CANs may, in fact, be WANs. The differences are often semantic. If two buildings are in a campus but are connected via Frame Relay, are they part of a WAN or part of a CAN? What if the Frame Relay is supplied as part of the campus infrastructure, and not through a telecom provider? Does that make a difference? If the campus is in a metropolitan area, can it be called a MAN?

Usually, a network's designers start calling it by a certain description that sticks for the life of the network. If a team of consultants builds a WAN and refers to it in the documentation as a MAN, the company will probably call it a MAN for the duration of its existence.

Add into all of this the idea that LANs may be connected with a CAN, and CANs may be connected with a WAN, and you can see how confusing it can be, especially to the uninitiated.

The point here is that a lot of terms are thrown around in this industry, and not everyone uses them properly. Additionally, as in this case, the definitions may be nebulous; this, of course, leads to confusion.

You must be careful about the terminology you use. If the CIO calls the network a WAN, but the engineers call the network a CAN, you must either educate whoever is wrong or opt to communicate with each party using its own language. This issue is more common than you might think. In the case of MAN versus WAN versus CAN, beware of absolutes. In other areas of networking, the terms are more specific.

For our purposes, we will define these network types as follows:

LAN
> A LAN is a network that is confined to a limited space, such as a building or floor. It uses short-range technologies such as Ethernet, Token Ring, and the like. A LAN is usually under the control of the company or entity that requires its use.

WAN

A WAN is a network that is used to connect LANs by way of a third-party provider. An example is a Frame Relay cloud (provided by a telecom provider) connecting corporate offices in New York, Boston, Los Angeles, and San Antonio.

CAN

A CAN is a network that connects LANs and/or buildings in a discrete area owned or controlled by a single entity. Because that single entity controls the environment, there may be underground conduits between the buildings that allow them to be connected by fiber. Examples include college campuses and industrial parks.

MAN

A MAN is a network that connects LANs and/or buildings in an area that is often larger than a campus. For example, a MAN might connect a company's various offices within a metropolitan area via the services of a telecom provider. Again, be careful of absolutes. Many companies in Manhattan have buildings or data centers across the river in New Jersey. These New Jersey sites are considered to be in the New York metropolitan area, so they are part of the MAN, even though they are in a different state.

Terminology and language are like any protocol: be careful how you use the terms you throw around in your daily life, but don't be pedantic to the point of annoying other people by telling them when and how they're wrong. Instead, listen to those around you and help educate them. A willingness to share knowledge is what separates the average IT person from the good one.

## CHAPTER 2

Hubs and Switches

Hubs

In the beginning of Ethernet, 10Base-5 used a very thick cable that was hard to work with (it was nicknamed *thick-net*). 10Base-2, which later replaced 10Base-5, used a much smaller cable, similar to that used for cable TV. Because the cable was much thinner than that used by 10Base-5, 10Base-2 was nicknamed *thin-net*. These cable technologies required large metal couplers called N connectors (10Base-5) and BNC connectors (10Base-2). These networks also required special terminators to be installed at the end of cable runs. When these couplers or terminators were removed, the entire network would stop working. These cables formed the physical backbones for Ethernet networks.

With the introduction of Ethernet running over unshielded twisted pair (UTP) cables terminated with RJ45 connectors, hubs became the new backbones in most installations. Many companies attached hubs to their existing thin-net networks to allow greater flexibility as well. Hubs were made to support UTP and BNC 10Base-2 installations, but UTP was so much easier to work with that it became the de facto standard.

A *hub* is simply a means of connecting Ethernet cables together so that their signals can be repeated to every other connected cable on the hub. Hubs may also be called *repeaters* for this reason, but it is important to understand that while a hub is a repeater, a repeater is not necessarily a hub.

A repeater repeats a signal. Repeaters are usually used to extend a connection to a remote host or to connect a group of users who exceed the distance limitation of 10Base-T. In other words, if the usable distance of a 10Base-T cable is exceeded, a repeater can be placed inline to increase the usable distance.

I was surprised to learn that there is no specific distance limitation included in the 10Base-T standard. While 10Base-5 and 10Base-2 do include distance limitations (500 meters and 200 meters, respectively), the 10Base-T spec instead describes certain characteristics that a cable should meet.

Category-5e cable specifications (TIA/EIA-568-B.2-2001) designate values based on 100m cable, but to be painfully accurate, the cable must meet these values at 100m. It is one thing to say, "Propagation delay skew shall not exceed 45 ns/100m." It is quite another to say, "The cable must not exceed 100m."

Semantics aside, keeping your Cat-5e cable lengths within 100m is a good idea.

Segments are divided by repeaters or hubs. Figure 2-1 shows a repeater extending the distance between a server and a personal computer.

A hub is like a repeater, except that while a repeater may have only two connectors, a hub can have many more; that is, it repeats a signal over many cables as opposed to just one. Figure 2-2 shows a hub connecting several computers to a network.

In Ethernet network design, repeaters and hubs are treated the same way. The 5-4-3 rule of Ethernet design states that between any two nodes on an Ethernet network, there can be only five segments, connected via four repeaters, and only three of the segments can be populated. This rule, which seems odd in the context of today's networks, was the source of much pain for those who didn't understand it.

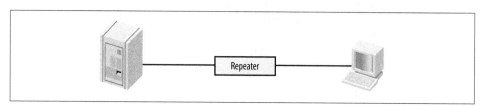

Figure 2-1. Repeater extending a single 10Base-T link

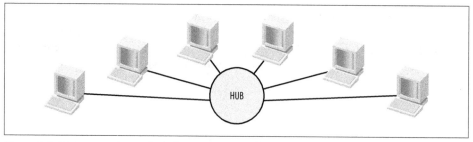

Figure 2-2. Hub connecting multiple hosts to a network

As hubs became less expensive, extra hubs were often used as repeaters in more complex networks. Figure 2-3 shows an example of how two remote groups of users could be connected using hubs on each end and a repeater in the middle.

Hubs are very simple devices. Any signal received on any port is repeated out every other port. Hubs are purely physical and electrical devices, and do not have a presence on the network (except possibly for management purposes). They do not alter frames or make decisions based on them in any way.

Figure 2-4 illustrates how hubs operate. As you might imagine, this model can become problematic in larger networks. The traffic can become so intensive that the network becomes saturated—if someone prints a large file, everyone on the network will suffer while the file is transferred to the printer over the network.

If another device is already using the wire, the sending device will wait a bit and then try to transmit again. When two stations transmit at the same time, a *collision* occurs. Each station records the collision, backs off again, and then retransmits. On very busy networks, a lot of collisions will occur.

With a hub, more stations are capable of using the network at any given time. Should all of the stations be active, the network will appear to be slow because of the excessive collisions.

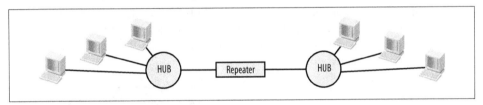

Figure 2-3. Repeater joining hubs

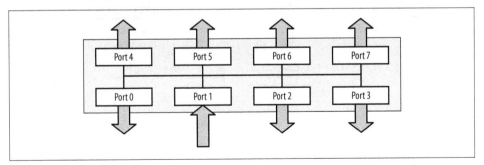

Figure 2-4. Hubs repeat inbound signals to all ports, regardless of type or destination

Collisions are limited to network segments. An Ethernet network segment is a section of network where devices can communicate using Layer-2 MAC addresses. To communicate outside an Ethernet segment, an additional device, such as a router, is required. Collisions are also limited to *collision domains*. A collision domain is an area of an Ethernet network where collisions can occur. If one station can prevent another from sending because it is using the network, these stations are in the same collision domain.

A *broadcast domain* is the area of an Ethernet network where a broadcast will be propagated. Broadcasts stay within a Layer-3 network (unless forwarded), which is usually bordered by a Layer-3 device such as a router. Broadcasts are sent through switches (Layer-2 devices) but stop at routers.

 Many people mistakenly think that broadcasts are contained within switches or virtual LANs (VLANs). I think this is because they are so contained in a properly designed network. If you connect two switches with a crossover cable—one configured with VLAN 10 on all ports and the other configured with VLAN 20 on all ports—hosts plugged into each switch will be able to communicate if they are on the same IP network. Broadcasts and IP networks are not limited to VLANs, though it is very tempting to think so.

Figure 2-5 shows a network of hubs connected via a central hub. When a frame enters the hub on the bottom left on Port 1, the frame is repeated out every other port on that hub, which includes a connection to the central hub. The central hub in turn repeats the frame out every port, propagating it to the remaining hubs in the network. This design replicates the backbone idea, in that every device on the network will receive every frame sent on the network.

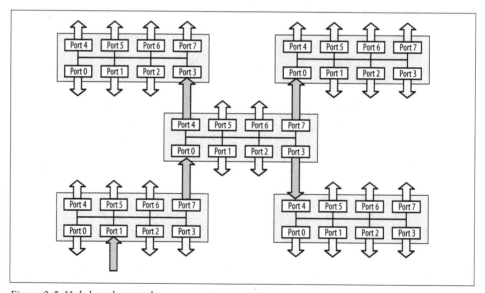

Figure 2-5. Hub-based network

In large networks of this type, new problems can arise. *Late collisions* occur when two stations successfully test for a clear network and then transmit, only to encounter a collision. This condition can occur when the network is so large that the propagation of a transmitted frame from one end of the network to the other takes longer than the test used to detect whether the network is clear.

One of the other major problems when using hubs is the possibility of *broadcast storms*. Figure 2-6 shows two hubs connected with two connections. A frame enters the network on Hub 1 and is replicated on every port, which includes the two connections to Hub 2, which now repeats the frame out all of its ports, including the two ports connecting the two switches. Once Hub 1 receives the frame, it again repeats it out every interface, effectively causing an endless loop.

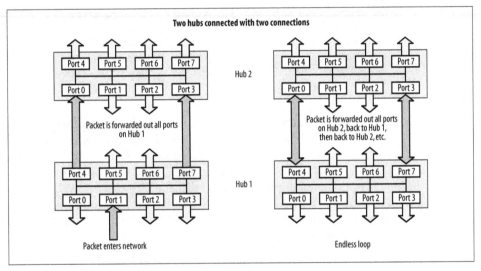

Figure 2-6. Broadcast storm

Anyone who's ever lived through a broadcast storm on a live network knows how much fun it can be—especially if you consider your boss screaming at you to be fun. It's extra special fun when your boss's boss joins in. Symptoms of a broadcast storm include every device essentially being unable to send any frames on the network due to constant network traffic, all status lights on the hubs staying on constantly instead of blinking normally, and (perhaps most importantly) senior executives threatening you with bodily harm.

The only way to resolve a broadcast storm is to break the loop. Shutting down and restarting the network devices will just start the cycle again. Because hubs are not generally manageable, it can be quite a challenge to find a Layer-2 loop in a crisis.

Hubs have a lot of drawbacks, and modern networks rarely employ them. Hubs have long since been replaced by *switches*, which offer greater speed, automatic loop detection, and a host of additional features.

Switches

The next step in the evolution of Ethernet was the switch. Switches differ from hubs in that switches play an active role in how frames are forwarded. Remember that a hub simply repeats every signal it receives via any of its ports out every other port. A switch, in contrast, keeps track of which devices are on which ports, and forwards frames only to the devices for which they are intended.

What we refer to as a *packet* in TCP/IP is called a *frame* when speaking about hubs, bridges, and switches. Technically, they are different things, since a TCP packet is encapsulated with Layer-2 information to form a frame. However, the terms "frames" and "packets" are often thrown around interchangeably (I'm guilty of this myself). To be perfectly correct, always refer to frames when speaking of hubs and switches.

When other companies began developing switches, Cisco had all of its energies concentrated in routers, so it did not have a solution that could compete. Hence, Cisco did the smartest thing it could do at the time—it acquired the best of the new switching companies, like Kalpana, and added their devices to the Cisco lineup. As a result, Cisco switches did not have the same operating system that their routers did. While Cisco routers used the Internetwork Operating System (IOS), the Cisco switches sometimes used menus, or an operating system called *CatOS* (Cisco calls its switch line *Catalyst*; thus, the Catalyst Operating System was CatOS).

A quick note about terminology: the words "switching" and "switch" have multiple meanings, even in the networking world. There are Ethernet switches, Frame Relay switches, Layer-3 switches, multilayer switches, and so on. Here are some terms that are in common use:

Switch
> The general term used for anything that can switch, regardless of discipline or what is being switched. In the networking world, a switch is generally an Ethernet switch. In the telecom world, a switch can be many things, none of which we are discussing in this chapter.

Ethernet switch
> Any device that forwards frames based on their Layer-2 MAC addresses using Ethernet. While a hub repeats all frames to all ports, an Ethernet switch forwards frames only to the ports for which they are destined. An Ethernet switch creates a collision domain on each port, while a hub generally expands a collision domain through all ports.

Layer-3 switch

This is a switch with routing capabilities. Generally, VLANs can be configured as virtual interfaces on a Layer-3 switch. True Layer-3 switches are rare today; most switches are now multilayer switches.

Multilayer switch

Similar to a Layer-3 switch, but may also allow for control based on higher layers in packets. Multilayer switches allow for control based on TCP, UDP, and even details contained within the data payload of a packet.

Switching

In Ethernet, switching is the act of forwarding frames based on their destination MAC addresses. In telecom, switching is the act of making a connection between two parties. In routing, switching is the process of forwarding packets from one interface to another within a router.

Switches differ from hubs in one very fundamental way: a signal that comes into one port is *not* replicated out every other port on a switch as it is in a hub (unless, as we'll see, the packet is destined for all ports). While modern switches offer a variety of more advanced features, this is the one that makes a switch a switch.

Figure 2-7 shows a switch with paths between Ports 4 and 6, and Ports 1 and 7. The beauty is that frames can be transmitted along these two paths simultaneously, which greatly increases the perceived speed of the network. A dedicated path is created from the source port to the destination port for the duration of each frame's transmission. The other ports on the switch are not involved at all.

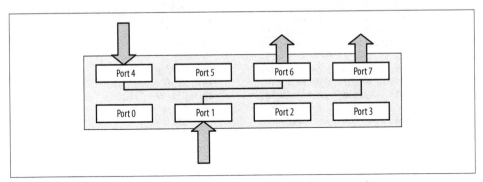

Figure 2-7. A switch forwards frames only to the ports that need to receive them

So, how does the switch determine where to send the frames being transmitted from different stations on the network? Every Ethernet frame contains the source and destination MAC address for the frame. The switch opens the frame (only as far as it needs to), determines the source MAC address, and adds that MAC address to a table if it is not already present. This table, called the *content-addressable memory table* (or CAM table) in CatOS, and the *MAC address table* in IOS, contains a map of which MAC addresses have been discovered on which ports. The switch then determines the frame's destination MAC address and checks the table for a match. If a match is found, a path is created from the source port to the appropriate destination port. If there is no match, the frame is sent to all ports.

When a station using IP needs to send a packet to another IP address on the same network, it must first determine the MAC address for the destination IP address. To accomplish this, IP sends out an Address Resolution Protocol (ARP) request packet. This packet is a broadcast, so it is sent out all switch ports. The ARP packet, when encapsulated into a frame, now contains the requesting station's MAC address, so the switch knows which port to assign as the source. When the destination station replies that it owns the requested IP address, the switch knows which port the destination MAC address is located on (the reply frame will contain the replying station's MAC address).

Running the `show mac-address-table` command on an IOS-based switch displays the table of MAC addresses and corresponding ports. Multiple MAC addresses on a single port usually indicates that the port in question is a connection to another switch or networking device:

```
Switch1-IOS>sho mac-address-table
Legend: * - primary entry
        age - seconds since last seen
        n/a - not available

    vlan   mac address     type    learn    age    ports
------+---------------+--------+-----+----------+------------------------
 *    24   0013.bace.e5f8  dynamic  Yes       165   Gi3/4
 *    24   0013.baed.4881  dynamic  Yes        25   Gi3/4
 *    24   0013.baee.8f29  dynamic  Yes        75   Gi3/4
 *     4   0013.baeb.ff3b  dynamic  Yes         0   Gi2/41
 *    24   0013.baee.8e89  dynamic  Yes       108   Gi3/4

 *    18   0013.baeb.01e0  dynamic  Yes         0   Gi4/29
 *    24   0013.2019.3477  dynamic  Yes       118   Gi3/4
 *    18   0013.bab3.a49f  dynamic  Yes        18   Gi2/39
 *    18   0013.baea.7ea0  dynamic  Yes         0   Gi7/8
 *    18   0013.bada.61ca  dynamic  Yes         0   Gi4/19
 *    18   0013.bada.61a2  dynamic  Yes         0   Gi4/19
 *     4   0013.baeb.3993  dynamic  Yes         0   Gi3/33
```

From the preceding output, you can see that if the device with the MAC address `0013.baeb.01e0` attempts to talk to the device with the MAC address `0013.baea.7ea0`, the switch will set up a connection between ports Gi4/29 and Gi7/8.

 You may notice that I specify the command show in my descriptions, and then use the shortened version sho while entering commands. Cisco devices allow you to abbreviate commands, so long as the abbreviation cannot be confused with another command.

This information is also useful if you need to figure out where a device is connected to a switch. First, get the MAC address of the device you're looking for. Here's an example from Solaris:

```
[root@unix /]$ifconfig -a
lo0: flags=1000849<UP,LOOPBACK,RUNNING,MULTICAST,IPv4> mtu 8232 index 1
        inet 127.0.0.1 netmask ff000000
dmfe0: flags=1000843<UP,BROADCAST,RUNNING,MULTICAST,IPv4> mtu 1500 index 2
        inet 172.16.1.9 netmask ffff0000 broadcast 172.16.255.255
        ether 0:13:ba:da:d1:ca
```

Then, take the MAC address (shown on the last line) and include it in the IOS command `show mac-address-table | include` *mac-address*:

```
Switch1-IOS>sho mac-address-table | include 0013.bada.d1ca
 *  18  0013.bada.d1ca  dynamic Yes         0  Gi3/22
```

> Note the format when using MAC addresses, as different systems display MAC addresses differently. You'll need to convert the address to the appropriate format for IOS or CatOS. IOS displays each group of two-byte pairs separated by a period. Solaris and most other operating systems display each octet separated by a colon or hyphen (CatOS uses a hyphen as the delimiter when displaying MAC addresses in hexadecimal). Some systems may also display MAC addresses in decimal, while others use hexadecimal.

The output from the preceding command shows that port Gi3/22 is where our server is connected.

In NX-OS, the command is the same as IOS, though the interface names reflect the Nexus hardware (in this case, a 5010 with a 2148T configured as FEX100):

```
NX-5K-1(config-if)# sho mac-address-table
VLAN      MAC Address      Type     Age       Port
---------+-----------------+-------+---------+-----------------------------
100       0005.9b74.b811   dynamic 0         Po100
100       0013.bada.d1ca   dynamic 40        Eth100/1/2
Total MAC Addresses: 2
```

On a switch running CatOS, this works a little differently because the `show cam` command contains an option to show a specific MAC address:

```
Switch1-CatOS: (enable)sho cam 00-00-13-ba-da-d1-ca
* = Static Entry. + = Permanent Entry. # = System Entry. R = Router Entry.
X = Port Security Entry $ = Dot1x Security Entry

VLAN  Dest MAC/Route Des    [CoS]  Destination Ports or VCs / [Protocol Type]
----  ------------------    -----  -------------------------------------------
20    00-13-ba-da-d1-ca            3/48 [ALL]
Total Matching CAM Entries Displayed  =1
```

Switch Types

Cisco switches can be divided into two types: fixed-configuration and modular switches. Fixed-configuration switches are smaller—usually one rack unit (RU) in size. These switches typically contain nothing but Ethernet ports and are designed for situations where larger switches are unnecessary.

Examples of fixed-configuration switches include the Cisco 2950, 3550, and 3750 switches. The 3750 is capable of being *stacked*. Stacking is a way of connecting multiple switches together to form a single logical switch. This can be useful when you need more than the maximum number of ports available on a single fixed-configuration switch (48). The limitation of stacking is that the backplane of the stack is limited to 32 or 64 gigabits per second (Gbps). For comparison, some of the chassis-based modular switches can support 720 Gbps on their backplanes. These large modular switches are usually more expensive than a stack of fixed-configuration switches, however.

The benefits of fixed-configuration switches include:

Price
> Fixed-configuration switches are generally much less expensive than their modular cousins.

Size
> Fixed-configuration switches are usually only 1 RU in size. They can be used in closets and in small spaces where chassis-based switches do not fit. Two switches stacked together are still smaller than the smallest chassis switch.

Weight
> Fixed-configuration switches are lighter than even the smallest chassis switches. Two people, at minimum, are required to install most chassis-based switches.

Power
> Fixed-configuration switches are all capable of operating on normal household power, and hence can be used almost anywhere. The larger chassis-based switches require special power supplies and AC power receptacles when fully loaded with modules. Many switches are also available with DC power options.

On the other hand, Cisco's larger, modular chassis-based switches have the following advantages over their smaller counterparts:

Expandability
> Larger chassis-based switches can support hundreds of Ethernet ports, and the chassis-based architecture allows the processing modules (supervisors) to be upgraded easily. Supervisors are available for the 6500 chassis that provide 720 Gbps of backplane speed. While you can stack up to seven 3750s for an equal number of ports, remember that the backplane speed of a stack is limited to 32 Gbps.

Flexibility

The Cisco 6500 chassis will accept modules that provide services outside the range of a normal switch. Such modules include:

- Firewall Services Modules (FWSMs)
- Intrusion Detection System Modules (IDSMs)
- Application Control Engines (ACE) modules
- Network Analysis Modules (NAMs)
- WAN modules (FlexWAN)

Redundancy

Some fixed-configuration switches support a power distribution unit, which can provide some power redundancy at additional cost. However, Cisco's chassis-based switches all support multiple power supplies (older 4000 chassis switches actually required three power supplies for redundancy and even more to support VoIP). Most chassis-based switches support dual supervisors as well.

Speed

The Cisco 6500 chassis employing Supervisor-720 (Sup-720) processors supports up to 720 Gbps of throughput on the backplane. The fastest backplane in a fixed-configuration switch—the Cisco 4948—supports only 48 Gbps. The 4948 switch is designed to be placed at the top of a rack in order to support the devices in the rack. Due to the specialized nature of this switch, it cannot be stacked and is therefore limited to 48 ports.

Chassis-based switches do have some disadvantages. They can be very heavy, take up a lot of room, and require a lot of power. If you need the power and flexibility offered by a chassis-based switch, however, the disadvantages are usually just considered part of the cost of doing business.

Cisco's two primary chassis-based Catalyst switches are the 4500 series and the 6500 series. There is an 8500 series as well, but these switches are rarely seen in corporate environments.

The Nexus switches can fit in either camp depending on the model. The Nexus 7000 chassis switch is available in a 10-slot or 18-slot chassis. These models have all the benefits and drawbacks of any other chassis switch, though as of this writing the 7000 does not support many service modules. Word on the street is that this will change as the product line evolves.

The Nexus 5000, having only one (5010) or two (5020) expansion modules can be expanded through the use of fabric extenders (FEXs). FEXs appear to be physical switches, but are actually more like a module connected to the 5000s. The Nexus 2000 switches act as FEXs. With the capability to connect up to twelve 48-port FEXs to a single (or pair of) Nexus 5000s, each Nexus 5000 behaves more like a 12-slot chassis than a fixed-configuration switch. The Nexus hardware chapter will go into more detail regarding Nexus expandability.

Planning a Chassis-Based Switch Installation

Installing chassis-based switches requires more planning than installing smaller switches. There are many elements to consider when configuring a chassis switch. You must choose the modules (sometimes called *blades*) you will use and then determine what size power supplies you need. You must decide whether your chassis will use AC or DC power and what amperage the power supplies will require. Chassis-based switches are large and heavy, so you must ensure that there is adequate rack space. Here are some of the things you need to think about when planning a chassis-based switch installation.

Rack space

Chassis switches can be quite large. The 6513 switch occupies 19 RU of space. The NEBS version of the 6509 takes up 21 RU. The 10-slot Nexus 7010 consumes 21 RU as well, while the 18-slot model 7018 requires 25 RU. A seven-foot telecom rack is 40 RU, so these larger switches use up a significant portion of the available space.

 Be careful when planning rack space for Nexus switches. The Nexus 5000 series is as deep as a rack-mount server and requires the full depth of a cabinet for mounting. The Nexus 5000 switches cannot be mounted in a standard two-post telecom rack.

The larger chassis switches are very heavy and should be installed near the bottom of the rack whenever possible. Smaller chassis switches (such as the 4506, which takes up only 10 RU) can be mounted higher in the rack.

 Always use a minimum of two people when lifting heavy switches. Often, a third person can guide the chassis into the rack. The chassis should be moved only after all the modules and power supplies have been removed.

Power

Each module will draw a certain amount of power (measured in watts). When you've determined which modules will be present in your switch, you must add up the power requirements for all of them. The result will determine what size power supplies you should order. For redundancy, each power supply in the pair should be able to provide all the power necessary to run the entire switch, including all modules. So, if your modules require 3,200 watts in total, you'll need two 4,000-watt power supplies for redundant power. You can use two 3,000-watt power supplies instead, but they will both be needed to power all the modules. Should one power supply fail, some modules will be shut down to conserve power.

Depending on where you install your switch, you may need power supplies capable of using either AC or DC power. In the case of DC power supplies, make sure you specify *A and B feeds*. For example, if you need 40 amps of DC power, you'd request *40 amps DC—A and B feeds*. This means that you'll get two 40-amp power circuits for failover purposes. Check the Cisco documentation regarding grounding information. Most collocation facilities supply positive ground DC power.

For AC power supplies, you'll need to specify the voltage, amperage, and socket needed for each feed. Each power supply typically requires a single feed, but some will take two or more. You'll need to know the electrical terminology regarding plugs and receptacles. All of this information will be included in the documentation for the power supply, which is available on Cisco's website. For example, the power cord for a power supply may come with a NEMA L6-20P plug, which will require NEMA L6-20R receptacles. The P and R on the ends of the part numbers describe whether the part is a *plug* or a *receptacle* (the NEMA L6-20 is a twist-lock 250-volt AC 16-amp connector).

The power cables will connect to the power supplies via a large rectangular connector. This plug will connect to a receptacle on the power supply, which will be surrounded by a clamp. Always tighten this clamp to avoid the cable popping out of the receptacle when stressed.

Cooling

Many chassis switches are cooled from side to side: the air is drawn in on one side, pulled across the modules, and blown out the other side. Usually, rackmounting the switches allows for plenty of airflow. Be careful if you will be placing these switches in cabinets, though. Cables are often run on the sides of the switches, and if there are a lot of them, they can impede the airflow.

The NEBS-compliant 6509 switch moves air vertically and the modules sit vertically in the chassis. With this switch, you can see the air vents plainly on the front of the chassis. Take care to keep them clear. All Nexus switches are designed for front-to-back airflow to facilitate hot-/cold-aisle data-center designs. Be careful when mounting these switches. Some people like to have the Ethernet ports in the front of the rack. With Nexus, this position is a bad idea, as air will flow in the wrong direction in the rack.

I once worked on a project where we needed to stage six 6506 switches. We pulled them out of their crates and put them side by side on a series of pallets. We didn't stop to think that the heated exhaust of each switch was blowing directly into the input of the next switch. By the time the air got from the intake of the first switch to the exhaust of the last switch, it was so hot that the last switch shut itself down. Always make sure you leave ample space between chassis switches when installing them.

Installing and removing modules

Modules for chassis-based switches are inserted into small channels on both sides of the slot. Be very careful when inserting modules, as it is very easy to miss the channels and get the modules stuck. Many modules—especially service modules like FWSMs, IDSMs, CSMs and ACE—are densely packed with components. I've seen $40,000 modules ruined by engineers who forced them into slots without properly aligning them. Remember to use a static strap, too.

> Anytime you're working with a chassis or modules, you should use a static strap. They're easy to use, and come with just about every piece of hardware these days. I know you feel like a dork using them, but imagine how you'll feel when you trash a $400,000 switch.

Routing cables

When routing cables to modules, remember that you may need to remove the modules in the future. Routing 48 Ethernet cables to all those modules in a chassis switch can be a daunting task. Remember to leave enough slack in the cables so that each module's cables can be moved out of the way to slide the module out. When one of your modules fails, you'll need to pull aside all the cables attached to that module, replace the module, and place all the cables back into their correct ports. The more planning you do ahead of time, the easier this task will be.

## CHAPTER 3

Autonegotiation

When I get called to a client's site to diagnose a network slowdown or a "slow" device, the first things I look at are the error statistics and the autonegotiation settings on the switches as well as the devices connected to them. If I had to list the most common problems I've seen during my years in the field, autonegotiation issues would be in the top five, if not number one.

Why is autonegotiation such a widespread problem? The truth is, too many people don't really understand what it does and how it works, so they make assumptions that lead to trouble.

What Is Autonegotiation?

Autonegotiation is the feature that allows a port on a switch, router, server, or other device to communicate with the device on the other end of the link to determine the optimal duplex mode and speed for the connection. The driver then dynamically configures the interface to the values determined for the link. Let's examine the configuration parameters:

Speed
> Speed is the rate of the interface, usually listed in megabits per second (Mbps). Common Ethernet speeds include 10 Mbps, 100 Mbps, and 1,000 Mbps. 1,000 Mbps Ethernet is also referred to as *Gigabit Ethernet*. Many switches now support 10 Gbps Ethernet, and 100 Gbps is on the horizon as well.

Duplex
> Duplex refers to how data flows on the interface. On a half duplex interface, data can only be transmitted or received at any given time. A conversation on a two-way radio is usually half-duplex—each person must push a button to talk and, while talking, that person cannot listen. A full-duplex interface, on the other hand, can send and receive data simultaneously. A conversation on a telephone is full duplex.

How Autonegotiation Works

First, let's cover what autonegotiation does *not* do: when autonegotiation is enabled on a port, it does not automatically determine the configuration of the port on the other side of the Ethernet cable and then match it. This is a common misconception that often leads to problems.

Autonegotiation is a protocol and, as with any protocol, it only works if it's running on both sides of the link. In other words, if one side of a link is running autonegotiation and the other side of the link is not, autonegotiation *cannot* determine the speed and duplex configuration of the other side. If autonegotiation *is* running on the other side of the link, the two devices decide *together* on the best speed and duplex mode. Each interface advertises the speeds and duplex modes at which it can operate, and the best match is selected (higher speeds and full duplex are preferred).

The confusion exists primarily because autonegotiation always seems to work. This is because of a feature called *parallel detection*, which kicks in when the autonegotiation process fails to find autonegotiation running on the other end of the link. Parallel detection works by sending the signal being received to the local 10Base-T, 100Base-TX, and 100Base-T4 drivers. If any one of these drivers detects the signal, the interface is set to that speed.

Parallel detection determines only the link speed, not the supported duplex modes. This is an important consideration because the common modes of Ethernet have differing levels of duplex support:

10Base-T
> 10Base-T was originally designed without full-duplex support. Some implementations of 10Base-T support full duplex, but many do not.

100Base-T
> 100Base-T has long supported full duplex, which has been the preferred method for connecting 100 Mbps links for as long as the technology has existed. However, the default behavior of 100Base-T is usually half duplex, and full-duplex support must be set manually.

1000Base-T
> Gigabit Ethernet has a much more robust autonegotiation protocol than 10M or 100M Ethernet. Gigabit interfaces should be left to autonegotiate in most situations.

10 Gigabit
> 10 Gigabit (10G) connections are generally dependent on fiber transceivers or special copper connections that differ from the RJ-45 connections seen on other Ethernet types. The hardware usually dictates how 10G connects. On a 6500, 10G interfaces usually require XENPAKs, which only run at 10G. On a Nexus 5000 switch, some of the ports are 1G/10G and can be changed with the speed command.

Because of the lack of widespread full-duplex support on 10Base-T and the typical default behavior of 100Base-T, when autonegotiation falls through to the parallel detection phase (which only detects speed), the safest thing for the driver to do is to choose half-duplex mode for the link.

As networks and networking hardware evolve, higher-speed links with more robust negotiation protocols will likely make negotiation problems a thing of the past. That being said, I still see 20-year-old routers in service, so knowing how autonegotiation works will be a valuable skill for years to come.

When Autonegotiation Fails

When autonegotiation fails on 10/100 links, the most likely cause is that one side of the link has been set to 100/full and the other side has been set to autonegotiation. This results in one side being 100/full and the other side being 100/half.

Figure 3-1 shows a half-duplex link. In a half-duplex environment, the receiving (RX) line is monitored. If a frame is present on the RX link, no frames are sent until the RX line is clear. If a frame is received on the RX line while a frame is being sent on the transmitting (TX) line, a collision occurs. Collisions cause the collision error counter to be incremented—and the sending frame to be retransmitted—after a random back-off delay. This may seem counterintuitive in a modern switched environment, but remember that Ethernet was originally designed to work over a single wire. Switches and twisted pair came along later.

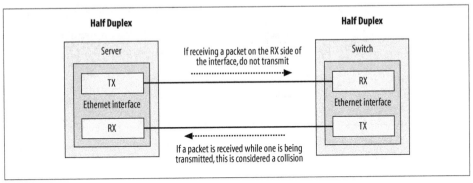

Figure 3-1. Half duplex

Figure 3-2 shows a full-duplex link. In full-duplex operation, the RX line is not monitored, and the TX line is always considered available. Collisions do not occur in full-duplex mode because the RX and TX lines are completely independent.

When one side of the link is full duplex and the other side is half duplex, a large number of collisions will occur on the half-duplex side. Because the full-duplex side sends frames without checking the RX line, if it's a busy device, chances are it will be sending

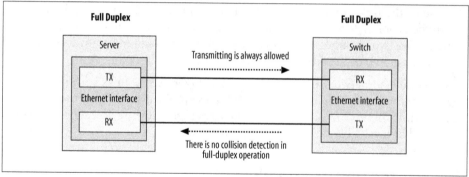

Figure 3-2. Full duplex

frames constantly. The other end of the link, being half duplex, will listen to the RX line and will not transmit unless the RX line is available. It will have a hard time getting a chance to transmit and will record a high number of collisions, making the device appear to be slow on the network. The issue may not be obvious, because a half-duplex interface normally shows collisions, while a full-duplex interface does not. Since full duplex means never having to test for a clear-to-send condition, a full-duplex interface will not record any errors in this situation. The problem should present itself as excessive collisions, but only on the half-duplex side.

Figure 3-3 shows a link where autonegotiation has failed.

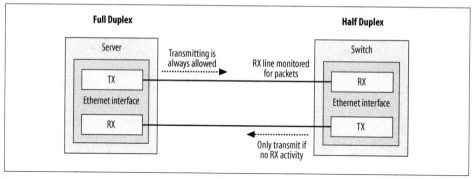

Figure 3-3. Common autonegotiation failure scenario

In the real world, if you see that an interface that is set to autonegotiation has negotiated to 100/half, chances are the other side is set to 100/full. 100 Mbps interfaces that do not support full duplex are rare, so properly configured autonegotiation ports should almost never end up configured for half duplex.

Autonegotiation Best Practices

Using autonegotiation to your advantage is as easy as remembering one simple rule:

> Make sure that both sides of the link are configured the same way.

If one side of the link is set to autonegotiation, make sure the other side is also set to autonegotiation. If one side is set to 100/full, make sure the other side is also set to 100/full.

 Be careful about using 10/full, as full duplex is not supported on all 10Base-T Ethernet devices.

Gigabit Ethernet uses a substantially more robust autonegotiation mechanism than the one described in this chapter. Gigabit Ethernet should thus always be set to autonegotiation, unless there is a compelling reason not to do so (such as an interface that will not properly negotiate). Even then, this should be considered a temporary workaround until the misbehaving part can be replaced.

Configuring Autonegotiation

For Cisco switches, autonegotiation is enabled by default. You can configure the speed and duplex mode manually with the **speed** and **duplex** interface commands in IOS.

You cannot set the duplex mode without first setting the speed. The switch will complain if you attempt to do so:

```
2950(config-if)#duplex half
Duplex can not be set until speed is set to non-auto value
```

Additionally, gigabit switches may give you further warnings about trying to configure half duplex on gigabit ports:

```
SW-3750(config-if)#duplex half

% Duplex cannot be set to half when speed autonegotiation subset contains 1Gbps
```

To set the speed of the interface, use the **speed** command. If the interface has previously been configured, you can return it to autonegotiation with the **auto** keyword:

```
SW-3750(config-if)#speed ?
  10    Force 10 Mbps operation
  100   Force 100 Mbps operation
  1000  Force 1000 Mbps operation
  auto  Enable AUTO speed configuration
```

Once you've set the speed, you can set the duplex mode to auto, full, or half:

```
SW-3750(config-if)#duplex ?
  auto  Enable AUTO duplex configuration
  full  Force full duplex operation
  half  Force half-duplex operation
```

On NX-OS, the commands are the same as the IOS equivalent:

```
NX-5K(config)#int e1/5
NX-5K(config-if)#speed ?
  10    Force 10 Mbps operation
  100   Force 100 Mbps operation
  1000  Force 1000 Mbps operation
  auto  Enable AUTO speed configuration
NX-5K(config-if)#
NX-5K(config-if)#speed 1000
NX-5K(config-if)#duplex full
```

## CHAPTER 4

VLANs

Virtual LANs, or VLANs, are virtual separations within a switch that provide distinct logical LANs that each behave as if they were configured on a separate physical switch. Before the introduction of VLANs, one switch could serve only one LAN. VLANs enabled a single switch to serve multiple LANs. Assuming no vulnerabilities exist in the switch's operating system, there should be no way for a frame that originates on one VLAN to make its way to another.

> When I wrote the first edition of *Network Warrior*, I had not yet learned of VLAN-hopping exploits. There are ways to circumvent the VLAN barrier. Attacks such as switch spoofing and double tagging are methods used to gain access to one VLAN from another. Though reading data from another VLAN is not so easy, denial-of-service attacks could be accomplished through VLAN hopping, especially where trunks interconnect switches. Don't rely on VLANs as your sole means of security, especially in high-risk environments.

Connecting VLANs

Figure 4-1 shows a switch with multiple VLANs. The VLANs have been numbered 10, 20, 30, and 40. In general, VLANs can be named or numbered; Cisco's implementation uses numbers to identify VLANs by default. The default VLAN is numbered 1. If you plug a number of devices into a switch without assigning its ports to specific VLANs, all the devices will reside in VLAN 1.

Frames cannot leave the VLANs from which they originate. This means that in the example configuration, Jack can communicate with Jill, and Bill can communicate with Ted, but Bill and Ted cannot communicate with Jack or Jill in any way.

For a packet on a Layer-2 switch to cross from one VLAN to another, an outside router must be attached to each of the VLANs to be routed. Figure 4-2 shows an external router connecting VLAN 20 with VLAN 40. Assuming a proper configuration on the

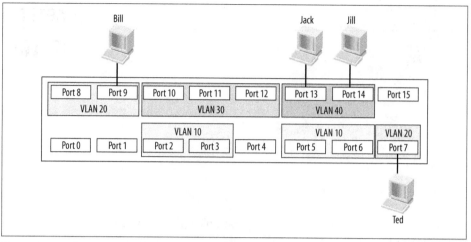

Figure 4-1. VLANs on a switch

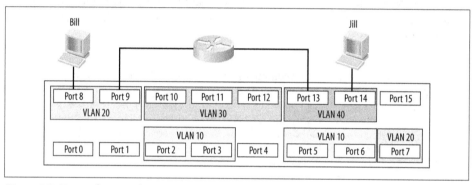

Figure 4-2. External routing between VLANs

router, Bill will now be able to communicate with Jill, but neither workstation will show any indication that they reside on the same physical switch.

When expanding a network using VLANs, you face the same limitations. If you connect another switch to a port that is configured for VLAN 20, the new switch will be able to forward frames only to or from VLAN 20. If you wanted to connect two switches, each containing four VLANs, you would need four links between the switches: one for each VLAN. A solution to this problem is to deploy *trunks* between switches. Trunks are links that carry frames for more than one VLAN.

Figure 4-3 shows two switches connected with a trunk. Jack is connected to VLAN 20 on Switch B, and Diane is connected to VLAN 20 on Switch A. Because there is a trunk connecting these two switches together, assuming the trunk is allowed to carry traffic for all configured VLANs, Jack will be able to communicate with Diane. Notice that the ports to which the trunk is connected are not assigned VLANs. These ports are *trunk ports* and, as such, do not belong to a single VLAN.

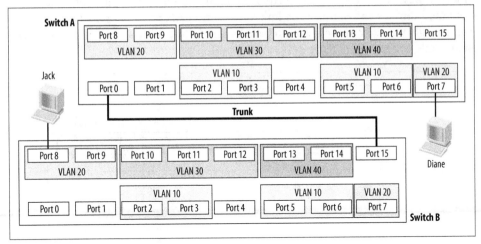

Figure 4-3. Two switches connected with a trunk

Trunks also allow another possibility with switches. Figure 4-2 shows how two VLANs can be connected with a router, as if the VLANs were separate physical networks. Imagine you want to route between *all* of the VLANs on the switch. How would you go about implementing such a design? Traditionally, the answer would be to provide a single connection from the router to each network to be routed. On this switch, each network is a VLAN, so you'd need a physical connection between the router and each VLAN.

As you can see in Figure 4-4, with this setup, four interfaces are being used both on the switch and on the router. Smaller routers rarely have four Ethernet interfaces, though, and Ethernet interfaces on routers can be costly. Additionally, users buy switches with a certain port density in mind. In this configuration, a quarter of the entire switch has been used up just for routing between VLANs.

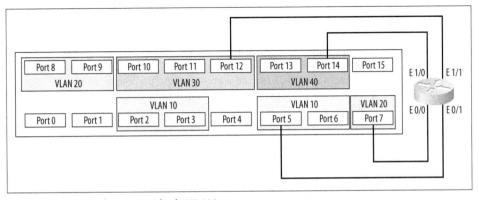

Figure 4-4. Routing between multiple VLANs

Another way to route between VLANs is commonly known as the *router-on-a-stick* configuration. Instead of running a link from each VLAN to a router interface, you can run a single trunk from the switch to the router. All the VLANs will then pass over a single link, as shown in Figure 4-5.

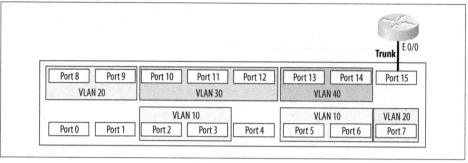

Figure 4-5. Router on a stick

Deploying a router on a stick saves a lot of interfaces on both the switch and the router. The downside is that the trunk is only one link, and the total bandwidth available on that link is only 10 Mbps. In contrast, when each VLAN has its own link, each VLAN has 10 Mbps to itself. Also, don't forget that the router is passing traffic between VLANs, so chances are each frame will be seen twice on the same link—once to get to the router, and once to get back to the destination VLAN.

> When I edited this chapter for the second edition, I briefly contemplated updating all the drawings to bring them more in line with currently common interface speeds. I decided against it because the last time I saw anyone doing router on a stick, the fastest switches only had 10M interfaces. It had nothing to do with me being too lazy to change the drawings.
>
> To be painfully accurate, running a trunk to a firewall and having the firewall perform default gateway functions for multiple VLANs employs the same principle, so you could argue that I'm just too lazy after all. I would then counter with the fact that the latest switching technology from Cisco, the Nexus line, has done away with interface names that describe their speed, and instead names all Ethernet interfaces as "*e slot/port*". Therefore, I'm not lazy, but rather forward-thinking.
>
> Then I started writing the VoIP chapter where, lo and behold, I configured router on a stick in order to get my Voice-VLAN trunked to the router. Good thing I didn't pull the router-on-a-stick section. It looks like I was being forward-thinking after all.

Figure 4-6 shows conceptually how the same design would be accomplished with a Layer-3 switch. Because the switch contains the router, no external links are required.

With a Layer-3 switch, every port can be dedicated to devices or trunks to other switches.

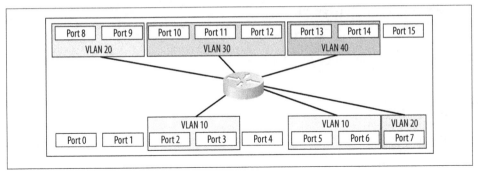

Figure 4-6. Layer-3 switch

Configuring VLANs

VLANs are typically configured via the CatOS or IOS command-line interpreter (CLI), like any other feature. However, some IOS models, such as the 2950 and 3550 switches, have a configurable *VLAN database* with its own configuration mode and commands. This can be a challenge for the uninitiated, especially because the configuration for this database is completely separate from the configuration for the rest of the switch. Even a write erase followed by a reload will not clear the VLAN database on these switches. Configuring through the VLAN database is a throwback to older models that offered no other way to manage VLANs. Luckily, all newer switches (including those with a VLAN database) offer the option of configuring the VLANs through the normal IOS CLI. Switches like the 6500, when running in native IOS mode, only support IOS commands for switch configuration. The Nexus line does not have a configurable VLAN database.

 Cisco recommends that you configure the VLAN Trunking Protocol (VTP) as a first step when configuring VLANs. This idea has merit, as trunks will not negotiate without a VTP domain. However, setting a VTP domain is not required to make VLANs function on a single switch. Configuring VTP is covered later (see Chapter 5, *Trunking* and Chapter 6, *VLAN Trunking Protocol*).

CatOS

For CatOS, create a VLAN with the set vlan command:

```
Switch1-CatOS# (enable)set vlan 10 name Lab-VLAN
VTP advertisements transmitting temporarily stopped,
and will resume after the command finishes.
Vlan 10 configuration successful
```

There are a lot of options when creating a VLAN, but for the bare minimum, this is all you need. To show the status of the VLANs, execute the `show vlan` command:

```
Switch1-CatOS# (enable)sho vlan
VLAN Name                             Status    IfIndex Mod/Ports, Vlans
---- -------------------------------- --------- ------- -----------------------
1    default                          active    7       1/1-2
                                                        2/1-2
                                                        3/5-48
                                                        6/1-48
10   Lab-VLAN                         active    112
20   VLAN0020                         active    210     3/1-4
1002 fddi-default                     active    8
1003 token-ring-default               active    11
1004 fddinet-default                  active    9
1005 trnet-default                    active    10
1006 Online Diagnostic Vlan1          active    0       internal
1007 Online Diagnostic Vlan2          active    0       internal
1008 Online Diagnostic Vlan3          active    0       internal
1009 Voice Internal Vlan              active    0       internal
1010 Dtp Vlan                         active    0       internal
1011 Private Vlan Reserved Vlan       suspend   0       internal
1016 Online SP-RP Ping Vlan           active    0       internal
```

Notice that VLAN 10 has the name you assigned; VLAN 20's name, which you did not assign, defaulted to VLAN0020. The output shows which ports are assigned to VLAN 20 and that most of the ports still reside in VLAN 1 (because VLAN 1 is the default VLAN, all ports reside there by default).

There are no ports in VLAN 10 yet, so add some, again using the `set vlan` command:

```
Switch1-CatOS# (enable)set vlan 10 6/1,6/3-4
VLAN 10 modified.VLAN 1 modified.
VLAN  Mod/Ports
---- -----------------------
10   6/1,6/3-4
```

You've now added ports 6/1, 6/3, and 6/4 to VLAN 10. Another `show vlan` will reflect these changes:

```
Switch1-CatOS# (enable)sho vlan
VLAN Name                             Status    IfIndex Mod/Ports, Vlans
---- -------------------------------- --------- ------- -----------------------
1    default                          active    7       1/1-2
                                                        2/1-2
                                                        3/5-48
                                                        6/2,6/5-48
10   Lab-VLAN                         active    112     6/1,6/3-4
20   VLAN0020                         active    210     3/1-4
1002 fddi-default                     active    8
1003 token-ring-default               active    11
1004 fddinet-default                  active    9
1005 trnet-default                    active    10
1006 Online Diagnostic Vlan1          active    0       internal
1007 Online Diagnostic Vlan2          active    0       internal
1008 Online Diagnostic Vlan3          active    0       internal
```

```
1009 Voice Internal Vlan           active    0      internal
1010 Dtp Vlan                      active    0      internal
1011 Private Vlan Reserved Vlan    suspend   0      internal
1016 Online SP-RP Ping Vlan        active    0      internal
```

The output indicates that VLAN 1 was modified as well. This is because the ports had to be removed from VLAN 1 to be added to VLAN 10.

IOS Using VLAN Database

This method is included for the sake of completeness. Older switches that require this method of configuration are no doubt still deployed. IOS switches that support the VLAN database, such as the 3750, actually display this message when you enter VLAN database configuration mode:

```
3750-IOS#vlan database
% Warning: It is recommended to configure VLAN from config mode,
  as VLAN database mode is being deprecated. Please consult user
  documentation for configuring VTP/VLAN in config mode.
```

 If you have an IOS switch with active VLANs, but no reference is made to them in the running configuration, it's possible they were configured in the VLAN database. Another possibility is that they were learned via VTP (we will cover this in Chapter 6). On 3750s, when the switch is in VTP server mode, even when you configure VLANs in CLI, they do not appear in the running configuration.

Since you're more likely to see the VLAN database in older switches, I'll continue with examples from a 2950, though they all behave pretty similarly. If you find any switch configured using the VLAN database, my advice is to convert it to an IOS configuration.

To configure VLANs in the VLAN database, you must enter VLAN database configuration mode with the command vlan database. Requesting help (?) lists the commands available in this mode:

```
2950-IOS#vlan database
2950-IOS(vlan)# ?
VLAN database editing buffer manipulation commands:
  abort  Exit mode without applying the changes
  apply  Apply current changes and bump revision number
  exit   Apply changes, bump revision number, and exit mode
  no     Negate a command or set its defaults
  reset  Abandon current changes and reread current database
  show   Show database information
  vlan   Add, delete, or modify values associated with a single VLAN
  vtp    Perform VTP administrative functions.
```

To create a VLAN, give the vlan command followed by the VLAN number and name:

```
2950-IOS(vlan)#vlan 10 name Lab-VLAN
VLAN 10 added:
    Name: Lab-VLAN
```

You can show the VLANs configured from within VLAN database mode with the command show. You have the option of displaying the current database (show cur rent), the differences between the current and proposed database (show changes), or the proposed database as it will look after you apply the changes using the apply command or exit VLAN database configuration mode. The default behavior of the show command is show proposed:

```
2950-IOS(vlan)#show
  VLAN ISL Id: 1
    Name: default
    Media Type: Ethernet
    VLAN 802.10 Id: 100001
    State: Operational
    MTU: 1500
    Backup CRF Mode: Disabled
    Remote SPAN VLAN: No

  VLAN ISL Id: 10
    Name: Lab-VLAN
    Media Type: Ethernet
    VLAN 802.10 Id: 100010
    State: Operational
    MTU: 1500
    Backup CRF Mode: Disabled
    Remote SPAN VLAN: No
```

Nothing else is required to create a simple VLAN. The database will be saved upon exit:

```
2950-IOS(vlan)#exit
APPLY completed.
Exiting....
```

Now, when you execute the show vlan command in IOS, you'll see the VLAN you've created:

```
2950-IOS#sho vlan
```

VLAN	Name	Status	Ports
1	default	active	Fa0/1, Fa0/2, Fa0/3, Fa0/4
			Fa0/5, Fa0/6, Fa0/7, Fa0/8
			Fa0/9, Fa0/10, Fa0/11, Fa0/12
			Fa0/13, Fa0/14, Fa0/15, Fa0/16
			Fa0/17, Fa0/18, Fa0/19, Fa0/20
			Fa0/21, Fa0/22, Fa0/23, Fa0/24
			Gi0/1, Gi0/2
10	Lab-VLAN	active	
1002	fddi-default	active	
1003	token-ring-default	active	

```
1004 fddinet-default                active
1005 trnet-default                  active
```

Adding ports to the VLAN is accomplished in IOS interface configuration mode, and is covered in the next section.

IOS Using Global Commands

Adding VLANs in IOS is relatively straightforward when all of the defaults are acceptable, which is usually the case. Here I'll revert to a 3750, since you're likely to encounter modern switches using this method.

First, enter configuration mode. From there, issue the vlan command with the identifier for the VLAN you're adding or changing. Next, specify a name for the VLAN with the name subcommand (as with CatOS, a default name of VLANxxxx is used if you do not supply one):

```
3750-IOS#conf t
Enter configuration commands, one per line. End with CNTL/Z.
3750-IOS(config)# vlan 10
3750-IOS(config-vlan)# name Lab-VLAN
```

Exit configuration mode and then issue the show vlan command to see the VLANs present:

```
3750-IOS#sho vlan

VLAN Name                             Status    Ports
---- -------------------------------- --------- -------------------------------
1    default                          active    Gi1/0/1, Gi1/0/2, Gi1/0/3
                                                Gi1/0/4, Gi1/0/5, Gi1/0/6
                                                Gi1/0/7, Gi1/0/8, Gi1/0/9
                                                Gi1/0/10, Gi1/0/11, Gi1/0/12
                                                Gi1/0/13, Gi1/0/14, Gi1/0/15
                                                Gi1/0/16, Gi1/0/17, Gi1/0/18
                                                Gi1/0/21, Gi1/0/22, Gi1/0/23
                                                Gi1/0/24, Gi1/0/25, Gi1/0/26
                                                Gi1/0/27, Gi1/0/28, Gi1/0/29
                                                Gi1/0/30, Gi1/0/31, Gi1/0/32
                                                Gi1/0/33, Gi1/0/34, Gi1/0/35
                                                Gi1/0/36, Gi1/0/37, Gi1/0/38
                                                Gi1/0/39, Gi1/0/40, Gi1/0/41
                                                Gi1/0/42, Gi1/0/43, Gi1/0/44
                                                Gi1/0/46, Gi1/0/49, Gi1/0/50
                                                Gi1/0/51, Gi1/0/52
10   Lab-VLAN                         active
100  VLAN0100                         active
200  VLAN0200                         active
300  VLAN0300                         active

VLAN Name                             Status    Ports
---- -------------------------------- --------- -------------------------------
1002 fddi-default                     act/unsup
1003 token-ring-default               act/unsup
```

```
1004 fddinet-default                    act/unsup
1005 trnet-default                       act/unsup

VLAN Type  SAID      MTU  Parent RingNo BridgeNo Stp BrdgMode Trans1 Trans2
---- ----- --------- ---- ------ ------ -------- ---- -------- ------ ------
1    enet  100001    1500 -      -      -        -    -        0      0
10   enet  100010    1500 -      -      -        -    -        0      0
100  enet  100100    1500 -      -      -        -    -        0      0
200  enet  100200    1500 -      -      -        -    -        0      0
300  enet  100300    1500 -      -      -        -    -        0      0
1002 fddi  101002    1500 -      -      -        -    -        0      0
1003 tr    101003    1500 -      -      -        -    -        0      0
1004 fdnet 101004    1500 -      -      -        ieee -        0      0
1005 trnet 101005    1500 -      -      -        ibm  -        0      0

Remote SPAN VLANs
-------------------------------------------------------------------------------


Primary Secondary Type              Ports
------- --------- ----------------- ----------------------------------------
```

You assign ports to VLANs in IOS in interface configuration mode. Each interface must be configured individually with the `switchport access` command (this is in contrast to the CatOS switches, which allow you to add all the ports at once with the `set vlan` command):

```
3750-IOS(config)#int g1/0/1
3750-IOS(config-if)#switchport access vlan 10
3750-IOS(config-if)#int g1/0/2
3750-IOS(config-if)#switchport access vlan 10
```

Modern versions of IOS allow you to apply commands to multiple interfaces with the `interface range` command. Using this command, you can accomplish the same result as before while saving some precious keystrokes:

```
3750-IOS(config)#interface range g1/0/1 - 2
3750-IOS(config-if-range)#switchport access vlan 10
```

Now, when you execute the `show vlan` command, you'll see that the ports have been assigned to the proper VLAN:

```
3750-IOS#sho vlan

VLAN Name                            Status    Ports
---- ------------------------------- --------- -------------------------------
1    default                         active    Gi1/0/3, Gi1/0/4, Gi1/0/5
                                               Gi1/0/6, Gi1/0/7, Gi1/0/8
                                               Gi1/0/9, Gi1/0/10, Gi1/0/11
                                               Gi1/0/12, Gi1/0/13, Gi1/0/14
                                               Gi1/0/15, Gi1/0/16, Gi1/0/17
                                               Gi1/0/18, Gi1/0/21, Gi1/0/22
                                               Gi1/0/23, Gi1/0/24, Gi1/0/25
                                               Gi1/0/26, Gi1/0/27, Gi1/0/28
                                               Gi1/0/29, Gi1/0/30, Gi1/0/31
```

```
                                          Gi1/0/32, Gi1/0/33, Gi1/0/34
                                          Gi1/0/35, Gi1/0/36, Gi1/0/37
                                          Gi1/0/38, Gi1/0/39, Gi1/0/40
                                          Gi1/0/41, Gi1/0/42, Gi1/0/43
                                          Gi1/0/44, Gi1/0/46, Gi1/0/49
                                          Gi1/0/50, Gi1/0/51, Gi1/0/52
10    Lab-VLAN              active        Gi1/0/1, Gi1/0/2
100   VLAN0100             active
200   VLAN0200             active
300   VLAN0300             active
1002  fddi-default         act/unsup
```

Nexus and NX-OS

NX-OS uses a command interface similar to IOS. NX-OS behaves a little bit differently, especially concerning the configuration of interfaces. The methods used for configuring VLANs are very similar to IOS. First we create the VLAN with the vlan *vlan-#* command:

```
NX-7K-1-Cozy(config)# vlan 10
```

Once you've created the VLAN, enter VLAN configuration mode and name the VLAN with the name *vlan-name* command:

```
NX-7K-1-Cozy(config-vlan)# name Lab-VLAN
```

One of the cool features of NX-OS is that you no longer need the do command to run show commands from configuration mode. This behavior is similar to the PIX and ASA configuration mode, and is a most welcome change. Here, I've executed the show vlan command from within VLAN configuration mode:

```
NX-7K-1-Cozy(config-if)# sho vlan

VLAN Name                             Status    Ports
---- -------------------------------- --------- -------------------------------
1    default                          active    Po1, Po10
10   Lab-VLAN                         active    Po1, Eth3/2

VLAN Type
---- -----
1    enet
10   enet

Remote SPAN VLANs
-------------------------------------------------------------------------------

Primary  Secondary  Type            Ports
-------  ---------  --------------- -------------------------------------------
```

Another new feature in NX-OS is the capability to configure a range of interfaces without using the interface-range command. Simply enter the range you want to configure as if you were using the interface-range command in IOS:

```
NX-7K-1-Cozy(config-vlan)# int e3/1 - 2
```

This automatically puts us into interface range configuration mode. Now we assign the ports to a VLAN the same way we would in IOS—using the switchport access vlan *vlan#* command:

```
NX-7K-1-Cozy(config-if-range)# switchport access vlan 10
Warning: command rejected, Eth3/1 not a switching port
Warning: command rejected, Eth3/2 not a switching port
```

Now there's a message you don't see on a Catalyst switch by default. The Nexus 7000 switch behaves differently than a catalyst. By default, all switch ports are router ports! To perform switch port commands on a Nexus port, you must first put them into switchport mode with the switchport command:

```
NX-7K-1-Cozy(config-if-range)# int e3/1 - 2
NX-7K-1-Cozy(config-if-range)# switchport
NX-7K-1-Cozy(config-if-range)# no shut
```

Now that we have placed the ports into switchport mode, we can assign them to a VLAN without further interruption:

```
NX-7K-1-Cozy(config-if-range)# switchport access vlan 10
NX-7K-1-Cozy(config-if-range)#
```

The show vlan command now shows our ports assigned to VLAN 10. Notice once more how I've executed a show command from within configuration mode. I love this feature!

```
NX-7K-1-Cozy(config-if-range)# sho vlan

VLAN Name                             Status    Ports
---- -------------------------------- --------- -------------------------------

1    default                          active
10   Lab-VLAN                         active    Eth3/1, Eth3/2


VLAN Type
---- -----
1    enet
10   enet


Remote SPAN VLANs
-------------------------------------------------------------------------------


Primary Secondary Type            Ports
------- --------- --------------- -------------------------------------------
```

## CHAPTER 5

Trunking

A *trunk*, using Cisco's terminology, is an interface or link that can carry frames for multiple VLANs at once. As you saw in the previous chapter, a trunk can connect two switches so that devices in VLANs on one switch can communicate with devices in the same VLANs on another switch. Unless there is only one VLAN to be connected, switches are connected at Layer 2 using trunks. Figure 5-1 shows two switches connected with a trunk.

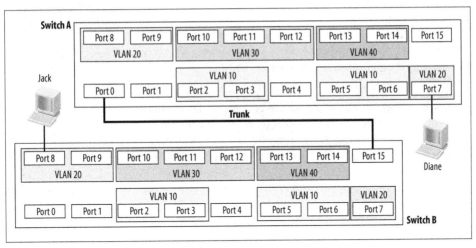

Figure 5-1. A trunk connecting two switches

Trunking is generally related to switches, but routers, firewalls, and all manner of devices can connect with trunks as well. The router-on-a-stick scenario described in Chapter 4 requires a router to communicate with a trunk port on a switch.

How Trunks Work

Figure 5-2 is a visual representation of a trunk. VLANs 10, 20, 30, and 40 exist on both sides of the trunk. Any traffic from VLAN 10 on Switch 1 that is destined for VLAN 10 on Switch 2 must traverse the trunk (of course, the reverse is true as well).

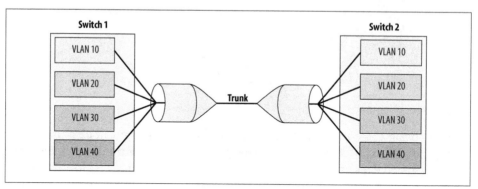

Figure 5-2. Visual representation of a trunk

For the remote switch to determine how to forward the frame, the frame must contain a reference to the VLAN to which it belongs. IP packets have no concept of VLANs, though, nor do TCP, UDP, ICMP, or any other protocol above Layer 2. Remember that a VLAN is a Layer-2 concept, so any reference to a VLAN would happen at the data-link layer. Ethernet was invented before VLANs, so there is no reference to VLANs in any Ethernet protocols, either.

To mark, or *tag*, frames to be sent over a trunk, both sides must agree to a protocol. Currently, the protocols for trunking supported on Cisco switches are Cisco's Inter-Switch Link (ISL) and the IEEE standard 802.1Q. Not all Cisco switches support both protocols. For example, the Cisco 2950 and 4000 switches only support 802.1Q. To determine whether a switch can use a specific trunking protocol, use the IOS or NX-OS command `show interface capabilities`, or the CatOS command `show port capabilities`:

```
NX-7K-1-Cozy(config)# sho interface capabilities | inc Trunk
Ethernet3/1
  Trunk encap. type:     802.1Q
```

As you can see from the preceding output, the Nexus supports only the open standard, 802.1Q. Here, you can see that a 3750 supports both 802.1Q and ISL:

```
3750-IOS#sho int g1/0/45 capabilities | inc Trunk
  Trunk encap. type:     802.1Q,ISL
  Trunk mode:            on,off,desirable,nonegotiate
```

ISL differs from 802.1Q in a couple of ways. First, ISL is a Cisco-proprietary protocol, whereas 802.1Q is an IEEE standard. Second, ISL encapsulates Ethernet frames within an ISL frame, while 802.1Q alters existing frames to include VLAN tags. Furthermore,

ISL is capable of supporting only 1,000 VLANs, while 802.1Q is capable of supporting 4,096.

On switches that support both ISL and 802.1Q, either may be used. The protocol is specific to each trunk. While both sides of the trunk must agree on a protocol, you may configure ISL and 802.1Q trunks on the same switch and in the same network.

ISL

To add VLAN information to a frame to be sent over a trunk, ISL encapsulates the entire frame within a new frame. An additional header is prepended to the frame and a small suffix is added to the end. The header contains information regarding the VLAN number and some other information, while the footer includes a checksum of the frame. A high-level overview of an ISL frame is shown in Figure 5-3.

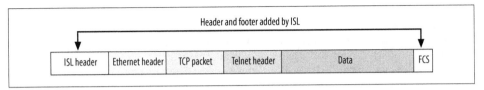

Figure 5-3. ISL encapsulated frame

The frame check sequence (FCS) footer is in addition to the FCS field already present in Ethernet frames. The ISL FCS frame computes a checksum based on the frame including the ISL header; the Ethernet FCS checksum does not include this header.

 Adding more information to an Ethernet frame can be problematic. If an Ethernet frame has been created at the maximum size of 1,518 bytes, ISL will add an extra 30 bytes, for a total frame size of 1,548 bytes. These frames may be counted as "giant" frame errors, though Cisco equipment has no problem accepting them.

802.1Q

802.1Q takes a different approach to VLAN tagging. Instead of adding more headers to a frame, 802.1Q inserts data into existing headers. An additional four-byte tag field is inserted between the Source Address and Type/Length fields. Because 802.1Q has altered the frame, the FCS of the frame is altered to reflect the change.

Because only four bytes are added, the maximum size for an 802.1Q frame is 1,522 bytes. This may result in "baby giant" frame errors, though the frames will still be supported on Cisco devices.

Which Protocol to Use

Why are there two protocols at all? There is a history at work here. Cisco developed and implemented ISL before 802.1Q existed. Older switches from Cisco only support ISL. Oddly enough, other switches, like the Nexus, only support 802.1Q. In some cases, the blade within a switch chassis may be the deciding factor. As an example, some 10 Gb blades available for the Catalyst 6509 only support 802.1Q, while the switch itself supports 802.1Q and ISL; in this case, 802.1Q must be used.

In many installations, you can use either protocol, and the choice is not important. When you're trunking between Cisco switches, there is no real benefit of using one protocol over the other, except for the fact that 802.1Q can support 4,096 VLANs, whereas ISL can only support 1,000. Some purists may argue that ISL is better because it doesn't alter the original frame, and some others may argue that 802.1Q is better because the frames are smaller and there is no encapsulation. What usually ends up happening is that whoever installs the trunk uses whichever protocol he is used to.

 Cisco has recommendations on how to set up trunks between Cisco switches. This document (Cisco document ID 24067) is titled "System Requirements to Implement Trunking."

When you're connecting Cisco switches to non-Cisco devices, the choice is 802.1Q. Remember, there are no restrictions regarding protocol choice on a switch that supports both. If you need to connect a 3Com switch to your Cisco network, you can do so with an 802.1Q trunk even if your Cisco network uses ISL trunks elsewhere. The trunking protocol is local to each individual trunk. If you connect to a 3Com switch using 802.1Q, the VLANs on that switch will still be accessible on switches connected using ISL elsewhere.

The Cisco Nexus line, which appears to embrace open standards more than previous devices, does not support ISL.

Trunk Negotiation

Some Cisco switches support the Dynamic Trunking Protocol (DTP). This protocol attempts to determine which trunking protocols are supported on each side and to establish a trunk, if possible.

 Trunk negotiation includes the VLAN Trunking Protocol (VTP) domain name in the process. For DTP to successfully negotiate, both switches must have the same VTP domain name. See Chapter 6 for details on configuring VTP domains.

An interface running DTP sends frames every 30 seconds in an attempt to negotiate a trunk. If a port has been manually set to either "trunk" or "prevent trunking," DTP is unnecessary and can be disabled. The IOS command `switchport nonegotiate` disables DTP:

```
3750-IOS(config-if)#switchport mode trunk
3750-IOS(config-if)#switchport nonegotiate
```

 Many networking engineers prefer to issue the `switchport nonegotiate` command to all ports as a security precaution. If someone were to attach a rogue switch to the network and manage to negotiate a trunk, she would potentially have access to every VLAN on the switch. I prefer to disable all ports by default so that any attached device requires human intervention to gain access to the network. Both approaches have merit, and they can even be used together.

Figure 5-4 shows the possible `switchport` modes. Remember, not all switches support all modes. A port can be set to the mode `access`, which means it will never be a trunk; `dynamic`, which means the port may become a trunk; or `trunk`, which means the port will be a trunk regardless of any other settings.

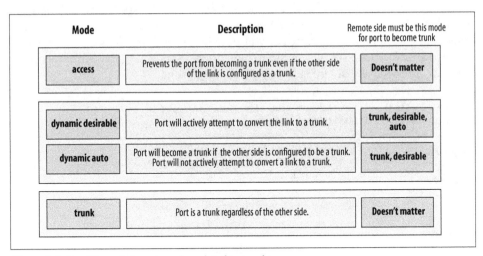

Mode	Description	Remote side must be this mode for port to become trunk
access	Prevents the port from becoming a trunk even if the other side of the link is configured as a trunk.	Doesn't matter
dynamic desirable	Port will actively attempt to convert the link to a trunk.	trunk, desirable, auto
dynamic auto	Port will become a trunk if the other side is configured to be a trunk. Port will not actively attempt to convert a link to a trunk.	trunk, desirable
trunk	Port is a trunk regardless of the other side.	Doesn't matter

Figure 5-4. Possible switch port modes related to trunking

The two `dynamic` modes, `desirable` and `auto`, refer to the method in which DTP will operate on the port. `desirable` indicates that the port will initiate negotiations and try to make the link a trunk. `auto` indicates that the port will listen for DTP but will not actively attempt to become a trunk.

The default mode for most Cisco switches is `dynamic auto`. A port in this condition will automatically become a trunk should the remote switch port connecting to it be hard-coded as a trunk or set to `dynamic desirable`.

Configuring Trunks

Configuring a trunk involves determining which port will be a trunk, which protocol the trunk will run, and whether and how the port will negotiate. Optionally, you may also wish to limit which VLANs are allowed on the trunk link.

IOS

The Cisco 3750 is an excellent example of an IOS switch. This section will walk you through configuring one of the Gigabit ports to be an 802.1Q trunk using a 3750 switch.

You might think the first step is to specify that the port is a trunk, but as you're about to see, that's not the case:

```
3750-IOS(config-if)#switchport mode trunk
Command rejected: An interface whose trunk encapsulation is "Auto" can not be
configured to "trunk" mode.
```

On an IOS switch capable of both ISL and 802.1Q, you must specify a *trunk encapsulation* before you can configure a port as a trunk (`trunk encapsulation` is an unfortunate choice for the command because, as you now know, 802.1Q does not encapsulate frames like ISL does; still, you must follow Cisco's syntax). Once you've chosen a trunking protocol, you are free to declare the port a trunk:

```
3750-IOS(config)#int g1/0/45
3750-IOS(config-if)#switchport trunk encapsulation dot1q
3750-IOS(config-if)#switchport mode trunk
```

 Should you wish to subsequently remove trunking from the interface, you'd use the command `switchport mode access`.

By default, all VLANs on a switch are included in a trunk. But you may have 40 VLANs and only need to trunk 3 of them. Because broadcasts from all allowed VLANs will be sent on every trunk port, excluding unneeded VLANs can save a lot of bandwidth on your trunk links. You can specify which VLANs are able to traverse a trunk with the `switchport trunk allowed` command. These are the options for this command:

```
3750-IOS(config-if)#switchport trunk allowed vlan ?
  WORD    VLAN IDs of the allowed VLANs when this port is in trunking mode
  add     add VLANs to the current list
  all     all VLANs
  except  all VLANs except the following
```

```
none    no VLANs
remove  remove VLANs from the current list
```

To allow only one VLAN (VLAN 100, in this case) on a trunk, use a command like this:

```
3750-IOS(config-if)#switchport trunk allowed vlan 100
```

As you can see from the output of the show interface trunk command, only VLAN 100 is now allowed. IOS has removed the others:

```
3750-IOS#sho int trunk

Port       Mode            Encapsulation  Status      Native vlan
Gi1/0/45   on              802.1q         trunking    1

Port       Vlans allowed on trunk
Gi1/0/45   100

Port       Vlans allowed and active in management domain
Gi1/0/45   100

Port       Vlans in spanning tree forwarding state and not pruned
Gi1/0/45   100
```

If you want to allow all VLANs except VLAN 100, do it with the following command:

```
3750-IOS(config-if)#switchport trunk allowed vlan except 100
```

This command will override the previous command specifying VLAN 100 as the only allowed VLAN, so now all VLANs *except* VLAN 100 will be allowed. Reexecuting the switchport trunk allowed vlan 100 command would again reverse the state of the VLANs allowed on the trunk. show interface trunk shows the status:

```
3750-IOS#sho int trunk

Port       Mode            Encapsulation  Status      Native vlan
Gi1/0/45   on              802.1q         trunking    1

Port       Vlans allowed on trunk
Gi1/0/45   1-99,101-4094

Port       Vlans allowed and active in management domain
Gi1/0/45   1

Port       Vlans in spanning tree forwarding state and not pruned
Gi1/0/45   none
```

VLANs 1-99 and 101-4096 are now allowed on the trunk. Let's say you want to remove VLANs 200 and 300 as well. Using the remove keyword, you can do just that:

```
3750-IOS(config-if)#switchport trunk allowed vlan remove 200
3750-IOS(config-if)#switchport trunk allowed vlan remove 300
```

The output of show interface trunk now shows that all VLANs—except 100, 200, and 300—are allowed on the trunk:

```
3750-IOS#sho int trunk

Port         Mode          Encapsulation  Status        Native vlan
Gi1/0/45     on            802.1q         trunking      1

Port         Vlans allowed on trunk
Gi1/0/45     1-99,101-199,201-299,301-4094

Port         Vlans allowed and active in management domain
Gi1/0/45     1

Port         Vlans in spanning tree forwarding state and not pruned
Gi1/0/45     1
```

CatOS

You configure a trunk on a CatOS switch via the set trunk command. Options for the set trunk command are as follows:

```
Switch1-CatOS# (enable)set trunk 3/1 ?
  none                      No vlans
  <mode>                    Trunk mode (on,off,desirable,auto,nonegotiate)
  <type>                    Trunk type (isl,dot1q,dot10,lane,negotiate)
  <vlan>                    VLAN number
```

The mode on indicates that the port has been hardcoded to be a trunk, and the mode off indicates that the port will never be a trunk. The modes desirable and auto are both dynamic and refer to the method with which DTP will operate on the port. desirable indicates that the port will initiate negotiations and try to make the link a trunk. auto indicates that the port will listen for DTP, but will not actively attempt to become a port. You can use the mode nonegotiate to turn off DTP in the event that either on or off has been chosen as the mode on the opposing port.

The trunk types isl and dotq1 specify ISL and 802.1Q as the protocols, respectively; negotiate indicates that DTP should be used to determine the protocol. The trunk types dot10 and lane are for technologies such as ATM, and will not be covered here.

One of the nice features of CatOS is that it allows you to stack multiple arguments in a single command. This command sets the port to mode desirable and the protocol to 802.1Q:

```
Switch1-CatOS# (enable)set trunk 3/5 desirable dot1q
Port(s)  3/1 trunk mode set to desirable.
Port(s)  3/1 trunk type set to dot1q.
Switch1-CatOS# (enable)
2006 May 23 11:29:31 %ETHC-5-PORTFROMSTP:Port 3/5 left bridge port 3/5
2006 May 23 11:29:34 %DTP-5-TRUNKPORTON:Port 3/5 has become dot1q trunk
```

The other side of the link was not configured, but the trunk became active because the default state of the ports on the other side is auto.

The command to view trunk status on CatOS is show port trunk:

```
Switch1-CatOS#sho port trunk
* - indicates vtp domain mismatch
# - indicates dot1q-all-tagged enabled on the port
$ - indicates non-default dot1q-ethertype value
Port      Mode          Encapsulation  Status       Native vlan
--------  -----------   -------------  -----------  -----------
   3/5    desirable     dot1q          trunking     1
  15/1    nonegotiate   isl            trunking     1
  16/1    nonegotiate   isl            trunking     1


Port      Vlans allowed on trunk
--------  --------------------------------------------------------------
   3/5    1-4094
  15/1    1-4094
  16/1    1-4094


Port      Vlans allowed and active in management domain
--------  --------------------------------------------------------------
   3/5    1,10,20
  15/1
  16/1


Port      Vlans in spanning tree forwarding state and not pruned
--------  --------------------------------------------------------------
   3/5    1,10,20
  15/1
  16/1
```

The trunks 15/1 and 16/1 shown in this output are internal trunks. On a 6500 switch running CatOS, trunks exist from the supervisors to the multilayer switch feature cards (MSFCs). The MSFCs are known as slots 15 and 16 when two supervisors are installed.

To specify which VLANs can traverse a trunk, use the same set trunk command and append the VLANs you wish to allow. CatOS works a little differently from IOS in that it will not remove all of the active VLANs in favor of ones you specify:

```
Switch-2# (enable)set trunk 3/5 100
Vlan(s) 100 already allowed on the trunk
Please use the 'clear trunk' command to remove vlans from allowed list.
```

Remember that all VLANs are allowed by default. Preventing a single VLAN from using a trunk is as simple as using the clear trunk command:

```
Switch-2# (enable)clear trunk 3/5 100
Removing Vlan(s) 100 from allowed list.
Port  3/5 allowed vlans modified to 1-99,101-4094.
```

You don't have to use a show trunk command to see which VLANs are allowed, because the clear trunk tells you the new status of the port.

To limit a CatOS switch so that only one VLAN is allowed, disallow all the remaining VLANs. Just as you removed one VLAN with the clear trunk command, you can remove all of the VLANs *except* the one you want to allow:

```
Switch-2# (enable)clear trunk 3/5 1-99,101-4094
Removing Vlan(s) 1-99,101-4094 from allowed list.
Port  3/5 allowed vlans modified to 100.
```

Finally, a show trunk will show you the status of the trunks. As you can see, only VLAN
100 is now allowed on trunk 3/5:

```
Switch-2# (enable)sho trunk
* - indicates vtp domain mismatch
# - indicates dot1q-all-tagged enabled on the port
$ - indicates non-default dot1q-ethertype value
Port      Mode         Encapsulation  Status        Native vlan
--------  -----------  -------------  ------------  -----------
 3/5      auto         dot1q          trunking      1
15/1      nonegotiate  isl            trunking      1
16/1      nonegotiate  isl            trunking      1


Port      Vlans allowed on trunk
--------  ------------------------------------------------------------------
 3/5      100
15/1      1-4094
16/1      1-4094


Port      Vlans allowed and active in management domain
--------  ------------------------------------------------------------------
 3/5
15/1
16/1


Port      Vlans in spanning tree forwarding state and not pruned
--------  ------------------------------------------------------------------
 3/5
15/1
16/1
```

Nexus and NX-OS

Remembering that NX-OS on a Nexus 7000 places interfaces in routed mode by default,
we must first issue the switchport interface command:

```
NX-7K-1-Cozy(config-if)# int e3/2
NX-7K-1-Cozy(config-if)# switchport
```

Now we put the port into trunk mode with the switchport mode trunk interface
command:

```
NX-7K-1-Cozy(config-if)# switchport mode ?
  access  Port mode access
  trunk   Port mode trunk

NX-7K-1-Cozy(config-if)# int e3/2
NX-7K-1-Cozy(config-if)# switchport mode trunk
```

We limit the VLANs allowed over the trunk with the switchport trunk allowed vlan
interface command:

```
NX-7K-1-Cozy(config-if)# switchport trunk allowed vlan ?
  <1-3967,4048-4093>  VLAN IDs of the allowed VLANs when this port in trunking
                      mode
  add                 Add VLANs to the current list
  all                 All VLANs
  except              All VLANs except the following
  none                No VLANs
  remove              Remove VLANs from the current list
```

This works similarly to the IOS version of the command. Here, if we allow VLAN 100, all other VLANs are prohibited.

```
NX-7K-1-Cozy(config-if)# switchport trunk allowed vlan 100
```

You can see which VLANs are allowed over the trunk with the show interface trunk command. The output of the command differs from IOS, but the information is all there.

```
NX-7K-1-Cozy(config-if)# sho int trunk

--------------------------------------------------------------------------------
Port        Native  Status          Port
            Vlan                    Channel
--------------------------------------------------------------------------------
Eth3/2      1       trunking        --
Eth8/1      1       trnk-bndl       Po1
Eth8/2      1       trnk-bndl       Po1
Po1         1       trunking        --


--------------------------------------------------------------------------------
Port        Vlans Allowed on Trunk
--------------------------------------------------------------------------------
Eth3/2      100
Eth8/1      1-3967,4048-4093
Eth8/2      1-3967,4048-4093
Po1         1-3967,4048-4093


--------------------------------------------------------------------------------
Port        Vlans Err-disabled on Trunk
--------------------------------------------------------------------------------
Eth3/2      none
Eth8/1      none
Eth8/2      none
Po1         none


--------------------------------------------------------------------------------
Port        STP Forwarding
--------------------------------------------------------------------------------
Eth3/2      none
Eth8/1      none
Eth8/2      none
Po1         1,10
```

## CHAPTER 6

VLAN Trunking Protocol

In complex networks, managing VLANs can be time-consuming and error-prone. The VLAN Trunking Protocol (VTP) is a means whereby VLAN names and numbers can be managed at central devices, with the resulting configuration distributed automatically to other devices. Take, for example, the network shown in Figure 6-1. This typical three-tier network is composed completely of Layer-2 switches. There are 12 switches in all: 2 in the core, 4 in the distribution layer, and 6 in the access layer (a real network employing this design might have hundreds of switches).

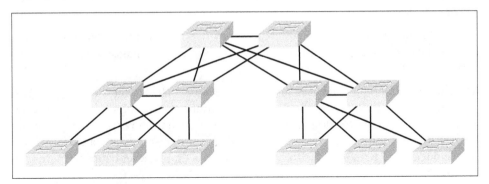

Figure 6-1. Three-tier switched network

Let's assume the network has 10 VLANs throughout the entire design. That's not so bad, right? Here's what a 10-VLAN configuration might look like on a 2950:

```
vlan 10
 name IT
!
vlan 20
 name Personnel
!
vlan 30
 name Accounting
!
vlan 40
```

```
 name Warehouse1
!
vlan 50
 name Warehouse2
!
vlan 60
 name Shipping
!
vlan 70
 name MainOffice
!
vlan 80
 name Receiving
!
vlan 90
 name Lab
!
vlan 100
 name Production
```

Now, consider that every switch in the design needs to have information about every VLAN. To accomplish this, you'll need to enter these commands exactly the same each time into every switch. Sure, you can copy the whole thing into a text file and paste it into each switch, but the process still won't be fun. Look at the VLAN names. There are two warehouses, a lab, a main office—this is a big place! You'll have to haul a laptop and a console cable out to each switch, and the whole process could take quite a while.

Now, add into the equation the possibility that you'll need to add or delete a VLAN at some point or change the name of one of them. You'll have to make the rounds all over again each time there's a change.

I can hear you thinking, "But I can just telnet to each switch to make the changes!" Yes, you can, but when you change the VLAN you're connected through, you'll be back out there working on the consoles—and this time you'll have the foreman threatening you with whatever tool he happened to find along the way because the network's been down since you mucked it up (don't worry; things like that almost never happen...more than once).

While the Telnet approach is an option, you need to be very careful about typos. Human error has to be the primary cause of outages worldwide. Fortunately, there's a better way: VTP.

VTP allows VLAN configurations to be managed on a single switch. Those changes are then propagated to every switch in the VTP domain. A *VTP domain* is a group of connected switches with the same VTP domain string configured. Interconnected switches with differently configured VTP domains will not share VLAN information. A switch can only be in one VTP domain; the VTP domain is null by default.

Switches with mismatched VTP domains will not negotiate trunk protocols. If you wish to establish a trunk between switches with mismatched VTP domains, you must have their trunk ports set to mode trunk. See Chapter 5 for more information.

The main idea of VTP is that changes are made on *VTP servers*. These changes are then propagated to *VTP clients*, and any other VTP servers in the domain. Switches can be configured manually as VTP servers, VTP clients, or the third possibility, *VTP transparent*. A VTP transparent switch receives and forwards VTP updates but does not update its configuration to reflect the changes they contain. Some switches default to VTP server, while others default to VTP transparent. VLANs cannot be locally configured on a switch in client mode.

There is actually a fourth state for a VTP switch: off. A switch in VTP mode off will not accept VTP packets, and therefore will not forward them either. This can be handy if you want to stop the forwarding of VTP updates at some point in the network. VTP mode off is not available on all switches, and is usually seen on large chassis switches like 6500s or Nexus 7000s.

Figure 6-2 shows a simple network with four switches. SW1 and SW2 are both VTP servers. SW3 is set to VTP transparent, and SW4 is a VTP client. Any changes to the VLAN information on SW1 will be propagated to SW2 and SW4. The changes will be passed through SW3 but will not be acted upon by that switch. Because the switch does not act on VTP updates, its VLANs must be configured manually if users on that switch are to interact with the rest of the network.

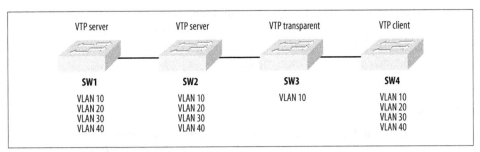

Figure 6-2. VTP modes in action

Looking at Figure 6-2, it is important to understand that both VTP servers can accept and disseminate VLAN information. This leads to an interesting problem. If someone makes a change on SW1, and someone else simultaneously makes a change on SW2, which one wins?

Every time a change is made on a VTP server, the configuration is considered *revised*, and the configuration revision number is incremented by one. When changes are made, the server sends out VTP updates (called *summary advertisements*) containing the revision numbers. The summary advertisements are followed by *subset advertisements*, which contain specific VLAN information.

When a switch receives a VTP update, the first thing it does is compare the VTP domain name in the update to its own. If the domains are different, the update is ignored. If they are the same, the switch compares the update's configuration revision number to its own. If the revision number of the update is lower than or equal to the switch's own revision number, the update is ignored. If the update has a higher revision number, the switch sends an *advertisement request*. The response to this request is another summary advertisement, followed by subset advertisements. Once it has received the subset advertisements, the switch has all the information necessary to implement the required changes in the VLAN configuration.

 When a switch's VTP domain is null, if it receives a VTP advertisement over a trunk link, it will inherit the VTP domain and VLAN configuration from the switch on the other end of the trunk. This will happen only over manually configured trunks, as DTP negotiations cannot take place unless a VTP domain is configured. Be careful of this behavior, as it can cause serious heartache, nausea, and potential job loss if you're not (or the person before you wasn't).

Switches also send advertisement requests when they are reset and when their VTP domains are changed.

To answer the question posed earlier, assuming that both SW1 and SW2 started with the same configuration revision number, whichever switch submits the change first will "win," and have its change propagated throughout the domain, as it will be the first switch to advertise a higher configuration revision number. The changes made on the other switch will be lost, having effectively been overwritten. There will be no indication that these changes were lost or even made.

VTP Pruning

On large or congested networks, VTP can create a problem when excess traffic is sent across trunks needlessly. Take, for example, the network shown in Figure 6-3. The switches in the gray box all have ports assigned to VLAN 100, while the rest of the switches do not. With VTP active, all of the switches will have VLAN 100 configured, and as such will receive broadcasts initiated on that VLAN. However, those without ports assigned to VLAN 100 have no use for the broadcasts.

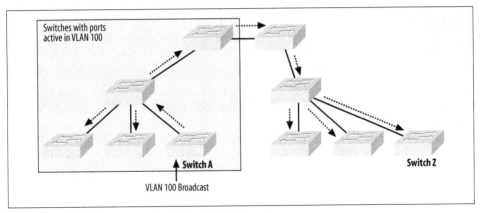

Figure 6-3. Broadcast sent to all switches in VTP domain

On a busy VLAN, broadcasts can amount to a significant percentage of traffic. In this case, all that traffic is being needlessly sent over the entire network, and is taking up valuable bandwidth on the interswitch trunks.

VTP pruning prevents traffic originating from a particular VLAN from being sent to switches on which that VLAN is not *active* (i.e., switches that do not have ports connected and configured for that VLAN). With VTP pruning enabled, the VLAN 100 broadcasts will be restricted to switches on which VLAN 100 is actively in use, as shown in Figure 6-4.

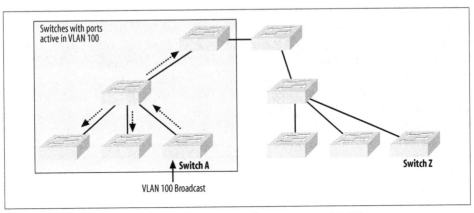

Figure 6-4. VTP pruning limits traffic to switches with active ports in VLANs

 Cisco documentation states that pruning is not designed to work with switches in VTP transparent mode.

Dangers of VTP

VTP offers a lot of advantages, but it can have some pretty serious drawbacks, too, especially if you're not careful.

Imagine a network in an active office. The office is in Manhattan and spans 12 floors in a skyscraper. There is a pair of 6509s in the core, a pair of 4507Rs on each floor in the distribution layer, and 3750 access-layer switches throughout the environment. The total number of switches is close to 100. VTP is deployed with the core 6509s being the only VTP servers. The rest of the switches are all configured as VTP clients. All in all, this is a pretty well-built system, very similar to the one shown in Figure 6-1 (but on a grander scale).

Now, say that somewhere along the way, someone needed some switches for the lab and managed to get a couple of 3750s of his own. These 3750s were installed in the lab but were not connected into the network. For months, the 3750s in the lab stayed as a standalone pair, trunked only to each other. The VLAN configuration was changed often, as is usually the case in a lab environment. More importantly, the lab was created as a mirror of the production network, including the same VTP domain.

Then, months after the 3750s were installed, some knucklehead decided that the lab needed to connect to the main network. He successfully created a trunk to one of the distribution-layer 4507R switches. Within a minute, the entire network was down. Remember the angry foreman with the threatening pipe wrench? He's got nothing on a financial institution's CTO on a rampage!

What went wrong? Remember that many switches are VTP servers by default. Remember, also, that when a switch participating in VTP receives an update that has a higher revision number than its own configuration's revision number, the switch will implement the new scheme. In our scenario, the lab's 3750s had been functioning as a standalone network with the same VTP domain as the regular network. Multiple changes were made to their VLAN configurations, resulting in a high configuration revision number. When these switches, which were VTP servers, were connected to the more stable production network, they automatically sent out updates. Each switch on the main network, including the core 6509s, received an update with a higher revision number than its current configuration. Consequently, they all requested the VLAN configuration from the rogue 3750s and implemented that design.

What's especially scary in this scenario is that the people administering the lab network may not even have been involved in the addition of the rogue 3750s to the production network. If they were involved, they might have recognized the new VLAN scheme as coming from the lab. If not, troubleshooting this problem could take some time.

The lesson here is that VTP can be dangerous if it is not managed well. In some cases, such as in smaller networks that are very stable, VTP should not be used. A good example of a network that should not use VTP is an ecommerce website. Changes to the VLAN design should occur rarely, if ever, so there is little benefit to deploying VTP.

In larger, more dynamic environments where VTP is of use, you must follow proper procedures to ensure that unintended problems do not occur. In the preceding example, security measures such as enabling VTP passwords (discussed in the next section) would probably have prevented the disaster. More importantly, perhaps, connecting rogue switches to a production network should not be allowed without change-control procedures being followed. A good way to prevent the connection of rogue switches is to shut down all switch ports that are not in use. This policy forces people to request that ports be turned up when they want to connect devices to a switch.

Configuring VTP

To use VTP, you must configure a VTP domain. You'll also need to know how to set the mode on your switches. Further configuration options include setting VTP passwords and configuring VTP pruning.

VTP Domains

The default VTP domain is null. Bear this in mind when implementing VTP, because trunks negotiated using the null VTP domain will break if you assign a different domain to one side.

 This behavior differs from switch to switch. For example, the Catalyst 5000 will not negotiate trunks unless a VTP domain has been set for each switch.

On some switches, such as the Cisco 6500, the null domain will be overwritten if a VTP advertisement is received over a trunk link, and the switch will inherit the VTP domain from the advertisement. If a VTP domain has been previously configured, this will not occur.

Also, once you've changed a switch's VTP domain to something other than null, there is no way to change it back to null short of erasing the configuration and rebooting.

IOS

Set or change the VTP domain in IOS with the `vtp domain` command:

```
3750-IOS(config)#vtp domain GAD-Lab
Changing VTP domain name from NULL to GAD-Lab
2w0d: %DTP-5-DOMAINMISMATCH: Unable to perform trunk negotiation on port Gi1/0/20
    because of VTP domain mismatch.
```

In this case, changing the domain results in a VTP domain mismatch that will prevent trunk negotiation from occurring on port G1/0/20.

CatOS

You can set or change the VTP domain on CatOS with the set vtp domain command:

```
Switch1-CatOS# (enable)set vtp domain GAD-Lab
VTP domain GAD-Lab modified
```

In this case, I resolved the trunk issue, so no error was reported. Had my change resulted in a VTP domain mismatch, the switch would have alerted me with a similar message to the one reported on the IOS switch.

NX-OS

VTP is a feature in NX-OS that must be enabled before use (see Chapter 18 for more information on features):

```
NX-7K-1-Daisy(config)# feature vtp
```

As of this writing, Nexus 7000s will only operate in transparent mode, while Nexus 5000s will only operate in VTP mode off. Since the Nexus will not actively participate in VTP, there is no reason to set a VTP password:

```
NX-7K-1-Daisy(config)# vtp mode ?
  transparent  Set the device to transparent mode
```

This Cisco documentation (*http://www.cisco.com/en/US/docs/switches/datacenter/ nexus5000/sw/configuration/guide/cli/VLANs.html*) has this to say about VTP on Nexus 5000s:

> VLAN Trunking Protocol (VTP) mode is OFF. VTP BPDUs are dropped on all interfaces of a Cisco Nexus 5000 Series switch, which partitions VTP domains if other switches have VTP turned on.

You can see details regarding VTP on a Nexus 7000 with the show vtp status command:

```
NX-7K-1-Daisy(config)# sho vtp status
VTP Version                     : 2
Configuration Revision          : 0
Maximum VLANs supported locally : 1005
VTP Operating Mode              : Transparent
VTP Domain Name                 : accounting
VTP Pruning Mode                : Disabled
VTP V2 Mode                     : Enabled
VTP Traps Generation            : Disabled
```

VTP Mode

Chances are, you will need to change the default VTP mode on one or more switches in the VTP domain. When this is the case, you'll need the relevant commands for IOS and CatOS.

IOS

There are three VTP modes on an IOS-based switch: `server`, `client`, and `transparent`. They are set using the `vtp mode` command:

```
3750-IOS(config)#vtp mode ?
  client       Set the device to client mode.
  server       Set the device to server mode.
  transparent  Set the device to transparent mode.
```

Setting a switch to the mode already in use results in an error message:

```
3750-IOS(config)#vtp mode server
Device mode already VTP SERVER.
```

Changing the VTP mode results in a simple message showing your change:

```
3750-IOS(config)#vtp mode transparent
Setting device to VTP TRANSPARENT mode.
```

CatOS

CatOS has an additional mode: `off`. This mode is similar to `transparent` mode in that advertisements are ignored, but they are not forwarded as they would be using `transparent`. The modes are set using the `set vtp mode` command:

```
Switch1-CatOS# (enable)set vtp mode ?
  client            VTP client mode
  off               VTP off
  server            VTP server mode
  transparent       VTP transparent mode
```

Changing the VTP mode on a CatOS switch results in a status message indicating that the VTP domain has been modified:

```
Switch1-CatOS# (enable)set vtp mode transparent
Changing VTP mode for all features
VTP domain GAD-Lab modified
```

Unlike with IOS, setting the mode to the one already in use does not result in an error message.

NX-OS

The only modes available for Nexus are `transparent` and `off`. The 5000 will only run in off and the 7000 will only run in `transparent` mode. As a result, the modes cannot be changed:

```
NX-7K-1-Cozy(config)# vtp mode ?
  transparent  Set the device to transparent mode
```

VTP Password

Setting a VTP password ensures that only switches configured with the same VTP password will be affected by VTP advertisements.

IOS

In IOS, you can set a password for VTP with the `vtp password` command:

```
3750-IOS(config)#vtp password MilkBottle
Setting device VLAN database password to MilkBottle
```

There is no option to encrypt the password, but the password is not displayed in the configuration. To show the password, execute the `show vtp password` command from the enable prompt:

```
3750-IOS#sho vtp password
VTP Password: MilkBottle
```

To remove the VTP password, negate the command:

```
3750-IOS(config)#no vtp password
Clearing device VLAN database password.
```

CatOS

Set the password for VTP in CatOS with the `set vtp passwd` command:

```
Switch1-CatOS# (enable)set vtp passwd MilkBottle
Generating the secret associated to the password.
VTP domain GAD-Lab modified
```

To encrypt the password so it cannot be read in the configuration, append the word hidden to the command:

```
Switch1-CatOS# (enable)set vtp passwd MilkBottle hidden
Generating the secret associated to the password.
The VTP password will not be shown in the configuration.
VTP domain GAD-Lab modified
```

To clear the password on a CatOS switch, set the password to the number zero:

```
Switch1-CatOS# (enable)set vtp passwd 0
Resetting the password to Default value.
VTP domain GAD-Lab modified
```

NX-OS

NX-OS does not support VTP passwords, since the switches only run in transparent or off mode.

VTP Pruning

VTP pruning must be enabled or disabled throughout the entire VTP domain. Failure to configure VTP pruning properly can result in instability in the network.

By default, all VLANs up to VLAN 1001 are eligible for pruning, except VLAN 1, which can never be pruned. VTP does not support the extended VLANs above VLAN 1001, so VLANs higher than 1001 cannot be pruned. CatOS allows the pruning of VLANs 2–1000.

If you enable VTP pruning on a VTP server, VTP pruning will automatically be enabled for the entire domain.

IOS

VTP pruning is enabled with the **vtp pruning** command on IOS. This can only be done when in VTP server mode:

```
3750-IOS(config)#vtp pruning
Pruning switched on
```

Disabling VTP pruning is done by negating the command (no vtp pruning).

To show which VLANs are eligible for pruning on a trunk, execute the show inter face *interface-id* switchport command:

```
3750-IOS#sho int g1/0/15 switchport
Name: Gi1/0/15
Switchport: Enabled
Administrative Mode: dynamic auto
Operational Mode: down
Administrative Trunking Encapsulation: negotiate
Negotiation of Trunking: On
Access Mode VLAN: 1 (default)
Trunking Native Mode VLAN: 1 (default)
Administrative Native VLAN tagging: enabled
Voice VLAN: none
Administrative private-vlan host-association: none
Administrative private-vlan mapping: none
Administrative private-vlan trunk native VLAN: none
Administrative private-vlan trunk Native VLAN tagging: enabled
Administrative private-vlan trunk encapsulation: dot1q
Administrative private-vlan trunk normal VLANs: none
Administrative private-vlan trunk associations: none
Administrative private-vlan trunk mappings: none
Operational private-vlan: none
Trunking VLANs Enabled: ALL
Pruning VLANs Enabled: 2-1001
Capture Mode Disabled
Capture VLANs Allowed: ALL

Protected: false
Unknown unicast blocked: disabled
Unknown multicast blocked: disabled
Appliance trust: none
```

You configure which VLANs are eligible for pruning at the interface level in IOS. Use the command switchport trunk pruning vlan on each trunking interface on the switch where pruning is desired:

```
3750-IOS(config-if)#switchport trunk pruning vlan ?
  WORD    VLAN IDs of the allowed VLANs when this port is in trunking mode
  add     add VLANs to the current list
  except  all VLANs except the following
```

```
none    no VLANs
remove  remove VLANs from the current list
```

All VLANs are eligible for pruning by default. If you configure VLAN 100 to be eligible for pruning, IOS considers this to mean *only* VLAN 100 should be eligible:

```
3750-IOS(config-if)#switchport trunk pruning vlan 100
```

No message is displayed indicating that you have just disabled pruning for VLANs 2–99 and 101–1001. You have to look at the interface again to see:

```
3750-IOS#sho int g1/0/15 switchport | inc Pruning
Pruning VLANs Enabled: 100
```

You can add VLANs to the list of pruning-eligible VLANs with the add keyword and remove them with the remove keyword:

```
3750-IOS(config-if)#switchport trunk pruning vlan add 20-30
3750-IOS(config-if)#switchport trunk pruning vlan remove 30
```

You can also specify that all VLANs except one or more that you list be made eligible for pruning with the switchport trunk pruning vlan except *vlan-id* command.

Remember to double-check your work with the show interface *interface-id* switch port command. Adding and removing VLANs can quickly get confusing, especially with IOS managing VTP pruning on an interface basis.

CatOS

CatOS gives you a nice warning about running VTP in the entire domain when you enable VTP pruning. Pruning is enabled with the set vtp pruning enable command:

```
Switch1-CatOS# (enable)set vtp pruning enable
This command will enable the pruning function in the entire management domain.
All devices in the management domain should be pruning-capable before enabling.
Do you want to continue (y/n) [n]? y
VTP domain GAD-Lab modified
```

Disabling pruning results in a similar prompt. To disable VTP pruning on CatOS, use the set vtp pruning disable command:

```
Switch1-CatOS# (enable)set vtp pruning disable
This command will disable the pruning function in the entire management domain.
Do you want to continue (y/n) [n]? y
VTP domain GAD-Lab modified
```

Once pruning has been enabled, VLANs 2–1000 are eligible for pruning by default. To remove a VLAN from the list of eligible VLANs, use the clear vtp pruneeligible command. Unlike IOS, CatOS manages pruning-eligible VLANs on a switch level as opposed to an interface level:

```
Switch1-CatOS# (enable)clear vtp pruneeligible 100
Vlans 1,100,1001-4094 will not be pruned on this device.
VTP domain GAD-Lab modified.
```

To add a VLAN back into the list of VLANs eligible for pruning, use the set vtp
pruneeligible command:

```
Switch1-CatOS# (enable)set vtp pruneeligible 100
Vlans 2-1000 eligible for pruning on this device.
VTP domain GAD-Lab modified.
```

NX-OS

NX-OS does not support VTP pruning, since the switches only run in modes
transparent or off.

## CHAPTER 7

Link Aggregation

EtherChannel

EtherChannel is the Cisco term for the technology that enables the bonding of up to eight physical Ethernet links into a single logical link. Cisco originally called Ether-Channel *Fast EtherChannel* (FEC), as it was only available on Fast Ethernet at the time. The technology is also called *Gigabit EtherChannel* (GEC), or more generically, just *Port Channel*. The non-Cisco term used for link aggregation is generally *Link Aggregation*, or LAG for short.

With EtherChannel, the single logical link's speed is equal to the aggregate of the speeds of all the physical links used. For example, if you were to create an EtherChannel out of four 100 Mbps Ethernet links, the EtherChannel would have a speed of 400 Mbps. This sounds great, and it is, but the idea is not without problems. For one thing, the increased capacity is not truly the aggregate of the physical link speeds in all situations. For example, on an EtherChannel composed of four 1 Gbps links, each conversation will still be limited to 1 Gbps by default.

The default behavior is to assign one of the physical links to each packet that traverses the EtherChannel, based on the packet's destination MAC address. This means that if one workstation talks to one server over an EtherChannel, only one of the physical links will be used. In fact, all of the traffic destined for that server will traverse a single physical link in the EtherChannel. This means that a single user will only ever get 1 Gbps from the EtherChannel at a time. This behavior can be changed to send each packet over a different physical link, but as you'll see, there are limits to how well this works for applications like VoIP. The benefit arises when there are multiple destinations, which can each use a different path.

EtherChannels are referenced by different names in NX-OS, IOS, and CatOS. As Figure 7-1 shows, on a switch running CatOS, an EtherChannel is called a *channel*, while on a switch running IOS or NX-OS, an EtherChannel is called a *port channel interface*. The command to configure an EtherChannel on CatOS is `set port channel`, and the commands to view channels include `show port channel` and `show channel`.

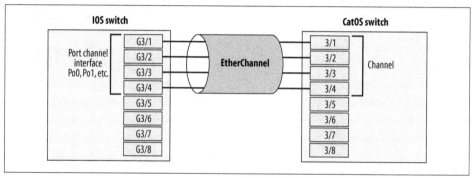

Figure 7-1. EtherChannel on IOS and CatOS

EtherChannels on IOS and NX-OS switches are actually virtual interfaces, and they are referenced like any other interfaces (for example, `interface port-channel 0` or `int po0`).

There is another terminology problem that can create many headaches for network administrators. While a group of physical Ethernet links bonded together is called an *EtherChannel* in Cisco parlance, Unix admins sometimes refer to the same configuration as a *trunk*. Of course, in the Cisco world the term "trunk" refers to something completely different: a link that labels frames with VLAN information so that multiple VLANs can traverse it. Some modern Unixes sometimes create a *bond* interface when performing link aggregation, and Windows admins often use the term *teaming* when combining links.

EtherChannel Load Balancing

As stated earlier, EtherChannel, by default, does not truly provide the aggregate speed of the included physical links. EtherChannel gives the *perceived* speed of the combined links by passing certain packets through certain physical links. By default, the physical link used for each packet is determined using the packet's destination MAC address. The algorithm used is Cisco-proprietary, but it is deterministic in that packets with the same destination MAC address will always travel over the same physical link. This ensures that packets sent to a single destination MAC address never arrive out of order.

The hashing algorithm for determining the physical link to be used may not be public, but the weighting of the links used in the algorithm is published. What is important here is the fact that a perfect balance between the physical links is not necessarily assured.

The hashing algorithm takes the destination MAC address (or another value, as you'll see later), and hashes that value to a number in the range of 0–7. The same range is used regardless of how many links are actually in the EtherChannel. Each physical link is assigned one or more of these eight values, depending on how many links are in the EtherChannel. This is why there is a maximum of eight physical links in an EtherChannel.

Figure 7-2 shows how packets are distributed according to this method. Notice that the distribution is not always even. This is important to understand, because link usage statistics—especially graphs—will bear it out.

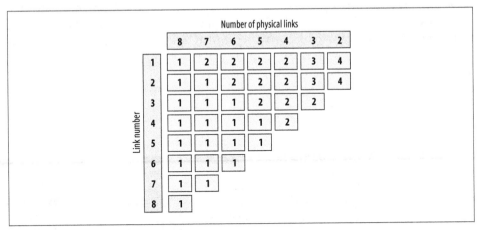

Figure 7-2. *EtherChannel physical link balancing*

On an EtherChannel with eight physical links, each link is assigned a single value. On an EtherChannel with six links, two of the links are assigned two values, and the remaining four links are each assigned one value. This means two of the links (assuming a theoretical perfect distribution) will receive twice as much traffic as the other four. Having an EtherChannel thus does not imply that all links are used equally. Indeed, it should be obvious looking at Figure 7-2 that the only possible way to distribute traffic equally across all links in an EtherChannel (again, assuming a perfect distribution) is to design one with eight, four, or two physical links. Regardless of the information used to determine the link, the method will still hash the value to a number in the range of 0–7, which will be used to assign a link according to this table.

You can change the method the switch uses to determine which path to assign. The default behavior is to use the destination MAC address. However, depending on the version of the software and hardware in use, the options may include:

- The source MAC address
- The destination MAC address
- The source and destination MAC addresses
- The source IP address
- The destination IP address
- The source and destination IP addresses
- The source port
- The destination port

- The source and destination ports

The reasons for changing the default behavior vary by circumstance. Figure 7-3 shows a relatively common layout: a group of users connected to Switch A reach a group of servers on Switch B through an EtherChannel. By default, the load-balancing method will be based on the destination MAC address in each packet. The issue here is one of usage patterns. You might think that with the MAC addresses being unique, the links will be used equally. However, the reality is that it is very common for one server to receive a good deal more traffic than others.

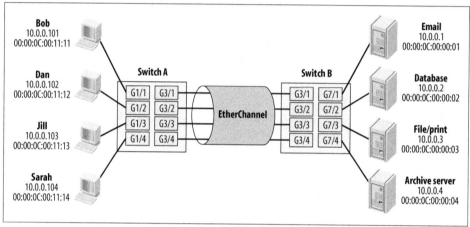

Figure 7-3. EtherChannel load-balancing factors

Let's assume the email server in this network is receiving more than 1 Gbps of traffic, while the other servers average about 50 Mbps. Using the destination MAC address method will cause packets to be lost on the EtherChannel, because every packet destined for the email server's MAC address will ride on the same physical link within the EtherChannel. Overflow does not spill over to the other links—when a physical link becomes saturated, packets are dropped.

 This point deserves a special note. I've seen many networking engineers, some with years of experience, who firmly believe that an EtherChannel will automatically spill traffic over from one physical link to another when the first link becomes oversubscribed. This is not the case.

In the case of one server receiving the lion's share of the traffic, destination MAC address load balancing does not make sense. Given this scenario, balancing with the source MAC address might make more sense.

Another important point to remember is that the load-balancing method is only applied to packets being *transmitted* over the EtherChannel. This is not a two-way function. While changing the method to the source MAC address on Switch A might be a good idea, it would be a terrible idea on Switch B, given that the email server is the most-used server. Remember, when packets are being returned from the email server, the source MAC address is that of the email server itself. So, if we use the source MAC address to determine load balancing on Switch B, we'll end up with the same problem we were trying to solve.

In this circumstance, the solution is to have the source MAC address load balancing on Switch A and the destination MAC address load balancing on Switch B. If all your servers are on one switch and all your users are on another, as in this example, this solution will work. Unfortunately, the real world seldom provides such simple problems. A far more common scenario is that all of the devices are connected in one large switch, such as a 6509. Changing the load-balancing algorithm is done on a chassis-wide basis, so with all the devices connected to a single switch, you're out of luck.

Figure 7-4 shows an interesting problem. Here we have a single server connected to Switch A via an EtherChannel, and a single network attached storage (NAS) device that is also attached to Switch A via an EtherChannel. All of the filesystems for the server are mounted on the NAS device, and the server is heavily used—it's a database server that serves more than 5,000 users at any given time. The bandwidth required between the server and the NAS device is in excess of 2 Gbps.

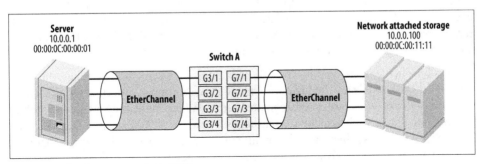

Figure 7-4. Single server to single NAS

Unfortunately, there is no easy solution to this problem. We can't use the destination MAC address or the source MAC address for load balancing, because in each case there is only one address, and it will always be the same. For the same reason, we can't use a combination of source and destination MAC addresses or the source and/or destination IP addresses. And we can't use the source or destination port numbers, because once they're negotiated, they don't change. One possibility, assuming the drivers support it, is to change the server and/or NAS device so each link has its own MAC address, but the packets will still be sourced from and destined for only one of those addresses.

The only solutions for this problem are manual load balancing or faster links. Splitting the link into four 1 Gbps links, each with its own IP network, and mounting different filesystems on each link will solve the problem. However, that's too complicated for my tastes. A better solution, if available, might be to use a faster physical link, such as 10 Gbps Ethernet.

Configuring and Managing EtherChannel

The device on the other end of the EtherChannel is usually the determining factor in how the EtherChannel is configured. One design rule that must always be applied is that each link participating in an EtherChannel must have the same configuration. The descriptions can be different, but all of the physical links must be the same type and speed, and they must all be in the same VLAN. If they are trunks, they must all be configured with the same trunk parameters.

EtherChannel protocols

EtherChannel can negotiate with the device on the other side of the link. Two protocols are supported on Cisco devices. The first is the Link Aggregation Control Protocol (LACP), which is defined in IEEE specification 802.3ad. LACP is used when you're connecting to non-Cisco devices, such as servers. The other protocol used in negotiating EtherChannel links is the Port Aggregation Control Protocol (PAgP). Since PAgP is Cisco-proprietary, it is used only when you're connecting two Cisco devices via an EtherChannel. Each protocol supports two modes: a passive mode (auto in PAgP and passive in LACP), and an active mode (desirable in PAgP and active in LACP). Alternatively, you can set the mode to on, thus forcing the creation of the EtherChannel. The available protocols and modes are outlined in Figure 7-5.

Generally, when you are configuring EtherChannels between Cisco switches, the ports will be EtherChannels for the life of the installation. Setting all interfaces in the EtherChannel on both sides to desirable makes sense. When connecting a Cisco switch to a non-Cisco device such as a Unix machine, use the active LACP setting. Also be aware that some devices use their own channeling methods and require the Cisco side of the EtherChannel to be set to on because they don't negotiate with the other sides of the links.

CatOS example

Creating an EtherChannel in CatOS is relatively straightforward once you know what you need. As an example, we'll create the EtherChannel shown in Figure 7-1. Because the devices on both sides are Cisco switches, we will configure the ports on both sides to be desirable (running PAgP and initiating negotiation):

```
set port name        3/1  Link #1 in Channel
set port name        3/2  Link #2 in Channel
set port name        3/3  Link #3 in Channel
set port name        3/4  Link #4 in Channel

set vlan 20    3/1-4

set port channel 3/1-4 mode desirable
```

Assuming the other side is set properly, this is all we need to get an EtherChannel
working. The names are not necessary, of course, but everything should be labeled and
documented regardless of perceived need.

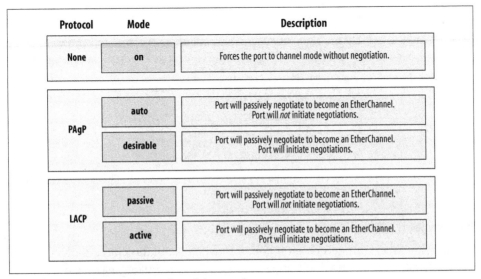

Figure 7-5. EtherChannel protocols and their modes

Now that we've configured an EtherChannel, we need to be able to check on its status.
First, let's look at the output of show port channel:

```
Switch-2-CatOS: (enable)sho port channel
Port  Status      Channel              Admin Ch
                  Mode                 Group Id
----- ----------  -------------------- ----- -----
 3/1 connected   desirable              74   770
 3/2 connected   desirable              74   770
 3/3 connected   desirable              74   770
 3/4 connected   desirable              74   770
```

The show channel info command shows a very similar output to show port channel,
but contains even more information. In most cases, this command is far more useful,
as it shows the channel ID, admin group, interface type, duplex mode, and VLAN
assigned all in one display:

```
Switch-2-CatOS: (enable)sho channel info
Chan Port  Status      Channel                Admin Speed Duplex Vlan
id                     mode                   group
---- ----- ----------  --------------------   ----- ----- ------ ----
 770  3/1  connected   desirable                 74 a-1Gb a-full   20
 770  3/2  connected   desirable                 74 a-1Gb a-full   20
 770  3/3  connected   desirable                 74 a-1Gb a-full   20
 770  3/4  connected   desirable                 74 a-1Gb a-full   20
```

The show channel command shows a very brief output indicating which ports are assigned to which channels:

```
Switch-2-CatOS: (enable)sho channel
Channel Id   Ports
-----------  ---------------------------------------------------
770          3/1-4
```

show channel traffic is another very useful command. This command shows how the
links have been used, with the traffic distribution reported as actual percentages:

```
Switch-2-CatOS: (enable)sho channel traffic
ChanId Port  Rx-Ucst Tx-Ucst Rx-Mcst Tx-Mcst Rx-Bcst Tx-Bcst
------ ----- ------- ------- ------- ------- ------- -------
   770  3/1   21.80%  18.44%  87.48%  87.70%  26.49%  21.20%
   770  3/2   34.49%  37.97%   4.02%   4.98%  19.38%  11.73%
   770  3/3   21.01%  23.47%   3.99%   3.81%  29.46%  28.60%
   770  3/4   22.66%  20.06%   4.13%   2.79%  23.69%  38.32%
```

Notice that the percentages do not always add up to 100 percent. This tool is not about
specifics, but rather trends.

IOS example

Configuring EtherChannels on an IOS-based switch is not difficult, although, as discussed earlier, if you're used to CatOS switches, the terminology may seem a bit odd.
The major difference is that a port-channel virtual interface is created. This actually
gives you a lot of leeway: you can configure this interface with an IP address if you wish
(assuming your switch supports Layer 3), or just leave it as a normal switch port. Remember that each interface must be configured with identical settings, with the exception of the description. I like to configure meaningful descriptions on all my physical
ports. This helps keep me track of how the interfaces are assigned, as the show inter
face command does not indicate whether an interface is a member of an EtherChannel.

Again, we'll design the EtherChannel shown in Figure 7-1 as an example, so there are
Cisco switches on both sides of the links:

```
interface Port-channel1
 description 4G Etherchannel Po1
 no ip address
 switchport
 switchport access vlan 20

interface GigabitEthernet3/1
 description Link #1 in Po1
```

```
 no ip address
 switchport
 channel-group 1 mode desirable

interface GigabitEthernet3/2
 description Link #2 in Po1
 no ip address
 switchport
 channel-group 1 mode desirable

interface GigabitEthernet3/3
 description Link #3 in Po1
 no ip address
 switchport
 channel-group 1 mode desirable

interface GigabitEthernet3/4
 description Link #4 in Po1
 no ip address
 switchport
 channel-group 1 mode desirable
```

On IOS switches, the quick way to see the status of an EtherChannel is to use the show
etherchannel summary command. CatOS users may be frustrated by the complexity of
the output. First, you must figure out the codes, as outlined in the included legend;
then, you can determine the status of your EtherChannel. In this example, the Ether-
Channel is Layer2 and is in use (Po1(SU)). The individual physical links are all active,
as they have (P) next to their port numbers:

```
Switch-1-IOS#sho etherchannel summary
Flags:  D - down         P - in port-channel
        I - stand-alone s - suspended
        H - Hot-standby (LACP only)
        R - Layer3       S - Layer2
        U - in use       f - failed to allocate aggregator

        u - unsuitable for bundling
Number of channel-groups in use: 1
Number of aggregators:           1

Group  Port-channel  Protocol    Ports
------+-------------+-----------+-------------------------------------------------
1      Po1(SU)       PAgP        Gi3/1(P)  Gi3/2(P)   Gi3/3(P)    Gi3/4(P)
```

A more useful command, though missing the real status of the interfaces, is the show
etherchannel command. This command is interesting in that it shows the number of
bits used in the hash algorithm for each physical interface, as illustrated previously in
Figure 7-3. Also of interest in this command's output is the fact that it displays the last
time at which an interface joined the EtherChannel:

```
Switch-1-IOS #sho etherchannel 1 port-channel
                Port-channels in the group:
                ---------------------
```

```
Port-channel: Po1
------------

Age of the Port-channel    = 1d:09h:22m:37s
Logical slot/port    = 14/6          Number of ports = 4
GC                   = 0x00580001    HotStandBy port = null
Port state           = Port-channel Ag-Inuse
Protocol             =    PAgP

Ports in the Port-channel:

Index  Load   Port    EC state           No of bits
------+------+------+------------------+-----------
  1     11    Gi3/1   Desirable-Sl      2
  2     22    Gi3/2   Desirable-Sl      2
  0     44    Gi3/3   Desirable-Sl      2
  3     88    Gi3/4   Desirable-Sl      2

Time since last port bundled:    1d:09h:21m:08s   Gi3/4
```

Because EtherChannels are assigned virtual interfaces on IOS, you can show the interface information as if it were a physical or virtual interface. Notice that the bandwidth is set to the aggregate speed of the links in use, but the duplex line shows the interface as Full-duplex, 1000Mb/s. The hardware is listed as EtherChannel, and there is a line in the output identifying the members of this EtherChannel as Gi3/1, Gi3/2, Gi3/3, and Gi3/4:

```
Switch-1-IOS#sho int port-channel 1
Port-channel1 is up, line protocol is up (connected)
  Hardware is EtherChannel, address is 0011.720a.711d (bia 0011.720a.711d)
  Description: 4G Etherchannel Po1
  MTU 1500 bytes, BW 4000000 Kbit, DLY 10 usec,
     reliability 255/255, txload 1/255, rxload 1/255
  Encapsulation ARPA, loopback not set
  Full-duplex, 1000Mb/s
  input flow-control is off, output flow-control is unsupported
  Members in this channel: Gi3/1 Gi3/2 Gi3/3 Gi3/4
  ARP type: ARPA, ARP Timeout 04:00:00
  Last input never, output never, output hang never
  Last clearing of "show interface" counters 30w6d
  Input queue: 0/2000/1951/0 (size/max/drops/flushes); Total output drops: 139
  Queueing strategy: fifo
  Output queue: 0/40 (size/max)
  5 minute input rate 3906000 bits/sec, 628 packets/sec
  5 minute output rate 256000 bits/sec, 185 packets/sec
     377045550610 packets input, 410236657639149 bytes, 0 no buffer
     Received 66730119 broadcasts (5743298 multicast)
     0 runts, 0 giants, 0 throttles
     0 input errors, 0 CRC, 0 frame, 1951 overrun, 0 ignored
     0 watchdog, 0 multicast, 0 pause input
     0 input packets with dribble condition detected
     255121177828 packets output, 159098829342337 bytes, 0 underruns
     0 output errors, 0 collisions, 0 interface resets
     0 babbles, 0 late collision, 0 deferred
```

```
    0 lost carrier, 0 no carrier, 0 PAUSE output
    0 output buffer failures, 0 output buffers swapped out
```

Because the individual links are physical, these interfaces can be shown in the same manner as any physical interface on an IOS device via the show interface command:

```
Switch-1-IOS#sho int g3/1
GigabitEthernet5/1 is up, line protocol is up (connected)
  Hardware is C6k 1000Mb 802.3, address is 0011.7f1a.791c (bia 0011.7f1a.791c)
  Description: Link #1 in Po1
  MTU 1500 bytes, BW 1000000 Kbit, DLY 10 usec,
     reliability 255/255, txload 1/255, rxload 1/255
  Encapsulation ARPA, loopback not set
  Full-duplex, 1000Mb/s
  input flow-control is off, output flow-control is off
  Clock mode is auto
  ARP type: ARPA, ARP Timeout 04:00:00
  Last input 00:00:45, output 00:00:03, output hang never
  Last clearing of "show interface" counters 30w6d
  Input queue: 0/2000/1054/0 (size/max/drops/flushes); Total output drops: 0
  Queueing strategy: fifo
  Output queue: 0/40 (size/max)
  5 minute input rate 924000 bits/sec, 187 packets/sec
  5 minute output rate 86000 bits/sec, 70 packets/sec
     190820216609 packets input, 207901078937384 bytes, 0 no buffer
     Received 48248427 broadcasts (1757046 multicast)
     0 runts, 0 giants, 0 throttles
     0 input errors, 0 CRC, 0 frame, 1054 overrun, 0 ignored
     0 watchdog, 0 multicast, 0 pause input
     0 input packets with dribble condition detected
     129274163672 packets output, 80449383231904 bytes, 0 underruns
     0 output errors, 0 collisions, 0 interface resets
     0 babbles, 0 late collision, 0 deferred
     0 lost carrier, 0 no carrier, 0 PAUSE output
     0 output buffer failures, 0 output buffers swapped out
```

Notice that the output does not mention the fact that the interface is a member of an EtherChannel, other than in the description. This reinforces the notion that all ports should be labeled with the description command.

NX-OS example

You create and manage port channels in NX-OS in almost the same way as in IOS:

```
NX-7K-1-Cozy(config)# int e3/10-11
NX-7K-1-Cozy(config-if-range)# channel-group 10
```

Once the channel group is created, we can view it with the show interface command:

```
NX-7K-1-Cozy(config-if-range)# sho int po 10
port-channel10 is down (No operational members)
  Hardware: Port-Channel, address: 0026.9807.95c2 (bia 0000.0000.0000)
  MTU 1500 bytes, BW 100000 Kbit, DLY 10 usec,
     reliability 255/255, txload 1/255, rxload 1/255
  Encapsulation ARPA
  auto-duplex, auto-speed
```

```
Input flow-control is off, output flow-control is off
Switchport monitor is off
Members in this channel: Eth3/10, Eth3/11
Last clearing of "show interface" counters never
30 seconds input rate 0 bits/sec, 0 packets/sec
30 seconds output rate 0 bits/sec, 0 packets/sec
Load-Interval #2: 5 minute (300 seconds)
  input rate 0 bps, 0 pps; output rate 0 bps, 0 pps
L3 in Switched:
  ucast: 0 pkts, 0 bytes - mcast: 0 pkts, 0 bytes
L3 out Switched:
  ucast: 0 pkts, 0 bytes - mcast: 0 pkts, 0 bytes
RX
  0 unicast packets  0 multicast packets  0 broadcast packets
  0 input packets  0 bytes
  0 jumbo packets  0 storm suppression packets
  0 runts  0 giants  0 CRC  0 no buffer
  0 input error  0 short frame  0 overrun  0 underrun  0 ignored
  0 watchdog  0 bad etype drop  0 bad proto drop  0 if down drop
  0 input with dribble  0 input discard
  0 Rx pause
TX
  0 unicast packets  0 multicast packets  0 broadcast packets
  0 output packets  0 bytes
  0 jumbo packets
  0 output error  0 collision  0 deferred  0 late collision
  0 lost carrier  0 no carrier  0 babble
  0 Tx pause
0 interface resets
```

A cool command to see which links are part of which port channels is `show interface brief`. This is not the `show ip interface brief` command that you may be accustomed to using. Check out the last column, which displays what port channel each interface is associated with:

```
NX-7K-1-Cozy(config-if-range)# sho int brie
```

Ethernet Interface	VLAN	Type	Mode	Status	Reason	Speed	Port Ch #
Eth3/1	1	eth	trunk	down	Link not connected	auto(D)	--
Eth3/2	10	eth	access	down	Link not connected	auto(D)	--
Eth3/3	--	eth	routed	down	Administratively down	auto(D)	--
Eth3/4	--	eth	routed	down	Administratively down	auto(D)	--
Eth3/5	--	eth	routed	down	Administratively down	auto(D)	--
Eth3/6	--	eth	routed	down	Administratively down	auto(D)	--
Eth3/7	--	eth	routed	down	Administratively down	auto(D)	--
Eth3/8	--	eth	routed	down	Administratively down	auto(D)	--
Eth3/9	--	eth	routed	down	Administratively down	auto(D)	--
Eth3/10	**--**	**eth**	**routed**	**down**	**Administratively down**	**auto(D)**	**10**
Eth3/11	**--**	**eth**	**routed**	**down**	**Administratively down**	**auto(D)**	**10**
Eth3/12	--	eth	routed	down	Administratively down	auto(D)	--

```
[-- output truncated --]
```

These commands are great, but they come at a price. The `show etherchannel` commands you may be used to from IOS are not available on NX-OS, at least as of this writing.

Cross-Stack EtherChannel

Sometimes you can create an EtherChannel across two physical switches. For example, when 3750s are stacked, the stack becomes a single logical entity and each physical switch acts like a blade. Configuring an EtherChannel across two physical switches in the stack is possible, and even recommended to eliminate single physical failure points. Nothing special is required to accomplish this once the stack has been configured— just configure each port to be in the same port-channel group:

```
3750-IOS(config)#int range g1/0/1 , g2/0/1
3750-IOS(config-if-range)#channel-group 10 mode on
Creating a port-channel interface Port-channel 10
```

Cisco calls this *cross-stack EtherChannel*, and it has some interesting capabilities and limitations. For example, you can have 16 ports in a cross-stack EtherChannel, with 8 active and 8 in standby. You cannot use PAgP, though, so your modes are confined to `active`, `passive`, and `on`.

Multichassis EtherChannel (MEC)

Multichassis EtherChannel (MEC) is very similar to cross-stack EtherChannel in principle. The difference is that the feature known as MEC is found on the Catalyst 6500 VSS switches. VSS is a clustering technology that allows multiple 6500 chassis to be configured as a single logical switch. This is similar in principle to a 3750 switch stack. For MEC to be possible, VSS must be properly configured and the switches active in the VSS cluster. See Chapter 17 for more information on VSS configuration.

Once VSS is running, creating MECs is as easy as it is on 3750s. Here, I've created a 20 Gb MEC between two 6500s clustered with VSS:

```
VSS(config)#int range ten 1/3/2 , ten 2/3/2
VSS(config-if-range)#channel-group 500 mode on
```

Virtual Port Channel

Virtual Port Channel (vPC) is the multichassis port-channel solution for Nexus switches. While the end result is similar, the method used is significantly different than MEC. The main difference has to do with the fact you cannot cluster multiple Nexus switches into a VSS pair the way you can with 6500 VSS switches. Having multiple physical links connecting to two physical switches appear as a single logical link is complicated, and it can take some getting used to when you start to work with the technology. The logical differences are shown in Figure 7-6.

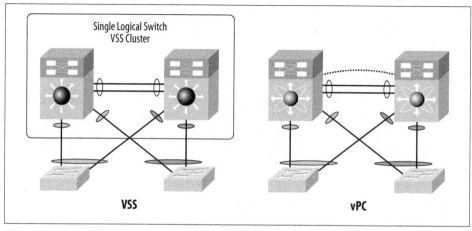

Figure 7-6. VSS MEC versus Nexus vPC

VSS and vPC accomplish the same goal, but in vastly different ways. With VSS, a cluster is configured so that two physical 6500s appear to be a single logical switch (single control plane, single data plane). With Nexus and vPC, the Nexus 5000 or 7000 switches remain separate physical and logical entities (separate control plane, single data plane). The EtherChannel terminates to two separate physical switches on the network side while appearing to be connected to one logical device. If that sounds confusing, that's because it is. The good news is that once it clicks, it's pretty straightforward and easy to configure.

While MEC relies on the VSS cluster to be up and running, vPC requires specific vPC features to be enabled and configured on the Nexus switches. This original configuration only needs to be done once for each switch in the pair, after which multiple vPCs can be configured with relative ease.

Initial vPC Configuration

The following steps are required for each of the two Nexus switches that will take part in the vPC. There can be only two Nexus switches in a vPC as of this writing.

First, enable the vPC feature with the feature vpc command:

```
NX-5k-1(config)# feature vpc
```

Before configuring anything else regarding vPCs, you must first establish a vPC domain. The domain number must match for all switches working with the configured vPCs:

```
NX-5K-1(config-if)# vpc domain 1
```

vPCs require a link between the vPC peer switches, called a *peer keepalive link*. This link is in addition to the port channel between the switches in which the VLAN trunks ride. The peer keepalive link must be a routed link, in that an IP address is used on each side. The link can be over an existing IP network, but Cisco suggests that it be established over the management interface. This is especially important on the Nexus 5000s, since there are no Layer-3 interfaces except for the management interface. I'm not a huge fan of putting what amounts to critical (criticality is in the eye of the be-holder) connections on the management network, but this example shows how to do so. The management VRF is used by default on the 5000 (see Chapter 18 for more information regarding VRFs):

```
NX-5K-1(config-vpc)# peer-keepalive destination 10.10.10.2
```

On a Nexus 7000, this link can be any interface, since they all default to routing mode anyway. Here is the configuration for a point-to-point link between two Nexus 7000s. First we configure NX-7K-1:

```
NX-7K-1(config-if-range)# int e3/1
NX-7K-1(config-if)# ip address 10.255.255.1/24

NX-7K-1 (config-vpc-domain)# peer-keepalive destination 10.255.255.2
```

And now the other switch, named NX-7K-2:

```
NX-7K-2(config-if-range)# int e3/1
NX-7K-2(config-if)# ip address 10.255.255.2/24

NX-7K-2 (config-vpc-domain)# peer-keepalive destination 10.255.255.1
```

vPC requires that a link—preferably a trunk—between the vPC peers be defined as a peer link. This link will be used for the traversal of traffic necessary to utilize the ether channel. Generally, this link is the main interswitch link between the two switches. The vPC peer link must be a multi–10 G bps EtherChannel according to the documentation, but of course it will work with only one physical link. This command is the same on both the 5000 and the 7000. Here, port channel 1 is used as the peer link:

```
NX-5K-1(config-if)# int po 1
NX-5K-1(config-if)# vpc peer-link

Please note that spanning tree port type is changed to "network" port type on vPC
peer-link.This will enable spanning tree Bridge Assurance on vPC peer-link provided
the STP Bridge Assurance (which is enabled by default) is not disabled.
```

A vPC domain is the area in which vPCs reside. The domain must be the same for each switch participating in the vPC. Remember, there can be only two switches in the do-main. In our example, each 5K is assigned vPC Domain 1.

This may seem daunting, but the good news is that all of these vPC commands need only be entered once. Once the pair of Nexus switches is configured to support vPCs, adding a vPC is very simple.

Adding a vPC

With everything else ready to go, the EtherChannels on each 5K that are to be linked into a single vDC must be tagged with a vPC ID. The ID is up to you, but a good rule to follow is to tag the EtherChannel with the same number as the channel itself.

Technically, you could bond port channel 10 on 5K1 with port channel 20 on 5K2, and tag it with vPC ID 30, but if you do, every networking engineer who works on the switches after you will want to hunt you down and kill you. Let's endeavor to keep them all the same.

First the configuration on NX-5K-1:

```
NX-5K-1(config)# int po 10
NX-5K-1(config-if)#vpc 10
```

And the same configuration on NX-5K-2:

```
NX-5K-2(config)# int po 10
NX-5K-2(config-if)#vpc 10
```

Though the concept can be difficult to grasp, once you've set up the original vPC architecture, the configuration for adding a vPC is that simple. There are limitations with vPCs that we'll see in Chapter 18, the most important having to do with how fabric extenders are connected.

Since vPCs create a single data link across two separate switches, the switches must agree that the vPC is possible. To do so, they communicate with each other and will refuse to bring up a vPC if the two switches are configured differently. Luckily, there is a quick way to see if there is a problem. Using the show vpc consistency-parame ters command will show you if there's a problem that's keeping your vPC from coming up. The global version will show you system settings that need to match:

```
NX-5K-1# sho vpc consistency-parameters global

    Legend:
        Type 1 : vPC will be suspended in case of mismatch

Name                        Type  Local Value              Peer Value
----------------            ----  ----------------------   ----------------------
QoS                         1     ([], [3], [], [], [],    ([], [3], [], [], [],
                                  [])                      [])
Network QoS (MTU)           1     (1538, 2240, 0, 0, 0,    (1538, 2240, 0, 0, 0,
                                  0)                       0)
Network Qos (Pause)         1     (F, T, F, F, F, F)       (F, T, F, F, F, F)
Input Queuing (Bandwidth)   1     (50, 50, 0, 0, 0, 0)     (50, 50, 0, 0, 0, 0)
Input Queuing (Absolute     1     (F, F, F, F, F, F)       (F, F, F, F, F, F)
Priority)
Output Queuing (Bandwidth)  1     (50, 50, 0, 0, 0, 0)     (50, 50, 0, 0, 0, 0)
Output Queuing (Absolute    1     (F, F, F, F, F, F)       (F, F, F, F, F, F)
Priority)
STP Mode                    1     Rapid-PVST               Rapid-PVST
STP Disabled                1     None                     None
STP MST Region Name         1     ""                       ""
STP MST Region Revision     1     0                        0
STP MST Region Instance to  1
  VLAN Mapping
STP Loopguard               1     Disabled                 Disabled
STP Bridge Assurance        1     Enabled                  Enabled
STP Port Type, Edge         1     Normal, Disabled,        Normal, Disabled,
```

```
BPDUFilter, Edge BPDUGuard          Disabled              Disabled
STP MST Simulate PVST        1      Enabled               Enabled
Allowed VLANs                -      1-10,50-90,94-97      1-10,50-90,94-97
```

You can also use the `interface` *interface-name* keywords to get interface-specific data regarding vPC consistency:

```
NX-5K-1# sho vpc consistency-parameters interface po4

    Legend:
        Type 1 : vPC will be suspended in case of mismatch

Name                       Type  Local Value            Peer Value
-------------              ----  -----------------      -----------------
STP Port Type               1    Edge Trunk Port        Edge Trunk Port
STP Port Guard              1    None                   None
STP MST Simulate PVST       1    Default                Default
lag-id                      1    [(1, 2-a0-98-13-6-10,  [(1, 2-a0-98-13-6-10,
                                 1, 0, 0), (7f9b,       1, 0, 0), (7f9b,
                                 0-23-4-ee-be-1, 8005,  0-23-4-ee-be-1, 8005,
                                 0, 0)]                 0, 0)]
mode                        1    active                 active
Speed                       1    10 Gb/s                10 Gb/s
Duplex                      1    full                   full
Port Mode                   1    trunk                  trunk
Native Vlan                 1    1                      1
Shut Lan                    1    No                     No
Allowed VLANs               -    3-7,9                  3-7,9
```

You can get a status for all your vPCs with the `show vpc` command:

```
NX-5K-1# sho vpc
Legend:
                (*) - local vPC is down, forwarding via vPC peer-link

vPC domain id                    : 1
Peer status                      : peer adjacency formed ok
vPC keep-alive status            : peer is alive
Configuration consistency status: success
vPC role                         : secondary

vPC Peer-link status
---------------------------------------------------------------------
id   Port   Status Active vlans
--   ----   ------ --------------------------------------------------
1    Po1    up     1-100,300-400

vPC status
----------------------------------------------------------------------
id     Port         Status Consistency Reason                    Active vlans
------ -----------  ------ ----------- ------------------------- -----------
2      Po2          up     success     success                   1-10,50-90
                                                                 ,94-97
3      Po12         up     success     success                   1-10,50-90
                                                                 ,94-97
4      Po13         up     success     success                   3-7,9
```

5	Po14	up	success	success		3-7,9
6	Po15	up	success	success		3-7,9
7	Po16	down*	success	success		

If you think all of this configuration matching looks like a pain, you're absolutely right. One of the biggest problems I've seen with Nexus vPCs is in environments where they need to be changed often. I worked in a data center where VLANs were constantly being added or removed from trunks as new virtual machines were added to blade servers. To add a VLAN to a trunk, we would issue the `switchport trunk allowed vlan vlan-number` command. As you can see from the preceding output, the number of allowed VLANs is a consistency parameter for vPCs. This means when we added it to the NX-5K-1 switch, the vPC would break until we could get the command added to the other switch in the pair. Even if we set up two SSH windows, one to each switch, and hit Enter at the same time, the vPCs would break.

Here's a similar example, where I changed the spanning tree port type on the vPC. Before I could get to the second switch in the pair, the vPC broke with the following message:

```
2010 May 11 19:51:38 NX-5k-1 %ETHPORT-5-IF_ERROR_VLANS_SUSPENDED: VLANs 3-7,9
on Interface port-channel14 are being suspended. (Reason: vPC type-1 configuration
incompatible - STP interface port type inconsistent)
```

Cisco's answer to this problem is a feature called *config-sync*. See Chapter 18 for more information.

## CHAPTER 8

Spanning Tree

The Spanning Tree Protocol (STP) is used to ensure that no Layer-2 loops exist in a LAN. As you'll see in this chapter, Layer-2 loops can cause havoc.

 Spanning tree is designed to prevent loops among bridges. A *bridge* is a device that connects multiple segments within a single collision domain. Switches are considered bridges—hubs are not. While the spanning tree documentation always refers to bridges generically, my examples will show switches. Switches are generally the devices in which you will encounter spanning tree.

When a switch receives a broadcast, it repeats the broadcast on every port (except the one on which it was received). In a looped environment, the broadcasts are repeated forever. The result is called a *broadcast storm*, and it will quickly bring a network to a halt.

Figure 8-1 illustrates what can happen when there's a loop in a network.

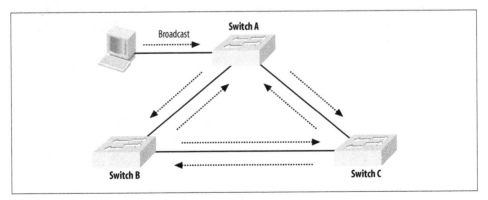

Figure 8-1. Broadcast storm

The computer on Switch A sends out a broadcast frame. Switch A then sends a copy of the broadcast to Switch B and Switch C. Switch B repeats the broadcast to Switch C, and Switch C repeats the broadcast to Switch B; Switch B and Switch C also repeat the broadcast back to Switch A. Switch A then repeats the broadcast it heard from Switch B to Switch C and the broadcast it heard from Switch C to Switch B. This progression will continue indefinitely until the loop is somehow broken. Spanning tree is an automated mechanism used to discover and break loops of this kind.

 Spanning tree was developed by Dr. Radia Perlman of Sun Microsystems, Inc., who summed up the idea in a poem titled "Algorhyme" that's based on Joyce Kilmer's "Trees":

> I think that I shall never see
> A graph more lovely than a tree.
> A tree whose crucial property
> Is loop-free connectivity.
> A tree which must be sure to span.
> So packets can reach every LAN.
> First the Root must be selected
> By ID it is elected.
> Least cost paths from Root are traced
> In the tree these paths are placed.
> A mesh is made by folks like me
> Then bridges find a spanning tree.

Broadcast Storms

In the network shown in Figure 8-2, there's a simple loop between two switches. Switch A and Switch B are connected to each other with two links: F0/14 and F0/15 on Switch A are connected to the same ports on Switch B. I've disabled spanning tree, which is enabled by default, to demonstrate the power of a broadcast storm. Both ports are trunks. There are various devices on other ports on the switches, which create normal broadcasts (such as ARP and DHCP broadcasts). There is nothing unusual about this network, aside from spanning tree being disabled.

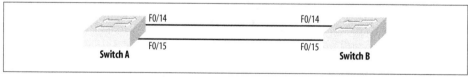

Figure 8-2. Simple Layer-2 loop

Interface F0/15 has already been configured and is operating properly. The output from the `show interface f0/15` command shows the input and output rates to be very low (both are around 1,000 bits per second and 2–3 packets per second):

```
3550-IOS#sho int f0/15
FastEthernet0/15 is up, line protocol is up (connected)
  Hardware is Fast Ethernet, address is 000f.8f5c.5a0f (bia 000f.8f5c.5a0f)
  MTU 1500 bytes, BW 100000 Kbit, DLY 100 usec,
     reliability 255/255, txload 1/255, rxload 1/255
  Encapsulation ARPA, loopback not set
  Keepalive set (10 sec)
  Full-duplex, 100Mb/s, media type is 10/100BaseTX
  input flow-control is off, output flow-control is unsupported
  ARP type: ARPA, ARP Timeout 04:00:00
  Last input 00:00:10, output 00:00:00, output hang never
  Last clearing of "show interface" counters never
  Input queue: 0/75/0/0 (size/max/drops/flushes); Total output drops: 0
  Queueing strategy: fifo
  Output queue: 0/40 (size/max)
  5 minute input rate 1000 bits/sec, 2 packets/sec
  5 minute output rate 1000 bits/sec, 3 packets/sec
     5778444 packets input, 427859448 bytes, 0 no buffer
     Received 5707586 broadcasts (0 multicast)
     0 runts, 0 giants, 0 throttles
     0 input errors, 0 CRC, 0 frame, 0 overrun, 0 ignored
     0 watchdog, 5707585 multicast, 0 pause input
     0 input packets with dribble condition detected
     2597516 packets output, 213866427 bytes, 0 underruns
```

A useful tool when you're troubleshooting a broadcast storm is the show processes cpu history command. This command displays an ASCII histogram of the CPU utilization over the past 72 hours. It produces three graphs:

- CPU percent per second (last 60 seconds)
- CPU percent per minute (last 60 minutes)
- CPU percent per hour (last 72 hours)

Here is the output from the show process cpu history command on switch B, which shows 0–3 percent CPU utilization over the course of the last minute (the remaining graphs have been removed for brevity):

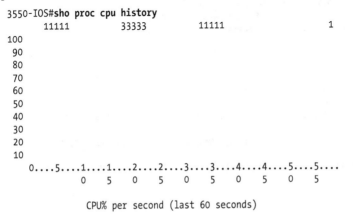

```
3550-IOS#sho proc cpu history
        11111           33333          11111                        1
  100
   90
   80
   70
   60
   50
   40
   30
   20
   10
    0....5....1....1....2....2....3....3....4....4....5....5....
              0    5    0    5    0    5    0    5    0    5

          CPU% per second (last 60 seconds)
```

The numbers on the left side of the graph are the CPU utilization percentages. The numbers on the bottom are seconds in the past (0 = the time of command execution). The numbers on the top of the graph show the integer values of CPU utilization for that time period on the graph. For example, according to the preceding graph, CPU utilization was normally 0 percent, but increased to 1 percent 5 seconds ago and to 3 percent 20 seconds ago. When the values exceed 10 percent, you'll see visual peaks in the graph itself.

This switch is a 3550 and has routing protocol neighbors (EIGRP, in this case), so it's an important device that is providing Layer-3 functionality:

```
3550-IOS#sho ip eigrp neighbors
IP-EIGRP neighbors for process 55
H   Address            Interface      Hold Uptime    SRTT   RTO  Q     Seq Type
                                      (sec)          (ms)        Cnt   Num
0   10.55.1.10         Fa0/13         14  00:25:30      1    200  0     27
2   10.55.10.3         Vl10           13  1w0d         18    200  0     25
```

Now I'll turn up interface F0/14 as a trunk:

```
3550-IOS(config)#int f0/14
3550-IOS(config-if)# switchport
3550-IOS(config-if)# switchport trunk encapsulation dot1q
3550-IOS(config-if)# switchport mode trunk
```

There are now two trunks connecting Switch A and Switch B. Remember that I've disabled spanning tree. Mere seconds after I converted F0/14 to a trunk, the input and output rates on F0/15 have shot up from 1,000 bits per second and 2–3 packets per second to 815,000 bits per second and 1,561 packets per second:

```
3550-IOS#sho int f0/15 | include minute
  5 minute input rate 815000 bits/sec, 1565 packets/sec
  5 minute output rate 812000 bits/sec, 1561 packets/sec
```

Ten seconds later, the input and output have more than doubled to 2.7 Mbps and over 4,500 packets per second:

```
3550-IOS#sho int f0/15 | include minute
  5 minute input rate 2744000 bits/sec, 4591 packets/sec
  5 minute output rate 2741000 bits/sec, 4587 packets/sec
```

Now I start to get warning messages on the console. The EIGRP neighbors are bouncing:

```
1w0d: %DUAL-5-NBRCHANGE: IP-EIGRP(0) 55: Neighbor 10.55.1.10 (FastEthernet0/13) is
down: holding time expire
1w0d: %DUAL-5-NBRCHANGE: IP-EIGRP(0) 55: Neighbor 10.55.1.10 (FastEthernet0/13) is
up: new adjacency
1w0d: %DUAL-5-NBRCHANGE: IP-EIGRP(0) 55: Neighbor 10.55.10.3 (Vlan10) is down: retry
limit exceeded
1w0d: %DUAL-5-NBRCHANGE: IP-EIGRP(0) 55: Neighbor 10.55.10.3 (Vlan10) is up: new
adjacency
```

A quick look at the CPU utilization for the past minute explains why. The histogram shows that for the last 25 seconds, CPU utilization has been at 99 percent. The trouble started 40 seconds ago, which is when I enabled the second trunk:

```
3550-IOS#sho proc cpu hist

        99999999999999999999999993333399999966666
        99999999999999999999999999999999993333311111
   100  *************************     *****
    90  *************************     *****
    80  *************************     *****
    70  *************************     *****
    60  *************************     **********
    50  *************************     **********
    40  ****************************************
    30  ****************************************
    20  ****************************************
    10  ****************************************
     0....5....1....1....2....2....3....3....4....4....5....5....
         0    5    0    5    0    5    0    5    0    5

        CPU% per second (last 60 seconds)
```

CPU utilization rocketed to 99 percent within seconds of the loop being created. The switch is expending most of its processing power forwarding broadcasts through the loop. As a result, all other processes start to suffer. Using Telnet or SSH to administer the switch is almost impossible at this point. Even the console is beginning to show signs of sluggishness.

Within five minutes, the two links are at 50 percent utilization. They are also sending and receiving in excess of 70,000 packets per second:

```
3550-IOS#sho int f0/15
FastEthernet0/15 is up, line protocol is up (connected)
  Hardware is Fast Ethernet, address is 000f.8f5c.5a0f (bia 000f.8f5c.5a0f)
  MTU 1500 bytes, BW 100000 Kbit, DLY 100 usec,
     reliability 255/255, txload 143/255, rxload 143/255
  Encapsulation ARPA, loopback not set
  Keepalive set (10 sec)
  Full-duplex, 100Mb/s, media type is 10/100BaseTX
  input flow-control is off, output flow-control is unsupported
  ARP type: ARPA, ARP Timeout 04:00:00
  Last input 00:00:00, output 00:00:00, output hang never
  Last clearing of "show interface" counters never
  Input queue: 0/75/0/0 (size/max/drops/flushes); Total output drops: 0
  Queueing strategy: fifo
  Output queue: 0/40 (size/max)
  5 minute input rate 56185000 bits/sec, 71160 packets/sec
  5 minute output rate 56277000 bits/sec, 70608 packets/sec
     48383882 packets input, 112738864 bytes, 0 no buffer
     Received 48311185 broadcasts (0 multicast)
     0 runts, 0 giants, 0 throttles
     0 input errors, 0 CRC, 0 frame, 0 overrun, 0 ignored
     0 watchdog, 36608855 multicast, 0 pause input
```

```
0 input packets with dribble condition detected
45107032 packets output, 4212355164 bytes, 356 underruns
0 output errors, 0 collisions, 1 interface resets
0 babbles, 0 late collision, 0 deferred
0 lost carrier, 0 no carrier, 0 PAUSE output
361 output buffer failures, 0 output buffers swapped out
```

Remember that the baseline traffic load for this interface was 1,000 bits per second and 2–3 packets per second. Of the traffic we're seeing now, 99.9 percent is recycled broadcasts. This is a broadcast storm. Rest assured that experiencing one on a live network—particularly one for which you are responsible—is not fun. The storm occurs quickly and affects services immediately.

Because this example takes place in a lab environment, I am having fun (though my wife would no doubt have some interesting comments regarding what I consider fun), but all good things must come to an end. Within seconds of disabling one of the trunks, EIGRP stabilizes, and the network problems disappear. I can now telnet to the switch with ease. The CPU returns almost immediately back to normal utilization rates of 0–1 percent:

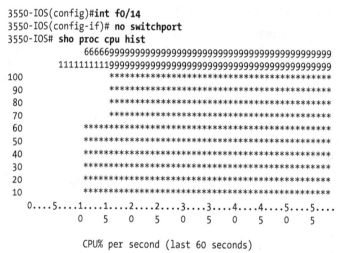

```
3550-IOS(config)#int f0/14
3550-IOS(config-if)# no switchport
3550-IOS# sho proc cpu hist

            6666699999999999999999999999999999999999999999999
            1111111111999999999999999999999999999999999999999999
    100        *****************************************
     90        *****************************************
     80        *****************************************
     70        *****************************************
     60     *******************************************
     50     *******************************************
     40     *******************************************
     30     *******************************************
     20     *******************************************
     10     *******************************************
        0....5....1....1....2....2....3....3....4....4....5....5....
             0    5    0    5    0    5    0    5    0    5

              CPU% per second (last 60 seconds)
```

This example shows how devastating a broadcast storm can be. When the switches involved become unresponsive, diagnosing the storm can become very difficult. If you can't access the switch via the console, SSH, or Telnet, the only way to break the loop is by disconnecting the offending links. If you're lucky, the looped port's activity lights will be flashing more than those of the other ports. In any case, you won't be having a good day.

MAC Address Table Instability

Another problem caused by a looped environment is MAC address tables (CAM tables in CatOS) being constantly updated. Take the network in Figure 8-3, for example. With

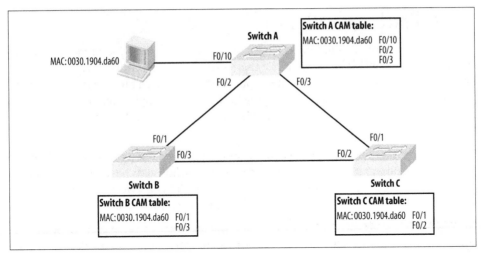

Figure 8-3. MAC address table inconsistencies

all of the switches interconnected and spanning tree disabled, Switch A will assume the MAC address for the PC directly connected to it is sourced from a different switch. This happens very quickly during a broadcast storm and, in the rare instances when you see this behavior without a broadcast storm, chances are things are about to get very bad very quickly.

With this network in place and spanning tree disabled, I searched for the MAC address of the PC on Switch A using the show mac-address-table | include 0030.1904.da60 command. I repeated the command as fast as I could and got the following results:

```
3550-IOS#sho mac-address-table | include 0030.1904.da60
    1    0030.1904.da60    DYNAMIC    Fa0/10
3550-IOS# sho mac-address-table | include 0030.1904.da60
    1    0030.1904.da60    DYNAMIC    Fa0/10
3550-IOS# sho mac-address-table | include 0030.1904.da60
    1    0030.1904.da60    DYNAMIC    Fa0/2
3550-IOS# sho mac-address-table | include 0030.1904.da60
    1    0030.1904.da60    DYNAMIC    Fa0/3
3550-IOS# sho mac-address-table | include 0030.1904.da60
    1    0030.1904.da60    DYNAMIC    Fa0/2
3550-IOS# sho mac-address-table | include 0030.1904.da60
```

This switch is directly connected to the device in question, yet at different times it seems to believe that the best path to the device is via Switch B or Switch C.

Remember that a switch examines each packet that arrives on a port and assigns the packet's source MAC address to that port in its MAC address/CAM table. Because devices can and do move, the switch will assume that the last port on which the MAC address was observed is where the address now resides. Because the broadcast packets originating from the PC are constantly cycling through the looped network, wherever the packet comes into the switch is where the switch will believe that MAC address belongs.

Preventing Loops with Spanning Tree

The obvious way to prevent loops is to follow the same advice a doctor might give you when you complain, "It hurts when I do this"—don't do it! Of course, in the real world, there are many variables that are out of your control. I've seen more than one network go down because someone decided to plug both network drops under his desk into the little switch he brought in from home. Heck, I've seen network administrators do it themselves.

Having more than one link between switches is a good idea in terms of redundancy—in fact, it's recommended. The trick is to have only one link active at a time (or combine them into a single logical link). If you configure two links between two switches and shut one down, you'll solve the loop problem, but when the live link fails, you'll need to manually bring up the second link.

Spanning tree is a protocol designed to discover network loops and break them before they can cause any damage. Properly configured, spanning tree is an excellent tool that should always be enabled on any network. Improperly configured, however, it can cause subtle problems that can be hard to diagnose.

How Spanning Tree Works

Spanning tree elects a *root bridge* (switch) in the network. The root bridge is the bridge that all other bridges need to reach via the shortest path possible. Spanning tree calculates the cost for each path from each bridge in the network to the root bridge. The path with the lowest cost is kept intact, while all others are broken. Spanning tree breaks paths by putting ports into a *blocking* state.

Every bridge on the network that supports spanning tree sends out frames called *bridge protocol data units* (BPDUs) every two seconds. The format of the BPDU frame is shown in Figure 8-4.

These frames contain the information necessary for switches in the network to perform the following functions:

Elect a root bridge
> When a switch boots, it assumes that it is the root bridge and sets the root ID to the local bridge ID in all outgoing BPDUs. If it receives a BPDU that has a lower root ID, the switch considers the switch identified by the root ID in the BPDU to be the root switch. The local switch then begins using that root ID in the BPDUs it sends.
>
> Every bridge has a *bridge ID*. The bridge ID is a combination of the bridge priority and the bridge's MAC address. The bridge priority is a configurable two-byte field with a default value of 32,768. The lower the bridge ID value is, the more likely it is that the bridge will become the root bridge (the bridge with the lowest bridge ID becomes the root bridge).

The *root ID* is similarly composed of two fields: the root priority and the root MAC address. The root priority is also configured with a value of 32768 (0×8000) by default. Should there be a tie between root priorities, the lower root MAC address is used to break the tie.

Determine the best path to the root bridge

If BPDUs from the root bridge are received on more than one port, there is more than one path to the root bridge. The best path is considered to be via the port on which the BPDU with the lowest *path cost* was received.

Path costs are determined by adding each bridge's port priority to the initial path cost as BPDUs are forwarded from bridge to bridge.

Determine the root port on each bridge

The *root port* is the port on the switch that has the shortest path to the root bridge. The root bridge does not have root ports; it only has designated ports.

Determine the designated port on each segment

The *designated port* is the port on the segment that has the shortest path to the root bridge. On segments that are directly connected to the root bridge, the root bridge's ports are the designated ports.

Elect a designated bridge on each segment

The bridge on a given segment with the designated port is considered the *designated bridge*. The root bridge is the designated bridge for all directly connected segments. In the event that two bridges on a segment have root ports, the bridge with the lowest bridge ID becomes the designated bridge.

Block nonforwarding ports

Ports that have received BPDUs, and are neither designated nor root ports, are placed into a *blocking* state. These ports are administratively up but are not allowed to forward traffic (though they still send and receive BPDUs).

 Always configure a switch to be the root bridge. Letting the switches configure themselves is dangerous, because they will choose the switch with the lowest MAC address, which will usually be a switch other than the one it should be. As a general rule, you should not let networking devices make critical decisions using default values. It will cause your network to behave in unexpected ways and will cause you to fail higher-level certification exams, which are designed to catch you in exactly this way. Usually, the device that should be the root bridge will be obvious. The root bridge should generally be one of the core switches in your design.

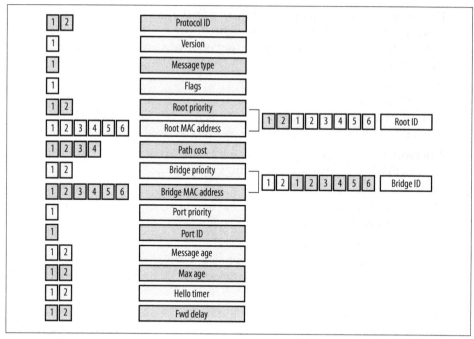

Figure 8-4. BPDU format

Every port on a switch goes through a series of spanning tree states when it is brought online, as illustrated in the flowchart in Figure 8-5. These states transition in a pattern depending on the information learned from BPDUs received on the port.

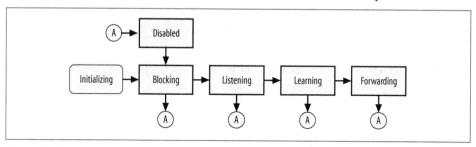

Figure 8-5. Spanning tree port states

These are the spanning tree states:

Initializing

A port in the initializing state has either just been powered on or taken out of the administratively down state.

Blocking

A port in the blocking state is essentially unused. It does not forward or receive frames, with the following exceptions:

- The port receives and processes BPDUs.
- The port receives and responds to messages relating to network management.

Listening

The listening state is similar to the blocking state, except that in this state, BPDUs are sent as well as received. Frame forwarding is still not allowed, and no addresses are learned.

Learning

A port in the learning state still does not forward frames, but it does analyze frames that come into the port and retrieve the MAC addresses from those frames for inclusion in the MAC address/CAM table. After the frames are analyzed, they are discarded.

Forwarding

The forwarding state is what most people would consider the "normal" state. A port in this state receives and transmits BPDUs, analyzes incoming packets for MAC address information, and forwards frames from other switch ports. When a port is in the forwarding state, the device or network attached to the port is active and able to communicate.

Disabled

A port in the disabled state does not forward frames and does not participate in spanning tree. It receives and responds to only network-management messages.

Per-VLAN Spanning Tree

Because VLANs can be pruned from trunks (as discussed in Chapter 6), it is possible that some VLANs may form loops while others do not. For this reason, Cisco switches now default to a multiple-VLAN form of spanning tree called *Per-VLAN Spanning Tree* (PVST). PVST allows for a spanning tree instance for each VLAN when used with ISL trunks. Per-VLAN Spanning Tree Plus (PVST+) offers the same features when used with 802.1Q trunks.

By default, all VLANs will inherit the same values for all spanning tree configurations. However, each VLAN can be configured differently. For example, each VLAN may have a different spanning tree root bridge. See more detail on different types of spanning tree in Cisco switches at the end of this chapter.

Managing Spanning Tree

Spanning tree is enabled by default. To see its status, use the show spanning-tree command in IOS and NX-OS:

```
Cat-3550#sho spanning-tree

VLAN0001
  Spanning tree enabled protocol ieee
```

```
Root ID      Priority     24577
             Address      0009.43b5.0f80
             Cost         23
             Port         20 (FastEthernet0/20)
             Hello Time   2 sec  Max Age 20 sec  Forward Delay 15 sec

Bridge ID    Priority     32769  (priority 32768 sys-id-ext 1)
             Address      000f.8f5c.5a00
             Hello Time   2 sec  Max Age 20 sec  Forward Delay 15 sec
             Aging Time 300

Interface         Role Sts Cost      Prio.Nbr Type
----------------- ---- --- --------- -------- --------------------------------
Fa0/13            Altn BLK 19         128.13   P2p
Fa0/14            Altn BLK 19         128.14   P2p
Fa0/15            Altn BLK 19         128.15   P2p
Fa0/20            Root FWD 19         128.20   P2p
Fa0/23            Desg FWD 19         128.23   P2p
[-text removed-]
```

The bolded text shows the priority and MAC address of the root bridge, as well as which port the switch is using to get there (this is the root port). This is very useful information when you're trying to figure out where the root bridge is on a network. By running this command on every switch in the network, you should be able to map your connections and figure out which switch is the root.

Here is the output from the show spanning-tree command from a Nexus 7000 that is operating as the STP root:

```
NX-7K-1-Cozy# sho spanning

VLAN0001
  Spanning tree enabled protocol rstp
  Root ID      Priority     32769
               Address      0026.9807.95c2
               This bridge is the root
               Hello Time  2  sec  Max Age 20 sec  Forward Delay 15 sec

  Bridge ID    Priority     32769  (priority 32768 sys-id-ext 1)
               Address      0026.9807.95c2
               Hello Time  2  sec  Max Age 20 sec  Forward Delay 15 sec

Interface         Role Sts Cost      Prio.Nbr Type
----------------- ---- --- --------- -------- --------------------------------
Po1               Desg FWD 1          128.4096 (vPC peer-link) Network P2p
Po10              Desg FWD 1          128.4105 (vPC) P2p
[-text removed-]
```

Switch-specific information is located below the root information, and below the local switch information is information specific to each port on the switch that is actively participating in spanning tree. This information will be repeated for every VLAN.

In CatOS, the equivalent command is show spantree. The command produces very similar information, with a slightly different layout:

```
CatOS-6509: (enable)sho spantree
VLAN 1
Spanning tree mode          RAPID-PVST+
Spanning tree type          ieee
Spanning tree enabled

Designated Root             00-00-00-00-00-00
Designated Root Priority    0
Designated Root Cost        0
Designated Root Port        1/0
Root Max Age   0  sec  Hello Time 0  sec   Forward Delay 0  sec

Bridge ID MAC ADDR          00-00-00-00-00-00
Bridge ID Priority          32768
Bridge Max Age 20 sec  Hello Time 2  sec   Forward Delay 15 sec

Port                    State         Role Cost      Prio Type
----------------------- ------------- ---- --------- ---- --------------------
  1/1                   not-connected -              4    32
  1/2                   not-connected -              4    32
  2/1                   not-connected -              4    32
  2/2                   not-connected -              4    32
[-text removed-]
```

Notice that the designated root MAC address is all zeros. This indicates that the switch considers itself to be the root bridge.

To get a summary of spanning tree, use the IOS command show spanning-tree summary. This command shows you the status of features like UplinkFast and BackboneFast (discussed in the following section):

```
Cat-3550#sho spanning-tree summary
Switch is in pvst mode
Root bridge for: VLAN0002, VLAN0200
Extended system ID           is enabled
Portfast Default             is disabled
PortFast BPDU Guard Default  is disabled
Portfast BPDU Filter Default is disabled
Loopguard Default            is disabled
EtherChannel misconfig guard is enabled
UplinkFast                   is disabled
BackboneFast                 is disabled
Configured Pathcost method used is short

Name                    Blocking Listening Learning Forwarding STP Active
----------------------- -------- --------- -------- ---------- ----------
VLAN0001                   3         0        0         2          5
VLAN0002                   0         0        0         5          5
VLAN0003                   2         0        0         2          4
VLAN0004                   2         0        0         2          4
VLAN0010                   2         0        0         2          4
VLAN0100                   2         0        0         2          4
VLAN0200                   0         0        0         4          4
----------------------- -------- --------- -------- ---------- ----------
7 vlans                   11         0        0        19         30
```

Here is the same command as seen on a Nexus 5000:

```
NX-5K-1# sho spanning-tree summ
Switch is in rapid-pvst mode
Root bridge for: none
Port Type Default                         is disable
Edge Port [PortFast] BPDU Guard Default  is disabled
Edge Port [PortFast] BPDU Filter Default is disabled
Bridge Assurance                          is enabled
Loopguard Default                         is disabled
Pathcost method used                      is short


Name                 Blocking Listening Learning Forwarding STP Active
-------------------- -------- --------- -------- ---------- ----------
VLAN0001                    0         0        0          1          1
VLAN0100                    0         0        0          2          2
-------------------- -------- --------- -------- ---------- ----------
2 vlans                     0         0        0          3          3
```

In CatOS, the summary command is show spantree summary:

```
CatOS-6509: (enable)sho spantree summ
Spanning tree mode: RAPID-PVST+
Runtime MAC address reduction: disabled
Configured MAC address reduction: disabled
Root switch for vlans: 20.
Global loopguard is disabled on the switch.
Global portfast is disabled on the switch.
BPDU skewing detection disabled for the bridge.
BPDU skewed for vlans:  none.
Portfast bpdu-guard disabled for bridge.
Portfast bpdu-filter disabled for bridge.
Uplinkfast disabled for bridge.
Backbonefast disabled for bridge.

Summary of connected spanning tree ports by vlan

VLAN Blocking Listening Learning Forwarding STP Active
----- -------- --------- -------- ---------- ----------
  20         0         0        0          1          1

      Blocking Listening Learning Forwarding STP Active
----- -------- --------- -------- ---------- ----------
Total        0         0        0          1          1
```

An excellent command in IOS is show spanning-tree root, which shows you the information regarding the root bridge for every VLAN:

```
Cat-3550#sho spanning-tree root


                                  Root   Hello Max Fwd
Vlan                  Root ID     Cost   Time  Age Dly Root Port
---------------- -------------------- --------- ----- --- --- ------------
VLAN0001         24577 0009.43b5.0f80    23     2    20  15  Fa0/20
VLAN0002         32770 000f.8f5c.5a00     0     2    20  15
```

```
VLAN0003        32771 000d.edc2.0000        19    2    20   15  Fa0/13
VLAN0004        32772 000d.edc2.0000        19    2    20   15  Fa0/13
VLAN0010        32778 000d.edc2.0000        19    2    20   15  Fa0/13
VLAN0100        32868 000d.edc2.0000        19    2    20   15  Fa0/13
VLAN0200        32968 000f.8f5c.5a00         0    2    20   15
```

And the same command from a Nexus 7000:

```
NX-7K-1-Cozy# sho spanning-tree root

                                Root Hello Max Fwd
Vlan                Root ID     Cost Time  Age Dly  Root Port
---------------- -------------------- ------- ----- --- ---  ----------------
VLAN0001        32769 0026.9807.95c2    0    2    20  15  This bridge is root
VLAN0010        32778 0026.9807.95c2    0    2    20  15  This bridge is root
```

There is no equivalent command in CatOS.

Additional Spanning Tree Features

Spanning tree was originally designed for bridges with few ports. With the advent of
Ethernet switches, some enhancements were made to spanning tree. These commonly
seen enhancements helped make spanning tree more palatable by decreasing the time
a host needs to wait for a port, and decreasing the convergence time in a Layer-2
network.

PortFast

PortFast is a feature on Cisco switches that allows a port to bypass all of the other
spanning tree states (see Figure 8-5, shown earlier) and proceed directly to the forwarding state. PortFast should be enabled only on ports that will not have switches
connected. Spanning tree takes about 30 seconds to put a normal port into the forwarding state, which can cause systems using DHCP to time out and not get an IP
address (on a Windows machine, a default IP address may be used). Enabling the Port-
Fast feature on a port alleviates this problem, but you should be very careful when using
this feature. If a switch were to be connected to a port configured with PortFast active,
a loop could occur that would not be detected.

To enable PortFast on an IOS switch, use the `spanning-tree portfast` interface command. The switch will deliver a nice warning about the dangers of PortFast when you
enable the feature:

```
Cat-3550(config-if)#spanning-tree portfast
%Warning: portfast should only be enabled on ports connected to a single
  host. Connecting hubs, concentrators, switches, bridges, etc... to this
  interface when portfast is enabled, can cause temporary bridging loops.
  Use with CAUTION

%Portfast has been configured on FastEthernet0/20 but will only
  have effect when the interface is in a non-trunking mode.
```

To disable PortFast on an interface in IOS, simply negate the command. There is no fanfare when disabling PortFast:

```
Cat-3550(config-if)#no spanning-tree portfast
Cat-3550(config-if)#
```

On a CatOS switch, the command to enable PortFast is set spantree portfast <mod/port> enable. Executing this command will also result in a nice message about the dangers of PortFast:

```
CatOS-6509: (enable)set spantree portfast 3/10 enable

Warning: Connecting Layer 2 devices to a fast start port can cause
temporary spanning tree loops. Use with caution.

Spantree port  3/10 fast start enabled.
```

To disable PortFast, use the same command with disable instead of enable:

```
CatOS-6509: (enable)set spantree portfast 3/10 disable
Spantree port  3/10 fast start disabled.
```

On Nexus, PortFast is configured using the spanning-tree port type edge interface command:

```
NX-5K-1(config-if)# spanning-tree port type edge
Warning: Edge port type (portfast) should only be enabled on ports connected
to a single host. Connecting hubs, concentrators, switches, bridges, etc...
to this interface when edge port type (portfast) is enabled, can cause
temporary bridging loops. Use with CAUTION

Edge Port Type (Portfast) has been configured on Ethernet100/1/12 but will
only have effect when the interface is in a non-trunking mode.
```

For servers that require trunks, a special type of PortFast is offered. To configure a trunk to a server with PortFast, use the spanning-tree port type edge trunk interface command:

```
NX-5K-1(config-if)# spanning-tree port type edge trunk
Warning: Edge port type (portfast) should only be enabled on ports connected
to a single host. Connecting hubs, concentrators, switches, bridges, etc... to
this interface when edge port type (portfast) is enabled, can cause temporary
bridging loops. Use with CAUTION
```

BPDU Guard

Ports configured for PortFast should never receive BPDUs as long as they are connected to devices other than switches/bridges. If a PortFast-enabled port is connected to a switch, a bridging loop will occur. To prevent this, Cisco developed a feature called *BPDU Guard*. BPDU Guard automatically disables a port configured for PortFast in the event that it receives a BPDU. The port is not put into blocking mode, but is put into the *ErrDisable* state. Should this happen, the interface must be reset. BPDU Guard is enabled with the spanning-tree bpduguard enable command in IOS:

```
Cat-3550(config-if)#spanning-tree bpduguard enable
```

To disable this feature, change the enable keyword to disable.

In CatOS, use the set spantree bpdu-guard <*mod/port*> enable (or disable) command:

```
CatOS-6509: (enable)set spantree bpdu-guard 3/10 enable
Spantree port  3/10 bpdu guard enabled.
```

FEXs on Nexus systems have BPDU Guard on by default and should not be removed. This is to prevent you from connecting a switch to the FEX, since they are designed for host connectivity only.

UplinkFast

UplinkFast is a feature designed for access-layer switches. These switches typically have links to other switches to connect to the distribution layer. Normally, when the link on the designated port fails, a port with an alternate path to the root bridge is cycled through the spanning tree listening and learning states until it returns to the forwarding state. Only then can the port pass traffic. This process can take 45 seconds or more.

UplinkFast allows a blocked uplink port to bypass the listening and learning states when the designated port fails. This allows the network to recover in five seconds or less. This feature affects all VLANs on the switch. It also sets the bridge priority to 49,152 to ensure that the switch will not become the root bridge.

Figure 8-6 shows where UplinkFast would be applied in a simple network. Switches A and B would be either core or distribution switches. Switch C would be an access-layer switch. The only links to other switches on Switch C are to the distribution or core.

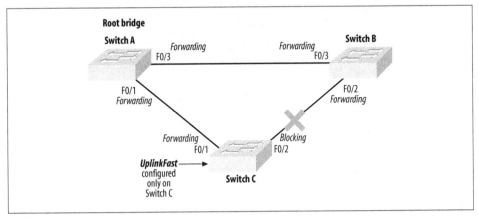

Figure 8-6. UplinkFast example

UplinkFast should be configured only on access-layer switches. It should never be enabled on distribution-layer or core switches, because it prevents the switch from becoming the root bridge, which is usually counterindicated in core switches.

To configure UplinkFast on a CatOS switch, use the set spantree uplinkfast enable command:

```
CatOS-6509: (enable)set spantree uplinkfast enable
VLANs 1-4094 bridge priority set to 49152.
The port cost and portvlancost of all ports set to above 3000.
Station update rate set to 15 packets/100ms.
uplinkfast all-protocols field set to off.
uplinkfast enabled for bridge.
```

When disabling UplinkFast, be careful, and remember that a lot of other values were changed when you enabled the feature:

```
CatOS-6509: (enable)set spantree uplinkfast disable
uplinkfast disabled for bridge.
Use clear spantree uplinkfast to return stp parameters to default.
```

That last line of output is important. If you're moving a switch from an access-layer role to a role in which you want it to become the root bridge, you'll need to change the priorities back to their defaults.

Here's what happens when I follow the switch's advice:

```
CatOS-6509: (enable)clear spantree uplinkfast
This command will cause all portcosts, portvlancosts, and the
bridge priority on all vlans to be set to default.
Do you want to continue (y/n) [n]? y
VLANs 1-4094 bridge priority set to 32768.
The port cost of all bridge ports set to default value.
The portvlancost of all bridge ports set to default value.
uplinkfast all-protocols field set to off.
uplinkfast disabled for bridge.
```

The values are not necessarily set to what they were before I enabled UplinkFast—they are returned to their defaults.

When configuring UplinkFast on IOS switches, there are no scary messages like there are in CatOS:

```
Cat-3550(config)#spanning-tree uplinkfast
Cat-3550(config)#
```

That's it. Simple! But don't let the simplicity fool you—enabling UplinkFast changes priorities in IOS, too. Unlike in CatOS, however, disabling the feature in IOS (via no spanning-tree uplinkfast) automatically resets the priorities to their defaults. Again, this might not be what you want or expect, so be careful.

BackboneFast

When a switch receives a BPDU advertising a root bridge that's less desirable than the root bridge it already knows about, the switch discards the BPDU. This is true as long as the switch knows about the better root bridge. If the switch stops receiving BPDUs for the better root bridge, it will continue to believe that bridge is the best bridge until the max_age timeout is exceeded. max_age defaults to 20 seconds.

Figure 8-7 shows a network with three switches. All of these switches are core or distribution switches, though they could also be access-layer switches. Switch A is the root bridge. Through normal convergence, the F0/2 port on Switch C is blocking, while all the others are forwarding.

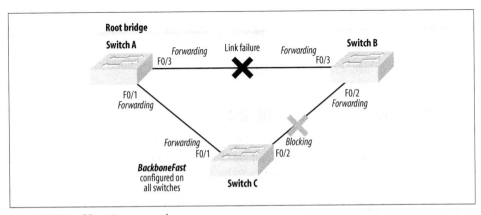

Figure 8-7. BackboneFast example

Say an outage occurs that brings down the F0/3 link between Switch A and Switch B. This link is not directly connected to Switch C. The result is an *indirect link failure* on Switch C. When Switch B recognizes the link failure, it knows that it has no path to the root and starts advertising itself as the root. Until this point, Switch B had been advertising BPDUs showing the more desirable Switch A as the root. Switch C still has that information in memory, and refuses to believe that the less desirable Switch B is the root until the max_age timeout expires.

After 20 seconds, Switch C will accept the BPDU advertisements from Switch B and start sending its own BPDUs to Switch B. When Switch B receives the BPDUs from Switch C, it will understand that there is a path to Switch A (the more desirable root bridge) through Switch C, and accepts Switch A as the root bridge again. This process takes upward of 50 seconds with the default spanning tree timers.

BackboneFast adds functionality that detects indirect link failures. It actively discovers paths to the root by sending out *root link query* PDUs after a link failure. When it discovers a path, it sets the max_age timer to 0 so the port can cycle through the normal listening, learning, and forwarding states without waiting an additional 20 seconds.

If BackboneFast is used, it must be enabled on every switch in the network.

Enabling BackboneFast on an IOS switch is as simple as using the `spanning-tree back bonefast` global command:

```
Cat-3550(config)#spanning-tree backbonefast
Cat-3550(config)#
```

Negating the command disables the feature.

To enable BackboneFast on a CatOS switch, use the `set spantree backbonefast enable` command:

```
CatOS-6509: (enable)set spantree backbonefast enable
Backbonefast enabled for all VLANs
```

To disable this feature, change the `enable` keyword to `disable`.

Common Spanning Tree Problems

Spanning tree can be a bit of a challenge when it misbehaves. More to the point, spanning tree problems can be hard to diagnose if the network is not properly designed. Here are a couple of common problems and how to avoid them.

Duplex Mismatch

A bridge still receives and processes BPDUs on ports, even when they are in a blocked state. This allows the bridge to determine that a path to the root bridge is still available should the primary path fail.

If a port in the blocking state stops receiving BPDUs, the bridge no longer considers the port to be a path to the root bridge. In this case, the port should no longer be blocked, so the bridge puts the port into the forwarding state. Would this ever happen in the real world? It's happened to me more than once.

A common spanning tree problem is shown in Figure 8-8. Here, two switches are connected with two links: F0/0 on Switch A is connected to F0/0 on Switch B, and F0/1 on Switch A is connected to F0/1 on Switch B. Switch A is the root bridge. All ports are in the forwarding state, except for F0/1 on Switch B, which is blocking. The network is stable because spanning tree has broken the potential loop. The arrows show BPDUs being sent.

Port F0/0 on Switch A is the only port that is set to autonegotiation. Autonegotiation has determined that the port should be set to 100 Mbps and half-duplex mode. The

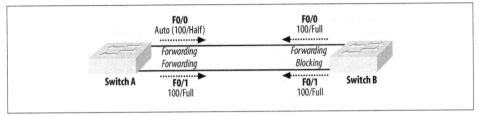

Figure 8-8. Spanning tree half-duplex problem

other ports are all hardcoded to 100/full. Spanning tree is sending BPDUs out of all ports and is receiving them on all ports—even the one that is blocking.

> Always make sure both sides of an Ethernet link are configured the same way regarding speed and duplex. See Chapter 3 for details.

When a port is in half-duplex mode, it listens for collisions before transmitting. A port in full-duplex mode does not. When a half-duplex port is connected with a full-duplex port, the full-duplex port will send continuously, causing the half-duplex port to encounter many collisions. After a collision, the port will perform the back-off algorithm, and wait to resend the packet that collided. In our example, the half-duplex port is the active link with data being sent across it. When the data rate gets high, the collision problem gets worse, resulting in frames—including BPDUs—being dropped.

Switch B will listen for BPDUs over the two links shown in Figure 8-8. If it doesn't see any BPDUs over the F0/0 link for a set amount of time, Switch B will no longer consider the F0/0 link to be a valid path to the root bridge. Because this was the primary path to the root bridge, and the root bridge can no longer be seen, Switch B will change F0/1 from blocking to forwarding to reestablish a path to the root bridge. At this point, there are no blocking ports on the two links connecting the switches, and a bridging loop exists.

Unidirectional Links

When a link is able to transmit in one direction but not another, the link is said to be *unidirectional*. While this can happen with copper Ethernet, the problem most often occurs with fiber.

A common issue when installing fiber plants is the cross-connection of individual fibers. Should a fiber pair be split, one fiber strand can end up on a different port or switch from the other strand in the pair.

Figure 8-9 shows four switches. Switch A is supposed to be connected to Switch B by two pairs of fiber—one between the G0/1 ports on each switch and another between the G0/2 ports on each switch. Somewhere in the cabling plant, the fiber pair for the

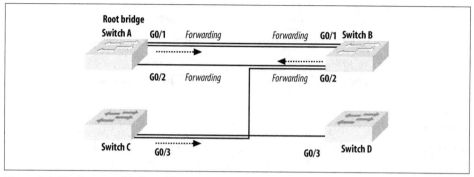

Figure 8-9. Unidirectional link problem

G0/2 link has been split. Though the pair terminates correctly on Switch B, Switch A has only one strand from the pair. The other strand has been routed to Switch C and connected to port G0/3.

Fiber interfaces test for link integrity by determining whether there is a signal on the RX side of the pair. Switch B's port G0/2 has link integrity because its RX is active from Switch C, Switch A's port G0/2 has link integrity because its RX is active from Switch B, and Switch C's port G0/3 has link integrity because its RX is active from Switch D.

Spanning tree is sending BPDUs out each interface on Switch A and Switch B because the links are active. Switch A is the root bridge. Switch B is only receiving BPDUs from the root bridge on one port: G0/1. Because Switch B is not receiving BPDUs from the root bridge on port G0/2, spanning tree does not block the port. Broadcasts received on Switch B on G0/1 will be retransmitted out G0/2. A loop is born.

This problem can be difficult to uncover. A bridging loop causes mayhem in the network because the CPU utilization on network devices can quickly reach 100 percent, causing outages. The first thing inexperienced engineers try is rebooting one or more devices in the network. In the case of a unidirectional link, rebooting will not resolve the issue. When that fails, the loop is usually detected, and the engineer shuts down one of the links. But when he shuts down the link, the proof of the unidirectional link is often lost.

 Physical layer first! Always suspect that something physical is wrong when diagnosing connectivity problems. It can save you hours of headaches, especially if all the other clues don't seem to add up to anything substantial. Also, don't assume that it works today just because it worked yesterday. It doesn't take much for someone to crush a fiber strand when closing a cabinet door.

With the latest versions of IOS and CatOS, unidirectional link problems are handled by a protocol called Unidirectional Link Detection (UDLD). UDLD is enabled by default and should be left on. If you see UDLD errors, look for issues similar to what I've just described.

Bridge Assurance

Nexus includes a fun little enhancement called *bridge assurance* (BA), which is designed to prevent loops in your topology. Wait, isn't spanning tree designed for this purpose? Yes, it is, but bridge assurance makes your network foolproof! If you believe that, I've got a bridge to sell you, along with a book on why nerds shouldn't use puns.

Bridge assurance is designed to prevent unidirectional links, but it behaves differently than Unidirectional Link Detection (UDLD).

Let's start with this blurb from the Cisco Nexus documentation:

> Bridge Assurance is enabled by default and can only be disabled globally. Also, Bridge Assurance can be enabled only on spanning tree network ports that are point-to-point links. Finally, both ends of the link must have Bridge Assurance enabled.

> With Bridge Assurance enabled, BPDUs are sent out on all operational network ports, including alternate and backup ports, for each hello time period. If the port does not receive a BPDU for a specified period, the port moves into the blocking state and is not used in the root port calculation. Once that port receives a BPDU, it resumes the normal spanning tree transitions.

Here's what you need to remember: BA is always on unless globally disabled, and BPDUs are sent out every operational networking port when it's enabled. More to the point, if you don't manage BA properly, it will break your network. While that's true of spanning tree as well, we've all become used to how STP operates. BA changes the rules a bit.

BA is only supported by Rapid PVST+ and MST. This is important, because for BA to work properly, it must be enabled and configured on both sides of a link. If you plug your Nexus 5K into a 2960 that's running PVST, BA may disable the link to the 2960.

With Nexus, spanning tree ports are identified as *normal*, *host*, or *network*. A host port is analogous to `spanning-tree portfast` in IOS. A network port is a port that is not connected to a host but is connected to another BA-capable switch. While you might be tempted to make all your trunk ports spanning tree network ports, be careful. I had a client for whom we connected a Nexus 5K to a 6509. The 6509 supported bridge assurance, but we weren't paying attention when we configured the interswitch link. The Nexus side got configured for spanning tree port type *network* (it was a network port, after all), but what we didn't count on was the 6509 running PVST. As a result, the Nexus blocked many of our VLANs. Changing the trunk port to spanning tree type *normal* solved the problem.

Designing to Prevent Spanning Tree Problems

Proper design can help minimize spanning tree problems. One of the simplest ways to help keep trouble to a minimum is to document and know your network. If you have to figure out how your network operates when there's a problem, the problem may last longer than your job.

Use Routing Instead of Switching for Redundancy

The saying used to be, "Switch when you can and route when you have to." But in today's world of fast Layer-3 switching, this mantra no longer holds. With Layer-3 switches, you can route at switching speeds.

For many people, Layer-3 redundancy is easier to understand than Layer-2 redundancy. As long as the business needs are met and the end result is the same, using routing to solve your redundancy concerns is perfectly acceptable.

 If you decide to use routing instead of switching, don't turn off spanning tree. Spanning tree will still protect against loops you might have missed. If you're using switches—even Layer-3 switches—spanning tree can be a lifesaver if someone plugs in a switch where it doesn't belong.

Always Configure the Root Bridge

Don't let spanning tree elect the root bridge dynamically. Decide which switch in your network should be the root, and configure it with a bridge priority of 1. If you let the switches decide, not only may they choose one that doesn't make sense, but switches added later may assume the role of root bridge. This will cause the entire network to reconverge and cause links to change states as the network discovers paths to the new root bridge.

I once saw a large financial network in a state of confusion because the root bridge was a switch under someone's desk. The root bridge had not been configured manually, and when this rogue switch was added to the network, all the switches reconverged to it because it had the lowest MAC address of all the switches. While this may not sound like a big deal on the surface, the problem manifested itself because the main trunk between the core switches, which was the link farthest from the root bridge, became blocked.

## CHAPTER 9

Routing and Routers

Routing is a term with multiple meanings in different disciplines. In general, it refers to determining a path for something. In telecom, a call may be routed based on the number being dialed or some other identifier. In either case, a path is determined for the call.

Mail is also routed—I'm not talking about email here (though email is routed, too)—but rather, snail mail. When you write an address and a zip code on a letter, you are providing the means for the post office to route your letter. You provide a destination and, usually, a source address, and the post office determines the best path for the letter. If there is a problem with the delivery of your letter, the return address is used to route it back to you. The exact path the letter takes to get from its source to its destination doesn't really matter; all you care about is that it (hopefully) makes it in a timely fashion, and in one piece.

In the IP world, packets or frames are forwarded on a local network by switches, hubs, or bridges. If the address of the destination is not on the local network, the packet must be forwarded to a *gateway*. The gateway is responsible for determining how to get the packet to where it needs to be. RFC 791, titled INTERNET PROTOCOL, defines a gateway thusly:

2.4. Gateways

Gateways implement Internet protocol to forward datagrams between networks. Gateways also implement the Gateway to Gateway Protocol (GGP) [7] to coordinate routing and other Internet control information.

In a gateway the higher level protocols need not be implemented and the GGP functions are added to the IP module.

When a station on a network sends a packet to a gateway, the station doesn't care *how* the packet gets to its destination—just that it does (at least, in the case of TCP). Much like a letter in the postal system, each packet contains its source and destination addresses so routing can be accomplished with ease.

In the realm of semantics and IP, a gateway is a device that forwards packets to a destination other than the local network. For all practical purposes, a gateway is a router. Router is the term I will generally use in this book, although you will also see the phrase *default gateway*.

 In the olden days of data communication, a "gateway" was a device that translated one protocol to another. For example, if you had a device that converted a serial link into a parallel link, that device would be called a gateway. Similarly, a device that converted Ethernet to Token Ring might be called a gateway. Nowadays, such devices are called *media converters*. (This wouldn't be the first time I've been accused of harkening back to the good old days—pull up a rocker here on the porch, and have a mint julep while I spin you a yarn.)

Routers usually communicate with each other by means of one or more *routing protocols*. These protocols let the routers learn information about networks other than the ones directly connected to them.

Network devices used to be limited to bridges and routers. Bridges, hubs, and switches operated only on Layer 2 of the OSI stack, and routers only on Layer 3. Now these devices are often merged into single devices, and routers and switches often operate on all seven layers of the OSI stack.

In today's world, where every device seems to be capable of anything, when should you pick a router rather than a switch? Routers tend to be WAN-centric, while switches tend to be LAN-centric. If you're connecting T1s, you probably want a router. If you're connecting Ethernet, you probably want a switch.

Routing Tables

Routing is a fundamental process common to almost every network in use today. Still, many engineers don't understand how routing works. While the Cisco certification process should help you understand how to configure routing, in this section, I'll show you what you need to know about routing in the real world. I'll focus on the foundations, because that's what most engineers seem to be lacking—we spend a lot of time studying the latest technologies and sometimes forget the core principles on which everything else is based.

In a Cisco router, the routing table is called the *route information base* (RIB). When you execute the command `show ip route`, the output you receive is a formatted view of the information in the RIB.

Each routing protocol has its own table of information. For example, EIGRP has the topology table, and Open Shortest Path First (OSPF) has the OSPF database. Each protocol makes decisions about which routes will be held in its database. Routing protocols use their own metrics to determine which route is best, and the metrics vary widely. The metric value is determined by the routing protocol from which the route was learned. Thus, the same link may have very different metrics depending on the protocol used. For example, the same path may be described with a metric of 2 in the Routing Information Protocol (RIP), 200 in OSPF, and 156160 in EIGRP.

 Routing protocols and metrics are covered in more detail in Chapter 10.

If the same route is learned from two sources within a single routing protocol, the one with the best metric will win. Should the same route be learned from two routing protocols within a single router, the protocol with the lowest administrative distance will win. The *administrative distance* is the value assigned to each routing protocol to allow the router to prioritize routes learned from multiple sources. The administrative distances for the various routing protocols are shown in Table 9-1.

Table 9-1. Routing protocols and their administrative distances

Route type	Administrative distance
Connected interface	0
Static route	1
Enhanced Interior Gateway Routing Protocol (EIGRP) summary route	5
External Border Gateway Protocol (BGP)	20
Internal EIGRP	90
Interior Gateway Routing Protocol (IGRP)	100
Open Shortest Path First (OSPF)	110
Intermediate System-Intermediate System (IS-IS)	115
Routing Information Protocol (RIP)	120
Exterior Gateway Protocol (EGP)	140
On Demand Routing (ODR)	160
External EIGRP	170
Internal BGP	200
Unknown	255

 Spanning tree, discussed in Chapter 8, isn't really a routing protocol, because the protocol doesn't care about the data being passed; spanning tree is only concerned with loops and with preventing them from a physical and Layer-2 perspective. In other words, spanning tree is concerned more with determining that all possible paths within its domain are loop-free than with determining the paths along which data should be sent.

When a packet arrives at a router, the router determines whether the packet needs to be forwarded to another network. If it does, the router checks the RIB to see whether it contains a route to the destination network. If there is a match, the packet is adjusted and forwarded out the proper interface to where it belongs (see Chapter 15 for more information on this process). If no match is found in the RIB, the packet is forwarded to the default gateway, if one exists. If no default gateway exists, the packet is dropped.

Originally, the destination network was described by a network address and a subnet mask. Today, destination networks are often described by a network address and a prefix length. The network address is an IP address that references a network. The prefix length is the number of bits set to 1 in the subnet mask. Networks are described in the format *network-address/prefix-length*. For example, the network 10.0.0.0 with a subnet mask of 255.0.0.0 would be described as 10.0.0.0/8. When shown in this format, the route is called simply a *prefix*. The network 10.0.0.0/24 is said to be a longer prefix than the network 10.0.0.0/8. The more bits that are used to identify the network portion of the address, the longer the prefix is said to be.

The RIB may include multiple routes to the same network. For example, in Figure 9-1, R2 learns the network 10.0.0.0 from two sources: R1 advertises the route 10.0.0.0/8, and R3 advertises the route 10.0.0.0/24. Because the prefix lengths are different, these are considered to be different routes. As a result, they will both end up in the routing table.

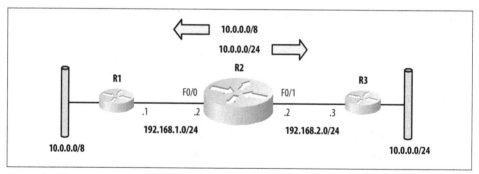

Figure 9-1. Same network with different prefix lengths

Here are the routes as seen in R2:

```
10.0.0.0/8 is variably subnetted, 2 subnets, 2 masks
D       10.0.0.0/8 [90/30720] via 192.168.1.1, 00:12:01, FastEthernet0/0
D       10.0.0.0/24 [90/30720] via 192.168.2.3, 00:12:01, FastEthernet0/1
```

When a packet is received in R2, the destination IP address is matched against the routing table. If R2 receives a packet destined for 10.0.0.1, which route will it choose? There are two routes in the table that seem to match: 10.0.0.0/8 and 10.0.0.0/24. The route with the longest prefix length (also called the *most specific* route) is the more desirable route. Thus, when a packet destined for 10.0.0.1 arrives on R2, it will be forwarded to R3. The important thing to realize about this example is that there may be legitimate addresses within the 10.0.0.0/24 range behind R1 that R2 will never be able to access.

 Technically, 10.0.0.0/8 is a network and 10.0.0.0/24 is a subnet. Read on for further clarification.

Route Types

The routing table can contain six types of routes:

Host route
> A host route is a route to a host. In other words, the route is not to a network. Host routes have a subnet mask of 255.255.255.255 and a prefix length of /32.

Subnet
> A subnet is a portion of a major network. The subnet mask is used to determine the size of the subnet. 10.10.10.0/24 (255.255.255.0) is a subnet.

Summary (group of subnets)
> A summary route is a single route that references a group of subnets. 10.10.0.0/16 (255.255.0.0) would be a summary, provided that subnets with longer masks (such as 10.10.10.0/24) existed.

Major network
> A major network is any classful network, along with its native mask. 10.0.0.0/8 (255.0.0.0) is a major network.

Supernet (group of major networks)
> A supernet is a single route that references a group of major networks. For example, 10.0.0.0/7 is a supernet that references 10.0.0.0/8 and 11.0.0.0/8.

Default route
> A default route is shown as 0.0.0.0/0 (0.0.0.0). This route is also called the *route of last resort*. This is the route that is used when no other route matches the destination IP address in a packet.

The IP Routing Table

To show the IP routing table, use the show ip route command:

```
R2#sho ip route
Codes: C - connected, S - static, I - IGRP, R - RIP, M - mobile, B - BGP
       D - EIGRP, EX - EIGRP external, O - OSPF, IA - OSPF inter area
       N1 - OSPF NSSA external type 1, N2 - OSPF NSSA external type 2
       E1 - OSPF external type 1, E2 - OSPF external type 2, E - EGP
       i - IS-IS, su - IS-IS summary, L1 - IS-IS level-1, L2 - IS-IS level-2
```

```
        ia - IS-IS inter area, * - candidate default, U - per-user static route
        o - ODR, P - periodic downloaded static route

Gateway of last resort is 11.0.0.1 to network 0.0.0.0

        172.16.0.0/16 is variably subnetted, 6 subnets, 2 masks
D          172.16.200.0/23 is a summary, 00:56:18, Null0
C          172.16.200.0/24 is directly connected, Loopback2
C          172.16.201.0/24 is directly connected, Serial0/0
C          172.16.202.0/24 is directly connected, Loopback3
C          172.16.100.0/23 is directly connected, Loopback4
D          172.16.101.0/24 [90/2172416] via 11.0.0.1, 00:53:07, FastEthernet0/1
C       10.0.0.0/8 is directly connected, FastEthernet0/0
C       11.0.0.0/8 is directly connected, FastEthernet0/1
        192.168.1.0/32 is subnetted, 1 subnets
D          192.168.1.11 [90/156160] via 11.0.0.1, 00:00:03, FastEthernet0/1
S*      0.0.0.0/0 [1/0] via 11.0.0.1
D       10.0.0.0/7 is a summary, 00:54:40, Null0
```

The first block of information is shown every time the command is executed. In the interest of brevity, I will remove it from most of the examples in this book. This block is a key that explains the codes listed down the left side of the routing table.

The next line lists the default gateway, if one is present:

```
Gateway of last resort is 11.0.0.1 to network 0.0.0.0
```

If there are two or more default gateways, they will all be listed. This is common when the default gateway is learned from a routing protocol that allows equal-cost load sharing. If two links provide access to the advertised default and they both have the same metric, they will both be listed as default routes. In this case, packets will be equally balanced between the two links using per-packet load balancing.

If no default gateway has been configured or learned, you'll instead see this message:

```
Gateway of last resort is not set
```

The next block of text contains the rest of the routing table:

```
        172.16.0.0/16 is variably subnetted, 6 subnets, 2 masks
D          172.16.200.0/23 is a summary, 00:56:18, Null0
C          172.16.200.0/24 is directly connected, Loopback2
C          172.16.201.0/24 is directly connected, Serial0/0
C          172.16.202.0/24 is directly connected, Loopback3
C          172.16.100.0/23 is directly connected, Loopback4
D          172.16.101.0/24 [90/2172416] via 11.0.0.1, 00:53:07, FastEthernet0/1
C       10.0.0.0/8 is directly connected, FastEthernet0/0
C       11.0.0.0/8 is directly connected, FastEthernet0/1
        192.168.1.0/32 is subnetted, 1 subnets
D          192.168.1.11 [90/156160] via 11.0.0.1, 00:00:03, FastEthernet0/1
S*      0.0.0.0/0 [1/0] via 11.0.0.1
D       10.0.0.0/7 is a summary, 00:54:40, Null0
```

Let's examine a single entry from the routing table, so you can see what's important:

```
D          172.16.101.0/24 [90/2172416] via 11.0.0.1, 00:53:07, FastEthernet0/1
```

First is the route code. In this case it's D, which indicates the route was learned via EIGRP (you can look this up in the block of codes at the top of the show ip route output).

Next is the route itself. In this example, the route is to the subnet 172.16.101.0/24. After that are two numbers in brackets: the first number is the administrative distance (see Table 9-1) and the second number is the metric for the route. The metric is determined by the routing protocol from which the route was learned (in this case, EIGRP).

The next piece of information is the next hop the router needs to send packets to in order to reach this subnet. In this case, via 11.0.0.1 indicates that packets destined for the subnet 172.16.101.0/24 should be forwarded to the IP address 11.0.0.1. Finally, you have the age of the route (00:53:07), followed by the interface out which the router will forward the packet (FastEthernet0/1).

I've built the sample router so that the routing table will have one of each type of route. Again, those route types are *host*, *subnet*, *summary*, *major network*, *supernet*, and *default*. The following sections explain the types in more detail. I'll show the routing table entries for each type in bold.

Host Route

A host route is simply a route with a subnet mask of all ones (255.255.255.255), or a prefix length of /32. In the sample routing table, the route to 192.168.1.11 is a host route:

```
       172.16.0.0/16 is variably subnetted, 6 subnets, 2 masks
D         172.16.200.0/23 is a summary, 00:56:18, Null0
C         172.16.200.0/24 is directly connected, Loopback2
C         172.16.201.0/24 is directly connected, Serial0/0
C         172.16.202.0/24 is directly connected, Loopback3
C         172.16.100.0/23 is directly connected, Loopback4
D         172.16.101.0/24 [90/2172416] via 11.0.0.1, 00:53:07, FastEthernet0/1
C      10.0.0.0/8 is directly connected, FastEthernet0/0
C      11.0.0.0/8 is directly connected, FastEthernet0/1
       192.168.1.0/32 is subnetted, 1 subnets
D         192.168.1.11 [90/156160] via 11.0.0.1, 00:00:03, FastEthernet0/1
S*     0.0.0.0/0 [1/0] via 11.0.0.1
D      10.0.0.0/7 is a summary, 00:54:40, Null0
```

Notice that the route is shown to be a part of a larger network (in this case, 192.168.1.0). We know this because the host route is indented under the major network. The router will attempt to show you which classful (major) network contains the route. If the router knows about only a single subnet mask, it will assume the network has been divided equally with that mask. In this case, the router has assumed that the major network 192.168.1.0/24 has been equally subnetted, with each subnet having a /32 mask. Hence, the natively /24 network 192.168.1.0 is shown as 192.168.1.0/32.

Subnet

Subnets are indented under their source major networks. In our example, the major network 172.16.0.0/16 has been subnetted; in fact, it has been subnetted under the rules of Variable Length Subnet Masks (VLSM), which allow each subnet to have a different subnet mask (within certain limits—see Chapter 34 for more detail). The route in the middle that is not in bold is a summary route, which I'll cover next:

```
   172.16.0.0/16 is variably subnetted, 6 subnets, 2 masks
D        172.16.200.0/23 is a summary, 00:56:18, Null0
C        172.16.200.0/24 is directly connected, Loopback2
C        172.16.201.0/24 is directly connected, Serial0/0
C        172.16.202.0/24 is directly connected, Loopback3
C        172.16.100.0/23 is directly connected, Loopback4
D        172.16.101.0/24 [90/2172416] via 11.0.0.1, 00:53:07, FastEthernet0/1
C     10.0.0.0/8 is directly connected, FastEthernet0/0
C     11.0.0.0/8 is directly connected, FastEthernet0/1
      192.168.1.0/32 is subnetted, 1 subnets
D        192.168.1.11 [90/156160] via 11.0.0.1, 00:00:03, FastEthernet0/1
S*    0.0.0.0/0 [1/0] via 11.0.0.1
D     10.0.0.0/7 is a summary, 00:54:40, Null0
```

Summary (Group of Subnets)

The term *summary* is used in the routing table to represent any group of routes. Technically, according to the Cisco documentation, a summary is a group of subnets, while a supernet is a group of major networks. Both are called summaries in the routing table. Thus, while the example routing table shows two summary entries, only the first is technically a summary route:

```
   172.16.0.0/16 is variably subnetted, 6 subnets, 2 masks
D        172.16.200.0/23 is a summary, 00:56:18, Null0
C        172.16.200.0/24 is directly connected, Loopback2
C        172.16.201.0/24 is directly connected, Serial0/0
C        172.16.202.0/24 is directly connected, Loopback3
C        172.16.100.0/23 is directly connected, Loopback4
D        172.16.101.0/24 [90/2172416] via 11.0.0.1, 00:53:07, FastEthernet0/1
C     10.0.0.0/8 is directly connected, FastEthernet0/0
C     11.0.0.0/8 is directly connected, FastEthernet0/1
      192.168.1.0/32 is subnetted, 1 subnets
D        192.168.1.11 [90/156160] via 11.0.0.1, 00:00:03, FastEthernet0/1
S*    0.0.0.0/0 [1/0] via 11.0.0.1
D     10.0.0.0/7 is a summary, 00:54:40, Null0
```

The last entry in the routing table, which is also reported as a summary, is a group of major networks and is technically a supernet.

The differentiation between supernets and summary routes is primarily an academic one. In the real world, both are routinely called summary routes or aggregate routes. Different routing protocols use different terms for groups of routes, be they subnets or major networks—BGP uses the term "aggregate," while OSPF uses the term "summary."

The destination for both summary routes is `Null0`. `Null0` as a destination indicates that packets sent to this network will be dropped. The summary routes point to `Null0` because they were created within EIGRP on this router.

The `Null0` route is there for the routing protocol's use. The more specific routes must also be included in the routing table because the local router must use them when forwarding packets. The specific routes will not be advertised in the routing protocol; only the summary will be advertised. We can see this if we look at an attached router:

```
     172.16.0.0/16 is variably subnetted, 4 subnets, 2 masks
D       172.16.200.0/23 [90/156160] via 11.0.0.2, 04:30:21, FastEthernet0/1
D       172.16.202.0/24 [90/156160] via 11.0.0.2, 04:30:21, FastEthernet0/1
D       172.16.100.0/23 [90/156160] via 11.0.0.2, 04:30:21, FastEthernet0/1
C       172.16.101.0/24 is directly connected, Serial0/0
```

On the connected router, the summary route for 172.16.200.0/23 is present, but the more specific routes 172.16.200.0/24 and 172.16.201.0/24 are not.

Major Network

A major network is a network in its native form. For example, the 10.0.0.0/8 network has a native subnet mask of 255.0.0.0. The network 10.0.0.0/8 is therefore a major network. Referencing 10.0.0.0 with a prefix mask longer than /8 changes the route to a subnet, while referencing it with a mask shorter than /8 changes the route to a supernet.

Two major networks are shown in the routing table:

```
     172.16.0.0/16 is variably subnetted, 6 subnets, 2 masks
D       172.16.200.0/23 is a summary, 00:56:18, Null0
C       172.16.200.0/24 is directly connected, Loopback2
C       172.16.201.0/24 is directly connected, Serial0/0
C       172.16.202.0/24 is directly connected, Loopback3
C       172.16.100.0/23 is directly connected, Loopback4
D       172.16.101.0/24 [90/2172416] via 11.0.0.1, 00:53:07, FastEthernet0/1
C    10.0.0.0/8 is directly connected, FastEthernet0/0
C    11.0.0.0/8 is directly connected, FastEthernet0/1
     192.168.1.0/32 is subnetted, 1 subnets
D       192.168.1.11 [90/156160] via 11.0.0.1, 00:00:03, FastEthernet0/1
S*   0.0.0.0/0 [1/0] via 11.0.0.1
D    10.0.0.0/7 is a summary, 00:54:40, Null0
```

172.16.0.0/16 is also shown, but only as a reference to group all of the subnets underneath it. The entry for 172.16.0.0/16 is not a route.

Supernet (Group of Major Networks)

A supernet is a group of major networks. In this example, there is a route to 10.0.0.0/7, which is a group of the major networks 10.0.0.0/8 and 11.0.0.0/8:

```
         172.16.0.0/16 is variably subnetted, 6 subnets, 2 masks
D           172.16.200.0/23 is a summary, 00:56:18, Null0
C           172.16.200.0/24 is directly connected, Loopback2
C           172.16.201.0/24 is directly connected, Serial0/0
C           172.16.202.0/24 is directly connected, Loopback3
C           172.16.100.0/23 is directly connected, Loopback4
D           172.16.101.0/24 [90/2172416] via 11.0.0.1, 00:53:07, FastEthernet0/1
C        10.0.0.0/8 is directly connected, FastEthernet0/0
C        11.0.0.0/8 is directly connected, FastEthernet0/1
         192.168.1.0/32 is subnetted, 1 subnets
D           192.168.1.11 [90/156160] via 11.0.0.1, 00:00:03, FastEthernet0/1
S*       0.0.0.0/0 [1/0] via 11.0.0.1
D        10.0.0.0/7 is a summary, 00:54:40, Null0
```

Notice the route is again destined to Null0. Sure enough, on a connected router we will only see the summary and not the more specific routes:

```
D        10.0.0.0/7 [90/30720] via 11.0.0.2, 04:30:22, FastEthernet0/1
```

Default Route

The default route, or "route of last resort," is displayed in a special place above the routing table, so it can easily be seen:

```
Gateway of last resort is 11.0.0.1 to network 0.0.0.0

         172.16.0.0/16 is variably subnetted, 6 subnets, 2 masks
D           172.16.200.0/23 is a summary, 00:56:18, Null0
C           172.16.200.0/24 is directly connected, Loopback2
C           172.16.201.0/24 is directly connected, Serial0/0
C           172.16.202.0/24 is directly connected, Loopback3
C           172.16.100.0/23 is directly connected, Loopback4
D           172.16.101.0/24 [90/2172416] via 11.0.0.1, 00:53:07, FastEthernet0/1
C        10.0.0.0/8 is directly connected, FastEthernet0/0
C        11.0.0.0/8 is directly connected, FastEthernet0/1
         192.168.1.0/32 is subnetted, 1 subnets
D           192.168.1.11 [90/156160] via 11.0.0.1, 00:00:03, FastEthernet0/1
S*       0.0.0.0/0 [1/0] via 11.0.0.1
D        10.0.0.0/7 is a summary, 00:54:40, Null0
```

In this case, the default route is a static route, as indicated by the S in the first column, but it could be learned from a routing protocol as well. The asterisk next to the S indicates that this route is a candidate for the default route. There can be more than one candidate, in which case there will be multiple entries with asterisks. There can even be multiple default routes, but only one will be listed in the first line.

This output shows a router with two active default gateways, though only one is listed in the first line:

```
Gateway of last resort is 10.0.0.1 to network 0.0.0.0

      20.0.0.0/24 is subnetted, 1 subnets
S        20.0.0.0 [1/0] via 10.0.0.1
      10.0.0.0/24 is subnetted, 3 subnets
C        10.0.0.0 is directly connected, FastEthernet0/0
C     192.168.1.0/24 is directly connected, FastEthernet0/1
S*    0.0.0.0/0 [1/0] via 10.0.0.1
                [1/0] via 10.0.0.2
```

When in doubt, look at the 0.0.0.0/0 entry in the routing table, as it will always have the most accurate information.

Virtual Routing and Forwarding

Nexus switches and newer versions of IOS support something called Virtual Routing and Forwarding (VRF) instances. Each VRF is a self-contained routing table within the same router. Within a Nexus 7000, you can have multiple VRFs within a single Virtual Device Context (VDC). On the Nexus 5000, which as of this writing does not support VDCs or routing, you can still have multiple VRFs. In fact, by default, the management network resides in a management VRF, while other traffic is in the default VRF. In IOS 15.x, you may also configure VRFs.

On the Nexus platform, two VRFs exist by default—*management* and *default*:

```
NX-7K-1-Daisy# sho vrf
VRF-Name                VRF-ID   State   Reason
default                      1   Up      --
management                   2   Up      --
```

Creating a new VRF is as simple as specifying one with the vrf context *vrf-name* command. Here, I'll create two new VRFs, named Earth and Mars:

```
NX-7K-1-Daisy(config)# vrf context Earth
NX-7K-1-Daisy(config)# vrf context Mars
```

Now we can see the additional VRFs with the show vrf command:

```
NX-7K-1-Daisy(config)# sho vrf
VRF-Name                VRF-ID   State   Reason
Earth                        3   Up      --
Mars                         5   Up      --
default                      1   Up      --
management                   2   Up      --
```

Interfaces can be assigned to VRFs. Remember that in Nexus 7000 switches, interfaces default to routed mode, so we don't need to configure them as such. You apply interfaces to VRFs with the vrf member *vrf-name* interface command:

```
NX-7K-1-Daisy(config)# int e3/25
NX-7K-1-Daisy(config-if)# vrf member Earth
NX-7K-1-Daisy(config-if)# ip address 10.0.0.1/24
```

Now I'll assign a different interface to another VRF:

```
NX-7K-1-Daisy(config-if)# int e3/26
NX-7K-1-Daisy(config-if)# vrf member Mars
NX-7K-1-Daisy(config-if)# ip address 10.0.0.1/24
```

Notice that I have two interfaces in the same router configured with the same IP address. This is possible because they each belong to a different VRF. The routing tables in VRFs Earth and Mars are completely separate from each other. This is a pretty powerful feature that adds another layer of virtualization to the Nexus platform.

VRFs are a distinctly Layer-3 idea, so you cannot assign a VLAN to a VRF, but you can assign a VLAN interface to one.

VRFs can be frustrating if you're not used to them. In our example, the command sho ip route won't show any of our configured interfaces. This is because the default VRF is named *default*. Since there are multiple routing tables now, if you want to see the routing table within a specific VRF, you must specify the VRF within your show command:

```
NX-7K-1-Daisy# sho ip route vrf Earth
IP Route Table for VRF "Earth"
'*' denotes best ucast next-hop
'**' denotes best mcast next-hop
'[x/y]' denotes [preference/metric]

10.0.0.0/24, ubest/mbest: 1/0, attached
    *via 10.0.0.1, Eth3/25, [0/0], 02:49:03, direct
10.0.0.1/32, ubest/mbest: 1/0, attached
    *via 10.0.0.1, Eth3/25, [0/0], 02:49:03, local
```

Most Layer-3 relayed commands support the VRF keyword in the Nexus, as shown here:

```
NX-7K-1-Daisy# sho ip eigrp neighbors vrf Earth
IP-EIGRP neighbors for process 0 VRF Earth

IP-EIGRP neighbors for process 100 VRF Earth
H   Address                Interface      Hold  Uptime  SRTT   RTO  Q   Seq
                                          (sec)         (ms)        Cnt Num
0   10.0.0.2               Eth3/25        11    00:00:50 3     200   0   2
```

Even the ping command supports the VRF keyword:

```
NX-7K-1-Daisy# ping 10.0.0.2 vrf Earth
PING 10.0.0.2 (10.0.0.2): 56 data bytes
Request 0 timed out
64 bytes from 10.0.0.2: icmp_seq=1 ttl=254 time=0.884 ms
64 bytes from 10.0.0.2: icmp_seq=2 ttl=254 time=0.538 ms
64 bytes from 10.0.0.2: icmp_seq=3 ttl=254 time=0.597 ms
64 bytes from 10.0.0.2: icmp_seq=4 ttl=254 time=0.6 ms
```

To make things easier, you can change the current VRF so that all subsequent commands apply to that VRF. You do this with the routing-context command, which is not a configuration command:

```
NX-7K-1-Daisy# routing-context vrf Earth
NX-7K-1-Daisy%Earth#
```

This changes our prompt by appending the name of the VRF after a percent sign to remind us where we are. Now when we run the show ip route (or any other) command, it is applied to the current routing context, which is Earth:

```
NX-7K-1-Daisy%Earth# sho ip route
IP Route Table for VRF "Earth"
'*' denotes best ucast next-hop
'**' denotes best mcast next-hop
'[x/y]' denotes [preference/metric]

10.0.0.0/24, ubest/mbest: 1/0, attached
    *via 10.0.0.1, Eth3/25, [0/0], 05:01:14, direct
10.0.0.1/32, ubest/mbest: 1/0, attached
    *via 10.0.0.1, Eth3/25, [0/0], 05:01:14, local
200.200.200.0/24, ubest/mbest: 1/0
    *via 10.0.0.2, Eth3/25, [90/130816], 00:21:50, eigrp-100, internal
```

To change back to the default VRF, use the routing-context vrf default command, which results in our prompt returning to normal:

```
NX-7K-1-Daisy%Earth# routing-context vrf default
NX-7K-1-Daisy#
```

## CHAPTER 10

Routing Protocols

A *routing protocol* is a means whereby devices exchange information about the state of the network. The information collected from other devices is used to make decisions about the best path for packets to flow to each destination network.

Routing protocols are both protocols and applications. The protocols themselves sit at Layer 3 in the OSI model, while the applications that make the routing decision run at Layer 7. Many routing protocols exist, though only a few are in common use today. Older protocols are rarely used, though some networks may contain legacy devices that support only those protocols. Some firewalls and servers may support a limited scope of routing protocols—most commonly Routing Information Protocol (RIP) and Open Shortest Path First (OSPF)—but for the sake of simplicity, I will refer to all devices that participate in a routing protocol as *routers*.

Routing protocols allow networks to be dynamic and resistant to failure. If all routes in a network were static, the only form of dynamic routing we would be able to employ would be the *floating static route*. A floating static route becomes active only if another static route is removed from the routing table. Here's an example:

```
ip route 0.0.0.0 0.0.0.0 192.168.1.1 1
ip route 0.0.0.0 0.0.0.0 10.0.0.1 2
```

The primary default route points to 192.168.1.1 and has a metric of 1. The second default route points to 10.0.0.1 and has a metric of 2.

Routes with the best metrics are inserted into the routing table, so in this case, the first route will win. Should the network 192.168.1.0 become unavailable, all routes pointing to it will be removed from the routing table. At this time, the default route to 10.0.0.1 will be inserted into the routing table, since it now has the best metric for the 0.0.0.0/0 network.

The floating static route allows routes to change if a directly connected interface goes down, but it cannot protect routes from failing if a remote device or link fails. *Dynamic* routing protocols usually allow all routers participating in the protocol to learn about any failures on the network through regular communication between routers.

Communication Between Routers

Routers need to communicate with one another to learn the state of the network. One of the original routing protocols, the RIP, sent out updates about the network using broadcasts. This was fine for smaller networks, but as networks grew, these broadcasts became troublesome. Every host on a network listens to broadcasts, and with RIP, the broadcasts can be quite large.

Most modern routing protocols communicate on broadcast networks using *multicast packets*. Multicast packets have specific IP and corresponding MAC addresses that reference predetermined groups of devices.

Because routing is usually a dynamic process, existing routers must be able to discover new routers to add their information into the tables that describe the network. For example, all EIGRP (Enhanced Internal Gateway Routing Protocol) routers within the same domain must be able to communicate with each other. Defining specific neighbors is not necessary with this protocol, because they are discovered dynamically.

> Most interior gateway protocols discover neighbors dynamically. BGP (Border Gateway Protocol) does not discover neighbors. Instead, BGP must be configured to communicate with each neighbor manually.

The Internet Assigned Numbers Authority (IANA) shows all multicast addresses in use at *http://www.iana.org/assignments/multicast-addresses*. Some of the more common multicast addresses include:

```
224.0.0.0   Base Address (Reserved)            [RFC1112,JBP]
224.0.0.1   All Systems on this Subnet         [RFC1112,JBP]
224.0.0.2   All Routers on this Subnet               [JBP]
224.0.0.4   DVMRP    Routers                   [RFC1075,JBP]
224.0.0.5   OSPFIGP  OSPFIGP All Routers       [RFC2328,JXM1]
224.0.0.6   OSPFIGP  OSPFIGP Designated Routers [RFC2328,JXM1]
224.0.0.9   RIP2 Routers                       [RFC1723,GSM11]
224.0.0.10  IGRP Routers                          [Farinacci]
224.0.0.12  DHCP Server / Relay Agent             [RFC1884]
224.0.0.18  VRRP                                  [RFC3768]
224.0.0.102 HSRP                                   [Wilson]
```

The list shows that all IGRP (Internal Gateway Routing Protocol) routers, including Enhanced IGRP routers, will listen to packets sent to the address 224.0.0.10.

> Not all routing protocols use multicasts to communicate. Because BGP does not discover neighbors, it has no need for multicasts, and instead uses unicast packets. Many other routing protocols can also be configured to assign neighbors statically. This usually results in unicast messages, instead of multicasts, being sent to specific routers.

There may be more than one type of routing protocol on a single network. In the Ethernet network shown in Figure 10-1, for example, there are five routers, three of which are running OSPF, and two of which are running EIGRP. There is no reason for the EIGRP routers to receive OSPF updates, or vice versa. Using multicasts ensures that only the routers running the same routing protocols communicate with and discover each other.

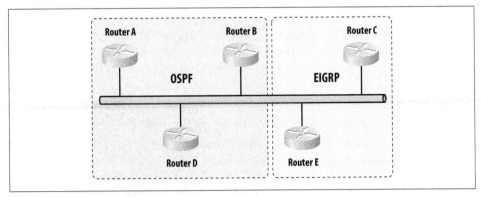

Figure 10-1. Multiple routing protocols on a single Ethernet network

A network may also contain multiple instances of the same routing protocol. These separate areas of control are called *autonomous systems* in EIGRP, and *domains* in OSPF (although the term autonomous system is often used incorrectly). In EIGRP, each instance is referenced with an autonomous system number (ASN). OSPF is more complicated to configure in this way, and is outside the realm of this book. OSPF on Cisco routers is configured with a *process-ID*, but this ID is locally significant to the router. Within a single router, routes between multiple OSPF processes are not automatically redistributed, but two OSPF routers, each with a different process-ID, will form a neighbor adjacency (assuming everything else required is in place). The process-ID in OSPF does not reference the domain.

Figure 10-2 shows a network with two EIGRP processes active. Because the multicast packets sent by an EIGRP router will be destined for all EIGRP routers, all EIGRP routers will listen to the updates. The updates contain the autonomous-system-ID, so the individual routers can determine whether to retain or discard them. RIP does not support the idea of separate processes, so any router running RIP will receive and process updates from all other RIP routers on the network.

When there are two autonomous systems on the same network, the routes learned in each may or may not be shared between the processes by default. One of the features of EIGRP is automatic redistribution between processes. For routes to be shared with other protocols, one of the routers must participate in both processes and be configured to share the routes between them.

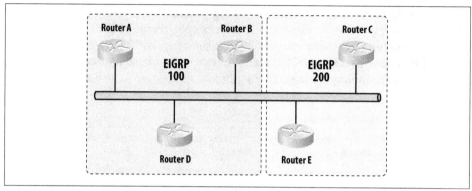

Figure 10-2. Two EIGRP processes on a single network

The act of passing routes from one process or routing protocol to another process or routing protocol is called *redistribution*. An example of multiple EIGRP routing processes being redistributed is shown in Figure 10-3.

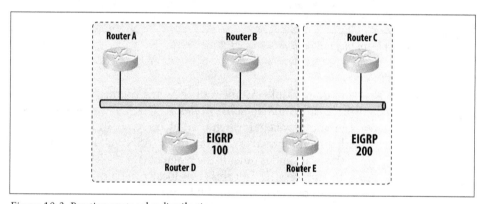

Figure 10-3. Routing protocol redistribution

In Figure 10-2, we have two EIGRP autonomous systems, but there is no way for the processes to learn each other's routes. In Figure 10-3, Router E is configured to be a member of EIGRP 100 and EIGRP 200. Router E thus redistributes routes learned on each AS into the other process.

When a route is learned within a routing process, the route is said to be *internal*. When a route is learned outside the routing process and redistributed into the process, the route is said to be *external*. Internal routes are usually considered to be more reliable than external routes, based on a metric called *administrative distance* (described later in the chapter). Exceptions include BGP, which prefers external routes over internal ones, and OSPF, which does not assign different administrative distances to internal versus external routes.

Metrics and Protocol Types

The job of a routing protocol is to determine the best path to a destination network. The best route is chosen based on a protocol-specific set of rules. RIP uses the number of hops (routers) between networks, whereas OSPF calculates the cost of a route based on the bandwidth of all the links in the network. EIGRP uses links' reported bandwidths and delays to determine the best path, by default, and you can configure it to use a few more factors as well. Each of these protocols determines a value for each route. This value is usually called a *metric*. Routes with lower metrics are more desirable.

Perhaps the simplest form of metric to understand is the one used by RIP: hop count. In RIP, the hop count is simply the number of routers between the router determining the path and the network to be reached.

Let's consider an example. In Figure 10-4, there are two networks, labeled 10.0.0.0 and 20.0.0.0. Router A considers 20.0.0.0 to be available via two paths: one through Router B and one through Router E. The path from Router A through Router B traverses Routers B, C, and D, resulting in a hop count of three for this path. The path from Router A through Router E traverses routers E, F, G, and D, resulting in a hop count of four for this path.

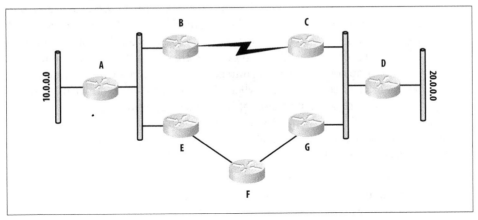

Figure 10-4. Example of metrics in routing protocols

Lower metrics always win, so Router A will consider the path through Router B to be the better path. This router will be added to the routing table with a metric of 3.

Using hop count as a metric has a limitation that can cause suboptimal paths to be chosen. Looking at Figure 10-5, you can see that the link between Routers B and C is a T1 running at 1.54 Mbps, while the links between Routers E, F, and G are all direct fiber links running at 1 Gbps. That means the path through Routers E, F, and G will be substantially faster than the link between Routers B and C, even though that link has fewer hops. However, RIP doesn't know about the bandwidth of the links in use, and takes into account only the number of hops.

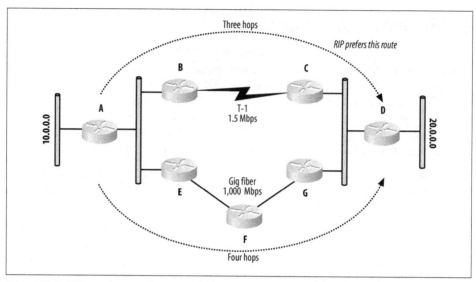

Figure 10-5. RIP uses hops to determine the best routes

A protocol such as RIP is called a *distance-vector* routing protocol, as it relies on the distance to the destination network to determine the best path. Distance-vector protocols suffer from another problem, called *counting to infinity*. Protocols such as RIP place an upper limit on the number of hops allowed to reach a destination. Hop counts that exceed this number are considered to be unreachable. In RIP, the maximum hop count is 15, with a hop count of 16 being unreachable. As you might imagine, this does not scale well in modern environments, where there may easily be more than 16 routers in a given path. A more modern version of RIP, called RIP version 2 (RIPv2 or RIP2), raises the limit to 255 hops, with 256 being unreachable. However, since RIPv2 still doesn't understand the states and capabilities of the links that join the hops together, most networks employ newer, more robust routing protocols instead.

Routing protocols such as OSPF are called *link-state* routing protocols. These protocols include information about the links between the source router and destination network, as opposed to simply counting the number of routers between them.

OSPF adds up the *cost* of each link. You determine the cost of a link by dividing 100,000,000 by the bandwidth of the link in bits per second (bps). The costs of some common links are therefore:

    100 Mbps (100,000,000 / 100,000,000 bps) = 1
    10 Mbps (100,000,000 / 10,000,000 bps) = 10
    1.5 Mbps (100,000,000 / 1,540,000 bps) = 64 (results are rounded)

Figure 10-6 shows the same network used in the RIP example. This time, OSPF is determining the best path to the destination network using bandwidth-based metrics. The metric for the T1 link is 64, and the metric for the gigabit link path is 4. Because

---

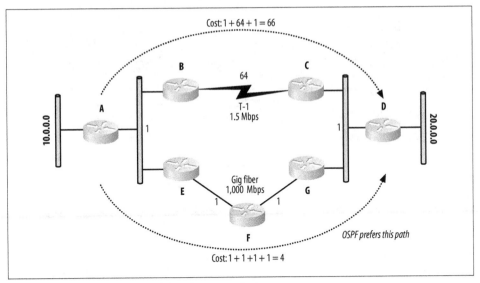

Figure 10-6. OSPF uses bandwidth to determine the best routes

the metric for the link through Routers E, F, and G is lower than that for the link through Routers B and C, this path is inserted into the routing table.

EIGRP uses a more complicated formula for determining costs. It can include bandwidth, delay, reliability, effective bandwidth, and maximum transmission unit (MTU) in its calculation of a metric. EIGRP is considered to be a *hybrid* protocol.

Administrative Distance

Networks often have more than one routing protocol active. In such situations, there is a high probability that the same networks will be advertised by multiple routing protocols. Figure 10-7 shows a network in which two routing protocols are running: the top half of the network is running RIP, and the bottom half is running OSPF. Router A will receive routes for the network 20.0.0.0 from RIP and OSPF. RIP's route has a better metric, but, as we've seen, OSPF has a better means of determining the proper path. So, how is the best route determined?

Routers choose routes based on a predetermined set of rules. One of the factors in deciding which route to place in the routing table is *administrative distance*. Administrative distance is a value assigned to every routing protocol. In the event of two protocols reporting the same route, the routing protocol with the lowest administrative distance will win, and its version of the route will be inserted into the RIB.

The administrative distances of the various routing protocols are shown in Table 10-1.

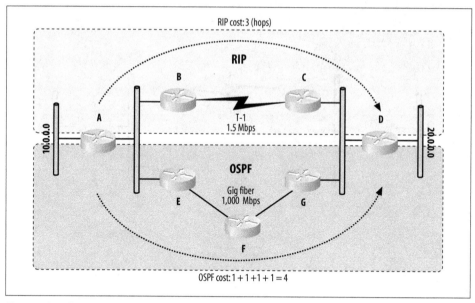

Figure 10-7. Competing routing protocols

Table 10-1. Administrative distances of routing protocols

Route type	Administrative distance
Connected interface	0
Static route	1
EIGRP summary route	5
External BGP	20
Internal EIGRP	90
IGRP	100
OSPF	110
IS-IS	115
RIP	120
EGP	140
ODR	160
External EIGRP	170
Internal BGP	200
Unknown	255

A static route to a connected interface has an administrative distance of 0, and is the only route that will override a normal static route. A route sourced with an administrative distance of 255 is not trusted, and will not be inserted into the routing table.

Looking at Table 10-1, you can see that RIP has an administrative distance of 120, while OSPF has an administrative distance of 110. This means that even though the RIP route has a better metric in Figure 10-7, the route inserted into the routing table will be the one provided by OSPF.

Specific Routing Protocols

Entire books have been written on each of the routing protocols discussed in this chapter. My goal is not to teach you everything you need to know about the protocols, but rather to introduce them and show you what you need to know to get them operational. I'll also include some of the commands commonly used to troubleshoot these protocols.

Routing protocols are divided into types based on their purpose and how they operate. The major division between routing protocols is that of internal gateway protocols versus external gateway protocols.

An *internal gateway protocol*, or IGP, is designed to maintain routes within an *autonomous system*. An autonomous system is any group of devices controlled by a single entity. An example might be a company or a school, but the organization does not need to be that broad—an autonomous system could be a floor in a building or a department in a company. Examples of IGPs include RIP, EIGRP, and OSPF.

An *external gateway protocol*, or EGP, is designed to link autonomous systems together. The Internet is the prime example of a large-scale EGP implementation. The autonomous systems—groups of devices controlled by individual service providers, schools, companies, etc.—are each self-contained. They are controlled internally by IGPs and are interconnected using an EGP (in the case of the Internet, BGP).

Figure 10-8 shows how different autonomous systems might be connected. Within each circle is an autonomous system. The IGP running in each autonomous system is unrelated to the external gateway protocol. The EGP knows only that a certain network is owned by a certain autonomous system. Let's say that 1.0.0.0/8 is within ASN 1, 2.0.0.0/8 is within ASN 2, 3.0.0.0/8 is within ASN 3, and so on. For a device in ASN 1 to get to the network 10.0.0.0/8, the path might be through autonomous systems 1, 2, 3, 9, and 10. It might also be through autonomous systems 1, 2, 7, 8, 9, and 10, or even 1, 2, 7, 8, 3, 9, and 10. As with a distance-vector IGP counting hops, the fewer the number of autonomous systems traversed, the more appealing the route.

The important thing to remember with EGPs is that they really don't care how many routers there are or what the speeds of the links are. The only thing an EGP cares about is traversing the least possible number of autonomous systems to arrive at a destination.

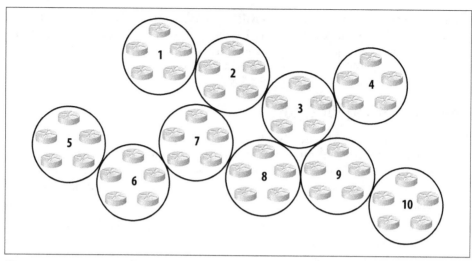

Figure 10-8. Interconnected autonomous systems

Before we go any further, let's define some key routing terms:

Classful routing protocol

A classful routing protocol is one that has no provision to support subnets. The natural state of the network is always advertised. For example, the network 10.0.0.0 will always be advertised with a subnet mask of 255.0.0.0 (/8), regardless of what subnet mask is actually in use. RIPv1 and IGRP are classful routing protocols.

Classless routing protocol

A classless routing protocol is one that includes subnet masks in its advertisements. All modern protocols are classless. EIGRP and OSPF are classless routing protocols.

Poison reverse

If a router needs to tell another router that a network is no longer viable, one of the methods it might employ is *route poisoning*. Consider RIPv1 as an example. Recall that a metric of 16 is considered unreachable. A router can send an update regarding a network with a metric of 16, thereby *poisoning* the entry in the routing table of the receiving router. When a router receives a poison update, it returns the same update to the sending router. This reflected route poisoning is called *poison reverse*. Distance-vector routing protocols (including the hybrid protocol EIGRP) use route poisoning, while link-state protocols such as OSPF do not.

Split horizon

Split horizon is a technique used by many routing protocols to prevent routing loops. When split horizon is enabled, routes that the routing protocol learns are not advertised out the same interfaces from which they were learned. This rule can be problematic in virtual circuit topologies, such as Frame Relay or ATM. If a route is learned on one permanent virtual circuit (PVC) in a Frame Relay interface, chances are the other PVC needs the update but will never receive it, because both PVCs exist on the same physical interface. Frame Relay subinterfaces are often the preferred method of dealing with split horizon issues.

Convergence

A network is said to be *converged* when all of the routers in the network have received and processed all updates. Essentially, this condition exists when a network is stable. Anytime a link's status changes, the routing protocols must propagate that change, whether through timed updates or triggered updates. With timed updates, if updates are sent but no changes need to be made, the network has converged.

As mentioned earlier, many routing protocols exist, but luckily, only a few are in widespread use. Each has its own idiosyncrasies. In the following sections, I'll cover the basic ideas behind the more common protocols and show how to configure them for the most typical scenarios. There is no right or wrong way to configure routing protocols, though some ways are certainly better than others. When designing any network, remember that simplicity is a worthy goal that will save you countless hours of troubleshooting misery.

RIP

RIP is the simplest of the routing protocols in use today. While I like to tell my clients that *simple is good*, I don't consider RIP to be simple goodness.

RIP broadcasts all the routes it knows about every 30 seconds, regardless of the statuses of any other routers in the network. Because RIP uses broadcasts, every host on the network listens to the updates, even though few can process them. On larger networks, the updates can be quite large and consume a lot of bandwidth on expensive WAN links.

Another issue with RIP is the fact that it does not use triggered updates. A *triggered update* is one that is sent when the network changes; *nontriggered (timed) updates* are sent on a regular schedule. Coupled with the fact that updates are sent only every 30 seconds, this behavior causes RIP networks to converge very slowly. Slow convergence is not acceptable in most modern networks, which require failover and convergence in seconds. A RIP network with only five routers may take two minutes or more to converge.

RIP is a classful protocol, which means subnet masks are not advertised. This is also an unacceptable limitation in most networks. Figure 10-9 illustrates one of the most common pitfalls of using classful protocols such as RIP. Router A is advertising its directly connected network 10.10.10.0/24, but because RIP is classful, it advertises the network without the subnet mask. Without a subnet mask, the receiving router must assume the entire network is included in the advertisement. Consequently, upon

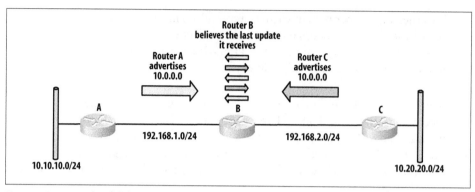

Figure 10-9. RIP classful design problem

receiving the advertisement for 10.0.0.0 from Router A, Router B inserts the entire 10.0.0.0/8 network into its routing table. Router C has a different 10 network attached: 10.20.20.0/24. Again, RIP advertises the 10.0.0.0 network from Router C without a subnet mask. Router B has now received another advertisement for 10.0.0.0/8. The network is the same, the protocol is the same, and the hop count is the same. When a newer update is received for a route that has already been inserted into the routing table, the newer update is considered to be more reliable and is inserted into the routing table, overwriting the previous entry. This means each time Router B receives an update from Router A or Router C, it will change its routing table to show that network 10.0.0.0 is behind the router from which it received the update.

You might be tempted to say that the networks behind Routers A and C in Figure 10-9 are different, but from RIP's point of view, you would be wrong. Technically, the *networks* behind Routers A and C are the same. They are both part of the 10.0.0.0/8 network. The routers are connected to different *subnets* within the 10.0.0.0/8 network, which is why RIP has a problem with the design.

The only other type of network that RIP understands is a host network. RIP can advertise a route for a /32 or 255.255.255.255 network. Because RIP does not include subnet masks in its updates, a route is determined to be a host route when the address of the network is anything other than a normal network address.

Configure routing protocols in IOS using the `router` command. The protocol name is included in the command, which puts the router into router configuration mode:

```
Router-A (config)#router rip
Router-A (config-router)#
```

On modern routers that support RIPv2, if you wish to use RIPv1, you must specify it explicitly in the router configuration, because RIPv2 is used by default:

```
router rip
 version 1
```

By default, no interfaces are included in the routing protocol. This means no interfaces will have routing updates sent on them, and any routing updates received on the interfaces will be ignored.

To enable interfaces in a routing protocol, specify the networks that are configured on the interfaces you wish to include by using the network command in router configuration mode:

```
Router-A (config)#router rip
Router-A (config-router)# network 10.10.10.0
```

With a classful protocol like RIP, you must be careful, because, as an example, including the network 10.0.0.0 will include every interface configured with a 10.x.x.x IP address, regardless of subnet mask. RIP does not allow the inclusion of a subnet or inverse mask in the network statements. You can enter a network other than 10.0.0.0, but IOS will convert the entry into the full classful network.

The preceding entry results in the following being displayed in the configuration:

```
router rip
 network 10.0.0.0
```

The configuration that would include all interfaces for Router A as shown in Figure 10-10 is as follows:

```
router rip
 version 1network 10.0.0.0
 network 192.168.1.0
 network 192.168.2.0
```

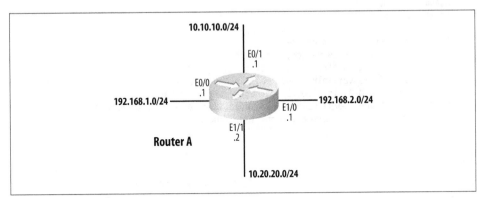

Figure 10-10. Routing protocol network interfaces

One entry covers both the 10.10.10.0 and 10.20.20.0 networks, but the 192.168 networks each require their own network statements. This is because 192.x.x.x networks are class C networks, while 10.x.x.x networks are class A networks.

You won't always want to include every interface that the network statement encompasses. In the preceding example, we might want to allow RIP on E0/0, but not on

E1/1. This can be accomplished with the use of the `passive-interface` command, which removes an interface from the broader range specified by the `network` command:

```
router rip
 version 1
 passive-interface Ethernet1/1
 network 10.0.0.0
```

The `passive-interface` command causes RIP to stop sending updates on the specified interface. The router will continue to receive and process RIP updates received on the interface, though.

Routes learned via RIP are identified in the routing table with an R in the first column. This example shows the network 172.16.0.0/16 learned via RIP. The actual network in use is 172.16.100.0/24, but because RIP is classful, the router assumes the entire 172.16.0.0/16 network is there as well:

```
R3#sho ip route
[text removed]

Gateway of last resort is 192.168.1.2 to network 0.0.0.0
R    172.16.0.0/16 [120/1] via 10.10.10.4, 00:00:21, Ethernet0/0
     10.0.0.0/8 is variably subnetted, 2 subnets, 2 masks
C       10.10.10.0/24 is directly connected, Ethernet0/0
C       10.100.100.100/32 is directly connected, Loopback0
C    192.168.1.0/24 is directly connected, Ethernet1/0
S*   0.0.0.0/0 [254/0] via 192.168.1.2
```

Here we see an example of a host route being received by RIP:

```
R4#sho ip route
[text removed]

Gateway of last resort is not set
     172.16.0.0/32 is subnetted, 1 subnets
C       172.16.1.1 is directly connected, Loopback0
     10.0.0.0/8 is variably subnetted, 2 subnets, 2 masks
C       10.10.10.0/24 is directly connected, Ethernet0/0
R       10.100.100.100/32 [120/1] via 10.10.10.3, 00:00:21, Ethernet0/0
C    192.168.1.0/24 is directly connected, Ethernet0/1
```

RIPv2

RIP was updated in the mid-1990s to reflect the widespread use of Classless Internet Domain Routing (CIDR) and Variable Length Subnet Masks (VLSM). The new protocol, RIP version 2, operates similarly to RIP version 1 in that it still uses hops as its only metric. However, it does have some significant advantages over RIPv1, including:

- RIPv2 supports classless routing by including subnet masks in network advertisements.
- RIPv2 supports triggered updates.

- Updates in RIPv2 are sent using the multicast address 224.0.0.9 instead of as broadcasts.
- Neighbors can be configured with RIPv2. When a neighbor is configured, updates are sent to that neighbor using unicasts, which can further reduce network traffic.
- RIPv2 supports authentication between routers.

> Even though RIPv2 supports subnets, it still only accepts classful addresses in the network command, so be careful when determining which networks and interfaces you've included. Use the passive-interface command to limit the scope of the network command, if necessary.

RIPv2 is classless and advertises routes including subnet masks, but it summarizes routes by default. This means that if you have a 10.10.10.0/24 network connected to your router, it will still advertise 10.0.0.0/8, just like RIPv1. The first thing you should do when configuring RIPv2 is turn off autosummarization with the router command no auto-summary:

```
R3(config)#router rip
R3(config-router)# no auto-summary
```

The routing table in a Cisco router makes no distinction between RIPv1 and RIPv2. Both protocols are represented by a single R in the routing table. Cisco routers default to RIPv1, so you should enable version 2 if you want it, and if you're using RIP, you probably do.

EIGRP

EIGRP is a classless enhancement to IGRP, which supports only classful networks. EIGRP, like IGRP, is a Cisco-proprietary routing protocol, which means that only Cisco routers can use this protocol. If you throw a Juniper or Nortel router into your network, it will not be able to communicate with your Cisco routers using EIGRP.

EIGRP is a very popular routing protocol because it's easy to configure and manage. With minimal configuration and design, you can get an EIGRP network up and running that will serve your company for years to come.

The ease of configuring EIGRP is also the main reason I see so many misbehaving EIGRP networks in the field. A network engineer builds a small network for his company. As time goes on, the network gets larger and larger, and the routing environment gets more and more complicated. EIGRP manages the routing on the network quite nicely, until one day things start to go wrong. The engineer who built the network can't figure out what's wrong, and consultants are called in who completely redesign the network.

This is not to say that EIGRP is not a good routing protocol; I believe it is a very strong protocol. My point is that it's almost too easy to configure. You can throw two EIGRP routers on an Ethernet LAN with minimal configuration, and they will communicate and share routes. You can do the same with 10 or 20 or 100 routers, and they will all communicate and share routes. You can add 100 serial links with remote sites using EIGRP, and they will all communicate and share routes. The routing table will be a mess and the routers may be converging constantly, but the packets will flow. Eventually, however, the default settings may fail to work properly because the default configurations are not designed to scale in massive networks.

When EIGRP is configured properly on a network with a well-designed IP address scheme, it can be an excellent protocol for even a large network. When configured with multiple processes, it can scale very well.

EIGRP is a hybrid routing protocol that combines features from distance-vector protocols with features usually seen in link-state protocols. EIGRP uses triggered updates, so updates are sent only when changes occur. Bandwidth and delay are used as the default metrics, and although you can add other attributes to the equation, it is rarely a good idea to do so. EIGRP converges very quickly, even in large networks. A network that might take minutes to converge with RIP will converge in seconds with EIGRP.

To configure EIGRP, enter into router configuration mode with the `router eigrp autonomous-system-number` command. The autonomous system number identifies the instance of EIGRP. A router can have multiple instances of EIGRP running on it, each with its own database containing routes. The router will choose the best route based on criteria such as metrics, administrative distance, and so on. This behavior is different from that of RIP in that RIP runs globally on the router.

Figure 10-11 shows a router with two instances of EIGRP active. Each instance is referenced by an ASN. Routes learned in one process are not shared with the other process, by default. Each process is essentially its own routing protocol. For a route learned in one process to be known to the other, the router must be configured for redistribution. EIGRP will redistribute IGRP routes automatically within the same ASN (redistribution is covered in detail in Chapter 11).

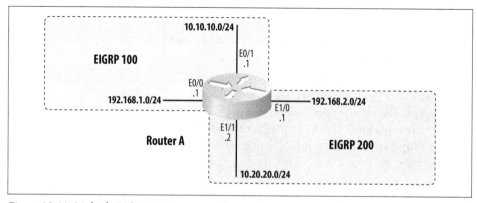

Figure 10-11. Multiple EIGRP instances

As with all IGPs, you list the interfaces you wish to include using the network command. EIGRP, like RIP, will automatically convert a classless network into the classful equivalent. The difference is that with EIGRP, you can add an inverse subnet mask to make the entry more specific. The following commands add all interfaces with addresses in the 10.0.0.0 network to the EIGRP 100 process:

```
Router-A(config)#router eigrp 100
Router-A(config-router)# network 10.0.0.0
```

But in the example in Figure 10-11, we'd like to add only the interface with the network 10.10.10.0/24. The subnet mask for a /24 network is 255.255.255.0, and the inverse subnet mask is 0.0.0.255 (inverse subnet masks are also called wildcard masks, and are discussed in Chapter 23). So, to add only this interface, we'd use the following net work command:

```
Router-A(config-router)#network 10.10.10.0 0.0.0.255
```

After executing this command, the running configuration will still contain the less specific 10.0.0.0 network statement:

```
router eigrp 100
 network 10.10.10.0 0.0.0.255
 network 10.0.0.0
```

Both commands will take effect. Be careful of this, as it can cause no end of frustration. In this example, it will cause the interface E1/1 to be included in EIGRP 100, which is not what we want. We need to remove the less specific network command by negating it:

```
router eigrp 100
 no network 10.0.0.0
```

It's a very good practice to enable only the specific interface you wish to add in any routing process that supports it. You can do this by specifying the IP address on the interface with an all-zeros mask. In our example, the command is network 10.10.10.1 0.0.0.0. This prevents surprises should network masks change or interfaces be renumbered. Thus, my preferred configuration for EIGRP on the router shown in Figure 10-11 is:

```
router eigrp 100
 network 10.10.10.1 0.0.0.0
 network 192.168.1.1 0.0.0.0
 !
router eigrp 200
 network 10.20.20.1 0.0.0.0
 network 192.168.2.1 0.0.0.0
```

EIGRP summarizes routes the same way RIP does, but because EIGRP is a classless protocol, we can disable this behavior with the no auto-summary command:

```
Router-A(config-router)#no auto-summary
```

There are very few instances where you'd want to leave autosummary on, so you should get into the habit of disabling it.

EIGRP operates by sending out hello packets using the multicast IP address 224.0.0.10 on configured interfaces. When a router running EIGRP receives these hello packets, it checks to see if the hello contains a process number matching an EIGRP process running locally. If it does, a handshake is performed. If the handshake is successful, the routers become *neighbors*.

Unlike RIP, which broadcasts routes to anyone who'll listen, EIGRP routers exchange routes only with neighbors. Once a *neighbor adjacency* has been formed, update packets are sent to the neighbor directly using unicast packets.

A useful command for EIGRP installations is `eigrp log-neighbor-changes`. This command displays a message to the console/monitor/log (depending on your logging configuration) every time an EIGRP neighbor adjacency changes state:

```
1d11h: %DUAL-5-NBRCHANGE: IP-EIGRP 100: Neighbor 10.10.10.4 (Ethernet0/0) is up:
new adjacency
```

On large networks, this can be annoying during a problem, but it can easily be disabled if needed.

To see the status of EIGRP neighbors on a router, use the `show ip eigrp neighbors` command:

```
R3#sho ip eigrp neighbors
IP-EIGRP neighbors for process 100
H   Address              Interface    Hold Uptime   SRTT   RTO Q  Seq Type
                                      (sec)         (ms)       Cnt Num
1   10.10.10.5           Et0/0         14 00:00:19    4   200 0  1
0   10.10.10.4           Et0/0         13 00:02:35    8   200 0  3
```

This command's output should be one of the first things you look at if you're having problems, because without a neighbor adjacency, EIGRP routers will not exchange routes.

Routes learned via internal EIGRP have an administrative distance of 90 and are marked with a single D in the first column of the routing table. Routes learned via external EIGRP have an administrative distance of 170 and are marked with the letters D EX at the beginning of the route:

```
R3#sho ip route
[text removed]

Gateway of last resort is 192.168.1.2 to network 0.0.0.0

     5.0.0.0/32 is subnetted, 1 subnets
D EX    5.5.5.5 [170/409600] via 10.10.10.5, 00:00:03, Ethernet0/0
     10.0.0.0/8 is variably subnetted, 2 subnets, 2 masks
C       10.10.10.0/24 is directly connected, Ethernet0/0
C       10.100.100.100/32 is directly connected, Loopback0
C    192.168.1.0/24 is directly connected, Ethernet1/0
```

```
D    192.168.3.0/24 [90/2195456] via 10.10.10.5, 00:08:42, Ethernet0/0
S*   0.0.0.0/0 [254/0] via 192.168.1.2
```

EIGRP stores its information in three databases: the route database, the topology database, and the neighbor database. Viewing the topology database can be a tremendous help when troubleshooting routing problems. Not only can you see what EIGRP has put into the routing table, but you can also see what EIGRP considers to be alternate possibilities for routes:

```
R3#sho ip eigrp topology
IP-EIGRP Topology Table for AS(100)/ID(10.100.100.100)

Codes: P - Passive, A - Active, U - Update, Q - Query, R - Reply,
       r - reply Status, s - sia Status

P 5.5.5.5/32, 1 successors, FD is 409600
        via 10.10.10.5 (409600/128256), Ethernet0/0
P 10.10.10.0/24, 1 successors, FD is 281600
        via Connected, Ethernet0/0
P 192.168.3.0/24, 1 successors, FD is 2195456
        via 10.10.10.5 (2195456/2169856), Ethernet0/0
```

OSPF

In a nutshell, the premise of the OSPF routing protocol is that the shortest or fastest path that is available is the one that will be used.

OSPF is the routing protocol of choice when:

- There are routers from vendors other than Cisco in the network.
- The network requires segmentation into areas or zones.
- You want to avoid proprietary protocols.

OSPF is a link-state routing protocol. The metric it uses is bandwidth. The bandwidth of each link is calculated by dividing 100,000,000 by the bandwidth of the link in bits per second. Thus, a 100 Mbps link has a metric or "cost" of 1, a 10 Mbps link has a cost of 10, and a 1.5 Mbps link has a cost of 64. A 1 Gbps (or faster) link also has a cost of 1 because the cost cannot be lower than 1. The costs for each link in the path are added together to form a metric for the route.

In networks that include links faster than 100 Mbps, the formula for link cost can be changed using the `auto-cost reference-bandwidth` command. The default reference bandwidth is 100. In other words, by default, a 100 Mbps link has a cost of 1. To make a 1,000 Mbps link have a cost of 1, change the reference bandwidth to 1,000:

```
R3(config)#router ospf 100
R3(config-router)# auto-cost reference-bandwidth 1000
```

If you change the reference bandwidth, you must change it on every router communicating in the OSPF process. Failure to do so will cause unstable networks and unpredictable routing behavior.

OSPF classifies routers according to their function in the network. These are the types of OSPF routers:

Internal router
An internal router resides completely within a single area within a single OSPF autonomous system.

Area border router (ABR)
An ABR resides in more than one area within a single OSPF autonomous system.

Autonomous system border router (ASBR)
An ASBR connects to multiple OSPF autonomous systems, or to an OSPF autonomous system and another routing protocol's autonomous system.

Backbone routers
Backbone routers in area zero. Area zero is considered the backbone in an OSPF network.

Designated router (DR)
The DR is the router on a broadcast network that is elected to do the brunt of the OSPF processing. The DR will update all the other routers in the area with routes.

Backup designated router (BDR)
The BDR is the router most eligible to become the DR should the DR fail.

Unlike other routing protocols, OSPF does not send routes, but rather *link state advertisements* (LSAs). Each OSPF router determines which routes to use based on an internal database compiled from these LSAs. There are six LSA types:

Router LSAs (type 1)
Router LSAs are sent by every OSPF router into each connected area. These advertisements describe the router's links within the area.

Network LSAs (type 2)
Network LSAs are sent by DRs and describe the routers connected to the network from which the LSA was received.

Summary LSAs for ABRs (type 3)
Summary LSAs for ABRs are sent by ABRs. These advertisements describe interarea routes for networks. They are also used to advertise summary routes.

Summary LSAs for ASBRs (type 4)
Summary LSAs for ASBRs are sent by ASBRs and ABRs. These advertisements describe links to ASBRs.

Autonomous System External (ASE) LSAs (type 5)

ASE LSAs are sent by ASBRs and ABRs. These advertisements describe networks external to the autonomous system. They are sent everywhere except to stub areas.

Not So Stubby Area (NSSA) LSAs (type 7)

NSSA LSAs are sent by NSSA ASBRs. Since type-5 LSAs are not allowed within the NSSA, type-7 LSAs are sent instead and stay within the NSSA. Type-7 LSAs get converted to type-5 LSAs by NSSA ASRs for advertisement into the backbone.

OSPF separates networks into areas. The core area, which all other areas must connect with, is area zero. One of OSPF's perceived benefits is that it forces you to design your network in such a way that there is a core with satellite areas. You can certainly build an OSPF network with only an area zero, but such a design usually doesn't scale well.

There are two main types of areas: *backbone* and *nonbackbone*. Area zero is the backbone area; all other areas are nonbackbone areas. Nonbackbone areas are further divided into the following types:

Normal area

An OSPF area that is not area zero and is not configured as one of the other types. No special configuration is required.

Stub area

An OSPF area that does not allow ASE LSAs. When an area is configured as a stub, no O E1 or O E2 routes will be seen in the area.

Totally stubby area (TSA)

An OSPF area that does not allow type-3, -4, or -5 LSAs, except for the default summary route. TSAs see only a default route and routes local to the areas themselves.

Not so stubby area (NSSA)

No type-5 LSAs are allowed in an NSSA. Type-7 LSAs that convert to type 5 at the ABR are allowed.

NSSA totally stub area

NSSA totally stub areas are a combination of totally stubby and not so stubby areas. This area type does not allow type-3, -4, or -5 LSAs, except for the default summary route; it does allow type-7 LSAs that convert to type 5 at the ABR.

On Ethernet and other broadcast networks, OSPF elects a router to become the designated router and another to be the backup designated router. Calculating OSPF routes can be CPU-intensive, especially in a dynamic network. Having one router that does the brunt of the work makes the network more stable and allows it to converge faster. The DR calculates the best paths, then propagates that information to its neighbors within the network that are in the same area and OSPF process.

OSPF dynamically elects the DR through a relatively complicated process. The first step involves the router interface's OSPF *priority*. The default priority is 1, which is the lowest value an interface can have and still be elected the DR. A value of 0 indicates that the router is ineligible to become the DR on the network. Setting the priority higher increases the chances that the router will be elected the DR. The OSPF interface priority is configured using the interface command `ip ospf priority`. The valid range is 0–255.

Ideally, you should plan which router is to become the DR and set its priority accordingly. Usually, there is an obvious choice, such as a hub or core router, or perhaps just the most powerful router on the network. The designated router will be doing more work than the other routers, so it should be the one with the most horsepower. If your design includes a hub router, that router will need to be the DR, because it will be the center of the topology.

If the OSPF interface priority is not set, resulting in a tie, the router will use the OSPF router ID to break the tie. Every router has an OSPF router ID. This ID can be configured manually with the `router-id` command. If the router ID is not configured manually, the router will assign it based on the IP address of the highest-numbered loopback address, if one is configured. If a loopback address is not configured, the router ID will be the highest IP address configured on the router. The only ways to change the router ID are to remove and reinstall the OSPF configuration or to reboot the router. Be careful, and think ahead when planning your network IP scheme.

 When first deploying OSPF, engineers commonly make the mistake of neglecting the priority and router ID when configuring the routers. Left to its own devices, OSPF will usually pick routers that you would not choose as the DR and BDR.

A common network design using OSPF is to have a WAN in the core as area zero. Figure 10-12 shows such a network. Notice that all of the areas are designated with the same OSPF process number. Each area borders on area zero, and there are no paths between areas other than via area zero. This is a proper OSPF network design.

Area zero does not have to be fully meshed when you're using technologies such as Frame Relay. This is in part because OSPF recognizes the fact that there are different types of networks. OSPF knows that networks supporting broadcasts act differently from networks that are point-to-point and thus have only two active IP addresses. OSPF supports the following network types:

Point-to-point
> A point-to-point network is one with only two nodes on it. A common example is a serial link between routers, such as a point-to-point T1. No DR is chosen in a point-to-point network, because there are only two routers on the network. This is the default OSPF network type on serial interfaces with PPP or HDLC encapsulation.

Point-to-multipoint
> In a point-to-multipoint network, one hub router connects to all the other routers, but the other routers only connect to the hub router. Specifically, the remote

routers are assumed to be connected with virtual circuits, though only one IP network is used. No neighbors are configured and no DR is chosen. Area 0 in Figure 10-12 could be configured as a point-to-multipoint OSPF network.

Broadcast

A broadcast network is an Ethernet, Token Ring, or FDDI network. Any number of hosts may reside on a broadcast network, and any host may communicate directly with any other host. A DR must be chosen and neighbors must be discovered or configured on a broadcast network. A broadcast network uses multicasts to send hello packets to discover OSPF routers. This is the default OSPF network type for Ethernet and Token Ring networks.

Nonbroadcast multiaccess (NBMA)

In a nonbroadcast multiaccess network, all nodes may be able to communicate with one another, but they do not share a single medium. Examples include Frame Relay, X.25, and Switched Multimegabit Data Service (SMDS) networks. Because NBMA networks do not use multicasts to discover neighbors, you must manually configure them. Area 0 in Figure 10-12 could be configured as an NBMA network. This is the default OSPF network type on serial interfaces with Frame Relay encapsulation.

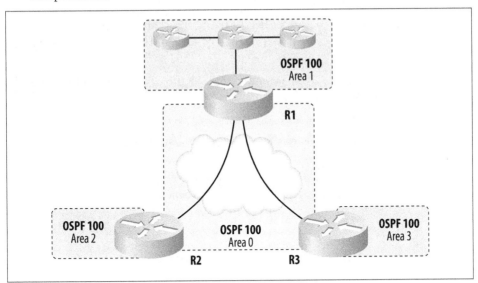

Figure 10-12. Simple OSPF network

OSPF enables interfaces using the network router command. It is a classless protocol, so you must use inverse subnet masks to limit the interfaces included. Unlike with EIGRP, you must include the inverse mask. If you do not, OSPF will not assume a classful network, but will instead report an error:

```
R3(config-router)#network 10.10.10.0
% Incomplete command.
```

In addition to the inverse mask, you must also specify the area in which the network resides:

```
R3(config-router)#network 10.10.10.0 0.0.0.255 area 0
```

My preference is to specifically configure interfaces so there are no surprises. You do this with an inverse mask of 0.0.0.0:

```
R3(config-router)#network 10.10.10.1 0.0.0.0 area 0
```

OSPF routes are marked by the letter O in the first column of the routing table:

```
R3#sho ip route
[Text Removed]

Gateway of last resort is 192.168.1.2 to network 0.0.0.0

      192.192.192.0/30 is subnetted, 1 subnets
C        192.192.192.4 is directly connected, Serial0/0
      172.16.0.0/32 is subnetted, 1 subnets
O IA     172.16.1.1 [110/11] via 10.10.10.4, 00:00:09, Ethernet0/0
      10.0.0.0/24 is subnetted, 1 subnets
C        10.10.10.0 is directly connected, Ethernet0/0
C     192.168.1.0/24 is directly connected, Ethernet1/0
S*    0.0.0.0/0 [254/0] via 192.168.1.2
```

Various OSPF route types are described in the routing table. They are: O (OSPF), O IA (OSPF interarea), O N1 (OSPF NSSA external type 1), and O N2 (OSPF NSSA external type 2).

OSPF stores its routes in a database, much like EIGRP. The command to show the database is show ip ospf database:

```
R3#sho ip ospf database

            OSPF Router with ID (192.192.192.5) (Process ID 100)

                Router Link States (Area 0)
    Link ID         ADV Router      Age       Seq#        Checksum Link count
    192.192.192.5   192.192.192.5   1769      0x8000002A 0x00C190 1

                Summary Net Link States (Area 0)

    Link ID         ADV Router      Age       Seq#        Checksum
    192.192.192.4   192.192.192.5   1769      0x8000002A 0x003415

                Router Link States (Area 1)

    Link ID         ADV Router      Age       Seq#        Checksum Link count
    192.192.192.5   192.192.192.5   1769      0x8000002A 0x00B046 1

                Summary Net Link States (Area 1)

    Link ID         ADV Router      Age       Seq#        Checksum
    10.10.10.0      192.192.192.5   1769      0x8000002A 0x0002A2
```

```
OSPF Router with ID (192.168.1.116) (Process ID 1)
```

If all of this seems needlessly complicated to you, you're not alone. The complexity of OSPF is one of the reasons many people choose EIGRP instead. If you're working in a multivendor environment, however, EIGRP is not an option.

BGP

BGP is a very different protocol from the others described here. The most obvious difference is that BGP is an external gateway protocol, while all the previously discussed protocols were internal gateway protocols. BGP can be hard to understand for those who have only ever dealt with internal protocols like EIGRP and OSPF, because the very nature of the protocol is different. As BGP is not often seen in the corporate environment, I'll cover it only briefly here.

BGP does not deal with hops or links, but rather with autonomous systems. A network in BGP is referred to as a *prefix*. A prefix is advertised from an autonomous system. BGP then propagates that information through the connected autonomous systems until all the autonomous systems know about the prefix.

Routes in BGP are considered most desirable when they traverse the least possible number of autonomous systems. When a prefix is advertised, the autonomous system number is prefixed onto the autonomous system *path*. This path is the equivalent of a route in an internal gateway protocol. When an autonomous system learns of a prefix, it learns of the path associated with it. When the autonomous system advertises that prefix to another autonomous system, it prepends its own ASN to the path. As the prefix is advertised to more and more autonomous systems, the path gets longer and longer. The shorter the path, the more desirable it is.

Figure 10-13 shows a simple example of BGP routing in action. The network 10.0.0.0/8 resides in AS 105, which advertises this prefix to AS 3 and AS 2. The path for 10.0.0.0/8 within AS 3 and AS 2 is now 10.0.0.0/8 AS105. AS 2 in turn advertises the prefix to AS 1, prepending its own ASN to the path. AS 1 now knows the path to 10.0.0.0/8 as 10.0.0.0/8 AS2, AS105. Meanwhile, AS 3 advertises the prefix to AS 100, which then knows the path to 10.0.0.0/8 as 10.0.0.0/8 AS3, AS105.

On the other side of the world, AS 102 receives two paths:

```
> 10.0.0.0/8 AS1, AS2, AS105
  10.0.0.0/8 AS101, AS100, AS3, AS105
```

The > on the first line indicates that BGP considers this the preferred path. The path is preferred because it is the shortest path among the known choices.

What makes BGP so confusing to newcomers is the many attributes that can be configured. A variety of weights can be attributed to paths, with names like local preference, weight, communities, and multiexit discriminator. To make matters worse, many of these attributes are very similar in function.

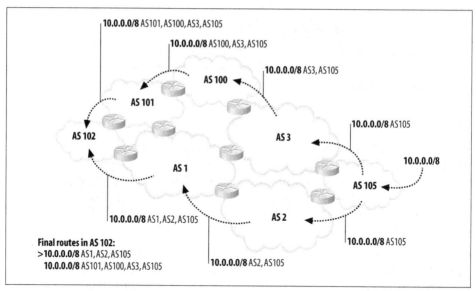

10.0.0.0/8 AS101, AS100, AS3, AS105

10.0.0.0/8 AS100, AS3, AS105

10.0.0.0/8 AS3, AS105

AS 100

AS 101

10.0.0.0/8 AS105

AS 102

AS 3

10.0.0.0/8

AS 1

AS 105

10.0.0.0/8 AS1, AS2, AS105

AS 2

Final routes in AS 102:
>**10.0.0.0/8** AS1, AS2, AS105
  10.0.0.0/8 AS101, AS100, AS3, AS105

10.0.0.0/8 AS2, AS105

10.0.0.0/8 AS105

Figure 10-13. Routing in BGP

The protocol also functions differently from other protocols. For example, the net
work statement, which is used to enable interfaces in other protocols, is used in BGP to
list the specific networks that can be advertised.

BGP does not discover neighbors; they must be configured manually. There can only
be one autonomous system on any given router, though it may communicate with
neighbors in other autonomous systems.

BGP is the routing protocol of the Internet. Many of the major service providers allow
anonymous Telnet into *route servers* that act just like Cisco routers. Do an Internet
search for the term "looking-glass routers," and you should find plenty of links. These
route servers are an excellent way to learn more about BGP, as they are a part of the
largest network in the world and have active routes to just about every public network
on Earth. Unless you're working at a tier-1 service provider, where else could you get
to poke around with a BGP router that has 20 neighbors, 191,898 prefixes, and
3,666,117 paths? I have a pretty cool lab, but I can't compete with that! Here is the
output from an actual route server:

```
route-server>sho ip bgp summary
BGP router identifier 10.1.2.5, local AS number 65000
BGP table version is 208750, main routing table version 208750
191680 network entries using 19359680 bytes of memory
3641563 path entries using 174795024 bytes of memory
46514 BGP path attribute entries using 2605064 bytes of memory
42009 BGP AS-PATH entries using 1095100 bytes of memory
4 BGP community entries using 96 bytes of memory
0 BGP route-map cache entries using 0 bytes of memory
0 BGP filter-list cache entries using 0 bytes of memory
BGP using 197854964 total bytes of memory
```

```
Dampening enabled. 2687 history paths, 420 dampened paths
191529 received paths for inbound soft reconfiguration
BGP activity 191898/218 prefixes, 3666117/24554 paths, scan interval 60 secs
```

Neighbor	V	AS	MsgRcvd	MsgSent	TblVer	InQ	OutQ	Up/Down	State/PfxRcd
10.0.0.2	4	7018	0	0	0	0	0	never	Idle (Admin)
12.0.1.63	4	7018	45038	188	208637	0	0	03:04:16	0
12.123.1.236	4	7018	39405	189	208637	0	0	03:05:02	191504
12.123.5.240	4	7018	39735	189	208637	0	0	03:05:04	191504
12.123.9.241	4	7018	39343	189	208637	0	0	03:05:03	191528
12.123.13.241	4	7018	39617	188	208637	0	0	03:04:20	191529
12.123.17.244	4	7018	39747	188	208637	0	0	03:04:58	191505
12.123.21.243	4	7018	39441	188	208637	0	0	03:04:28	191528
12.123.25.245	4	7018	39789	189	208637	0	0	03:05:07	191504
12.123.29.249	4	7018	39602	188	208637	0	0	03:04:16	191505
12.123.33.249	4	7018	39541	188	208637	0	0	03:04:16	191528
12.123.37.250	4	7018	39699	188	208637	0	0	03:04:26	191529
12.123.41.250	4	7018	39463	188	208637	0	0	03:04:19	191529
12.123.45.252	4	7018	39386	188	208637	0	0	03:04:20	191505
12.123.133.124	4	7018	39720	188	208637	0	0	03:04:20	191528
12.123.134.124	4	7018	39729	188	208637	0	0	03:04:22	191529
12.123.137.124	4	7018	39480	188	208637	0	0	03:04:15	191528
12.123.139.124	4	7018	39807	188	208637	0	0	03:04:24	191528
12.123.142.124	4	7018	39748	188	208637	0	0	03:04:22	191505
12.123.145.124	4	7018	39655	188	208637	0	0	03:04:23	191529

 These route servers can get pretty busy and very slow. If you find yourself waiting too long for a response to a query, either wait a bit and try again, or try another route server.

Choose your favorite public IP network (doesn't everyone have one?) and see how the paths look from the looking-glass router. If you don't have a favorite, choose one that you can easily figure out, like one in use by www.cisco.com or www.oreilly.com:

```
[bossman@myserver bossman]$nslookup www.oreilly.com
Server:  localhost
Address:  127.0.0.1

Name:    www.oreilly.com
Addresses:  208.201.239.36, 208.201.239.37
```

Once you have the address, you can do a lookup for the network:

```
route-server>sho ip bgp 208.201.239.0
BGP routing table entry for 208.201.224.0/19, version 157337
Paths: (19 available, best #15, table Default-IP-Routing-Table)
  Not advertised to any peer
  7018 701 7065, (received & used)
    12.123.137.124 from 12.123.137.124 (12.123.137.124)
      Origin IGP, localpref 100, valid, external, atomic-aggregate
      Community: 7018:5000
  7018 701 7065, (received & used)
    12.123.33.249 from 12.123.33.249 (12.123.33.249)
```

```
                Origin IGP, localpref 100, valid, external, atomic-aggregate
                Community: 7018:5000
       7018 701 7065, (received & used)
         12.123.29.249 from 12.123.29.249 (12.123.29.249)
                Origin IGP, localpref 100, valid, external, atomic-aggregate
                Community: 7018:5000
       7018 701 7065, (received & used)
         12.123.41.250 from 12.123.41.250 (12.123.41.250)
                Origin IGP, localpref 100, valid, external, atomic-aggregate
                Community: 7018:5000
       7018 701 7065, (received & used)
         12.123.1.236 from 12.123.1.236 (12.123.1.236)
                Origin IGP, localpref 100, valid, external, atomic-aggregate, best
                Community: 7018:5000
```

## CHAPTER 11

Redistribution

Redistribution is the process of injecting routes into a routing protocol from outside the realm of the protocol. For example, if you had a router that was running EIGRP and OSPF, and you needed the routes learned by EIGRP to be advertised in OSPF, you would redistribute the EIGRP routes into OSPF. Another common example is the redistribution of static or connected routes. Because static routes are entered manually, and not learned, they must be redistributed into a routing protocol if you wish them to be advertised.

As Figure 11-1 shows, routes learned through EIGRP are not automatically advertised out of the OSPF interfaces. To accomplish this translation of sorts, you must configure redistribution within the protocol where you wish the routes to appear.

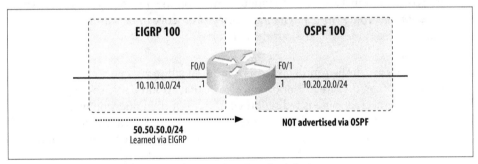

Figure 11-1. Most routing protocols do not redistribute by default

One of the main reasons protocols do not redistribute routes automatically is that different protocols have vastly different metrics. OSPF, for example, calculates the best route based on the bandwidth of the links. EIGRP, on the other hand, uses bandwidth and delay (by default) to form a very different metric. While the router could assume you wanted to redistribute, and assign a standard metric to the learned routes, a better approach is to allow you to decide whether and how routes should be redistributed.

There are two steps to redistributing routes. First, you must configure a metric. This allows the routing protocol to assign a metric that it understands to the incoming routes. Second, add the `redistribute` command. The exact commands used for these purposes vary widely between protocols, and they'll be discussed individually in the sections that follow.

One reason to redistribute routes might be the inclusion of a firewall that must participate in dynamic routing but cannot use the protocol in use on the network. For example, many firewalls support RIP, but not EIGRP. To dynamically route between an EIGRP router and a RIP-only firewall, you must redistribute between RIP and EIGRP on the router.

The best rule to remember when redistributing is to keep it simple. It's easy to get confused when routes are being sent back and forth between routing protocols. Keeping the design as simple as possible will help keep the network manageable. You can create some pretty interesting problems when redistribution isn't working properly. The simpler the design is, the easier it is to troubleshoot.

Redistribution is about converting one protocol's routes into a form that another protocol can understand. You do this by assigning new metrics to the routes as they pass into the new protocol. Because the routes must adhere to the metrics of the new protocol, the key to understanding redistribution is understanding metrics.

When a protocol redistributes routes from any source, they become *external* routes in the new protocol. Routes can be redistributed from a limited number of sources:

Static routes
> Routes that have been entered manually into the configuration of the router doing the redistribution can be redistributed into routing protocols. Injecting static routes on one router into a dynamic routing protocol can be a useful way of propagating those routes throughout the network.

Connected routes
> Routes that are in the routing table as a result of a directly connected interface on the router doing the redistribution can also be redistributed into routing protocols. When a connected route is redistributed, the network in question will be inserted into the routing protocol, but the interfaces configured within that network will not advertise or listen for route advertisements. You can use this as an alternative to the `network` command when such behavior is desired.

Other routing protocols
> Routes can be learned dynamically from other routing protocols that are active on the router doing the redistribution. Routes from any routing protocol can be redistributed into any other routing protocol. An example of redistributing between routing protocols is OSPF redistributing into EIGRP.

The same routing protocol from a different autonomous system or process
> Protocols that support autonomous systems, such as EIGRP, OSPF, and BGP, can redistribute among these systems. An example of a single protocol redistributing between autonomous systems is EIGRP 100 redistributing into EIGRP 200.

Regardless of which protocol you redistribute into, you can still only do it from one of the sources just listed. When redistributing routes, you use the command `redistribute` —followed by the route source—within the protocol receiving the route.

> Redistribution is configured on the protocol for which the routes are destined, not the one from which they are sourced. No configuration is required on the protocol providing the routes.

Redistributing into RIP

We'll start with RIP because it has the simplest metric and, therefore, the simplest configuration.

A common problem with configuring routing protocols is the inclusion of static routes. Because the routes are static, they are, by definition, not dynamic. But if they're statically defined, why include them in a dynamic routing protocol at all?

Figure 11-2 shows a simple network where redistribution of a static route is required. R1 has a directly connected interface on the 50.50.50.0/24 network, but is not running a routing protocol. R2 has a static route pointing to R1 for the 50.50.50.0/24 network. R2 and R3 are both communicating using RIPv2. In this case, R3 cannot get to the 50.50.50.0/24 network because R2 has not advertised it.

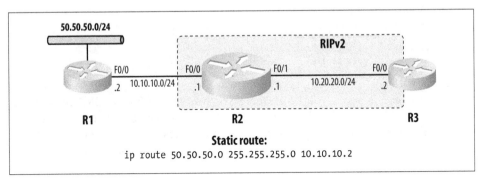

Figure 11-2. Redistributing a static route into RIPv2

For RIP to advertise the static route to R3, the route must be redistributed into RIP. Here is the full RIP configuration for R2:

```
router rip
 version 2
 redistribute static metric 1
 network 10.0.0.0
 no auto-summary
```

Notice the `metric` keyword on the `redistribute` command. This defines the RIP metric for all static routes injected into RIP. Another way to accomplish this is with the `default-metric` command:

```
router rip
 version 2
 redistribute static
 network 10.0.0.0
 default-metric 3
 no auto-summary
```

Here, the default metric is set to 3. If you set a default metric as shown here, you don't need to include a metric when you use the `redistribute static` command. The router will automatically assign the default metric you've specified to all redistributed static routes.

You can see a protocol's default metric with the `show ip protocols` command:

```
R2#sho ip protocols
Routing Protocol is "rip"
  Sending updates every 30 seconds, next due in 2 seconds
  Invalid after 180 seconds, hold down 180, flushed after 240
  Outgoing update filter list for all interfaces is not set
  Incoming update filter list for all interfaces is not set
  Default redistribution metric is 3
  Redistributing: static, rip
  Default version control: send version 2, receive version 2
  Automatic network summarization is not in effect
  Maximum path: 4
  Routing for Networks:
    10.0.0.0
  Routing Information Sources:
    Gateway         Distance      Last Update
  Distance: (default is 120)
```

Be careful with default metrics, because they apply to all routes redistributed into the routing protocol, regardless of the source. If you now redistribute EIGRP into RIP, the metric assigned in RIP will be 3 because that is the configured default. You can override the default metric by specifying a metric on each `redistribute` command. Here, I have specified a default metric of 5, but I've also configured EIGRP routes to have a metric of 1 when redistributed into RIP:

```
router rip
 version 2
 redistribute static
 redistribute eigrp 100 metric 1
 network 10.0.0.0
 default-metric 5
 no auto-summary
```

Here is the routing table on R3 after the final configuration on R2:

```
R3#sho ip route
[text removed]
```

```
Gateway of last resort is not set

     192.192.192.0/30 is subnetted, 1 subnets
C       192.192.192.4 is directly connected, Serial0/0
     50.0.0.0/24 is subnetted, 1 subnets
R       50.50.50.0 [120/5] via 10.20.20.1, 00:00:07, Ethernet1/0
     10.0.0.0/24 is subnetted, 2 subnets
R       10.10.10.0 [120/1] via 10.20.20.1, 00:00:10, Ethernet1/0
C       10.20.20.0 is directly connected, Ethernet1/0
```

The route 50.50.50.0/24 is in the routing table and has a metric of 5. The route below it is a result of the network 10.0.0.0 statement on R2. This route is not a product of redistribution, and so has a normal RIP metric.

Another common issue is the need to advertise networks that are connected to a router but are not included in the routing process. Figure 11-3 shows a network with three routers, all of which are participating in RIPv2. R1 has a network that is not included in the RIP process. The configuration for R1's RIP process is as follows:

```
router rip
 version 2
 network 10.0.0.0
 no auto-summary
```

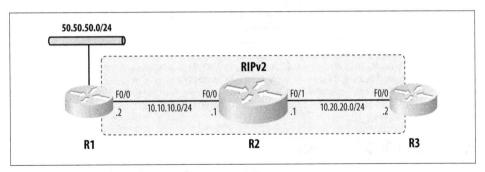

Figure 11-3. Redistributing connected routes into RIP

There are no routers on the 50.50.50.0/24 network, so enabling RIP on that interface would add useless broadcasts on that network. Still, R3 needs to be able to get to the network. To add 50.50.50.0/24 to the advertisements sent out by R1, we must redistribute connected networks into RIP using the redistribute connected command on R1:

```
router rip
 version 2
 redisribute connected metric 1
 network 10.0.0.0
 no auto-summary
```

While sending useless broadcasts may seem trivial, remember that RIP sends broadcasts that include the entire routing table. Only 25 destinations can be included in a single RIP update packet. On a network with 200 routes, each update will be composed of eight large broadcast packets, each of which will need to be processed by every device on the network. That's potentially 12k of data every 30 seconds.

If that's not enough proof for you, consider this: RIP updates are classified as *control* packets (IP precedence 6 or DSCP 48). That means that they have a higher precedence than voice RTP (Real-Time Protocol) packets, which are classified as *express forwarding* packets (IP precedence 5 or DSCP 40). Put simply, RIP updates can easily affect voice quality on VOIP-enabled networks.

Now R3 can see the 50.50.50.0/24 network in its routing table because it's been advertised across the network by RIP:

```
R3#sho ip route
[text removed]

Gateway of last resort is not set

     192.192.192.0/30 is subnetted, 1 subnets
C       192.192.192.4 is directly connected, Serial0/0
     50.0.0.0/24 is subnetted, 1 subnets
R       50.50.50.0 [120/2] via 10.20.20.1, 00:00:05, Ethernet1/0
     10.0.0.0/24 is subnetted, 2 subnets
R       10.10.10.0 [120/1] via 10.20.20.1, 00:00:24, Ethernet1/0
C       10.20.20.0 is directly connected, Ethernet1/0
     192.168.1.0/29 is subnetted, 1 subnets
R       192.168.1.0 [120/2] via 10.20.20.1, 00:00:24, Ethernet1/0
```

Redistributing into EIGRP

EIGRP was designed to automatically redistribute IGRP routes from the same ASN. You can disable this behavior with the `no redistribute igrp` *autonomous-system* command:

```
router eigrp 100
  no redistribute igrp 100
```

You redistribute routes into EIGRP in the same way as you do with RIP. It only looks harder because the metric in EIGRP is more complicated than that in RIP; whereas RIP only uses hop count as a metric, EIGRP uses the combined bandwidth and delay values from all the links in the path. In fact, EIGRP uses more than just these two measurements, but, by default, the other metrics are disabled. However, with redistribution, you must specify them, so let's take a look at what they should be.

As with RIP, you can use the `default-metric` command to specify the metric of redistributed routes, or you can specify the metric on each `redistribute` command line.

Here are the arguments required for the `default-metric` command in EIGRP, and the allowed ranges of values:

- Bandwidth in Kbps: 1–4,294,967,295
- Delay in 10-microsecond units: 0–4,294,967,295
- Reliability metric, where 255 is 100 percent reliable: 0–255
- Effective bandwidth metric (loading), where 255 is 100 percent loaded: 1–255
- Maximum Transmission Unit (MTU) metric of the path: 1–4,294,967,295

How you configure these values will depend largely on your needs at the time. Remember that redistributed routes are external routes, so they will always have a higher administrative distance than internal routes in EIGRP. Such routes will be advertised with an administrative distance of 170.

You need to make redistributed routes appear as though they are links, because that's what EIGRP understands. If you wanted to make redistributed routes appear as 100 Mbps Ethernet links, configure the default metric like this:

```
R3(config-router)#default-metric 100000 10 255 1 1500
```

The appropriate values to use in these commands are not always obvious. For example, the bandwidth is presented in Kbps, not bps (a 100 Mbps link is 100,000 Kbps). This reflects the way bandwidth is displayed in the `show interface` command:

```
R2#sho int f0/0 | include BW
  MTU 1500 bytes, BW 100000 Kbit, DLY 100 usec,
```

Conversely, notice how the `show interface` command shows the delay of an interface:

```
R2#sho int f0/0 | include DLY
  MTU 1500 bytes, BW 100000 Kbit, DLY 100 usec,
```

Here, the delay is shown in microseconds, but when you specify the delay in redistribution, you must use 10-microsecond units. That is, to achieve a delay of 100 microseconds, you specify a delay value of 10.

When I configure redistribution, I always make the reliability 255, loading 1, and MTU 1500. In fact, I usually make the redistributed routes appear as 100 Mbps links, as shown previously. Keep it simple. While there may be instances where you'll want to alter these values, those instances will be rare.

The method of specifying a default metric and overriding it with a specific metric described earlier in the section "Redistributing into RIP" on page 149 is also valid with EIGRP. Here, I've specified a default metric reflecting a 100 Mbps link with a delay of 100 microseconds, and I'm redistributing OSPF process 100 with a metric reflecting a 1,000 Mbps link with a delay of 50 microseconds:

```
router eigrp 100
 redistribute ospf 100 metric 1000000 5 255 1 1500
 network 10.0.0.0
```

```
default-metric 100000 10 255 1 1500
no auto-summary
```

When redistributing OSPF routes into another protocol, you can limit the types of routes that are redistributed. For example, you can redistribute only OSPF internal routes, while ignoring all OSPF external routes. You do so by using the match keyword with the redistribute ospf command:

```
R2(config-router)#redistribute ospf 100 match ?
  external      Redistribute OSPF external routes
  internal      Redistribute OSPF internal routes
  nssa-external Redistribute OSPF NSSA external routes
```

When matching external routes, you can also differentiate between OSPF type-1 and type-2 routes:

```
R2(config-router)#redistribute ospf 100 match external ?
  1             Redistribute external type 1 routes
  2             Redistribute external type 2 routes
  external      Redistribute OSPF external routes
  internal      Redistribute OSPF internal routes
  match         Redistribution of OSPF routes
  metric        Metric for redistributed routes
  nssa-external Redistribute OSPF NSSA external routes
  route-map     Route map reference
  <cr>
```

Finally, you can combine route types with the match keyword. As an example, I have configured this router to redistribute OSPF routes from process 100 into EIGRP 100, but to include only internal routes and external type-2 routes:

```
R2(config-router)#redistribute ospf 100 match internal external 2
```

Because I have not specified a metric, the default metric will be used. I could have added a metric to the specific redistribution as well.

You redistribute RIP into EIGRP in the same way as redistributing OSPF, but there is no option for matching route types, because RIP does not support the many types of routes that OSPF does:

```
router eigrp 100
 redistribute rip metric 100000 100 255 1 1500
```

Redistributing into OSPF

You redistribution into OSPF in the same way as in the other protocols. The metric for an OSPF route is a derivative of the bandwidths of the links contained in the route. Set the default metric in OSPF to 10 Mbps as follows:

```
R3(config-router)#default-metric 10
```

There are no other options. The metric can have a value of 1–16,777,214, with 1 being 100 Mbps (assuming default settings).

If you do not specify a default metric or a metric on the `redistribute` command line, OSPF will assign a metric of 20 to all redistributed routes, except those from BGP, which will be assigned a metric of 1.

While all redistributed routes are external, OSPF supports two types of external routes, which are cleverly described as *type-1* and *type-2* external routes. Type-1 routes are designated with `O E1` in the routing table, while type-2 routes are designated with `O E2`. `E1` routes include the metric as set at the point of redistribution, plus the metric of all the links within the OSPF autonomous system. `E2` routes only include the metric set at the point of redistribution. Figure 11-4 illustrates how the OSPF metrics change throughout a simple network depending on the external route type in use.

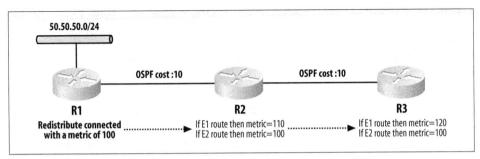

Figure 11-4. OSPF external route types

Redistribution into OSPF defaults to type-2 routes. Which type should you use? That depends on your needs at the time. Generally, in smaller networks (less than, say, 10 routers), `E2` routes may be easier to maintain, as they have the same value anywhere in the OSPF autonomous system. But to me, `E1` routes function more logically because they increment with each hop, as do most other metrics.

To set the route type, add the `metric-type` keyword to the `redistribute` command:

```
R3(config-router)#redistribute eigrp 100 metric-type ?
  1   Set OSPF External Type 1 metrics
  2   Set OSPF External Type 2 metrics
```

The metric type and the metric can be added onto one command line:

```
R3(config-router)#redistribute eigrp 100 metric-type 2 metric 100
```

In practice, every time you redistribute into OSPF, you should include the keyword `subnets`:

```
R3(config-router)#redistribute eigrp 100 metric 100 subnets
```

Without the `subnets` keyword, OSPF will redistribute only routes that have not been subnetted. In the world of VLSM, where practically all networks are subnets, it is rare that you will not want subnets to be redistributed.

If you do not include the subnets keyword on modern versions of IOS, you will be warned about your probable mistake:

```
R3(config-router)#redistribute eigrp 100 metric 100
% Only classful networks will be redistributed
```

Mutual Redistribution

The term *mutual redistribution* refers to when a router redistributes between two routing protocols in both directions instead of just one. Often, we redistribute because there is a device or entity we wish to connect with that doesn't support the routing protocol we have chosen to use. We need to share routes between protocols, but, if you will, the protocols don't speak the same language.

Figure 11-5 shows a network in which every subnet needs to be reached by every other subnet. The problem here is that the network on the left is using OSPF and the network on the right is using EIGRP. For a host on 50.50.50.0 to route to a host on the 70.70.70.0 network, EIGRP routes will need to be redistributed into OSPF. Conversely, if hosts on the 70.70.70.0 network wish to talk with the hosts on 50.50.50.0, OSPF routes will need to be redistributed into EIGRP. Because there is only one router connecting these two domains together, redistribution must occur in both directions.

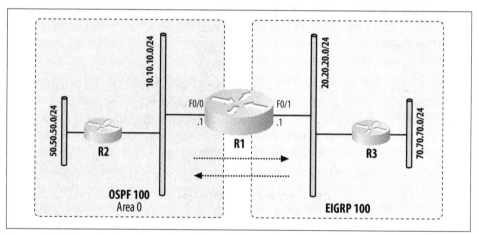

Figure 11-5. Mutual redistribution

To accomplish mutual redistribution on one router, simply configure both protocols for redistribution into the other:

```
router eigrp 100
 redistribute ospf 100
 network 20.20.20.0 0.0.0.255
 default-metric 100000 100 255 1 1500
 no auto-summary
!
```

```
router ospf 100
  redistribute eigrp 100 metric 100 subnets
  network 10.10.10.0 0.0.0.255 area 0
  default-metric 10
```

The configuration is simple. I've followed the steps outlined in the preceding sections by establishing a default metric in each protocol, then redistributed accordingly. Nothing more needs to be done when there is only one router doing mutual redistribution.

Redistribution Loops

Things can get interesting when multiple routers are redistributing. Routes redistributed from one routing protocol into another can be redistributed back into the originating protocol, which can cause some pretty strange results. All of the original metrics will have been lost, so the route will inherit whatever metric was configured during redistribution.

Figure 11-6 shows a network with three routers. R3 has a network attached that is being advertised in EIGRP 100 by way of the `redistribute connected` command (50.50.50.0/24). R1 is redistributing from OSPF into EIGRP (from left to right in the figure), and R2 is redistributing from EIGRP to OSPF (from right to left in the figure).

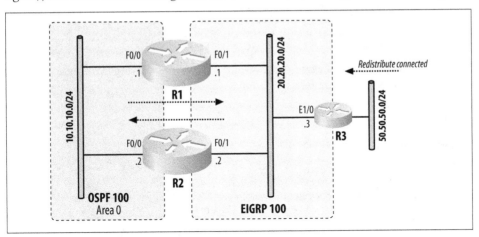

Figure 11-6. Redistribution loop

The network 50.50.50.0/24 will be advertised from R3 to R1 and R2 through EIGRP. R2 will in turn redistribute the route into OSPF 100. R2 now has an entry for 50.50.50.0.24 in the OSPF database as well as the EIGRP topology table. Because the route was originally redistributed into EIGRP, it has an administrative distance of 170 when it gets to R2. R2 advertises the route to R1 via OSPF, which has an administrative distance of 110. So, even though R1 has also learned of the route from R3, where it originated, it will prefer the route from R2 because of the more attractive administrative distance.

Here are the IP routing tables from each router. Router R1 has learned the route for 50.50.50.0/24 from router R2 via OSPF:

```
R1#sho ip route
[text removed]

Gateway of last resort is not set

     50.0.0.0/24 is subnetted, 1 subnets
O E2    50.50.50.0 [110/10] via 10.10.10.2, 00:16:28, FastEthernet0/0
     20.0.0.0/24 is subnetted, 1 subnets
C        20.20.20.0 is directly connected, FastEthernet0/1
     10.0.0.0/24 is subnetted, 1 subnets
C        10.10.10.0 is directly connected, FastEthernet0/0
```

R2 has learned the route from EIGRP as an external route from R3. The route is external because it was originally redistributed into EIGRP on R3:

```
R2#sho ip route
[text removed]

Gateway of last resort is not set

     50.0.0.0/24 is subnetted, 1 subnets
D EX    50.50.50.0 [170/156160] via 20.20.20.3, 00:17:30, FastEthernet0/1
     20.0.0.0/24 is subnetted, 1 subnets
C        20.20.20.0 is directly connected, FastEthernet0/1
     10.0.0.0/24 is subnetted, 1 subnets
C        10.10.10.0 is directly connected, FastEthernet0/0
```

R3 shows only its two connected routes and the network from the OSPF side, as it was redistributed into EIGRP on R2:

```
R3#sho ip route
[text removed]

Gateway of last resort is not set

     50.0.0.0/24 is subnetted, 1 subnets
C        50.50.50.0 is directly connected, Loopback0
     20.0.0.0/24 is subnetted, 1 subnets
C        20.20.20.0 is directly connected, Ethernet1/0
     10.0.0.0/24 is subnetted, 1 subnets
D EX    10.10.10.0 [170/537600] via 20.20.20.1, 00:00:15, Ethernet1/0
```

The key to this example lies in the fact that EIGRP has a higher administrative distance for external routes (170) than it does for internal routes (90). OSPF only has one administrative distance for all routes (110).

This type of problem can cause no end of headaches in a production environment. If you don't have experience using redistribution in complex environments, this is a very easy mistake to make. Symptoms of the problem include routes pointing to places you don't expect. Look carefully at the design and follow the route back to its source to see where the problem starts. In networks where you're redistributing between different autonomous systems using the same routing protocol, you may see routes flip-flop back and forth between sources. This behavior can be caused by each autonomous system reporting the same metric, in which case the router will update its routing table each time it receives an update.

In the present example, one way to resolve the problem is to stop redistributing the connected route and include the interface into EIGRP with the network command. Using this approach, the route becomes an internal route with an administrative distance of 90, which is more desirable than OSPF's administrative distance of 110.

Limiting Redistribution

When designing complex networks with multiple redistribution points, you must somehow limit redistribution so that loops are prevented. Next I'll show you my method of choice, which involves tagging routes and filtering with route maps.

Route Tags

Many routing protocols—for example, EIGRP, OSPF, and RIPv2 (but not RIPv1)—allow you *tag* routes with values when redistributing them. The route tags are nothing more than numbers within the range of 0–4,294,967,295 (unfortunately, the tags cannot be alphanumeric). Route tags do not affect the protocol's actions; the tag is simply a field to which you can assign a value to use elsewhere.

To set a route tag when redistributing into OSPF, add the tag *tag#* keyword to the redistribute command:

```
R2(config-router)#redistribute eigrp 100 metric 10 subnets tag 2
```

This command will redistribute routes from EIGRP 100 into OSPF. The OSPF metric will be 10, and the tag will be 2. To see the tags in OSPF routes, use the show ip ospf database command. Redistributed routes will be external routes. The last column will be the tags for these routes:

```
R2#sho ip ospf dat

            OSPF Router with ID (10.10.10.2) (Process ID 100)

                Router Link States (Area 0)

Link ID         ADV Router      Age      Seq#       Checksum Link count
10.10.10.2      10.10.10.2      128      0x80000002 0x00F5BA 1
20.20.20.1      20.20.20.1      129      0x80000002 0x009DD9 1

                Net Link States (Area 0)

Link ID         ADV Router      Age      Seq#       Checksum
10.10.10.1      20.20.20.1      129      0x80000001 0x00B5CA

                Type-5 AS External Link States
```

```
Link ID        ADV Router      Age      Seq#       Checksum Tag
20.20.20.0     10.10.10.2      4        0x80000001 0x00D774 2
20.20.20.0     20.20.20.1      159      0x80000001 0x002DF9 0
50.50.50.0     10.10.10.2      4        0x80000001 0x009B56 2
```

To set a route tag in EIGRP, you need to use route maps. Luckily for those of you who have a route-map phobia, the method I'll show you is one of the simplest ways to deploy them.

> Route maps are cool! There, I said it. Route maps are quite powerful, and if you have a fear of them, I suggest you spend some time playing around with them. The fear is usually based in confusion between route maps and access lists and how they interact. It will be well worth your time to learn more about route maps. They can get you out of a technical corner (such as a redistribution loop) when no other option exists. See Chapter 14 for more information.

To apply a tag to a redistributed route in EIGRP, you must first create a route map, and then call it in a redistribute command line. Route maps in their simplest form consist of a line including the route map name, a permit or deny statement, and a number, followed by descriptions of one or more actions to carry out. Here's a simple route map:

```
route-map TAG-EIGRP permit 10
  set tag 3
```

The first line lists the name of the route map, the keyword permit, and the number 10 (this is the default; the numbers are used to order multiple entries in a route map, and as there's only one entry here, it doesn't really matter what the number is). The keyword permit says to perform the actions specified below the opening line. The next line shows the action to be taken for this route map entry, which is "Set the tag to a value of 3."

Once you've created the TAG-EIGRP route map, you can call it using the route-map keyword and the route map's name in the EIGRP redistribute command:

```
R2(config-router)#redistribute connected route-map TAG-EIGRP
```

This command redistributes connected routes into EIGRP using the default metric and applies the tag set in the TAG-EIGRP route map.

To see whether your tag has been implemented, look in the EIGRP topology table for the specific routes you believe should be tagged. To illustrate, I've applied this route map to R3 in the network shown in Figure 11-6. Here's what R2's EIGRP topology table looks like for the route 50.50.50.0/24:

```
R2#sho ip eigrp top
IP-EIGRP Topology Table for AS(100)/ID(10.10.10.2)

Codes: P - Passive, A - Active, U - Update, Q - Query, R - Reply,
       r - reply Status, s - sia Status
```

```
P 10.10.10.0/24, 1 successors, FD is 28160
        via Redistributed (281600/0)
P 20.20.20.0/24, 1 successors, FD is 28160
        via Connected, FastEthernet0/1
P 50.50.50.0/24, 1 successors, FD is 156160, tag is 3
        via 20.20.20.3 (156160/128256), FastEthernet0/1
```

And here is the detail for 50.50.50.0/24 on R3. The source is *Rconnected*, which means it was learned from the `redistributed connected` command:

```
R3#sho ip eigrp top 50.50.50.0/24
IP-EIGRP (AS 100): Topology entry for 50.50.50.0/24
  State is Passive, Query origin flag is 1, 1 Successor(s), FD is 128256
  Routing Descriptor Blocks:
  0.0.0.0, from Rconnected, Send flag is 0x0
      Composite metric is (128256/0), Route is External
      Vector metric:
        Minimum bandwidth is 10000000 Kbit
        Total delay is 5000 microseconds
        Reliability is 255/255
        Load is 1/255
        Minimum MTU is 1514
        Hop count is 0
      External data:
        Originating router is 50.50.50.1 (this system)
        AS number of route is 0
        External protocol is Connected, external metric is 0
        Administrator tag is 3 (0x00000003)
```

The last line shows the *administrator tag* as 3, indicating that routes redistributed into EIGRP (specifically, redistributed connected routes) have been marked with a tag of 3.

EIGRP doesn't do anything with this information other than store it. So what does tagging do for you? Just as you can set a tag to apply when redistributing routes into a routing protocol, you can also test for a tag, and permit or deny redistributions based on it. Call me a nerd, but I think that's pretty cool.

To check for an incoming route tag, you again must use a route map. You must do this for all routing protocols, including OSPF.

Looking back at the example from Figure 11-6, consider that we've now set a tag of 3 for the connected route 50.50.50.0/24 on R3. If we could prevent this route from being advertised into OSPF, that would solve the problem, because R1 would never learn of the route improperly.

On R2, when we redistribute into OSPF, we need to tell the router to call a route map. We're no longer setting the tag with the `redistribute` command, as we'll set it in the route map. If I'm checking for a tag using a route map, I always set it there, too. It's easier for me to understand things when I do everything in one place. I've also seen problems where setting a tag with the **tag** keyword and then checking for it with route maps doesn't work very well. Here, I'm telling the router to redistribute EIGRP 100 routes into OSPF 100, assign them a metric of 10, and apply whatever logic is included in the route map No-EIGRP-Tag3:

```
router ospf 100
  redistribute eigrp 100 metric 10 subnets route-map No-EIGRP-Tag3
```

Here's how I've designed the route map:

```
route-map No-EIGRP-Tag3 deny 10
  match tag 3
!
route-map No-EIGRP-Tag3 permit 20
  set tag 2
```

This one's a little more complicated than the last route map, but it's still pretty simple. The first line is a deny entry. It's followed by an instruction that says, "Match anything with a tag of 3." The match coming after the deny can be confusing, but the more you play with route maps, the more this will make sense. The next entry doesn't match anything; it permits everything and then sets a tag of 2 for the routes. Taken together, the route map essentially says, "Match anything with a tag of 3 and deny it," then "Match everything else and set the tag to 2."

Now when we look at the OSPF database on router R2, we'll see that the route for 50.50.50.0/24 is gone. The route to 20.20.20.0/24 that was learned from R1 is still there, however, because it was not tagged with a 3:

```
R2#sho ip ospf database

            OSPF Router with ID (10.10.10.2) (Process ID 100)

                Router Link States (Area 0)

Link ID        ADV Router      Age      Seq#       Checksum Link count
10.10.10.2     10.10.10.2      769      0x80000002 0x00F5BA 1
20.20.20.1     20.20.20.1      770      0x80000002 0x009DD9 1

                Net Link States (Area 0)

Link ID        ADV Router      Age      Seq#       Checksum
10.10.10.1     20.20.20.1      771      0x80000001 0x00B5CA

                Type-5 AS External Link States

Link ID        ADV Router      Age      Seq#       Checksum Tag
20.20.20.0     10.10.10.2      224      0x80000001 0x00D774 2
20.20.20.0     20.20.20.1      800      0x80000001 0x002DF9 0
```

The route still exists in the EIGRP topology table on R2; it just wasn't redistributed into OSPF because of our cool route map.

In the routing table on R1, we'll now see that 50.50.50.0/24 is pointing to R3 the way we want it to:

```
R1#sho ip route
[text removed]
```

```
Gateway of last resort is not set

     50.0.0.0/24 is subnetted, 1 subnets
D EX    50.50.50.0 [170/156160] via 20.20.20.3, 00:00:16, FastEthernet0/1
     20.0.0.0/24 is subnetted, 1 subnets
C       20.20.20.0 is directly connected, FastEthernet0/1
     10.0.0.0/24 is subnetted, 1 subnets
C       10.10.10.0 is directly connected, FastEthernet0/0
```

A Real-World Example

Today's networks are often designed with high availability as a primary driver. When you're designing networks with no single points of failure, a scenario like the one shown in Figure 11-7 is a real possibility.

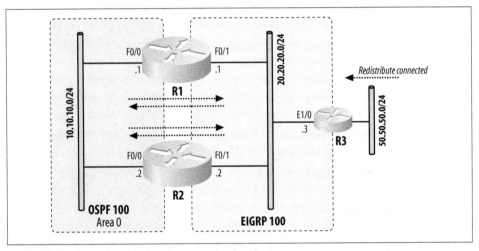

Figure 11-7. Two routers performing mutual redistribution

Here, we have two routers doing mutual redistribution (both are redistributing EIGRP into OSPF, and OSPF into EIGRP). You've already seen what can happen when each one is only redistributing in one direction. The probability of router-induced mayhem is pretty strong here, but this kind of design is very common, for the reasons already discussed.

To make this scenario work, we'll again use route tags, but this time we'll add some flair (you can never have too much flair).

The idea behind this technique is simple: routes sent from one protocol into another will not be advertised back to the protocol from which they came.

I like to tag my routes with the number of the router I'm working on. That's not always possible, especially if you've named your router something clever, like Boston-PoP-Router or Michelle. Another option is to tag your routes with the administrative distance of the routing protocols they came from—90 for EIGRP, and so on. Still another is to use autonomous system numbers. Whatever you choose, make sure it's obvious, if possible. And always document what you've done so others can understand your brilliance.

Using the administrative distance as a tag, here is the configuration for R1:

```
router eigrp 100
 redistribute ospf 100 route-map OSPF-to-EIGRP
 network 20.20.20.0 0.0.0.255
 default-metric 100000 100 255 1 1500
 no auto-summary
!
router ospf 100
 log-adjacency-changes
 redistribute eigrp 100 subnets route-map EIGRP-to-OSPF
 network 10.10.10.0 0.0.0.255 area 0
 default-metric 100
!
route-map EIGRP-to-OSPF deny 10
 match tag 110
!
route-map EIGRP-to-OSPF permit 20
 set tag 90
!
route-map OSPF-to-EIGRP deny 10
 match tag 90
!
route-map OSPF-to-EIGRP permit 20
 set tag 110
```

The route maps are the same on R2 because the same rules apply, and we need to test for any routes redistributed from other routers.

When a route is redistributed from OSPF into EIGRP, it will be assigned a tag of 110. Routes redistributed from EIGRP into OSPF will be assigned a tag of 90. When a route tagged with 90 is seen in OSPF, we'll know it was sourced from EIGRP, because the tag value will have been set to 90. When this route then comes to be redistributed into EIGRP from OSPF on the other router, the route map will deny it. Thus, a route cannot be redistributed into EIGRP if it originated in EIGRP. OSPF-sourced routes are similarly blocked from redistribution back into OSPF.

While this design does prevent routing loops, it does not solve the problem of R3's 50.50.50.0/24 network being advertised through the wrong protocol. R2 is now pointing back to OSPF for this network:

```
R2#sho ip route
[text removed]
```

```
Gateway of last resort is not set

     50.0.0.0/24 is subnetted, 1 subnets
O E2    50.50.50.0 [110/100] via 10.10.10.1, 00:11:50, FastEthernet0/0
     20.0.0.0/24 is subnetted, 1 subnets
C       20.20.20.0 is directly connected, FastEthernet0/1
     10.0.0.0/24 is subnetted, 1 subnets
C       10.10.10.0 is directly connected, FastEthernet0/0
```

Every network is different, and there will always be challenges to solve. In this case, we might have been better off with the first design, where each router was only redistributing in one direction, even though that design is not very resilient.

The way to solve the problem and provide multiple mutual redistribution points is to combine the two scenarios. With route maps, we can match multiple tags, so in addition to denying any routes already redistributed into EIGRP on R2, we can also match on the 3 tag we set on R3:

```
route-map EIGRP-to-OSPF deny 10
 match tag 110 3
!
route-map EIGRP-to-OSPF permit 20
 set tag 90
```

The line match tag 110 3 means, "Match on tag 110 or 3." Now R2 has the right routes:

```
R2#sho ip route
[text removed]

Gateway of last resort is not set

     50.0.0.0/24 is subnetted, 1 subnets
D EX    50.50.50.0 [170/156160] via 20.20.20.3, 00:00:01, FastEthernet0/1
     20.0.0.0/24 is subnetted, 1 subnets
C       20.20.20.0 is directly connected, FastEthernet0/1
     10.0.0.0/24 is subnetted, 1 subnets
C       10.10.10.0 is directly connected, FastEthernet0/0
```

Another method

Here's another method to use, which I like for its elegance: because redistributed routes are external, only allow internal routes to be redistributed. Once a route is redistributed and becomes external, it won't be redistributed again.

When you're redistributing OSPF routes into another protocol, this is simple. The keyword match in the redistribute command lets you match on route type:

```
router eigrp 100
 redistribute ospf 100 match internal
 network 20.20.20.0 0.0.0.255
 default-metric 100000 100 255 1 1500
 no auto-summary
```

When redistributing other protocols, you must resort to route maps:

```
router ospf 100
 redistribute eigrp 100 route-map Only-Internal subnets
 network 10.10.10.0 0.0.0.255 area 0
 default-metric 100
 !
route-map Only-Internal permit 10
 match route-type internal
```

This solution solves both our problems. As the 50.50.50.0/24 route is an external route by nature of its original redistribution into R3, it will not be redistributed into OSPF. What once required many lines of code and multiple route maps has now been accomplished with one keyword and a single two-line route map. Simple is good.

Here is the final routing table from R2:

```
R2#sho ip route
[text removed]

Gateway of last resort is not set

     50.0.0.0/24 is subnetted, 1 subnets
D EX    50.50.50.0 [170/156160] via 20.20.20.3, 00:13:30, FastEthernet0/1
     20.0.0.0/24 is subnetted, 1 subnets
C       20.20.20.0 is directly connected, FastEthernet0/1
     10.0.0.0/24 is subnetted, 1 subnets
C       10.10.10.0 is directly connected, FastEthernet0/0
```

As long as you keep things simple, tagging and filtering redistributed routes is easy. The more complicated the network is, the harder it is to keep all the redistributed networks behaving properly. Additionally, a more complex network might not allow this last solution because there might be valid external routes that need to be redistributed.

## CHAPTER 12

Tunnels

A *tunnel* is a means whereby a local device can communicate with a remote device as if the remote device were local as well. There are many types of tunnels. Virtual Private Networks (VPNs) are tunnels. Generic Routing Encapsulation (GRE) creates tunnels. Secure Shell (SSH) is also a form of tunnel, though different from the other two. Let's take a closer look at these three types:

GRE

GRE tunnels allow remote networks to appear to be locally connected. GRE offers no encryption, but it does forward broadcasts and multicasts. If you want a routing protocol to establish a neighbor adjacency or exchange routes through a tunnel, you'll probably need to configure GRE. GRE tunnels are often built within VPN tunnels to take advantage of encryption. GRE is described in RFCs 1701 and 2784.

VPN

VPN tunnels also allow remote networks to appear as if they were locally connected. VPN encrypts all information before sending it across the network, but it will not usually forward multicasts and broadcasts. Consequently, GRE tunnels are often built within VPNs to allow routing protocols to function. VPNs are often used for remote access to secure networks.

There are two main types of VPNs: *point-to-point* and *remote access*. Point-to-point VPNs offer connectivity between two remote routers, creating a virtual link between them. Remote access VPNs are single-user tunnels between a user and a router, firewall, or *VPN concentrator* (a specialized VPN-only device).

Remote access VPNs usually require VPN client software to be installed on a personal computer. The client communicates with the VPN device to establish a personal virtual link.

SSH

SSH is a client/server application that allows secure connectivity to servers. In practice, it is usually used just like Telnet. The advantage of SSH over Telnet is that it encrypts all data before sending it. While not originally designed to be a tunnel in the sense that VPN or GRE would be considered a tunnel, SSH can be used to access remote devices in addition to the one to which you have connected. While this does not have a direct application on Cisco routers, the concept is similar to that of VPN and GRE tunnels, and thus worth mentioning. I use SSH to access my home network instead of a VPN.

Tunnels can encrypt data so that only the other side can see it, as with SSH; or they can make a remote network appear local, as with GRE; or they can do both, as is the case with VPN.

GRE tunnels will be used for the examples in this chapter because they are the simplest to configure and the easiest to understand. GRE tunnels are solely a means of connecting remote networks as if they were local networks—they enable a remote interface on another router to appear to be directly connected to a local router, even though many other routers and networks may separate them. GRE does not encrypt data.

GRE Tunnels

To create a GRE tunnel, you must create virtual interfaces on the routers at each end, and the tunnel must begin and terminate at existing routable IP addresses. The tunnel is not a physical link—it is logical. As such, it must rely on routes already in place for its existence. The tunnel will behave like a physical link in that it will need an IP address on each side of the link. These will be the tunnel interface IPs. In addition, as the link is virtual, the tunnel will need to be told where to originate and terminate. The source and destination must be existing IP addresses on the routers at each end of the tunnel.

The best way to guarantee that the tunnel's source and destination points are available is to use the loopback interfaces on each end as targets. This way, if there are multiple paths to a router, the source and destination points of the tunnel are not dependent on any single link, but rather on a logical interface on the router itself.

 Loopback interfaces are different from loopback IP addresses. A loopback interface can have any valid IP address assigned to it. A loopback interface on a router is a logical interface within the router that is always up. It can be included in routing protocols and functions like any other interface, with the exception that a loopback interface is always up/up (interface is enabled and the line protocol is active). You can configure multiple loopback interfaces on a router.

Figure 12-1 shows an example of a simple network in which we will build a GRE tunnel. Four routers are connected. They are all running EIGRP, with all connected networks redistributed into the routing table. This example demonstrates how the path from Router A to the network 10.20.20.0/24 on Router D will change with the addition of a GRE tunnel.

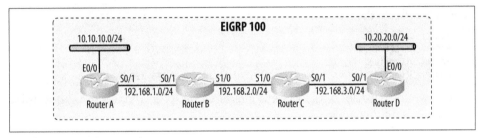

Figure 12-1. Simple network

Given the network in Figure 12-1, the routing table on Router A looks like this:

```
Router-A#sho ip route

Gateway of last resort is not set

      10.0.0.0/24 is subnetted, 2 subnets
D        10.20.20.0 [90/3196416] via 192.168.1.2, 03:39:06, Serial0/1
C        10.10.10.0 is directly connected, Ethernet0/1
C     192.168.1.0/24 is directly connected, Serial0/1
D     192.168.2.0/24 [90/2681856] via 192.168.1.2, 03:39:06, Serial0/1
D     192.168.3.0/24 [90/3193856] via 192.168.1.2, 03:39:06, Serial0/1
```

All routes except the connected routes are available through Serial0/1. Now we'll add a tunnel between Router A and Router D. Because we prefer to link tunnels to loopback interfaces, we will add one to each router. Figure 12-2 shows the network as we will create it.

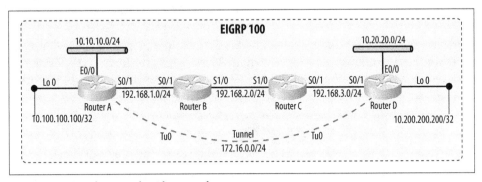

Figure 12-2. Simple network with a tunnel

First, we will add the loopback interfaces on Router A:

```
Router-A#conf t
Enter configuration commands, one per line. End with CNTL/Z.
Router-A(config)# int lo 0
Router-A(config-if)# ip address 10.100.100.100 255.255.255.255
```

Next, we will add the loopback interfaces on Router D:

```
Router-D#conf t
Enter configuration commands, one per line. End with CNTL/Z.
Router-D(config)# int lo 0
Router-D(config-if)# ip address 10.200.200.200 255.255.255.255
```

Because we are redistributing connected interfaces in EIGRP, they are now both visible in Router A's routing table:

```
Router-A#sho ip route

Gateway of last resort is not set

     10.0.0.0/8 is variably subnetted, 4 subnets, 2 masks
D       10.20.20.0/24 [90/3196416] via 192.168.1.2, 03:50:27, Serial0/1
C       10.10.10.0/24 is directly connected, Ethernet0/1
C       10.100.100.100/32 is directly connected, Loopback0
D EX    10.200.200.200/32 [170/3321856] via 192.168.1.2, 00:00:52, Serial0/1
C     192.168.1.0/24 is directly connected, Serial0/1
D     192.168.2.0/24 [90/2681856] via 192.168.1.2, 03:50:27, Serial0/1
D     192.168.3.0/24 [90/3193856] via 192.168.1.2, 03:50:27, Serial0/1
```

Now that the loopback addresses are visible in the routing table, it's time to create the tunnel. The process is simple. We'll begin by creating the virtual interfaces for each side of the tunnel. Tunnel interfaces are numbered like all interfaces in IOS, with the first being tunnel 0:

```
Router-A(config)#int tunnel ?
  <0-2147483647>  Tunnel interface number

Router-A(config)#int tunnel 0
Router-A(config-if)#
23:23:39: %LINEPROTO-5-UPDOWN: Line protocol on Interface Tunnel0, changed state to
down
```

Tunnels must have existing routable IP addresses as their beginning and endpoints, and these must be configured on both routers. The *source* of the tunnel is the local side, and the *destination* is the remote side (from the viewpoint of the router being configured):

```
Router-A(config-if)#ip address 172.16.0.1 255.255.255.0
Router-A(config-if)# tunnel source loopback 0
Router-A(config-if)# tunnel destination 10.200.200.200
23:25:15: %LINEPROTO-5-UPDOWN: Line protocol on Interface Tunnel0, changed state to up
```

As soon as we add the destination IP address to the tunnel, the tunnel interface comes up on Router A:

```
Router-A#sho int tu0
Tunnel0 is up, line protocol is up
  Hardware is Tunnel
  Internet address is 172.16.0.1/24
  MTU 1514 bytes, BW 9 Kbit, DLY 500000 usec,
     reliability 255/255, txload 1/255, rxload 1/255
  Encapsulation TUNNEL, loopback not set
```

```
    Keepalive not set
    Tunnel source 10.100.100.100 (Loopback0), destination 10.200.200.200
    Tunnel protocol/transport GRE/IP, key disabled, sequencing disabled
    Checksumming of packets disabled, fast tunneling enabled
    Last input never, output never, output hang never
    Last clearing of "show interface" counters never
    Input queue: 0/75/0/0 (size/max/drops/flushes); Total output drops: 0
    Queueing strategy: fifo
    Output queue :0/0 (size/max)
    5 minute input rate 0 bits/sec, 0 packets/sec
    5 minute output rate 0 bits/sec, 0 packets/sec
        0 packets input, 0 bytes, 0 no buffer
        Received 0 broadcasts, 0 runts, 0 giants, 0 throttles
        0 input errors, 0 CRC, 0 frame, 0 overrun, 0 ignored, 0 abort
        0 packets output, 0 bytes, 0 underruns
        0 output errors, 0 collisions, 0 interface resets
        0 output buffer failures, 0 output buffers swapped out
```

Notice that although Router A indicates that the interface is up, because Router D does not yet have a tunnel interface, nothing can be sent across the link. Be careful of this, as you may get confused under pressure. The tunnel network 172.16.0.0/24 is even active in Router A's routing table (it will not be found on Router D at this time):

```
Router-A#sho ip route

Gateway of last resort is not set

     172.16.0.0/24 is subnetted, 1 subnets
C        172.16.0.0 is directly connected, Tunnel0
     10.0.0.0/8 is variably subnetted, 4 subnets, 2 masks
D        10.20.20.0/24 [90/3196416] via 192.168.1.2, 04:25:38, Serial0/1
C        10.10.10.0/24 is directly connected, Ethernet0/1
C        10.100.100.100/32 is directly connected, Loopback0
D EX     10.200.200.200/32 [170/3321856] via 192.168.1.2, 00:36:03, Serial0/1
C     192.168.1.0/24 is directly connected, Serial0/1
D     192.168.2.0/24 [90/2681856] via 192.168.1.2, 04:25:39, Serial0/1
D     192.168.3.0/24 [90/3193856] via 192.168.1.2, 04:25:39, Serial0/1
```

To terminate the tunnel on Router D, we need to add the tunnel interface there. We'll use the same commands we used on Router A, but reverse the source and destination:

```
Router-D(config)#int tu 0
23:45:13: %LINEPROTO-5-UPDOWN: Line protocol on Interface Tunnel0, changed state to
down
Router-D(config-if)# ip address 172.16.0.2 255.255.255.0
Router-D(config-if)# tunnel source lo 0
Router-D(config-if)# tunnel destination 10.100.100.100
Router-D(config-if)#
23:47:06: %LINEPROTO-5-UPDOWN: Line protocol on Interface Tunnel0, changed state to up
```

Now we have a live link between these routers, which appear to be directly connected. However, the Ethernet network on Router D, which was known through the serial link, is still known through the serial link, and not the tunnel. If the tunnel is theoretically directly connected to both routers, why isn't the tunnel the preferred path?

Digging into our EIGRP expertise, we can use the show ip eigrp topology command to see what EIGRP knows about the paths:

```
Router-A#sho ip eigrp top
5d18h: %SYS-5-CONFIG_I: Configured from console by console
IP-EIGRP Topology Table for AS(100)/ID(192.168.1.1)

Codes: P - Passive, A - Active, U - Update, Q - Query, R - Reply,
       r - reply Status, s - sia Status
P 10.20.20.0/24, 1 successors, FD is 3196416
        via 192.168.1.2 (3196416/2684416), Serial0/1
        via 172.16.0.2 (297246976/28160), Tunnel0
P 10.10.10.0/24, 1 successors, FD is 281600
        via Connected, Ethernet0/1
P 192.168.1.0/24, 1 successors, FD is 2169856
        via Connected, Serial0/1
```

Both paths appear in the table, but the distance on the tunnel path is huge compared with that of the serial interface. To find out why, let's take a look at the virtual tunnel interface:

```
Router-A#sho int tu 0
Tunnel0 is up, line protocol is up
  Hardware is Tunnel
  Internet address is 172.16.0.1/24
  MTU 1514 bytes, BW 9 Kbit, DLY 500000 usec,
     reliability 255/255, txload 1/255, rxload 1/255
  Encapsulation TUNNEL, loopback not set
  Keepalive not set
  Tunnel source 10.100.100.100 (Loopback0), destination 10.200.200.200
  Tunnel protocol/transport GRE/IP, key disabled, sequencing disabled
  Checksumming of packets disabled,  fast tunneling enabled
  Last input 00:00:00, output 00:00:00, output hang never
  Last clearing of "show interface" counters never
  Input queue: 0/75/0/0 (size/max/drops/flushes); Total output drops: 0
  Queueing strategy: fifo
  Output queue :0/0 (size/max)
  5 minute input rate 0 bits/sec, 0 packets/sec
  5 minute output rate 0 bits/sec, 0 packets/sec
     88293 packets input, 7429380 bytes, 0 no buffer
     Received 0 broadcasts, 0 runts, 0 giants, 0 throttles
     0 input errors, 0 CRC, 0 frame, 0 overrun, 0 ignored, 0 abort
     80860 packets output, 6801170 bytes, 0 underruns
     0 output errors, 0 collisions, 0 interface resets
     0 output buffer failures, 0 output buffers swapped out
```

Take a look at the bandwidth and delay for the tunnel interface. The defaults are an extremely low speed and an extremely high delay, and because EIGRP uses these metrics to determine feasible distance, the tunnel appears to be a much less desirable path than the existing serial links. This is beneficial because the tunnel is built over what could potentially be a multitude of links and routers. A tunnel is a software device, which means that the processing delay for the interface is variable (unlike with a physical interface). Tunnels should not be the most desirable paths by default.

To prove that the tunnel is running and to show how the virtual link behaves, here is a traceroute from Router A to the closest serial interface on Router D, which is 192.168.3.2 on S0/1:

```
Router-A#trace 192.168.3.2

Type escape sequence to abort.
Tracing the route to 192.168.3.2

  1 192.168.1.2 4 msec 4 msec 0 msec
  2 192.168.2.2 4 msec 4 msec 4 msec
  3 192.168.3.2 4 msec 4 msec 4 msec
Router-A#
```

And here's a traceroute to the remote end of the tunnel on Router D (172.16.0.2), which is on the same router some three physical hops away:

```
Router-A#trace 172.16.0.2

Type escape sequence to abort.
Tracing the route to 172.16.0.2

  1 172.16.0.2 4 msec 4 msec 4 msec
Router-A#
```

The other end of the tunnel appears to the router to be the other end of a wire or link, but in reality, the tunnel is a logical construct composed of many intermediary devices that are not visible. Specifically, the tunnel hides the fact that Routers B and C are in the path.

GRE Tunnels and Routing Protocols

The introduction of a routing protocol across a GRE tunnel can cause some interesting problems. Take, for example, our network, now altered as shown in Figure 12-3. This time, we have the links between the routers updating routes using RIPv2. The other interfaces on Router A and Router D are included in RIP using the `redistribute con nected` command. EIGRP is running on all interfaces on Routers A and D with the exception of the serial links, which are running RIPv2.

While this may look a bit odd, consider the possibility that the Routers B and C are owned and operated by a service provider. We cannot control them, and they only run RIPv2. We run EIGRP on our routers (A and D) and want to route between them using EIGRP.

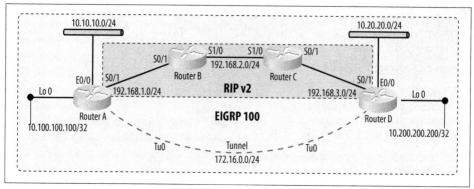

Figure 12-3. Recursive routing example

Here are the pertinent configurations for Router A and Router D (remember, in this scenario, Routers B and C are beyond our control):

Router A:

```
interface Loopback0
 ip address 10.100.100.100 255.255.255.255
!
interface Tunnel0
 ip address 172.16.0.1 255.255.255.0
 tunnel source Loopback0
 tunnel destination 10.200.200.200
!
interface Ethernet0/0
 ip address 10.10.10.1 255.255.255.0
!
interface Serial0/1
 ip address 192.168.1.1 255.255.255.0

router eigrp 100
 network 10.10.10.0 0.0.0.255
 network 10.100.100.0 0.0.0.255
 network 172.16.0.0 0.0.0.255
 no auto-summary
!
router rip
 version 2
 redistribute connected
 passive-interface Ethernet0/0
 passive-interface Loopback0
 passive-interface Tunnel0
 network 192.168.1.0
 no auto-summary
```

Router D:

```
interface Loopback0
 ip address 10.200.200.200 255.255.255.255
!
interface Tunnel0
 ip address 172.16.0.2 255.255.255.0
 tunnel source Loopback0
 tunnel destination 10.100.100.100
!
interface Ethernet0/0
 ip address 10.20.20.1 255.255.255.0
!
interface Serial0/1
 ip address 192.168.3.2 255.255.255.0
!
router eigrp 100
 network 10.20.20.0 0.0.0.255
 network 10.200.200.0 0.0.0.255
 network 172.16.0.0 0.0.0.255
 no auto-summary
!
router rip
 version 2
 redistribute connected
 passive-interface FastEthernet0/0
 passive-interface Loopback0
 passive-interface Tunnel0
 network 192.168.3.0
 no auto-summary
```

Everything looks fine, and in fact the tunnel comes up right away, but shortly after it does, we start seeing these errors on the console:

```
1d01h: %LINEPROTO-5-UPDOWN: Line protocol on Interface Tunnel0, changed state to up
1d01h: %TUN-5-RECURDOWN: Tunnel0 temporarily disabled due to recursive routing
1d01h: %LINEPROTO-5-UPDOWN: Line protocol on Interface Tunnel0, changed state to down
```

The error message Tunnel0 temporarily disabled due to recursive routing is a result of the destination of the tunnel being learned through the tunnel itself. With the tunnel manually shut down on Router A, the loopback interface on Router D is known through RIP, as expected:

```
Router-A#sho ip route

Gateway of last resort is not set

     10.0.0.0/8 is variably subnetted, 4 subnets, 2 masks
R       10.20.20.0/24 [120/3] via 192.168.1.2, 00:00:07, Serial0/1
C       10.10.10.0/24 is directly connected, Ethernet0/1
C       10.100.100.100/32 is directly connected, Loopback0
R       10.200.200.200/32 [120/3] via 192.168.1.2, 00:00:07, Serial0/1
C     192.168.1.0/24 is directly connected, Serial0/1
R     192.168.2.0/24 [120/1] via 192.168.1.2, 00:00:07, Serial0/1
R     192.168.3.0/24 [120/2] via 192.168.1.2, 00:00:07, Serial0/1
```

Once we bring the tunnel up and EIGRP starts working, the remote loopback becomes known through the tunnel:

```
Router-A#sho ip route

Gateway of last resort is not set

     172.16.0.0/24 is subnetted, 1 subnets
C       172.16.0.0 is directly connected, Tunnel0
     10.0.0.0/8 is variably subnetted, 4 subnets, 2 masks
D       10.20.20.0/24 [90/297246976] via 172.16.0.2, 00:00:04, Tunnel0
C       10.10.10.0/24 is directly connected, Ethernet0/1
C       10.100.100.100/32 is directly connected, Loopback0
D       10.200.200.200/32 [90/297372416] via 172.16.0.2, 00:00:04, Tunnel0
C     192.168.1.0/24 is directly connected, Serial0/1
R     192.168.2.0/24 [120/1] via 192.168.1.2, 00:00:00, Serial0/1
R     192.168.3.0/24 [120/2] via 192.168.1.2, 00:00:00, Serial0/1
```

Once this occurs, the routers on both sides immediately recognize the problem and shut down the tunnel. The EIGRP route is lost and the RIP route returns. The router will then bring the tunnel back up and the cycle will continue indefinitely until something is changed.

The reason for the recursive route problem is the administrative distances of the protocols in play. RIP has an administrative distance of 120, while EIGRP has an administrative distance of 90. When the protocol with the better administrative distance learns the route, that protocol's choice is placed into the routing table. Figure 12-4 shows how Router A learns the different routing protocols.

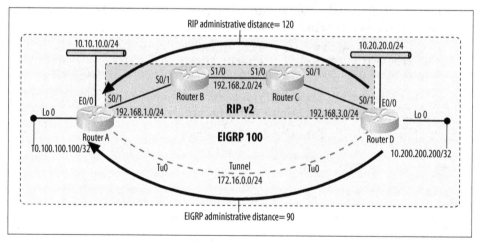

Figure 12-4. EIGRP route learned through tunnel

In the case of the tunnel running EIGRP, the issue is that the route to the remote end of the tunnel is known through the tunnel itself. The tunnel relies on the route to the remote loopback interface, but also provides it. This is not allowed, so the router shuts down the tunnel. Unfortunately, it then brings the tunnel back up, which causes the routes to constantly change and the tunnel to become unstable.

The solutions to this problem are either to stop using tunnels (recommended in this case) or to filter the remote side of the tunnel so it is not included in the routing protocol being run through the tunnel (EIGRP). Installing a VPN would work as well, as the VPN would hide the "public" networks from the "inside" of either side, thus alleviating the problem. Looking at our configurations, we can see the problem is that we've included the loopback networks in our EIGRP processes. Removing them solves our recursive route problems:

```
Router-A (config)#router eigrp 100
Router-A(config-router)# no network 10.100.100.0 0.0.0.255
```

Here's the new configuration for Router A:

```
router eigrp 100
 network 10.10.10.0 0.0.0.255
 network 172.16.0.0 0.0.0.255
 no auto-summary
```

We'll do the same on Router D for its loopback network, and then we'll be able to see the desired result on Router A. Now the route to the remote loopback address has been learned through RIP, and the route to the remote Ethernet has been learned through EIGRP:

```
Router-A#sho ip route

Gateway of last resort is not set

     172.16.0.0/24 is subnetted, 1 subnets
C       172.16.0.0 is directly connected, Tunnel0
     10.0.0.0/8 is variably subnetted, 4 subnets, 2 masks
D       10.20.20.0/24 [90/297246976] via 172.16.0.2, 00:03:23, Tunnel0
C       10.10.10.0/24 is directly connected, Ethernet0/1
C       10.100.100.100/32 is directly connected, Loopback0
R       10.200.200.200/32 [120/3] via 192.168.1.2, 00:00:11, Serial0/1
C     192.168.1.0/24 is directly connected, Serial0/1
R     192.168.2.0/24 [120/1] via 192.168.1.2, 00:00:12, Serial0/1
R     192.168.3.0/24 [120/2] via 192.168.1.2, 00:00:12, Serial0/1
```

GRE tunnels are not usually a good idea, because they complicate networks. If someone were troubleshooting the network we just built, the tunnel would only add complexity. Usually, introducing a GRE tunnel into a network without a clear need is the result of poor planning or design. Routing across a VPN is one of the few legitimate needs for a GRE tunnel (IPSec, the protocol widely used in VPN, does not forward multicast or broadcast packets, so GRE is required).

Running a GRE tunnel through a VPN tunnel can get you the routing protocol link you need. Why not just run the GRE tunnel? Remember that GRE does not encrypt data. Figure 12-5 shows a common layout incorporating GRE over VPN.

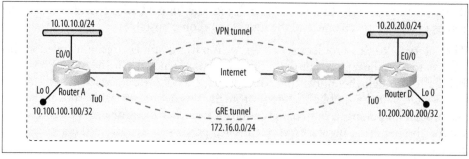

Figure 12-5. GRE through VPN

The configuration for this example is identical with regard to EIGRP and the tunnel. The difference is that in this case, there is no RIP in the middle. Routes to the remote end of the VPN tunnel are default routes for the VPN concentrators because they will have public IP addresses. The VPN concentrators will provide the capability to see the remote router's loopback address through static routes.

This is a relatively common application of GRE, and one that is necessary when you're running routing protocols over a VPN. The risk of recursive routing is still present, though, so you must take care to prevent the remote loopback networks from being included in the EIGRP routing processes.

GRE and Access Lists

GRE is a protocol on the same level as TCP and UDP. When configuring a firewall to allow GRE, you do not configure a port like you would for Telnet or SSH. Instead, you must configure the firewall to allow protocol 47. Cisco routers offer the keyword gre for configuring access lists:

```
R1(config)#access-list 101 permit ?
  <0-255>  An IP protocol number
  ahp      Authentication Header Protocol
  eigrp    Cisco's EIGRP routing protocol
  esp      Encapsulation Security Payload
  gre      Cisco's GRE tunneling
  icmp     Internet Control Message Protocol
  igmp     Internet Gateway Message Protocol
  igrp     Cisco's IGRP routing protocol
  ip       Any Internet Protocol
  ipinip   IP in IP tunneling
  nos      KA9Q NOS compatible IP over IP tunneling
  ospf     OSPF routing protocol
  pcp      Payload Compression Protocol
  pim      Protocol Independent Multicast
  tcp      Transmission Control Protocol
  udp      User Datagram Protocol
```

PIX firewalls also support the keyword gre:

```
PIX(config)#access-list In permit gre host 10.10.10.10 host 20.20.20.20
```

The Point-to-Point Tunneling Protocol (PPTP) uses GRE, so if you're using this protocol for VPN access, you will need to allow GRE on your firewall.

## CHAPTER 13

First Hop Redundancy

When designing a network, eliminating single points of failure should be a priority for any network engineer or architect. While it may be easy to assume that having two of every device will provide redundancy, how does one go about truly making the devices redundant?

Devices like firewalls and load balancers have redundancy and fault-tolerance features built into their operating systems, which even go so far as to transfer configuration changes from the primary to the secondary devices. Cisco routers don't really have that level of functionality, though, and with good reason. While you may wish to have two routers be a failover default gateway for a LAN, those two routers may have different serial links connected to them, or perhaps a link from one Internet provider connects to one router, while a link from a different provider connects to the other. The router configurations will not be the same, so configuration sync will not be practical.

Usually, on routers we're looking for the capability of one device to take over for another device on a specific network. Routers generally support multiple protocols and connect many types of technologies, and each technology can be configured with the failover method preferred for it. In the case of Ethernet, the methods most often used are the Hot Standby Router Protocol (HSRP) and the Virtual Router Redundancy Protocol (VRRP). HSRP is Cisco-specific, while VRRP is nonproprietary and thus available on other vendors' equipment as well. There is a new addition to the first hop redundancy game called the Gateway Load Balancing Protocol, or GLBP, which is also Cisco-proprietary. In this chapter, I will cover HSRP and GLBP.

HSRP

HSRP works by configuring one or more routers with `ip standby` commands on the interfaces that will be part of an *HSRP group*. In HSRP's simplest form, two routers will each have one interface on a network. One of the routers will be the primary and one will be the secondary. If the primary fails, the secondary will take over.

The details of Cisco's HSRP can be found in RFC 2281, which is titled "Cisco Hot Standby Router Protocol (HSRP)."

Figure 13-1 shows a simple design with a redundant pair of routers acting as a default gateway. The normal design in such a case would dictate that one router is a primary and one is a secondary (or, in HSRP terms, one is *active* and one is *standby*). However, this figure does not contain enough information for us to determine how the network is behaving. Which router is actually forwarding packets? Are they both forwarding packets? Is one router a primary and the other a secondary?

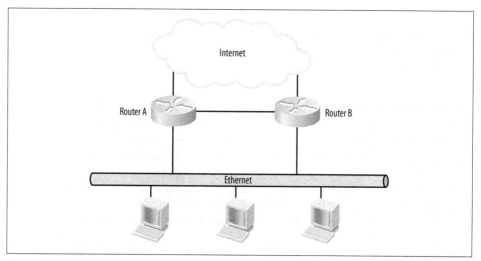

Figure 13-1. Simple HSRP design

To configure HSRP for this network, we'll need to determine three things ahead of time: the IP address of Router A's Ethernet interface, the IP address of Router B's Ethernet interface, and a virtual IP address (VIP) that will act as the gateway for the devices on the network.

The IP addresses of the router interfaces never change, and neither does the VIP. The only thing that changes in the event of a failure is who owns the VIP. The VIP is active on whichever router has the highest priority. The priority defaults to a value of 100 and can be configured to any value between 0 and 255.

All routers that are in the same HSRP group (the default group is 0) send out HSRP packets to the multicast address 224.0.0.2 using UDP port 1985. All HSRP packets have a time-to-live (TTL) of 1, so they will not escape the local Ethernet segment.

When a router with an interface running HSRP starts that interface (or anytime the interface comes up), HSRP sends out hello packets and waits to see if any other HSRP routers are found. If more than one HSRP router is found, the routers negotiate to determine which one should become the active router. The router with the highest priority becomes the active router, unless there is a tie, in which case the router with the highest configured IP address becomes the active router.

In our example, we'll apply the three IP addresses needed, as shown in Figure 13-2.

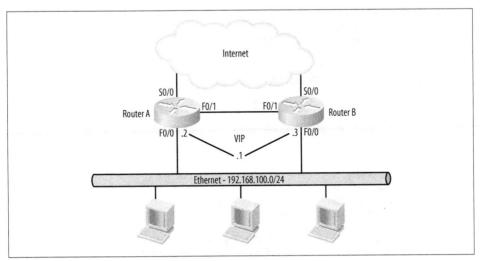

Figure 13-2. IP addresses assigned

We can now create the simplest HSRP configuration:

Router A:

```
interface f0/0
 ip address 192.168.100.2 255.255.255.0
 standby ip 192.168.100.1
 standby preempt
```

Router B:

```
interface f0/0
 ip address 192.168.100.3 255.255.255.0
 standby ip 192.168.100.1
 standby priority 95
 standby preempt
```

On each router, we assign the IP address to the interface as usual. We also assign the same standby IP address to both—this is the VIP.

Notice that only Router B has a standby priority statement. Remember that the default priority is 100, so by setting Router B to a priority of 95, we have made Router B the standby (since 95 is lower than 100).

Finally, both router configurations contain the command standby preempt. By default, HSRP does not reinstate the primary as the active router when it comes back online.

To enable this behavior, you must configure the routers to preempt. This means that when a router with a higher priority than the active router comes online, the active router will allow the higher-priority router to become active.

To view the status of HSRP on the routers, we can execute the show standby command:

Router A:

```
Router-A>sho standby
FastEthernet0/0 - Group 0
  Local state is Active, priority 100, may preempt
  Hellotime 3 sec, holdtime 10 sec
  Next hello sent in 0.412
  Virtual IP address is 192.168.100.1 configured
  Active router is local
  Standby router is 192.168.100.3 expires in 7.484
  Virtual mac address is 0000.0c07.ac00
  2 state changes, last state change 23w3d
```

Router B:

```
Router-B>sho standby
FastEthernet0/0 - Group 0
  Local state is Standby, priority 95, may preempt
  Hellotime 3 sec, holdtime 10 sec
  Next hello sent in 1.398
  Virtual IP address is 192.168.100.1 configured
  Active router is 192.168.100.2 priority 100 expires in 9.540
  Standby router is local
  2 state changes, last state change 23w3d
```

Router A's output reflects that Router A is active with a priority of 100 and may preempt. We can also see that the VIP is 192.168.100.1 and that the standby router is 192.168.100.3. With more than two routers participating, it may not be obvious without this information which router is the standby router.

One important aspect of HSRP that many people miss is that if more than two routers are participating, once active and standby routers have been elected, the remaining routers are neither active nor standby until the standby router becomes active. RFC 2281 states:

> To minimize network traffic, only the active and the standby routers send periodic HSRP messages once the protocol has completed the election process. If the active router fails, the standby router takes over as the active router. If the standby router fails or becomes the active router, another router is elected as the standby router.

HSRP Interface Tracking

While HSRP is a wonderful solution that enables recovery from router or Ethernet interface failures, its basic functionality falls short in another area. Figure 13-3 depicts a more complex problem than the one described previously. In this scenario, the serial link connecting Router A to the Internet has failed. Because the router and Ethernet

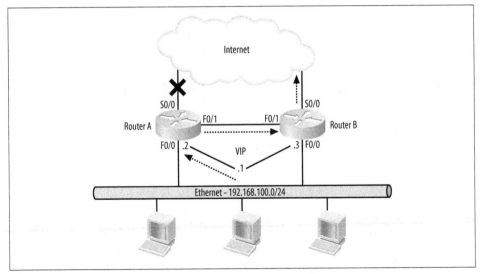

Figure 13-3. Primary Internet link failure without interface tracking

interfaces are still up, HSRP is still able to send and receive hello packets, and Router A remains the active router.

The network is resilient, so the packets will still get to the Internet via the F0/1 interfaces. But why add another hop when we don't need to? If we could somehow influence the HSRP priority based on the status of another interface, we could fail the VIP from Router A over to Router B based on the status of S0/0. *HSRP interface tracking* allows us to do exactly that.

By adding a couple of simple commands to our HSRP configurations, we can create a design that will allow the Ethernet interfaces to failover in the result of a serial interface failure:

Router A:

```
interface f0/0
 ip address 192.168.100.2 255.255.255.0
 standby ip 192.168.100.1
 standby preempt
 standby track Serial0/0 10
```

Router B:

```
interface f0/0
 ip address 192.168.100.3 255.255.255.0
 standby ip 192.168.100.1
 standby priority 95
 standby preempt
 standby track Serial0/0 10
```

On each router, we have added the `standby track Serial0/0 10` command to the Ethernet interface. This command tells HSRP to decrement the Ethernet interface's priority by 10 if the Serial0/0 interface goes down.

 I've seen many networks where one router has a priority of 100 and the other has a priority of 90. When a tracked interface on the primary fails, this will result in a tie, which will cause IOS to assign the router with the highest configured IP address as the active router. While this may not seem like a problem with only two routers, traffic may not flow where you expect it to in this situation.

Adding a priority decrement value is a very handy feature. If each router had three links to the Internet, for instance, you could decrement the priority by 3 for each tracked interface. In our example, if one link went down, Router A would remain active, but if two serial links went down, we would decrement its priority by a total of 6, bringing it down to 94; this would be lower than Router B's priority of 95, so Router B would become the active router. In other words, with two routers, each containing three links to the Internet, the one with the most serial links up would become the active router (of course, a router or Ethernet interface failure would still affect the routers in the same way as the basic example).

When HSRP Isn't Enough

HSRP is an awesome tool, and coupled with interface tracking, it can be the means for near-total redundancy. There are situations, however, where HSRP is not enough. The example I will show here is one of my favorite interview questions, because usually only someone with real-world experience in complex networks has seen it.

Figure 13-4 shows a deceptively simple HSRP setup. Two locations, New York and Los Angeles, are connected via two T1s. The routers on either side are connected via the F0/1 interfaces, and HSRP is implemented with interface tracking on the F0/0 interfaces. The idea here is that if either of the primary routers should fail, the secondary routers will take over for them. Additionally, should the primary T1 link fail, the secondary link will take over, because interface tracking is enabled.

Here are the primary Ethernet configurations for each router:

NY-Primary:

```
interface f0/0
 ip address 10.10.10.2 255.255.255.0
 standby ip 10.10.10.1
 standby preempt
 standby track Serial0/0 10
```

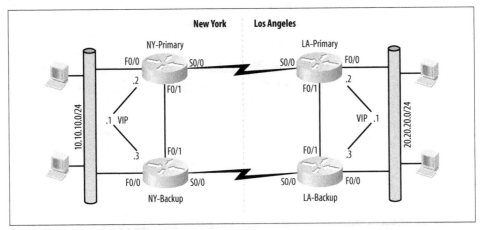

Figure 13-4. Two-link failover scenario using HSRP

NY-Secondary:

```
interface f0/0
 ip address 10.10.10.3 255.255.255.0
 standby ip 10.10.10.1
 standby priority 95
 standby preempt
 standby track Serial0/0 10
```

LA-Primary:

```
interface f0/0
 ip address 20.20.20.2 255.255.255.0
 standby ip 20.20.20.1
 standby preempt
 standby track Serial0/0 10
```

LA-Secondary:

```
interface f0/0
 ip address 20.20.20.3 255.255.255.0
 standby ip 20.20.20.1
 standby priority 95
 standby preempt
 standby track Serial0/0 10
```

Should the T1 connecting NY-Primary with LA-Primary go down completely, the NY and LA routers will recognize the failure and the secondary routers will take over. But real-world problems tend to be more complex than theoretical ones, and this design doesn't work as well as we'd like. Figure 13-5 shows what can go wrong.

Assume that the link between New York and Los Angeles suffers a partial outage. Something has happened to cause the serial interface on NY-Primary to enter a state of up/down, but the serial interface on LA-Primary has stayed up/up. I've seen this more than once on different kinds of circuits.

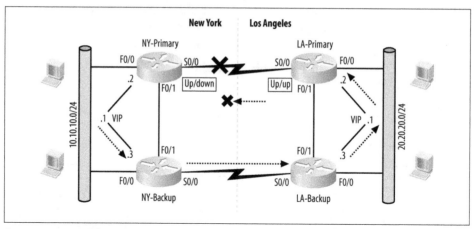

Figure 13-5. HSRP limitations

 Metropolitan Area Ethernet (Metro-E) is susceptible to this condition. Because the Metro-E link is usually a SONET transport that's converted to Ethernet, link integrity is local to each side. If you unplug one side of a Metro-E circuit, the far side will not go down with most installations.

HSRP responds to the down interface on the New York side by making the NY-Backup router active, because we're tracking the serial interface on NY-Primary. Packets are forwarded to NY-Backup and then across the T1 to LA-Backup, which forwards them to their destinations. The return packets have a problem, though. As the LA-Primary router does not recognize the link failure on the primary T1, it has remained the active router. Return packets are sent to the LA-Primary router, and because it believes the link is still up, it forwards the packets out the S0/0 interface, where they die because the other side of the link is down.

A more robust solution to a link-failover scenario is to incorporate an interior gateway protocol running on all of the routers. A protocol like OSPF or EIGRP establishes neighbor adjacencies across links. When a link fails, the routing protocol knows that the remote neighbor is unavailable and removes the link from the routing table.

The solution therefore includes a routing protocol in addition to HSRP. Figure 13-6 shows the same network, but with EIGRP included. Now when the NY-Primary side of the primary links fails, EIGRP loses the neighbor adjacency between NY-Primary and LA-Primary and removes the link from each router's routing table. Because EIGRP alters the routing tables, it can route around the failed link, even though one side reports an up/up condition. HSRP is still required in this design, as EIGRP has no means of making two routers appear to be a single gateway on the local Ethernet segments.

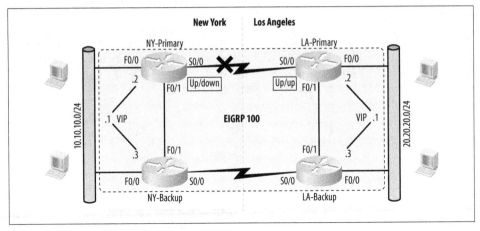

Figure 13-6. Better failover design using EIGRP

Nexus and HSRP

As with many protocols on Nexus, you must first enable the HSRP feature with the `feature hsrp` command.

NX-OS adds some functionality to HSRP when you're using vPCs. In short, when a packet is received on a routed (nonswitch) port and is destined for the HSRP VIP configured on the router, the packet will terminate on that router, even if it is not the active HSRP router. Packets received on Layer-2 interfaces will be forwarded to the active router.

Why is this important? First, this will help to eliminate traffic on interrouter links. Second, if you're not aware of this behavior, you may go quite mad trying to figure out where traffic is flowing when you think it works the traditional way. You have been warned.

vPCs between two Nexus switches will forward traffic through both the active and standby routers. Cisco documentation recommends that you configure the HSRP active router to be the same device as the primary vPC peer.

GLBP

GLBP (Gateway Load Balancing Protocol) is similar to HSRP and VRRP, but with the addition of load balancing between group members. With HSRP and VRRP, there is only one active member, while the other member or members forward no traffic. With GLBP, each member may forward traffic and can even be weighted. Weighting the gateway members allows you to have, for example, three gateways active with 50% of traffic going to one and 25% going to each of the other two. You can have a maximum of 1,024 GLBP groups per router interface with up to four virtual forwarders per group. Let's look at an example.

Figure 13-7 shows a simple network containing five hosts with three routers. Each of these three routers will participate in GLBP, and we will actively forward traffic through all three. We'll configure R1 to take 50% of the load, while R2 and R3 will take 25% each.

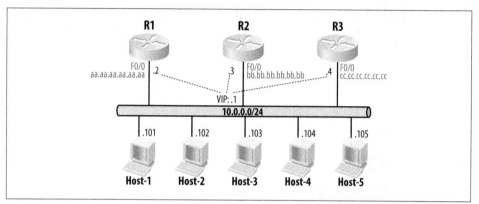

Figure 13-7. GLBP example network

Gateways configured with GLBP are called *forwarders*. Any router that is forwarding packets is called an Active Virtual Forwarder (AVF). One of the routers will be elected as the Active Virtual Gateway (AVG). The AVG has the responsibility for controlling the group and essentially being the brain of the operations. The AVG will control the load-balancing operations, respond to ARP requests, and assign virtual MAC addresses to AVFs. Be careful with terminology here, because the term *active* means something different with HSRP.

The AVG in a GLBP group is determined through priorities. The AVG priority can be preempted so that a higher-priority member takes control when it comes online.

Load balancing can be done based on round-robin, weighted load balancing, or host-dependent methods. We'll use weighted load balancing to allocate a percentage of traffic flow. Host-dependent is a means whereby the same virtual MAC address is always delivered to the same host MAC address. This method allows hosts to always use the same physical gateway unless the gateway goes offline. If no load balancing is specified, GLBP behaves like HSRP, and the AVG acts as the only forwarder.

Saying things like "percentage of traffic flow" and "load balancing" is useful, especially when you're talking to executives, but the phrases are technically inaccurate. GLBP does not load-balance traffic, but rather it load-*shares* by changing which gateway is advertised when an ARP request is made. Why is this distinction important? Let's say that Host-5 in Figure 13-7 is the corporate email server. If all the other hosts are just workstations, there is a high probability that, regardless of how GLBP distributes its virtual MAC addresses, the email server will consume most of the resources. Here's another way to look at this: though R1 will be the default gateway for 50% of the hosts, if the mail server is assigned to use R3 as its gateway, R3 will likely see 99% of the traffic flow.

Let's look at a sample configuration based on our example. Here are the basic GLBP configs for our three routers:

R1 configuration:

```
interface FastEthernet0/0
 ip address 10.0.0.2 255.255.255.0
 glbp 10 ip 10.0.0.1
 glbp 10 preempt
 glbp 10 weighting 50
 glbp 10 load-balancing weighted
```

Without a configured value, R1 will default to a priority of 100.

R2 configuration:

```
interface FastEthernet0/0
 ip address 10.0.0.3 255.255.255.0
 glbp 10 ip 10.0.0.1
 glbp 10 priority 50
 glbp 10 preempt
 glbp 10 weighting 25
 glbp 10 load-balancing weighted
```

R3 configuration:

```
interface Ethernet0/0
 ip address 10.0.0.4 255.255.255.0
 glbp 10 ip 10.0.0.1
 glbp 10 priority 25
 glbp 10 preempt
 glbp 10 weighting 25
 glbp 10 load-balancing weighted
```

On Nexus, you must first enable GLBP with the `feature glbp` command.

Weighting is used both for load distribution and object tracking (see the next section). The weighting value can be between 1 and 254, which means you can configure a single router with a weight over 100. How does the router distribute load when the weighting values can all be over 100?

The Cisco documentation has this to say:

> The amount of load directed to an AVF is dependent upon the weighting value advertised by the gateway containing that AVF.
>
> Each Virtual Forwarder in a gateway uses the current weighting value of that gateway, regardless of how many Virtual Forwarders are active in that gateway.

and:

> This is the ability [of] GLBP to place a weight on each device when calculating the amount of load sharing that will occur through MAC assignment. Each GLBP router in the group will advertise its weighting and assignment; the AVG will act based on that value.
>
> For example, if there are two routers in a group and router A has double the forwarding capacity of router B, the weighting value of router A should be configured to be double the amount of router B.

The weighting is determined by dividing the individual router's weight by the sum of all the weights in the group. For example, if we configure our three gateways with weights of 50/25/25, it will result in the following distribution:

R1: 50 / (50+25+25) = .50 (50%)
R2: 25 / (50+25+25) = .25 (25%)
R3: 25 / (50+25+25) = .25 (25%)

If you're going to use weighted load balancing, I recommend keeping your values as simple as possible. As we'll see, these values can be altered with object tracking, so keeping them simple is in your best interest.

As you can see, the configuration is very similar to HSRP. It's a little different when looking at the active interfaces though. Here is the output from show glbp on R1:

```
R1#sho glbp
FastEthernet0/0 - Group 10
  State is Active
    8 state changes, last state change 00:09:19
  Virtual IP address is 10.0.0.1
  Hello time 3 sec, hold time 10 sec
    Next hello sent in 1.496 secs
  Redirect time 600 sec, forwarder time-out 14400 sec
  Preemption enabled, min delay 0 sec
  Active is local
  Standby is 10.0.0.3, priority 50 (expires in 9.496 sec)
  Priority 100 (default)
  Weighting 50 (configured 50), thresholds: lower 1, upper 50
  Load balancing: weighted
  Group members:
    0012.43b9.2020 (10.0.0.4)
    0012.43b9.2c70 (10.0.0.2) local
```

```
    001c.588b.f6a8 (10.0.0.3)
  There are 3 forwarders (1 active)
  Forwarder 1
    State is Listen
      8 state changes, last state change 00:00:45
    MAC address is 0007.b400.0a01 (learnt)
    Owner ID is 001c.588b.f6a8
    Redirection enabled, 597.840 sec remaining (maximum 600 sec)
    Time to live: 14397.840 sec (maximum 14400 sec)
    Preemption enabled, min delay 30 sec
    Active is 10.0.0.3 (primary), weighting 25 (expires in 7.840 sec)
  Forwarder 2
    State is Active
      1 state change, last state change 00:00:44
    MAC address is 0007.b400.0a02 (default)
    Owner ID is 0012.43b9.2c70
    Redirection enabled
    Preemption enabled, min delay 30 sec
    Active is local, weighting 50
  Forwarder 3
    State is Listen
    MAC address is 0007.b400.0a03 (learnt)
    Owner ID is 0012.43b9.2020
    Redirection enabled, 599.836 sec remaining (maximum 600 sec)
    Time to live: 14399.836 sec (maximum 14400 sec)
    Preemption enabled, min delay 30 sec
    Active is 10.0.0.4 (primary), weighting 25 (expires in 9.836 sec)
```

GLBP is a useful protocol, but I find it pretty frustrating to troubleshoot. Look at the paragraph for the active forwarder:

```
  Forwarder 2
    State is Active
      1 state change, last state change 00:00:44
    MAC address is 0007.b400.0a02 (default)
    Owner ID is 0012.43b9.2c70
    Redirection enabled
    Preemption enabled, min delay 30 sec
    Active is local, weighting 50
```

We can tell that forwarder 2 is active, but we don't know which router is forwarder 2. We didn't name them 1,2,3, yet the router has labeled them as such. GLBP does tell us what the MAC address of the owner is, and we can cross-reference that with the group members listed earlier in the output:

```
  Group members:
    0012.43b9.2020 (10.0.0.4)
    0012.43b9.2c70 (10.0.0.2) local
    001c.588b.f6a8 (10.0.0.3)
```

Call me old and get off my lawn, but I believe that information should all be within the forwarder paragraph. Irritations aside, GLBP is invaluable if you would like to utilize more than one gateway at a time while being able to have a single virtual gateway address.

Another nice GLBP command is `show glbp brief`, which gives a simpler overview of how GLBP is configured and operating:

```
R1#sho glbp brief
Interface  Grp Fwd Pri State   Address          Active router  Standby router
Fa0/0      10  -   100 Active  10.0.0.1         local          10.0.0.3
Fa0/0      10  1   -   Listen  0007.b400.0a01   10.0.0.3       -
Fa0/0      10  2   -   Active  0007.b400.0a02   local          -
Fa0/0      10  3   -   Listen  0007.b400.0a03   10.0.0.4       -
```

Object Tracking in GLBP

Like HSRP's interface tracking, GLBP can be configured to track the status of another interface. Even better, GLBP uses something called *object tracking*, which lets you track much more than simple up/down status.

First we need to configure an object to track. Here, I'll configure a new object, number 2, which is the line-protocol status on F0/1:

```
R1(config)#track 2 interface FastEthernet0/1 line-protocol
```

 Object tracking is a powerful tool that can track more than just interface status. For example, you can use it to track response times across a link using the Response Time Reporter (RTR), and then disable a gateway in GLBP when response times get too high. You can also use object tracking for many protocols other than GLBP. But be careful with it, because though it's very powerful, you can make your router configuration so complicated that someone else will have a hard time figuring out what's going on during an outage.

Once we've defined the object, we can reference it with the GLBP `weighting` parameter:

```
R1(config-if)# glbp 10 weighting track 2 decrement 10
```

Now, when object 2 (line-protocol) goes down, the weight will decrement by 10. But that's not all. We can track more than one object. Let's add another, this time pointing to a serial interface:

```
R1(config)#track 3 interface s0/0/0 line-protocol
```

Now let's add that to the interface's GLBP group:

```
R1(config-if)# glbp 10 weighting track 3 decrement 10
```

Here's the configuration of f0/0 so far:

```
interface FastEthernet0/0
 ip address 10.0.0.2 255.255.255.0
 glbp 10 ip 10.0.0.1
 glbp 10 preempt
 glbp 10 weighting 50
 glbp 10 load-balancing weighted
```

```
glbp 10 weighting track 2 decrement 10
glbp 10 weighting track 3 decrement 10
end
```

And our objects being tracked:

```
track 2 interface FastEthernet0/1 line-protocol
track 3 interface Serial0/0/0 line-protocol
```

Now, should either f0/1 or s0/0/0 suffer a line-protocol outage, the GLBP gateway will drop its weight by 10. Should they both go offline, the weight will drop by 20. But wait—this is not HSRP, and lowering the weight will only reduce the traffic flow to this router. To make this work the way we want, we need to tell GLBP that if the weight falls below a certain threshold, this router should no longer be used as a forwarder. We do this by adding the lower and upper keywords to the glbp weighting command:

```
R1(config-if)# glbp 10 weighting 50 lower 35 upper 45
```

Now, should the weight drop below 35, GLBP will stop using this forwarder. Be careful, though, because as I've configured this, should only one interface come back online, GLBP will not enable this forwarder, since the upper threshold is 45.

Let's look at the output from show glbp with one interface up after both tracked interfaces have failed:

```
R1#sho glbp
FastEthernet0/0 - Group 10
  State is Active
    8 state changes, last state change 21:47:52
  Virtual IP address is 10.0.0.1
  Hello time 3 sec, hold time 10 sec
    Next hello sent in 1.756 secs
  Redirect time 600 sec, forwarder time-out 14400 sec
  Preemption enabled, min delay 0 sec
  Active is local
  Standby is 10.0.0.3, priority 50 (expires in 8.932 sec)
  Priority 100 (default)
  Weighting 40, low (configured 50), thresholds: lower 35, upper 45
    Track object 2 state Up decrement 10
    Track object 3 state Down decrement 10
  Load balancing: weighted

[--output truncated--]

  Forwarder 2
    State is Listen
      6 state changes, last state change 00:05:40
    MAC address is 0007.b400.0a02 (default)
    Owner ID is 0012.43b9.2c70
    Redirection enabled
    Preemption enabled, min delay 30 sec
    Active is 10.0.0.4 (secondary), weighting 25 (expires in 8.816 sec)
```

If we wanted GLBP to enable the forwarder with even one of the tracked links online, then we should make the lower and upper thresholds both 35:

```
R1(config-if)# glbp 10 weighting 50 lower 35 upper 35
```

Now, with one link up after a dual-link failure, our gateway is an active forwarder:

```
R1#sho glbp
FastEthernet0/0 - Group 10
  State is Active
    11 state changes, last state change 00:08:52
  Virtual IP address is 10.0.0.1
  Hello time 3 sec, hold time 10 sec
    Next hello sent in 1.200 secs
  Redirect time 600 sec, forwarder time-out 14400 sec
  Preemption enabled, min delay 0 sec
  Active is local
  Standby is 10.0.0.3, priority 50 (expires in 9.212 sec)
  Priority 100 (default)
  Weighting 40 (configured 50), thresholds: lower 35, upper 35
    Track object 2 state Up decrement 10
    Track object 3 state Down decrement 10
  Load balancing: weighted
  Group members:
    0012.43b9.2020 (10.0.0.4)
    0012.43b9.2c70 (10.0.0.2) local
    001c.588b.f6a8 (10.0.0.3)
  There are 3 forwarders (1 active)

[--output truncated--]

  Forwarder 2
    State is Active
      7 state changes, last state change 00:00:06
    MAC address is 0007.b400.0a02 (default)
    Owner ID is 0012.43b9.2c70
    Redirection enabled
    Preemption enabled, min delay 30 sec
    Active is local, weighting 40
```

## CHAPTER 14

Route Maps

Route maps are the bane of many people studying for certification exams. I think the reason for this lies in the way route maps are designed. They're a little bit backward when compared with more common features, like access lists. Why do I consider them backward? Let's take a look.

An access list gives the function of each entry in the entry itself. For example, this line permits any IP packet from any source to any destination:

```
access-list 101 permit ip any any
```

The syntax is pretty straightforward and self-documenting. Access list 101 permits IP packets from anywhere to anywhere. Simple!

In contrast, a route map written to accomplish the same thing might look like this:

```
route-map GAD permit 10
 match ip address 101
```

To determine what the route map is for, you have to see what access list 101 is doing, and then figure out how the route map is applying it. This route map also permits any IP packet from any source to any destination, but unlike the access list above, its purpose is not obvious.

Why add a route map to an already simple access list? First, there are instances where an access list is not directly available for use. BGP, for example, makes use of route maps and, in many cases, does not support direct application of access lists. Second, route maps are far more flexible than access lists. They allow you to match on a whole list of things that access lists cannot:

```
R1(config)#route-map GAD permit 10
R1(config-route-map)# match ?
  as-path        Match BGP AS path list
  clns           CLNS information
  community      Match BGP community list
  extcommunity   Match BGP/VPN extended community list
  interface      Match first hop interface of route
  ip             IP specific information
  length         Packet length
```

```
    metric      Match metric of route
    route-type  Match route-type of route
    tag         Match tag of route
```

Route maps are particularly useful in routing protocols. Using route maps, you can filter based on route types, route tags, prefixes, packet size, and even the source or next hop of the packet.

Route maps can also alter packets, while access lists cannot. The set route map command allows you to change all sorts of things in a packet as it's being sent. You can change the interface to which the packet is being sent, the next hop of the packet, and quality of service (QoS) values such as IP precedence:

```
R1(config-route-map)#set ?
    as-path          Prepend string for a BGP AS-path attribute
    automatic-tag    Automatically compute TAG value
    clns             OSI summary address
    comm-list        Set BGP community list (for deletion)
    community        BGP community attribute
    dampening        Set BGP route flap dampening parameters
    default          Set default information
    extcommunity     BGP extended community attribute
    interface        Output interface
    ip               IP specific information
    level            Where to import route
    local-preference BGP local preference path attribute
    metric           Metric value for destination routing protocol
    metric-type      Type of metric for destination routing protocol
    origin           BGP origin code
    tag              Tag value for destination routing protocol
    weight           BGP weight for routing table
```

The IP-specific items that can be changed are accessed under the ip category:

```
R1(config-route-map)#set ip ?
    default     Set default information
    df          Set DF bit
    next-hop    Next hop address
    precedence  Set precedence field
    qos-group   Set QOS Group ID
    tos         Set type of service field
```

Policy routing is the term for using a route map to change information regarding where a packet is routed. Use care when policy routing, as policy-routing scenarios can involve process switching (which can put a serious strain on the router's CPU). Process switching is discussed in Chapter 15.

Building a Route Map

Route maps are named and built from *clauses*. The name is included in each clause, and the clauses are numbered to specify the order in which they should be evaluated and to allow you to include or omit only certain steps without having to reenter the entire route map. The default clause number is 10, and it's good practice to number your clauses in intervals of 10. This allows you to insert multiple clauses without needing to redesign the entire route map. You can enter individual clauses at any time. The parser will insert them in the proper order within the configuration.

Each clause can be either a `permit` or a `deny` clause, with `permit` being the default. How the `permit` and `deny` values affect the processing of the route map depends on the route map's application. The next section presents an example of policy routing using route maps.

Within each clause, there are two basic types of commands:

`match`
Selects routes or packets based on the criteria listed.

`set`
Modifies information in either packets or routing protocol tables based on the criteria listed.

`match` commands are evaluated in order of entry within the clause. `match` entries can be evaluated in two ways: multiple `match` entries on a single line will be considered logical OR tests, while multiple `match` entries on separate lines will be considered logical AND tests.

This code configures the route map GAD with the default clause values of `permit` and 10. The first `match` tests for the IP address matching access list 101 OR 102 OR 103. The second `match` tests for the packet between 200 and 230 bytes in length:

```
route-map GAD permit 10
 match ip address 101 102 103
 match length 200 230
 set ip next-hop 10.10.10.10
```

By nature of the way route maps operate, any of the three access lists (ACLs) can be matched, AND the packet length must match the second test for the `set` command to be executed. If no match is made, no action is taken for this clause, and the next higher-numbered clause in the route map is evaluated.

If no `match` command is present in the clause, all packets or routes match. In this case, the `set` command is executed on every packet or route.

If no `set` command is present, no action is taken beyond the scope of the clause itself. This is useful when limiting redistribution in routing protocols—because you don't want to change anything, there doesn't need to be a `set` command. The route map will permit route redistribution until a `deny` clause is encountered.

The following route map can be applied to a `redistribute` statement. It will permit any routes that match access list 101 OR access list 102, while denying all others:

```
route-map GAD permit 10
 match ip address 101 102
route-map GAD deny 20
```

We used to be able to do AND operations in route maps by putting each ACL reference on its own match line. The first edition of *Network Warrior* shows such an example. Doing so on modern revisions of IOS will result in the router changing your entries to make the route map perform an OR operation on the ACLs. For example, here's the original code from the first edition:

```
R1-PBX(config)#route-map GAD permit 10
R1-PBX(config-route-map)#match ip address 101
R1-PBX(config-route-map)#match ip address 102
R1-PBX(config-route-map)#route-map GAD deny 20
```

And here's how the router converts this configuration:

```
route-map GAD permit 10
 match ip address 101 102
 !
route-map GAD deny 20
```

Similarly, we could use a route map to deny only certain routes while permitting all others by simply reversing the permit and deny clauses:

```
route-map GAD deny 10
 match ip address 101 102
route-map GAD permit 20
```

Policy Routing Example

Policy routing is the act of routing packets using some intelligence other than normal routing. For example, with policy routing, you can send packets to a different destination than the one determined by the routing protocol running on the router. It does have some limitations, but this feature can get you out of some interesting jams. Figure 14-1 illustrates an example that comes from a real problem I encountered.

Two companies, Company 1 and Company 2, partnered together. To save money, they decided they would build each branch such that it would be a single office that connected directly to both companies' headquarters. To save more money, they decided they would split the cost of a single router for each branch. One Ethernet interface connected the workers from Company 1, while another Ethernet interface connected the workers from Company 2. The workers from each company, although sitting in the same office, could not interact with workers from the other company using the network. We had to put access lists on the Ethernet interfaces to prevent interaction between the two networks.

This design is an excellent example of politics and money trumping best-practice engineering. Still, our job was not to judge, but rather to make the network function the way the client wanted it to function.

To further complicate the issue, employees were only supposed to use the Frame Relay link purchased by their respective companies. The problem with this mandate was that

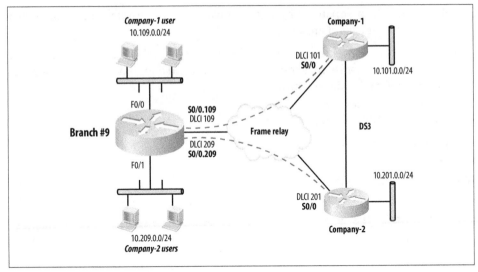

Figure 14-1. Policy routing example

each company's branch employees used servers at both companies' headquarters. In other words, if a Company 1 user at Branch #9 needed to use a server at Company 2 headquarters, that user was not allowed to use the link that connected Branch #9 to Company 2. Instead, he was to use the link provided by Company 1, so that Company 1 could route (and attempt to secure) the request across the DS3 link between the two companies' headquarters. This needed to be done across more than 300 branches, all of which were configured the same way. We were not allowed to add hardware.

Here is the routing table from the Branch-9 router:

```
Branch-9#sho ip route
[- text removed -]

     172.16.0.0/24 is subnetted, 2 subnets
C       172.16.201.0 is directly connected, Serial0/0.209
C       172.16.101.0 is directly connected, Serial0/0.109
     10.0.0.0/24 is subnetted, 4 subnets
C       10.109.0.0 is directly connected, FastEthernet0/0
D       10.101.0.0 [90/2172416] via 172.16.101.1, 00:16:02, Serial0/0.109
D       10.201.0.0 [90/2172416] via 172.16.201.1, 00:16:06, Serial0/0.209
C       10.209.0.0 is directly connected, FastEthernet1/0
```

As you can see, the routing protocol (EIGRP, in this case) is doing what it is designed to do. The network 10.101.0.0/24 is available through the shortest path—the direct link on S0/0.109. The 10.201.0.0/24 network is similarly available through the shortest path, which is found on S0/0.209.

The problem is that routing is based on destination addresses. When a user on either of the locally connected Ethernet networks wants to get to either of the companies' HQ networks, the router doesn't care where the packets originate from; the routing protocol simply provides the best path to the destination networks. With route maps and policy routing, we were able to change that.

The configuration for the Ethernet links on Branch #9 is simple (I've removed the access lists that prevent inter-Ethernet communication to avoid any confusion, as these ACLs are not germane to this discussion):

```
interface FastEthernet0/0
 ip address 10.109.0.1 255.255.255.0

interface FastEthernet0/1
 ip address 10.209.0.1 255.255.255.0
```

We needed to add a policy map on each Ethernet interface that told the router to alter the next hop of each packet sent to the HQ offices based on the source address contained in the packet.

First, we had to define our route maps. The logic for the route maps is shown in this snippet of pseudocode:

```
IF {the source network is 10.109.0.0/24
      AND the destination is 10.201.0.0/24}
THEN send the packet out interface S0/0.109

IF {the source network is 10.209.0.0/24
      AND the destination is 10.101.0.0/24}
THEN send the packet out interface S0/0.209
```

In route map terms, we needed to *match* the destination address of the packet and then *set* the next hop. These route maps would then be applied to the input interfaces to accomplish our goal.

To match IP addresses in route maps, you need to specify and include access lists. We made two access lists to match the destination networks. Access list 101 matched the 10.101.0.0/24 network (Company 1), and access list 102 matched the 10.201.0.0/24 network (Company 2):

```
access-list 101 permit ip any 10.101.0.0 0.0.0.255
access-list 101 remark <[ Company-1 Network ]>
!
access-list 102 permit ip any 10.201.0.0 0.0.0.255
access-list 102 remark <[ Company-2 Network >]
```

Now let's revisit our pseudocode and update it with router configuration information:

```
IF {the source network is 10.109.0.0/24 (int F0/0)
      AND the destination is 10.201.0.0/24 (ACL 102)}
THEN send the packet out interface S0/0.109

IF {the source network is 10.209.0.0/24 (int F0/1)
      AND the destination is 10.101.0.0/24 (ACL 101)}
THEN send the packet out interface S0/0.209
```

With the destination networks defined, we were able to create route map clauses to match against them. After matching the destination network, we needed to change the interface to which the packet would switch within the router. The first route map forced packets destined for Company 1's HQ network to go across Company 1's link:

```
route-map Company-1 permit 10
 match ip address 102
 set interface Serial0/0.109
```

The second forced traffic destined for Company 2's HQ network over Company 2's link:

```
route-map Company-2 permit 10
 match ip address 101
 set interface Serial0/0.209
```

In this example, the source-network part of our pseudocode is matched by applying our route map to the interface attached to the network in question. We do this with the `ip policy` interface command.

We used some fall-through logic here. We knew that Company 1's users' packets headed to Company 1's headquarters would route properly without alteration, as would Company 2's users' packets headed to Company 2's headquarters. The only time we needed to interfere was when either company's users accessed a server at the other company's headquarters—then, and only then, we needed to force the packets to take the other link. To accomplish this, we applied the Company 2 route map to the Company 1 Ethernet interface, and vice versa. We did this on the Branch #9 router:

```
interface FastEthernet0/0
 description <[ Company-1 Users ]>
 ip address 10.109.0.1 255.255.255.0
 ip policy route-map Company-1
 half-duplex

interface FastEthernet0/1
 description <[ Company-2 Users ]>
 ip address 10.209.0.1 255.255.255.0
 ip policy route-map Company-2
 half-duplex
```

 Policy routing takes place when a packet is received on an interface. For this reason, the policy must be placed on the Ethernet interfaces in this example.

Monitoring Policy Routing

Once policy routing is configured, how do you know it's working? In the preceding source-routing example, we altered the way packets routed, but the IP routing table didn't change. Normally, we would look at the routing table to determine where a router is sending packets, but with policy routing in place, the routing table is no longer the most reliable source of information.

Policy routing overrides the routing table, which can be confusing when you're troubleshooting routing problems. If your packets are not routing the way you expect them to, check for policy routing on your interfaces.

To see which policies are applied to which interfaces, use the show ip policy command:

```
Branch-9#sho ip policy
Interface          Route map
FastEthernet0/0    Company-1
FastEthernet0/1    Company-2
```

Another method for determining whether policy routing is enabled is using the show ip interface command. This command creates a lot of output, so filtering with include Policy is useful for our purposes:

```
Branch-9#sho ip int f0/0 | include Policy
  Policy routing is enabled, using route map Company-1
  BGP Policy Mapping is disabled
```

The problem with these commands is that they only show that a policy is applied, not how it's working. The command show route-map will show you all the route maps configured on the router, as well as some useful statistics regarding how many times the route map has been used for policy routing. This information is cumulative, so you can only assume the route map is working the way you want it to if the counters are incrementing:

```
Branch-9#sho route-map
route-map Company-1, permit, sequence 10
  Match clauses:
    ip address (access-lists): 102
  Set clauses:
    interface Serial0/0.109
    ip next-hop 172.16.101.1
  Policy routing matches: 626 packets, 65304 bytes
route-map Company-2, permit, sequence 10
  Match clauses:
    ip address (access-lists): 101
  Set clauses:
    interface Serial0/0.209
  Policy routing matches: 656 packets, 68624 bytes
```

Another option you can use to determine whether a router is acting on enabled policies is the debug ip policy command.

Take care when using debug, as it can impact the operation of the router. Remember that policy routing is applied to every packet that comes into an interface. Test this in a lab before you try it in a production network.

Here, a workstation on Company 2's user network in Branch #9 is pinging Company 1's HQ network (10.101.0.1):

```
D       10.101.0.0 [90/2172416] via 172.16.101.1, 03:21:29, Serial0/0.109
```

According to the routing table, these packets should route through S0/0.109. But, when the user pings 10.101.0.1, the debug output tells a different story:

```
04:49:24: IP: s=10.209.0.2 (FastEthernet0/1), d=10.101.0.1, len 100, FIB policy match
04:49:24: IP: s=10.209.0.2 (FastEthernet0/1), d=10.101.0.1, g=172.16.101.1, len 100,
FIB policy routed
04:49:25: IP: s=10.209.0.2 (FastEthernet0/1), d=10.101.0.1, len 100, FIB policy match
04:49:25: IP: s=10.209.0.2 (FastEthernet0/1), d=10.101.0.1, g=172.16.101.1, len 100,
FIB policy routed
04:49:25: IP: s=10.209.0.2 (FastEthernet0/1), d=10.101.0.1, len 100, FIB policy match
04:49:25: IP: s=10.209.0.2 (FastEthernet0/1), d=10.101.0.1, g=172.16.101.1, len 100,
FIB policy routed
04:49:25: IP: s=10.209.0.2 (FastEthernet0/1), d=10.101.0.1, len 100, FIB policy match
04:49:25: IP: s=10.209.0.2 (FastEthernet0/1), d=10.101.0.1
Branch-9#, g=172.16.101.1, len 100, FIB policy routed
04:49:25: IP: s=10.209.0.2 (FastEthernet0/1), d=10.101.0.1, len 100, FIB policy match
04:49:25: IP: s=10.209.0.2 (FastEthernet0/1), d=10.101.0.1, g=172.16.101.1, len 100,
FIB policy routed
```

Notice the entries in bold, each of which corresponds to a single ping packet. First, we see an FIB policy match entry. This indicates that one of the match statements in our route map was successful. The following line contains the phrase FIB policy routed. This indicates that the packet was policy-routed instead of being routed as it would normally.

Here's an example of packets that did not match the route map and, as such, were routed normally:

```
04:52:35: IP: s=10.209.0.2 (FastEthernet0/1), d=10.201.0.1, len 100, FIB policy
rejected(no match) - normal forwarding
04:52:35: IP: s=10.209.0.2 (FastEthernet0/1), d=10.201.0.1, len 100, FIB policy
rejected(no match) - normal forwarding
04:52:35: IP: s=10.209.0.2 (FastEthernet0/1), d=10.201.0.1, len 100, FIB policy
rejected(no match) - normal forwarding
04:52:35: IP: s=10.209.0.2 (FastEthernet0/1), d=10.201.0.1, len 100, FIB policy
rejected(no match) - normal forwarding
04:52:35: IP: s=10.209.0.2 (FastEthernet0/1), d=10.201.0.1, len 100, FIB policy
rejected(no match) - normal forwarding
```

Again, I've highlighted the entry for a single packet. This time, we see the phrase FIB policy rejected(no match) - normal forwarding, which indicates that the packet did not match any clauses in the route map and was forwarded by normal means.

 See Chapter 11 for another example of route maps in action.

## CHAPTER 15

Switching Algorithms in Cisco Routers

The term *switching*, when used in the context of routers, describes the process of moving packets from one interface to another within a router. Packets in transit arrive at one interface and must be moved to another, based on routing information stored in the router.

Routing is the process of choosing paths and forwarding packets to destinations outside the physical router. *Switching* is the internal forwarding of packets between interfaces.

Just as there are different routing protocols for determining the external paths for packets, there are different internal methods for switching. These switching algorithms, or *paths*, are a valuable way to increase (or decrease) a router's performance.

One of the biggest factors in how fast a packet gets from its source to its destination is the processing delay present in each router along the way. Different switching methods have vastly different impacts on a router's performance. Choosing the right one—and knowing what to look for when there's a problem—will help the savvy administrator keep a network running at peak performance.

A router must move packets from one interface to another, just like a switch. The decisions about how to move packets from one interface to another are based on the *routing information base* (RIB), which is built manually or by Layer-3 routing protocols. The RIB is essentially the routing table (see Chapter 9 for details). Nexus switches may have multiple RIBs called Virtual Route Forwarding (VRF) instances. See Chapter 18 for more details regarding VRFs.

There are many types of switching within a Cisco router. They are divided into two categories: *process switching* and *interrupt context switching*. Process switching involves the processor calling a process that accesses the RIB, and waiting for the next scheduled execution of that process to run. Interrupt context switching involves the processor interrupting the current process to switch the packet. Interrupt context switching is further divided into three types:

- Fast switching
- Optimum switching

- Cisco Express Forwarding (CEF)

Each method uses different techniques to determine the destination interface. Generally speaking, the process of switching a packet involves the following steps:

1. Determine whether the packet's destination is reachable.
2. Determine the next hop to the destination and to which interface the packet should be switched to get there.
3. Rewrite the MAC header on the packet so it can reach its destination.

While the information in this chapter may not benefit you in the day-to-day operation of your network, knowing how the different choices work will help you understand why you should choose one path over another. Knowledge of your router's switching internals will also help you understand why your router behaves differently when you choose different switching paths.

Figure 15-1 shows a simplified view of the inside of a router. There are three interfaces, all of which have access to input/output memory. When a packet comes into an interface, the router must decide to which interface the packet should be sent. Once that decision is made, the packet's MAC headers are rewritten and the packet is sent on its way.

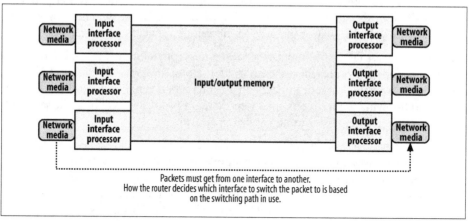

Figure 15-1. Router switching requirements

The routing table contains all the information necessary to determine the correct interface, but process switching must be used to retrieve data from the routing table, and this is inefficient. Interrupt context switching is typically preferred.

The number of steps involved in forwarding a packet varies with the switching path used. The method of storing and retrieving next-hop and interface information also differs in each of the switching paths. Additionally, various router models operate differently in terms of memory and where the decisions are made.

Process Switching

The original method for determining to which interface a packet should be forwarded is called *process switching*. This may be the easiest method to understand, because it behaves in a way you'd probably expect.

With process switching, when a packet comes in, the scheduler calls a process that examines the routing table, determines which interface the packet should be switched to, and then switches the packet. This happens for every packet seen on every interface. Figure 15-2 shows the following steps for process switching:

1. The interface processor detects a packet and moves the packet to the input/output memory.

2. The interface processor generates a *receive interrupt*. During this time, the central processor (CPU) determines the packet type (IP) and copies it to the processor memory, if necessary (this is platform-dependent). The processor then places the packet on the appropriate process's input queue and releases the interrupt. The process for IP packets is titled *ip_input*.

3. When the scheduler next runs, it notices the presence of a packet in the input queue for the *ip_input* process and schedules the process for execution.

4. When the *ip_input* process runs, it looks up the next hop and output interface information in the RIB. The *ip_input* process then consults the ARP cache to retrieve the Layer-2 address for the next hop.

5. The process rewrites the packet's MAC header with the appropriate addresses, then places the packet on the output queue of the appropriate interface.

6. The packet is moved from the output queue of the outbound interface to the transmit queue of the outbound interface. Outbound QoS happens in this step.

7. The output interface processor notices the packet in its queue and transfers the packet to the network media.

There are a couple of key points in this process that make it particularly slow. First, the processor waits for the next scheduled execution of the *ip_input* process. Second, when the *ip_input* process finally runs, it references the RIB, which is a very slow process. The *ip_input* process runs at the same priority level as other processes on the router, such as routing protocols and the HTTP web server interface.

The benefit of process switching is that it is available on every Cisco router platform, regardless of size or age. Packets sourced from or destined to the router itself, such as SNMP traps from the router and Telnet packets destined for the router, are always process-switched.

As you can imagine, on large routers or routers that move a lot of packets, process switching can be very taxing. Even on smaller routers, process switching can cause

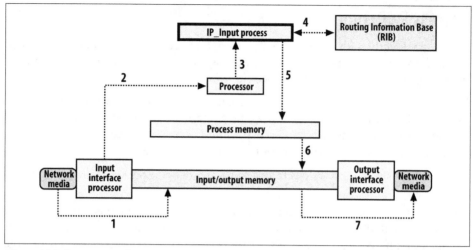

Figure 15-2. Process switching

performance problems. I've seen 2600-series routers serving only a single T1 average 60–80 percent CPU utilization while using process switching.

Process switching should never be used as the switching method of choice. Any of the other methods will produce significantly better performance.

Interrupt Context Switching

Interrupt context switching is much faster than process switching. The increase in speed is largely due to the fact that the *ip_input* process is rarely called. Interrupt context switching instead interrupts the process currently running on the router to switch the packet. Interrupt context switching usually bypasses the RIB, and works with parallel tables, which are built more efficiently (the details of these tables differ according to the switching path in use). You also save a considerable amount of time because the processor no longer has to wait for a process to complete.

The general steps for interrupt context switching are shown in Figure 15-3.

Interrupt context switching is a broad description that encompasses various switching paths—fast switching, optimum switching, and CEF—and includes the following steps:

1. The interface processor detects a packet and moves the packet into input/output memory.

2. The interface processor generates a receive interrupt. During this time, the central processor (CPU) determines the packet type (IP) and begins to switch the packet.

3. The processor searches the route cache for the following information and uses it to rewrite the packet's MAC header:

a. Is the destination reachable?

b. What should the output interface be?

c. What is the next hop?

d. What should the MAC addresses be converted to?

4. The packet is copied to either the transmit queue or the output queue of the outbound interface. The receive interrupt is ended, and the originally running process continues.

5. The output interface processor notices the packet in its queue and transfers the packet to the network media.

The obvious difference is that there are only five steps, as opposed to seven for process switching. The big impact comes from the fact that the currently running process on the router is interrupted, as opposed to waiting for the next scheduled execution of the *ip_input* process.

The RIB is also bypassed entirely in this model, and the necessary information is retrieved from other sources. In the example shown in Figure 15-3, the source is called the *route cache*. As you'll see, each switching path has its own means of determining, storing, and retrieving this information. The different methods are what separate the individual switching paths within the interrupt context switching group.

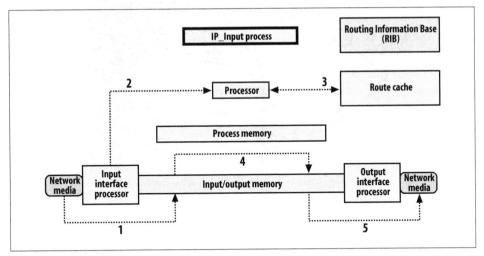

Figure 15-3. Interrupt context switching

Fast Switching

Fast switching process-switches the first packet in a conversation, then stores the information learned about the destination for that packet in a table called the route cache.

Fast switching uses the *binary tree* format for recording and retrieving information in the route cache.

Figure 15-4 shows an example of a binary tree as it might be viewed for fast switching. Each branch of the tree appends a 0 or a 1 to the previous level's value. Starting at 0 (the root), the next branch to the right contains a 0 on the bottom and a 1 on the top. Each of those nodes again branches, appending a 0 on the bottom branch and a 1 on the top branch. Eight levels of the tree are shown in Figure 15-4, but an actual tree used for IP addresses would have 32 levels, corresponding to the bits within an IP address.

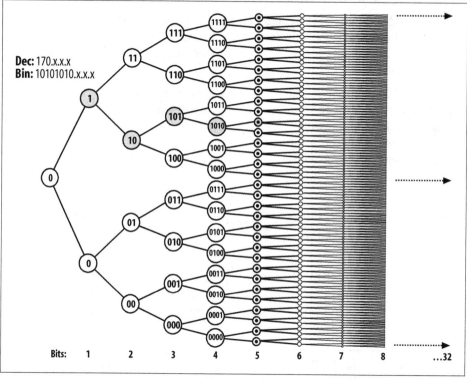

Figure 15-4. Fast-switching binary tree

The nodes marked in gray in Figure 15-4 match an IP address of 170.x.x.x (the binary value of 170 is 10101010—this should make the example easier to visualize). The IP address is only 170.x.x.x, because I couldn't fit any more visible nodes beyond eight bits in the drawing.

The benefit of this design, as compared to searching the RIB, is speed. Information regarding the next hop and MAC address changes is stored within each node. Since the tree is very deterministic, finding specific entries is very quick.

The drawbacks of this implementation include the sheer size of the table and the fact that while the data for each address is stored within the nodes, the size of the data is not static. Because each node may be a different size, the table can be inefficient.

The route cache is not directly related to the routing table, and it is updated only when packets are process-switched. In other words, the route cache is updated only when the first packet to a destination is switched. From that point, the route cache is used, and the remaining packets are fast-switched. To keep the data in the route cache current, 1/20th of the entire route cache is *aged out* (discarded) every minute. This information must be rebuilt using process switching.

Because the ARP table is not directly related to the contents of the route cache, changes to it result in parts of the route cache being invalidated. Process switching must also be used to resolve these differences.

Optimum Switching

Optimum switching uses a *multiway tree* instead of a binary tree to record and retrieve information in the route cache. For the purposes of IP addresses, a multiway tree is much faster because each octet can only be one of 256 values. A binary tree is designed to support any type of value, so there is no limit to its potential size.

Figure 15-5 shows a multiway tree as it might appear for optimum switching. The root branches into 256 nodes, numbered 0–255. Each node then branches into an additional 256 nodes. This pattern continues for four levels—one for each octet. The nodes in gray show how an IP address would be matched. The example used here is the address 3.253.7.5.

This type of tree is much faster for IP address lookups than a binary tree, because the table is optimized for the IP address format. Information for each route (prefix) or IP address is stored within the final node, as shown in Figure 15-6. Because the size of this information can be variable, and each node may or may not contain information, the overall table size is also variable. This is a drawback: searching the tree is not as efficient as it might be if every node were of a known static size.

Because the relevant data is stored in the nodes and has no direct relationship to the RIB or the ARP cache, entries are aged and rebuilt through process switching in the same manner used with fast switching.

Optimum switching is available only on high-end routers, such as models in the 7500 and 7600 series.

CEF

CEF is the switching path of choice on any router that supports it. Almost all modern routers and switches default to CEF switching, especially in the data-center space.

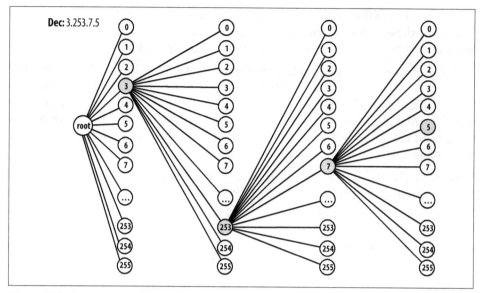

Figure 15-5. Optimum-switching multiway tree

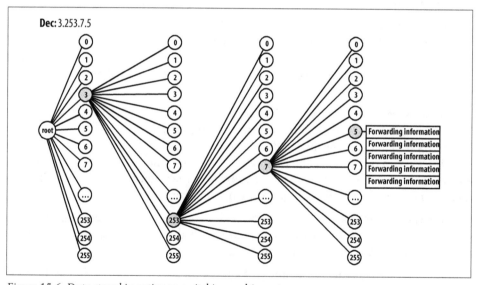

Figure 15-6. Data stored in optimum-switching multiway tree

CEF takes the ideas behind the optimum-switching multiway tree a step further by introducing the concept of a *trie*. The initial concept is the same as for a multiway or binary tree, but the data is not stored within the nodes. Rather, each node becomes a pointer to another table, which contains the data.

The term *trie* comes from the word *retrieve*, and is pronounced like *tree*. Some prefer the pronunciation *try* to differentiate the term from the word "tree."

In CEF, this trie is called the *forwarding table*. Each node is the same static size and contains no data. Instead, the node's position in the trie is itself a reference to another table, called the *adjacency table*. This table stores the pertinent data, such as MAC header substitution and next-hop information for the nodes. Figure 15-7 shows a representation of the CEF tables.

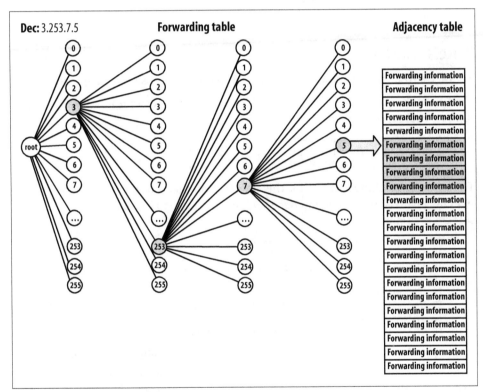

Figure 15-7. *CEF forwarding and adjacency tables*

One of the biggest advantages of CEF is the fact that the tables are built without process switching. Both tables can be built without waiting for a packet to be sent to a destination. Also, as the forwarding table is built separately from the adjacency table, an error in one table does not cause the other to become stale. When the ARP cache changes, only the adjacency table changes, so aging or invalidation of the forwarding table is not required.

CEF supports load balancing over equal-cost paths, as you'll see in the next section. Load balancing at the switching level is far superior to load balancing by routing protocols, as routing protocols operate at a much higher level. The latest versions of IOS incorporate CEF switching into routing protocol load balancing, so this has become less of an issue.

Configuring and Managing Switching Paths

Configuring switching paths is done both globally and at the interface level, allowing you the flexibility of configuring different switching paths on each interface. For example, you may want to disable CEF on an interface to see whether it's causing problems.

Process Switching

To force a router to use process switching, turn off all other switching methods.

Here, I'm showing the performance of a Cisco 2621XM router with about 600k of traffic running over serial interface s0/1:

```
R1#sho int s0/1 | include minute
   5 minute input rate 630000 bits/sec, 391 packets/sec
   5 minute output rate 627000 bits/sec, 391 packets/sec
```

The normal switching method for this interface on this router is CEF. To see which switching path is running on interface s0/1, use the show ip interface s0/1 | include switching command:

```
R1#sho ip interface s0/1 | include switching
  IP fast switching is enabled
  IP fast switching on the same interface is enabled
  IP Flow switching is disabled
  IP CEF switching is enabled
  IP CEF Fast switching turbo vector
  IP multicast fast switching is enabled
  IP multicast distributed fast switching is disabled
```

Notice that fast switching and CEF are both enabled. CEF will try to switch the packet first. If CEF cannot switch the packet, it will *punt* the packet to the next best available switching path—fast switching. If fast switching cannot process the packet, the router will process-switch the packet. If all the other switching paths are turned off, the router must process-switch all packets.

To disable all interrupt context switching paths, use the interface command no ip route-cache:

```
R1(config-if)#no ip route-cache
R1(config-if)# ^Z
R1# sho ip interface s0/1 | include switching
  IP fast switching is disabled
```

```
IP fast switching on the same interface is disabled
IP Flow switching is disabled
IP CEF switching is disabled
IP Fast switching turbo vector
IP multicast fast switching is disabled
IP multicast distributed fast switching is disabled
```

I've done this for all interfaces on the router. Now let's look at the CPU utilization on the router with the command show processes cpu history:

```
R1#sho proc cpu hist
```

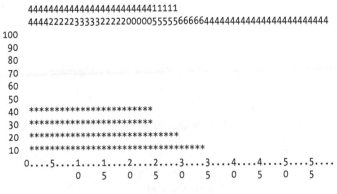

CPU% per second (last 60 seconds)

The router was running at an average of 4 percent CPU utilization with CEF running. When I disabled all route caching, the router reverted to process switching for all packets. For just 600k of traffic, the router is now using 40 percent of its CPU cycles to forward the packets.

When a router is process-switching most of its IP packets, the top process will always be *ip_input*. You can verify this by executing the command show processes cpu sorted:

```
R1#sho proc cpu sort
CPU utilization for five seconds: 48%/20%; one minute: 44%; five minutes: 40%
 PID Runtime(ms)   Invoked   uSecs   5Sec   1Min   5Min TTY Process
  31 177614152 132817658    1337 26.60% 24.06% 21.94%   0 IP Input
   3     60540     20255    2988  1.47%  0.22%  0.05%   0 Exec
   4   1496508    210836    7097  0.16%  0.06%  0.05%   0 Check heaps
   1         0         1       0  0.00%  0.00%  0.00%   0 Chunk Manager
   2     12488    328220      38  0.00%  0.00%  0.00%   0 Load Meter
   5       220       332     662  0.00%  0.00%  0.00%   0 Pool Manager
   6         0         2       0  0.00%  0.00%  0.00%   0 Timers
   7         0         8       0  0.00%  0.00%  0.00%   0 Serial Backgroun
   8     12108    327897      36  0.00%  0.00%  0.00%   0 ALARM_TRIGGER_SC
```

This is a good troubleshooting step if you have a router or multilayer switch that is running slowly. If you see *ip_input* taking up the majority of available CPU time (as shown here), you need to ask yourself why the router is process switching. Check your config and look for problems.

Packets that are malformed can cause a router to process-switch. I've seen Metropolitan Area Ethernet carrier equipment muck up Ethernet packets just enough that the router had to process-switch them. I've seen the same thing when an ASIC in a switch fails. My point is that external devices or events, not just events internal to the router, can cause the router to fall back on process switching.

Fast Switching

On an interface that is currently process-switching, the interface command `ip route-cache` enables fast switching:

```
R1(config)#int s0/1
R1(config-if)# ip route-cache
```

This turns on fast switching without enabling CEF:

```
R1#sho ip int s0/1 | include swi
 IP fast switching is enabled
 IP fast switching on the same interface is enabled
 IP Flow switching is disabled
 IP CEF switching is disabled
 IP Fast switching turbo vector
 IP multicast fast switching is enabled
 IP multicast distributed fast switching is disabled
```

On an interface that is running CEF, turning off CEF will result in the interface running fast switching:

```
R1(config)#int s0/1
R1(config-if)# no ip route-cache cef
```

You cannot disable fast switching without also disabling CEF, but you can enable fast switching without enabling CEF.

Continuing with the example in the previous section, as soon as I enable fast switching again on the process-switching router, the CPU utilization drops back down to normal levels:

```
R1#sho proc cpu hist

            2222244444444444444444444444444444444444444444444
      444444444444000007777711111888889999988888999993333344446
 100
  90
  80
  70
  60
  50          *****      ******************             *
  40          ****************************************************
```

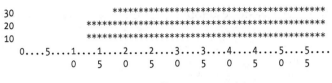

```
30                    *****************************************
20                    *****************************************
10                    *****************************************
    0....5....1....1....2....2....3....3....4....4....5....5....
         0    5    0    5    0    5    0    5    0    5
```

                    CPU% per second (last 60 seconds)

CEF

CEF is enabled by default on all modern Cisco routers, but in the event that you need to enable it on an older router, or if it has been disabled, there are two places you can configure it. First, using the global command `ip cef`, you can enable CEF on every interface that supports it:

```
R1(config)#ip cef
```

Negating the command disables CEF globally:

```
R1(config)#no ip cef
```

To enable or disable CEF on a single interface, use the interface command `ip route-cache cef`:

```
R1(config)#int s0/1
R1(config-if)# ip route-cache cef
```

Negating the command disables CEF on the interface.

CEF will load-balance packets across equal-cost links. By default, load balancing will be done on a per-destination basis. This means every packet for a single destination will use the same link. CEF also allows you to configure load balancing on a per-packet basis. This can be beneficial if, for example, there is only one host on the far end of the links or there is a large server that consumes the majority of the bandwidth for any single link.

Certain protocols, such as VoIP, cannot tolerate per-packet load balancing, because packets may arrive out of order. When using such protocols, always ensure that load balancing is performed per destination, or use a higher-level protocol such as Multilink-PPP.

To change an interface to load-balance using the per-packet method, use the `ip load-sharing per-packet` interface command:

```
R1(config-if)#ip load-sharing per-packet
```

To reconfigure an interface for per-destination load balancing, use the `ip load-sharing per-destination` interface command:

```
R1(config-if)#ip load-sharing per-destination
```

To show the CEF tables in an easy-to-read format, use the show ip cef command:

```
R1#sho ip cef
Prefix                 Next Hop           Interface
0.0.0.0/32             receive
10.1.1.0/24            attached           Loopback1
10.1.1.0/32            receive
10.1.1.1/32            receive
10.1.1.255/32          receive
10.2.2.0/24            attached           Loopback2
10.2.2.0/32            receive
10.2.2.2/32            receive
10.2.2.255/32          receive
10.3.3.0/24            192.168.1.2        Serial0/1
10.4.4.0/24            192.168.1.2        Serial0/1
10.5.5.0/24            attached           FastEthernet0/1
10.5.5.0/32            receive
10.5.5.1/32            10.5.5.1           FastEthernet0/1
10.5.5.5/32            receive
10.5.5.255/32          receive
10.10.10.0/24          192.168.1.2        Serial0/1
192.168.1.0/24         attached           Serial0/1
192.168.1.0/32         receive
192.168.1.1/32         receive
192.168.1.255/32       receive
224.0.0.0/4            drop
224.0.0.0/24           receive
255.255.255.255/32     receive
```

Usually, you won't need to look into what CEF is doing unless Cisco TAC tells you to. About the only time I've needed this command was when we had a CEF bug that caused packets to be sent out interfaces other than the ones indicated in the routing table. As a general rule, you should never disable CEF.

## CHAPTER 16

Multilayer Switches

Switches, in the traditional sense, operate at Layer 2 of the OSI stack. The first multilayer switches were called *Layer-3 switches* because they added the capability to route between VLANs. These days, switches can do just about anything a router can do, including protocol testing and manipulation all the way up to Layer 7. Thus, we now refer to switches that operate above Layer 2 as *multilayer switches*.

The core benefit of the multilayer switch is the capability to route between VLANs, which is made possible through the addition of virtual interfaces within the switch. These virtual interfaces are tied to VLANs, and are called *switched virtual interfaces* (SVIs).

Figure 16-1 illustrates the principles behind routing within a switch. First, you assign ports to VLANs. Then, you create SVIs, which allow IP addresses to be assigned to the VLANs. The virtual interface becomes a virtual router interface, thus allowing the VLANs to be routed.

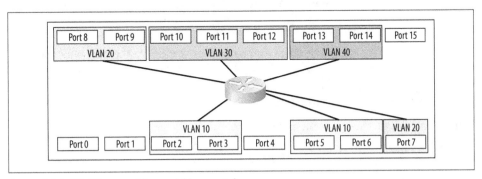

Figure 16-1. VLANs routed from within a switch

Most multilayer switches today do not have visible routers. The router is contained within the circuitry of the switch itself or in the supervisor (i.e., the CPU) of a modular switch. Older switch designs, like the Cisco 4000 chassis switch, have a Layer-3 module that was added to make the switch multilayer-capable. Such modules are no longer needed, since Layer-3 functionality is included with most supervisors.

On chassis-based switches with older supervisor modules, the router is a separate device with its own operating system. The router in these switches is a daughter card on the supervisor called the *multilayer switch function card* (MSFC). On these devices, Layer-2 operations are controlled by the CatOS operating system, while Layer-3 routing operations are controlled by the IOS operating system. This configuration, called *hybrid mode*, can be a bit confusing at first. To some people, having a separate OS for each function makes more sense than combining them. For most people, however, the single-OS model—called *native mode* on the chassis switches—is probably easier. Nexus switches run NX-OS, which is similar to IOS.

On a chassis-based switch in hybrid mode, physical interfaces and VLANs must be configured in CatOS. To route between them, you must move to IOS and create the SVIs for the VLANs you created in CatOS.

Another option for some switches is to change a switch port into a router port—that is, to make a port directly addressable with a Layer-3 protocol such as IP. To do this, you must have a switch that is natively IOS or running in IOS native mode. Nexus 7000 switch ports default to router mode.

Sometimes, I need to put a Layer-3 link between two multilayer switches. Configuring a port, a VLAN, and an SVI involves a lot of steps, especially when you consider that the VLAN will never have any ports included aside from the interswitch link. In such cases, converting a switch port to a router port is simpler.

You cannot assign an IP address to a physical interface when it is configured as a switch port (the default state for most Catalyst switches):

```
3750-IOS(config)#int g1/0/17
3750-IOS(config-if)#ip address 10.10.10.1 255.255.255.0
                       ^
% Invalid input detected at '^' marker.
```

To convert a multilayer switch port to a router port, configure the port with the command no switchport:

```
3750-IOS(config)#int g1/0/17
3750-IOS(config-if)#no switchport
```

Once you've done this, you can assign an IP address to the physical interface:

```
3750-IOS(config)#int g1/0/17
3750-IOS(config-if)#ip address 10.10.10.1 255.255.255.0
```

On Nexus 7000 switches, the ports default to routed mode. To make them switchports, issue the switchport interface command:

```
NX-7K-1(config)# int e8/1-2
NX-7K-1(config-if-range)# switchport
```

Ethernet ports on routers tend to be expensive, and they don't offer very good port density. The addition of switch modules, which provide a few interfaces, has improved their port densities, but nothing beats the flexibility of a multilayer switch when it comes to Ethernet.

 Watch out when using switches as routers. I once designed a nationwide MPLS network and, since all the handoffs were Metro Ethernet, decided that we could save some money by using existing 3750s for termination at the branches. Everything went great until I tried to configure low-latency queuing (LLQ) for QoS. Since switches aren't routers, they usually don't support WAN-type QoS, but rather LAN-type CoS. The configuration commands for LLQ weren't supported on the 3750. I was out of luck and had to go ask for more hardware late in the project.

Configuring SVIs

Switch virtual interfaces are configured differently depending on the switch platform and operating systems installed. Let's take a look.

IOS (4500, 6500, 3550, 3750, etc.)

Here is the output of the command show ip interface brief from a 3750:

```
3750-IOS#sho ip int brief
Interface             IP-Address    OK? Method Status                Protocol
Vlan1                 unassigned    YES NVRAM  administratively down down
GigabitEthernet1/0/1  unassigned    YES unset  down                  down
GigabitEthernet1/0/2  unassigned    YES unset  down                  down
GigabitEthernet1/0/3  unassigned    YES unset  down                  down
[-- text removed --]
GigabitEthernet1/0/47 unassigned    YES unset  up                    up
GigabitEthernet1/0/48 unassigned    YES unset  up                    up
GigabitEthernet1/0/49 unassigned    YES unset  down                  down
GigabitEthernet1/0/50 unassigned    YES unset  down                  down
GigabitEthernet1/0/51 unassigned    YES unset  down                  down
GigabitEthernet1/0/52 unassigned    YES unset  down                  down
Port-channel1         unassigned    YES unset  down                  down
```

The first interface is a switched virtual interface for VLAN 1. This SVI cannot be removed on a 3750, as it is used for management by default. Looking at the VLAN table with the show vlan command, we can see there are three VLANs configured in addition to the default VLAN 1:

```
3750-IOS#sho vlan
```

VLAN	Name	Status	Ports
1	default	active	Gi1/0/1, Gi1/0/2, Gi1/0/3
			Gi1/0/4, Gi1/0/5, Gi1/0/6
			Gi1/0/7, Gi1/0/8, Gi1/0/9

```
                                              Gi1/0/10, Gi1/0/11, Gi1/0/13
                                              Gi1/0/14, Gi1/0/15, Gi1/0/16
[ -- Text Removed --]
                                              Gi1/0/44, Gi1/0/45, Gi1/0/46
                                              Gi1/0/49, Gi1/0/50, Gi1/0/51
                                              Gi1/0/52
2    VLAN0002                  active         Gi1/0/12
3    VLAN0003                  active
4    VLAN0004                  active

VLAN Name                      Status    Ports
---- ------------------------- --------- -------------------------------
100  VLAN0100                  active
1002 fddi-default              act/unsup
1003 token-ring-default        act/unsup
1004 fddinet-default           act/unsup
1005 trnet-default             act/unsup
```

These VLANs are strictly Layer 2, in that the switch will not route between them. For the switch to access these VLANs at higher layers, we need to create an SVI for each one.

 To create SVIs on a Nexus 7000, you must first enable the feature with the `feature interface-vlan` global command.

The only step required to create an SVI is to define it. Simply by entering the global configuration command `interface vlan *vlan#*`, you will create the SVI. The *vlan#* does not need to match an existing VLAN. For example, defining an SVI for VLAN 200, which does not exist on our switch, will still result in the SVI being created. We can even assign an IP address to the interface and enable it with the `no shutdown` command:

```
3750-IOS(config)#int vlan 200
3750-IOS(config-if)#
00:11:40: %LINEPROTO-5-UPDOWN: Line protocol on Interface Vlan200, changed state to
down
3750-IOS(config-if)#ip address 10.200.0.1 255.255.255.0
3750-IOS(config-if)#no shut
```

The interface will initially be down/down because there is no VLAN at Layer 2 to support it. The hardware type is *EtherSVI*, indicating that this is a logical SVI:

```
3750-IOS#sho int vlan 200
Vlan200 is down, line protocol is down
  Hardware is EtherSVI, address is 001c.b0a9.6541 (bia 001c.b0a9.6541)
  Internet address is 10.200.0.1/24
  MTU 1500 bytes, BW 1000000 Kbit, DLY 10 usec,
     reliability 255/255, txload 1/255, rxload 1/255
  Encapsulation ARPA, loopback not set
  ARP type: ARPA, ARP Timeout 04:00:00
  Last input never, output never, output hang never
  Last clearing of "show interface" counters never
  Input queue: 0/75/0/0 (size/max/drops/flushes); Total output drops: 0
```

```
Queueing strategy: fifo
Output queue: 0/40 (size/max)
5 minute input rate 0 bits/sec, 0 packets/sec
5 minute output rate 0 bits/sec, 0 packets/sec
    0 packets input, 0 bytes, 0 no buffer
    Received 0 broadcasts (0 IP multicasts)
    0 runts, 0 giants, 0 throttles
    0 input errors, 0 CRC, 0 frame, 0 overrun, 0 ignored
    0 packets output, 0 bytes, 0 underruns
    0 output errors, 0 interface resets
    0 output buffer failures, 0 output buffers swapped out
```

Once we add VLAN 200 to the switch, the interface comes up:

```
3750-IOS(config-if)#vlan 200

3750-IOS#sho ip int brie | include Vlan200
Vlan200            10.200.0.1     YES manual up                 up
```

We have not assigned any ports to this VLAN, but the SVI for the VLAN is up and operating at Layer 3. We can even ping the new interface:

```
3750-IOS#ping 10.200.0.1

Type escape sequence to abort.
Sending 5, 100-byte ICMP Echos to 10.200.0.1, timeout is 2 seconds:
!!!!!
```

If we were so inclined, we could also add routing protocols and do almost anything else we would normally do with an interface operating at Layer 3.

What's the point of having an SVI without any physical ports assigned to it? One example might be to create a management network other than VLAN 1 for all your devices. You wouldn't need any physical ports assigned to the VLAN except for a trunk port to your other switches. This way, you could keep your management traffic on a separate VLAN from your production traffic. You may also have VLANs attached to your switch via trunks, in which case you might use the switch as a default gateway, even though there are no ports dedicated to the VLAN.

Hybrid Mode (4500, 6500)

On a switch supporting hybrid IOS mode, IOS is not an integral part of the switch's function. CatOS is used for switching, which is integral to the operation of Layer 2. IOS is used only to manage the MSFC and Layer 3.

You create a VLAN in CatOS, but create an SVI for the VLAN in IOS. You name the VLAN in CatOS, but add a description to the SVI in IOS. You must configure anything that is related to Layer-2 functionality in CatOS; Layer-3 and above functions must be configured in IOS.

On an IOS-only switch, there is always a VLAN 1 virtual interface. This is not the case in hybrid-mode switches, because VLAN 1 does not, by default, require Layer-3 functionality.

I've created two VLANs on a 6509 running in hybrid mode here:

```
CatOS-6509: (enable)sho vlan

VLAN Name                             Status    IfIndex Mod/Ports, Vlans
---- -------------------------------- --------- ------- ------------------------
1    default                          active    9       1/1-2
                                                        2/1-2
                                                        3/5-48
                                                        4/1-48
                                                        5/1-48
10   Lab-VLAN                         active    161
20   VLAN0020                         active    162     3/1-4
1002 fddi-default                     active    10
1003 token-ring-default               active    13
1004 fddinet-default                  active    11
1005 trnet-default                    active    12
```

The first, VLAN 10, I have named Lab-VLAN. The second, VLAN 20, has the default name of VLAN0020. To configure these VLANs in IOS, we must first connect to the MSFC using the session command. This command must be followed by the number of the module to which we'd like to connect. The number can be determined with the show module command:

```
CatOS-6509: (enable)sho mod
Mod Slot Ports Module-Type              Model              Sub Status
--- ---- ----- ------------------------ ------------------ --- -------
1   1    2     1000BaseX Supervisor     WS-X6K-SUP2-2GE    yes ok
15  1    1     Multilayer Switch Feature WS-F6K-MSFC2      no  ok
2   2    2     1000BaseX Supervisor     WS-X6K-SUP2-2GE    yes standby
16  2    1     Multilayer Switch Feature WS-F6K-MSFC2      no  ok
3   3    48    10/100BaseTX Ethernet    WS-X6348-RJ-45     no  ok
4   4    48    10/100BaseTX Ethernet    WS-X6348-RJ-45     no  ok
5   5    48    10/100BaseTX Ethernet    WS-X6348-RJ-45     no  ok
```

The first MSFC is reported as being in slot 15. This is normal when the supervisor is in slot 1, as the MSFC is a daughter card on the supervisor. The switch assigns an internal slot number to the MSFC. We can now connect to the MSFC:

```
CatOS-6509: (enable)session 15
Trying Router-15...
Connected to Router-15.
Escape character is '^]'.

MSFC-6509> en
MSFC-6509#
```

Another way to get to the MSFC is with the `switch console` command.

Now that we're in IOS, let's see what the MSFC thinks about the two VLANs:

```
MSFC-6509#sho ip int brief
Interface                IP-Address      OK? Method Status        Protocol
```

There are no SVIs active on the MSFC—not even VLAN 1. Let's add an SVI for VLAN 20 and see what happens:

```
MSFC-6509#conf t
Enter configuration commands, one per line. End with CNTL/Z.
MSFC-6509(config)# int vlan 20
MSFC-6509(config-if)# ip address 10.20.20.1 255.255.255.0
MSFC-6509(config-if)# no shut
MSFC-6509(config-if)# ^Z
MSFC-6509#
17w2d: %LINK-3-UPDOWN: Interface Vlan20, changed state to down
17w2d: %LINEPROTO-5-UPDOWN: Line protocol on Interface Vlan20, changed state to down
MSFC-6509#
MSFC-6509# sho ip int brief
Interface                IP-Address      OK? Method Status        Protocol
Vlan20                   10.20.20.1      YES manual down          down
```

The SVI is now there, but it won't come up. The SVI will not come up unless there is an active port in the VLAN in Layer 2. I often forget this fact and, after adding the SVIs, go off to create my VLANs, only to find that none of them will come up. To illustrate the point, I'll assign an IP address to the CatOS management interface SC0 and place it in VLAN 20. This will put an active device in the VLAN:

```
CatOS-6509: (enable)set int sc0 20 10.20.20.20 255.255.255.0
Interface sc0 vlan set, IP address and netmask set.
```

Now, with something active in VLAN 20, the VLAN 20 SVI comes up in the MSFC:

```
MSFC-6509#sho ip int brief
Interface                IP-Address      OK? Method Status        Protocol
Vlan20                   10.20.20.1      YES manual up            up
```

NX-OS (Nexus 7000, 5000)

Configuring a Nexus for SVIs is very similar to doing so in IOS. The main difference that gets me every time I'm configuring one for the first time is that, by default, SVIs are not allowed:

```
NX-7K-1(config)# int vlan 10
                     ^
Invalid command (interface name) at '^' marker.
```

As with many technologies on the Nexus platform, SVIs must be enabled. The specific feature that needs to be enabled is called `interface-vlan`:

```
NX-7K-1(config)# feature interface-vlan
```

Once this feature is enabled, we're free to configure the SVI as we would in IOS:

```
NX-7K-1(config)# int vlan 10
NX-7K-1(config-if)# ip address 10.10.10.10.24
```

Multilayer Switch Models

Cisco offers a variety of multilayer switch models. The line between them has become fuzzy, though, because routers like the 7600 series can take some of the 6500-series switching modules. The 3800 and 2800 series of routers also support a small switching module capable of supporting multiple Ethernet interfaces. These modules actually behave as if they were a separate 3750 switch.

Still, there is no magic all-in-one device. You must choose either a switch with limited routing capabilities or a router with limited switching capabilities. The difference is primarily in how the system internals are designed and which modules are supported. A router is designed differently from a switch, though this is also becoming less true if you consider devices like the CSR-1 (fortunately, the average networking engineer will likely never encounter these behemoths). A router is generally more WAN-centric, whereas a switch is usually more LAN-centric. There are no modules that allow T1 WAN connectivity for the 6500 switches. While you can put 6500-series Ethernet modules in a 7600 router, the backplane capacity is not as high in the router as it is in the switch.

Multilayer switches are divided by chassis type. On the lower end are the single rack unit (1 RU) models that are designed for wiring closets and small installations. Some of these switches can be stacked in a number of ways depending on the model. Some 1 RU models have increased backplane speeds and even support 10 Gbps uplinks.

Next in the hierarchy are the small chassis-based switches. This group is composed of the models in the 4500 range. These switches are designed for larger wiring closets, or even small core functions. They can support multiple power supplies and supervisors and are designed for high-availability installations.

The 6500 switches used to occupy the high end of the spectrum. Available in multiple chassis sizes, these switches are very popular due to their expandability, flexibility, and performance. The Cisco Nexus line is now the cutting edge of the Cisco data-center class of switches.

 For more information on switch types, refer to Chapter 2. Cisco 6500-series switches are discussed in more detail in Chapter 17, and the 3750 is the focus of Chapter 19. Chapter 18, which covers Nexus switches, is also included for your reading pleasure.

A quick word is in order about choosing the right device for the job. Many of my clients buy what I call closet switches for use in their data centers. A great example of this is the Cisco 3750. This is a very attractive switch because it can be stacked, allowing for pretty decent port densities. You must be careful, though, as this model switch is really designed for end-user connectivity. Sure, the purpose of the switch is to forward packets, and the switch doesn't care what's connected to it, but the 3750 has only one power supply. This can be mitigated with Redundant Power System (RPS) add-ons and multichassis EtherChannel, but the RPS is an add-on device that consumes a rack unit. Consider, also, that the 3750 only supports 127 spanning tree instances. With the default installation of RPVST, you will not be able to add a 128th VLAN and have spanning tree protect you from loops. Trust me when I tell you that this is not a fun situation in which to find yourself.

Cisco has switches to support the higher availability demands found in the data center. Switches like the 4900 series come with dual power supplies and are designed for top-of-rack installations. The Nexus line is designed specifically for data centers and includes proper front-to-back airflow along with dual power supplies. Nexus 5000 and 5500 switches allow you to add FEXs for port densities exceeding the 6509, but some models don't support Layer 3.

Where possible, try to avoid using the wrong switch to save a few bucks. You'll just end up paying someone like me in a few years to get you out of the corner you've painted yourself into. Believe me, paying for the better switch is cheaper.

## CHAPTER 17

Cisco 6500 Multilayer Switches

The Cisco 6500 is possibly the most widely deployed enterprise-class switch in the world. The balance of expandability, power, capabilities, and port density offered by this switch is hard to beat. The 6500 series comes in sizes ranging from 3 to 13 slots. There are even versions that are Network Equipment Building System (NEBS)-compliant for use in telecom infrastructures that must meet these stringent specifications.

The 6500 architecture has been around for some time, but because it was developed with expandability in mind, the switch that originally supported only 32 Gbps on the backplane now routinely supports 720 Gbps. There is even a way to cluster two 6500s together for a theoretical speed of 1,440 Gbps, though as we'll see, I find that claim to be more marketing than reality.

The versatility of the 6500 platform has been a prime driver for this series' placement in a wide variety of positions in an even wider array of solutions. 6509 switches are often at the center of enterprise networks, at the access layer of large companies, as the core of ecommerce websites, and even as the telecom gateways for large VoIP implementations.

Likewise, the flexibility of the 6500 platform has made it prevalent in smaller companies. The 6500 series includes Firewall Services Modules (FWSMs), Content Switching Modules (CSMs), and Network Analysis Modules (NAMs). The entire network infrastructure, as well as all security, load-balancing, and monitoring hardware, can be contained in a single chassis.

With the addition of a multilayer-switch feature card (included in the latest supervisors), the 6500 becomes a multilayer switch. With the addition of IOS running natively, the 6500 becomes a router with the potential for more than 300 Ethernet interfaces while retaining the functionality and speed of a switch.

When running in native IOS mode, a 6500 operates very similarly to the smaller 3550 and 3750 switches, but with more flexibility and power. Figure 17-1 shows how a typical multitiered ecommerce website can benefit from using a 6509 chassis-based solution rather than a series of individual components.

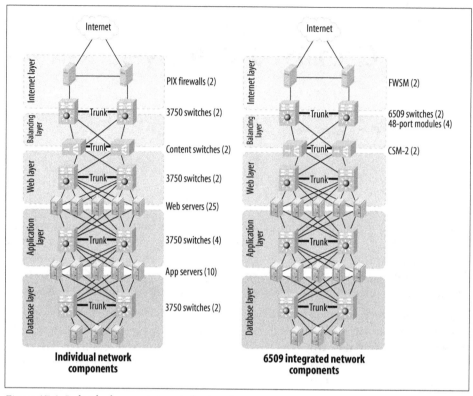

Figure 17-1. Individual versus integrated network components

First, because all of the layers can be consolidated into a single device using VLANs, many of the switches are no longer needed and are replaced with Ethernet modules in the 6509 chassis.

Second, because some layers do not need a lot of ports, ports can be better utilized. A module is not dedicated to a specific layer, but can be divided in any way needed. If we allocated a physical switch to each layer, there would be many unused ports on each switch, especially at the upper layers.

Another benefit is that because the components are included in a single chassis, there are fewer maintenance contracts to manage (though modules like the FWSM and Application Content Engines [ACE] require their own contracts). Additionally, because all of the devices are now centralized, there only needs to be one pair of power outlets for each switch. The tradeoff here is that the power will no doubt be 220V 20A or more.

Some of the new power supplies for the 6500e chassis require multiple power feeds per supply. The 6,000-watt AC power supply requires two power outlets per supply. The 8,700-watt AC power supply requires three outlets per supply, resulting in a total of six outlets per chassis!

The main advantages are supportability and speed. Each module is available through the switch itself in addition to its own accessibility, and, in the case of the ACE module, the configuration is a part of the Cisco IOS for the switch itself (assuming native IOS). Each module is hot-swappable, with the only limitation being that some modules must be shut down before being removed. Also, because the modules communicate with each other over the backplane, they offer substantial increases in speed over their standalone counterparts. The FWSM, for example, is capable of more than 5.5 Gbps of throughput. Only recently, with the introduction of the ASA 5580-40, has a standalone appliance exceeded this throughput with a whopping 10 Gbps. The ASA 5580-20 is only capable of 2.5 Gbps. While this processing difference has a lot to do with the design of the FWSM and ASA firewalls, remember that standalone devices must communicate through Ethernet interfaces, while service modules communicate directly over the backplane of the switch. This has become less of an issue with larger ASAs that support 10 Gb Ethernet.

6500-series switches are designed to be highly redundant. They support dual power supplies and dual supervisors. The supervisor MSFCs can run as individual routers or in single-router mode. The power supplies can be configured in a failover mode or a combined mode to allow more power for hungry modules.

Combine this switch's features, scalability, and resilience with the additional fault tolerance of a high-availability network design, and you've got a world-class architecture at your fingertips. Though the Nexus is becoming the switch of choice in the data center, it cannot yet match the versatility of the 6500.

Architecture

The 6500-series switches are an evolution of the 6000 series. The 6000-series switch contains only a 32 Gbps backplane bus, whereas the 6500 series contains an additional bus called the *fabric bus* or *crossbar switching bus*. This bus allows backplane speeds to be boosted up to 720 Gbps and beyond.

The addition of the crossbar switching fabric in the 6500 series also provides an amazing amount of flexibility in the new chassis. Legacy modules from the 6000 chassis can still be used, as the 32 Gbps bus in the 6500 is identical to the one found in the 6000 series. However, with the addition of a *Switch Fabric Module* (SFM), newer fabric-enabled modules are able to take advantage of the new bus.

The SFM is essentially a 16-port switch that connects each fabric-enabled module via the fabric bus. Because the SFM is a switch unto itself, modules communicate concurrently, in much the same way that multiple computers can communicate on a switched Ethernet network. By contrast, the 32 Gbps bus operates in such a way that all modules receive all packets, regardless of the destination module (similar to the way computers communicate on an Ethernet network connected with a hub).

Because it controls the crossbar fabric bus, the SFM can only reside in certain slots. One of the major downsides to this design is that a highly redundant installation requires two slots for the supervisors and an additional two slots for the SFMs. In a nine-slot chassis, this leaves only five slots for line cards or service modules.

The Supervisor-720 solves the slot density problem by incorporating the SFM into the supervisor module. Now, a highly resilient installation requires only two slots for supervisors. However, because the Supervisor-720 includes the SFM's functionality, it must reside in the SFM's slots. For example, on a redundant 6509, the Supervisor-2 modules reside in slots 1 and 2, while the SFMs reside in slots 5 and 6. Supervisor-720 modules must reside in slots 5 and 6, which frees up slots 1 and 2 for line cards or service modules.

Buses

The 6500-series switch backplane is composed of the following four buses:

D bus
> The data bus, or D bus, is used by the EARL chipset to transfer data between modules. The speed of the D bus is 32 Gbps. The D bus is shared much like a traditional Ethernet network in that all modules receive all frames that are placed on the bus. When frames need to be forwarded from a port on one module to a port on another module, assuming the crossbar fabric bus is not in use or available to the modules, they will traverse this bus.

R bus
> The results bus, or R bus, handles communication between the modules and the switching logic on the supervisors. The speed of the R bus is 4 Gbps.

C bus
> The control bus, or C bus, is also sometimes referred to as the *Ethernet Out-of-Band Channel* (EOBC). The C bus is used for communication between the line cards and the network management processors on the supervisors. The C bus is actually a 100 Mbps half-duplex network. Line-control code downloads to the line cards on this bus.

Crossbar fabric bus
> *Crossbar* is a type of switching technology where each node is connected to every other node by means of intersecting paths. An alternative switching fabric is the fully interconnected model, where each port is directly connected to every other port.
>
> Figure 17-2 shows visual representations of such switching fabrics. The term *fabric* is used to describe the mesh of connections in such designs, as logically, the connections resemble interwoven strands of fabric.

The crossbar fabric shown in Figure 17-2 shows one black intersection. This is an active connection, whereas the other connections are inactive. The active connection shown here indicates that port 2 is communicating with port 3.

The crossbar fabric bus, combined with a Supervisor-2 and an SFM is capable of 256 Gbps and 30 million packets per second (Mpps). With the addition of a distributed forwarding card, this combination is capable of 210 Mpps. With a Supervisor-720 module, the crossbar fabric supports up to 720 Gbps. When distributed Cisco Express Forwarding (dCEF) interface modules are used, a Sup-720-equipped 6500 is capable of 400 Mpps.

The SFM is what provides the actual switch fabric between all the fabric-enabled modules (recall that the SFM's functionality is included in the Supervisor-720, so in this case, a separate module is not required). The module is actually a switch in and of itself that uses the backplane fabric bus as a communication channel between the modules. For this reason, the speed of a 6500 can change with a new supervisor module.

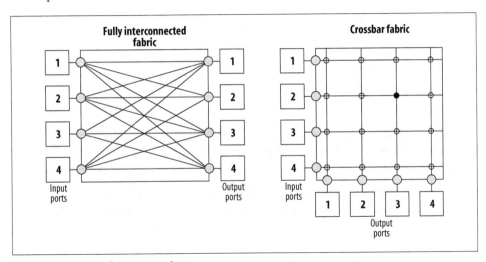

Figure 17-2. Switch fabric examples

Figure 17-3 shows a visual representation of the backplane in a 6509 chassis. Looking at the chassis from the front, you would see each slot's connectors as shown. There are two backplane circuit boards separated by a vertical space. To the left of the space (at the back of the chassis) are the power connectors and the crossbar fabric bus. To the right of the space are the D, R, and C buses. A 6000 chassis would look the same to the right of the space, but have no crossbar fabric bus to the left.

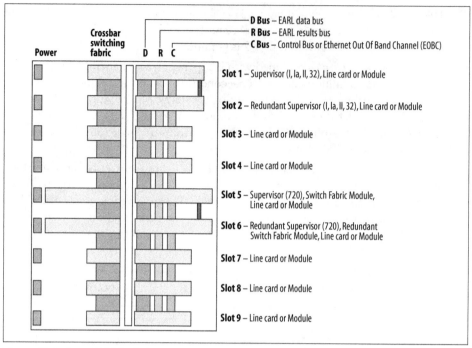

Figure 17-3. Cisco 6509 backplanes

Certain slots are capable of taking specific modules, while other slots are not. The breakdown of slots in a 6509 is as follows:

Slot 1

Slot 1 is capable of housing supervisor modules 1, 1A, and 2; line cards; or service modules. If there is only one Sup-1, Sup-1A, or Sup-2 in the chassis, it should reside in slot 1.

Slot 2

Slot 2 is capable of housing supervisor modules 1, 1A, and 2; line cards; or service modules. This slot is used for the redundant supervisor module if a failover pair is installed. Though a single supervisor can be installed in this slot, the first slot is generally used for single-supervisor installations.

Slot 3

Slot 3 is capable of housing any line card or module, with the exception of supervisors or SFMs.

Slot 4

Slot 4 is capable of housing any line card or module, with the exception of supervisors or SFMs.

Slot 5

> Slot 5 is capable of housing an SFM or a supervisor incorporating an SFM, such as the Supervisor-720. This slot may also support any line card or module, with the exception of supervisors that would normally be placed in slot 1 or 2. In the 6513 chassis, this slot is for line cards, as the supervisors reside in slots 7 and 8 in a 6513.

Slot 6

> Slot 6 is capable of housing an SFM or a supervisor incorporating an SFM, such as the Supervisor-720. This slot may also support any line card or module, with the exception of supervisors that would normally be placed in slot 1 or 2. This slot is used for the redundant fabric module or supervisor module if a failover pair is installed. Though a single fabric module or supervisor can be installed in this slot, slot 5 is generally used for single-supervisor/SFM installations. In the 6513 chassis, this slot is for line cards, as the supervisors reside in slots 7 and 8 in a 6513.

Slot 7

> Slot 7 is capable of housing any line card or module, with the exception of supervisors or SFMs. In the 6513 chassis, this slot is used for supervisors and is treated like slot 5/6 in a 6509.

Slot 8

> Slot 8 is capable of housing any line card or module, with the exception of supervisors or SFMs. In the 6513 chassis, this slot is used for supervisors and is treated like slot 5/6 in a 6509.

Slot 9

> Slot 9 is capable of housing any line card or module, with the exception of supervisors or SFMs.

The 6506-chassis slots are allocated the same way, with the obvious difference that there are no slots 7, 8, and 9; the 6513-chassis slots are allocated similarly, though Sup-720s must reside in slots 7 and 8 instead of 5 and 6. The additional slots (10–13) can house any line card or service module apart from supervisors or SFMs. These last four slots in the 6513 chassis cannot support certain fabric-only blades. Consult the Cisco documentation for specifics when ordering cards for this chassis.

Enhanced Chassis

A series of enhanced 6500 chassis, identified by an *e* at the end of the chassis part number, is also available. An example of an enhanced chassis is the 6500e. The enhanced chassis are designed to allow more power to be drawn to the line cards. The advent of Power over Ethernet (PoE) line cards for VoIP applications was one of the key drivers for this evolution. The enhanced chassis use high-speed fans to cool these power-hungry modules.

The e-series chassis also provide a redesigned backplane that allows for a total of 80 Gbps of throughput per slot. This represents a theoretical doubling of the capacity of the standard 6500 chassis (40 Gbps of throughput per slot), though at the time of this writing, there are no line cards or supervisors that support this speed. The new architecture will allow eight 10 Gbps ports per blade with no oversubscription. Cisco now only produces the enhanced chassis models, though the standard chassis models are still available though the secondhand market.

Vertical Enhanced Chassis

A special version of the enhanced 6500 chassis is now available. This chassis, named the 6509-V-E, supports 80 Gbps per slot and includes features previously found on the NEBS chassis. Features of this chassis include front-to-back airflow and vertical module orientation.

Supervisors

Chassis-based switches do not have processors built into them like smaller switches do. Instead, the processor is on a module, which allows the hardware to be swapped and upgraded with ease. The processor for a Cisco chassis-based switch is called a supervisor. Supervisors are also commonly referred to as *sups* (pronounced like "soups").

Over the years, different supervisor models have been introduced to offer greater speed and versatility. Increased functionality has also been made available via add-on daughter cards, which are built into the later supervisor models.

MSFC

Supervisors offer Layer-2 processing capabilities, while an add-on daughter card—called a multilayer switch feature card—supports Layer-3 and higher functionality. Supervisor models 1 and 2 offer the MSFC as an add-on, while later models include the MSFC as an integral part of the supervisor.

When you're running hybrid-mode IOS on the 6500 chassis, the MSFC is considered a separate device regardless of the supervisor model. In CiscoView, the MSFC appears as a small router icon to the left of the supervisor, where the fan tray resides. Figure 17-4 shows the CiscoView representation of a Supervisor-720 with the MSFC on the left.

Different versions of the MSFC are referenced as MSFC1, MSFC2, and MSFC3. The MSFC2 is paired with the Supervisor-2, while the MSFC3 is part of the Supervisor-720.

PFC

The *policy feature card* (PFC) is a daughter card that supports QoS functions in hardware, drastically improving performance where QoS is needed. No direct configuration of the PFC is required. The three generations of the PFC are named PFC1, PFC2, and

PFC3. The PFC2 is paired with the Supervisor-2, and the PFC3 is an integral part of the Supervisor-720.

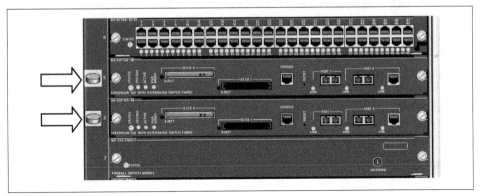

Figure 17-4. CiscoView representation of Supervisor-720 and MSFC

Models

Supervisor models most commonly seen today include:

Supervisor-1A
> This is the slowest and oldest of the supervisor modules, capable of supporting 32 Gbps and 15 Mpps (the Supervisor-1A replaced the original Supervisor Engine, also called the Supervisor-1). The Supervisor-1A is end-of-life but may still be seen in older installations. When coupled with a PFC and an MSFC, the Sup-1A is capable of Layer-2 to Layer-4 forwarding, as well as enhanced security and QoS. The Supervisor-1A was an excellent solution for wiring closets or networks that did not require the throughput and speed of the Supervisor-2. If you find one in the wild today, it should be replaced.

Supervisor-2
> This model was the standard in backbone and ecommerce website switching until the Supervisor-720 was released. The Supervisor-2 is capable of 30 Mpps and 256 Gbps when paired with an SFM. When coupled with a PFC2 and an MSFC2, the Supervisor-2's forwarding capability increases to 210 Mpps, and it is capable of Layer-2 to Layer-4 forwarding as well as enhanced security and QoS. This module is also pretty old now and should be replaced where possible.

Supervisor-32
> This is the latest replacement for the Supervisor-1A. Any existing Supervisor-1As should be replaced with Supervisor-32s. This model differs from the other supervisors in that it includes eight 1 Gbps small-form-factor GBIC ports or two 10 Gbps Ethernet XENPAK-based ports. Other supervisors will offer, at most, two 1 Gbps ports.

Supervisor-720

This model represents a major upgrade to the aging Supervisor-2 architecture. Capable of 400 Mpps and a blazing 720 Gbps, this supervisor is designed for bandwidth-hungry installations and critical core implementations. The Supervisor-720 includes the PFC3 and MSFC3 as well as new accelerated CEF and dCEF capabilities. Fabric-only modules are capable of 40 Gbps throughput when coupled with a Sup-720.

Supervisor-720-10G VSS

This supervisor is similar to the Sup-720, but includes two 10 Gb Ethernet ports. It also supports a new feature called Virtual Switching System (VSS). VSS allows two 6500s to be clustered together into a single logical switch. Similar in principle to the stacking technology found on Cisco 3750s, VSS allows EtherChannels to be split between two physical switches. Details of VSS are included later in this chapter.

Modules

Modules for the 6500 chassis are designed to support one or both of the chassis backplanes. A module that does not support the crossbar fabric is considered *nonfabric-enabled*. One that supports the 32 Gbps D bus and the fabric bus is considered to be *fabric-enabled*. A module that uses only the fabric bus and has no connection to the D bus is considered to be *fabric-only*.

Supervisors do not have the same connectors for insertion into the backplane as SFMs. Supervisor-720 modules that include the SFM's functionality have large connectors that can mate only with the receptacles in slots 5 and 6. The connectors for a Sup-720 are shown in Figure 17-5.

Figure 17-5. Supervisor-720 connectors

Nonfabric-enabled modules have connectors on only one side, for connection to the D bus. Modules from a 6000 chassis are nonfabric-enabled, since there is no crossbar fabric bus in the 6000 series.

A fabric-enabled module has two connectors on the back of the blade: one for the D bus and one for the crossbar fabric bus.

An example of such a blade (in this case, a 16-port gigabit fiber module) is shown in Figure 17-6.

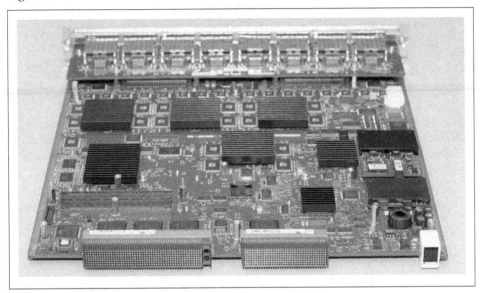

Figure 17-6. Fabric-enabled blade connectors

Modules that are fabric-only have a single connector on the fabric side, with no connector on the D bus side.

 Be very careful when inserting modules into chassis-based switches such as the 6500 series. Many of the components on the modules are quite tall. As a result, they can impact the chassis and be damaged by improper or forced insertion. Supervisor modules and service modules such as CSMs, ACE modules, and the FWSMs are particularly susceptible to this problem due to the large quantity of components incorporated into these devices. Some of these modules retail for more than $50,000, and you probably don't want to be the one who has to admit to breaking them.

Module interaction

When fabric-enabled or fabric-only blades are placed in a chassis with nonfabric-enabled blades, the supervisor must make compromises to facilitate the interaction between the different buses. Specifically, if there is a nonfabric-enabled module in the chassis, the Supervisor-720 will not be able to run at 720 Gbps speeds.

Here is an example of a 6509 that is filled with fabric-only 10/100/1000 Mb model 6748 Ethernet modules and two Sup-720 supervisors:

```
6509-1#sho mod
Mod Ports Card Type                                    Model             Serial No.
--- ----- ----------------------------------------     --------------    ----------
  1   48  CEF720 48 port 10/100/1000mb Ethernet        WS-X6748-GE-TX    SAL05340V5X
  2   48  CEF720 48 port 10/100/1000mb Ethernet        WS-X6748-GE-TX    SAL09347ZXK
  3   48  CEF720 48 port 10/100/1000mb Ethernet        WS-X6748-GE-TX    SAL05380V5Y
  4   48  CEF720 48 port 10/100/1000mb Ethernet        WS-X6748-GE-TX    SAL092644CJ
  5    2  Supervisor Engine 720 (Active)               WS-SUP720-3B      SAL05304AZV
  6    2  Supervisor Engine 720 (Hot)                  WS-SUP720-3B      SAL09295RWB
  7   48  CEF720 48 port 10/100/1000mb Ethernet        WS-X6748-GE-TX    SAL05340Z9H
  8   48  CEF720 48 port 10/100/1000mb Ethernet        WS-X6748-GE-TX    SAL0938145M
  9   48  CEF720 48 port 10/100/1000mb Ethernet        WS-X6748-GE-TX    SAL053415EC
```

The command show fabric switching-mode demonstrates how each module is communicating with the system. The output shows that all of the modules are using the crossbar switching bus and the Sup-720 is operating in dCEF mode, which allows forwarding at up to 720 Gbps:

```
6509-1#sho fabric switching-mode
Fabric module is not required for system to operate
Modules are allowed to operate in bus mode
Truncated mode allowed, due to presence of aCEF720  module

Module Slot      Switching Mode
    1               Crossbar
    2               Crossbar
    3               Crossbar
    4               Crossbar
    5                 dCEF
    6               Crossbar
    7               Crossbar
    8               Crossbar
    9               Crossbar
```

Each fabric-only module has two 20 Gbps connections to the crossbar fabric bus, as we can see with the show fabric status or show fabric utilization command. Notice that the supervisors each have only one 20 Gbps connection to the fabric bus:

```
6509-1#sho fabric util
  slot     channel      speed     Ingress %     Egress %
    1          0          20G          1            0
    1          1          20G          0            2
    2          0          20G          1            0
    2          1          20G          0            0
    3          0          20G          1            0
    3          1          20G          0            0
    4          0          20G          0            0
    4          1          20G          0            0
    5          0          20G          0            0
```

```
6      0      20G      0      0
7      0      20G      0      0
7      1      20G      0      0
8      0      20G      0      0
8      1      20G      0      0
9      0      20G      0      0
9      1      20G      0      0
```

For comparison, here is a 6509 operating with two Supervisor-720s, one fabric-only module, a couple of fabric-enabled modules, and one nonfabric-enabled module:

```
6509-2#sho mod
Mod Ports Card Type                          Model              Serial No.
--- ----- ------------------------------------ ------------------ ----------
  1    48 CEF720 48 port 10/100/1000mb Ethernet WS-X6748-GE-TX     SAL04654F2K
  4     8 Network Analysis Module              WS-SVC-NAM-2       SAD093002B6
  5     2 Supervisor Engine 720 (Active)       WS-SUP720-3B       SAL0485498A
  6     2 Supervisor Engine 720 (Hot)          WS-SUP720-3B       SAL09358NE6
  7     6 Firewall Module                      WS-SVC-FWM-1       SAD042408DF
  8     4 CSM with SSL                         WS-X6066-SLB-S-K9  SAD094107YN
  9     8 Intrusion Detection System           WS-SVC-IDSM-2      SAD048102CG
```

The module in slot 1 is the same as the Ethernet modules in the previous example. This module is fabric-only. Modules 4, 7, and 9 are all fabric-enabled, while module 8 is nonfabric-enabled. The output from the show fabric switching-mode command reveals that the single nonfabric-enabled blade has caused the supervisor to revert to a slower operating mode:

```
6509-2#sho fabric switching-mode
Global switching mode is Truncated
dCEF mode is not enforced for system to operate
Fabric module is not required for system to operate
Modules are allowed to operate in bus mode
Truncated mode is allowed, due to presence of aCEF720, Standby supervisor module

Module Slot      Switching Mode
    1                Crossbar
    4                Crossbar
    5                     Bus
    6                Crossbar
    7                Crossbar
    8                     Bus
    9                Crossbar
```

In this case, the module in question is a CSM, which, prior to the release of the ACE, was one of the more expensive modules available. Remember that cost does not equate to speed. The CSM was an excellent device, and I highly recommended it for situations where load balancing was a necessity, but in the case of extremely high throughput requirements, this service module may become a bottleneck. In the case of website architecture, it would be extremely rare for more than 32 Gbps to be flowing through the frontend. Such throughput would be possible in the case of balancing large application server farms or databases on the backend. The ACE module has replaced the

CSM for load-balancing needs, but this example shows how the older, slower card impacts the entire switch.

Using the show fabric status command on this switch indicates that not all fabric-enabled modules are created equal. The fabric-only module in slot 1 has two 20 Gbps channels to the fabric bus. The Network Analysis Module (NAM) in slot 4 is fabric-enabled, but connects with only one 8 Gbps channel, as do the FWSM and IDS modules in slots 7 and 9:

```
6509-2#sho fabric status
   slot    channel    speed    module        fabric
                                status        status
     1         0        20G       OK            OK
     1         1        20G       OK            OK
     4         0         8G       OK            OK
     5         0        20G       OK            OK
     6         0        20G       OK            OK
     7         0         8G       OK            OK
     9         0         8G       OK            OK
```

The lesson here is that it's important to understand how your modules interoperate. Even though a module may be a "fabric blade," it may not perform the same way as another fabric-enabled module. Knowing how the different modules operate can help you understand your current setup and design future solutions.

Module types

6500-series modules are generally divided into line cards and service modules. A line card offers connectivity, such as copper or fiber Ethernet. Service modules offer functionality. Examples of service modules include FWSMs and ACE.

Service modules dramatically enhance the usefulness of the 6500 switch. In one chassis, you can have a complete web server architecture, including Ethernet ports, DS3 Internet feeds, firewalls, IDSs, and load balancing. All devices will be configurable from the single chassis, and all will be powered from the same source. For redundancy, two identically configured chassis can be deployed with complete failover functionality that will provide no single point of failure.

Ethernet modules. Ethernet modules are available in many flavors and speeds. Some offer simple connectivity, while others offer extreme speed with 40 Gbps or even 80 Gbps connections to the crossbar fabric bus.

Connectivity options for Ethernet modules include RJ-45, GBIC, small-form-factor GBIC, XENPAK, SFP and even Amphenol connectors for direct connection to patch panels. Port density ranges from 4-port 10 Gbps XENPAK-based modules to 48-port 1,000 Mbps RJ-45 modules, and even 96-port RJ-21 connector modules supporting 10/100 Mbps. Options include PoE and dCEF capabilities.

FWSMs. FWSMs provide firewall services, just as a PIX firewall appliance would. At this time, the FWSM is the only device still current in the PIX product line. All other PIX firewall appliances have been replaced with ASA models incorporating either better speed, a wider feature set, or both. Because the interfaces on an FWSM are switched virtual interfaces (SVIs), the FWSM is not limited to physical connections like an appliance is. There can be hundreds of interfaces on an FWSM, each corresponding to a VLAN in the switch. The FWSM is also capable of over 5 Gbps of throughput, as compared with 1.7 Gbps on the PIX 535, which used to be the top-of-the line appliance. Now with the ASA 5580-40 supporting 10 Gbps, this is not nearly as impressive as it used to be.

The FWSM supports multiple contexts, which allows for virtual firewalls that can serve different functions, be supported by different parties, or both. One example where this might be useful is for a service provider who wishes to provide individual firewalls to customers while having only a single physical device. While this is also something that used to be FWSM-specific, many of the ASA appliances now support contexts as well.

The FWSM is a separate device in the chassis. To administer the FWSM, you must first connect to it. Here, I'm connecting to an FWSM in slot 8:

```
Switch-IOS#session slot 8 proc 1
The default escape character is Ctrl-^, then x.
You can also type 'exit' at the remote prompt to end the session
Trying 127.0.0.81 ... Open

User Access Verification

Password:
Type help or '?' for a list of available commands.
Switch-IOS-FWSM > en
Password: ********
Switch-IOS-FWSM #
```

If the FWSM is running in single-context mode, you will be able to run all PIX commands as if you were in any other PIX firewall. If the FWSM is running in multiple-context mode, you will be in the system context and will need to change to the proper context to make your changes. Do this with the changeto context command:

```
Switch-IOS-FWSM#sho context
Context Name     Class      Interfaces        URL
 admin           default                      disk:/admin.cfg
*EComm           default    vlan20,30         disk:/Ecomm.cfg
Switch-IOS-FWSM# changeto context EComm
Switch-IOS-FWSM/EComm#
```

At this point, you will be in the EComm context and, assuming you're used to PIX firewalls, everything should look very familiar:

```
Switch-IOS-FWSM/EComm#sho int
Interface Vlan20 "outside", is up, line protocol is up
        MAC address 0008.4cff.b403, MTU 1500
        IP address 10.1.1.1, subnet mask 255.255.255.0
                Received 90083941155 packets, 6909049206185 bytes
                Transmitted 3710031826 packets, 1371444635 bytes
                Dropped 156162887 packets
```

```
Interface Vlan30 "inside", is up, line protocol is up
    MAC address 0008.4cff.b403, MTU 1500
    IP address 10.10.10.1, subnet mask 255.255.255.0
        Received 156247369908 packets, 214566399699153 bytes
        Transmitted 2954364369 packets, 7023125736 bytes
        Dropped 14255735 packets
```

CSMs. The CSMs from Cisco are an excellent alternative to standalone content switches. The CSM is capable of 4 Gbps of throughput and is available with an SSL accelerator daughter card.

 The CSMs have been replaced with the newer fabric-enabled ACE module.

CSM integration with the 6500 running native IOS is very smooth. All of the CSM commands are included in the switch's CLI. The commands for the CSM are included under the module CSM *module#* command. The command expands to the full module contentswitchingmodule *module#* in the configuration:

```
Switch-IOS (config)#mod csm 9
Switch-IOS (config-module-csm)#
```

One big drawback of CSMs is that they are not fabric-enabled. While this is not an issue in terms of the throughput of the blade itself, it becomes an issue if the switch containing the CSM will also be serving the servers being balanced. The CSM is a 32 Gbps blade. Inserting it into a switch that is using the fabric backplane will cause the supervisor to revert to bus mode instead of faster modes such as dCEF. A switch with a Supervisor-720, fabric-only Ethernet modules, and a CSM will not run at 720 Gbps, because of the CSM's limited backplane connections.

CSM blades will operate in a stateful failover design. The pair of CSMs can sync their configurations, provided they are running version 4.2(1) or later. They can be synced with the hw-module csm *module#* standby config-sync command:

```
Switch-IOS#hw-module csm 9 standby config-sync
Switch-IOS#
May  5 17:12:14: %CSM_SLB-6-REDUNDANCY_INFO: Module 9 FT info: Active: Bulk sync
started
May  5 17:12:17: %CSM_SLB-4-REDUNDANCY_WARN: Module 9 FT warning: FT configuration
might be out of sync.
May  5 17:12:24: %CSM_SLB-4-REDUNDANCY_WARN: Module 9 FT warning: FT configuration
back in sync
May  5 17:12:26: %CSM_SLB-6-REDUNDANCY_INFO: Module 9 FT info: Active: Manual bulk
sync completed
```

NAM. Cisco's NAM is essentially a remote monitoring (RMON) probe and packet-capture device that allows you to monitor any port, VLAN, or combination of the two as if you were using an external packet-capture device.

The NAM is controlled through a web browser, which can be tedious when you're looking at large capture files. The benefit of the web-based implementation is that no extra software is required. The NAM may also be used from anywhere the network design allows.

The interface of the packet-capture screen should be familiar to anyone who has used products such as Ethereal. Each packet is broken down as far as possible, and there is an additional window showing the ASCII contents of the packets.

One limitation of the packet capture is the lack of smart alarm indications such as those found in high-end packet-capture utilities. Many other features are available on the NAM, as it operates as an RMON probe.

The NAM is an excellent troubleshooting tool, and because it's always there, it can be invaluable during a crisis (it's unlikely that someone will borrow the blade out of your production 6509, though stranger things have happened). Its ability to capture more than one session at a time makes the NAM blade an excellent addition to your arsenal of tools. With the capability to capture from RSPAN sources (see Chapter 18), the NAM blade can analyze traffic on any switch on your network.

A sample screen from the NAM interface is shown in Figure 17-7.

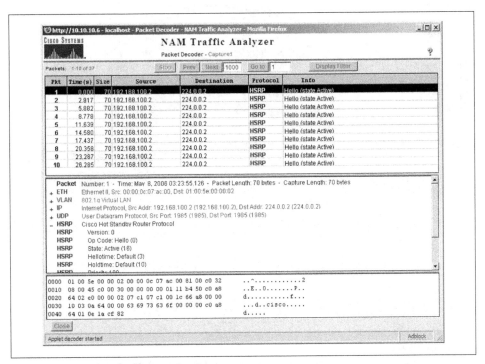

Figure 17-7. NAM packet capture detail

Intrusion Detection System modules. You can add intrusion detection functionality to the 6500-series chassis by introducing an intrusion detection system module (IDSM). These modules are actually preconfigured Linux servers that reside on a blade. They act like IDS appliances, but have the added capability of sampling data streams at wire speed because they are connected to the crossbar fabric bus.

You can manage these modules through an onboard secure web interface, shown in Figure 17-8, though Cisco recommends managing them through another application such as VPN/Security Management Solution (VMS), Cisco Security Manager, or Cisco Security Monitoring, Analysis, and Response System (MARS).

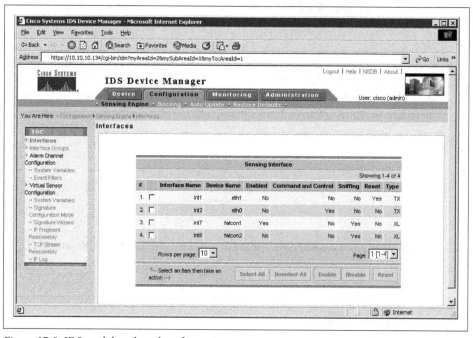

Figure 17-8. IDS module onboard configuration

You perform the basic configuration of the module via the switch itself by connecting to the module with the `session slot` *module#* `processor` *processor#* command. The *processor#* is usually 1:

```
Switch-IOS-1#session slot 9 proc 1
The default escape character is Ctrl-^, then x.
You can also type 'exit' at the remote prompt to end the session
Trying 127.0.0.91 ... Open
login: cisco
Password:
***NOTICE***
This product contains cryptographic features and is subject to United States
and local country laws governing import, export, transfer and use. Delivery
of Cisco cryptographic products does not imply third-party authority to import,
```

```
export, distribute or use encryption. Importers, exporters, distributors and
users are responsible for compliance with U.S. and local country laws. By using
this product you agree to comply with applicable laws and regulations. If you
are unable to comply with U.S. and local laws, return this product immediately.

A summary of U.S. laws governing Cisco cryptographic products may be found at:
http://www.cisco.com/wwl/export/crypto
If you require further assistance please contact us by sending email to
export@cisco.com.
Switch-IOS-1-IDS#
```

Configuration of the IDSM is quite different from that of other devices, and is a topic for a book unto itself.

FlexWAN modules. FlexWAN modules allow the connection of WAN links such as T1s as well as high-speed links such as DS3s up to OC3s.

There are two types of FlexWAN modules: FlexWAN and Enhanced FlexWAN. The primary differences between the two versions are CPU speed, memory capacity, and connection to the crossbar fabric bus.

Enhanced FlexWAN modules use the same WAN port adapters used in the Cisco 7600-series routers. The module is Layer-3 specific and requires either a Supervisor-720 or a Supervisor-2 with an MSFC to operate. When running in hybrid IOS mode, the Flex-WAN interfaces are not visible to Layer 2 with CatOS.

Communication Media Modules. The Communication Media Module (CMM) provides telephony integration into 6500-series switches. This fabric-enabled module contains three slots, which accept a variety of *port adapters*.

The port adapters available for the CMM include Foreign eXchange Service (FXS) modules for connection to analog phones, modems, and fax machines; T1/E1 CAS and PRI gateway modules; conferencing and transcoding port adapters that allow conferencing services; and Unified Survivable Remote Site Telephony (SRST) modules that will manage phones and connections should the connection to a Unified Call Manager become unavailable.

The port adapters can be mixed and matched in each CMM installed. A 6500-series chassis can be filled with CMMs and a supervisor, providing large port density for VoIP connectivity.

CatOS Versus IOS

Cisco Catalyst switches originally did not run IOS—the early chassis-based switches were CatOS-based. This was because the technology for these switches came from other companies that Cisco acquired, such as Crescendo, Kalpana, and Grand Junction.

CatOS may appear clunky to those who have used only IOS, but there are some distinct advantages to using CatOS in a switching environment. One of these advantages can also be considered a disadvantage: when a Catalyst 6500 runs CatOS and also has an

MSFC for Layer-3 functionality, the MSFC is treated like a separate device. The switch runs CatOS for Layer-2 functionality, and the MSFC runs IOS for Layer-3 and above functionality. This separation can be easier to understand for people who do not have experience with IOS Layer-3 switches, but for those who are used to IOS-based switches like Catalyst 3550s and 3750s, the need to switch between operating systems can be burdensome and confusing.

 Because all of the new Cisco Layer-3 switches (such as the 3550 and the 3750) run only IOS, learning the native IOS way of thinking is a smart move, as that's clearly the direction Cisco has taken. At one point, Cisco actually announced plans to discontinue CatOS, but there was such an uproar from die-hard CatOS users that the plans were scrubbed. I still see CatOS out in the field, but they are disappearing.

Another advantage of CatOS over IOS is the concise way in which it organizes information. An excellent example is the show port command in CatOS:

```
Switch-CatOS#sho port

Port  Name                 Status      Vlan       Duplex Speed Type
----- -------------------- ----------  ---------- ------ ----- ------------
 1/1  Trunk                connected   trunk        full  1000 1000BaseSX
 1/2  Trunk                connected   trunk        full  1000 1000BaseSX
 2/1  Trunk                connected   trunk        full  1000 1000BaseSX
 2/2  Trunk                connected   trunk        full  1000 1000BaseSX
 3/1  Web-1-E1             connected   20         a-full a-100 10/100BaseTX
 3/2  Web-2-E1             connected   20         a-full a-100 10/100BaseTX
 3/3  Web-3-E1             connected   20           full   100 10/100BaseTX
 3/4  Web-4-E1             connected   20           full   100 10/100BaseTX
 3/5  Web-5-E1             connected   20         a-full a-100 10/100BaseTX
 3/6  Web-6-E1             connected   20         a-full a-100 10/100BaseTX
 3/7  Web-7-E1             connected   20         a-full a-100 10/100BaseTX
 3/8  App-1-E1             connected   40         a-full a-100 10/100BaseTX
 3/9  App-2-E1             connected   40         a-full a-100 10/100BaseTX
 3/10 App-3-E1             connected   40         a-full a-100 10/100BaseTX
 3/11 App-4-E1             connected   40         a-full a-100 10/100BaseTX
 3/12                      notconnect               full   100 10/100BaseTX
 3/13                      notconnect               full   100 10/100BaseTX
 3/14 DB-1-E1              connected   50           full   100 10/100BaseTX
 3/15 DB-2-E1              connected   50         a-full a-100 10/100BaseTX
 3/16 DB-3-E1              connected   50         a-full a-100 10/100BaseTX
```

Here, on one screen, we can see the port, the port's name (if any), its status, which VLAN it is associated with, the speed and duplex mode, the autonegotiation status, and the port type. In the first edition of this book, I wrote the following bit of know-it-all goodness:

IOS has nothing that directly compares to this command. Instead, the user must piece together the information from multiple sources.

Of all the errata, comments, and feedback I got, this line triggered the biggest response. Readers pointed out that the `show interface status` IOS command looked a whole lot like the CatOS `show port` command. When I got the first such comment, I fired up my lab and typed out the command. Imagine my surprise when, after 25 years of hard time in the industry, I learned of this wonderful command. The better lesson is to never write in absolutes, for they will surely come back to haunt you. Thank you to all of you who pointed this out to me:

```
3750-IOS#sho int status

Port       Name              Status       Vlan   Duplex  Speed Type
Gi1/0/1    Cozy-Server       notconnect   1        auto   auto 10/100/1000BaseTX
Gi1/0/2    Daisy-Server      notconnect   1        auto   auto 10/100/1000BaseTX
Gi1/0/3    Annie-Server      notconnect   1        auto   auto 10/100/1000BaseTX
Gi1/0/4    Guinness-Server   disabled     1        auto   auto 10/100/1000BaseTX
Gi1/0/5                      notconnect   1        auto   auto 10/100/1000BaseTX
Gi1/0/6                      notconnect   1        auto   auto 10/100/1000BaseTX
Gi1/0/7                      notconnect   1        auto   auto 10/100/1000BaseTX
Gi1/0/8                      notconnect   1        auto   auto 10/100/1000BaseTX
Gi1/0/9                      notconnect   1        auto   auto 10/100/1000BaseTX
Gi1/0/10                     notconnect   1        auto   auto 10/100/1000BaseTX
Gi1/0/11                     notconnect   1        auto   auto 10/100/1000BaseTX
 --More--
```

I'll still include one of my most-used commands for gathering information, though, since it includes IP addresses:

```
Switch-IOS#sho ip int brief
Interface            IP-Address      OK? Method Status                Protocol
Vlan1                unassigned      YES NVRAM  administratively down  down
Vlan20               10.10.20.2      YES manual up                     up
Vlan40               10.10.40.2      YES manual up                     up
Vlan50               10.10.50.2      YES manual up                     up
GigabitEthernet1/1   unassigned      YES unset  up                     up
GigabitEthernet1/2   unassigned      YES unset  up                     up
GigabitEthernet1/3   unassigned      YES unset  up                     up
GigabitEthernet1/4   unassigned      YES unset  up                     up
```

IOS tends to be a bit wordy. For example, the output of the IOS `show interface` *interface#* command, which shows the pertinent information for interfaces, looks like this:

```
Switch-IOS#sho int g3/1
GigabitEthernet3/1 is up, line protocol is up (connected)
  Hardware is C6k 1000Mb 802.3, address is 0015.6356.62bc (bia 0015.6356.62bc)
  Description: Web-1-E1
  MTU 1500 bytes, BW 1000000 Kbit, DLY 10 usec,
     reliability 255/255, txload 1/255, rxload 1/255
  Encapsulation ARPA, loopback not set
  Full-duplex, 1000Mb/s
  input flow-control is off, output flow-control is on
  Clock mode is auto
  ARP type: ARPA, ARP Timeout 04:00:00
  Last input never, output 00:00:47, output hang never
  Last clearing of "show interface" counters never
  Input queue: 0/2000/2/0 (size/max/drops/flushes); Total output drops: 2
```

```
Queueing strategy: fifo
Output queue: 0/40 (size/max)
5 minute input rate 456000 bits/sec, 91 packets/sec
5 minute output rate 110000 bits/sec, 81 packets/sec
   714351663 packets input, 405552413403 bytes, 0 no buffer
   Received 15294 broadcasts, 0 runts, 0 giants, 0 throttles
   2 input errors, 0 CRC, 0 frame, 0 overrun, 0 ignored
   0 input packets with dribble condition detected
   656796418 packets output, 97781644875 bytes, 0 underruns
   2 output errors, 0 collisions, 2 interface resets
   0 babbles, 0 late collision, 0 deferred
   0 lost carrier, 0 no carrier
   0 output buffer failures, 0 output buffers swapped out
```

The output from the CatOS command show port *port#* is much easier to read, especially when you're glancing quickly for a specific tidbit of information. The tradeoff is that the command provides less information than the IOS version:

```
Switch-CatOS: (enable)sho port 3/1
* = Configured MAC Address

Port  Name                  Status      Vlan        Duplex Speed Type
----- --------------------- ----------  ----------  ------ ----- ------------
 3/1  Web-1-E1              connected   20            auto  auto  10/100BaseTX

Port  AuxiliaryVlan AuxVlan-Status      InlinePowered       PowerAllocated
                                    Admin Oper   Detected  mWatt mA @42V
----- ------------- ---------------  ----- ------ --------  ----- --------
 3/1  none          none             -     -      -         -     -


Port  Security Violation Shutdown-Time Age-Time Max-Addr Trap     IfIndex
----- -------- --------- ------------- -------- -------- -------- -------
 3/1  disabled shutdown              0        0        1 disabled       5

Port  Num-Addr Secure-Src-Addr     Age-Left Last-Src-Addr    Shutdown/Time-Left
----- -------- -----------------   -------- ---------------- ------------------
 3/1         0               -            -                -         -        -

Port  Flooding on Address Limit
----- ------------------------
 3/1                 Enabled
--More--
```

Many people prefer the output of the commands on CatOS switches, but as a consultant, I have no real preference and must work with whatever the client has at the time.

One of the big features found in CatOS that was not available in IOS until very recently is show top. Executing the command show top 5 util all back interval 60 instructs the switch to run a Top-N report in the background for the five most utilized ports and save the report for viewing. When the report is done, a message is displayed indicating that it is ready to be viewed:

```
Switch-CatOS: (enable)show top 5 util all back interval 60
Switch-CatOS: (enable) 2006 May 07 12:47:00 EST +00:00 %MGMT-5-TOPN_START:Report 3
started by telnet/20.20.20.100/GAD
```

Notice that because I specified the background option, I can do other things while the report is running:

```
Switch-CatOS: (enable)
Switch-CatOS: (enable)
Sec-6505-1-TOP: (enable)dir
-#- -length- -----date/time------ name
  2 10518855 May 2  2006 02:27:09 cat6000-supk8.7-7-9.bin
 15    82230 May 2  2006 08:21:55 switch.cfg

4604208 bytes available (11386576 bytes used)
Switch-CatOS: (enable)
Switch-CatOS: (enable)
Switch-CatOS: (enable) 2006 May 07 12:48:01 EST +00:00 %MGMT-5-TOPN_AVAILABLE:Report 3
available: (enable) 2006 May 07 12:48:01 EST +00:00 %MGMT-5-TOPN_AVAILABLE:Report 3
available
```

While I was looking at the flash directory, my report finished. The switch told me that the report generated was report #3. I can view it using this command:

```
Switch-CatOS: (enable)sho top report 3
Start Time:     May 07 2006 12:47:00
End Time:       May 07 2006 12:48:01
PortType:       all
Metric:         util
```

Port	Band-width	Uti %	Bytes (Tx + Rx)	Pkts (Tx + Rx)	Bcst (Tx + Rx)	Mcst (Tx + Rx)	Error (Rx)	Over flow
3/14	100	0	624014	1126	89	89	0	0
3/15	100	0	105347	590	6	32	0	0
3/16	100	0	889310	2319	89	99	0	0
3/8	100	0	536246	3422	97	41	0	0
3/9	100	0	315228	2094	0	405	0	0

The show top feature also provides the capability to run a report showing the Top-N error-producing ports, which is a tremendously useful tool when you suspect autonegotiation issues. To run an error-based Top-N report on CatOS, execute the command show top error all back interval 60.

> IOS versions 12.2(18)SXE and later for the Catalyst 6500 allow Top-N reports to be generated. The results are very similar to those generated by CatOS, but the commands to run the reports are different. To run a Top-N report on IOS, execute the collect top command.

Installing VSS

This section outlines the commands used to enable VSS from a pair of standalone 6509-V-E switches. We will build a cluster with the configuration shown in Figure 17-9.

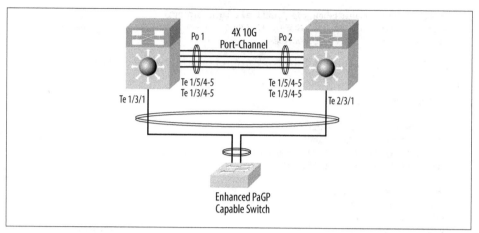

Figure 17-9. VSS layout including PaGP-capable switch

Since the switches start as standalone switches, we need to start configuring them individually. Once we've done that, I'll show the matching configuration for the switch on the right. First, we need to put the switch into stateful failover mode, which we do as follows:

```
6509-VE-Left#conf t
Enter configuration commands, one per line.  End with CNTL/Z.
6509-VE-Left(config)#redundancy
6509-VE-Left(config-red)#mode ?
  rpr  Route Processor Redundancy
  sso  Stateful Switchover
6509-VE-Left(config-red)#mode sso
```

You can view the redundancy state with the show redundancy states command:

```
6509-VE-Left#sho redundancy states
       my state = 13 -ACTIVE
     peer state = 1  -DISABLED
           Mode = Simplex
           Unit = Primary
        Unit ID = 5

Redundancy Mode (Operational) = sso
Redundancy Mode (Configured)  = sso
Redundancy State              = Non Redundant
    Maintenance Mode = Disabled
 Communications = Down      Reason: Simplex mode

   client count = 135
client_notification_TMR = 30000 milliseconds
         keep_alive TMR = 9000 milliseconds
       keep_alive count = 0
   keep_alive threshold = 18
           RF debug mask = 0x0
```

If the router will be running OSPF, you should add the following commands to the OSPF configuration. (We're not concerned with that here, so I'm not actually adding it.)

```
router ospf process-id
  nsf
  exit
```

Now we need to configure a switch virtual domain. The domain is a number in the range 1–255:

```
6509-VE-Left(config)#switch virtual domain ?
  <1-255>  Virtual switch domain number
```

The domain will need to match on both switches. Here I configure the domain to be 100:

```
6509-VE-Left(config)#switch virtual domain 100
Domain ID 100 config will take effect only
after the exec command 'switch convert mode virtual' is issued
```

I will number the switch on the left to be number 1, while the switch on the right will be number 2. Feel free to apply your own preferences as you see fit:

```
6509-VE-Left(config-vs-domain)#switch 1
```

You can configure one of the switches to have a higher priority and, using preempt, set one switch to always be preferred. I'm not a fan of this design, however, since failover occurs only by reloading the active switch. Cisco even discourages this in its best practices document (see the end of this chapter for a link). The VSS system does not function like Cisco firewalls, where the active unit can be changed without rebooting. If you'd like to configure preemption, assign a priority to the switch with the switch *switch-number* priority *priority-value* command:

```
6509-VE-Left(config-vs-domain)#switch 1 priority ?
  <1-255>  Virtual switch priority value

6509-VE-Left(config-vs-domain)#switch 1 priority 105
```

If you want to enable preemption, use the switch *switch-number* preempt command. Even the switch will tell you that it's a bad idea:

```
6509-VE-Left(config-vs-domain)#switch 1 preempt ?
  <15-20>  Delay in minutes before standby takes over as active. Default is 15
           minutes
  <cr>
```

The default delay is 15 minutes:

```
6509-VE-Left(config-vs-domain)#switch 1 preempt

Please note that Preempt configuration will make the ACTIVE switch with lower
priority to reload forcefully when preempt timer expires.

The default preempt timer is 15 minutes. It is set to the approximate time required
to bring up all linecards in a fully loaded chassis. Once the preempt timer starts,
the standby switch with higher priority will take over as active after 15 minutes.
```

If you change your mind, just negate the command. There is no fanfare when you do this:

```
6509-VE-Left(config-vs-domain)#no switch 1 preempt
```

When using VSS, you can manually set the MAC addresses to be used by the virtual switch, but the easier way to go in most installations is to let the switch assign virtual MACs from a predetermined range. Do this with the `mac-address use-virtual` command:

```
6509-VE-Left(config-vs-domain)#mac-address ?
  H.H.H        Manually set router mac address
  use-virtual  Use mac-address range reserved for Virtual Switch System

6509-VE-Left(config-vs-domain)#mac-address use-virtual
```

The link that connects the two switches together and acts like a stacking cable is called the *virtual switch link* (VSL). This link should have as many high-speed links as you can spare, and they should be distributed across multiple modules. They should also be installed in powers of two for optimal hashing. You don't want this link to fail, so make it as resilient as possible. For our design, we've got four 10 Gb Ethernet links making up the VSL.

 The VSL EtherChannel must be *different* on each switch so that when the two switches merge, they will be able to differentiate which side of the link belongs to which physical switch. This is the only time you'll need to have a different configuration for a single port channel with VSS. Watch out for this, since it seems to be counterintuitive to everyone I've taught.

I've configured Po10 on the left and Po20 on the right. These port channels must be assigned as the SVL using the `switch virtual link core-switch-number` command. The core-switch-number is the switch number we configured in the switch virtual domain section:

```
6509-VE-Left(config)#int port-channel 10
6509-VE-Left(config-if)#switch virtual link 1
```

Let's add some physical ports to the port channel:

```
6509-VE-Left(config)#int range ten 3/4-5 , ten 5/4-5
6509-VE-Left(config-if-range)#channel-group 10 mode on
6509-VE-Left(config-if-range)#no shut
```

We can now make VSS active. This will cause the switch to reboot and come up in VSS mode. From here on out, you will need to specify ports as chassis/module/port:

```
6509-VE-Left#switch convert mode virtual
*Sep 22 19:07:10.968: %SYS-5-CONFIG_I: Configured from console by console
This command will convert all interface names
to naming convention "interface-type switch-number/slot/port",
save the running config to startup-config and
```

```
reload the switch.
Do you want to proceed? [yes/no]: yes
Converting interface names
Building configuration...
[OK]
Saving converted configuration to bootflash: ...
Destination filename [startup-config.converted_vs-20090922-190952]

[-- lots of boring boot stuff removed --]

Initializing as Virtual Switch ACTIVE processor

[-- more boring boot stuff removed --]

*Sep 22 19:11:46.399: %VS_PARSE-4-NO_VSL_CONFIG: No VSL interface is configured
*Sep 22 19:11:45.836: %PFREDUN-6-ACTIVE: Initializing as ACTIVE processor for
this switch

*Sep 22 19:11:46.584: %VSLP-5-RRP_NO_PEER: No VSLP peer found. Resolving role
as Active
*Sep 22 19:11:47.023: %VSLP-2-VSL_DOWN:   VSL links down and not ready for any
traffic

*Sep 22 19:11:49.716: %OIR-SW1_SP-6-CONSOLE: Changing console ownership to
route processor
```

After more boring boot stuff, the switch comes online, at which point we can see that
all of the interfaces have been renumbered to include the chassis, just like a 3750 stack:

```
6509-VE-Left#sho ip int brie

Interface               IP-Address      OK? Method Status                Protocol
Vlan1                   unassigned      YES NVRAM  administratively down  down
GigabitEthernet1/1/1    unassigned      YES NVRAM  administratively down  down
GigabitEthernet1/1/2    unassigned      YES NVRAM  administratively down  down
GigabitEthernet1/1/3    unassigned      YES NVRAM  administratively down  down
[-- output truncated --]
```

The output of show redundancy indicates that it is running in simplex mode, which
means that though we're running in VSS, we don't have a partner. That will be resolved
when we configure and reboot the right switch:

```
6509-VE-Left#sho redundancy
Redundant System Information :
------------------------------
       Available system uptime = 3 minutes
Switchovers system experienced = 0
             Standby failures = 0
       Last switchover reason = none

                Hardware Mode = Simplex
    Configured Redundancy Mode = sso
    Operating Redundancy Mode = sso
             Maintenance Mode = Disabled
               Communications = Down        Reason: Simplex mode
[-- output truncated --]
```

We can see the status of the VSS cluster with the show switch virtual role command:

```
6509-VE-Left#sho switch virtual  role

Switch Switch Status  Preempt     Priority  Role    Session ID
       Number         Oper(Conf) Oper(Conf)         Local  Remote
--------------------------------------------------------------------
LOCAL   1     UP      FALSE(N )  100(100)   ACTIVE   0      0


In dual-active recovery mode: No
```

Based on the configuration we've created for the left switch, here's the configuration for the right switch:

```
redundancy
 mode sso

switch virtual domain 100
 switch 2
 switch 2 priority 100
 mac-address use-virtual

int port-channel 20
 switch virtual link 2

int range ten 3/4-5 , ten 5/4-5
 channel-group 20 mode on
 no shut
```

After I add this configuration, the switches will be capable of melding into a single logical switch. Once the switches have been converted to VSS mode, each needs to again be rebooted. When the switches have been configured for VSS, the 10 Gbps VSL link will be recognized and brought online before other module initializations. This is only important during the initial configuration and should not be a concern during normal operation.

When booting a VSS cluster, you can see these links come up before the rest of the switch. Here's a snippet of output from a booting VSS pair:

```
*Sep 23 15:23:47.856: %PFREDUN-6-ACTIVE: Initializing as ACTIVE
processor for this switch

*Sep 23 15:23:53.912: %VSL_BRINGUP-6-MODULE_UP: VSL module in
slot 5 switch 1 brought up

*Sep 23 15:24:28.191: %VSLP-5-RRP_ROLE_RESOLVED: Role resolved
as STANDBY by VSLP

*Sep 23 15:24:28.195: %VSL-5-VSL_CNTRL_LINK:  New VSL Control
Link  5/5

*Sep 23 15:24:28.712: %VSLP-5-VSL_UP:  Ready for control traffic
```

```
*Sep 23 15:25:01.363: %OIR-SW1_SPSTBY-6-CONSOLE: Changing console
ownership to route processor
```

To see if your virtual link is up, use the show switch virtual link command. This output shows an active virtual link:

```
6509-VE-Right#sho switch virtual link
VSL Status : UP
VSL Uptime : 4 minutes
VSL SCP Ping : Pass
VSL ICC Ping : Pass
VSL Control Link : Te2/5/5
```

You can also use the show switch virtual link detail command to get more specific information. It spits out a lot of data, so I'm not going to include the output here.

To see the status of the virtual switch cluster, use the show switch virtual role command. In this example, I've run the command from the switch on the right:

```
6509-VE-Right#sho switch virtual role
```

Switch	Switch Number	Status	Preempt Oper(Conf)	Priority Oper(Conf)	Role	Session ID Local	Remote
LOCAL	2	UP	FALSE(N)	100(100)	ACTIVE	0	0
REMOTE	1	UP	FALSE(N)	100(100)	STANDBY	5555	5649

Once the VSS system comes online and the switches become a single logical switch, you'll be able to configure the system only from the active supervisor:

```
6509-VE-Right-sdby>
Standby console disabled
```

At this point, it makes sense to just name the logical system instead of confusing ourselves with a name that no longer makes any sense (they're both 6509-VE-Right at this point). Here, I've moved the console cable back to the switch on the left and, as you can see, the hostname makes it look like it's the switch on the right. Once you're in VSS mode, the configuration applies to the logical cluster, not the physical switch:

```
6509-VE-Right(config)#hostname VSS
VSS(config)#exit
VSS#
```

Other Recommended VSS Commands

Per the Cisco documentation, the mac-address-table synchronize command should be included for the VSS cluster. You can find more information in the Cisco document located at *http://www.cisco.com/en/US/docs/switches/lan/catalyst6500/ios/12.2SX/con figuration/guide/vss.html#wp1131059*:

```
VSS(config)#mac-address-table synchronize
% Current OOB activity time is [160] seconds
% Recommended aging time for all vlans is at least three times the
```

```
activity interval and global aging time will be changed automatically
if required
```

VSS dual-active detection

Access switches with the proper IOS level can support enhanced PAgP messages that allow the detection of a dual-active scenario. *Dual-active*, also called *split-brain* by many people, describes the situation where both physical switches become active. This is a problem because both switches will own the same IP address. That's a bad thing, and we should work hard to defend against the condition. There are multiple ways to do this. If you've got all Cisco switches, Cisco recommends using enhanced PAgP. If you've got other vendor's switches, then you can use another method:

```
VSS#sho switch virtual dual-active ?
  bfd         Dual-active bfd summary
  fast-hello  Dual-active fast-hello summary
  pagp        Dual-active pagp summary
  summary     Dual-active config summary
```

Cisco has enhanced PAgP to sense a dual-active situation when a third switch is connected to the VSS cluster. To use this feature, you must have the minimum IOS version installed on the third switch as outlined in Table 17-1.

Table 17-1. Minimum IOS requirements

Device series	Minimum IOS required
Catalyst 3750	IOS 12.2(46)SE
Catalyst 4500	IOS 12.2(44)SE
Catalyst 6500	IOS 12.2(33)SXH
Catalyst 6500 VSS	IOS 12.2(33)SXH1

By default, PAgP dual-active detection is enabled on the VSS pair. However, the enhanced messages are sent only on port channels with trust mode enabled. To enable trust mode, you *must* shut down the port channel being trusted, if it already exists. Once the port channel interface is shut down, configure the switch virtual domain. Here, I'm configuring po30, the MEC connecting the third switch to the VSS pair as shown in Figure 17-9:

```
VSS(config)#int po30
VSS(config-if)# shut
VSS(config)#switch virtual domain 100
VSS(config-vs-domain)#dual-active detection pagp
VSS(config-vs-domain)#dual-active detection pagp trust channel-group 30
VSS(config)#int po30
VSS(config-if)#no shut
```

To see the status of dual-active detection, use the show switch virtual dual-active summary command:

```
VSS#sho switch virtual dual-active summary
Pagp dual-active detection enabled: Yes
Bfd dual-active detection enabled: Yes
Fast-hello dual-active detection enabled: Yes

No interfaces excluded from shutdown in recovery mode

In dual-active recovery mode: No
```

You can also get the status of dual-active detection links with the show switch virtual dual-active pagp command:

```
VSS#sho switch virtual dual-active pagp
PAgP dual-active detection enabled: Yes
PAgP dual-active version: 1.1

Channel group 100 dual-active detect capability w/nbrs
Dual-Active trusted group: Yes
            Dual-Active    Partner         Partner  Partner
Port        Detect Capable Name            Port     Version
Gi1/1/1     No             None            None     N/A
Gi2/1/1     No             None            None     N/A
```

VSS Failover Commands

The only way in which a VSS cluster will transfer active status to the standby switch is by reloading the active chassis. Reloading the active chassis with no actual configuration loaded except for the VSS VSL link takes almost 15 minutes in the systems I've tested; however, the standby supervisor takes over active duties in under one second.

Remember that only the active chassis will accept commands. The console prompt on the secondary chassis will have "-sdby" appended to the hostname. The secondary switch will report the following if you attempt to configure it:

```
VSS-sdby>en
Standby console disabled
```

Always reload a VSS switch with care. If you mean to reboot only one chassis, you might just reboot the entire cluster and, as I've been told, that's not good.

 If the reload command is issued on the active chassis, the entire cluster (both switches) will reload. You will get a helpful warning message, but how often do any of us really read those?

To reboot the standby switch from the active console, use the redundancy reload peer command:

```
VSS# redundancy reload peer
Reload peer [confirm]
```

To reboot only the active switch and thus cause a failover, use the `redundancy reload shelf` command:

```
VSS# redundancy reload shelf
Reload this shelf[confirm]
```

Alternatively, you can reload either switch by appending the shelf (switch) number to the same command:

```
VSS# redundancy reload shelf 2
Reload the entire remote shelf[confirm]
```

To specifically force a failover, use the `redundancy force-switchover` command. The active switch will be reloaded to force the switchover. I don't know of a way to force a switchover without reloading the active chassis, so don't do this lightly—remember, it will take up to 15 minutes to reload the chassis:

```
VSS# redundancy force-switchover
This will reload the active unit and force switchover to standby[confirm]
```

To see when the last failover occurred, use the `show redundancy switchover` command:

```
VSS#sho redundancy switchover
Switchovers this system has experienced         : 2
Last switchover reason                          : active unit removed
Uptime since this supervisor switched to active : 2 hours, 14 minutes
Total system uptime from reload                 : 3 hours, 32 minutes
```

Miscellaneous VSS Commands

Hardware-specific commands will usually have a new modifier to allow the user to view either switch's equipment. For example, the `show module` command now includes the `switch` modifier:

```
VSS#sho module switch ?
  <1-2>    Virtual switch number
  all      show all linecard module information
  version  show all linecard version information
  |        Output modifiers
  <cr>
```

Take care here, because the output of the `show module` command only includes information for the active chassis and does not indicate which chassis is being displayed. To show the modules for both switches, use the `show module switch all` command.

Similarly, the `show environment` command now includes a switch modifier, though this command defaults to showing both switches without the modifier:

```
VSS#sho env switch ?
  <1-2>   Virtual switch number
```

VSS Best Practices

Cisco has a document outlining its VSS best practices. The document should be required reading if you're going to take on a VSS install or existing VSS environment. You can find the document at *http://www.cisco.com/en/US/products/ps9336/products_tech_note09186a0080a7c837.shtml*.

## CHAPTER 18

Cisco Nexus

At the time of this writing, the Cisco Nexus product line is composed of four levels of devices: 7000, 5000, 2000, and 1000, though the 1000-level is usually a server appliance (1010) or a virtual switch (1000v). I will concentrate mostly on the hardware devices 7000–2000 in this chapter. As with most Cisco products, Nexus devices named with a larger number are larger and more powerful.

One of the selling points for the Nexus platform is something called *unified fabric*. Unified fabric provides the ability to combine traditional networking with storage networking in a single connector. This can be a pretty big deal, since we could have a pair of Nexus 7000s instead of a pair of Catalyst 6500s and a pair of MDS 9000 fabric switches in a data center. This chapter will focus on the networking aspect of Nexus switches, and will largely ignore storage. Though I'm sure there are companies out there eagerly pursuing this idea, in the few years that I've been working with Nexus, I've yet to see it in action. So far, I've built three large-scale data centers, and we worked with Cisco to understand FCoE (Fibre Channel over Ethernet), but we just couldn't get buy-in from the executives.

Nexus switches use NX-OS as their operating system. NX-OS was designed from its roots in MDS storage devices, but looks and feels mostly like IOS. I say "mostly" because there are subtle differences that will baffle you as you learn it. This book is filled with such examples, so have fun while you learn and see if you can find them all.

Nexus Hardware

Nexus networking devices come in three flavors; 7000, 5000, and 2000. The 7000 series are large chassis switches similar in purpose to the 6500 Catalysts (and MDS-9000 storage switches). The 5000 is a top-of-rack solution with 10 Gb interfaces in abundance. The 2000 FEXs are designed to be extensions to the 7000 and 5000 switches.

Nexus 7000

Nexus 7000s are currently available in two models: the 7010 and the 7018. As with other Cisco chassis switches, the model number reflects the number of slots within the chassis. These switches are shown in Figure 18-1. Additional models are being released that contain four slots and six slots. At the time of this writing, they were not yet available.

Figure 18-1. Nexus 7018 and 7010; courtesy of Cisco Systems, Inc.; unauthorized use not permitted

One big thing to remember when designing your data center around these switches is the way the air flows. The Nexus 7010, like the rest of the Nexus line, is designed so that air flows front to back. This allows the switch to be mounted so the front of the chassis is in the cold aisle.

The 7018 chassis, however, is designed such that the air flows from side to side. I've asked multiple people at Cisco about this, and their reply is the same as the reasoning in the documentation. The 7018 is designed to be placed at the end of the row of racks, apparently mounted sideways. I've never seen a switch mounted in such a fashion, though I'm sure someone has done it somewhere. This is a pretty big deal, and I've had execs discount hardware for no reason other than side-to-side airflow. The original

6509 and 6509E had side-to-side airflow, too. These execs would only use the 6509-V-E or older NEBS chassis, because they employed a "proper" airflow design. If you do mount these monsters in a cabinet, consider keeping the cabinets to either side empty, since they require significant airflow for proper cooling. From what I've seen, it looks like the new four- and six-slot chassis Nexus 7000s will also incorporate side-to-side airflow.

The Nexus 7000s are built around something called *midplane architecture*. A switch like a 6509 is built with a backplane architecture. *Backplane* means that all modules, power supplies, and fans are installed from the front, connecting internally to the back of the switch. The 7000s are designed in such a way that power and fans are installed from the back, while modules are installed from the front. Additionally, the fabric modules for the 7000s are installed in the rear. The connectors for all these modules are in the middle of the switch—hence *midplane*.

Nexus 7000s are designed to minimize failure points. As you can see in Figure 18-2, there are three power supplies, five fabric modules, two fabric fan trays, and two system fan trays. With dual supervisors, these switches are pretty well suited for a high-availability network.

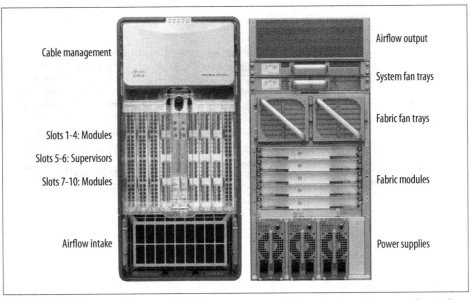

Figure 18-2. Nexus 7010 front and back; images courtesy of Cisco Systems, Inc.; unauthorized use not permitted

It may seem odd to have the fabric modules separate when we made such a big deal out of them being included in the 6500 supervisors. On the 6500, there were only two fabric modules (one on each supervisor). On the 7010, we can have five. Why is this important? Because each fabric module adds switching capacity, and with five slots, they can offer N+1 redundancy. That means that although we need only four, we can have five installed so that if one fails, there is no outage or degradation in capacity. Additionally, we can upgrade the capacity of the switch by adding more powerful fabric modules without having to shut down the switch. In a true high-availability network, this type of architecture is a must. Phone guys have been laughing at us for years because while networking equipment rarely incorporated these features, phone systems have used them for decades.

Nexus 5000

There are three Nexus 5000 switches available at this time. They are the 5010, 5020, and the 5548. The 5010 is a one-rack-unit (1 RU) switch with twenty 10 Gbps ports and a single expansion port. The 5020 is a 2 RU switch with forty 10 Gbps ports and two expansion ports. The 5548 is a 1 RU switch with thirty-two 10 Gbps ports and one expansion port. The expansion ports on the 5010 and 5020 are the same, while the 5549 expansion port is different. The 5548 is capable of forty-eight 10 Gbps ports with a throughput of 960 Gbps, which equates to wire speed on all forty-eight 10 Gbps interfaces. The Nexus 5000 family is shown in Figure 18-3.

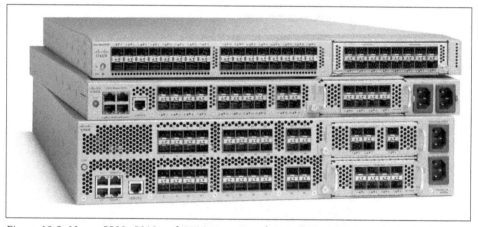

Figure 18-3. Nexus 5500, 5010 and 5020; courtesy of Cisco Systems, Inc.; unauthorized use not permitted

Though they all have dual power supplies, the 5010 and 5020 switches have the power connectors on the same side as the data ports. The hot-swappable portion of the power supply is found (and removed) from the opposite end of the switch.

These switches are designed with front-to-back airflow, but many people are surprised that in a properly designed hot-/cold-aisle data center, it seems that these switches need to be installed backward. What I mean by this is that the end of the switches with the ports is actually the back of the switch. Remember, these switches are designed to be mounted on the top of server racks, so the ports would be on the same end as the server ports. When mounting switches in racks by themselves (center-of-row methodology), many people seem to want to mount them the other way around.

Another thing to watch out for with these switches is that they need to extend a few inches beyond the rails on the back, which means they will extend beyond any air barriers you may have on the backs of the racks. The reason for this is, again, airflow. The backs of the 5010s are slightly slanted on top. This slant contains the air vents necessary for air to escape the chassis, as shown in Figure 18-4. The device shown is actually a 2148 FEX, but the 5010s are built the same way.

Figure 18-4. A 2148 FEX as seen from the side; notice the airflow vent on top

When you've installed the switches, be careful not to stuff cables into the space between them, as this will impede proper airflow and cooling. This is not a concern with the 5020 since it has more space on the back panel for air vents.

Though the Nexus 5000s were designed to be data-center switches, many of them seem to have some pretty significant limitations. For example, as of version 5.0 of NX-OS, the 5010 and 5020s don't support SVIs or routing, and support only 512 VLANs. These limitations can seem maddening, and rightly so. Still, the switches were designed for one purpose, and that is to connect many servers to the switching (and storage) fabric in a data center. For this purpose, they work very well. Just don't think you'll use a pair of 5000s as the core in your Enterprise LAN, as they simply aren't designed for that purpose. The newer 5548 does support L3 with the addition of a field-upgradable daughter card. It also supports over 4,000 VLANs, 16 ports per port channel, and a variety of other enhancements. My advice, if you're looking at Nexus 5000s, is to go for the newer models.

The 5000 series of switches marks a serious departure from traditional 1 RU switches in the Cisco lineup; they must be mounted in a server rack. Though the previous photos do not make it readily apparent, these switches are very deep and will fill the entire depth of a server cabinet. These switches simply cannot be mounted in standard two-post telecom racks. Remember, they were designed for use in a data center, and that's really where they belong. Figure 18-5 shows a Nexus 5010 underneath a Catalyst 2950 for scale. Notice the depth of the 5010. The 5010 is about three times deeper than the 2950.

The 5000-series switch contains four RJ-45 connectors on the left side. These are labeled Mgmt-0, Mgmt-1, L1, and L2. The only port that is configurable at this time is the Mgmt-0 interface. The rest are there for future expansion. The console port works as you'd expect. These four ports are found on the opposite end of the 5548 switch.

Figure 18-5. Catalyst 2960 on top of a Nexus 5010

The Nexus line is designed to be highly available. To that end, the dual power supplies and single fan tray are hot-swappable. Figure 18-6 shows a Nexus 5510 with its power supplies and fan trays removed.

Nexus 2000

The Nexus 2000 devices are not switches, but rather fabric extenders. FEXs can be thought of as external blades for Nexus switches. With a Nexus 5000, you can connect up to 12 FEXs. That's like having a 14-slot chassis when using a 5020, and the "slots" don't have to be in the same rack as the "supervisor." You can link two Nexus 5000s together, thereby making 24 FEXs available for dual-homing servers. This can be an amazingly flexible design, though it is not without its drawbacks, as we'll see in the configuration section. Newer Nexus models and versions of NX-OS support even more FEXs.

Because the FEXs are not switches, they have no intelligence of their own. They don't even have console ports. To use a FEX, you must connect it to a higher-tier Nexus

Figure 18-6. Nexus 5010 with power supplies and fan trays removed

switch like a 5000 or 7000. If you think of them like external blades for these switches, you'll understand FEXs pretty well.

Beware of the original 2148 48-port 1 Gbps FEXs, because they have a couple of serious limitations. The most maddening is their inability to support EtherChannels within a single FEX, though the fact that they have Gigabit ports that don't support 100 Mbps or 10 Mbps is a close second. Cisco has phased them out and is now selling the much-improved 2248 FEX, which resolves these issues. Just remember that you'll need to be on NX-OS code revision 4.2(1)N1(1) or later on the 5000 to use the 2248.

The 2000s also require the same rack-mount airflow tolerances mentioned in the 5000 section. A FEX mounted in an airflow-controlled rack is shown in Figure 18-7.

FEXs are not, and should not be considered, switches. Their primary purpose is to connect hosts to the network. This distinction is further clarified by the nature of the interfaces on a FEX, which are described as *host ports* or *fabric ports*:

Host ports
> Host ports are designed to connect servers (hosts) to the network. To this end, host ports have spanning tree BPDU Guard enabled, which will error-disable the port should another switch be connected. This is an important thing to understand, as the BPDU Guard cannot be disabled on a FEX.

Fabric ports
> A fabric port's sole purpose is to connect to a 5000 or 7000. It is not directly configurable, but is instead utilized when the connected port on the 5000 is placed into fabric mode. This will be detailed in a later section. Fabric ports are 10 Gbps only and cannot be used for hosts.

Figure 18-7. A 2148 FEX mounted in a cabinet with an airflow barrier above it

FEXs come in three varieties as of this writing. They are:

- Nexus 2148T GE Fabric Extender
- Nexus 2232PP 10 GE Fabric Extender
- Nexus 2248TP GE Fabric Extender

As listed previously, all of the Nexus devices are designed with data-center needs in mind. To that end, they all have dual hot-swappable power supplies and fan trays.

Figure 18-8 shows the front of a 2148T FEX with the dual power supplies and single fan tray removed.

Nexus 1000 Series

The Nexus 1000 series resides at or near the server level. There are two main models: the 1000V virtual switch for use with VMware and the 1010V appliance.

The Nexus 1000V switch is a software switch for use with VMware, especially in support of cloud computing architectures. The 1010 Virtual Services Appliance (VSA) is essentially a VSM that controls the VMware virtual switches within Unified Computing System (UCS) or other vendors' servers. Figure 18-9 shows a Cisco Nexus 1010 VSA. These devices are not covered further in this chapter.

Figure 18-8. Nexus 2148 FEX with power supplies and fan tray removed

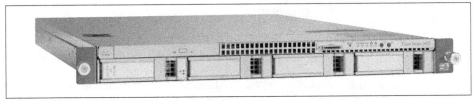

Figure 18-9. Cisco Nexus 1010 VSA; courtesy of Cisco Systems, Inc.; unauthorized use not permitted

NX-OS

NX-OS is the operating system for Nexus switches. NX-OS was written from the ground up to be a modular, scalable, and resilient operating system for the next generation of data center switches.

NX-OS looks like IOS. It's similar enough to make you feel comfortable but just different enough to be interesting and utterly frustrating until you get used to it. Many of the commands are the same, but the output of those commands is not what you'd expect if you've spent any time with IOS. Many of the commands are different entirely, and in some cases, contradict commands you may know from other Cisco devices.

There are web pages devoted to the many differences between IOS and NX-OS, and I could probably fill a book with such lists. Instead, I'll concentrate on the common things that seem to trip people up when they first learn NX-OS. Some of these are my favorite "So you think you know Nexus?" questions during an interview, so if you get the job, send me a thank you.

NX-OS Versus IOS

Since NX-OS is Linux-based, it benefits from many of the features that Linux users have come to enjoy, not the least of which is stability and modularity. The first thing that usually frustrates people is the modularity of NX-OS. Nexus is designed to be efficient and, to that end, the operating system does not load unnecessary modules. For example, if you want to run OSPF, you'll need to load the OSPF module. This is a departure from IOS, where everything is loaded regardless of need. As you might imagine, loading all the code for OSPF, BGP, and a myriad of other features you might not need can be wasteful. If you've ever compiled your own Linux kernel for speed and reliability, you'll recognize the benefits of this methodology.

Modules of code are called *features* in NX-OS. To load a module, use the feature command. To see which features are available, use the show feature command. Here is a list of features from a Nexus 5000:

```
NX-5K-1# sho feature
Feature Name          Instance   State
--------------------  --------   --------
tacacs                1          disabled
lacp                  1          enabled
interface-vlan        1          enabled
private-vlan          1          disabled
udld                  1          disabled
vpc                   1          enabled
fcoe                  1          disabled
fex                   1          enabled
```

As I was working on this section, I typed a command in the wrong config mode. The Nexus is smart enough to know how stupid I am, and further felt the need to comment as it showed me the answer I was really looking for. Here, I tried to use the feature command while in interface configuration mode:

```
NX-7K-1(config-if)# feature ?
*** No matching command found in current mode, matching in (config) mode ***
  bgp           Enable/Disable Border Gateway Protocol (BGP)
  cts           Enable/Disable CTS
  dhcp          Enable/Disable DHCP Snooping
[--output truncated--]
```

Here is the list of features from a Nexus 7000. As you can see, the bigger switch has a far more robust feature set:

```
NX-7K-1(config)# feature ?

  bgp           Enable/Disable Border Gateway Protocol (BGP)
  cts           Enable/Disable CTS
```

```
dhcp              Enable/Disable DHCP Snooping
dot1x             Enable/Disable dot1x
eigrp             Enable/Disable Enhanced Interior Gateway Routing Protocol
                  (EIGRP)
eou               Enable/Disable eou(l2nac)
glbp              Enable/Disable Gateway Load Balancing Protocol (GLBP)
hsrp              Enable/Disable Hot Standby Router Protocol (HSRP)
interface-vlan    Enable/Disable interface vlan
isis              Enable/Disable IS-IS Unicast Routing Protocol (IS-IS)
lacp              Enable/Disable LACP
msdp              Enable/Disable Multicast Source Discovery Protocol (MSDP)
netflow           Enable/Disable NetFlow
ospf              Enable/Disable Open Shortest Path First Protocol (OSPF)
ospfv3            Enable/Disable Open Shortest Path First Version 3 Protocol
                  (OSPFv3)
pbr               Enable/Disable Policy Based Routing(PBR)
pim               Enable/Disable Protocol Independent Multicast (PIM)
pim6              Enable/Disable Protocol Independent Multicast (PIM) for IPv6
port-security     Enable/Disable port-security
private-vlan      Enable/Disable private-vlan
rip               Enable/Disable Routing Information Protocol (RIP)
```

There are some features here that may surprise you. For example, if you want to use SVIs, you need to enable that feature with the `feature interface-vlan` command. Things that you might take for granted, like HSRP, are features on the Nexus, which makes sense given that the SVIs needed to even consider HSRP are features. The first thing I tell junior engineers when they work on Nexus is this: if what you're doing doesn't work, check for an unloaded feature. This nails everyone (myself included) at least a few times before it sinks in.

No more speed-related interface names

Every Ethernet interface is named *Ethernet* in NX-OS. No more FastEthernet, GigabitEthernet, or TenGigabitEthernet. Every interface, regardless of speed, is now just *Ethernet*. This is maddening to those of us who have been using IOS since version 9. Once again, though, Cisco didn't ask for my input when designing its new OS. It took a while, but I no longer see hundreds of 10-megabit interfaces when I look at the configuration of a Nexus switch.

 I'm sure this won't be a problem for younger, hipper engineers who never worked with Cisco 2501 routers. Heck, I used to work on AGS routers with internal PC-type expansion slots and no command-line parser. That was before the days of 100-megabit Ethernet, though. Now get off my lawn.

No hidden configuration in NX-OS

When an interface function is changed (L2 to L3, for example), IOS will sometimes keep the configuration for the original mode, which will reappear when the function changes back to the original. NX-OS does not do this.

Interface status displays operational state along with a reason

I like this feature a lot. A show interface will output the status of the interface and, if the interface is down, it will report the reason:

```
NX-7K-1-Cozy(config-if-range)# sho int e7/3
Ethernet7/3 is down (SFP not inserted)
  Hardware: 10000 Ethernet, address: 0026.9807.95c2 (bia 5475.d09a.81de)
  MTU 1500 bytes, BW 10000000 Kbit, DLY 10 usec,
    reliability 255/255, txload 1/255, rxload 1/255
[---output truncated---]
```

The show interface brief command

I don't know about you, but the show ip int brief command is probably in the top 10 list of commands I use daily. I was flummoxed when it didn't work the way I expected it to, and I stared blankly at the screen for quite some time, using the up arrow again and again, hoping that somehow the output would change. After snapping out of my confusion, I did the unthinkable and read the manual, where I discovered the show interface brief command:

```
NX-7K-1-Daisy# sho int brief
```

Ethernet Interface	VLAN	Type	Mode	Status	Reason	Speed	Port Ch #
Eth3/25	--	eth	routed	up	none	1000(D)	--
Eth3/26	--	eth	routed	up	none	1000(D)	--
Eth3/27	--	eth	routed	down	Link not connected	auto(D)	--
Eth3/28	--	eth	routed	down	Administratively down	auto(D)	--
Eth3/29	--	eth	routed	down	Administratively down	auto(D)	--
Eth3/30	1	eth	access	up	none	1000(D)	10
Eth3/31	--	eth	routed	down	Administratively down	auto(D)	--
Eth3/32	--	eth	routed	down	Administratively down	auto(D)	--
Eth3/33	--	eth	routed	down	Administratively down	auto(D)	--
Eth3/34	--	eth	routed	down	Administratively down	auto(D)	--
Eth3/35	--	eth	routed	down	Administratively down	auto(D)	--
Eth3/36	--	eth	routed	down	Administratively down	auto(D)	-

This command is pretty slick. It doesn't show the description, but it shows the VLAN used, the up/down status, the speed, and the port channel number for which the interface is a member. In the preceding example, you can see that interface e3/30 is a member of port channel 10.

No more write memory

Cisco has been threatening for years to no longer support the write memory command, but for those of us who have been around for too many years, we're used to it. Sadly, the Nexus no longer supports this command:

```
NX-5K-1# write ?
  erase  Destroys the configuration on persistent media
```

You must now run the copy running startup command to save your configuration. You get a cool little progress meter that moves as the config is saved, so you've got that going for you, which is nice:

```
NX-5K-1# copy running-config startup-config
[####################################] 100%
```

No more do command

The do command is no longer required. NX-OS allows any nonconfig command to be executed while in config mode:

```
NX-5K-2(config-if)# sho int po 100 switchport

Name: port-channel100
  Switchport: Enabled
  Switchport Monitor: Not enabled
  Operational Mode: access
  Access Mode VLAN: 1 (default)
  [--output truncated--]
```

No more show arp

The show arp command has been replaced with show ip arp. Makes sense, considering that ARP is an IP-related protocol. Some switches support both show arp and show ip arp, but the Nexus does not. Additionally, you may need to specify a VRF (see "Virtual Routing and Forwarding" on page 281 for more information):

```
NX-7K-1-Daisy# sho ip arp vrf Earth

IP ARP Table for context Earth
Total number of entries: 1
Address       Age       MAC Address     Interface
10.0.0.2      00:09:39  0026.981b.f043  Ethernet3/25
```

No more interface range command

What? I love that command! How dare they remove one of the most useful commands ever! Take it easy—the command may be gone, but the functionally remains, and it's better than ever. The functionality is now included without needing the command. How? Simply include the range when using the interface command and the switch will enter interface-range mode:

```
NX-7K-1-Cozy(config-vlan)# int e3/1 - 2
NX-7K-1-Cozy(config-if-range)#
```

Slash notation supported on all IPv4 and IPv6 commands

I think this is very cool, but I lament the fact that engineers who already can't do subnetting in their heads will have one more argument against learning. Ah, progress. Didn't I tell you to get off my lawn?

```
NX-7K-1-Cozy(config)# int 3/10
NX-7K-1-Cozy(config-int)# ip address 10.255.255.2/24
```

Two CLI help levels

From within the NX-OS CLI, you can still use the question mark to show all of the commands available at the current level. Here's a short example, which will seem familiar to anyone with experience using the bash shell in Unix. First, I'll use what would be called *tab completion* in Unix. I'll type the first few letters of a command, then press Tab to see what my options are:

```
NX-7K-1-Cozy(config)# tacacs<TAB>
tacacs+         tacacs-server
```

This is nice because it's quick and simple. If you'd like the traditional IOS-like description for each available command, simply use the question mark like you always have:

```
NX-7K-1-Cozy(config)# tacacs?
  tacacs+         Enable tacacs+
  tacacs-server  Configure TACACS+ server related parameters
```

Routing configuration mostly within interfaces

Router processes are still started globally:

```
NX-7K-1-Cozy(config)# router ospf 100
```

However, the majority of routing protocol commands now reside within interface configuration mode:

```
NX-7K-1-Cozy(config-router)# int e3/10
NX-7K-1-Cozy(config-if)# ip router ospf 100 area 0
NX-7K-1-Cozy(config-if)# ip ospf hello-interval 5
```

BGP commands still reside within the BGP block since they are neighbor-related.

Many more pipe options

NX-OS has many more useful commands to pipe into your show commands than IOS does. Here's the list from a Nexus 7000:

```
Daisy-Cozy# sho run | ?
  cut     Print selected parts of lines.
  diff    Show difference between current and previous invocation (creates
          temp files: remove them with 'diff-clean' command and dont use it
```

```
                on commands with big outputs, like 'show tech'!)
egrep    Egrep - print lines matching a pattern
grep     Grep - print lines matching a pattern
head     Display first lines
human    Output in human format (if permanently set to xml, else it will turn
                on xml for next command)
last     Display last lines
less     Filter for paging
no-more  Turn-off pagination for command output
section  Show lines that include the pattern as well as the subsequent lines
                that are more indented than matching line
sed      Stream Editor
sort     Stream Sorter
tr       Translate, squeeze, and/or delete characters
uniq     Discard all but one of successive identical lines
vsh      The shell that understands cli command
wc       Count words, lines, characters
xml      Output in xml format (according to .xsd definitions)
begin    Begin with the line that matches
count    Count number of lines
end      End with the line that matches
exclude  Exclude lines that match
include  Include lines that match
```

Some great new additions include last, which is similar to the tail command in Unix; egrep, which gives Unix-lovers reason to cheer; and no-more, which allows you to capture pages of output without having to set term length 0. Spend some quality time playing around with these features, and you'll be frustrated when you have to go back to IOS and its boring, limited output options.

Nexus Iconography

Before I get into the details of Nexus design principles, I must introduce some new icons to describe these devices. Figure 18-10 shows the icons used in my network diagrams to describe traditional switches.

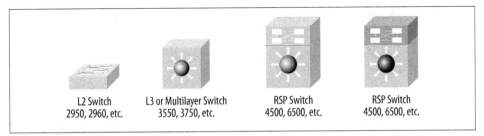

Figure 18-10. Traditional network icons in the Cisco style

Cisco has introduced new iconography to describe the Nexus line. The new icons are shown in Figure 18-11. Notice that all of the Nexus icons have the same atomic-looking pattern with arrows on the front or bottom of the icon.

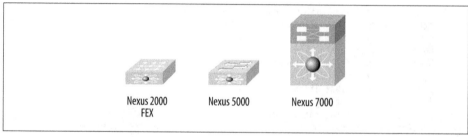

Nexus 2000
FEX

Nexus 5000

Nexus 7000

Figure 18-11. New Nexus icons

Nexus Design Features

The Nexus switches are designed from the ground up to be highly resilient and scalable. The Nexus architecture is built with the following features:

Management and control plane is separate from data plane
> In a nutshell, this means the act of forwarding packets is kept separate from the management and maintenance of the system. While you're SSHed into the switch, issuing commands, hardware is forwarding packets without any need to use the CPU. This allows you to do things like upgrade the switch's OS without interrupting packet flow.

Out-of-band management supported
> On the 5000s, there is a dedicated management interface that, on nonL3 models, is the only port that can be assigned an IP address. The management port is in its own VRF (see the section "Virtual Routing and Forwarding" on page 281 for more detail).

Lights-out management on 7000 series
> Similar to what servers have been doing for years, the Nexus 7000 series has a special port with its own processor that remains on even when the switch is powered off. This Connectivity Management Port (CMP) allows you to control the switch with *lights-out* capability that is completely independent of NX-OS.

High-speed backplane on 7000 series
> The original fabric modules released for the Nexus 7000-series switches provide up to 230 Gbps per slot with N+1 redundancy.

N+1 redundancy on 7000 series
> N+1 redundancy means that there is an additional module available in case of failure of the primary module. Thus if you require two fabric blades, you can install three, with the third being used for redundancy.

Hardware forwarding engines on every I/O module (7000 series)
> Every module contains distributed forwarding engines that allow the switch to forward packets without the need for CPU interaction once forwarding tables have been learned.

Scalability

The Nexus 7000 chassis was designed such that newer, more powerful fabric modules can be added without downtime. With new fabric modules, the available bandwidth per slot can increase. Additional features may be supported with new fabric modules as well.

Virtualization

Nexus supports VRF, virtual device contexts (VDC), virtual port channels (vPCs), all explained elsewhere in this chapter.

Resiliency

Nexus switches can be upgraded with no impact to packet flow under the proper conditions. Processes are run in separate protected-memory space. The control plane is separate from the data plane. All of these features and many others make the switch more resistant to failure. I've seen Nexus 7000s that were running at 100 percent CPU with no impact to the packet flowing through them. This is possible because routing tables are processed by the CPU, which then translates them to forwarding tables that are downloaded to hardware. Unless the forwarding tables change, the CPU is not involved in packet forwarding.

Integration of L3 routing, L2 switching, and SAN switching

Though the topic is not covered in this book, Nexus was designed from the ground up to incorporate storage networking including, but not limited to, FCoE.

Support for multiprocessor and multithreaded CPUs

Using multi-processor architectures allows you to take advantage of significantly increased processing power.

Virtual Routing and Forwarding

VRFs are separate and distinct routing processes within the same router. In a nutshell, a router can have multiple routing tables, each with its own set of routes and protocols. This is not a Nexus-specific feature. IOS version 15 supports VRFs as well.

 IOS version 15? I thought we were on 12.x. What happened to versions 13 and 14? Apparently, 13 is unlucky, as is 14 in some cultures, so Cisco jumped from 12 to 15. We now return you to our regularly scheduled Nexus chapter.

The Nexus 5000 comes with two VRFs by default: the default VRF and the management VRF. Here we assign a default route to the management VRF on a 5000. Notice that an IP address assigned to the management interface will reside in the management VRFs as well:

```
vrf context management
  ip route 0.0.0.0/0 10.1.1.1
```

Be careful with VRFs, especially on the 5000s. The 5000s do not, as of this writing, really support routing to begin with (the recently released 5500s will, with an additional daughter card). Their current iterations prefer to have the management IP address in the management VRF. This will likely burn you more than once because the management VRF is not the default VRF.

Here's a great example. Everyone loves the show ip interface brief command, so let's try it on a configured Nexus 5000:

```
NX-5K-1# sho ip int brie
IP Interface Status for VRF "default"
Interface          IP Address      Interface Status
```

Huh. That's odd. I know I configured the management interface, so why doesn't it show up? Because the default VRF is named "default" (clever huh?), but the management interface resides in the management VRF. To see it, we have to add vrf management to the show ip interface brief command:

```
NX-5K-1# sho ip int brie vrf management
IP Interface Status for VRF "management"
Interface          IP Address      Interface Status
mgmt0              10.10.10.1      protocol-up/link-up/admin-up
```

If you're thinking "That's dumb," you're not alone. Remember, though, the management VRF is designed to be out of band with the switch, and that's why it resides there. It makes sense, especially if you use a 7000 instead of a 5000, but it's different, so it can be frustrating. If you find that your command isn't working, think about your VRF and see if that helps. Even ping needs to have the VRF specified:

```
NX-5K-1# ping 10.10.10.2 vrf management
PING 10.10.10.2 (10.10.10.2): 56 data bytes
64 bytes from 10.10.10.2: icmp_seq=0 ttl=254 time=4.762 ms
64 bytes from 10.10.10.2: icmp_seq=1 ttl=254 time=8.052 ms
64 bytes from 10.10.10.2: icmp_seq=2 ttl=254 time=8.078 ms
64 bytes from 10.10.10.2: icmp_seq=3 ttl=254 time=8.168 ms
64 bytes from 10.10.10.2: icmp_seq=4 ttl=254 time=8.178 ms
```

Luckily, you can change the routing context used with the routing-context vrf *vrf-name* command:

```
NX-5K-1# routing-context vrf management
NX-5K-1%management#
```

Now, every command we issue will apply to the management VRF:

```
NX-5K-1%management # ping 10.10.10.2
PING 10.10.10.2 (10.10.10.2): 56 data bytes
64 bytes from 10.10.10.2: icmp_seq=0 ttl=254 time=4.762 ms
64 bytes from 10.10.10.2: icmp_seq=1 ttl=254 time=8.052 ms
64 bytes from 10.10.10.2: icmp_seq=2 ttl=254 time=8.078 ms
64 bytes from 10.10.10.2: icmp_seq=3 ttl=254 time=8.168 ms
64 bytes from 10.10.10.2: icmp_seq=4 ttl=254 time=8.178 ms
```

The downside is that it makes the command prompt pretty ugly, but that's the price we pay for being lazy typists. To change it back to the normal state, use the `routing-context vrf default` command:

```
NX-5K-1%management# routing-context vrf default
NX-5K-1#
```

VRFs can be very useful for accomplishing things like multitenancy in data centers. The ability to have 10 customers on the same switch, all with the same 10.10.10.0/24 address space, is a pretty nice benefit.

Virtual Device Contexts

The Nexus 7000s are capable of being split into multiple logical switches. If you're at all like me, you no doubt got very excited at the possibilities of running a pile of virtual switches within a single chassis. Naturally, I assumed that VDCs would be like firewall contexts in the ASA and FWSMs, where you can have up to 50 contexts. Naturally, I was wrong.

Only the 7000 series of Nexus switches supports VDCs at this time and, as of this writing, these powerful switches only support four VDCs. I thought that was an almost pointless number of contexts, so I asked some people in the know at Cisco why the seemingly silly limitation. The reply I got was that they wanted to make sure each context could have the full power and capabilities of a Nexus switch. The argument was that if they allowed 50 contexts—each supporting BGP, OSPF, EIGRP, tens of thousands of routes, and all the myriad possibilities a Nexus switch could include—the performance within the contexts would suffer. My argument would be to allow more contexts, provided certain features were disabled—just like on the ASAs. Perhaps this option will be available in the future, but as of this writing, we're stuck with a maximum of four contexts.

For our lab, I've taken two Nexus 7000s, built two VDCs within each, and interconnected them in a variety of ways. The two Nexus 7000s are named NX-7k-1 and NX-7k-2. The two VDCs in NX-7k-1 are named Cozy and Daisy, while the two VDCs in NX-7k-2 are named Annie and Guinness. These names reflect the names of my Newfoundland dogs. Since you didn't spend years living with these dogs learning their relationships to each other, perhaps a picture would help. Figure 18-12 shows the layout, the VDCs, and how they're all connected.

Let's get started. I've already configured the VDCs on NX-7K-1, so let's configure the Annie and Guinness VDCs on NX-7K-2.

I'll start by defining the VDC with the `vdc` command. I have to specify a name and a VDC number. VDC1 is the system VDC, so I have to start with 2:

```
NX-7K-2(config)# vdc Annie id 2

Note:  Creating VDC, one moment please ...
```

```
2010 May 27 00:05:57 NX-7K-2 %$ VDC-1 %$ %VDC_MGR-2-VDC_ONLINE: vdc 2 has come online
```

 Why don't we need to enable the VDC feature? I didn't write the code, but I speculate that the VDC feature is integral to the operating system. Even when you boot a 5010, which does not support multiple VDCs, it will report that it is booting VDC #1.

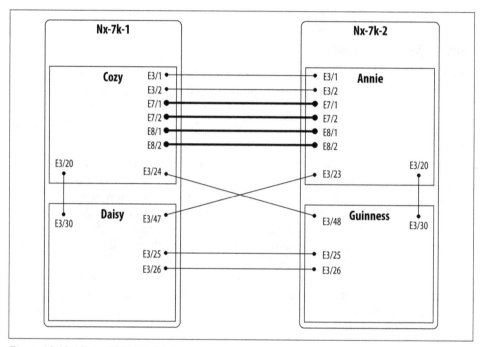

Figure 18-12. Nexus 7000 VDC Interconnects

Just like that, we have a VDC. But a router or switch, even a virtual one, is pretty useless without any interfaces, so let's allocate some. I'm going to allocate the first 24 ports from the 48-port blade in slot 3. You can allocate differently, but you must allocate interfaces in groups controlled by ASICs. As you'll see later in this chapter, those groups may seem odd. For now, let's keep it as simple as possible:

```
NX-7K-2(config-vdc)# allocate interface Ethernet3/1-24
Moving ports will cause all config associated to them in source vdc to be removed.
Are you sure you want to move the ports (y/n)? [yes]
```

This warning is telling me that these ports will be removed from the system context. If I had configured those interfaces within this context, bad things will happen when I yank them out and put them in another VDC. This is the equivalent of pulling half of the blade out of the virtual device NX-7K-2 and putting it into the virtual device Annie. It won't harm the switch, but anything connected to those ports will go offline.

Next, I'll allocate all 32 ports of the 10 GB blade:

```
NX-7K-2(config-vdc)# allocate interface Ethernet8/1-32
Moving ports will cause all config associated to them in source vdc to be removed.
Are you sure you want to move the ports (y/n)? [yes] y
```

A quick sanity check shows that we have two VDCs now—the original system context and Annie. We can show the VDCs configured with the show vdc command:

```
NX-7K-2(config-vdc)# sho vdc

vdc_id  vdc_name                    state          mac
------  --------                    -----          ----------
1       NX-7K-2                     active         00:26:98:1b:f0:41
2       Annie                       active         00:26:98:1b:f0:42
```

Now let's create the Guinness VDC, this time with an ID of 3:

```
NX-7K-2(config-vdc)# vdc Guinness id 3
Note:  Creating VDC, one moment please ...
2010 May 27 00:08:41 NX-7K-2 %$ VDC-1 %$ %VDC_MGR-2-VDC_ONLINE: vdc 3 has come online
```

Now I'll allocate interfaces. This VDC only gets the other half of the 48-port blade. There are no 10 Gbps ports in this VDC:

```
NX-7K-2(config-vdc)#   allocate interface Ethernet3/25-48
Moving ports will cause all config associated to them in source vdc to be removed.
Are you sure you want to move the ports (y/n)? [yes] y
```

And the preliminary configuration of our VDCs is done. Show VDC gives us a list of what's configured:

```
NX-7K-2(config-vdc)# sho vdc

vdc_id  vdc_name                    state          mac
------  --------                    -----          ----------
1       NX-7K-2                     active         00:26:98:1b:f0:41
2       Annie                       active         00:26:98:1b:f0:42
3       Guinness                    active         00:26:98:1b:f0:43
```

To see a detailed report of which ports have been allocated to which VDCs, I can use the show vdc membership command. Really, though, I like to just do a show run vdc and see the commands applied to the VDCs. All of the limit-resource commands shown are defaults; their use is outside the scope of this already large book:

```
NX-7K-2(config)# sho run vdc

!Command: show running-config vdc
!Time: Thu May 27 00:54:11 2010

version 4.2(4)
vdc NX-7K-2 id 1
  limit-resource vlan minimum 16 maximum 4094
  limit-resource monitor-session minimum 0 maximum 2
  limit-resource vrf minimum 16 maximum 200
  limit-resource port-channel minimum 0 maximum 768
  limit-resource u4route-mem minimum 32 maximum 32
```

```
    limit-resource u6route-mem minimum 16 maximum 16
    limit-resource m4route-mem minimum 58 maximum 58
    limit-resource m6route-mem minimum 8 maximum 8
vdc Annie id 2
  allocate interface Ethernet3/1-24
  allocate interface Ethernet8/1-32
  boot-order 1
  limit-resource vlan minimum 16 maximum 4094
  limit-resource monitor-session minimum 0 maximum 2
  limit-resource vrf minimum 16 maximum 200
  limit-resource port-channel minimum 0 maximum 768
  limit-resource u4route-mem minimum 8 maximum 8
  limit-resource u6route-mem minimum 4 maximum 4
  limit-resource m4route-mem minimum 8 maximum 8
  limit-resource m6route-mem minimum 2 maximum 2
vdc Guinness id 3
  allocate interface Ethernet3/25-48
  boot-order 1
  limit-resource vlan minimum 16 maximum 4094
  limit-resource monitor-session minimum 0 maximum 2
  limit-resource vrf minimum 16 maximum 200
  limit-resource port-channel minimum 0 maximum 768
  limit-resource u4route-mem minimum 8 maximum 8
  limit-resource u6route-mem minimum 4 maximum 4
  limit-resource m4route-mem minimum 8 maximum 8
  limit-resource m6route-mem minimum 2 maximum 2
```

Notice the boot-order command. With this command, I can specify the order in which VDCs should boot when the system is initialized.

Now that I've created our VDCs, I'll go ahead and actually use them. To access the VDCs from the system VDC, use the switchto vdc *vdc-name* command:

```
NX-7K-2(config-vdc)# switchto vdc Annie

        ---- System Admin Account Setup ----

Do you want to enforce secure password standard (yes/no) [y]:

   Enter the password for "admin":
   Confirm the password for "admin":

        ---- Basic System Configuration Dialog VDC: 2 ----
This setup utility will guide you through the basic configuration of
the system. Setup configures only enough connectivity for management
of the system.
[--output truncated--]
```

 If you're used to working with contexts on ASA security appliances, you'll be constantly annoyed by the fact that Cisco decided to use the switchto command on Nexus, while using the changeto command on the ASA.

Once I'm connected to the VDC, it appears as if I'm in a newly initialized Nexus switch, which is exactly what this is. The command prompt, by default, is the system-context hostname concatenated with the VDC name, separated by a hyphen. This behavior is configurable with the vdc combined-hostname command:

```
NX-7K-2-Annie#
```

Once within a VDC, if I want to get back to the system context, I can use the switch back command:

```
NX-7K-2-Annie# switchback
```

After I've configured some of the interfaces within the contexts on both chassis, the show CDP neighbors command executed from within the Annie VDC shows that it sees other contexts as devices, but only because I have physical Ethernet cables connecting them. There is no intraswitch communication between VDCs. The contexts have no idea that they are contexts, and no idea that other contexts are virtual:

```
NX-7K-2-Annie(config-if-range)# sho cdp neighbors
Capability Codes: R - Router, T - Trans-Bridge, B - Source-Route-Bridge
                  S - Switch, H - Host, I - IGMP, r - Repeater,
                  V - VoIP-Phone, D - Remotely-Managed-Device,
                  s - Supports-STP-Dispute

Device-ID           Local Intrfce Hldtme Capability  Platform      Port ID
NX-7K-1-Cozy(JAF1408BERL)
                    Eth3/1        140    R S I s     N7K-C7010     Eth3/1

NX-7K-1-Cozy(JAF1408BERL)
                    Eth3/2        140    R S I s     N7K-C7010     Eth3/2

NX-7K-1-Daisy(JAF1408BERL)
                    Eth3/23       172    R S I s     N7K-C7010     Eth3/47

NX-7K-1-Cozy(JAF1408BERL)
                    Eth7/1        179    R S I s     N7K-C7010     Eth7/1

NX-7K-1-Cozy(JAF1408BERL)
                    Eth7/2        179    R S I s     N7K-C7010     Eth7/2

NX-7K-1-Cozy(JAF1408BERL)
                    Eth8/2        123    R S I s     N7K-C7010     Eth8/2
```

Shared and Dedicated Rate-Mode

Some Nexus 10 Gb modules support something called *dedicated port mode*. In this mode, I can configure the switch to allow the maximum throughput on a port at the expense of three other ports. The way this works has to do with the way the modules are built. Ethernet ports are controlled by chips called Application-Specific Integrated Circuits (ASICs). These ASICs are responsible for port forwarding of a number of ports. On the 32-port 10 Gbps blade on the Nexus 7000, each ASIC controls four ports. What this means to you is that you can only get 10 Gbps of throughput for every four ports on the blade (4:1 oversubscription). This may sound like a terrible thing, but it's actually very common on modules of this type.

> I've seen interesting issues attributed to ASIC failures. Once, on a 6509, we had very strange problems with what seemed to be a random group of servers. The admin discovered that if he moved the server to a different port on the switch, the problem went away. When I started to dig into the physical connections, I discovered that the servers experiencing the problem were all connected within a contiguous range of six ports. These ports were all controlled by a single ASIC, which had gone bad. We migrated the servers off the offending ports, then made arrangements to get the blade replaced.

The Nexus 7000 allows you to dedicate all the ASIC's resources to one port on these modules in what is called *dedicated rate-mode*. When you do this, it disables all of the other ports controlled by that ASIC. The groups of ports are not contiguous; in other words, a single ASIC controls ports e1/1, 3, 5, and 7, while a different ASIC controls ports e1/2, 4, 6, and 8. This may seem odd until you look at the front of the blade. As you can see from Figure 18-13, the pattern corresponds to the physical layout of the ports on the blade. Ports 1, 3, 5, and 7 are all physically contiguous and share the same hardware connections (and therefore ASIC) within the module. This module even marks the ports that you can configure as dedicated ports.

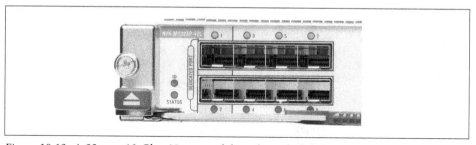

Figure 18-13. A 32-port 10 Gbps Nexus module with marked dedicated ports; courtesy of Cisco Systems, Inc.; unauthorized use not permitted

So why would we want to do this? Most devices rarely utilize the full capacity of an interface, which is why the ports share an ASIC. Certain devices do require a high utilization, though. Devices such as backup servers that pull in a lot of traffic from multiple sources are one example. Database servers are another. If your network is large, you may need to dedicate your uplink ports so that you can best utilize the available speed of your links.

To configure a port in dedicated mode, use the `rate-mode` interface command. The options are `dedicated` and `shared`:

```
NX-7K-1-Cozy(config-if)# rate-mode ?
  dedicated  Rate mode is dedicated
  shared     Rate mode is shared
```

When you're setting a port to dedicated mode, all of the ports in the port group must be in the admin-down state or you will get the following error:

```
NX-7K-1-Cozy(config-if)# rate-mode dedicated
ERROR: Ethernet7/1: all ports in the port-group must be in admin shut state
```

Here, I'll shut down all the ports in the first port group on module 7, then dedicate the ASIC to the first port:

```
NX-7K-1-Cozy(config-if)# int e7/1-4
NX-7K-1-Cozy(config-if-range)# shut
NX-7K-1-Cozy(config-if-range)# int e7/1
NX-7K-1-Cozy(config-if)# rate-mode dedicated
```

The switch now prevents me from bringing up the other ports in the port group:

```
NX-7K-1-Cozy(config-if)# int e7/3
NX-7K-1-Cozy(config-if)# no shut
ERROR: Ethernet7/3: Config not allowed, as first port in the port-grp is dedicated
```

The port will now have a dedicated (D) flag in the output of show int brief:

```
NX-7K-1-Cozy(config-if-range)# sho int brie  | beg Eth7
```

```
--------------------------------------------------------------------------------
Ethernet      VLAN   Type Mode    Status  Reason            Speed       Port
Interface                                                               Ch #
--------------------------------------------------------------------------------
Eth7/1        --     eth  routed up       none              10G(D) --
Eth7/2        --     eth  routed up       none              10G(S) --
Eth7/3        --     eth  routed down     SFP not inserted  auto(S) --
Eth7/4        --     eth  routed down     SFP not inserted  auto(S) -
[--output truncated--]
```

The interface will report that it is in dedicated rate mode:

```
X-7K-1-Cozy# sho int e7/1
Ethernet7/1 is up
  Hardware: 10000 Ethernet, address: 0026.9807.95c2 (bia 5475.d09a.81dc)
  MTU 1500 bytes, BW 10000000 Kbit, DLY 10 usec,
     reliability 255/255, txload 1/255, rxload 1/255
  Encapsulation ARPA
  full-duplex, 10 Gb/s, media type is 10g
  Beacon is turned off
  Auto-Negotiation is turned off
  Input flow-control is off, output flow-control is off
  Rate mode is dedicated
  Switchport monitor is off
  Last link flapped 00:03:48
[--output truncated--]
```

As you might expect from looking at the physical module, only the first port in a port group can be configured in dedicated rate mode:

```
NX-7K-1-Cozy(config-if)# int e7/1, e7/3, e7/5, e7/7
NX-7K-1-Cozy(config-if-range)# rate-mode dedicated
ERROR: Config not applied on all ports.
        Config allowed only on the first port in each port group.
```

On a Nexus 5548 switch, where all ports are capable of wire speed, each port is in dedicated mode and cannot be changed. Here's the output from a 5548's show int brief command, which shows each port with a (D) flag:

```
NX-5548# sho int brie


----------------------------------------------------------------------------
Ethernet      VLAN   Type Mode   Status  Reason                   Speed    Port
Interface                                                                  Ch #
----------------------------------------------------------------------------
Eth1/1        1      eth  access down    SFP validation failed    10G(D)   10
Eth1/2        1      eth  access down    SFP not inserted         10G(D)   10
Eth1/3        1      eth  access down    SFP not inserted         10G(D)   10
Eth1/4        1      eth  access down    SFP not inserted         10G(D)   10
Eth1/5        1      eth  access down    SFP not inserted         10G(D)   10
Eth1/6        1      eth  access down    SFP not inserted         10G(D)   10
Eth1/7        1      eth  access down    SFP not inserted         10G(D)   10
```

Configuring Fabric Extenders (FEXs)

There are two ways to attach FEXs to upstream switches. The first method is called *passthru* mode, and looks like the diagram in Figure 18-14. In this topology, each FEX should be thought of as a blade in the switch to which it is connected.

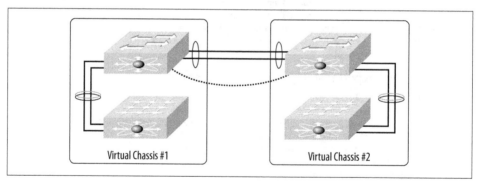

Virtual Chassis #1   Virtual Chassis #2

Figure 18-14. FEXs attached in passthru mode

The second topology for FEX attachment is called *crossover* mode, and is shown in Figure 18-15. This method looks more like a traditional multiswitch network, but remember, FEXs are not switches, they are fabric extenders. While this topology has merit in that each FEX is now connected to two upstream devices, the risks of such a design, in my opinion, outweigh this benefit. The only time I recommend crossover configuration is if the servers being connected to the FEXs will not be dual-homed.

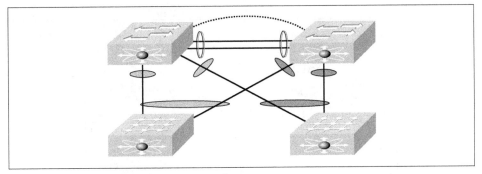

Figure 18-15. FEXs attached in crossover mode

 Watch out for older FEXs. The Nexus 2148 FEX does not allow Ether-
Channel bundles to be formed within a single FEX.

The drawback to the crossover design is that each upstream switch will think that the
FEX is an extension of its fabric, and in fact, it is. It becomes very easy to configure the
same physical FEX differently on each upstream switch, which can be catastrophic, not
to mention hard to troubleshoot. If such a design is warranted in your environment, I
strongly urge you to use the Nexus config-sync feature outlined later in this chapter.
Keep in mind that config-sync is available only on NX-OS version 5.0(2) and later.

Remember, FEXs do no switching of their own. All switching is done by the upstream
switches—in this example, a pair of Nexus 5000s. Even if two hosts connected to the
same FEX need to communicate, the frames will traverse the uplink, be switched on
the 5000, and be sent back down the uplink to the FEX. Instead of thinking of FEXs as
switches, it would be better to think of them as modules in a chassis switch. Once you
consider a 5K the supervisor and the FEXs to be modules, the passthru design makes
a lot more sense. You wouldn't cross-connect each blade on a chassis switch to the
supervisor of the other switch in a pair, would you?

You cannot attach a switch to a FEX. All FEX ports are configured with BPDU Guard,
which cannot be disabled. You can, however, connect a switch to the Nexus 5000, as
shown in Figure 18-16.

 OK, so you can connect a switch to a FEX, but to do so you must prevent
that switch from sending BPDUs. I'll spare you the "that's a bad idea"
speech.

Configuring the FEXs is pretty straightforward, so long as you understand how they
work. First, you must enable the FEX feature:

```
NX-5K-1(config)# feature fex
```

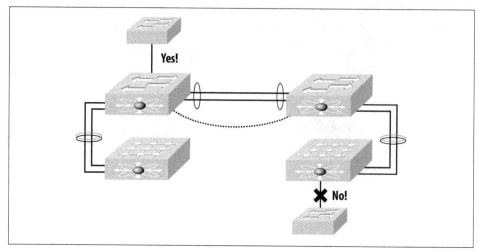

Figure 18-16. Switch connectivity with FEXs

Describing FEXs

After the FEX feature has been enabled, each FEX must then be described in the 5K. The FEXs are assigned numbers in the range of 100–199. The number is locally significant to the 5000 and is not shared outside the connected 5000. If you connect one FEX to two 5Ks, they can be named differently, so be careful because this will be very confusing:

```
NX-5K-1(config)# fex ?
  <100-199>  FEX number
```

Here is a config snippet from a configured FEX:

```
fex 100
  description FEX0100
  type "Nexus 2148T"
```

The description in this case was added automatically by the switch and can be changed. The type was also added by the switch upon discovery of the FEX and cannot be changed.

Physical connection

When connecting a port or ports on the 5K to the FEXs fabric ports, you must configure the 5K's ports as fabric ports using the `switchport mode fex-fabric` command. You must then assign the ports to the FEX using the `fex associate` *fex-number* command. When more than one uplink is used, the ports can be bonded into an EtherChannel:

```
interface Ethernet1/1
  switchport mode fex-fabric
  fex associate 100
  channel-group 10
```

The FEX associate command is what designates this FEX as FEX 100 within the switch.

 When a FEX is first recognized, it will likely need to download the proper microcode from the 5000 or 7000 to which it is connected. This process can take 10–15 minutes and will involve the FEX restarting. There may be no indication of this happening, so either go get some lunch or obsessively reenter the `show fex` command to see what's going on. You could do both, but make sure you don't leave any crumbs in the data center.

Pinning

Normally, with a 48-port 1 Gbps switch, assuming a 4×10 Gbps uplink EtherChannel totaling 40 Gbps, the uplink will have a possible oversubscription ratio of 4.8:1. Pinning allows us to assign banks of ports to individual uplinks instead of having all the ports share a single EtherChannel. Why would we do this? Read on.

 Why is the ratio 4.8:1 and not 1.2:1? After all, there is a 40 Gbps uplink and forty-eight 1 Gbps ports. The discrepancy is due to the nature of EtherChannel load balancing. Remember, an EtherChannel is not really a faster link, but rather multiple same-speed links balanced according to a predefined algorithm. See Chapter 7 for more information on how EtherChannel hashing works.

With four 10 Gbps uplinks, we can assign 12 ports to each 10 Gbps link, giving us an oversubscription ratio of 1.2:1. That's a potential four-to-one improvement in uplink speed. Sounds like a great idea. The downside of this increase in usable uplink is that should one of the uplinks fail, all 12 of the pinned ports will also be down. There is no dynamic healing like there is with an EtherChannel when pinning fabric ports.

Pinning can be done with one, two, or four links. On a 48-port FEX, the breakdown is as follows:

Pinning one
   All host ports use one uplink. This is the method used with an EtherChannel uplink.

Pinning two
   The first 24 ports use the first link and the second 24 ports use the second uplink.

Pinning four
   Each 12-port group uses its own uplink.

When using a FEX with all four uplinks bonded together, we must use a pinning of one, configured within the FEX configuration block:

```
fex 101
  pinning max-links 1
```

```
    description FEX0101
    type "Nexus 2148T"
```

If we wanted to abandon the idea of using an EtherChannel and instead get the most out of our bandwidth, we would use pinning four:

```
fex 101
    pinning max-links 4
    description FEX0101
    type "Nexus 2148T"
```

You will get an error if you try to configure your uplinks into a channel when pinning is set higher than one:

```
NX-5K-1(config-if-range)# channel-group 10
command failed: port not compatible [FEX pinning max-links not one]
```

FEX fabric uplinks using vPC

To configure a single FEX cross-connected to two Nexus 5000s (cross-connect design), we must use a vPC to bond the links together:

NX-5K-1:

```
interface port-channel 20
    switchport mode fex-fabric
    vpc 20
    fex associate 101
    speed 10000
```

NX-5K-2:

```
interface port-channel 20
    switchport mode fex-fabric
    vpc 20
    fex associate 101
    speed 10000
```

If this is confusing, read on, as vPCs are covered in the next section. Remember that the FEX configuration should be identical on both 5000s, or unpredictable results may occur.

Virtual Port Channel

A common requirement in networking is to dual-home devices. Switches connected to two other switches form a Layer-2 loop that can be disastrous for a network unless the loop is broken. Traditionally, spanning tree was used to find these loops and block one of the legs, thus preventing problems like broadcast storms. While Spanning Tree Protocol (STP) works well, it is slow and prohibits the use of one-half of the available bandwidth from the dual-homed switch. Figure 18-17 shows a traditional dual-home STP-based design. Notice that one of each of the links from the bottom switches is unavailable, since STP has blocked those links.

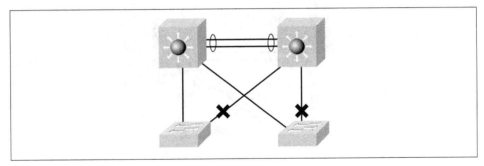

Figure 18-17. Traditional spanning tree design

In a 6500 environment using VSS supervisors, we can create a single logical switch from two physical switches. This new logical switch is called a *VSS cluster* (see Chapter 17 for more information). Since the two links from each bottom switch connect to a single logical switch, STP is not needed. A VSS cluster design is shown in Figure 18-18. The bottom switches see the VSS cluster as a single endpoint and can make a single port channel to that device. Cisco describes this as two switches with a single control plane.

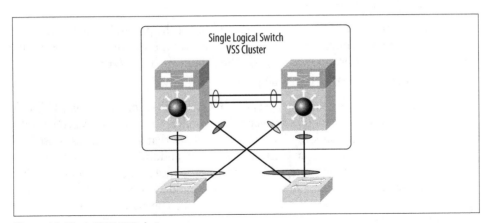

Figure 18-18. A 6500 VSS design

This solution is much cleaner, since spanning tree is not required. Each link can now be fully utilized, doubling the uplink speed from the bottom switches.

Nexus does not support VSS technology and instead uses vPCs. With vPCs, the top switches are not bonded into a single logical switch, but the bottom switches still see them as a single endpoint when creating port channels. Figure 18-19 shows two switches connected to two Nexus 7000s using vPCs for all connections. Cisco describes the Nexus vPC arrangement as two switches having one data plane and two control planes.

Let's walk though the steps needed to configure a vPC.

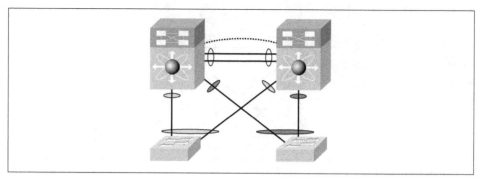

Figure 18-19. vPC design

First, you must enable the vPC feature:

```
NX-5k-1(config)# feature vpc
```

Before configuring anything else regarding vPCs, you must first establish a vPC domain. The domain number must match for all switches working with the configured vPCs:

```
NX-5K-1(config-if)# vpc domain 1
```

Though it's not required, I have configured one side of the pair to be the master with the vpc role priority command. The switch that acts as the spanning tree root should be the master. A lower priority value wins. The default value is 32768:

```
NX-5K-1(config-if)# role priority 1000
```

vPCs require a link between the vPC peer switches called a *peer keepalive link*. This link is in addition to the port channel between the switches in which the VLAN trunks reside. The peer keepalive link must be a routed link, in that an IP address is used on each side. The link can be over an existing IP network and, by default, Cisco suggests that it be established over the management interface. I'm not a huge fan of putting what amounts to critical (criticality is in the eye of the beholder) connections on the management network, but this example shows how to do so. The management VRF is used by default on a Nexus 5000:

```
NX-5K-1(config-vpc)# peer-keepalive destination 10.10.10.2
Note:
--------:: Management VRF will be used as the default VRF ::--------
```

On a Nexus 7000, this link can be any interface, since they all default to routing mode anyway. Here, I've configured e3/1 to be the peer keepalive link:

```
NX-7K-1(config)# int e3/1
NX-7K-1(config-if)# ip address 10.255.255.1/24
NX-7K-1 (config)# vpc domain 1
NX-7K-1 (config-vpc-domain)# peer-keepalive destination 10.255.255.2
```

Now let's configure the other side of the link on 7K-2:

```
NX-7K-2(config)# int e3/1
NX-7K-2(config-if)# ip address 10.255.255.2/24
```

And the vPC peer keepalive:

```
NX-7K-2 (config)# vpc domain 1
NX-7K-2 (config-vpc-domain)# peer-keepalive destination 10.255.255.1
```

vPC requires that a link—preferably a trunk—between the vPC peers be defined as a *peer link*. This link will be used for the traversal of traffic necessary to utilize the vPC. Generally, this link is the main interswitch link between the two switches. The vPC peer link must be a multi–10 Gbps EtherChannel according to the documentation. Indeed, it should be, but it will work with a single link if you need to test it in a lab. Regardless of the number of links, the interface must be a port channel. This command is the same on both the 5000 and the 7000. Here, port channel 1 is used as the peer link:

```
NX-5K-1(config-if)# int po 1
NX-5K-1(config-if)# vpc peer-link
Please note that spanning tree port type is changed to "network" port type on vPC
peer-link. This will enable spanning tree Bridge Assurance on vPC peer-link provided
the STP Bridge Assurance (which is enabled by default) is not disabled.
```

Once this is done, you must tag the EtherChannels on each 5K that are to be linked into a single VDC. A good rule to follow is to tag the EtherChannel with the same number as the channel itself:

```
interface port-channel 10
  vpc 10
```

 Please configure the vPC to be the same number as the port channel to which it is assigned. Having to debug a vPC where the numbers don't match is a puzzle that I don't enjoy solving when the CEO is barking at me to get the switch back up. Keep it simple.

Invariably, when your vPCs don't work, you'll wonder what in the Sam Hill is going on. Luckily, Cisco saw fit to include a command or two to help us figure out the problem.

vPCs rely on the configuration of each side of the link to match exactly, in much the way that an EtherChannel requires each of its component interfaces to match. The difference is that with vPCs, the configurations of two separate switches must match, and the requirements span more than just the interfaces in question.

There are two types of vPC compatibility parameters: type 1 and type 2. Type -1 parameters must match, or the vPC will not form (or will break if already formed). Type -2 parameters should match, but the vPCs should not break if they don't.

 I've worked in Nexus environments where changing type-2 parameters has caused vPCs to bounce or VLANs to be suspended. My recommendation is to change anything even remotely relating to vPCs during an approved change control window.

The first thing you should check when your vPCs don't work is the show vpc command. Here's an example of a vPC that's working. If you had 30 vPCs, each would be listed in the output of this command. Notice that the status of the peer link is shown as well.

 The output from these commands may differ based on the switch, OS revision, and features in use.

```
NX-7K-2-Annie(config-if)# sho vpc
Legend:
                (*) - local vPC is down, forwarding via vPC peer-link

vPC domain id                    : 100
Peer status                      : peer adjacency formed ok
vPC keep-alive status            : Suspended (Destination IP not reachable)
Configuration consistency status: success
Type-2 consistency status        : success
vPC role                         : secondary
Number of vPCs configured        : 1
Peer Gateway                     : Disabled
Dual-active excluded VLANs        : -

vPC Peer-link status
---------------------------------------------------------------------
id   Port   Status Active vlans
--   ----   ------ -----------------------------------------------------
1    Po1    up     1

vPC status
---------------------------------------------------------------------
id   Port   Status Consistency Reason                     Active vlans
--   ----   ------ ----------- ------------------------- ------------
10   Po10   up     success     success                   1
```

The next command you should grow to love when troubleshooting vPCs is the show vpc consistency-parameters command. When you specify the vPC you're struggling with, you will be treated to a list of every little detail concerning the items that must match. Here's the output for a working vPC:

```
NX-7K-2-Annie(config-if)# sho vpc consistency-parameters vpc 10

    Legend:
        Type 1 : vPC will be suspended in case of mismatch

Name                     Type Local Value             Peer Value
------------             ---- ----------------------- -----------------------
STP Port Type            1    Default                 Default
STP Port Guard           1    None                    None
STP MST Simulate PVST    1    Default                 Default
mode                     1    on                      on
Speed                    1    1000 Mb/s               1000 Mb/s
Duplex                   1    full                    full
```

```
Port Mode                     1     access              access
Native Vlan                   1     1                   1
MTU                           1     1500                1500
Allowed VLANs                 -     1                   1
Local suspended VLANs         -     -                   -
```

Now let's change something on one side and see what happens:

```
NX-7K-2-Annie(config-if)# int e3/23
NX-7K-2-Annie(config-if)# speed 100
```

The output of the show vpc command will show us that the vPC is now broken:

```
NX-7K-2-Annie(config-if)# sho vpc
Legend:
                (*) - local vPC is down, forwarding via vPC peer-link

vPC domain id                    : 100
Peer status                      : peer adjacency formed ok
vPC keep-alive status            : Suspended (Destination IP not reachable)
Configuration consistency status: failed
Configuration consistency reason: vPC type-1 configuration incompatible - STP gl
obal port type inconsistent
Type-2 consistency status        : success
vPC role                         : secondary
Number of vPCs configured        : 1
Peer Gateway                     : Disabled
Dual-active excluded VLANs       : -

vPC Peer-link status
---------------------------------------------------------------------
id   Port   Status Active vlans
--   ----   ------ ----------------------------------------------------
1    Po1    up      -

vPC status
---------------------------------------------------------------------
id   Port   Status Consistency Reason                    Active vlans
--   ----   ------ ----------- ------------------------- ------------
10   Po10   down*  failed      Global compat check failed -
```

The output of the show vpc consistency-parameters command now reports the issues:

```
NX-7K-2-Annie(config)# sho vpc consistency-parameters vpc 10

    Legend:
        Type 1 : vPC will be suspended in case of mismatch

Name                      Type  Local Value             Peer Value
------------              ----  ----------------------- -----------------------
STP Port Type             1     Default                 Default
STP Port Guard            1     None                    None
STP MST Simulate PVST     1     Default                 Default
mode                      1     on                      on
Speed                     1     100 Mb/s                1000 Mb/s
Duplex                    1     half                    full
Port Mode                 1     access                  access
```

```
Native Vlan              1    1                1
MTU                      1    1500             1500
Allowed VLANs            -    1                1
Local suspended VLANs    -    1                -
```

vPCs require more than just the interfaces to match. There is a whole laundry list of items that must be configured identically on both switches. To see the status of these items, add the global keyword to the show vpc consistency-parameters command. If any of the type-1 items are mismatched, your vPCs won't work.

 I've seen problems when working with vPCs in which the show vpc command reported a configuration mismatch where none existed. If this happens, remove the port channel interface and the channel group commands from the physical interfaces. When you replace them, the vPC will likely work. I've seen this behavior on 4.x and 5.x code on the 5Ks.

```
NX-7K-2-Annie(config)# sho vpc consistency-parameters global

Legend:
        Type 1 : vPC will be suspended in case of mismatch

Name                     Type  Local Value            Peer Value
-------------            ----  --------------------   -----------------------
STP Mode                 1     Rapid-PVST             Rapid-PVST
STP Disabled             1     None                   None
STP MST Region Name      1     " "                    " "
STP MST Region Revision  1     0                      0
STP MST Region Instance to 1
  VLAN Mapping
STP Loopguard            1     Disabled               Disabled
STP Bridge Assurance     1     Enabled                Enabled
STP Port Type, Edge      1     Normal, Disabled,      Normal, Disabled,
BPDUFilter, Edge BPDUGuard     Disabled               Disabled
STP MST Simulate PVST    1     Enabled                Enabled
Interface-vlan admin up  2                            -
Allowed VLANs            -     1,10                   1,10
Local suspended VLANs    -     -                      -
```

Config-Sync

Version 5.0(2)N1(1) of NX-OS on the 5000s introduced a feature called *config-sync*. This feature is useful because there are other features that require the configurations of two Nexus switches to be at least partially synchronized. Two examples that have bitten me are cross-connected FEXs (see "Configuring Fabric Extenders (FEXs)" on page 290) and vPCs (see "Virtual Port Channel" on page 294). vPCs in particular suffer from a maddening willingness to break anytime there is a configuration inconsistency between the two Nexus switches to which they are bound.

Imagine two Nexus 5010s, with large blade servers connecting via 10 Gbps trunks. The blade servers require redundancy, so we create a nice vPC between the two Nexus 5Ks. The blade server sees the EtherChannel, and everything works beautifully. The config for the blade chassis trunk might look something like this (replicated on each Nexus):

```
interface port-channel 10
  description BladeServer
  switchport mode trunk
  switchport trunk allowed vlan 10,20,30,40
  vpc 10
```

Everything is working fine, until one day we decide that we need to change the spanning tree port type. It doesn't matter why, other than that if this isn't changed in the next 10 minutes, you'll be fired. You know—a typically well-planned change. The spanning-tree port type edge trunk command is added to NX-5K-1 with some unfortunate results. As soon as we change the first 5K, the vPCs break:

```
NX-5K-1(config-if)# sho vpc
Legend:
                 (*) - local vPC is down, forwarding via vPC peer-link

vPC domain id                   : 1
Peer status                     : peer adjacency formed ok
vPC keep-alive status           : peer is alive
Configuration consistency status: success
Per-vlan consistency status     : success
Type-2 consistency status       : success
vPC role                        : primary
Number of vPCs configured       : 1
Peer Gateway                    : Disabled
Dual-active excluded VLANs      : -
Graceful Consistency Check      : Enabled

vPC Peer-link status
---------------------------------------------------------------------
id   Port   Status Active vlans
--   ----   ------ --------------------------------------------------
1    Po1    up     1

vPC status
----------------------------------------------------------------------------
id     Port         Status Consistency Reason                     Active vlans
------ ------------ ------ ----------- ------------------------- -----------
10     Po10         up     failed      vPC type-1 configuration   -
                                       incompatible - STP
                                       interface port type
                                       inconsistent
```

If that looks bad, it's because it is. The configuration of the vPC no longer matches between the switches, so the Nexus essentially disabled it. Now, in theory, the vPC should break, and one of the links will stay up, allowing traffic to flow. There should be no outage, but I've seen the server guys gripe every time we did this, and in the days before config-sync, that meant no changes outside of scheduled outages—and in this type of environment, there were never scheduled outages.

As soon as we added the command to the other switch, thereby making the configurations match again, the vPC came back online. No matter how quickly we thought we could configure both switches—even pressing the Enter key on two computers at the same moment—it wasn't fast enough, and the vPCs would go through this maddening process.

Config-sync is designed to alleviate this type of problem. In a nutshell, two Nexus switches are paired together over the mgmt0 interface. Configuration commands are loaded into a buffer on one of the switches, and when the `commit` command is executed, the commands are simultaneously entered on both switches. Sounds great, and it is, but there are some drawbacks.

The first thing to remember is that, as of this writing, only commands that have to do with vPCs and FEXs are supported. You cannot sync the configs of your Ethernet interfaces, for example.

The second thing to remember is that though your synced commands will show up in the output of `show run`, they're not really there. To work with config-sync, we must enter a new configuration mode called, surprisingly, `configure sync`:

```
NX-5K-1# configure sync
Enter configuration commands, one per line.  End with CNTL/Z.
NX-5K-1(config-sync)#
```

You might be tempted to think that anything you type here will be replicated to the other switch, but you'd be wrong. First, we haven't told it what the other switch is yet, and second, that would be too simple, and thus no fun.

Switch commands in sync mode are saved within a *switch profile*. You must configure the same switch profile on both switches that will be synced. Here, I've created a switch profile with the clever name GAD:

```
NX-5K-1(config-sync)# switch-profile GAD
Switch-Profile started, Profile ID is 1
NX-5K-1(config-sync-sp)#
```

You can only have one profile, and it must match on the other switch in the sync pair. So let's configure it on the other switch:

```
NX-5K-2# configure sync
Enter configuration commands, one per line.  End with CNTL/Z.
NX-5K-2(config-sync)# switch-profile GAD
Switch-Profile started, Profile ID is 1
NX-5K-2(config-sync-sp)#
```

We still haven't told each switch how to find its partner, so let's do so. First on NX-5K-1:

```
NX-5K-1(config-sync-sp)# sync-peers destination 10.0.0.2
```

And then on NX-5K-2:

```
NX-5K-2(config-sync-sp)# sync-peers destination 10.0.0.1
```

Those IP addresses correspond to the management interfaces on the Nexus 5000s.

Now here it gets a little weird for me. For commands to sync, they cannot exist in the running config. If you want to edit an existing switch config, you can import the running config, or parts thereof, into your switch profile. I recommend only doing this for the interfaces or FEXs for which you will be syncing, because otherwise you'll spend hours trying to figure out why it's not working. There are many commands that are not supported within config-sync and, as of now, the list is not well documented. Keep it simple, and stick to port channels and FEXs.

So I've decided that I'd like to sync port channel 10, which is already configured. Great—all I have to do is import it, and then I can use config-sync. The caveat here is that I cannot import a configuration after I've configured the config-sync peer. The good news is that I should only need to import once, since from that point on, I'll have config-sync managing my relevant interfaces and FEXs, assuming I was smart enough to import everything I needed up front. I'm showing you this specifically because it's wrong, and because it took me days of lab time and calls to Cisco TAC to figure it out.

Let's go ahead and import the configuration for port channel 10. Here, I'm importing on NX-5K-2, but I'll need to do it on both switches anyway:

```
NX-5K-2(config-sync-sp)# import interface po10
NX-5K-2(config-sync-sp-import)#
```

Seems simple enough. Anytime there are changes in the config-sync buffer, we should verify them. If the commands won't verify, they won't sync:

```
NX-5K-1(config-sync-sp-import)# verify
Failed: Verify Failed
```

I hate when that happens. That's not a very helpful message, either. How can we figure out what the problem is? The first step is to see what's in the buffer with the show switch-profile *profile-name* buffer command:

```
NX-5K-1(config-sync-sp-import)# sho switch-profile GAD buffer

switch-profile  : GAD
----------------------------------------------------------
Seq-no  Command
----------------------------------------------------------
1       interface port-channel10
1.1         switchport mode trunk
1.2         vpc 10
1.3         switchport trunk allowed vlan 10, 20, 30, 40
1.4         speed 1000
```

That all looks pretty good, but there's still no indication of why it's failing. Here's the output of the same command from NX-5K-1:

```
NX-5K-1(config-sync-sp-import)# sho switch-profile GAD buffer

switch-profile  : GAD
```

```
------------------------------------------------------------
Seq-no  Command
------------------------------------------------------------
1         interface port-channel10
1.1         switchport mode trunk
1.2         vpc 10
1.3         switchport trunk allowed vlan 10, 20, 30, 40
1.4         speed 1000
```

That looks identical. Just for fun, let's pull one of the lines out. Maybe the speed command isn't supported in config-sync (it is, but let's play). I'll do this with the buffer-delete command, followed by the line number I want to delete. I could also move lines with the buffer-move command. In this case, I want to delete line number 1.4:

```
NX-5K-1(config-sync-sp-import)# buffer-delete 1.4
NX-5K-1(config-sync-sp-import)# verify
Failed: Verify Failed
```

Nuts—it still doesn't verify. To get a better handle on what's going on, use the show switch-profile *profile-name* status command:

```
NX-5K-1(config-sync-sp-import)# sho switch-profile GAD status

switch-profile  : GAD
------------------------------------------------------------

Start-time:   5257 usecs after Mon Jan 17 20:53:21 2011
End-time: 980506 usecs after Mon Jan 17 20:53:21 2011

Profile-Revision: 1
Session-type: Import-Verify
Session-subtype: -
Peer-triggered: No
Profile-status: Verify Failed

Local information:
----------------
Status: Verify Failed

Error(s):

Peer information:
----------------
IP-address: 10.0.0.2
Sync-status: In sync
Status: Verify Failure
Error(s):
Following commands failed mutual-exclusion checks:
interface port-channel10
        switchport mode trunk
interface port-channel10
        vpc 10
interface port-channel10
        switchport trunk allowed vlan 10, 20, 30, 40
```

Here it says that it verified locally, but failed remotely. Let's cut to the chase—this simple configuration won't verify, because it's been imported and we have a peer configured.

 When working with config-sync, if you want to import existing configuration from the running config, you must disable the sync-peer. If you do not, the config will never verify, and you will not be able to commit it.

I'll remove the `sync-peers` command:

```
NX-5K-1(config-sync-sp-import)# no sync-peers dest 10.0.0.2
```

And watch the magic happen:

```
NX-5K-1(config-sync-sp-import)# verify
Verification Successful
```

 I have decided not to comment on this issue at this time, since I have nothing nice to say and my mother warned me to keep my mouth shut in such instances.

There are two verification checks that can fail. A *mutual-exclusion* (mutex) verification checks to make sure that the configuration you've entered in sync mode does not exist in the running config. Both switches are checked unless the peer is down or is not configured, in which case the mutex is done locally. *Merge checks* are done with the switch profile of the other switch to ensure that there are no conflicts. If either check results in a failure, the problem must be fixed manually.

Once we've got our interface configuration verified, we can `commit` it to the switch profile:

```
NX-5K-1(config-sync-sp-import)# commit
Verification successful...
```

After I jump through similar hoops on MX-5K-2, I've got the switches almost ready for syncing. Remember, I need to reestablish those sync-peer destination commands before I can sync between switches. I'll go ahead and do that on both switches. First, switch 1:

```
NX-5K-1(config-sync)# switch-profile GAD
Switch-Profile started, Profile ID is 1
NX-5K-1(config-sync-sp)# sync-peers destination 10.0.0.2
```

And then switch 2:

```
NX-5K-2(config-sync)# switch-profile GAD
Switch-Profile started, Profile ID is 1
NX-5K-2(config-sync-sp)# sync-peers destination 10.0.0.1
```

Now I can do what I came here to do in the first place. Remember the spanning-tree port type problem? I'll configure that, but this time I'll use config-sync. I'll need to be in config-sync mode, and within the switch profile:

```
NX-5K-2(config-sync)# switch-profile GAD
Switch-Profile started, Profile ID is 1
```

Once there, I just need to enter the commands that I'd like to sync. Remember, the commands must be for a vPC-related interface or FEX that has been either imported or input directly into config-sync mode. I only enter this on one of the switches:

```
NX-5K-1(config-sync-sp)# int po 10
NX-5K-1(config-sync-sp-if)# spanning-tree port type edge trunk
```

Now I'll see if I can verify:

```
NX-5K-1(config-sync-sp-if)# verify
Failed: Session Database already locked, Verify/Commit in Progress.
```

If you've been banging on this in a lab and have been dropping/adding the sync-peer like I have, you may see this message. You will also see this message if you telnet to the switch and try to verify or commit while someone else is verifying or committing. Wait a bit, make sure you're the only one making changes, and try again:

```
NX-5K-1(config-sync-sp)# verify
Verification Successful
```

Now that we're all verified, let's commit the change. This will commit it locally, and will also commit the configuration to the remote switch. It can take a few seconds, so don't worry if it seems hung for a bit:

```
NX-5K-1(config-sync-sp)# commit
Verification successful...
Proceeding to apply configuration. This might take a while depending on amount
of configuration in buffer.
Please avoid other configuration changes during this time.

Commit Successful
```

I made the change on NX-5K-1, so let's take a look at the port channel 10 interface on NX-5K-2 and see if my change has propagated. Hopefully, the other switch will have the spanning-tree port type edge trunk command:

```
NX-5K-1(config-sync)# sho run int po 10

!Command: show running-config interface port-channel10
!Time: Mon Jan 17 22:57:20 2011

version 5.0(2)N2(1)

interface port-channel10
  description BladeServer
  switchport mode trunk
  vpc 10
  switchport trunk allowed vlan 10,20,30,40
```

```
spanning-tree port type edge trunk
speed 1000
```

 Holy crap, it worked! That's an actual quote from the first time I saw config-sync work. Hey, you get a little goofy after sitting in a windowless lab for three days.

Config-sync is fun and all, but let's look at the dangers. The configuration you enter is visible in the running config, as we can plainly see from the example above, but it's not really there. The configuration we've entered exists in the config-sync database. You can see what's in this database by using the show running-config switch-profile command:

```
NX-5K-1# sho running-config switch-profile

switch-profile GAD
  sync-peers destination 10.0.0.2

  interface port-channel10
    spanning-tree port type edge trunk
```

Meanwhile, the running config looks normal, with only this line to reveal the dangers lurking beneath:

```
NX-5K-1# sho run | begin switch-profile
switch-profile GAD
  sync-peers destination 10.0.0.2
```

Doesn't look very dangerous, does it? Imagine that you've hired a new junior engineer. Better yet, imagine that you *are* the new junior engineer. Being the young, headstrong networking demigod that you are, you feel that the switch-profile command clearly has no purpose, so you decide to summarily delete it.

 Think this scenario is implausible? I can think of no fewer than five— no, wait—seven instances where junior engineers have come into a shop and decided that they would "clean things up," only to cause catastrophic outages. Don't be that guy:

```
NX-5K-1# conf sync
Enter configuration commands, one per line.  End with CNTL/Z.
NX-5K-1(config-sync)# no switch-profile GAD ?
  all-config    Deletion of profile, local and peer configurations
  local-config  Deletion of profile and local configuration
```

Hmm. That's odd. I'll pick local, because I wouldn't want to break anything:

```
NX-5K-1(config-sync)# no switch-profile GAD local-config
Verification successful...
Proceeding to delete switch-profile. This might take a while depending on
amount of configuration under a switch-profile.
```

```
Please avoid other configuration changes during this time.
Delete Successful
```

Uh oh. Let's take a look at the damage, shall we? First let's look at the port channel 10 interface that we synchronized earlier:

```
NX-5K-1(config-sync)# sho run int po10

interface port-channel10
  description BladeServer
  switchport mode trunk
  vpc 10
  switchport trunk allowed vlan 10,20,30,40
  speed 1000
```

Notice anything missing? That's right—the spanning-tree port type edge trunk command is gone. Since it was only deleted locally, that means the vPC is probably broken now. Sure enough:

```
NX-5K-1(config-sync)# sho vpc
Legend:
                (*) - local vPC is down, forwarding via vPC peer-link

vPC domain id                     : 1
Peer status                       : peer adjacency formed ok
vPC keep-alive status             : peer is alive
Configuration consistency status: success
Per-vlan consistency status       : success
Type-2 consistency status         : success
vPC role                          : primary
Number of vPCs configured         : 1
Peer Gateway                      : Disabled
Dual-active excluded VLANs        : -
Graceful Consistency Check        : Enabled

vPC Peer-link status
---------------------------------------------------------------------
id   Port   Status Active vlans
--   ----   ------ --------------------------------------------------
1    Po1    up     1

vPC status
---------------------------------------------------------------------
id     Port        Status Consistency Reason                  Active vlans
------ ----------- ------ ----------- -------------------------- -----------
10     Po10        up     failed      vPC type-1 configuration   -
                                      incompatible - STP
                                      interface port type
                                      inconsistent
```

Yeah, that's bad, but let's take this opportunity to examine one of the benefits of config-sync. Because we had synced the config to the other switch, and because all of the lines executed through config-sync are stored in a database on the other switch, we can get them all back with ease. All we have to do is configure the switch profile, configure the destination peer, and wait:

```
NX-5K-1# config sync
NX-5K-1(config-sync)# switch-profile GAD
Switch-Profile started, Profile ID is 1
NX-5K-1(config-sync-sp)# sync-peers destination 10.0.0.2
```

After a few seconds, it all comes back. Here we can see the lines in the running config (that aren't actually there):

```
NX-5K-1(config-sync-sp)# sho run int po 10

!Command: show running-config interface port-channel10
!Time: Mon Jan 17 23:05:25 2011

version 5.0(2)N2(1)

interface port-channel10
  description BladeServer
  switchport mode trunk
  vpc 10
  switchport trunk allowed vlan 10,20,30,40
  spanning-tree port type edge trunk
  speed 1000
```

And here we can see the lines back in the local switch's database:

```
NX-5K-1(config-sync-sp)# sho run switch-profile

switch-profile GAD
  sync-peers destination 10.0.0.2

  interface port-channel10
    spanning-tree port type edge trunk
```

There is one more thing to watch out for with config-sync, and that is the fact that once you've configured an interface or FEX using the feature, you may no longer configure it in config term mode:

```
NX-5K-1# conf t
Enter configuration commands, one per line.  End with CNTL/Z.
NX-5K-1(config)# int po 10
NX-5K-1(config-if)# no spanning-tree port type edge trunk

Error: Command is not mutually exclusive
```

Config-sync is a very useful tool. It is a bit cumbersome, though, especially when you're first getting used to it. I strongly recommend that you play with this in a lab setting first, or at least test it out on gear before it goes into production.

Configuration Rollback

One of the cool new features in Nexus is the ability to roll back configs with ease. As you probably know, IOS employs an additive CLI. That means commands are always added on top of what's there. There's no easy way to wipe out the entire config and load another without rebooting. This is especially a pain when you're in a lab environment, since the only way to clear the config is to use the write-erase command, reload, and then somehow enter the new configuration. This is time-consuming and clumsy, to use nice words.

 Rollback is supported on Nexus 5000s using NX-OS version 5.0(2)N1(1) and later.

Nexus allows us to roll back the entire box—VDCs and all—to a previously saved point. I've saved some configuration checkpoints, but before we list them, let's create a new one:

```
NX-7K-2# checkpoint 100526-1 description Before VDC Re-order
..........................Done
```

You can view your saved checkpoints with the `rollback running-config check point ?` exec command. This is not a config-mode command:

```
NX-7K-2# rollback running-config checkpoint ?
  100526-1  Checkpoint name
  GAD       Checkpoint name
  Clean     Checkpoint name
```

You can also get details about each saved checkpoint by using the `show checkpoint summary` command:

```
Annie# sho checkpoint summary
User Checkpoint Summary
--------------------------------------------------------------------------------
1) Clean:
Created by admin
Created at Thu, 01:29:40 20 May 2010
Size is 23,601 bytes
Description: None

2) GAD:
Created by gtac
Created at Thu, 08:27:05 20 May 2010
Size is 23,928 bytes
Description: None

3) 100526-1:
Created by gtac
Created at Wed, 23:55:30 26 May 2010
Size is 23,934 bytes
Description: Before VDC Re-order
```

You can view the contents of a checkpoint with the `show checkpoint` *checkpoint-name* command:

```
NX-7K-2# sho checkpoint GAD
--------------------------------------------------------------------------------
```

```
Name: GAD
!Command: Checkpoint cmd vdc 1

!Time: Thu May 20 01:29:40 2010

version 4.2(4)
poweroff module 1
poweroff module 2
poweroff module 9
power redundancy-mode combined force
feature interface-vlan
username admin password 5 $1$wlVidSSk$dMAUWLJLkkFPH3Dk7dEl7/  role network-admin
ip domain-lookup
ip host Annie 10.1.1.102
hostname Annie
ip access-list copp-system-acl-bgp
  10 permit tcp any gt 1024 any eq bgp
  20 permit tcp any eq bgp any gt 1024
ipv6 access-list copp-system-acl-bgp6
  10 permit tcp any gt 1024 any eq bgp
  20 permit tcp any eq bgp any gt 1024
ip access-list copp-system-acl-cts
[---output truncated---]
```

Take care when playing with rollback, as it will wreak havoc on a running system if you're not careful. Here I'll roll back the system to the GAD checkpoint:

```
NX-7K-2(config)# rollback running-config checkpoint GAD
Note: Applying config parallelly may fail Rollback verification
Collecting Running-Config
Generating Rollback Patch
Executing Rollback Patch
Generating Running-config for verification
Generating Patch for verification
Annie(config)#
```

Seems simple enough. The error message about applying config parallelly (not a real word) is a result of me rolling back the config while in config mode. The system is warning me that I really shouldn't do that. I'm stubborn (read: stupid), so I'm trudging on. Wait a minute, though—the hostname has changed. What else has changed?

```
Annie(config)# sho vdc

vdc_id  vdc_name              state          mac
------  --------              -----          ----------
1       Goober                active         00:26:98:1b:f0:41
```

Goober? What happened to the Annie and Guinness VDCs? They were wiped out when I did the config rollback.

 If you're going to play with configuration rollback and you're going to restore a previous configuration, always make a new checkpoint before you do anything else!

Holy panic attack—I need my VDCs back! Luckily, I made a checkpoint before I started all this. What was the name of that checkpoint again?

```
NX-7K-2# rollback running-config checkpoint ?
  100526-1  Checkpoint name
  GAD       Checkpoint name
  Clean     Checkpoint name
```

Restoring my configuration is as simple as rolling back to that checkpoint:

```
Annie(config)# rollback running-config checkpoint 100526-1
Note: Applying config parallelly may fail Rollback verification
Collecting Running-Config
Generating Rollback Patch
Executing Rollback Patch
Generating Running-config for verification
Generating Patch for verification
NX-7K-2(config)#
```

My hostname is back, but what about my VDCs?

```
NX-7K-2# sho vdc
```

```
vdc_id  vdc_name                    state          mac
------  --------                    -----          ----------
1       NX-7K-2                     active         00:26:98:1b:f0:41
2       Annie                       active         00:26:98:1b:f0:42
3       Guinness                    active         00:26:98:1b:f0:43
```

All present and accounted for.

Configuration rollback is a fabulous tool. I strongly recommend that you create a new checkpoint before making any major change. It might just save your job.

Upgrading NX-OS

You can upgrade a Nexus switch similarly to IOS, but there is a much better way. With NX-OS, the image files are very large. Version 4.2.1 for the 5000 was around 182 MB. Not only are the images large, but you must also install the proper kickstart image along with it. The kickstart images are usually around 20 MB.

Here I'll walk through the steps of upgrading the code on a Nexus 5020 from version 4.1 to 5.0. I use a TFTP server running on my MacBook Pro connected to the 5020 via the mgmt0 interface on the switch. First I'll start with the similar copy tftp: boot flash: statement:

```
NX-5K-1# copy tftp: bootflash:
```

The switch then prompts me for the new filename, which I give as follows:

```
Enter source filename: n5000-uk9-kickstart.5.0.2.N2.1.bin
```

This next prompt trips up people new to Nexus. It's asking for the VRF you want to use. The switch will default to the VRF named *default*, which is incorrect. We need to

---

tell it that we're using the management VRF. Remember, the Nexus likes to keep control and data planes separate, and the mgmt0 interface is a part of the management VRF:

```
Enter vrf (If no input, current vrf 'default' is considered): management
```

From here on, it should seem pretty familiar:

```
Enter hostname for the tftp server: 10.1.1.1

Trying to connect to tftp server......
Connection to Server Established.
```

The switch will then transfer the file. The same process must be completed for the main image file as well. If you're using TFTP as I've done, expect it to take a long time. Of course, you can also use FTP or even SCP directly from Cisco's website if you have an Internet connection to the switch.

Once the transfer is complete, the proper way to upgrade a Nexus is with the install all command. Not only can we install the kickstart and system images at once, but if the system conditions are right, we can do it without interrupting traffic flow. This will also update the BIOS and module images as needed. Let's walk through the process on a Nexus 5020.

The first thing we should do is make sure that our configuration won't be compromised when we upgrade. This nifty command will examine your config and report if anything will break upon upgrade (or downgrade, as the case may be):

```
NX-5K-1# sho incompatibility system n5000-uk9.5.0.2.N2.1.bin
No incompatible configurations
```

If you forget to do this, the system will do it for you during the install process and warn you with the following message:

```
"Running-config contains configuration that is incompatible with the new image
(strict incompatibility).
 Please run 'show incompatibility system <image>' command to find out which feature
needs to be disabled."
```

Now that I'm happy that I won't break the network, I can go ahead and install the images using the install command:

```
NX-5K-1# install all kickstart n5000-uk9-kickstart.5.0.2.N2.1.bin
system n5000-uk9.5.0.2.N2.1.bin

Verifying image bootflash:/n5000-uk9-kickstart.5.0.2.N2.1.bin for boot
variable "kickstart".
[###################] 100% -- SUCCESS

Verifying image bootflash:/n5000-uk9.5.0.2.N2.1.bin for boot variable "system".
[###################] 100% -- SUCCESS

Verifying image type.
[###################] 100% -- SUCCESS

Extracting "system" version from image bootflash:/n5000-uk9.5.0.2.N2.1.bin.
```

```
[####################] 100% -- SUCCESS

Extracting "kickstart" version from image
bootflash:/n5000-uk9-kickstart.5.0.2.N2.1.bin.
[####################] 100% -- SUCCESS

Extracting "bios" version from image bootflash:/n5000-uk9.5.0.2.N2.1.bin.
[####################] 100% -- SUCCESS

Notifying services about system upgrade.
[####################] 100% -- SUCCESS
```

If you cannot do a hitless upgrade, you will get this paragraph (or one similar, depending on the reason:

```
Compatibility check is done:
Module  bootable        Impact  Install-type  Reason
------  --------        --------------  ------------  ------
    1     yes      disruptive         reset  Current running-config is not
supported by new image
```

Luckily, we're in good shape, and got the following instead:

```
Compatibility check is done:
Module  bootable        Impact  Install-type  Reason
------  --------        --------------  ------------  ------
    1     yes  non-disruptive         reset
```

A disruptive upgrade means that the entire switch will reboot, ceasing all network traffic traversing the switch. A nondisruptive, or *hitless*, upgrade will reload the kernel, but packets will continue to flow during the process. This is possible because Nexus separates packet flow from CPU processing, or as the marketing docs say, the data plane is separate from the control plane.

Finally, we get the following chart, which tells us what's about to happen:

```
Images will be upgraded according to following table:
Module       Image      Running-Version             New-Version  Upg-Required
------  ----------  ----------------------  ----------------------  ------------
    1      system           4.2(1)N2(1)             5.0(2)N2(1)           yes
    1    kickstart           4.2(1)N2(1)             5.0(2)N2(1)           yes
    1        bios   v1.2.0(06/19/08)       v1.3.0(09/08/09)           yes
    1    power-seq                  v1.2                    v1.2            no
```

At this point, if your Nexus switch needs to be rebooted (disruptive upgrade), you will get the following message:

```
Switch will be reloaded for disruptive upgrade.
Do you want to continue with the installation (y/n)?  [n]
```

Ours does not, so we get this instead:

```
Do you want to continue with the installation (y/n)?  [n] y
```

We're then treated to a pile of descriptive process updates:

```
Install is in progress, please wait.

Notifying services about the upgrade.
[####################] 100% -- SUCCESS

Setting boot variables.
[####################] 100% -- SUCCESS

Performing configuration copy.
[####################] 100% -- SUCCESS

Module 1: Refreshing compact flash and upgrading bios/loader/bootrom/power-seq.
Warning: please do not remove or power off the module at this time.
Note: Power-seq upgrade needs a power-cycle to take into effect.
On success of power-seq upgrade, SWITCH OFF THE POWER to the system and then,
power it up.
[####################] 100% -- SUCCESS

Upgrade can no longer be aborted, any failure will result in a disruptive upgrade.

Requesting Line Cards to stop communication.
[####################] 100% -- SUCCESS

Requesting Sup Apps to stop communication.
[####################] 100% -- SUCCESS

Freeing memory in the file system.
[####################] 100% -- SUCCESS

Loading images into memory.
[####################] 100% -- SUCCESS

Saving supervisor runtime state.
[####################] 100% -- SUCCESS

Saving mts state.
 writing reset reason 88, <NULL>
[####################] 100% -- SUCCESS

Rebooting the switch to proceed with the upgrade.
```

This looks scary, but it's only informing us that the CPU-based processes are restarting. While we'll be kicked out of the switch, traffic will continue to flow during this process:

```
All telnet and ssh connections will now be terminated.
Starting new kernel
Calling kexec callback
Moving to new kernel
Calling into reboot_code_buffer code
Starting kernel...
Usage: init 0123456SsQqAaBbCcUu
INIT: version 2.85 booting
platform_type cmdline parameter not found. Asssuming Oregon.
I2C - Mezz present
sprom_drv_init_platform: nuova_i2c_register_get_card_index
autoneg unmodified, ignoring
```

```
autoneg unmodified, ignoring
Checking all filesystems..... done.
.
Loading system software
Uncompressing system image: bootflash:/n5000-uk9.5.0.2.N2.1.bin

Loading plugin 0: core_plugin...
Loading plugin 1: eth_plugin...
ethernet switching mode
INIT: Entering runlevel: 3
Exporting directories for NFS kernel daemon...done.
Starting NFS kernel daemon:rpc.nfsd.
rpc.mountddone.

Setting envvar: SYSMGR_SERVICE_NAME to muxif_service
Set envvar SYSMGR_SERVICE_NAME to muxif_service
/isan/bin/muxif_config: argc:2
muxif_init....vacl: ret: 0
Set name-type for VLAN subsystem. Should be visible in /proc/net/vlan/config
Added VLAN with VID == 4042 to IF -:muxif:-
2011 Jan  6 17:49:39 NX-5K-1 %$ VDC-1 %$ %USER-2-SYSTEM_MSG: CLIS: loading cmd
files begin  - clis
2011 Jan  6 17:50:07 NX-5K-1 %$ VDC-1 %$ Jan  6 17:50:07 %KERN-2-SYSTEM_MSG:
Starting kernel... - kernel
2011 Jan  6 17:50:07 NX-5K-1 %$ VDC-1 %$ Jan  6 17:50:07 %KERN-0-SYSTEM_MSG:
platform_type cmdline parameter not found. Asssuming Oregon. - kernel
2011 Jan  6 17:50:07 NX-5K-1 %$ VDC-1 %$ Jan  6 17:50:07 %KERN-0-SYSTEM_MSG:
I2C - Mezz present  - kernel
2011 Jan  6 17:50:07 NX-5K-1 %$ VDC-1 %$ Jan  6 17:50:07 %KERN-0-SYSTEM_MSG:
sprom_drv_init_platform: nuova_i2c_register_get_card_index  - kernel

Continuing with installation process, please wait.
The login will be disabled until the installation is completed.

Performing supervisor state verification.
[####################] 100% -- SUCCESS

Supervisor non-disruptive upgrade successful.
2011 Jan  6 17:50:40 NX-5K-1 %$ VDC-1 %$ %USER-2-SYSTEM_MSG: CLIS: loading cmd
files end  - clis
2011 Jan  6 17:50:40 NX-5K-1 %$ VDC-1 %$ %USER-2-SYSTEM_MSG: CLIS: init begin  - clis

Install has been successful.
NX-5K-1 login:
```

Again, from our viewpoint it looks like the switch rebooted, but this was a hitless upgrade, so only communication to the switch itself—such as SNMP, Telnet, SSH, etc.—was interrupted.

## CHAPTER 19

Catalyst 3750 Features

The Catalyst 3750 switch is the next step in the evolution of the very popular 3550 fixed-configuration switch. The 3550 was the first multilayer switch offered at its price to boast such a vast array of features. It was later succeeded by the 3560. The 3750 is a more powerful switch that introduced, among other things, a true stacking feature, which the 3560 lacks.

There is not enough room to cover all of the capabilities of the 3750 in one chapter, so I've focused on those features that I have found most useful in the field. I've purposely not included all the gory details of each feature discussed. Instead, I've covered what I believe you'll need to know to take advantage of these features.

Not all of the features I'll discuss are specific to the 3750. The commands may be identical on other models, but this chapter specifically includes examples taken from the 3750. As always, Cisco's documentation covers all the features in detail.

Stacking

One of the major shortcomings of the 3550 and 3560 switches is the way they are stacked. *Stacking* refers to linking together multiple switches, usually of the same type, to form a single logical switch with a single management IP address. Once you telnet or SSH to the IP address, you can control the stack as if it were a single device.

The 3550 uses a stacking design that requires modules called *stacking GBICs* to be used in one of the gigabit GBIC slots. This not only limits the stacking backplane speed to 1 Gbps, but also ties up the only gigabit slots on the otherwise 100 Mbps switches for stacking. So, when you stack your switches, you can no longer connect your uplinks at gigabit speeds. The 3560 uses a special SFP interconnect cable. It is available with 10/100/1000 RJ-45 ports, but using the stacking cables still occupies one of the fiber uplink ports.

The 3750 uses a more robust approach, incorporating special stacking cables that connect to the back of the switch chassis. This backplane connection is 32 Gbps (or higher, depending on model) and does not tie up any of the ports on the front of the switch. I won't go into the physical connection of a switch stack, as the Cisco documentation is more than adequate.

On a single 24-port 3750, the interfaces are numbered Gi1/0/1–Gi1/0/23. The interfaces are described as *interface-type stack-member#/module#/port#*. The *interface-type* is usually Gigabit Ethernet on a 3750, though some models support 10 Gb ports. The *stack-member#* is 1 for a standalone switch, and for a stacked switch, reflects the position the switch occupies in the stack. The *module#* on a 3750 is always 0. The *port#* is the physical port number on the switch. Thus, port 14 on the third switch in a stack would be numbered Gi3/0/14.

If you break a stack of 3750s and use them each independently, they may not renumber themselves. For example, here's a switch I pulled from a stack. It used to be switch 2, but now it's a standalone switch. The problem is, it still believes that it is switch 2:

```
IOS-3750#sho switch detail
Switch/Stack Mac Address : dc7b.94dd.2280
                                  H/W   Current
  Switch# Role  Mac Address    Priority Version State
  ----------------------------------------------------
  *2      Master dc7b.94dd.2280    1       0     Ready
```

While this may not seem like a big deal, the annoying part is that all the interfaces are numbered as if this switch was the second switch in a stack:

```
IOS-3750#sho ip int brie
Interface             IP-Address    OK? Method Status                Protocol
Vlan1                 unassigned    YES NVRAM  administratively down down
GigabitEthernet2/0/1  unassigned    YES unset  down                  down
GigabitEthernet2/0/2  unassigned    YES unset  down                  down
GigabitEthernet2/0/3  unassigned    YES unset  down                  down
[-- output truncated --]
```

This is pretty easy to fix, but I need to do it so rarely that I always forget how. All you need to do is issue the switch *switch-number* renumber *new-switch-number* command and reboot. Let's see that in action, because though it's a simple process, it may not work as you'd expect. Since this is switch 2 and I want it to be switch 1, I'll issue the switch 2 renumber 1 command:

```
IOS-3750(config)#switch 2 renumber 1
WARNING: Changing the switch number may result in a
configuration change for that switch.
The interface configuration associated with the old switch
number will remain as a provisioned configuration.
Do you want to continue?[confirm]
Changing Switch Number 2 to Switch Number 1
New Switch Number will be effective after next reboot
```

As it says, I need to reboot, so I write mem and reload. After I do so, my interfaces are properly named. Hooray!

```
IOS-3750#sho ip int brie
Interface          IP-Address    OK? Method Status                    Protocol
Vlan1              unassigned    YES NVRAM  administratively down down
GigabitEthernet1/0/1  unassigned    YES unset  down                      down
GigabitEthernet1/0/2  unassigned    YES unset  down                      down
GigabitEthernet1/0/3  unassigned    YES unset  down                      down
GigabitEthernet1/0/4  unassigned    YES unset  down                      down
[-- output truncated --]
```

But there's a problem. First, the output of show switch detail shows two switches, even though the switch is obviously switch 1:

```
IOS-3750#sho switch detail
Switch/Stack Mac Address : dc7b.94dd.2280
                                        H/W  Current
Switch# Role  Mac Address    Priority Version State
---------------------------------------------------------
*1      Master dc7b.94dd.2280    1      0      Ready
 2      Member 0000.0000.0000    0      0      Provisioned
```

That will make sense as soon as you look at the configuration and realize that the configuration for all your interfaces has disappeared. Well, technically, that isn't accurate. The configuration still exists for those interfaces, but the switch considers switch 2 to be absent, which is why the MAC address is all zeros and the status is "provisioned." You can see the interfaces in the configuration with other show commands:

```
IOS-3750#sho ip int brie | beg 1/0/50
GigabitEthernet1/0/50  unassigned    YES unset  down                      down
GigabitEthernet1/0/51  unassigned    YES unset  down                      down
GigabitEthernet1/0/52  unassigned    YES unset  down                      down
GigabitEthernet2/0/1   unassigned    YES unset  down                      down
GigabitEthernet2/0/2   unassigned    YES unset  down                      down
[-- output truncated --]
```

Just remember—this command will not renumber your interfaces and move the configurations. You'll need to do that yourself.

Interface Ranges

Interface ranges are a very useful addition to IOS. Instead of entering the same commands on multiple interfaces, you can specify a range of interfaces and then enter the commands only once. When you apply commands to an interface range, the parser will replicate the commands on each interface within the range. On a switch with 96 interfaces, this can save hours of time—especially during initial configurations.

Interface ranges are composed of lists of interfaces. You can specify interfaces individually or grouped in concurrent ranges. Individual interfaces are separated by commas, while ranges are shown as the starting and ending interfaces, separated by hyphens. Here, I'm accessing the two interfaces g1/0/10 and g1/0/12:

```
3750(config)#interface range g1/0/10 , g1/0/12
3750(config-if-range)#
```

Once you're in *config-if-range* configuration mode, all commands you enter will be applied to every interface you've included in the specified range.

Here, I'm accessing the range of ports g1/0/10 through (and including) g1/0/12. When specifying a range, for the second value I only need to include the significant value from the interface. That is, I don't need to type g/1/0/10 - g1/0/12, but only g1/0/10 - 12:

```
3750(config)#interface range g1/0/10 - 12
3750(config-if-range)#
```

To reference multiple ranges, separate them with commas. Here, I'm referencing the ranges g1/0/10 through g1/0/12 and g1/0/18 through g1/0/20:

```
3750(config)#interface range g1/0/10 - 12 , g1/0/18 - 20
3750(config-if-range)#
```

Not only can you specify lists of interfaces, but you can save lists of interfaces for future reference. To do this, define the interface range with the define interface-range *macro-name* command. Here, I've created a macro called Servers:

```
3750(config)#define interface-range Servers g1/0/10 , g1/0/12 - 14
3750(config)#
```

 Don't confuse these macros with another feature, called *smartport macros* (covered next). The two features are unrelated. To make matters even more confusing, you can apply a smartport macro to an interface-range macro. For the programmers out there, smartport macros are probably closer to the macros you're used to.

Once you've defined an interface-range macro, you can reference it with the interface range macro *macro-name* command:

```
3750(config)#interface range macro Servers
3750(config-if-range)#
```

Macros

Macros, called *smartport macros* by Cisco, are groups of commands saved with reference names. Macros are useful when you find yourself entering the same group of commands repeatedly. For example, say you're adding a lot of servers. Every time you add a server, you execute the same configuration commands for the switch interface to be used for that server. You could create a macro that would execute all of the commands automatically and then simply reference this macro every time you add a new server to the switch.

You create macros are created with the macro command. There are two types of macros: *global* and *interface*. An interface macro (the default type) is applied to one or more interfaces. To make a macro global, include the global keyword when creating it.

The way macros are created is a little strange, because the commands are not parsed as you enter them. As a result, you can enter invalid commands without causing errors. First, enter the macro name *macroname* command. Because you're not including the global keyword, this will be an interface macro. Then, enter the commands you'd like to include in the macro, one by one. These commands are not checked for syntax. When you're done entering commands, put an at sign (@) on a line by itself.

Here, I've created a macro named SetServerPorts. The commands included are spanning-tree portfast, hhhhhh (an invalid command), and description <[Server]>:

```
3750(config)#macro name SetServerPorts
Enter macro commands one per line. End with the character '@'.
spanning-tree portfast
hhhhhh
description <[ Server ]>
@
3750(config)#
```

 Inserting the description within <[and]> brackets does not accomplish anything special in IOS. This is just something I've done for years to make the descriptions stand out, both in the running config and in the output of show commands, such as show interface.

As you can see, the switch accepted all of the commands without a problem. The macro, including the bogus command, now appears in the running config:

```
!
macro name SetServerPorts
spanning-tree portfast
hhhhhh
description <[ Server ]>
@
!
```

When you apply a macro, the parser gets involved and applies syntax and validity checking to your commands. This is when you'll see errors if you've entered invalid commands. The macro will not terminate on errors, so be sure to watch out for them:

```
3750(config-if)#macro apply SetServerPorts
%Warning: portfast should only be enabled on ports connected to a single
 host. Connecting hubs, concentrators, switches, bridges, etc... to this
 interface  when portfast is enabled, can cause temporary bridging loops.
 Use with CAUTION

%Portfast has been configured on GigabitEthernet1/0/20 but will only
 have effect when the interface is in a non-trunking mode.
hhhhhh
```

```
          ^
% Invalid input detected at '^' marker.

3750(config-if)#
```

Notice that commands that do not generate output show no indication of being completed. This is because a macro is just a group of commands that are run when the macro is invoked. If you'd like more information about what your macro is doing when you run it, you can include the trace keyword. This will add a line indicating when each command in the macro is run:

```
3750(config-if)#macro trace SetServerPorts
Applying command... 'spanning-tree portfast'
%Warning: portfast should only be enabled on ports connected to a single
  host. Connecting hubs, concentrators, switches, bridges, etc... to this
  interface  when portfast is enabled, can cause temporary bridging loops.
  Use with CAUTION

%Portfast has been configured on GigabitEthernet1/0/20 but will only
  have effect when the interface is in a non-trunking mode.
Applying command... 'hhhhhh'
hhhhhh
      ^
% Invalid input detected at '^' marker.
Applying command... 'description <[ Server ]>'
3750(config-if)#
```

When you run a macro, a *macro description* is added to the interface or interfaces to which the macro has been applied. The configuration for the interface is altered to include the command macro description, followed by the name of the macro:

```
interface GigabitEthernet1/0/20
 description <[ Server ]>
 switchport mode access
 macro description SetServerPorts
 storm-control broadcast level bps 1g 900m
 spanning-tree portfast
```

You can add your own macro description with the macro description command, from within the macro, or from the command line:

```
3750(config-if)#macro description [- Macro Description -]

interface GigabitEthernet1/0/20
 description <[ Server ]>
 switchport mode access
 macro description SetServerPorts | [- Macro Description -]
 storm-control broadcast level bps 1g 900m
 spanning-tree portfast
```

As you can see, every time you run a macro or execute the macro description command, the description specified (or the macro name) is appended to the macro description command in the configuration of the interface to which it's applied. Iterations are separated with vertical bars.

An easier way to see where macros have been applied is with the `show parser macro description` command. Here, you can see that I ran the same macro repeatedly on the Gi1/0/20 interface:

```
SW2#sho parser macro description
Interface    Macro Description(s)
-------------------------------------------------------------
Gi1/0/20    SetServerPorts | SetServerPorts | SetServerPorts | [- Macro
Description -]
-------------------------------------------------------------
```

To see all the macros on the switch, use the `show parser macro brief` command:

```
3750#sho parser macro brief
    default global    : cisco-global
    default interface: cisco-desktop
    default interface: cisco-phone
    default interface: cisco-switch
    default interface: cisco-router
    default interface: cisco-wireless
    customizable      : SetServerPorts
```

Six macros are included in IOS by default, as you can see in the preceding output (the six listed default macros). You can use the `show parser macro name` *macroname* to view the details of any of the macros:

```
SW2#sho parser macro name cisco-desktop
Macro name : cisco-desktop
Macro type : default interface
# macro keywords $access_vlan
# Basic interface - Enable data VLAN only
# Recommended value for access vlan should not be 1
switchport access vlan $access_vlan
switchport mode access

# Enable port security limiting port to a single
# MAC address -- that of desktop
switchport port-security
switchport port-security maximum 1

# Ensure port-security age is greater than one minute
# and use inactivity timer
switchport port-security violation restrict
switchport port-security aging time 2
switchport port-security aging type inactivity

# Configure port as an edge network port
spanning-tree portfast
spanning-tree bpduguard enable
```

This macro contains some advanced features, such as variables and comments. See the Cisco documentation for further details on the macro feature.

If you've been wondering how to apply a smartport macro to an interface-range macro, here is your answer (assuming an interface-range macro named Workstations and a smartport macro named SetPortsPortfast):

```
SW2(config)#interface range macro Workstations
SW2(config-if-range)# macro apply SetPortsPortfast
```

Flex Links

Flex links are Layer-2 interfaces manually configured in primary/failover pairs. The Spanning Tree Protocol (STP, discussed in Chapter 8) normally provides primary/failover functionality, but it was designed for the sole purpose of preventing loops. Flex links ensure that there are backup links for primary links. Only one of the links in a flex-link pair will be forwarding traffic at any time.

Flex links are designed for, and should be used only on, switches that do not run spanning tree. Should flex links be configured on a switch running spanning tree, the flex links will not participate in STP.

Flex links are configured on the primary interface by specifying the backup interface with the switchport backup interface command:

```
interface GigabitEthernet1/0/20
 switchport access vlan 10
 switchport backup interface Gi1/0/21
!
interface GigabitEthernet1/0/21
 switchport access vlan 10
```

No configuration is necessary on the backup interface.

Neither of the links can be an interface that is a member of an EtherChannel. An EtherChannel *can* be a flex-link backup for another port channel. A single physical interface can be a backup to an EtherChannel as well. The backup link does not need to be the same type of interface as the primary. For example, a 100 Mbps interface can be a backup for a 1 Gbps interface.

Monitor flex links with the show interface switchport backup command:

```
3750#sho int switchport backup

Switch Backup Interface Pairs:

Active Interface        Backup Interface        State
------------------------------------------------------------------------
GigabitEthernet1/0/20   GigabitEthernet1/0/21   Active Down/Backup Down
```

Storm Control

Storm control prevents broadcast, multicast, and unicast storms from overwhelming a network. Storms can be the result of a number of issues, from bridging loops to virus outbreaks. With storm control, you can limit the amount of storm traffic that can come into a switch port. Outbound traffic is not limited.

With storm control enabled, the switch monitors the packets coming into the configured interface. It determines the amount of unicast, multicast, or broadcast traffic every 200 milliseconds, then compares that amount with a configured threshold. Packets that exceed the threshold are dropped.

This sounds straightforward, but the feature actually works differently from how many people expect. When I first learned of it, I assumed that the preceding description was accurate—that is, that at any given time, traffic of the type I'd configured for monitoring would be allowed to come into the switch until the threshold was met (similar to what is shown in Figure 19-1). The reality, however, is more complicated.

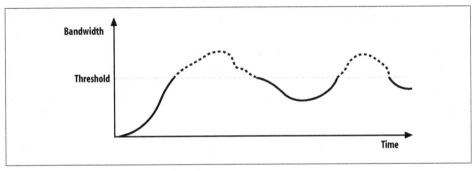

Figure 19-1. Incorrect storm-control model

In reality, the switch monitors the interface, accumulating statistics in 200 ms increments. If, at the end of 200 ms, the threshold has been exceeded, the configured (or default) action is taken for the next 200 ms increment.

Figure 19-2 shows how storm-control actually functions. Traffic is measured in 200 ms increments, shown on the graph as T0, T1, and so on. If the type of traffic being monitored does not surpass the configured threshold during a given interval, the next 200 ms interval is unaffected. In this example, when T1 is reached, the threshold has not been exceeded, so the next interval (ending with T2) is unaffected. However, the configured threshold is exceeded during the T2 interval, so the packets received during the next interval (T3) are dropped. The important distinction here is that during each interval, received packets or bytes are counted from the start of that interval only.

Traffic is still monitored on the interface during the interval in which packets are being dropped (packets are received but not passed on to other interfaces within the switch). If the packet rate again exceeds the configured threshold, packets for the next interval

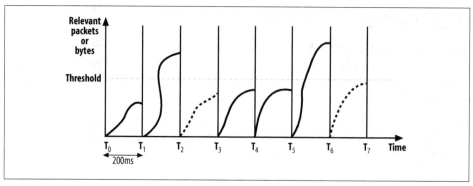

Figure 19-2. Actual storm-control function

are again dropped. If, however, the number of packets received is below the configured threshold, as is the case in the interval T3 in Figure 19-2, packets are allowed for the next interval.

Because packets are not received in a smooth pattern, understanding how storm control works will help you understand why it may cause intermittent communication failures in normal applications on a healthy network. For example, if you were to encounter a virus that sent enough broadcasts to trigger your configured storm control, chances are the port would stop forwarding all broadcasts because the threshold would constantly be exceeded. On the other hand, if you had a healthy network, but your normal broadcast traffic was hovering around the threshold, you would probably end up missing some broadcasts while passing others. Only by closely monitoring your switches can you be sure that you're not impeding normal traffic. If storm control is causing problems in an otherwise healthy network, you probably need to tune the storm-control parameters.

Configure storm control using the `storm-control` interface command:

```
3750(config-if)#storm-control ?
  action     Action to take for storm-control
  broadcast  Broadcast address storm control
  multicast  Multicast address storm control
  unicast    Unicast address storm control
```

 Storm control is available only on physical interfaces. While the commands are available on EtherChannel (port-channel) interfaces, they are ignored if configured.

Storm control has changed over the past few versions of IOS. Originally, the commands to implement this feature were `switchport broadcast`, `switchport multicast`, and `switchport unicast`. Older IOS versions and 3550 switches may still use these commands.

Additionally, the latest releases of IOS allow for some newer features. One such feature provides the ability to send an SNMP trap instead of shutting down the port. You can configure this with the `storm-control action` interface command:

```
3750(config-if)#storm-control action ?
  shutdown  Shutdown this interface if a storm occurs
  trap      Send SNMP trap if a storm occurs
```

Also, originally you could set thresholds only as percentages of the overall available bandwidth. Now, you have the option of configuring percentages, actual bits per second, or packets per second. Each storm-control type (broadcast, multicast, and unicast) can be configured with any of these threshold types:

```
3750(config-if)#storm-control broadcast level ?
  <0.00 - 100.00>  Enter rising threshold
  bps              Enter suppression level in bits per second
  pps              Enter suppression level in packets per second
```

A threshold (any type) of 0 indicates that no traffic of the configured type is allowed. A percentage threshold of 100 indicates that the configured type should never be blocked.

When configuring bits-per-second or packets-per-second thresholds, you can specify a value either alone or with a metric suffix. The suffixes allowed are k, m, and g, for *kilo*, *mega*, and *giga*, respectively:

```
3750(config-if)#storm-control broadcast level bps ?
  <0.0 - 10000000000.0>[k|m|g]  Enter rising threshold
```

Another new feature lets you specify a rising threshold and a falling threshold. When the rising threshold is passed, the configured type of packets will be dropped for the next interval. When the falling threshold is passed, the next interval will be allowed to pass the configured type of packets again.

Figure 19-3 shows an example of the effects of configuring rising and falling thresholds. The rising threshold is set higher than the falling threshold. This has a dramatic impact on the number of intervals dropping packets. When T2 exceeds the rising threshold, T3 drops packets, just as it did when only one threshold was configured. T3 does not exceed the rising threshold, but because it exceeds the falling threshold, packets are again dropped in T4. Once the rising threshold has been exceeded, traffic of the configured type will continue to be dropped as long as the falling threshold is exceeded. It is not until the interval ending at T5 that the level finally falls below the falling threshold, thus allowing packets of the configured type to be forwarded again during the next interval.

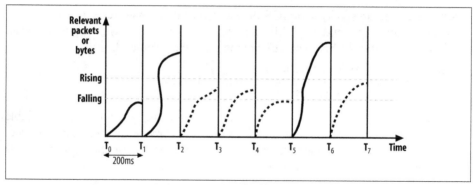

Figure 19-3. Rising and falling thresholds

The falling threshold is configured after the rising threshold. If no value is entered, the falling threshold is the same as the rising threshold:

```
3750(config-if)#storm-control broadcast level bps 100 ?
  <0.0 - 10000000000.0>[k|m|g]  Enter falling threshold
  <cr>
```

Here, I've configured the same thresholds using different forms of the same numbers. Either way is valid:

```
3750(config-if)#storm-control broadcast level bps 100000 90000
3750(config-if)# storm-control broadcast level bps 100m 90k
```

I think the simplest way to configure storm control is with percentages. This is also the only supported method for older versions of IOS:

```
3750(config-if)#storm-control multicast level 40.5 30
```

Be careful when configuring multicast storm control. When multicast packets are suppressed, routing protocols that use multicasts will be affected. Control traffic such as Cisco Discovery Protocol (CDP) packets will not be affected, though, and having CDP functioning while routing protocols are not can create confusion in the field during outages.

To monitor storm control, use the show storm-control command. The output is not extensive, but you probably won't need to know anything else:

```
3750#sho storm-control
Interface  Filter State   Upper        Lower        Current
---------  -------------  -----------  -----------  ----------
Gi1/0/20   Link Down          1g bps     900m bps      0 bps
Gi1/0/21   Link Down         50.00%       40.00%       0.00%
Gi1/0/22   Forwarding         1m pps     500k pps      0 pps
```

The Current column shows the current value for the interface. This should be the first place you look if you think you're dropping packets due to storm control. Remember that this is measured every 200 ms, so you may have to execute the command many times to see whether your traffic is spiking.

You can also run the command for specific storm-control types (broadcast, multicast, or unicast). The output is the same but includes only the type specified:

```
3750#sho storm-control unicast
Interface Filter State  Upper        Lower        Current
--------- ------------  -----------  -----------  ----------
Gi1/0/19  Link Down     50.00%       40.00%       0.00%
```

Finally, you can specify a particular interface by including the interface name:

```
3750#sho storm-control g1/0/20
Interface Filter State  Upper        Lower        Current
--------- ------------  -----------  -----------  ----------
Gi1/0/20  Link Down     1g bps       900m bps     0 bps
```

Port Security

Port security is the means whereby you can prevent network devices from using a port on your switch. At the port level, you can specify certain MAC addresses that you allow or deny the right to use the port. You can do this statically or dynamically. For example, you can tell the switch to allow only the first three stations that connect to use a port, and then deny all the rest. You can also tell the switch that only the device with the specified MAC address can use the switch port, or that any node *except* the one with the specified MAC address can use the switch port.

MAC addresses can be either manually configured or dynamically learned. Addresses that are learned can be saved. Manually configured addresses are called *static secure MAC addresses*; dynamically learned MAC addresses are termed *dynamic secure MAC addresses*; and saved dynamic MAC addresses are called *sticky secure MAC addresses*.

You enable port security with the switchport port-security interface command. This command can be configured only on an interface that has been set as a switchport. Trunks and interfaces that are dynamic (the default) cannot be configured with port security:

```
3750(config-if)#switchport port-security
Command rejected: GigabitEthernet1/0/20 is a dynamic port.
```

If you get this error, you need to configure the port for switchport mode access before you can continue:

```
3750(config-if)#switchport mode access
3750(config-if)# switchport port-security
```

You cannot configure port security on a port that is configured as a SPAN destination:

```
3750(config-if)#switchport port-security
Command rejected: GigabitEthernet1/0/20 is a SPAN destination.
```

Once you've enabled port security, you can configure your options:

```
3750(config-if)#switchport port-security ?
  aging       Port-security aging commands
  mac-address Secure mac address
  maximum     Max secure addresses
  violation   Security violation mode
  <cr>
```

Here, I'm configuring the interface to accept packets only from the MAC address 1234.5678.9012:

```
3750(config-if)#switchport port-security mac-address 1234.5678.9012
```

You might think you can run the same command to add another MAC address to the permitted device list, but when you do this, you'll get an error:

```
3750(config-if)#switchport port-security mac-address 1234.5678.1111
Total secure mac-addresses on interface GigabitEthernet1/0/20 has reached maximum
limit.
```

By default, only one MAC address can be entered. To increase the limit, use the switch port port-security maximum command. Once you've increased the maximum, you can add another MAC address:

```
3750(config-if)#switchport port-security maximum 2
3750(config-if)# switchport port-security mac-address 1234.5678.1111
```

 If you try to set the maximum to a number less than the number of secure MAC addresses already configured, you will get an error and the command will be ignored.

You can also enter the switchport port-security maximum command without specifying any MAC addresses. By doing this, you will allow a finite number of MAC addresses to use the port. For example, with a maximum of three, the first three learned MAC addresses will be allowed, while all others will be denied.

If you need the switch to discover MAC addresses and save them, use the sticky keyword. Sticky addresses are added to the running configuration:

```
3750(config-if)#switchport port-security mac-address sticky
```

 For the addresses to be retained, you must copy the running configuration to the startup configuration (or use the command write memory) before a reboot.

When you have a port configured with port security, and a packet arrives that is outside the scope of your configured limits, it's considered a violation. There are three actions the switch can perform in the event of a port-security violation:

Protect

When a violation occurs, the switch will drop any packets from MAC addresses that do not meet the configured requirements. No notification is given of this occurrence.

Restrict

When a violation occurs, the switch will drop any packets from MAC addresses that do not meet the configured requirements. An SNMP trap is generated, the log is appended, and the violation counter is incremented.

Shutdown

When a violation occurs, the switch will put the port into the *error-disabled* state. This action stops all traffic from entering and exiting the port. This action is the default behavior for port-security-enabled ports. To recover from this condition, reset the interface using either the shutdown and no shutdown commands, or the errdisable recovery cause psecure-violation command.

To change the port-security violation behavior, use the switchport port-security violation command:

```
3750(config-if)#switchport port-security violation ?
  protect   Security violation protect mode
  restrict  Security violation restrict mode
  shutdown  Security violation shutdown mode
```

Secure MAC addresses can be aged out based on either an absolute time or the time for which the addresses have been inactive. The latter option can be useful in dynamic environments, where there may be many devices connecting and disconnecting repeatedly. Say you have a room full of consultants. The first three to connect in the morning get to use the network, and the rest are out of luck. If one of the original three leaves early, you may want to free up his spot to allow someone else to use the network. Alternately, you may wish to ensure that only the first three consultants to connect can use the network for the entire day, regardless of what time they leave. This would penalize the rest of the consultants for being late. I've worked with execs who would love to be able to implement such a design to get consultants to come in early! To configure the type of aging employed, use the switchport port-security aging type command:

```
3750(config-if)#switchport port-security aging type ?
  absolute    Absolute aging (default)
  inactivity  Aging based on inactivity time period
```

The aging time is set in minutes with the time keyword:

```
3750(config-if)#switchport port-security aging time ?
  <1-1440>  Aging time in minutes. Enter a value between 1 and 1440
3750(config-if)# switchport port-security aging time 30
```

To see the status of port security, use the show port-security command. This command shows a nice summary of all ports on which port security is enabled, how many addresses are configured for them, how many have been discovered, and how many violations have occurred:

```
3750#sho port-security
Secure Port  MaxSecureAddr  CurrentAddr  SecurityViolation  Security Action
              (Count)        (Count)        (Count)
---------------------------------------------------------------------------
   Gi1/0/20          2            2                0          Shutdown
---------------------------------------------------------------------------
Total Addresses in System (excluding one mac per port)    : 1
Max Addresses limit in System (excluding one mac per port) : 6272
```

For more detail, use the show port-security interface command for a specific interface:

```
3750#sho port-security interface g1/0/20
Port Security                : Enabled
Port Status                  : Secure-down
Violation Mode               : Shutdown
Aging Time                   : 0 mins
Aging Type                   : Absolute
SecureStatic Address Aging   : Disabled
Maximum MAC Addresses        : 2
Total MAC Addresses          : 2
Configured MAC Addresses     : 2
Sticky MAC Addresses         : 0
Last Source Address:Vlan     : 0000.0000.0000:0
Security Violation Count     : 0
```

SPAN

Switched Port Analyzer (SPAN) allows traffic to be replicated to a port from a specified source. The traffic to be replicated can be from physical ports, virtual ports, or VLANs, but you cannot mix source types within a single SPAN session. The most common reason for SPAN to be employed is for packet capture. If you need to capture the traffic on VLAN 10, for example, you can't just plug a sniffer on a port in that VLAN, as the switch will only forward packets destined for the sniffer. However, enabling SPAN with the VLAN as the source, and the sniffer's port as the destination, will cause all traffic on the VLAN to be sent to the sniffer. SPAN is also commonly deployed when Intrusion Detection Systems (IDSs) are added to a network. IDS devices need to read all packets in one or more VLANs, and SPAN can get the packets to the IDS devices.

Using *Remote Switched Port Analyzer* (RSPAN), you can even send packets to another switch. RSPAN can be useful in data centers where a packet-capture device is permanently installed on one of many interconnected switches. With RSPAN, you can capture packets on switches other than the one with the sniffer attached (RSPAN configuration details are provided later in this section).

Configure SPAN with the monitor command. You can have more than one SPAN session, each identified with a session number:

```
3750(config)#monitor session 1 ?
  destination   SPAN destination interface or VLAN
  filter        SPAN filter
  source        SPAN source interface, VLAN
```

Having more than one SPAN session is useful when you have an IDS device on your network and you need to do a packet capture. The IDS device will require one SPAN session, while the packet capture will use another.

For a monitor session to be active, you must configure a source port or VLAN, and a destination port. Usually, I configure the destination port first because the packet-capture device is already attached. If you have port security set, you must disable it before you can use the port as a SPAN destination:

```
3750(config)#monitor session 1 destination interface g1/0/20
%Secure port can not be dst span port
```

Sessions can be numbered from 1 to 66, but you can only have two sessions configured at any given time on a 3750 switch. Here, I have two sessions configured (session 1 and session 10):

```
monitor session 1 source vlan 20 rx
monitor session 1 destination interface Gi1/0/10
!
monitor session 10 source vlan 10 rx
monitor session 10 destination interface Gi1/0/20
```

If you try to configure more than two SPAN sessions on a 3750 switch, you will get the following error:

```
3750(config)#monitor session 20 source int g1/0/10
% Platform can support a maximum of 2 source sessions
```

In this example, I've configured two VLANs to be the sources, both of which will have their packets reflected to interface Gi1/0/20:

```
monitor session 10 source vlan 20 rx
monitor session 10 source vlan 10
monitor session 10 destination interface Gi1/0/20
```

You can also monitor one or more interfaces. Multiple interfaces can be configured separately or on a single configuration line:

```
3750(config)#monitor session 11 source interface g1/0/11
3750(config)# monitor session 11 source interface g1/0/12
```

Entering the two preceding commands adds the following line to the configuration:

```
monitor session 11 source interface Gi1/0/11 - 12
```

The sources in a monitor session can be configured as either receive (rx), transmit (tx), or both. The default is both:

```
3750(config)#monitor session 1 source int g1/0/12 ?
  ,      Specify another range of interfaces
  -      Specify a range of interfaces
  both   Monitor received and transmitted traffic
```

```
rx    Monitor received traffic only
tx    Monitor transmitted traffic only
<cr>
```

Interfaces should usually be monitored in both directions, while VLANs should be monitored in only one direction.

 When capturing VLAN information, be careful if you see double packets. Remember that each packet will come into the VLAN on one port and exit on another. Using the default behavior of both when monitoring a VLAN will result in almost every packet being duplicated in your packet capture.

I can't tell you how many times I've been convinced that I'd stumbled onto some rogue device duplicating packets on the network, only to realize that I'd once again burned myself by monitoring a VLAN in both directions. The safest thing to do when monitoring VLANs is to monitor them only in the rx direction. Because the default is both, I like to think that I'm a victim of some inside joke at Cisco, as opposed to being a complete idiot.

To see which SPAN sessions are configured or active, use the show monitor command:

```
3750#sho monitor
Session 1
---------
Type              : Local Session
Source VLANs      :
    RX Only       : 20
Destination Ports : Gi1/0/22
    Encapsulation : Native
          Ingress : Disabled


Session 10
----------
Type              : Local Session
Source VLANs      :
    TX Only       : 20
    Both          : 10
Destination Ports : Gi1/0/20
    Encapsulation : Native
          Ingress : Disabled
```

To disable monitoring on a specific SPAN, you can delete the entire monitor session, remove all the sources, or remove the destination. All monitor commands can be negated:

```
3750(config)#no monitor session 11 source interface Gi1/0/11 - 12
```

You can remove all local SPAN, all RSPAN, or all SPAN sessions as a group by adding the local, remote, or all keywords:

```
3750(config)#no monitor session ?
  <1-66>  SPAN session number
  all     Remove all SPAN sessions in the box
  local   Remove Local SPAN sessions in the box
  remote  Remove Remote SPAN sessions in the box
```

You should always remove your SPAN sessions when you no longer need them. SPAN takes up system resources, and there can be confusion if someone plugs a device into the SPAN destination port.

RSPAN works the same way that SPAN does, with the exception that the destination interface is on another switch. The switches must be connected with an *RSPAN VLAN*. To create an RSPAN VLAN, configure a VLAN and add the remote-span command:

```
3750-1(config)#vlan 777
3750-1(config-vlan)# remote-span
```

If you're running VTP, you may not need to create the VLAN, but you will still need to configure it for RSPAN. In either case, the steps are the same. On the source switch, specify the destination as the RSPAN VLAN:

```
3750-1(config)#monitor session 11 destination remote vlan 777
```

You can enter a destination VLAN that has not been configured as an RSPAN VLAN, but, alas, it won't work.

Now, on the destination switch, configure the same VLAN as an RSPAN VLAN. Once you've done that, configure a monitor session to receive the RSPAN being sent from the source switch:

```
3750-2(config)#vlan 777
3750-2(config-vlan)# remote-span
3750-2(config)# monitor session 11 source remote vlan 777
```

There is no requirement for the monitor session numbers to be the same, but as I like to say, *simple is good*. If you have not configured the source switch to be the RSPAN source, you will get an error:

```
3750-2(config)#monitor session 11 source remote vlan 777
% Cannot add RSPAN VLAN as source for SPAN session 11 as it is not a RSPAN
Destination session
```

 When using RSPAN, don't use an existing trunk for your RSPAN VLAN. SPAN can create a large amount of traffic. When you're monitoring VLANs composed of multiple gigabit interfaces, the SPAN traffic can easily overwhelm a single gigabit RSPAN link. Whenever possible, set up a dedicated RSPAN VLAN link between the switches.

Voice VLAN

Voice VLAN allows the 3750 to configure a Cisco IP phone that's connected to the switch. The switch uses CDP to transfer information to the phone configuration regarding Class of Service (CoS) and the VLANs to be used for voice and data traffic. By default, this feature is disabled, which results in the phone not receiving configuration instructions from the switch. In this case, the phone will send voice and data over the default VLAN (VLAN 0 on the phone).

Cisco IP phones such as the model 7960 have built-in three-port switches. Port 1 on the built-in switch is the connection to the upstream switch (the 3750 we'll configure here). Port 2 is the internal connection to the phone itself. Port 3 is the external port, which usually connects to the user's PC.

By using the `switchport voice vlan` interface command, you can have the switch configure an IP phone that is connected to the interface being configured. You can specify a VLAN for voice calls originating from the phone, or you can have the switch tell the phone to use the regular data VLAN for voice calls (with or without setting CoS values):

```
3750(config-if)#switchport voice vlan ?
  <1-4094>  Vlan for voice traffic
  dot1p     Priority tagged on PVID
  none      Don't tell telephone about voice vlan
  untagged  Untagged on PVID
```

To set the VLAN, specify a VLAN number. The `dot1p` option tells the phone to set CoS bits in voice packets while using the data VLAN. The `untagged` option tells the phone to use the data VLAN without setting any CoS values.

To take advantage of voice VLANs, you need to tell the switch to trust the CoS values being sent by the phone. You do this with the `mls qos trust cos` interface command.

 The `mls qos trust cos` interface command will not take effect unless you globally enable quality of service (QoS) with the `mls qos` command.

Here is a sample interface configured to use VLAN 100 for data and VLAN 10 for voice. The switch will instruct the IP phone to use VLAN 10 for voice, and will trust the CoS values as set by the phone:

```
interface GigabitEthernet1/0/20
 switchport access vlan 100
 switchport voice vlan 10
 mls qos trust cos
```

Another nice aspect of the voice VLAN feature is that you can have the IP phone alter or trust any CoS values set by the device plugged into its external switch port (usually the user's PC). You configure this feature with the `switchport priority extend` interface

---

command. The options are cos and trust. When using the cos option, you may set the CoS field to whatever CoS value you like:

```
3750(config-if)#switchport priority extend ?
  cos    Override 802.1p priority of devices on appliance
  trust  Trust 802.1p priorities of devices on appliance
```

 I prefer to trust the PC's CoS values, as different software on the PC may have different values. For example, the user may wish to run a softphone application on the PC. Overriding the CoS values set by this software might lead to voice quality issues for the softphone.

Here, I've configured an interface to use VLAN 10 for voice while trusting the CoS values set by the user's PC and phone:

```
interface GigabitEthernet1/0/20
 switchport access vlan 100
 switchport voice vlan 10
 switchport priority extend trust
 mls qos trust cos
```

To see which VLAN is configured as the voice VLAN, use the show interface *interface-name* switchport command:

```
3750#sho int g1/0/20 switchport
Name: Gi1/0/20
Switchport: Enabled
Administrative Mode: static access
Operational Mode: down
Administrative Trunking Encapsulation: negotiate
Negotiation of Trunking: Off
Access Mode VLAN: 1 (default)
Trunking Native Mode VLAN: 1 (default)
Administrative Native VLAN tagging: enabled
Voice VLAN: 10 (Inactive)
Administrative private-vlan host-association: none
Administrative private-vlan mapping: none
Administrative private-vlan trunk native VLAN: none
Administrative private-vlan trunk Native VLAN tagging: enabled
Administrative private-vlan trunk encapsulation: dot1q
Administrative private-vlan trunk normal VLANs: none
Administrative private-vlan trunk private VLANs: none
Operational private-vlan: none
Trunking VLANs Enabled: ALL
Pruning VLANs Enabled: 2-1001
Capture Mode Disabled
Capture VLANs Allowed: ALL

Protected: false
Unknown unicast blocked: disabled
Unknown multicast blocked: disabled
Appliance trust: none
```

QoS

QoS is covered in detail in Chapter 31, and it's a topic that could easily fill an entire book. In this section, I will focus on some 3750-specific QoS features.

One of the useful features of the 3750 is support for *AutoQoS*, which makes certain assumptions about your network and configures the switch accordingly. While I'm not a fan of letting network devices assume anything, in this case, the assumptions are accurate most of the time. I have had no qualms about enabling AutoQoS on the 3750s I've installed in VoIP networks with hundreds of phones supported by Cisco Call Manager. The reason I'm OK with this is that Cisco's assumptions are built around the idea that you're using Call Manager, Cisco IP phones, and low-latency queuing on your network. Chances are, if you need QoS enabled on your switches, it's because you're implementing VoIP.

You can enable AutoQoS on an interface with the `auto qos voip` command:

```
3750(config-if)#auto qos voip ?
  cisco-phone       Trust the QoS marking of Cisco IP Phone
  cisco-softphone   Trust the QoS marking of Cisco IP SoftPhone
  trust             Trust the DSCP/CoS marking
```

There are three options: `cisco-phone`, `cisco-softphone`, and `trust`. The first two are used for interfaces connected to either hard- or softphones. When configured with these options, the QoS values received in packets will be trusted only if they're sourced from Cisco IP phones. The `trust` option enables QoS while trusting all packets' QoS values.

If you'd like to see what AutoQoS does, enable AutoQoS debugging with the `debug auto qos` command before you configure the interface:

```
3750#debug auto qos
3750# conf t
Enter configuration commands, one per line. End with CNTL/Z.
3750(config)# int g1/0/20
3750(config-if)# auto qos voip cisco-phone
3750(config-if)#
3d04h: mls qos map cos-dscp 0 8 16 26 32 46 48 56
3d04h: mls qos
3d04h: no mls qos srr-queue input cos-map
3d04h: no mls qos srr-queue output cos-map
3d04h: mls qos srr-queue input cos-map queue 1 threshold 3  0
3d04h: mls qos srr-queue input cos-map queue 1 threshold 2  1
3d04h: mls qos srr-queue input cos-map queue 2 threshold 1  2
3d04h: mls qos srr-queue input cos-map queue 2 threshold 2  4 6 7
3d04h: mls qos srr-queue input cos-map queue 2 threshold 3  3 5
3d04h: mls qos srr-queue output cos-map queue 1 threshold 3  5
3d04h: mls qos srr-queue output cos-map queue 2 threshold 3  3 6 7
3d04h: mls qos srr-queue output cos-map queue 3 threshold 3  2 4
3d04h: mls qos srr-queue output cos-map queue 4 threshold 2  1
3d04h: mls qos srr-queue output cos-map queue 4 threshold 3  0
[-Lots of text removed-]
```

The interface's configuration will look as follows:

```
interface GigabitEthernet1/0/20
 srr-queue bandwidth share 10 10 60 20
 srr-queue bandwidth shape  10  0  0  0
 queue-set 2
 auto qos voip cisco-phone
```

The changes to the switch's global configuration are a bit more extensive. Thankfully, AutoQoS does all the work for you:

```
mls qos map cos-dscp 0 8 16 26 32 46 48 56
mls qos srr-queue input bandwidth 90 10
mls qos srr-queue input threshold 1 8 16
mls qos srr-queue input threshold 2 34 66
mls qos srr-queue input buffers 67 33
mls qos srr-queue input cos-map queue 1 threshold 2  1
mls qos srr-queue input cos-map queue 1 threshold 3  0
mls qos srr-queue input cos-map queue 2 threshold 1  2
mls qos srr-queue input cos-map queue 2 threshold 2  4 6 7
mls qos srr-queue input cos-map queue 2 threshold 3  3 5
mls qos srr-queue input dscp-map queue 1 threshold 2  9 10 11 12 13 14 15
mls qos srr-queue input dscp-map queue 1 threshold 3  0 1 2 3 4 5 6 7
mls qos srr-queue input dscp-map queue 1 threshold 3  32
mls qos srr-queue input dscp-map queue 2 threshold 1  16 17 18 19 20 21 22 23
mls qos srr-queue input dscp-map queue 2 threshold 2  33 34 35 36 37 38 39 48
mls qos srr-queue input dscp-map queue 2 threshold 2  49 50 51 52 53 54 55 56
mls qos srr-queue input dscp-map queue 2 threshold 2  57 58 59 60 61 62 63
mls qos srr-queue input dscp-map queue 2 threshold 3  24 25 26 27 28 29 30 31
mls qos srr-queue input dscp-map queue 2 threshold 3  40 41 42 43 44 45 46 47
mls qos srr-queue output cos-map queue 1 threshold 3  5
mls qos srr-queue output cos-map queue 2 threshold 3  3 6 7
mls qos srr-queue output cos-map queue 3 threshold 3  2 4
mls qos srr-queue output cos-map queue 4 threshold 2  1
mls qos srr-queue output cos-map queue 4 threshold 3  0
mls qos srr-queue output dscp-map queue 1 threshold 3  40 41 42 43 44 45 46 47
mls qos srr-queue output dscp-map queue 2 threshold 3  24 25 26 27 28 29 30 31
mls qos srr-queue output dscp-map queue 2 threshold 3  48 49 50 51 52 53 54 55
mls qos srr-queue output dscp-map queue 2 threshold 3  56 57 58 59 60 61 62 63
mls qos srr-queue output dscp-map queue 3 threshold 3  16 17 18 19 20 21 22 23
mls qos srr-queue output dscp-map queue 3 threshold 3  32 33 34 35 36 37 38 39
mls qos srr-queue output dscp-map queue 4 threshold 1  8
mls qos srr-queue output dscp-map queue 4 threshold 2  9 10 11 12 13 14 15
mls qos srr-queue output dscp-map queue 4 threshold 3  0 1 2 3 4 5 6 7
mls qos queue-set output 1 threshold 1 138 138 92 138
mls qos queue-set output 1 threshold 2 138 138 92 400
mls qos queue-set output 1 threshold 3 36 77 100 318
mls qos queue-set output 1 threshold 4 20 50 67 400
mls qos queue-set output 2 threshold 1 149 149 100 149
mls qos queue-set output 2 threshold 2 118 118 100 235
mls qos queue-set output 2 threshold 3 41 68 100 272
mls qos queue-set output 2 threshold 4 42 72 100 242
mls qos queue-set output 1 buffers 10 10 26 54
mls qos queue-set output 2 buffers 16 6 17 61
mls qos
```

 If you're looking at someone else's router and you see all this stuff, resist the urge to think he's some sort of QoS genius. Chances are he just ran AutoQoS!

To see which interfaces have AutoQoS enabled, use the `show auto qos` global command:

```
3750#show auto qos
GigabitEthernet1/0/20
auto qos voip cisco-phone
```

To disable AutoQoS on an interface, use the `no auto qos voip` interface command. To disable AutoQoS globally, use the `no mls qos` command. Beware that this disables *all* QoS on the switch.

## CHAPTER 20

Telecom Nomenclature

The telecom world is a bit different from the data world, as endless telecom engineers will no doubt tell you. For example, a lot of the telecom infrastructure that exists today is the way it is because of standards that have been in place for upward of 100 years. Samuel Morse invented the telegraph in 1835. Alexander Graham Bell invented the telephone in 1876. In 1961, Bell Labs invented the T1 as a way to aggregate links between the central offices (COs) of the phone companies. It took almost 100 years to get from the first telephone to the invention of the T1.

In contrast, consider the data world: the ARPANET was started in 1969, Robert Metcalfe and David Boggs built the first Ethernet in 1973, and Vint Cerf and Bob Kahn published the original TCP/IP standard in 1974. Hayes introduced the first modem in 1977 (300 bps, baby!), and 3Com shipped the first 10 Mbps Ethernet card in 1981. The first commercial router was sold in 1983.

Let's think about that for a moment—the first commercial router was sold in 1983. Ask anyone around you if she can remember a time when there weren't phones.

The telecom world is built on standards that work and have worked for a very long time. How often does your phone stop working? The telecom infrastructure is so reliable that we expect reliable phone service even more than we expect reliable electrical service (cellular service is a whole different ball game, and does not apply to this discussion).

As with any technology, the engineers in the trenches (and their bosses behind the desks) like to sling the lingo. If you've spent your professional life around data equipment, telecom lingo might seem pretty foreign to you. To help bridge the gap between the data and telecom worlds, I've put together a list of terms that you might hear when dealing with telecom technologies.

Most telecom words and phrases have standard meanings defined in Federal Standard 1037C, titled "Telecommunications: Glossary of Telecommunication Terms." These definitions are often very simple and don't go into a lot of detail. The terms I'll cover here are the ones most often encountered in the life of a network administrator or engineer. If you need to know how to refer to circuit noise voltage measured with a psophometer that includes a CCIF weighting network, Federal Standard 1037C is a good place to look. Another excellent source that should be on the bookshelf of anyone in the telecom world is *Newton's Telecom Dictionary*, by Harry Newton (CMP Books).

The meanings of many widely used telecom terms have changed over time. Through regulation over the years, the functions of entities like IXCs and LECs (both defined in the following glossary) have changed. I will cover the original intended meanings in this text.

Telecom Glossary

ACD

ACD stands for Automatic Call Distributor. An ACD is usually found in a call center, where calls may come in from anywhere and need to be directed to the next available operator or queued until one is available.

Add/drop

The term add/drop is used in telecom to describe the capability of peeling off channels from a circuit and routing them elsewhere. An add/drop CSU/DSU can separate ranges of channels to discrete data ports, thus allowing a T1 to be split into two partial T1s. One can be used for voice and the other for data, or both can be used for either function and routed differently. You can make an add/drop device function like a non-add/drop device simply by assigning all of the channels to a single data port. However, add/drop adds cost to devices, so it should only be considered if the extra functionality is required.

Analog and digital

Would you like to have some fun? Ask someone in the computer field to define the word "analog." You might be surprised at some of the answers you receive.

Analog means, literally, *the same*. When one item is analogous to another, it is the same as the other item. In the telecom and data worlds, "analog" refers to a signal that is continuous in amplitude and time.

An analog signal is not composed of discrete values: any small fluctuation of the signal is important. Radio waves are analog, as are power waves. Sound is also analog. When you speak, you create waves of air that hit people's eardrums. The sound waves are an analog signal.

Digital refers to a signal that has discrete values. If you analyze a sound wave, and then assign a value to each sample of the wave at specific time intervals, you will create a digital representation of the analog wave.

Because digital involves discrete values and analog does not, converting analog signals to digital will always result in loss of information.

While increasing the rate at which the signal is sampled (among other things) can increase the quality of the final reproduction, technically, the signal cannot be reproduced exactly the same way.

Bandwidth

Bandwidth is one of those terms that is thrown around a lot by people who don't really know what it means. A range of frequencies is called a *band*. The width of the band is referred to as *bandwidth*. For those of you who aren't old enough to remember FM radios with analog dials, I've drawn one in Figure 20-1.

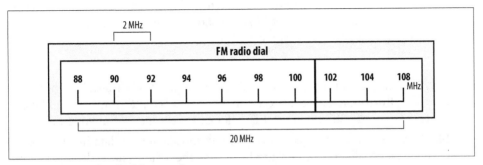

Figure 20-1. True bandwidth example

An FM radio dial displays the range of frequencies allocated by the US government for stereo radio broadcasts. The exact range of frequencies is 87.9 MHz to 107.9 MHz. The bandwidth of this range is 20 MHz. The frequency range of 90 MHz to 92 MHz inclusive has a bandwidth of 2 MHz.

What we're really referring to when we talk about bandwidth on digital links is the *throughput*. On a digital link, the number of possible state transitions per second is how we measure throughput.

Figure 20-2 shows how the number of state transitions can vary based on link speed. The signal on the left shows six possible state changes in the time depicted. Two concurrent equal values do not require a change of state, so only five state changes occurred, though six were possible. The signal on the right shows 19 possible state changes in the same amount of time (with 17 occurring). The signal on the right can be described as having more bits per second (bps) of throughput.

When someone says that a DS3 has more bandwidth than a T1, what he's really saying is that the DS3 will deliver higher throughput in that it is capable of 45 million bits per second (Mbps), as opposed to the T1's paltry (by comparison) 1.54 Mbps. In common usage, the terms bandwidth and throughput are

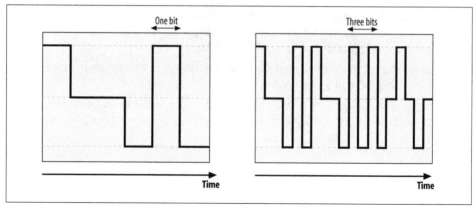

Figure 20-2. Digital state changes over time

interchangeable. A more accurate term to refer to links might be *data rate*, as a DS3 can deliver the same number of bits in a shorter amount of time than a T1. In simplest terms, a DS3 is faster than a T1.

BERT

> BERT stands for Bit Error Rate Test. You'll often hear "BERT test," although this is technically redundant because the T in BERT stands for test. Still, saying, "We're going to run some BERTs on the T1" will make everyone look at you funny.

> BERT tests are disruptive tests run on a link to validate the data integrity of the circuit. You usually run a BERT test by putting the remote end of the link in loopback and sending out a special pattern of ones and zeros. How the data is returned from the far-end loopback can help you determine whether certain types of problems exist in the line. Some of the common types of BERT tests you may hear mentioned include QRSS (Quasi-Random Signal Source), 3 in 24, 1:7 or 1 in 8, Min/Max, All Ones, and All Zeros. Each of these patterns stresses a link in a certain predictable way. A device used to perform BERT testing on a T1 is called a *T-Berd*.

Central Office (CO)

> The central office is where phone lines from residences or businesses physically terminate. COs have the necessary switching equipment to route calls locally or to another carrier as needed. When you make a call that is destined for somewhere other than your premises, the CO is the first stop.

> With technology like T1, the copper connection from your location will probably terminate at a CO, where it may be aggregated into part of a larger SONET system.

Channel bank

> A channel bank is a device that separates a T1 into 24 individual analog phone lines, and vice versa. Today, private branch exchanges (PBXs) usually take care of partitioning T1s into analog lines, thereby eliminating the need for a channel bank.

CSU/DSU

CSU stands for Channel Service Unit, and DSU stands for Data Service Unit. A CSU is responsible for interfacing with the WAN link, and a DSU is responsible for interfacing with data equipment such as routers. A CSU/DSU combines these functions into a single unit. Typically, an RJ-45-terminated cable will connect the *demarc* to the CSU/DSU, and a V.35 cable will connect the CSU/DSU to a router. The CSU/DSU is usually configurable to support all the common T1 signaling and framing options. Modern Cisco routers support WAN interface cards (WICs) that have integrated CSU/DSUs.

CPE

CPE is short for customer premises equipment (i.e., equipment that is located at the customer's premises). Examples include a PBX, phones, routers, and even cable modems. Traditionally, the term was used to describe equipment owned by a telephone service provider that resided at customer premises, but it has evolved to include equipment owned by anyone.

 Telecom engineers often shorten the word *premises* to *prem* when speaking.

DACCS

DACCS (pronounced *dacks*) stands for Digital Access Cross-Connect System. You may also see this as DAX, or DACS®, which is a registered trademark of AT&T.

A DACCS is a device that allows changes to the way voice channels are connected between trunks, through the use of software.

Figure 20-3 shows a logical representation of a DACCS in use. T1-A connects to the DACCS, and has 18 of its 24 channels in use. Those channels need to be routed to three different places. With the DACCS, we can link the first six channels (1–6) of T1-A to channels 1–6 on T1-B, the next six channels (7–12) of T1-A to channels 1–6 on T1-C, and the next six channels (13–18) of T1-A to channels 1–6 on T1-D. The channels do not have to be grouped, and may be mapped between links in any way, provided there are available channels on the links.

Demarc

Demarc (pronounced *dee-mark*) is a slang abbreviation for demarcation point. The demarcation point is the point where the telecom provider's responsibilities end and yours begin. Demarcs are often telecom closets or similar locations that can be secured to allow access for the telecom provider's engineers. If you need your T1s to terminate somewhere in your building other than the demarc, the telecom provider may install an *extended demark* to accommodate your needs.

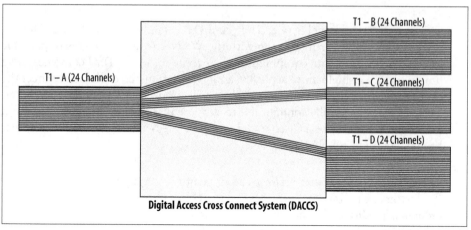

T1 – B (24 Channels)

T1 – A (24 Channels)

T1 – C (24 Channels)

T1 – D (24 Channels)

Digital Access Cross Connect System (DACCS)

Figure 20-3. DACCS

Digital signal hierarchy

The digital signal (DS) hierarchy describes the signaling rates of trunk links. These links are the physical links on which logical T-carriers are placed.

The carrier numbers grow larger as the number of multiplexed DS0s increases. DS0 is the smallest designation, and is the rate required for a single phone line. The hierarchy is shown in Table 20-1.

Table 20-1. Digital signal hierarchy

Designator	Carrier	Transmission rate	Voice channels
DS0	N/A	64 Kbps	1
DS1	T1	1.544 Mbps	24
DS2	T2	6.312 Mbps	96
DS3	T3	44.736 Mbps	672
DS4	T4	274.176 Mbps	4,032

E-carrier

The E-carrier hierarchy is similar to the US T-carrier hierarchy (described later), though the speeds are slightly different, as is the signaling. The European E-carrier hierarchy is shown in Table 20-2.

Table 20-2. European E-carrier hierarchy

Designator	Transmission rate	Voice channels
E0	64 Kbps	1
E1	2.048 Mbps	30
E2	8.448 Mbps	120
E3	34.368 Mbps	480

Designator	Transmission rate	Voice channels
E4	139.268 Mbps	1,920
E5	565.148 Mbps	7,680

ISDN

ISDN stands for Integrated Services Digital Network. ISDN is a form of digital transmission for voice and data. Unlike normal POTS lines or channelized T1 services—which use the voice path for signaling—ISDN uses a separate channel called the *data channel* for signaling, so the remaining channels (called *bearer channels*) can be used exclusively for voice. Because a separate channel is used for signaling, greater functionality is possible with ISDN.

The bearer channels are sometimes referred to as *B-channels*, and the data channel is sometimes referred to as the *D-channel*.

One of the benefits of ISDN is that it can support normal voice calls and ISDN digital calls. In the early 1990s, ISDN was considered to be the next big thing: it was supposed to revolutionize phone and data service. There are two types of ISDN links:

BRI

BRI is short for Basic Rate Interface. A BRI is an ISDN link composed of two 64 Kbps bearer channels and one 16 Kbps data channel.

PRI

PRI is short for Primary Rate Interface. A PRI is an ISDN T1 link composed of twenty-three 64 Kbps bearer channels, and one 64 Kbps data channel. PRIs are used a lot for connecting PBX systems, or at ISPs for dial-up lines.

While PRI circuits are used today for voice, BRI circuits, which were commonly used for data, have been widely replaced by cheaper alternatives such as DSL.

IXC

IXC stands for interexchange carrier. An IXC is a telephone company that supplies connections between local exchanges provided by local exchange carriers. Connecting between LATAs may involve IXCs.

J-carrier

The J-carrier hierarchy is much closer to the US T-carrier hierarchy (in terms of speed) than the European hierarchy, though the values change as the rates get faster. While J-carrier circuits may still be seen, most of the circuits I've worked on in Japan have actually been E1s or T1s.

The Japanese J-carrier hierarchy is shown in Table 20-3.

Table 20-3. Japanese J-carrier hierarchy

Designator	Transmission rate	Voice channels
J0	64 Kbps	1

Designator	Transmission rate	Voice channels
J1	1.544 Mbps	24
J2	6.312 Mbps	96
J3	32.064 Mbps	480
J4	397.200 Mbps	5,760

LATA

LATA (pronounced *lat-ah*) is short for local access and transport area. LATAs are geographically defined areas in which a telecom provider can provide local service. The Regional Bell Operating Companies (RBOCs), for example, were usually not permitted to provide services between LATAs (interLATA), but could provide services within a LATA (intraLATA).

LATAs come into play when point-to-point circuits like T1s are ordered. When a T1 starts and ends within the same LATA, the cost for the circuit is usually much lower than if the circuit starts in one LATA and ends in another. This is because IXCs must be involved to connect LATAs. To further complicate things, LATAs are geographic, and often do not mirror political boundaries such as county or state lines.

Latency

Latency is the term used to describe the amount of time it takes for data to be processed or moved. Latency has nothing to do with the throughput, bandwidth, or speed of a link. Latency has to do with distance, the speed of light, and the amount of time it takes for hardware to process data.

Latency on networks links is a combination of propagation delay and processing delay:

Propagation delay

Figure 20-4 shows three locations: New York, Cleveland, and Los Angeles. There are two links: one T1 between New York and Cleveland, and one T1 between New York and Los Angeles. Both links have the same speed (1.54 Mbps), but it takes longer for packets to get from New York to Los Angeles than it does for them to get from New York to Cleveland.

The discrepancy occurs because Los Angeles is a lot farther away from New York than Cleveland is. This form of latency is called *propagation delay*. Propagation delay is, to a large degree, a function of physics, and as such cannot be fixed, improved, or otherwise changed (no matter what your boss may want). To oversimplify, the speed at which electrons can transmit electrical impulses is limited. The speed at which photons can move in fiber is similarly limited.

Processing delay

Another form of latency is called processing delay, which is the time it takes for a device to process information. In contrast to propagation delay, which

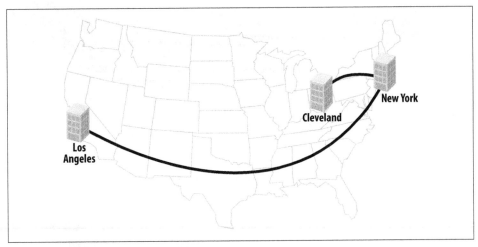

Figure 20-4. Different propagation delays

usually cannot be changed, processing delay is a function of the speed of the equipment in use.

Figure 20-5 shows two links: the top link is a direct connection between two modern Cisco 7609 routers, involving only the latest hardware; the bottom link connects the same two routers, but with a very old Cisco 2501 router in the middle.

Although the total distance between the two Cisco 7609s is the same from point to point in both cases, adding a Cisco 2501 in the middle of the second link increases the processing delay dramatically.

Another example of increasing processing delay occurs when you're using multilink PPP. Taking three 1.54 Mbps T1s and bonding them to form one logical 4.5 Mbps link sounds great, and it can be, but the added processing delay when you do so can be enormous.

As an example, notice the delay parameter in this show interface output from a T1 interface:

```
Router#sho int s0/1 | inc DLY
  MTU 1500 bytes, BW 1544 Kbit, DLY 20000 usec,
```

Compare that with the output from the same show interface command for a multilink interface:

```
Router#sho int multilink 1 | inc DLY
  MTU 1500 bytes, BW 100000 Kbit, DLY 100000 usec,
```

The delay for a multilink interface is five times that of a serial T1 interface.

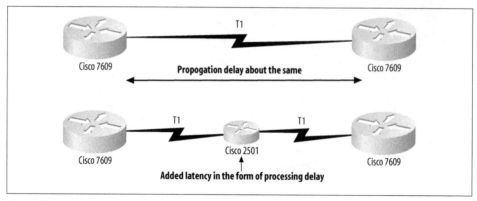

Figure 20-5. Processing delay

 The bandwidth and delay values shown for an interface are representative of the actual bandwidth and delay, provided they have not been modified. The bandwidth and delay values are configurable in IOS. The default values reflect the propagation delay well enough to illustrate the impact of multilink PPP.

LEC

LEC (pronounced *leck*) is short for local exchange carrier. A LEC is a phone company that provides local service, as opposed to an IXC, which interconnects LECs to provide long-distance service. Most of the largest LECs are RBOCs.

Local loop

The local loop (also referred to as the *last mile*) is the copper handoff for a circuit from the telecom facility to your facility. While a T1 may be converted and multiplexed into a larger circuit like a DS3 or SONET circuit, the last mile is usually copper.

Multiplexing

Multiplexing is the act of taking multiple signals and sharing them on a single signal. The act of converting twenty-four 64 Kbps channels into a single T1 is an example of multiplexing.

PBX

PBX is the abbreviation for private branch exchange. A PBX is essentially a phone system as most people know it; it offers a phone network to an entity such as an enterprise. Some of the main features of a PBX are the ability for many phones to share a limited number of public phone lines, and the ability to number individual extensions with, typically, three- or four-digit extension numbers. PBX systems have traditionally been large hardware devices with cryptic control systems and proprietary hardware. VoIP is often controlled by software versions of PBXs. Examples include Cisco's Unified Communications Manager (formerly Call Manager) and the open source product Asterisk.

POTS

POTS is short for the clever phrase *plain-old telephone service*. A POTS line is one into which you can plug in a normal analog phone or fax machine. Most home phone lines are POTS lines.

RBOC

RBOC (pronounced *are-bock*) is short for Regional Bell Operating Company.

In 1875, Alexander Graham Bell (and two others who agreed to finance his inventions) started the Bell Telephone Company. Bell Telephone later became known as the Bell System as it acquired controlling interests in other companies such as Western Electric. In 1885, American Telephone and Telegraph (AT&T) was incorporated to build and operate the US's original long-distance telephone network. In 1899, AT&T acquired Bell. For almost 100 years, AT&T and its Bell System operated as a legally sanctioned, though regulated, monopoly, building what was by all accounts the best telephone system in the world.

In 1984, however, a judge—citing antitrust monopoly issues—broke up AT&T's Bell System, known as Ma Bell. The resulting seven companies were known as the RBOCs, or, more commonly, the *Baby Bells*. AT&T remained a long-distance carrier, or IXC, during the divestiture. However, the Telecommunications Deregulation Act of 1996 allowed RBOCs (also called LECs) and long-distance companies to sell local, long-distance, and international services, making these lines very fuzzy.

Each of the original seven companies was given a region in which it was allowed to do business. The regions are shown in Figure 20-6.

Most of the original RBOCs are now part of SBC (formerly Southwestern Bell), which also acquired AT&T, bringing the entire dizzying affair one step closer to a monopoly again. Here's what's become of the seven original RBOCs:

Bell Atlantic
Bell Atlantic merged with NYNEX in 1996 to become Verizon.

Southwestern Bell
Southwestern Bell changed its name to SBC in 1995. SBC acquired PacBell in 1996, and has subsequently acquired Ameritech, Southern New England Telecommunications, and AT&T. SBC adopted the name AT&T following the acquisition of that company.

NYNEX
NYNEX merged with Bell Atlantic in 1996 to become Verizon.

Pacific Bell (PacBell)
PacBell was acquired by SBC in 1996.

BellSouth
BellSouth has been acquired by SBC/AT&T.

Ameritech
Ameritech was acquired by SBC in 1998.

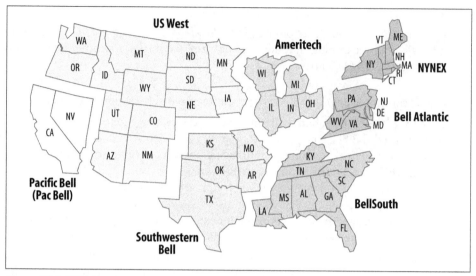

Figure 20-6. RBOC regions

US West

US West was acquired by Qwest Communications in 2000.

Smart jack

A smart jack is a device that terminates a digital circuit. It is considered "smart" because the phone company can control it remotely. Smart jacks also offer test points for equipment such as BERT testers. T1s are usually terminated at smart jacks. Larger installations have racks of smart jacks called smart jack racks.

SONET

SONET (pronounced like *bonnet*) is short for synchronous optical network. SONET is an ANSI standard for fiber-optic transmission systems. The equivalent European standard is called the synchronous digital hierarchy (SDH).

SONET is strictly optical, as its name suggests, and is very fast. SONET defines certain *optical carrier* levels, as shown in Table 20-4.

Table 20-4. Optical carrier levels

Optical carrier level	Line rate	Payload rate
OC1	51 Mbps	50 Mbps
OC3	155 Mbps	150 Mbps
OC12	622 Mbps	601 Mbps
OC48	2,488 Mbps	2,405 Mbps
OC192	9,953 Mbps	9,621 Mbps
OC768	39,813 Mbps	38,486 Mbps

T-carrier

T-carrier is the generic name for digital multiplexed carrier systems. The letter T stands for *trunk*, as these links were originally designed to trunk multiple phone lines between central offices. The T-carrier hierarchy is used in the US and Canada. Europe uses a similar scale called the European E-carrier hierarchy, and Japan uses a system titled the Japanese J-carrier hierarchy. The North American T-carrier hierarchy is shown in Table 20-5.

Table 20-5. North American T-carrier hierarchy

Designator	Transmission rate	Voice channels
T1	1.544 Mbps	24
T1C	3.152 Mbps	48
T2	6.312 Mbps	96
T3	44.736 Mbps	672
T4	274.176 Mbps	4,032

T-Berd

A T-Berd is a *T1 Bit Error Rate Detector*. The generic term is used for any device that will perform BERT tests on a T1. If you have a T1 that's misbehaving, the provider will probably send out an engineer with a T-Berd to perform invasive testing.

TDM

TDM stands for time-division multiplexing. A T1 link is a TDM link because its 24 channels are divided into time slots. A T1 link is a serial link, so one bit is sent at a time. The channels are cycled through at a high rate of speed, with each channel being dedicated to a slice of time.

## CHAPTER 21

T1

In the 1950s, the only method for connecting phone lines was with a pair of copper wires. For each phone line entering a building, there had to be a pair of copper wires. Wire congestion was a huge problem in central offices (COs) and under streets in metropolitan areas at the time. Imagine the CO of a large city, where tens of thousands of phone lines terminated, each requiring a pair of wires. These COs also needed to communicate with each other, which required even more wiring.

In 1961, Bell Labs in New Jersey invented the T1 as a means for digitally trunking multiple voice channels together between locations. The T1 delivered a 12:1 factor of relief from the congestion, as it could replace 24 two-wire phone lines with 4 wires. Back then, this was a major shift in thinking. Remember that at the time, digital technology was practically nonexistent. The first T1 went into service in 1962, linking Illinois Bell's Dearborn office in Chicago with Skokie, Illinois. Today, you would be hard-pressed to find a company that doesn't deploy multiple T1s.

In this chapter, I will go into detail about the design, function, and troubleshooting of T1s. While I usually try to simplify complex engineering topics, I feel that it's important to understand the principles of T1 operation. We live in a connected world, and much of that world is connected with T1s. Knowing how they work can save you countless hours of troubleshooting time when they break.

Understanding T1 Duplex

A full-duplex link can send and receive data at the same time. As anyone who's ever had a fight with his or her significant other over the phone can attest, both parties on a call can talk (or scream) at the same time. This is a full-duplex conversation. If only one person could talk at a time, the conversation would be half duplex. Using walkie-talkies, where you have to push a button to talk, is an example of a half-duplex conversation. While the button is depressed, typically, you cannot hear the person with whom you are speaking (although some high-end walkie-talkies can use one frequency for transmitting and another for receiving, thereby allowing full-duplex conversations).

T1s are full-duplex links. Voice T1s transmit and receive audio simultaneously, and data is sent and received simultaneously on WAN-link T1s. Still, I've met many people in the field who don't understand T1 duplex. This may have a lot to do with the way data flow across WAN links is commonly reported.

Figure 21-1 shows a T1 Internet link's bandwidth utilization as monitored by the Multi Router Traffic Grapher (MRTG). The numbers on the bottom of the graph are the hours of the day, with 0 being midnight, 2 being 2:00 a.m., and so on. The solid graph, which looks like an Arizona landscape, is the inbound data flow. The solid line in the foreground is the outbound data flow. This is a typical usage pattern for a heavily used T1 Internet link. The bulk of the data comes from the Internet. The requests to get that data are very small. At about 8:45 a.m., there's a spike in the outbound traffic—perhaps a large email message was sent at that time.

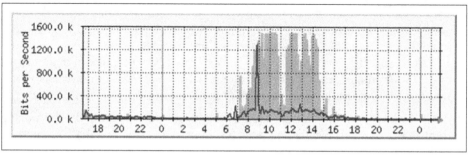

Figure 21-1. MRTG usage graph

The graph does not make obvious the duplex mode of the link. One could easily assume that the T1 was half duplex and switched from transmit to receive very quickly. If someone who didn't understand the technology only saw graphs like this one, he might conclude that a T1 can only send data in one direction at a time. You'd be surprised how common this misconception is.

Types of T1

Terminology is important when discussing any technology, and T1 is no exception. Many terms are commonly misused, even by people who have been in the industry for years. The terms *T1* and *DS1* are often thrown around interchangeably, although doing this can get you into trouble if you're talking with people who have a long history in telecommunications. You may also hear some people refer to a Primary Rate Interface (PRI) as a "digital T1," which is not strictly correct. All T1s are digital. The difference with PRI is that it uses digital signaling within the data channel as opposed to analog signaling within each voice channel. Even with an "analog" T1, each channel's audio must be converted to digital to be sent over the T1.

You may encounter a lot of conflicting information when learning about T1s. While there is a lot to learn, there are only a few basic types of T1s:

Channelized T1

A channelized T1 is a voice circuit that has 24 voice channels. Each channel contains its own signaling information, which is inserted into the data stream of the digitized voice. This is called *in-band signaling*. Provided the circuit has been provisioned correctly (see the upcoming sections "Encoding" on page 357 and "Framing" on page 359), with the use of an Add/Drop CSU/DSU, a channelized T1 can be used for data.

PRI

A PRI is a voice circuit that has 24 channels, one of which is dedicated to signaling. Thus, the number of available voice channels is 23. The voice channels are called *bearer channels*, and the signaling channel is called the *data channel*. This type of signaling is called *out-of-band signaling*.

Clear-channel T1

A clear-channel T1 is not framed in any way. There are no channels and no organization of the bits flowing through the link. Clear-channel T1s are a rarity, as most data links are provisioned with Extended Super Frame framing.

You can think of in-band signaling like pushing buttons on your phone during a call. The tones are in the voice path of the call. Tones are sent at the beginning of the call (sometimes you can hear them) from switch to switch (when CAS signaling is used) to provide signals for the switch to make decisions about how to route your call. There are also signals within the channel that are not audible. These signals are bits embedded in the voice data; they are called the *ABCD* bits and are used to report on the status of phones (e.g., off-hook/on-hook).

Out-of-band signaling, in contrast, works similarly to the FTP protocol: a channel is used to set up the call, and then a separate channel is chosen and used to deliver the payload (in this case, a voice call).

Encoding

Encoding refers to the method by which electrical signals are generated and decoded. There are two types of encoding in use on T1 links today: *Alternate Mark Inversion* (AMI), and *Binary Eight Zero Substitution* (B8ZS). Generally, AMI is used for voice circuits, and B8ZS is used for data. B8ZS can be used for voice, but AMI should not be used for data, for reasons noted next.

AMI

AMI is a method of encoding that inverts alternate marks. In T1 signaling, there are two possible states: mark and space. Simply put, a *mark* is a one and a *space* is a zero. On a T1, a space is 0V, and a mark is either +5V or –5V. AMI encodes the signal such that the polarity of each mark is the opposite of the one preceding it.

This allows for some interesting error-detection techniques. For example, Figure 21-2 shows two ones occurring in a row with the same polarity. This is considered an error (a *bipolar violation*, or BPV). If all ones were positive voltage, a voltage spike could be misconstrued as a valid one. As an added benefit, when the alternating marks are flipped, the average voltage of the physical line will always be 0V, making the physical T1 wires safe to handle.

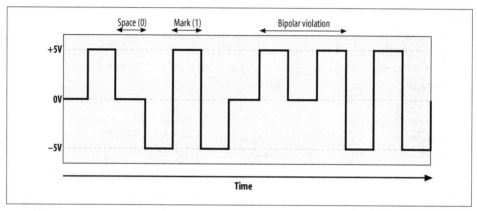

Figure 21-2. T1 AMI signaling

T1s are asynchronous links, meaning that only one side of the link provides clocking. The far side of the link must rely on the signal itself to determine where bits begin and end. Because the duration of a mark is known, synchronization can be achieved simply by receiving marks. When AMI is used, a long progression of spaces will result in a loss of synchronization. With no marks in the signal, the receiving end will eventually lose track of where bits begin and end.

The risk of an *all zeros* signal exists, so AMI sets every eighth bit to a 1, regardless of its original value. This ensures that there are enough signal transitions in the line (i.e., that the *ones density* of the signal stream is sufficiently high to ensure synchronization). As few as 16 zeros in a row can cause the remote end to lose synchronization.

Voice signals can easily absorb having every eighth bit set to 1. The human ear can't hear the difference if a single bit in the stream is changed. Data signals, though, cannot tolerate having any bits changed. If one bit is different in a TCP packet, the Cyclic Redundancy Check (CRC) will fail, and the packet will be resent (CRCs are not performed for UDP packets). Because of this limitation, AMI is not an acceptable encoding technique for use on data T1s.

B8ZS

B8ZS encoding was introduced to resolve the shortcomings of AMI. The idea behind B8ZS is that if eight zeros in a row are detected in a signal, those eight zeros are converted to a pattern including intentional BPVs. When the remote side sees this well-known pattern, it converts it back to all zeros.

Figure 21-3 shows how long strings of zeros are converted on the wire. The top signal consists of a one, followed by nine zeros, and then three ones. B8ZS takes the first eight zeros and converts them to a pattern including two BPVs. You would not see this pattern on a normal, healthy circuit. When the remote side receives the pattern, it converts it back into eight zeros. This technique allows data streams to contain as many consecutive zeros as necessary while maintaining ones density.

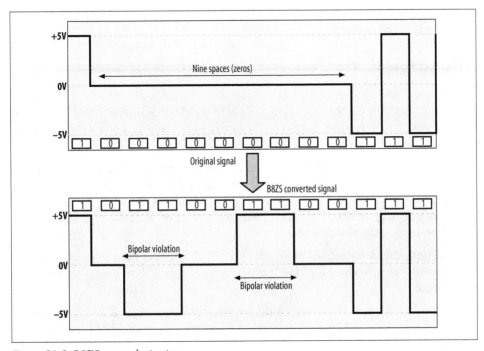

Figure 21-3. B8ZS zero substitution

Framing

Phone audio is sampled 8,000 times per second (i.e., at 8 kHz). Each sample is converted to an eight-bit value, with one of the bits used for signaling.

Figure 21-4 shows a single-channel sample, with one bit used for signaling. This is called *in-band signaling*.

When a T1 is configured as a PRI, all eight bits in each channel may be used for data, because one entire channel is reserved for signaling (as opposed to pulling one bit from each channel). This reduces the number of usable channels from 24 to 23, and is called *out-of-band signaling*.

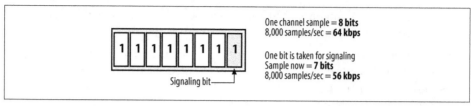

One channel sample = **8 bits**
8,000 samples/sec = **64 kbps**

One bit is taken for signaling
Sample now = **7 bits**
8,000 samples/sec = **56 kbps**

Signaling bit

Figure 21-4. One-channel sample

T1s use time-division multiplexing, which means that each channel is actually a group of serial binary values. The channels are relayed in order, but the receiving equipment needs to know when the first channel starts and when the last channel ends. The way this is done is called *framing*.

D4/Superframe

In standard voice framing, called *D4* or *superframe*, each eight-bit sample is relayed from each channel in order. One sample from channel one is relayed, then one sample from channel two is relayed, and so on, until all 24 channels have relayed one sample. The process then repeats.

For the receiving end to understand which channel is which, framing bits are added after each of the 24 channels has relayed one sample. Because each sample is 8 bits, and there are 24 channels, one iteration for all channels is 192 bits. With the addition of the framing bit, we have 193 bits. These 193-bit chunks are called *frames*. Each set of 12 frames is called a superframe.

The framing scheme is outlined in Figure 21-5. The T1 devices keep track of the frames by inserting the pattern 110111001000 into the framing bits over the span of a superframe.

When the framing bits do not match the expected sequence, the receiving equipment logs a *framing error*. When a T1 device reaches a certain threshold of framing errors, an alarm is triggered.

You may have seen a discrepancy in the reported speed of T1 links in your reading. Some texts will show a T1 to be 1.544 Mbps, while others may show 1.536 Mbps. This discrepancy is a result of the framing bits. Because the framing bits are used by the T1 hardware and are not available as data, they are considered overhead. Thus, 1.536 Mbps is the usable speed of a T1 when framing bits are taken into consideration.

Extended Super Frame

The D4/superframe standard was developed for voice and is not practical for data transmissions. One of the reasons D4 is unsuitable for data is the lack of error detection. To provide error-detection capabilities and to better use the framing bits, a newer framing standard called *Extended Super Frame* (ESF) was developed.

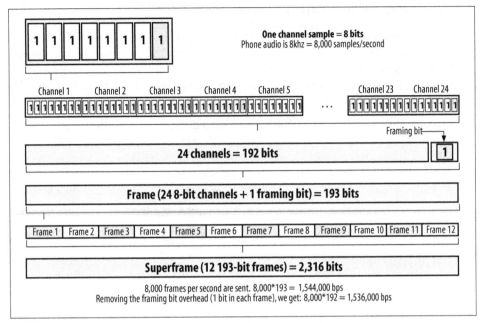

Figure 21-5. DS1 framing

ESF works under the same general principles as D4/superframe, except that an ESF is composed of 24 frames instead of 12. The framing bit of each frame is used to much greater effect in ESF than it is in D4. Instead of simply filling the framing bits with an expected pattern throughout the course of the superframe, ESF uses these bits as follows:

Frames 4, 8, 12, 16, 20, and 24 (every fourth frame)
These frames' framing bits are filled with the pattern 001011.

Frames 1, 3, 5, 7, 9, 11, 13, 15, 17, 19, 21, and 23 (every odd-numbered frame)
These frames' framing bits are used for a new, 4,000 bps virtual data channel. This channel is used for out-of-band communications between networking devices on the link.

Frames 2, 6, 10, 14, 18, and 22 (the remaining even-numbered frames)
These frames' framing bits are used to store a six-bit CRC value for each superframe.

Anytime a T1 circuit is ordered for use as a WAN link for data networks, the T1 should be provisioned with B8ZS encoding and ESF framing.

Performance Monitoring

CSU/DSUs convey the status of T1 links by reporting the incidence of a set of standard events. Some of the events and the alarms they trigger can be a bit confusing to data professionals who have not been exposed to the technology before. To make matters worse, most CSU/DSUs report errors using not words, but rather the well-known (to telecom engineers) abbreviations of the errors.

Different vendors often define performance events differently, and finding detailed descriptions of these events can be challenging. The event types are outlined in RFC 1232, titled "Definitions of Managed Objects for the DS1 Interface Type." This RFC defines the standards for use in SNMP traps and does not describe the electrical properties of these alarms. These descriptions are not binding for manufacturers, and thus may not be accurate for any given device. Still, the RFC does contain some of the clearest descriptions of these events.

Loss of Signal

Loss of signal (LOS) is the state where no electrical pulses have been detected in a preset amount of time. RFC 1232 describes LOS as:

> This event is declared upon observing 175 +/– 75 contiguous pulse positions with no pulses of either positive or negative polarity (also called keep alive).

In English, that means the line is dead. There are no alarms, no signals, etc. LOS is equivalent to having no cable in the T1 jack.

Out of Frame

An out-of-frame (OOF) condition (also called loss of frame, or LOF) indicates that a certain number of frames have been received with framing bits in error. In this case, the data cannot be trusted, because the synchronization between the two sides of the T1 is invalid. Excessive OOF errors will trigger a red alarm. An OOF condition is described in RFC 1232 as follows:

> An Out of Frame event is declared when the receiver detects two or more framing-bit errors within a 3 millisecond period, or two or more errors out of five or less consecutive framing-bits. At this time, the framer enters the Out of Frame State, and starts searching for a correct framing pattern. The Out of Frame state ends when reframe occurs.

Bipolar Violation

A BVP occurs when two mark signals (ones) occur in sequence with the same polarity. DS1 signaling specifies that each mark must be the opposite polarity of the one preceding it. When two marks occur with the same polarity (when not part of a B8ZS substitution), this is considered an error. Excessive BPVs will put the station into alarm. BPVs are described in RFC 1232 as follows:

> A Bipolar Violation, for B8ZS-coded signals, is the occurrence of a received bipolar violation that is not part of a zero-substitution code. It also includes other error patterns such as: eight or more consecutive zeros and incorrect parity.

CRC6

CRC6 is the Cyclic Redundancy Check (six-bit) mechanism for error checking in ESF. This error is a result of ESF reporting data integrity problems. CRC6 events are not described in RFC 1232.

Errored Seconds

Errored Second is a counter showing the number of seconds in a 15-minute interval during which errors have occurred. This counter provides a quick way to see whether there are problems. It also offers an indication of how "dirty" a T1 might be. If the number is high, there is a consistent problem. If it is low, there is probably a short-term (possibly repetitive) or intermittent problem. Errored Seconds are usually incremented when one or more errors occur in the span of one second. Errored Seconds are described in RFC 1232 as follows:

> An Errored Second is a second with one or more Code Violation Error Events OR one or more Out of Frame events. In D4 and G.704 section 2.1.3.2 (e.g., G.704 which does not implement the CRC), the presence of Bipolar Violations also triggers an Errored Second.

Extreme Errored Seconds

Sometimes also referred to as Severely Errored Seconds, this counter increments when a certain threshold of errors is passed in the span of one second. The threshold and the errors to be counted depend on the hardware implementation. You should not see Extreme Errored Seconds on a healthy link, but some Errored Seconds may occur on a normal circuit. Severely Errored Second events are described in RFC 1232 as follows:

> A Severely Errored Second is a second with 320 or more Code Violation Error Events OR one or more Out of Frame events.

Alarms

Alarms are serious conditions that require attention. Excessive errors can trigger alarms, as can hardware problems and signal disruption. The alarms are coded as colors. As with performance events, different vendors define alarms differently, and finding detailed descriptions of them can be challenging. RFC 1232 also describes most alarms, though again, they are described for use in SNMP, and the descriptions are not intended as a standard for hardware implementation.

Red Alarm

A red alarm is defined in RFC 1232 as follows:

> A Red Alarm is declared because of an incoming Loss of Signal, Loss of Framing, Alarm Indication Signal. After a Red Alarm is declared, the device sends a Yellow Signal to the far-end. The far-end, when it receives the Yellow Signal, declares a Yellow Alarm.

A red alarm is triggered when a local failure has been detected, or continuous OOF errors have been detected for more than x seconds (vendor-specific). The alarm is cleared after a specific amount of time has elapsed with no OOF errors detected (the amount of time varies by hardware).

When a device has a local red alarm, it sends out a yellow alarm.

Figure 21-6 shows a sample red alarm. Something has failed on Telecom Switch C. The switch triggers a local red alarm, and sends out the yellow alarm signal to alert its neighbors of the problem.

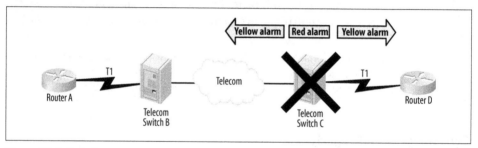

Figure 21-6. Red alarm

Figure 21-7 shows another red-alarm scenario. In this example, Telecom Switch C is sending garbled frames to Router D, which sees consecutive OOF problems and declares a red alarm. When Router D declares the red alarm, a yellow-alarm signal is sent back out the link.

The way these alarms behave can be a bit confusing. A red alarm generally indicates that something serious is happening on the local equipment, but in the example in Figure 21-7, Router D is receiving so many OOF errors that the signal is useless. Because Router D cannot figure out how to read the frames from the far side, it triggers a local red alarm and sends out a yellow alarm.

Yellow Alarm

A yellow alarm is also called a remote alarm indication (RAI) and indicates a remote problem. A yellow alarm is defined in RFC 1232 as follows:

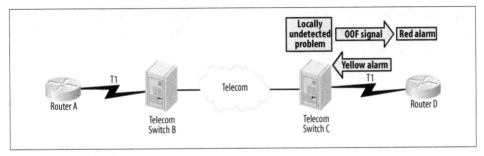

Figure 21-7. Yellow alarm

> A Yellow Alarm is declared because of an incoming Yellow Signal from the far-end. In effect, the circuit is declared to be a one way link.

One vendor specifies that a yellow alarm be declared for superframe links when bit six of all the channels has been zero for at least 335 ms, and that it be cleared when bit six of at least one channel is not zero for less than one to five seconds. For an ESF link, a yellow alarm is declared if the signal pattern occurs in at least 7 of 10 contiguous 16-bit pattern intervals, and is cleared if the pattern does not occur in 10 contiguous 16-bit pattern intervals.

Wow, what a mouthful! The simple truth is that unless you're designing T1 CSU/DSUs, you don't need to know all of that. Here's what you need to know: a yellow alarm does not necessarily indicate a problem with your device; rather, it's a problem being reported by the device to which you are connected.

Figure 21-8 shows a simple network. Router A has a T1 link to Router D. The T1 is actually terminated locally at the T1 provider's central office, where it is usually aggregated into a larger circuit, hauled to the remote CO, and then converted back to a T1 for delivery to the remote location. Telecom Switch B is fine, but Telecom Switch C has experienced a failure.

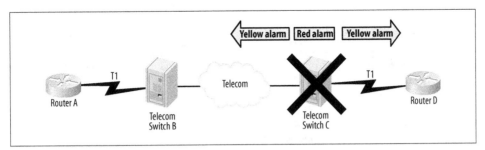

Figure 21-8. Another yellow alarm

Telecom Switch B receives a yellow alarm from Telecom Switch C. This alarm may be forwarded to Router A. When diagnosing the outage, remember that the presence of a yellow alarm usually indicates that some other device is at fault. Here, Telecom Switch C is the cause of the outage.

Watch out for assumptions. Router D will receive a yellow alarm, as might Router A. In this case, the admin for Router A may blame Router D (and vice versa), as he probably has no idea that telecom switches are involved.

Blue Alarm

A blue alarm is also called an alarm indication signal (AIS). There is no definition in RFC 1232 for this condition. A blue alarm is representative of a complete lack of an incoming signal and is indicated by a constant stream of unframed ones. You may hear someone say that the interface is receiving "all ones" when a blue alarm is active. If you're receiving a blue alarm, there is a good chance that a cable is disconnected or a device has failed.

Troubleshooting T1s

The first step in troubleshooting a T1 is to determine where the problem lies. Usually, it's cabling-, hardware-, or telco-related. Running some simple tests can help you determine what steps to take. All of these tests are invasive, which means you must take the T1 out of service to perform them.

Loopback Tests

Loopback tests involve setting one piece of equipment to a loopback state and sending data over the link. The data should return to you exactly as you sent it. When the data does not come back as expected, something has happened to alter it. Figure 21-9 shows how a loopback test might fail.

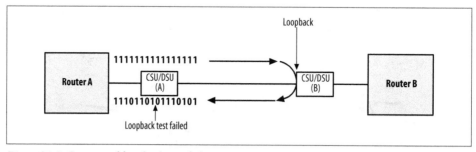

Figure 21-9. Conceptual loopback test failure

When you perform a loopback test, failed results won't typically be as clean as ones being changed into zeros. Usually, the problem is more electrical in nature, like the scenario shown in Figure 21-10, or framing errors cause the data to become entirely unreadable.

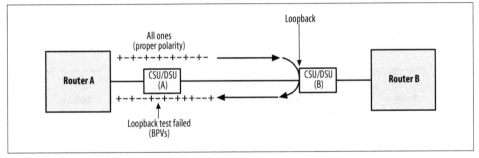

Figure 21-10. BPVs seen during loopback test

When you're performing loopback tests, the logical way to proceed is to start at one end of the link and move across it until the symptom appears.

CSU/DSUs generally offer the option of setting multiple types of loopback, which greatly assists in this process: you can usually set a loopback at the interface connecting the T1 to telco (called a *line loopback*), or after the signal has passed through the CSU/DSU's logic (called a *payload loopback*).

Many CSU/DSUs allow these loopbacks to be set in either direction, which can help you isolate the trouble.

 Telecom engineers look for *trouble* in a line when they troubleshoot. This may sound pedantic, but when you listen to telecom engineers troubleshooting, they will use very specific terms like *no trouble found* (which is often abbreviated as NTF). Remember, there are more than 100 years of standards at work here.

Let's look at an example. In Figure 21-11, Router A is connected to Router B by a T1 using two CSU/DSUs. From the point of view of CSU/DSU (A), we can see the possible loopback points available on the CSU/DSUs themselves.

Bear in mind that if we were to look from the point of view of CSU/DSU (B), all of the points would be reversed.

Not all models of CSU/DSU have all of these options, and not all CSU/DSUs call these loopback points by the same names.

The following list of terms describes the loopback points that are usually available. Remember that the descriptions are based on the network as seen from Router A in Figure 21-11:

Data port/DTE
This point loops the signal from the directly connected data device (in our case, Router A) back to that device without using the T1 framer logic. This tests the V.35 cable and the router.

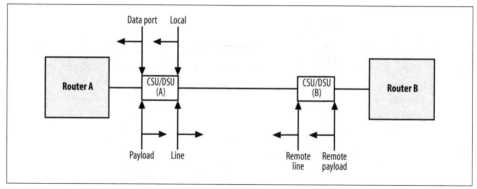

Figure 21-11. Loopback points in CSU/DSUs

Local

> This point loops the signal from the directly connected data device back to that device after it has been processed by the T1 framer logic. This tests the CSU/DSU, in addition to testing the physical connection to the router.

Payload

> This point loops the signal coming from the T1 back onto the T1 after it has been processed by the T1 framer logic. This test would be administered on the (B) side in our example, but the loopback would be set locally on CSU/DSU (A).

Line

> This point loops the signal coming from the T1 back onto the T1 before it has been processed by the T1 framer logic, effectively testing the T1 line without testing the CSU/DSU. In our example, a line loopback on CSU/DSU (A) would be tested from the (B) side, though the line loopback would be set locally on CSU/DSU (A).

Remote line

> Remote line loopback is a feature available on some CSU/DSUs that allows a local CSU/DSU to set a line loopback on the far-end device. In our example, though the loopback would exist on CSU/DSU (B), you'd enter the command to initiate the loopback on CSU/DSU (A).

Remote payload

> Remote payload loopback is a feature available on some CSU/DSUs that allows a local CSU/DSU to set a payload loopback on the far-end device. In our example, though the loopback would exist on CSU/DSU (B), you'd enter the command to initiate the loopback on CSU/DSU (A).

Say we're having problems with the T1 in Figure 21-11 and we need to troubleshoot. Looking at the error stats in CSU/DSU (A), we see many OOF, BPV, and CRC6 errors. Actual testing of the T1 line would typically proceed as shown in Figure 21-12.

First, we set a data port loopback on CSU/DSU (A) and send our tests. The tests all pass without error, indicating that the V.35 cable is good.

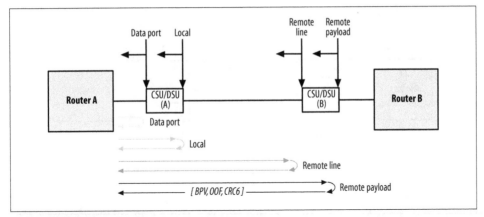

Figure 21-12. Loopback testing progression

Next, we clear the data port loopback on CSU/DSU (A) and set a local loopback. Again, we perform our tests and all packets return with no errors. We have now eliminated Router A, the V.35 cable, and 90 percent of CSU/DSU (A).

The next step is to clear the local loopback on CSU/DSU (A) and set a remote line loopback on CSU/DSU (B). Because this is a remote loopback, we'll set the loop from CSU/DSU (A). Alternatively, we could have called someone at the (B) location to manually set a line loopback on CSU/DSU (B). Again, we run our tests and all results are clean. We have now eliminated Router A, Router A's V.35 cable, CSU/DSU (A), and the T1 line itself (including all telco responsibility).

Now we clear the remote line loopback on CSU/DSU (B) and set a remote payload loopback on CSU/DSU (B)—again, administered from CSU/DSU (A). This time when we run our test, CSU/DSU (A) reports many BPV, OOF, and CRC6 errors. We have found the source of the trouble—CSU/DSU (B) is not functioning properly. By systematically moving our loopback point further and further away from one side of the link, we were able determine the point at which the trouble started to appear. Replacing CSU/DSU (B) solves our problem, and we're back in business.

Integrated CSU/DSUs

T1 WAN interface cards (WICs) with integrated CSU/DSUs are about the coolest thing to happen to routers in the past 15 years. Call me a nerd, but the idea of removing another physical piece of equipment for each T1 installed (as well as those horrible V.35 cables from equipment racks) is the closest thing to geek paradise I've ever seen.

The integrated CSU/DSU WICs serve the same purpose as standalone units, and they have the added benefit of being controlled via IOS from the router. Figure 21-13 shows the loopback points for a T1 CSU/DSU WIC as they are described in IOS.

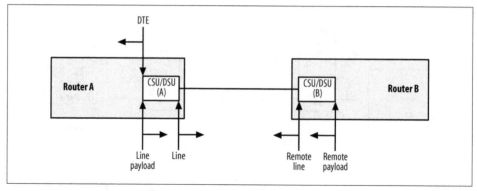

Figure 21-13. Integrated CSU/DSU loopback points

Some CSU/DSUs even include a feature that lets them run BERT tests. While this can be useful, if you're running BERT tests, you should probably call telco. Most problems discovered by BERT tests cannot be fixed with router configuration.

Configuring T1s

There are two steps involved in configuring T1s for use on a router. The first step is the configuration of the CSU/DSUs. The second step is the configuration of the router interface. When you're using integrated CSU/DSUs, the lines might seem blurred, but the concepts remain the same. Configuring the router interface is just like configuring any serial interface.

CSU/DSU Configuration

To get a T1 up and operational, you must do the following:

Configure both sides with the same encoding that matches the circuit's provisioned encoding
   Encoding options are AMI and B8ZS. Data T1s should always use B8ZS encoding. To configure encoding on a CSU/DSU WIC, use the `service-module t1 line code` interface command:

    ```
    Router(config)#int s0/1
    Router(config-if)# service-module t1 linecode b8zs
    ```

Configure both sides with the same framing that matches the circuit's provisioned framing
   Framing options are D4/SF and ESF. Data T1s should always use ESF framing. To configure framing on a CSU/DSU WIC, use the `service-module t1 framing` interface command:

    ```
    Router(config)#int s0/1
    Router(config-if)# service-module t1 framing esf
    ```

Configure how many channels will be used for the link, which channels will be used, and what speed they will be

If the T1 is being split or you have had fewer than 24 channels delivered to you, you must tell the CSU/DSU how many channels are in use. You do this for the CSU/DSU WIC with the `service-module t1 timeslots` interface command. Here, I've specified that channels 7–12 will be used at a speed of 64 Kbps:

```
Router(config)#int s0/1
Router(config-if)# service-module t1 timeslots 7-12 speed 64
```

By default, all channels are used with a speed of 64 Kbps per channel. In the event that you need to return a configured CSU/DSU WIC back to using all channels, you can do so with the `all` keyword:

```
Router(config)#int s0/1
Router(config-if)# service-module t1 timeslots all speed 64
```

Configure one side as the clock master and the other side as the slave

T1s are asynchronous, so only one side has an active clock. The other side will determine the clocking from the data stream itself using a technology called *phase-locked loop* (PLL). To configure clocking on a CSU/DSU WIC, use the `service-module t1 clock source` interface command. The options are `internal` and `line`:

```
Router(config)#int s0/1
Router(config-if)# service-module t1 clock source internal
```

`internal` means that the CSU/DSU will provide clocking (master), and `line` indicates that the clocking will be determined from the data stream on the line (slave). The default behavior is to use the line for clocking.

 Some environments may require that clocking be set to `line` on both ends. Check with your provider if you are unsure of your clocking requirements.

CSU/DSU Troubleshooting

Having a CSU/DSU integrated into a router is an excellent improvement over using standalone CSU/DSUs. Being able to telnet to the CSU/DSU is marvelous during an outage. Standalone CSU/DSUs often have serial ports on them that can be hooked to console servers, but the average corporate environment rarely uses this feature. Additionally, many companies use many different brands and models of CSU/DSUs, each with its own menus, commands, features, and quirks.

The Cisco T1 CSU/DSU WIC allows you to view CSU/DSU statistics by telneting to the router and issuing commands. The main command for troubleshooting a T1 CSU/DSU WIC is the `show service-module` *interface* command. This command outputs a wealth of information regarding the status of the CSU/DSU and the T1 circuit in general.

Let's look at the output of this command with a T1 that is not connected on the far end:

```
Router#sho service-module s0/1
Module type is T1/fractional
    Hardware revision is 0.112, Software revision is 0.2,
    Image checksum is 0x73D70058, Protocol revision is 0.1
Transmitter is sending remote alarm.
Receiver has loss of frame,
Framing is ESF, Line Code is B8ZS, Current clock source is line,
Fraction has 24 timeslots (64 Kbits/sec each), Net bandwidth is 1536 Kbits/sec.
Last user loopback performed:
    dte loopback
    duration 08:40:48
Last module self-test (done at startup): Passed
Last clearing of alarm counters 08:45:16
    loss of signal      :    1, last occurred 08:45:07
    loss of frame       :    2, current duration 00:01:38
    AIS alarm           :    0,
    Remote alarm        :    0,
    Module access errors :    0,
Total Data (last 34 15 minute intervals):
    2 Line Code Violations, 0 Path Code Violations
    1 Slip Secs, 200 Fr Loss Secs, 2 Line Err Secs, 0 Degraded Mins
    0 Errored Secs, 0 Bursty Err Secs, 0 Severely Err Secs, 200 Unavail Secs
Data in current interval (896 seconds elapsed):
    255 Line Code Violations, 255 Path Code Violations
    32 Slip Secs, 109 Fr Loss Secs, 34 Line Err Secs, 0 Degraded Mins
    0 Errored Secs, 0 Bursty Err Secs, 0 Severely Err Secs, 116 Unavail Secs
```

Here, we can see that the CSU/DSU is sending a remote alarm (yellow alarm) out the T1 because it's receiving loss-of-frame errors. More importantly, one loss-of-signal event occurred approximately 8 hours and 45 minutes ago. This T1 has not been up since the router booted. The last time the alarm stats were cleared was also 8 hours and 45 minutes ago.

This output essentially tells us that there's nothing on the other side of our circuit. Sure enough, the router on the far end is powered off. It also has an integrated CSU/DSU. After we power up the far-end router, let's clear the counters and see how the service module looks:

```
Router#clear counters s0/1
Clear "show interface" counters on this interface [confirm]
09:00:04: %CLEAR-5-COUNTERS: Clear counter on interface Serial0/1 by console
Router#
Router#sho service-module s0/1
Module type is T1/fractional
    Hardware revision is 0.112, Software revision is 0.2,
    Image checksum is 0x73D70058, Protocol revision is 0.1
Receiver has no alarms.
Framing is ESF, Line Code is B8ZS, Current clock source is line,
Fraction has 24 timeslots (64 Kbits/sec each), Net bandwidth is 1536 Kbits/sec.
Last user loopback performed:
    dte loopback
    duration 08:40:48
```

```
Last module self-test (done at startup): Passed
Last clearing of alarm counters 00:03:01
    loss of signal       :    0,
    loss of frame        :    0,
    AIS alarm            :    0,
    Remote alarm         :    0,
    Module access errors :    0,
Total Data (last 96 15 minute intervals):
    258 Line Code Violations, 257 Path Code Violations
    33 Slip Secs, 309 Fr Loss Secs, 37 Line Err Secs, 1 Degraded Mins
    1 Errored Secs, 1 Bursty Err Secs, 0 Severely Err Secs, 320 Unavail Secs
Data in current interval (153 seconds elapsed):
    0 Line Code Violations, 0 Path Code Violations
    0 Slip Secs, 0 Fr Loss Secs, 0 Line Err Secs, 0 Degraded Mins
    0 Errored Secs, 0 Bursty Err Secs, 0 Severely Err Secs, 0 Unavail Secs
```

This output looks a lot better. It includes the welcome phrase "receiver has no alarms," and it indicates that we've just cleared the alarms and no errors or alarms have been received since.

The last two paragraphs of the output are especially important. CSU/DSUs usually keep track of all the events that have occurred during the previous 24 hours. These events are recorded in 15-minute intervals and reported as such. The first paragraph (Total Data), while alarming, is not as important as the next paragraph (Data in current interval), which shows us the events that have occurred during the current interval. This can be a bit confusing, so let's take a closer look.

By using the command show service-module *interface* performance-statistics, we can see which events occurred during each of the last ninety-six 15-minute intervals:

```
Router#sho service-module s0/1 performance-statistics
Total Data (last 96 15 minute intervals):
    258 Line Code Violations, 257 Path Code Violations
    33 Slip Secs, 309 Fr Loss Secs, 37 Line Err Secs, 1 Degraded Mins
    1 Errored Secs, 1 Bursty Err Secs, 0 Severely Err Secs, 320 Unavail Secs
Data in current interval (380 seconds elapsed):
    0 Line Code Violations, 0 Path Code Violations
    0 Slip Secs, 0 Fr Loss Secs, 0 Line Err Secs, 0 Degraded Mins
    0 Errored Secs, 0 Bursty Err Secs, 0 Severely Err Secs, 0 Unavail Secs
Data in Interval 1:
    1 Line Code Violations, 2 Path Code Violations
    0 Slip Secs, 0 Fr Loss Secs, 1 Line Err Secs, 0 Degraded Mins
    1 Errored Secs, 1 Bursty Err Secs, 0 Severely Err Secs, 0 Unavail Secs
Data in Interval 2:
    255 Line Code Violations, 255 Path Code Violations
    32 Slip Secs, 109 Fr Loss Secs, 34 Line Err Secs, 0 Degraded Mins
    0 Errored Secs, 0 Bursty Err Secs, 0 Severely Err Secs, 116 Unavail Secs
Data in Interval 3:
    0 Line Code Violations, 0 Path Code Violations
    0 Slip Secs, 0 Fr Loss Secs, 0 Line Err Secs, 0 Degraded Mins
    0 Errored Secs, 0 Bursty Err Secs, 0 Severely Err Secs, 0 Unavail Secs
Data in Interval 4:
    0 Line Code Violations, 0 Path Code Violations
```

```
0 Slip Secs, 0 Fr Loss Secs, 0 Line Err Secs, 0 Degraded Mins
0 Errored Secs, 0 Bursty Err Secs, 0 Severely Err Secs, 0 Unavail Secs
```

The first paragraph shows the combined totals for all the intervals in memory. The maximum amount of time for which the CSU/DSU will record events is 24 hours (ninety-six 15-minute intervals), at which point the oldest interval's data is discarded. The output is arranged by interval, not by something more obvious like actual time. This is a throwback to the way standalone CSU/DSUs report historical information. The first interval listed is the current interval. The next interval, numbered as *Interval 1*, is the most recent interval. The intervals increment until they reach 96.

When looking at this information, search for patterns. If you see several line code violations, or any other error that shows up in all or most of the intervals, you've got a problem. You will see errors when a T1 bounces for any reason. Interval 2 in the preceding output shows some pretty severe errors, which are the result of me unplugging the T1 cable from the jack.

If you're seeing errors incrementing, start troubleshooting, and remember: physical layer first! Most problems are caused by a bad cable or piece of equipment.

I'm going to treat DS3 (Digital Signal 3) a little differently than I did T1s. While I believe knowledge of T1 framing and signaling is useful for a network engineer, I don't feel that the specifics are all that important when dealing with DS3s. For example, contrary to what many people will tell you (often adamantly), a DS3 is not defined as 28 DS1s. A DS3 is actually the result of multiplexing 7 DS2s. If you're saying to yourself, "There's no such thing as a DS2," you're not alone. A DS2 is a group of four DS1s, and is not seen outside of multiplexing.

While it may be interesting to know that a DS3 is composed of DS2s, that knowledge won't help you build or troubleshoot a network today. In this chapter, I'll explain what you do need to know about DS3s: simple theory, error conditions, how to configure them, and how to troubleshoot them.

A DS3 is not a T3. DS3 is the logical carrier sent over a physical T3 circuit. In practice, the terms are pretty interchangeable; most people will understand what you mean if you use either. However, from this point on, I'll refer to the circuit simply as a DS3, as we're really interested in the circuit, not the physical medium.

You'll encounter two flavors of DS3s: channelized and clear-channel. A *channelized DS3* has 672 DS0s, each capable of supporting a single POTS-line phone call. When a DS3 is channelized, Cisco will often refer to it as a "channelized T3." A *clear-channel DS3* has no channels and is used for pure data.

Framing

When I stated earlier that a DS3 is actually a group of seven DS2s multiplexed together, I was referring to a channelized DS3. When DS3s were designed in the 1960s, there really wasn't a need for data circuits like those we have today. DS3s were designed to handle phone calls, which is why they are multiplexed the way they are. DS3s require framing for the same reasons that DS1s do. The difference is that there can be multiple DS1s multiplexed within a DS3. Each of those DS1s has its own clocking, framing, and encoding that must be maintained within the DS3. The DS3 must also have its own clocking, framing, and encoding, which must not interfere with the multiplexed circuits within it. There are a couple of different framing methods you can use. Your choice should be dictated by the intended use.

M13

M13 (pronounced *M-one-three*, not *M-thirteen*) is short for *Multiplexed DS1 to DS3*. When a multiplexer builds a DS3, it goes through two steps: M12 and M23. The combination of these steps is referred to as M13. Figure 22-1 shows the steps involved in converting 28 DS1s into a single DS3.

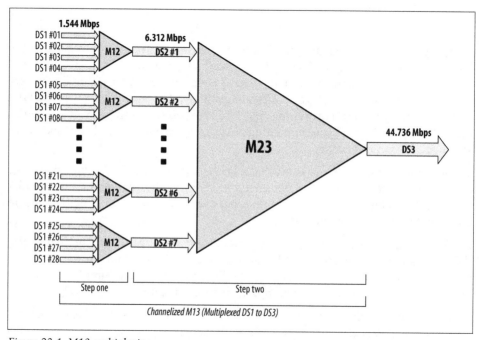

Figure 22-1. M13 multiplexing

Originally, DS3s were used for aggregating T1s. Imagine 28 T1s, all terminating at a CO but originating at 28 different locations at varying distances from it. Because the T1s are not related, they may be out of sync with each other. The original designers knew that this was a probability, so they designed the first stage of the multiplexing process to deal with the problem.

The speed of a T1 is generally reported as 1.544 Mbps. If you multiply 1.544 Mbps by 4, you get 6.176 Mbps. Why, then, is a DS2, which is four T1s, shown as 6.312 Mbps? To compensate for T1s that are not delivering bits in a timely manner (+/– 77 Hz), the M12 multiplexer stuffs bits into the signal to get them up to speed with the other T1s in the group.

Each T1 is brought up to a line rate of 1,545,796 bits per second after *bit stuffing*. In all, 128,816 additional framing and overhead bits are added, which brings the total to 6.312 Mbps (1,545,796 * 4 + 128,816). The receiving multiplexer removes the extra bits.

Overclocking the T1s ensures that the DS3 should never cause a timing problem with the individual T1s. Remember that each T1 will have its own clock master and slave. The DS3 needs to support its own clocking without interfering with that of the individual T1s (modern networks that use SONET in the core do not really have this problem, but this technology was designed many years ago, before SONET existed).

C-Bits

M13 framing is a bit outdated, because it assumes that DS2 links may be terminated from remote locations, just as DS1s are. In practice, DS2s are not deployed and, as a result, exist only within the multiplexer.

This means that the timing issues that require bit stuffing occur only at the M12 stage and never at the M23 stage. Still, the M13 framing process provides positions for bit stuffing at the M23 stage.

Another framing technique was developed to take advantage of the unused bits. The original purpose of these bits (called *C-bits*) was to signal the presence of bits stuffed at the M23 stage of the multiplexing process. *C-bit framing* uses the C-bits in the DS3 frame differently than originally planned.

One benefit of C-bit framing is the inclusion of *far-end block errors* (FEBEs) reporting. FEBEs (pronounced *FEE-bees*) are DS3-specific alarms that indicate the far end of the link has received a C-parity or framing error. Figure 22-2 shows how FEBEs are sent on a DS3 with SONET in the middle of the link.

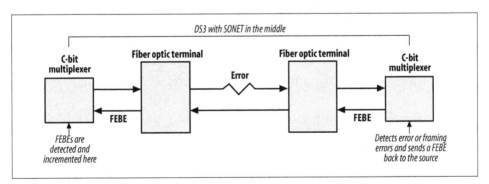

Figure 22-2. Far-end block errors

C-bit framing also allows for the introduction of *far-end out-of-frame* (FEOOF) signals. When a break is detected on the receiving interface of the remote end of the link, it sends a FEOOF signal back to the source. Figure 22-3 shows an example of FEOOFs in action.

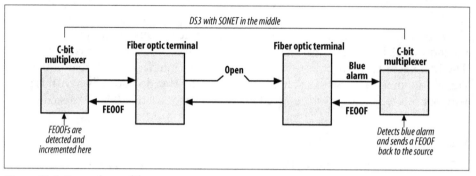

Figure 22-3. Far-end out-of-frame errors

Additional codes, called *far-end alarm and control* (FEAC) codes, are also available. They include:

- DS3 Equipment Failure—Service Affecting (SA)
- DS3 LOS/HBER
- DS3 Out-of-Frame
- DS3 AIS Received
- DS3 IDLE Received
- DS3 Equipment Failure—Non Service Affecting (NSA)
- Common Equipment Failure (NSA)
- Multiple DS1 LOS/HBER
- DS1 Equipment Failure (SA)
- Single DS1 LOS/HBER
- DS1 Equipment Failure (NSA)

FEAC codes are shown in the output of the show controllers command.

Clear-Channel DS3 Framing

Data links require the full capacity of the DS3 without any individual channels, as shown in Figure 22-4. Framing is still required, and either C-bit or M13 framing can be used to maintain clock synchronization between the two ends. The M12 and M23 steps are not needed, however, nor are the overhead bits introduced by them. These bits are used for pure data.

Because there's no multiplexing overhead, the amount of bandwidth available over a clear-channel DS3 is 44.2 Mbps.

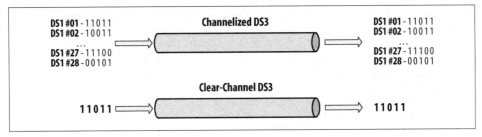

DS1 #01 - 11011
DS1 #02 - 10011
...
DS1 #27 - 11100
DS1 #28 - 00101

Channelized DS3

DS1 #01 - 11011
DS1 #02 - 10011
...
DS1 #27 - 11100
DS1 #28 - 00101

Clear-Channel DS3

11011

11011

Figure 22-4. Channelized versus clear-channel DS3

When using a DS3 for data links, use C-bit framing to gain the benefits of increased error reporting outlined previously.

Line Coding

DS-3 links support Alternate Mark Inversion (AMI), Bipolar Three Zero Substitution (B3ZS), and High-Density Bipolar Three (HDB3) line coding. AMI is the same as the AMI used on T1s, discussed in Chapter 21. B3ZS is similar to B8ZS, also discussed in Chapter 21, except that it replaces occurrences of three rather than eight consecutive zeros with a well-known bipolar violation. HDB3 is used primarily in Japan and Europe. The default line coding on Cisco DS3 interfaces is B3ZS. When channelized DS3s are used, the line coding may be AMI, depending on how the circuit was ordered. Usually B3ZS is preferred.

Configuring DS3s

Recall that there are two flavors of DS3: clear-channel and channelized. Typically, clear-channel DS3s are used for data links, and channelized DS3s are used for voice links. The configurations in this section assume an integrated CSU/DSU in all cases. If you have an older router that requires an external CSU/DSU, you'll probably have a High-Speed Serial Interface (HSSI—pronounced *hissy*), which still looks like a serial interface within IOS. The difference will be that you cannot configure framing on a HSSI port. Additionally, because the CSU/DSU (which counts and reports these errors) is an external device, you won't be able to see DS3 errors on a HSSI port.

Clear-Channel DS3

Configuring a clear-channel DS3 is a pretty boring affair. Specify the framing with the framing interface command, and then configure the interface like any other serial interface:

```
interface Serial3/1/0
 description DS3
 ip address 10.100.100.100 255.255.255.252
 framing c-bit
```

You show the status of the interface the same as you do for any other interface. The errors and counters are generic, and not DS3- or even telecom-specific:

```
7304#sho int s3/1/0
Serial3/1/0 is up, line protocol is up
  Hardware is SPA-4XT3/E3
  Description: DS3
  Internet address is 10.100.100.100/30
  MTU 4470 bytes, BW 44210 Kbit, DLY 200 usec,
      reliability 255/255, txload 1/255, rxload 1/255
  Encapsulation HDLC, crc 16, loopback not set
  Keepalive set (10 sec)
  Last input 00:00:02, output 00:00:01, output hang never
  Last clearing of "show interface" counters 6d03h
  Input queue: 0/75/0/0 (size/max/drops/flushes); Total output drops: 0
  Queueing strategy: fifo
  Output queue: 0/40 (size/max)
  5 minute input rate 101000 bits/sec, 179 packets/sec
  5 minute output rate 98000 bits/sec, 170 packets/sec
     81589607 packets input, 2171970011 bytes, 0 no buffer
     Received 61914 broadcasts (229394 IP multicast)
     1072 runts, 0 giants, 0 throttles
             0 parity
     1136 input errors, 10 CRC, 0 frame, 0 overrun, 0 ignored, 54 abort
     80620669 packets output, 1165631313 bytes, 0 underruns
     0 output errors, 0 applique, 0 interface resets
     0 output buffer failures, 0 output buffers swapped out
     0 carrier transitions
```

You find the real meaty information using the show controllers command:

```
7304#show controllers s3/1/0
Interface Serial3/1/0 (DS3 port 0)
  Hardware is SPA-4XT3/E3
  Framing is c-bit, Clock Source is Line
  Bandwidth limit is 44210, DSU mode 0, Cable length is 10 feet
  rx FEBE since last clear counter 792, since reset 3693

  No alarms detected.

  No FEAC code is being received
  MDL transmission is disabled

  PXF interface number = 0x12
SPA carrier card counters:
  Input: packets = 81583462, bytes = 6466441470, drops = 7
  Output: packets = 80614617, bytes = 5460208896, drops = 0
  Egress flow control status: XON
  Per bay counters:
  General errors: input = 0, output = 0
  SPI4 errors: ingress dip4 = 0, egress dip2 = 0

SPA FPGA Packet Counters:
  Transmit : 80614638, Drops : 0
  Receive : 81583490, Drops : 0
```

```
SPA FPGA Invalid Channel Packets:
  Transmit : 0, Receive : 0

SPA FPGA IPC Counters:
  Transmit : 1057496, Drops : 0
  Receive : 1057496, Drops : 0

SPA FPGA Packet Error Counters:
  202 Receive error packets

Framer(PM5383) Counters:
  Transmit :  80614555 packets, 1165231422 bytes
  Errors : 0 aborts, 0 underruns

  Receive : 81583399 packets, 2171463422 bytes
  Errors : 10 crc, 1072 runts, 0 giants, 54 aborts
```

This output shows a healthy clear-channel DS3. The framing is C-bit.

Notice that there are FEBEs shown. FEBEs may increment in small numbers over time without serious impact. The preceding output indicates that the counters were cleared six days ago. Since then, 792 FEBEs have accumulated, which translates to about 5.5 per hour (assuming an even distribution). Another possibility is that something happened within the past six days that caused FEBEs to increment in a short amount of time. In this case, it would be a good idea to clear the counters again and keep an eye on the interface. If FEBEs increment regularly, you might want to start troubleshooting further.

The show controllers output shows that there are no errors active and no FEAC codes have been received. This information indicates a relatively healthy clear-channel DS3.

 A known problem with the PA-A3-T3 and NM-1A-T3 modules results in the receiver being too sensitive (see Cisco bug ID CSCds15318). If you're seeing a large number of errors and you have a short cable, this might be the problem. Short of replacing the interface with a different model, Cisco recommends either reducing the transmit level of the device on the other end of the DS3 cable connected to your router, or installing attenuators on the line. These cards are pretty common, so watch out for this issue.

Channelized DS3

A channelized DS3 can be configured for voice, data, or both. Because the DS3 is channelized, individual T1s can be broken out as either data links or voice links. You do this in the controller configuration for the interface.

In this example, I've configured the first 10 T1s in the DS3 to be serial data links. I did this by assigning the desired number of DS0s to a *channel group*. Because my links will all be full T1s, I've assigned all 24 DS0s (referenced as *timeslots*) to each channel group.

However, because this is a channelized DS3, I could separate each T1 further by grouping DS0s together. Each group would get its own channel group number. Here's the controller configuration:

```
controller T3 2/0
 framing m23
 clock source line
 t1 1 channel-group 1 timeslots 1-24
 t1 2 channel-group 1 timeslots 1-24
 t1 3 channel-group 1 timeslots 1-24
 t1 4 channel-group 1 timeslots 1-24
 t1 5 channel-group 1 timeslots 1-24
 t1 6 channel-group 1 timeslots 1-24
 t1 7 channel-group 1 timeslots 1-24
 t1 8 channel-group 1 timeslots 1-24
 t1 9 channel-group 1 timeslots 1-24
 t1 10 channel-group 1 timeslots 1-24
 t1 1 clock source Line
 t1 2 clock source Line
 t1 4 clock source Line
 t1 6 clock source Line
 t1 7 clock source Line
 t1 8 clock source Line
 t1 9 clock source Line
 t1 10 clock source Line
 t1 11 clock source Line
 t1 12 clock source Line
 t1 13 clock source Line
 t1 14 clock source Line
 t1 15 clock source Line
 t1 16 clock source Line
 t1 17 clock source Line
 t1 18 clock source Line
 t1 19 clock source Line
 t1 20 clock source Line
 t1 21 clock source Line
 t1 22 clock source Line
 t1 23 clock source Line
 t1 24 clock source Line
 t1 25 clock source Line
 t1 26 clock source Line
 t1 27 clock source Line
 t1 28 clock source Line
```

Here, we have a DS3 connected to interface 2/0. This is a channelized DS3, so the framing is set to M23. The clock source defaults to Line. Unlike with T1s, this should normally be left alone, as clocking is usually provided from the SONET network upstream. Notice that there is a clock statement for the DS3 and additional clock statements for each T1 within the DS3.

Cisco supports only M23 and C-bit framing for channelized DS3s. When using M13 on telecom equipment, use M23 on your Cisco gear.

Once you have configured the controllers, you can configure the serial T1s as if they were regular T1s. The serial interfaces are a combination of the physical interfaces and the T1 numbers in the DS3, followed by a colon and the channel group assigned in the controller configuration:

```
interface Serial2/0/1:1
 description T1 #1
 ip address 10.220.110.1 255.255.255.252
!
interface Serial2/0/2:1
 description T1 #2
 ip address 10.220.120.1 255.255.255.252
!
interface Serial2/0/3:1
 description T1 #3
 ip address 10.220.130.1 255.255.255.252
!
interface Serial2/0/4:1
 description T1 #4
 ip address 10.220.140.1 255.255.255.252
```

You cannot create a serial interface larger than a T1 within a channelized DS3. If you need multimegabit speeds, you'll need to create multiple T1s, and either bundle them with Multilink-PPP or load-balance them using CEF or a routing protocol.

This router (a 7304) has both channelized and clear-channel interface cards. When you do a show version on a router like this, the output can be confusing because the number of serial interfaces includes the clear-channel DS3s and any T1s you've configured from your channelized DS3s. This router contains four channelized DS3s and four clear-channel DS3s. If a channelized DS3 is not configured at the controller level, it does not appear in the output of the show version command. Because we have four clear-channel DS3s, which are serial interfaces by default, and we've configured 10 T1s to be serial interfaces out of one of the channelized DS3s, the router reports a total of 14 serial interfaces:

```
7304#sho ver

[- Text Removed -]

1 FastEthernet interface
2 Gigabit Ethernet interfaces
14 Serial interfaces4 Channelized T3 ports
```

Here, we can see the individual serial interfaces on the router. Ten of them are logical (s2/0/1:1 – s/2/0/10:1), and four of them are physical (s3/1/0 – s3/1/3):

```
7304#sho ip int brie
Interface          IP-Address      OK? Method Status                    Protocol
FastEthernet0      unassigned      YES NVRAM  administratively down down
GigabitEthernet0/0 10.220.11.1     YES NVRAM  up                        up
GigabitEthernet0/1 10.220.12.1     YES NVRAM  up                        up
Serial2/0/1:1      10.220.110.1    YES NVRAM  up                        up
Serial2/0/2:1      10.220.120.1    YES NVRAM  up                        up
Serial2/0/3:1      10.220.130.1    YES NVRAM  up                        up
Serial2/0/4:1      10.220.140.1    YES NVRAM  up                        up
Serial2/0/5:1      unassigned      YES manual administratively down down
Serial2/0/6:1      unassigned      YES manual administratively down down
Serial2/0/7:1      unassigned      YES manual administratively down down
Serial2/0/8:1      unassigned      YES manual administratively down down
Serial2/0/9:1      unassigned      YES manual administratively down down
Serial2/0/10:1     unassigned      YES manual administratively down down
Serial3/1/0        10.100.100.100  YES manual up                        up
Serial3/1/1        unassigned      YES NVRAM  down                      down
Serial3/1/2        unassigned      YES NVRAM  down                      down
Serial3/1/3        unassigned      YES NVRAM  down                      down
```

The output of the show controllers command for a channelized DS3 is quite different from that for a clear-channel DS3. With a channelized DS3, you get a report of the line status for every 15-minute interval in the last 24 hours. The current alarm status and the framing and line coding are shown here in bold:

```
7304#sho controllers t3 2/0
T3 2/0 is up. Hardware is 2CT3+ single wide port adapter
  CT3 H/W Version: 0.2.2, CT3 ROM Version: 1.0, CT3 F/W Version: 2.5.1
  FREEDM version: 1, reset 0 resurrect 0
  Applique type is Channelized T3
  Description:
  No alarms detected.
  Framing is M23, Line Code is B3ZS, Clock Source is Line
  Rx-error throttling on T1's ENABLED
  Rx throttle total 99, equipment customer loopback
  Data in current interval (29 seconds elapsed):
     0 Line Code Violations, 0 P-bit Coding Violation
     0 C-bit Coding Violation, 0 P-bit Err Secs
     0 P-bit Severely Err Secs, 0 Severely Err Framing Secs
     0 Unavailable Secs, 0 Line Errored Secs
     0 C-bit Errored Secs, 0 C-bit Severely Errored Secs
  Data in Interval 1:
     0 Line Code Violations, 0 P-bit Coding Violation
     0 C-bit Coding Violation, 0 P-bit Err Secs
     0 P-bit Severely Err Secs, 0 Severely Err Framing Secs
     0 Unavailable Secs, 0 Line Errored Secs
     0 C-bit Errored Secs, 0 C-bit Severely Errored Secs
  Data in Interval 2:
     0 Line Code Violations, 0 P-bit Coding Violation
     0 C-bit Coding Violation, 0 P-bit Err Secs
     0 P-bit Severely Err Secs, 0 Severely Err Framing Secs
     0 Unavailable Secs, 0 Line Errored Secs
```

```
      0 C-bit Errored Secs, 0 C-bit Severely Errored Secs

[- Text Removed -]
```

## CHAPTER 23

Frame Relay

Frame Relay is a method of transporting digital information over a network. The data is formatted into frames, which are sent over a network of devices usually under the control of a telecommunications company. Diagrams depicting Frame Relay networks often display the network as a cloud, as the end user doesn't generally know (or care) how the network is actually designed. The end user only needs to know that *virtual circuits* (VCs) through the cloud will allow the delivery of frames to other endpoints in the cloud.

Whatever goes into one end of the VC should come out the other end. The far end appears as though it is on the other end of a physical cable, though in reality, the remote end is typically many hops away.

The VCs may be either *switched* or *permanent*. A Frame Relay permanent virtual circuit (PVC) is always up, even if it's not in use. A switched virtual circuit (SVC) is up only when it's needed. Most data networking deployments use PVCs.

Figure 23-1 shows a typical simple Frame Relay network using PVCs. Router A is connected to Router B with a PVC. Router A is also connected to Router C with a PVC. Router B and Router C are not connected to each other. The two PVCs terminate into a single interface on Router A.

Physically, each router is connected only to one of the provider's telecom switches. These switches are the entry and exit points into and out of the cloud.

Router A is connected with a DS3, while Routers B and C are connected to the cloud with T1s. Logically, Frame Relay creates the illusion that the routers on the far sides of the PVCs are directly connected.

In reality, there may be many devices in the cloud, any of which may be forwarding frames to the destination. Figure 23-2 shows what the inside of the cloud might look like.

Frame Relay functions in a manner similar to the Internet. When you send a packet to a remote website, you don't really care how it gets there. You have no idea how many devices your packets may pass through. All you know is what your default gateway is;

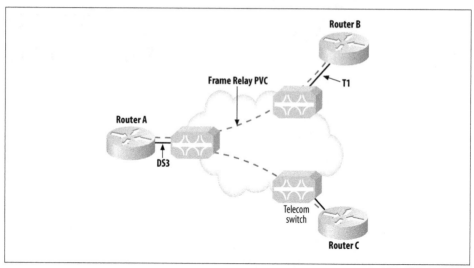

Figure 23-1. Simple Frame Relay WAN

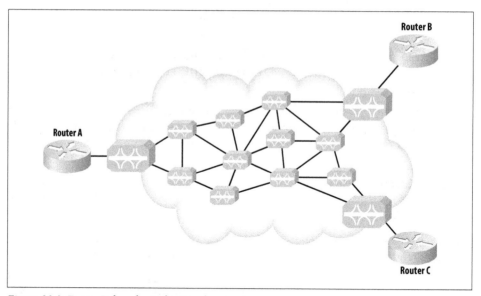

Figure 23-2. Frame Relay physical network

you let your Internet service provider worry about the rest. Frame Relay is similar in that you have no idea what the intermediary devices are or how they route your data. When you use Frame Relay, there are a finite number of destinations, all specified by you and provisioned by your telecom provider.

For Frame Relay to create the illusion of a direct connection, each end of the VC is given a Layer-2 address called a *data link control identifier* (DLCI, pronounced *dell-see*). These DLCIs (and your data) are visible only to the telecom switches that forward the frames and to your routers. Other customers connected to the Frame Relay cloud cannot see your DLCIs or your data. Your telecom provider will determine the DLCI numbers.

VCs can be combined in such a way that multiple endpoints terminate to a single DLCI. An example of this type of design is shown in Figure 23-3. Each VC can also have its own DLCI on both sides. How you design the Frame Relay PVCs will depend on your needs.

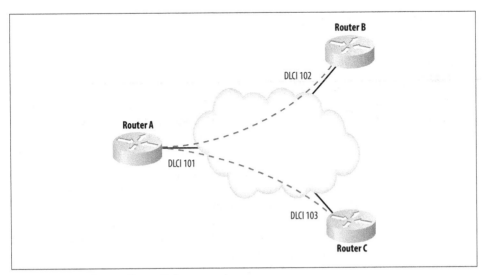

Figure 23-3. DLCIs in a Frame Relay network

DLCIs are mapped to IP addresses in Frame Relay networks in much the same way that Ethernet MAC addresses are mapped to IP addresses in Ethernet networks. Unlike with Ethernet, however, which learns MAC addresses dynamically, you'll usually have to map DLCIs to IP addresses yourself.

Ethernet networks use the Address Resolution Protocol (ARP) to determine how MAC addresses map to known IP addresses. Frame Relay uses a protocol called *Inverse ARP* to try to map IP addresses to known DLCIs. Frame Relay switches report on the statuses of all configured DLCIs on a regular basis.

 Be careful when configuring Frame Relay. There may be PVCs configured that you do not wish to enable, and Inverse ARP may enable those links without your knowledge.

The primary benefits of Frame Relay are cost and flexibility. A point-to-point T1 will cost more than a Frame Relay T1 link between two sites, especially if the sites are not in the same geographic location, or LATA. Also, with a point-to-point T1, 1.5 Mbps of dedicated bandwidth must be allocated between each point, regardless of the utilization of that bandwidth. In contrast, a Frame Relay link shares resources; on a Frame Relay link, if bandwidth is not being used in the cloud, other customers can use it.

The notion of shared bandwidth raises some questions. What if someone else is using the bandwidth and you suddenly need it? What if you're using the bandwidth and someone else suddenly needs it? Frame Relay introduces the idea of the *committed information rate* (CIR), which helps address these concerns.

Ordering Frame Relay Service

When you order a Frame Relay link, telco needs to know four pieces of information to provision the circuit. One of these is the CIR. Here are the requirements:

The addresses and phone numbers of the endpoints
> The street addresses—and, more importantly, phone numbers—in use at each endpoint are critical components of a circuit order. If the location does not have phone service, in most cases, it won't exist to telco.

The port speed
> The *port speed* is the size of the physical circuit you will deliver to each end. These physical links do not have to be the same size or type, but they must both be able to support the CIR requested for the Frame Relay link. The port speed can be anything from a 56 Kbps DDS circuit up to and exceeding a DS3. These days, the most common Frame Relay handoff is a full T1, though fractional T1s are still used as well. It all depends on the cost of the physical circuit.

The CIR
> The CIR is the rate of transfer that you want the carrier to provide. When requesting Frame Relay service, you specify the amount of bandwidth you want available, and the provider guarantees that, up to this level, all frames that are sent over this VC will be forwarded through the Frame Relay cloud to their intended destinations (additional frames may be dropped). The higher the CIR, the more the service will cost. A CIR is required for each VC.

The burst rate
> The burst rate is the maximum speed of the Frame Relay VC. Frames that exceed the CIR—but not the burst rate—are marked *discard-eligible* (DE). DE frames will be forwarded by the switches in the Frame Relay cloud as long as there is sufficient bandwidth to do so, but may be dropped at the discretion of the Frame Relay provider. Having a high burst rate is an inexpensive way to get more bandwidth for a lower cost. The burst rate is often a multiple of the CIR; you may hear the burst rate referred to as a "2× burst," which means the burst rate is twice the CIR. You can also order a VC with zero burst. A burst rate is required for each VC.

Figure 23-4 shows a bandwidth utilization graph for a Frame Relay link. The link is running locally over a T1 with a port speed of 1.5 Mbps. The CIR is 512 Kbps, and the

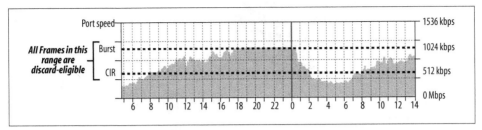

Figure 23-4. Frame Relay CIR and DE frames

link has been provisioned with a 2× burst. As you can see in the graph, as traffic exceeds the 2× burst threshold, it is discarded. This type of graph indicates that the link is saturated and needs to be upgraded. A good rule of thumb is to order more bandwidth when your link reaches 70 percent utilization. This circuit should have been upgraded long ago.

Frame Relay has fallen out of favor with many enterprises. Aggressive MPLS pricing by the major carriers along with features like Ethernet handoff have made MPLS more economical and therefore more popular. Frame Relay is still out there, though, so even if your job is to replace it with MPLS, you'll still need to understand how it works.

Frame Relay Network Design

Frame Relay links are more flexible than point-to-point links, because multiple links can be terminated at a single interface in a router. This opens up design possibilities allowing connectivity to multiple sites at a significant cost savings over point-to-point circuits.

Figure 23-5 shows three sites networked together with Frame Relay. On the left, Router B and Router C are both connected to Router A, but are not connected to each other. This design is often referred to as a *partial mesh* or *hub and spoke* network. In this network, Router B can communicate to Router C only through Router A.

On the right side of Figure 23-5 is an example of a *fully meshed* network. The difference here is that all sites are connected to all other sites. Router B can communicate directly with Router C in the fully meshed network.

Meshed networks are not strictly the domain of Frame Relay. As you can see in Figure 23-6, a fully meshed network can easily be created with point-to-point T1s.

In a Frame Relay network like the one shown on the left side of Figure 23-6, each location needs a router that can support a single T1. Each PVC can be configured as a separate virtual interface called a *subinterface*. Subinterfaces allow VCs to terminate into separate logical interfaces within a single physical interface.

With point-to-point links (T1s, in this case), each router must be able to support two T1 interfaces. Routers that support two T1s are generally more expensive than

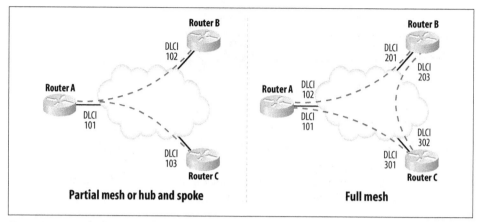

Figure 23-5. Meshed Frame Relay networks

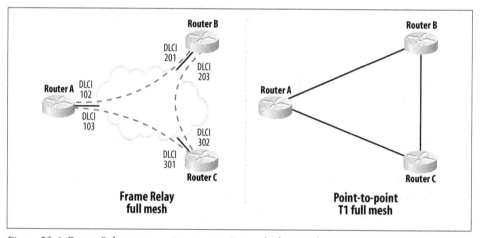

Figure 23-6. Frame Relay versus point-to-point T1 meshed networks

single-T1 routers. Additionally, point-to-point T1s cost more than Frame Relay T1 services, especially over long distances.

The example in Figure 23-6 is relatively simple, but what about larger networks? Figure 23-7 shows two networks, each with six nodes. On the left is a fully meshed network using Frame Relay, and on the right is a fully meshed network using point-to-point T1s.

With six nodes in the network, there must be five links on each router. With Frame Relay, you can accomplish this with a single T1 interface at each router, provided the bandwidth for all the links will total that of a T1 or less. When you're using point-to-point links, however, routers that can support five T1s are required. In addition to the hardware costs, the telecom costs for a network like this would be very high, especially over longer distances.

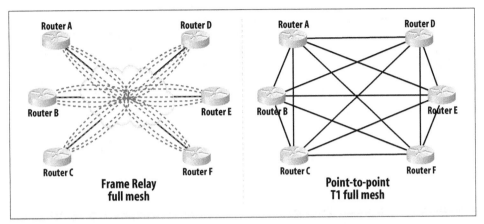

Figure 23-7. Six-node fully meshed networks

To figure out how many links are required to build a fully meshed network, use the formula N (N – 1) / 2, where N equals the number of nodes in the mesh. In our example, there are six nodes, so 6 (6 – 1) / 2 = 15 links are required.

Oversubscription

When designing Frame Relay networks, you must take care to ensure that the total amount of bandwidth being provisioned in all CIRs within a physical link does not exceed the port speed. A CIR represents guaranteed bandwidth, and it is technically impossible to guarantee bandwidth beyond the port speed. A Frame Relay link is considered *oversubscribed* when the total bandwidth of all the VCs within the link exceeds the port speed of the link. For example, having four PVCs each with a 512 Kbps CIR is possible on a T1, even though the total of all the CIRs is 2,048 Kbps. Some providers will allow this, while others will not.

 The burst rate has no bearing on the oversubscription of a link.

You should always plan carefully to ensure that the CIRs of your PVCs total no more than the port speed of your physical link. I use spreadsheets to keep me honest, but any form of documentation will do. Often, simple charts like the one in Figure 23-8 are the most effective.

There are no technical limitations preventing oversubscription. During the Internet boom, small ISPs often debated the ethics of oversubscription. Many ISPs routinely oversubscribed their Frame Relay links to save money and thereby increase profits.

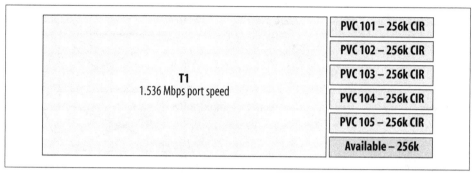

	PVC 101 – 256k CIR
	PVC 102 – 256k CIR
T1	PVC 103 – 256k CIR
1.536 Mbps port speed	PVC 104 – 256k CIR
	PVC 105 – 256k CIR
	Available – 256k

Figure 23-8. Subscription of a T1 using Frame Relay PVCs

Oversubscription is never good for customers, though: eventually, usage will increase to the point where packets are dropped.

 Be careful when ordering links from telecom providers. There are some providers who only provide 0 Kbps CIR Frame Relay links. They do this to provide links at lower costs than their competitors. The drawback is that all data sent over these links will be discard-eligible. Be specific when ordering, and know what you are buying.

Local Management Interface

In 1990, Cisco Systems, StrataCom, Northern Telecom, and Digital Equipment Corporation developed a set of enhancements to the Frame Relay protocol called the *Local Management Interface* (LMI). LMI provides communication between the data terminal equipment, or DTE devices (routers, in our examples), and the data communication equipment, or DCE devices (telecom switches, in our examples). One of the most useful enhancements in LMI is the exchange of status messages regarding VCs. These messages tell routers when a Frame Relay PVC is available.

LMI messages are sent on a predefined PVC. You can see the LMI type and PVC in use with the show interface command:

```
Router-A#sho int s0/0 | inc LMI
  LMI enq sent  85, LMI stat recvd 86, LMI upd recvd 0, DTE LMI up
  LMI enq recvd 0, LMI stat sent  0, LMI upd sent  0
  LMI DLCI 1023  LMI type is CISCO  frame relay DTE
```

Three forms of LMI are configurable on Cisco routers: cisco, ansi, and q933a (Annex A). The DCE device (telecom switch) usually determines the type of LMI. The default LMI type on Cisco routers is cisco. You can change the LMI type with the frame-relay lmi-type interface command:

```
Router-A(config-if)#frame-relay lmi-type ?
  cisco
```

```
ansi
q933a
```

Congestion Avoidance in Frame Relay

Frame Relay includes provisions for congestion avoidance. Included in the Frame Relay header are two bits titled *Forward-Explicit Congestion Notification* (FECN, pronounced *FECK-en*), and *Backward-Explicit Congestion Notification* (BECN, pronounced *BECK-en*). These flags are used to report congestion to the DTE devices (your routers).

The DCE devices (telecom switches) set the FECN bit when network congestion is found. When the receiving DTE device (your router) receives the FECN, it can then execute flow control, if so configured. The Frame Relay cloud does not perform any flow control; this is left up to the DTE devices on each end.

The Frame Relay switches set the BECN bit in frames when FECNs are found in frames traveling in the opposite direction. This allows the sending DTE device to know about congestion in the frames it is sending.

Figure 23-9 shows a Frame Relay network where congestion is occurring. A PVC exists between Router A and Router B. The PVC traverses the topmost Frame Relay switches in the drawing. Halfway through the cloud, a switch encounters congestion in Router B's direction. The switch marks packets moving forward (toward Router B) with FECNs, and packets moving in the opposite direction (toward Router A) with BECNs.

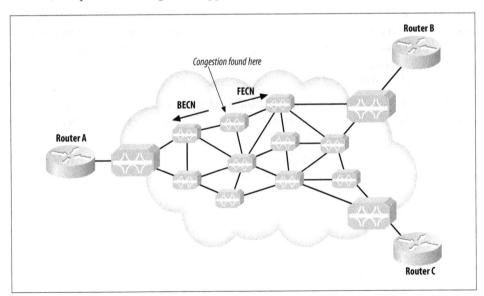

Figure 23-9. FECN and BECN example

Configuring Frame Relay

Once you understand how Frame Relay works, the mechanics of configuration are not very difficult to grasp. There are some interesting concepts, such as subinterfaces, that may be new to you; we'll cover those in detail here.

Basic Frame Relay with Two Nodes

Figure 23-10 shows a simple two-node Frame Relay network. Router A is connected to Router B using Frame Relay over a T1. The port speed is 1.536 Mbps, the CIR is 512 Kbps, and the burst rate is 2× (1,024 Kbps).

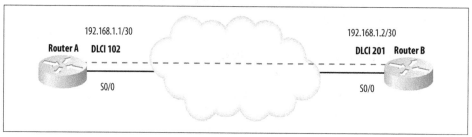

Figure 23-10. Two-node Frame Relay network

The first step in configuring Frame Relay is to configure Frame Relay encapsulation. There are two types of Frame Relay encapsulation: cisco and ietf. The default type is cisco, which is configured with the encapsulation frame-relay command:

```
interface Serial0/0
encapsulation frame-relay
```

You configure the ietf type with the encapsulation frame-relay ietf command. ietf Frame Relay encapsulation is usually used only when you're connecting Cisco routers to non-Cisco devices.

Once you've configured Frame Relay encapsulation and the interface is up, you should begin seeing LMI status messages. If the PVC has been provisioned, you can see it with the show frame-relay PVC command:

```
Router-A#sho frame pvc

PVC Statistics for interface Serial0/0 (Frame Relay DTE)

                Active     Inactive     Deleted      Static
    Local         0           0            0            0
    Switched      0           0            0            0
    Unused        0           1            0            0
DLCI = 102, DLCI USAGE = UNUSED, PVC STATUS = INACTIVE, INTERFACE = Serial0/0

    input pkts 0            output pkts 0        in bytes 0
    out bytes 0            dropped pkts 0        in pkts dropped 0
```

```
    out pkts dropped 0                out bytes dropped 0
    in FECN pkts 0        in BECN pkts 0            out FECN pkts 0
    out BECN pkts 0       in DE pkts 0              out DE pkts 0
    out bcast pkts 0      out bcast bytes 0
    switched pkts 0
    Detailed packet drop counters:
    no out intf 0         out intf down 0           no out PVC 0
    in PVC down 0         out PVC down 0            pkt too big 0
    shaping Q full 0      pkt above DE 0            policing drop 0
    pvc create time 00:19:12, last time pvc status changed 00:19:12
```

Notice that the information being sent relates status information about the local DLCI, not the remote side. LMI always reports on information critical to the local rather than the remote side of the link. The same output on Router B should show a similar report detailing the link from Router B's point of view:

```
Router-B#sho frame pvc

PVC Statistics for interface Serial0/0 (Frame Relay DTE)

             Active    Inactive    Deleted     Static
    Local      0          0           0          0
    Switched   0          0           0          0
    Unused     0          1           0          0
DLCI = 201, DLCI USAGE = UNUSED, PVC STATUS = ACTIVE, INTERFACE = Serial0/0

    input pkts 0          output pkts 0             in bytes 0
    out bytes 0           dropped pkts 0            in pkts dropped 0
    out pkts dropped 0                out bytes dropped 0
    in FECN pkts 0        in BECN pkts 0            out FECN pkts 0
    out BECN pkts 0       in DE pkts 0              out DE pkts 0
    out bcast pkts 0      out bcast bytes 0
    switched pkts 0
    Detailed packet drop counters:
    no out intf 0         out intf down 0           no out PVC 0
    in PVC down 0         out PVC down 0            pkt too big 0
    shaping Q full 0      pkt above DE 0            policing drop 0
    pvc create time 00:19:08, last time pvc status changed 00:19:08
```

Once you see that LMI is active, you can assign IP addresses to the interfaces like you would on any other type of interface. Here is the IP address configuration for Router A:

```
Router-A(config-if)#int s0/0
Router-A(config-if)# ip address 192.168.1.1 255.255.255.252
```

And here is the IP address configuration for Router B:

```
Router-B(config-if)#int s0/0
Router-B(config-if)# ip address 192.168.1.2 255.255.255.252
```

At this point, you can ping across the link:

```
Router-A#ping 192.168.1.2

Type escape sequence to abort.
Sending 5, 100-byte ICMP Echos to 192.168.1.2, timeout is 2 seconds:
.!!!!
```

Ping works because the router has determined from the IP subnet mask that this is a point-to-point link.

To see the status of the PVC and which IP address has been mapped, use the show frame-relay map command:

```
Router-A#sho frame map
Serial0/0 (up): ip 192.168.1.2 dlci 102(0x66,0x1860), dynamic,
                broadcast,, status defined, active
```

Basic Frame Relay with More Than Two Nodes

Figure 23-11 shows a slightly more complex Frame Relay network. There are three routers in this network. Router A has a PVC to Router B, and another PVC to Router C. Router B does not have a direct connection to Router C.

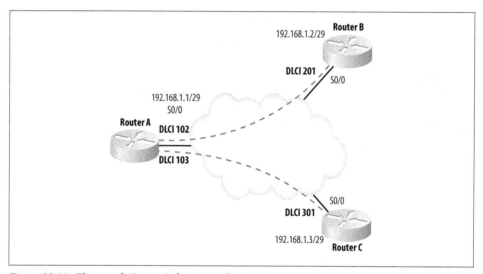

Figure 23-11. Three-node Frame Relay network

To accomplish this design, as in the previous example, begin by configuring Frame Relay encapsulation. This step is the same on all routers:

```
interface Serial0/0
  encapsulation frame-relay
```

The IP address configuration is nearly the same as well; the only difference is the subnet masks. Here are the configurations for the three routers:

Router A:

```
Router-A(config)#int s0/0
Router-A(config-if)# ip address 192.168.1.1 255.255.255.248
```

Router B:

```
Router-B(config)#int s0/0
Router-B(config-if)# ip address 192.168.1.2 255.255.255.248
```

Router C:

```
Router-C(config)#int s0/0
Router-C(config-if)# ip address 192.168.1.3 255.255.255.248
```

Performing these steps gives you a live Frame Relay network, which you can test as follows:

```
Router-A#ping 192.168.1.2

Type escape sequence to abort.
Sending 5, 100-byte ICMP Echos to 192.168.1.2, timeout is 2 seconds:
!!!!!
Success rate is 100 percent (5/5), round-trip min/avg/max = 56/57/60 ms

Router-A# ping 192.168.1.3

Type escape sequence to abort.
Sending 5, 100-byte ICMP Echos to 192.168.1.3, timeout is 2 seconds:
!!!!!
Success rate is 100 percent (5/5), round-trip min/avg/max = 56/57/60 ms
```

When there were only two nodes on the network, the routers were each able to determine the IP address of the far side by nature of the subnet mask. That's not the case here because there are more than two nodes.

When the subnet mask is other than 255.255.255.252, the routers will use Inverse ARP to determine which IP address belongs to which DLCI.

Beware of Inverse ARP on complex Frame Relay networks. Inverse ARP will discover all PVCs and their IP addresses, if they exist. This can cause unexpected or unwanted links to come online. Inverse ARP can be disabled with the no frame-relay inverse-arp command.

A better option for IP address-to-DLCI mappings is mapping them by hand, which you do with the frame-relay map interface command:

```
Router-A(config-if)#frame-relay map  ip 192.168.1.2 102 broadcast
Router-A(config-if)#frame-relay map  ip 192.168.1.3 103 broadcast
```

A mapping determined by Inverse ARP is considered a dynamic map, while a configured map is considered a static map.

Remember that each router only sees its own side of the PVC, so you are mapping the remote IP address to the local DLCI. Think of the local DLCI as pointing to the remote router. Take a look at the commands for Router B and Router C, and you'll see what I mean:

Router B:

```
Router-B(config-if)#frame-relay map ip 192.168.1.1 201 broadcast
```

Router C:

```
Router-C(config-if)#frame-relay map ip 192.168.1.1 301 broadcast
```

 At the end of each frame-relay map command, you'll notice the keyword broadcast. This keyword should be included anytime you execute this command. The broadcast keyword maps broadcasts, multicasts, and unicasts over the PVC. Broadcasts and multicasts are an integral part of most routing protocols, so if you have a Frame Relay WAN up and you can't figure out why EIGRP or OSPF isn't establishing adjacencies, check to make sure you've included the broadcast keyword in your map statements.

The way IP-DLCI mapping works includes one odd little side effect. With a network configured as you'd expect, you cannot ping your own Frame Relay interface:

```
Router-A#ping 192.168.1.1
Type escape sequence to abort.
Sending 5, 100-byte ICMP Echos to 192.168.1.1, timeout is 2 seconds:
.....
Success rate is 0 percent (0/5)
```

This can burn you during troubleshooting, because you may expect to be able to ping your own interface like you can with Ethernet. You cannot ping your own interface, because there is no predefined Layer-2 address. While Ethernet interfaces have permanent MAC addresses, Frame Relay interfaces do not. With Frame Relay, all Layer-2 addresses are configured manually.

To ping yourself, you must map your own IP address to a remote router. As odd as this seems, it will work—as soon as the packet arrives at the remote router, that router will send it back, because it has a mapping for your IP address. Because there is no local Layer-2 address, only a DLCI being advertised by the frame cloud, this is the only way to make it work. Beware that ping times to your local Frame Relay interface will actually reflect the round-trip time for the PVC you specify in the mapping. Here's an example:

```
Router-A(config-if)#frame-relay map ip 192.168.1.1 102

Router-A#ping 192.168.1.1

Type escape sequence to abort.
Sending 5, 100-byte ICMP Echos to 192.168.1.1, timeout is 2 seconds:
!!!!!
Success rate is 100 percent (5/5), round-trip min/avg/max = 112/112/112 ms
```

Notice the ping time compared with the previous example, where the remote side was pinged. Pinging yourself will take twice as long as pinging the remote side.

Local IP addresses mapped to remote DLCIs will not be locally available if the remote router fails or the PVC becomes unavailable. In this example, should Router B fail, Router A will no longer be able to ping its own S0/0 IP address, though Router A will still be able to communicate with Router C.

As a matter of best practice, I like to always map my DLCIs to IP addresses, even if the router can do it reliably on its own. Placing the DLCI information in the configuration makes the config easier to read and troubleshoot.

Frame Relay Subinterfaces

Sometimes, having two PVCs terminating on a single interface is not what you want, but, as you've seen, having a physical interface for each PVC is not beneficial for cost reasons. For example, with the network in Figure 23-11, each PVC terminates into a single interface. If you ran a routing protocol on these routers, Router B would advertise itself, but Router A would not advertise this route out to Router C, because of the split-horizon rule. Splitting the PVCs into separate interfaces would allow the routing protocol to advertise the route, because the split-horizon rule would no longer apply.

Cisco routers have a feature called *subinterfaces* that solves this problem. In a nutshell, subinterfaces allow you to configure virtual interfaces for each PVC. These virtual interfaces are named after the physical interfaces on which they are found. For example, a subinterface derived from S0/0 might be called S0/0.100. The subinterface number is user-definable, and can be within the range of 1 to 4,294,967,293. I like to name subinterfaces according to the DLCIs mapped to them.

There are two types of subinterfaces: point-to-point and multipoint. Point-to-point subinterfaces can have only one DLCI active on them, while multipoint subinterfaces can have many. Multipoint subinterfaces behave in much the same way that physical interfaces do: you can have a mix of point-to-point and multipoint subinterfaces on a physical interface. It is even possible to have some DLCIs assigned to subinterfaces, and others to the physical interface.

As mentioned earlier, one of the main benefits of Frame Relay subinterfaces is the elimination of split-horizon issues with routing protocols. Creating multiple point-to-point subinterfaces and assigning each of the PVCs to one of them allows each PVC to be considered a different interface. Subinterfaces are created with the global `inter face` command. Specify the name you'd like the subinterface to have, along with the keyword `point-to-point` or `multipoint`:

```
Router-A(config)#int s0/0.102 point-to-point
Router-A(config-subif)#
```

You're now in interface configuration mode for the newly created subinterface, and you can configure this subinterface as you would a physical interface.

Be careful when you choose your subinterface type. If you choose the wrong type by mistake, the only way to change it is to negate the defining command in the configuration, save the config minus the subinterface, and reboot the router. As a result, the following error message will be displayed when you remove a Frame Relay subinterface:

```
Not all config may be removed and may reappear after reactivating
the sub-interface.
```

You now need to assign specific VCs to the subinterface. You can do this with the `frame-relay interface-dlci` subinterface command, or by mapping a DLCI to a Layer-3 address with the `frame-relay map` subinterface command. If you're adding a subinterface after you've already configured the DLCI on the physical interface, you'll need to remove the maps on the physical interface before proceeding.

Mapping an IP address to a VC is a little different when you're using subinterfaces and the `interface-dlci` command:

```
interface Serial0/0.102 point-to-point
  frame-relay interface-dlci 102 protocol ip 192.168.1.2
```

I like this method because it shows that you've assigned the DLCI to the subinterface and that you've mapped it to an IP address. If you just use the `map` statement, it doesn't seem as obvious. Still, either way is acceptable.

On point-to-point subinterfaces, you don't really need to map IP addresses to DLCIs, as the router will know that the far end is the only other IP address available (assuming a network mask of 255.255.255.252). Remember that if you make point-to-point links with subinterfaces, each PVC will now require its own IP network.

Figure 23-12 shows the same network as Figure 23-11, only this time with each of the PVCs assigned to specific Frame Relay subinterfaces.

Routers B and C don't technically need subinterfaces in this scenario, but if you configured them on the physical interface, you need to change the configuration if you later added a PVC between Routers B and C. Configuring the subinterfaces now will potentially make life easier in the future.

Here are the configurations for the three routers:

Router A:

```
interface Serial0/0
 no ip address
 encapsulation frame-relay
!
interface Serial0/0.102 point-to-point
 ip address 192.168.1.1 255.255.255.252
 frame-relay interface-dlci 102 protocol ip 192.168.1.2
!
interface Serial0/0.103 point-to-point
 ip address 192.168.2.1 255.255.255.252
 frame-relay interface-dlci 103 protocol ip 192.168.2.2
```

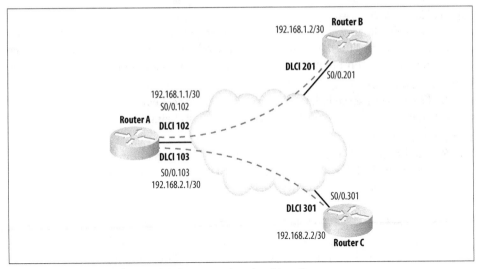

Figure 23-12. Three-node Frame Relay network with subinterfaces

Router B:

```
interface Serial0/0
 no ip address
 encapsulation frame-relay
!
interface Serial0/0.201 point-to-point
 ip address 192.168.1.2 255.255.255.252
 frame-relay interface-dlci 201 protocol ip 192.168.1.1
```

Router C:

```
interface Serial0/0
 no ip address
 encapsulation frame-relay
!
interface Serial0/0.301 point-to-point
 ip address 192.168.2.2 255.255.255.252
 frame-relay interface-dlci 301 protocol ip 192.168.2.1
```

Troubleshooting Frame Relay

Troubleshooting Frame Relay is quite simple once you understand how it works. Remember that most of the information regarding PVCs is delivered from the DCE device, which is usually the telecom switch on the far end of your physical link.

The key to any troubleshooting process is *problem isolation*. You need to identify where the problem lies so you can determine a corrective course of action. Follow these steps, and you'll quickly isolate where the trouble is:

Physical layer first!

Is the cable plugged in? Is the cable a known good cable? Is the cable on the other end plugged in? This may sound silly, but you'll feel pretty foolish if you call Cisco for help only to find that the cause of your woes was an unplugged cable.

Is the serial link up?

Make sure your serial link is up via a `show interface`. Leaving an interface in a shutdown state has a tendency to prevent traffic from being passed over it.

Are you receiving LMI?

Remember that LMI is sent from your locally connected telecom device. If you're not receiving LMI, you're not getting status messages regarding your VCs, so the router will not know that they exist. There are a couple of ways to see whether you're receiving LMI:

`show interface`

The output from a `show interface` command for a Frame Relay–encapsulated interface will include LMI counters. LMI updates are received every 10 seconds, so executing the command and then waiting 10 seconds or more and executing the command again should show an increase in the LMI counters:

```
Router-A#sho int s0/0 | include LMI
  LMI enq sent  186, LMI stat recvd 186, LMI upd recvd 0, DTE LMI up
  LMI enq recvd 0, LMI stat sent  0, LMI upd sent  0
  LMI DLCI 1023  LMI type is CISCO  frame relay DTE
Router-A#
Router-A#
Router-A# sho int s0/0 | include LMI
  LMI enq sent  188, LMI stat recvd 188, LMI upd recvd 0, DTE LMI up
  LMI enq recvd 0, LMI stat sent  0, LMI upd sent  0
  LMI DLCI 1023  LMI type is CISCO  frame relay DTE
```

`debug frame-relay lmi`

The `debug frame-relay lmi` command will show every LMI update sent and received on the Frame Relay interfaces. As always, be very careful when issuing debug commands on production devices. These commands can cause large or busy routers to stop functioning due to the increased CPU load. When you run the `debug frame-relay lmi` command, a small status message (which is not of much use) is sent every 10 seconds, and a summary of all the VCs present on the link is sent every 30 seconds. You'll recognize this message by the obvious inclusion of lines beginning with PVC or SVC:

```
Router-A#debug frame lmi
Frame Relay LMI debugging is on
Displaying all Frame Relay LMI data
Router-A#
00:33:05: Serial0/0(out): StEnq, myseq 197, yourseen 196, DTE up
00:33:05: datagramstart = 0×3CE9B74, datagramsize = 13
00:33:05: FR encap = 0×FCF10309
00:33:05: 00 75 01 01 01 03 02 C5 C4
00:33:05:
```

```
00:33:05: Serial0/0(in): Status, myseq 197, pak size 13
00:33:05: RT IE 1, length 1, type 1
00:33:05: KA IE 3, length 2, yourseq 197, myseq 197
00:33:15: Serial0/0(out): StEnq, myseq 198, yourseen 197, DTE up
00:33:15: datagramstart = 0x3CEA1B4, datagramsize = 13
00:33:15: FR encap = 0xFCF10309
00:33:15: 00 75 01 01 00 03 02 C6 C5
00:33:15:
00:33:15: Serial0/0(in): Status, myseq 198, pak size 53
00:33:15: RT IE 1, length 1, type 0
00:33:15: KA IE 3, length 2, yourseq 198, myseq 198
00:33:15: PVC IE 0x7 , length 0x6 , dlci 102, status 0x2 , bw 0
00:33:15: PVC IE 0x7 , length 0x6 , dlci 103, status 0x2 , bw 0
00:33:15: PVC IE 0x7 , length 0x6 , dlci 104, status 0x0 , bw 0
00:33:15: PVC IE 0x7 , length 0x6 , dlci 105, status 0x0 , bw 0
00:33:15: PVC IE 0x7 , length 0x6 , dlci 106, status 0x0 , bw 0
00:33:25: Serial0/0(out): StEnq, myseq 199, yourseen 198, DTE up
00:33:25: datagramstart = 0x3CEA574, datagramsize = 13
00:33:25: FR encap = 0xFCF10309
00:33:25: 00 75 01 01 01 03 02 C7 C6
```

In this example, the Frame Relay switch is advertising five PVCs. The status of each is 0x0 or 0x2. 0x0 means that the VC is configured on the Frame Relay switch, but is not active. This occurs most commonly because the far-end device is not configured (in other words, it's probably your fault, not telco's). A status of 0x2 indicates that the VC is configured and active. If the VC is not listed at all in the status message, either telco hasn't yet provisioned it, or it has been provisioned on the wrong switch or interface.

Are the VCs active on the router?

The command show frame-relay pvc will show the status of every known Frame Relay PVC on the router:

```
Router-A#sho frame pvc

PVC Statistics for interface Serial0/0 (Frame Relay DTE)

            Active      Inactive     Deleted      Static
Local        2             0            0            0
Switched     0             0            0            0
Unused       0             3            0            0
DLCI = 102, DLCI USAGE = LOCAL, PVC STATUS = ACTIVE, INTERFACE = Serial0/0.102

  input pkts 46           output pkts 55        in bytes 11696
  out bytes 14761         dropped pkts 0        in pkts dropped 0
  out pkts dropped 0          out bytes dropped 0
  in FECN pkts 0          in BECN pkts 0        out FECN pkts 0
  out BECN pkts 0         in DE pkts 0          out DE pkts 0
  out bcast pkts 45       out bcast bytes 13721
  pvc create time 00:44:07, last time pvc status changed 00:44:07
DLCI = 103, DLCI USAGE = LOCAL, PVC STATUS = ACTIVE, INTERFACE = Serial0/0.103

  input pkts 39           output pkts 47        in bytes 11298
  out bytes 13330         dropped pkts 0        in pkts dropped 0
```

```
out pkts dropped 0                    out bytes dropped 0
in FECN pkts 0         in BECN pkts 0           out FECN pkts 0
out BECN pkts 0        in DE pkts 0             out DE pkts 0
out bcast pkts 42      out bcast bytes 12810
pvc create time 00:39:13, last time pvc status changed 00:39:13
DLCI = 104, DLCI USAGE = UNUSED, PVC STATUS = INACTIVE, INTERFACE = Serial0/0

input pkts 0           output pkts 0            in bytes 0
out bytes 0            dropped pkts 0           in pkts dropped 0
out pkts dropped 0               out bytes dropped 0
in FECN pkts 0         in BECN pkts 0           out FECN pkts 0
out BECN pkts 0        in DE pkts 0             out DE pkts 0
out bcast pkts 0       out bcast bytes 0
switched pkts 0
Detailed packet drop counters:
no out intf 0          out intf down 0          no out PVC 0
in PVC down 0          out PVC down 0           pkt too big 0
shaping Q full 0       pkt above DE 0           policing drop 0
pvc create time 00:44:01, last time pvc status changed 00:44:01
```

[output truncated]

For every PVC, there is a paragraph that shows the status of the PVC and the interface on which it was discovered. Notice that PVCs that have been assigned to subinterfaces are shown to be active on those subinterfaces. All other PVCs are shown to be associated with the physical interfaces on which they were found. If a particular PVC is not shown here, you're probably not receiving LMI for that VC.

Each entry shows a status, which can be one of the following:

Active

> This status indicates that the PVC is up end to end and is functioning normally.

Inactive

> This status indicates that a PVC is defined by the telecom switch, but you do not have an active mapping for it. If this is the PVC you're trying to use, you probably forgot to map it or mapped it incorrectly.

Deleted

> This status indicates that you have a mapping active, but the PVC you've mapped to doesn't exist. An incorrect mapping may cause this problem.

Static

> This status indicates that no keepalive is configured on the Frame Relay interface of the router.

Is the PVC mapped to an interface?

> The show frame-relay map command shows a very concise report of the VCs that are mapped to interfaces:

```
Router-A#sho frame map
Serial0/0.103 (up): point-to-point dlci, dlci 103(0×67,0×1870), broadcast
          status defined, active
```

```
Serial0/0.102 (up): point-to-point dlci, dlci 102(0×66,0×1860), broadcast
            status defined, active
```

If a PVC is not listed here, but it is listed in the output of the show frame-relay
pvc command, you have a configuration problem.

## CHAPTER 24

MPLS

In my experience, there are two levels of involvement with MPLS (Multiprotocol Label Switching) networks. First, there are people who design and maintain the MPLS networks themselves. These people generally work for service providers such as AT&T, British Telecom, and the like. Second are the people who need to use MPLS in their corporate WANs. This chapter is written for the latter category—the people who need to employ an MPLS solution in their networks, not the people who actually design them. Why? Because the target audience for this book is composed mostly of the people who work with corporate networks on a daily basis. My goal is not to help you build an MPLS network from the ground up, it's to help you deploy MPLS as handed to you from a provider. As a result, you will not see a lot of jargon like *penultimate hop popping* (possibly my favorite tech term ever) used here. Really, you don't need to know this to make an MPLS WAN work for you. My goal, as always, is to help you get your job done.

In a nutshell, packets in an MPLS network are prefixed with an MPLS header (called a *label stack*). This header contains one or more *labels*, each of which contains a label value, a traffic-class field (used for quality of service [QoS]), a bottom-of-stack flag, and an 8-bit time-to-live (TTL) field. Sounds exciting, doesn't it? For most people using MPLS, none of this matters. Bear with me, though, because you need to understand some history.

The label stack is the only thing examined by the MPLS switches. Therefore, no traditional routing table lookups are required, which in theory makes this a much faster solution than more traditional IP-based solutions. In the time since MPLS was designed, hardware has evolved considerably, and one might argue that the speed gained from the more efficient protocol is only a small part of what makes MPLS successful.

When MPLS was being devised, the prevalent WAN technologies in use were ATM and Frame Relay, both of which suffered from some drawbacks. ATM especially suffered from severe overhead requirements that made it pretty unattractive. MPLS offered something more than simple speed and efficiency, though.

Because entire packets are prefixed with an MPLS header, the MPLS network can serve multiple networks as virtual networks within the MPLS cloud. Furthermore, there are no obvious virtual circuits in an MPLS network as seen from the customer device. An MPLS network, as seen from a customer's perspective, is like having a private Internet, with only the customer's desired endpoints being visible.

So let's cut to the chase. Why use MPLS over Frame Relay or ATM? I'll be honest with you—the number one reason that most companies deploy MPLS has nothing to do with technology. They make this decision because of cost. MPLS has been aggressively sold by the major carriers in the past few years, making it more attractive than its rival technologies. While MPLS used to be a specialty service reserved for those willing to pay for it, the major providers have made it mainstream through competitive pricing. I did a 300-node MPLS migration for a company that had reached the end of its Frame Relay contract. The price quoted for full T1 service to each location with dual OC3s at the head end was significantly less than the fractional T1 Frame Relay network with DS3s at the head end. The company got faster connections at every site for a significant reduction in cost—who wouldn't take that deal?

The challenge was getting the new WAN integrated with the existing network. MPLS uses a significantly different method of logical connectivity than Frame Relay, and migrating can be a challenge.

Frame Relay works on the fundamental principal of virtual circuits. With 300 locations connecting to one of two headquarters buildings, we had 300 virtual circuits to manage and maintain between two routers. Figure 24-1 shows the design as it was when it incorporated Frame Relay.

This design worked fine, but there were some pretty significant limitations. For example, should HQ-1 fail, the branches connected to it would be offline, since there was no dynamic failover to HQ-2. While each branch could have been connected to both HQ offices, this would require another Frame Relay PVC to be built at significant additional cost. Instead, loss of potentially one-half of the branches was considered to be an acceptable risk given the cost of full redundancy. ISDN lines were used as emergency backup links, which introduced more problems since ISDN usage was (and is) extremely expensive. This solution was designed before broadband was widely available, though, so we had to work with the cards we were dealt.

MPLS would allow us some significant improvements, not the least of which was an increase in speed. Perhaps the most important to us at the time, though, was that each branch could directly connect to both HQ locations without the need for an additional PVC. Not only that, but due to the nature of MPLS, every branch could communicate directly with every other branch without traversing the HQ locations. This would become important, since we were looking to implement a VoIP solution later on as well. Figure 24-2 shows the design using MPLS. Notice that the overall design has not really changed. Each branch and each HQ location still connects to the cloud. The difference is that there are no VCs from the customer's point of view. Each site truly connects to

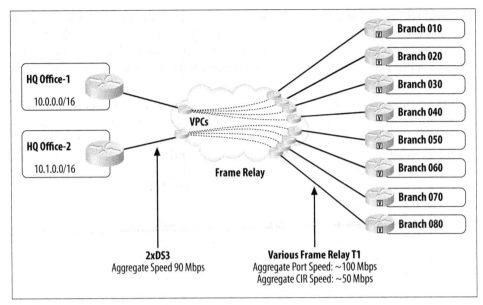

Figure 24-1. Multisite Frame Relay

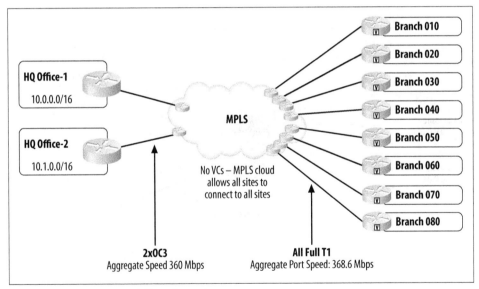

Figure 24-2. MPLS allows full-mesh topology

a cloud with no direct configured or learned virtual links to other locations. Notice that there are MPLS paths within the cloud and, indeed, this can get pretty complicated, but from the customer's point of view, there are no virtual circuits to configure, maintain, or monitor.

So how do the branches communicate if there are no links connecting them? There are two answers—the "how MPLS really works" answer, which involves switching in the cloud based on labels, and the "what you need to know" answer, which is much simpler. From each location's point of view, an IP routing protocol provides a next hop for the destination IP address.

Hold the phone! Didn't I say that IP routing tables weren't needed anymore? Yes, I did. At the level where the provider is forwarding packets, your IP routing table doesn't really matter. This entire WAN, BGP and all, is contained within a virtual network within the provider's MPLS network. Remember, the provider only cares about labels, and our network has no labels. The provider receives our packet, attaches a label to the packet, and forwards it through the cloud using that label. The contents of the packet are irrelevant. Only the label matters.

Figure 24-3 shows how this is possible. There are two customers using MPLS service from the same provider. Each customer is using the same IP space (10.0.0.0/16). Each customer also connects to the same MPLS environment, but neither customer can connect to the other's routers. Why? They each have their own labels. This is similar to a VPN in that each customer can only see its own equipment, even though they share the network beneath. You may hear people refer to MPLS networks as VPNs, but be careful with terminology, because with MPLS, there is usually no encryption involved.

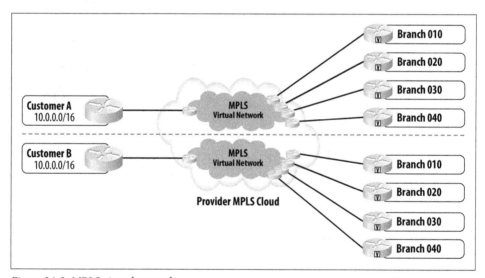

Figure 24-3. MPLS virtual networks

What matters to the customer is that all of this is transparent. There is no indication to the customer that there are any labels or virtual networks involved. The fact that the MPLS is involved is also (usually) completely transparent. For the most part, the only thing that appears to be different to most engineers turning up provider-supplied MPLS is that BGP is usually involved. We'll get to that in a moment.

One of the other big selling points for MPLS is the inherent support for QoS. Since one of the labels in the MPLS label stack is a traffic-class field, MPLS networks can be built to support true classes of service. The number of classes varies by provider, and each provider will generally offer different schemes for classification. The capability to support a strict priority queue makes MPLS very attractive for companies wishing to use VoIP across their WANs. For companies with thousands of nodes, MPLS can have a significant impact, especially where Frame Relay might have been used previously.

So how do you configure MPLS? In short, you don't. From a customer (versus a provider) viewpoint, you don't need to configure anything to make MPLS work—it all happens on the provider's equipment. This is a sharp contrast to both Frame Relay and ATM, where there are all sorts of things to know and configure. For most implementations of MPLS, you need to know BGP, and if you want to use QoS, you'll need to know how to configure that. Some providers that use BGP will allow you to use EIGRP instead of BGP, but I don't recommend this. Sure, it may be easier for you to understand if you have no experience with BGP, but you'll just be letting the provider do the BGP-EIGRP redistribution for you, and you'll lose control of how that's done. That might not be a big deal if you've got a simple MPLS environment, but with complex environments, redistribution can cause all sorts of problems if not properly managed.

Here is a sample MPLS router configuration for the router at branch number 10 from the preceding example.

First I'll design the QoS. We'll keep it simple. VoIP RTP and call control will get priority, and everything else will be dropped into the default queue. The priority queue can use up to 40 percent of the link, while call control will get 5 percent. See Chapters 31 and 32 for more detail on QoS:

```
class-map match-any VoIP-RTP
 match ip dscp ef
class-map match-any VoIP-Call-Control
 match ip dscp cs3
 match ip dscp af31
!
policy-map MPLS-QoS
 class VoIP-RTP
    priority percent 40
 class VoIP-Call-Control
    bandwidth percent 5
 class class-default
    fair-queue
```

Here's the configuration for the MPLS link. Notice that there's nothing MPLS-specific in this configuration:

```
interface Serial0/3/0
 description [ Branch 10 MPLS ]
 ip address 10.255.10.2 255.255.255.252
```

```
encapsulation ppp
auto qos voip trust
service-policy output MPLS-QoS
```

Here's the inside Ethernet interface:

```
interface FastEthernet0/0
description [ Branch 10 LAN ]
ip address 10.10.10.1 255.255.255.128
duplex auto
speed auto
auto qos voip trust
service-policy output MPLS-QoS
```

Next, I'll add a loopback address for routing, which will be useful for VPN failover (not shown here):

```
interface Loopback0
description [ Branch 10 Loopback ]
ip address 10.10.10.129 255.255.255.255
```

Finally, we need some BGP configuration so that we can learn and advertise routes through the cloud:

```
router bgp 65010
no synchronization
bgp log-neighbor-changes
network 10.10.10.0 mask 255.255.255.128
network 10.10.10.129 mask 255.255.255.255
aggregate-address 10.10.10.0 255.255.255.0 summary-only
neighbor 10.255.255.1 remote-as 65001
neighbor 10.255.255.1 update-source Serial0/3/0
neighbor 10.255.255.1 version 4
neighbor 10.255.255.1 prefix-list Aggregate out
no auto-summary
!
ip prefix-list Aggregate seq 5 permit 10.10.10.0/24
```

As you can see, there is nothing MPLS-specific about this configuration. No mention of labels, hop popping, or anything other than routing, QoS, and typical IP address entries.

## CHAPTER 25

Access Lists

The technical name for an access list is *access control list*. The individual entries in an access control list are called *access control entries*, or ACEs. The term access control list isn't often used in practice; you'll typically hear these lists referred to simply as access lists or ACLs.

Access lists do more than just control access. They are the means whereby Cisco devices categorize and match packets in any number of interesting ways. Access lists are used as simple filters to allow traffic through interfaces. They are also used to define "interesting traffic" for ISDN dialer maps, and are used in some route maps for matching.

Designing Access Lists

This chapter's focus will be less on the basics of access list design, and more on making you conscious of its benefits and pitfalls. The tips and tricks in this chapter should help you to write better, more efficient, and more powerful access lists.

 When you're creating access lists (or any configuration, for that matter), it's a good idea to create them first in a text editor, and then, once you've worked out all the details, try them in a lab environment. Anytime you're working on filters, you risk causing an outage.

Named Versus Numbered

Access lists on many Cisco devices can be either named or numbered. Named access lists are referenced with a name such as `GAD` or `RepelInvaders`. Numbered access lists are the older method, where each ACL is defined by a number such as `101`. Where possible, you should get in the habit of using named access lists. Some devices such as certain Nexus switches don't support numbered access lists at all.

Wildcard Masks

Wildcard masks (also called *inverse masks*) are used in many devices for creating access lists. These masks can be confusing, because they're the opposite, in binary, of normal subnet masks. In other words, the wildcard mask you would use to match a range that is described with a subnet mask of 255.255.255.0 would be 0.0.0.255.

Here's a simple rule that will solve most of the subnet/wildcard mask problems you'll see:

> Replace all 0s with 255s, and all 255s with 0s.

Table 25-1 shows how class A, B, and C subnet masks are written as wildcard masks.

Table 25-1. Classful wildcard masks

Subnet mask	Matching wildcard mask
255.0.0.0	0.255.255.255
255.255.0.0	0.0.255.255
255.255.255.0	0.0.0.255

While this may seem obvious, in the real world, networks are not often designed on classful boundaries. To illustrate my point, consider a subnet mask of 255.255.255.224. The equivalent wildcard mask works out to be 0.0.0.31.

Luckily, there is a trick to figuring out all wildcard masks, and it's easier than you might think. Here it is:

> The wildcard mask will be a derivative of the number of host addresses provided by the subnet mask minus one.

In the preceding example (the subnet mask 255.255.255.224), there are eight networks with 32 hosts in each (see Chapter 36 for help figuring out how many hosts are in a subnetted network), so 32 – 1 = 31. The wildcard mask is 0.0.0.31. Yes, it's really that simple.

All you really need to think about is the one octet that isn't a 0 or a 255. In the case of the wildcard mask being in a position other than the last octet, simply use the same formula and consider the number of hosts to be what it would be if the dividing octet were the last octet. Here's an example, using the subnet mask 255.240.0.0:

1. Replace all 0 octets with 255 and all 255 octets with 0 for a result of 0.240.255.255.
2. 240 in the last octet of a subnet mask (255.255.255.240) would yield 16 hosts.
3. 16 – 1 = 15. Replace this value for the octet not changed in step 1. The result is 0.15.255.255.
4. The wildcard mask is 0.15.255.255.

The more you work with inverse masks, the easier this becomes. Try a few for yourself, and you'll quickly get the hang of it.

To make things even more confusing, access lists in Cisco Adaptive Security Appliances (ASAs) don't use inverse masks, but instead use regular subnet masks. Here's a sample access list from a 5540 ASA:

```
access-list GAD extended permit tcp any 10.0.0.0 255.255.255.0 eq www
```

Here's the equivalent access list as configured in a 3750 switch:

```
ip access-list extended GAD
 permit tcp any 10.10.10.0 0.0.0.255 eq www
```

Notice the section in bold italics. On the ASA, a normal subnet mask is used to define the range. On the 3750, an inverse mask is used. Luckily, you'll get an error on either device if you do it the wrong way, but it's still an annoying inconsistency.

In NX-OS, access lists can use prefixes instead of subnet or inverse masks. I like this format the best and wish all platforms would adopt it:

```
ip access-list GAD
 10 permit tcp 10.10.10.0/24 any eq www
```

Where to Apply Access Lists

One of the most common questions I hear from junior engineers is, "Do I apply the access list inbound or outbound?" The answer is almost always *inbound*.

Figure 25-1 shows a simple router with two interfaces, E0 and E1. I've labeled the points where an access list could be applied. The thing to remember is that these terms are from the device's viewpoint.

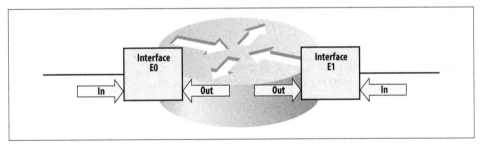

Figure 25-1. Access list application points

Usually, when you're trying to filter traffic, you want to prevent it from getting into the network, or even getting to the device in the first place. Applying access lists to the inbound side of an interface keeps the packets from entering the device, thus saving processing time. When a packet is allowed into a device, then switched to another interface only to be dropped by an outbound filter, resources used to switch the packet have been wasted.

Reflexive access lists, covered later in this chapter, are applied in both directions.

Figure 25-2 shows a small network connected to the Internet by a router. The router is filtering traffic from the Internet to protect the devices inside. As traffic comes from the Internet, it travels inbound on E1, is switched in the router to E0, and is then forwarded to the inside network. If the ACL is applied inbound on E1, the packets will be denied before the router has to process them any further. If the ACL is applied outbound on E0, the router must expend resources switching the packets between interfaces, only to then drop them.

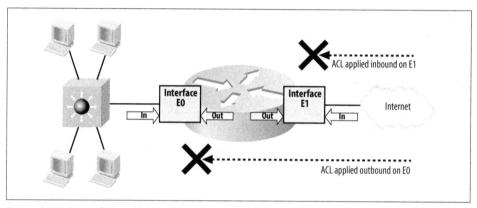

Figure 25-2. Access list application in a network

 Be careful when deleting access lists. If you delete an access list that is applied to an interface, the interface will deny all traffic. Always remove the relevant `access-group` commands before removing an access list.

Naming Access Lists

A quick word on naming access lists is in order. It's possible, and encouraged, to name access lists on Cisco routers with logical names rather than numbers, as it makes the configuration easier to read. The drawback of named access lists is that they cannot be used in many of the ways in which numbered access lists can be used. For example, route maps support named access lists, but dialer maps do not. ASA and PIX firewalls only support named access lists. That is, even if you create an access list named 10 on an ASA, it will be considered a named access list rather than a standard (numbered) access list. Nexus switches do not support numbered access lists.

When you name access lists, it makes sense to name them well. I've seen many installations of PIX firewalls where the inbound access list is named something like "out." Imagine troubleshooting this command:

```
access-group out in interface outside
```

If you're not used to configuring ASA or PIX firewalls, that command might be difficult to interpret. If the access list were instead named "Inbound," the command would be much more readable:

```
access-group Inbound in interface outside
```

The ability to quickly determine what a device is configured to do can save time during an outage, which can literally save your job. I like to begin my access list names with capital letters to help identify them in code. This is a personal preference that may or may not suit your style—I've worked with people who complain when they have to use the Shift key when typing.

Top-Down Processing

Access lists are processed from the top down, one line at a time. When a match is made, processing stops. This is an important rule to remember when building and troubleshooting access lists. A common mistake is to add a specific line to match something that's already been matched in a less specific line above it. Let's look at an example from a 3750 switch:

```
ip access-list extended GAD
  permit tcp any 10.10.10.0 0.0.0.255 eq www
  permit tcp any host 10.10.10.100 eq www
  permit tcp any host 10.10.10.100 eq domain
```

In this example, the second `permit` line will never be matched, because the IP address and protocol are matched in the previous line. Even so, in the event that the first line doesn't match, the second line will still be evaluated, wasting time and processing power. This is a very common problem in enterprise networks. On larger firewalls, where more than one person is administering the device, the problem can be severe. It may also be hard to spot, because it doesn't prevent protocols from working. This type of problem is usually uncovered during a network audit.

Most-Used on Top

Access lists should be built in such a way that the lines that are matched the most are at the beginning of the list. Recall that an ACL is processed until a match is made. Once a match is made, the remainder of the ACL is not processed. If you've only worked on routers with small ACLs, this may not seem like a big deal, but in real-world enterprise firewalls, ACLs can be extensive. I've worked on firewalls where there were over 50,000 rules in place. How many of those entries do you suppose were valid?

Here's an actual example from a PIX firewall. When my team built this small access list, we just added each line as we thought of it. This is a relatively common approach in the real world. We came up with a list of servers (web1, lab, web2), then listed each protocol to be allowed:

```
access-list Inbound permit tcp any host web1.gad.net eq www
access-list Inbound permit tcp any host web1.gad.net eq ssh
access-list Inbound permit udp any host web1.gad.net eq domain
access-list Inbound permit tcp any host web1.gad.net eq smtp
access-list Inbound permit tcp any host web1.gad.net eq imap4
access-list Inbound permit tcp any host lab.gad.net eq telnet
access-list Inbound permit tcp any host lab.gad.net eq 8080
access-list Inbound permit udp any host web2.gad.net eq domain
access-list Inbound permit tcp any host web2.gad.net eq smtp
access-list Inbound permit tcp any host web2.gad.net eq imap4
```

After letting the network run for a few days, we were able to see how our access list had fared by executing the show access-list command:

```
PIX#sho access-list
access-list cached ACL log flows: total 0, denied 0 (deny-flow-max 1024)
            alert-interval 300
access-list Inbound; 15 elements
access-list Inbound permit tcp any host web1.gad.net eq www (hitcnt=42942)
access-list Inbound permit tcp any host web1.gad.net eq ssh (hitcnt=162)
access-list Inbound permit udp any host web1.gad.net eq domain (hitcnt=22600)
access-list Inbound permit tcp any host web1.gad.net eq smtp (hitcnt=4308)
access-list Inbound permit tcp any host web1.gad.net eq imap4 (hitcnt=100)
access-list Inbound permit tcp any host lab.gad.net eq telnet (hitcnt=0)
access-list Inbound permit tcp any host lab.gad.net eq 8080 (hitcnt=1)
access-list Inbound permit udp any host web2.gad.net eq domain (hitcnt=10029)
access-list Inbound permit tcp any host web2.gad.net eq smtp (hitcnt=2)
access-list Inbound permit tcp any host web2.gad.net eq imap4 (hitcnt=0)
```

Look carefully at the hitcnt entries at the ends of the lines. They show how many times each line in the ACL has been hit. The hit counts indicate that this ACL was not built optimally. To build it better, take the preceding output and sort it by hitcnt, with the largest number first. The results look like this:

```
access-list Inbound permit tcp any host web1.gad.net eq www (hitcnt=42942)
access-list Inbound permit udp any host web1.gad.net eq domain (hitcnt=22600)
access-list Inbound permit udp any host web2.gad.net eq domain (hitcnt=10029)
access-list Inbound permit tcp any host web1.gad.net eq smtp (hitcnt=4308)
access-list Inbound permit tcp any host web1.gad.net eq ssh (hitcnt=162)
access-list Inbound permit tcp any host web1.gad.net eq imap4 (hitcnt=100)
access-list Inbound permit tcp any host web2.gad.net eq smtp (hitcnt=2)
access-list Inbound permit tcp any host lab.gad.net eq 8080 (hitcnt=1)
access-list Inbound permit tcp any host lab.gad.net eq telnet (hitcnt=0)
access-list Inbound permit tcp any host web2.gad.net eq imap4 (hitcnt=0)
```

This is an optimal design for this admittedly small access list. The entries with the most hits are now at the top of the list, and those with the fewest are at the bottom.

Beware of assumptions. You may think that SMTP should be high on your list because your firewall is protecting a mail server, but if you look at the preceding output, you'll see that DNS shows far more connections than SMTP. Check to see what's actually running on your network, and configure accordingly.

The problem with this approach can be a loss of readability. In this case, the original ACL is much easier to read and understand than the redesigned version. The second, more efficient ACL has an entry for web2 in the middle of all the entries for web1. This is easy to miss, and can make troubleshooting harder. Only you, as the administrator, can make the call as to the benefits or drawbacks of the current ACL design. In smaller ACLs, you may want to make some concessions for readability, but in the case of a 17-page access list, you'll find that putting the most-used lines at the top will have a significant impact on the operational speed of a heavily used firewall.

Using Groups in ASA and PIX ACLs

ASA and PIX firewalls now allow the use of *groups* in access lists. This is a huge benefit for access list creation because it allows for very complex ACLs with very simple configurations. Using groups in ACLs also allows you to change multiple ACLs by changing a group—when you change a group that is in use, the PIX will automatically change every instance where that group is applied. With complex access lists, using groups can help prevent mistakes, because you're less likely to forget an important entry: you don't have to make the addition in multiple places, you only have to remember to put it into the group.

Let's look at an example of groups in action. Here is the original ACL:

```
object-group service CCIE-Rack tcp
  description [< For Terminal Server Reverse Telnet >]
  port-object range 2033 2050

access-list Inbound permit tcp any host gto eq www
access-list Inbound permit tcp any host gto eq ssh
access-list Inbound permit tcp any host meg eq ssh
access-list Inbound permit tcp any host meg eq www
access-list Inbound permit tcp any host lab eq telnet
access-list Inbound permit tcp any host lab object-group CCIE-Rack
access-list Inbound permit udp any host ASA-Outside eq 5060
access-list Inbound permit tcp any host lab eq 8080
access-list Inbound permit udp any host meg eq domain
access-list Inbound permit udp any host gto eq domain
access-list Inbound permit tcp any host gto eq smtp
access-list Inbound permit tcp any host meg eq smtp
access-list Inbound permit tcp any host gto eq imap4
access-list Inbound permit tcp any host meg eq imap4
access-list Inbound permit esp any any
access-list Inbound permit icmp any any unreachable
```

```
access-list Inbound permit icmp any any time-exceeded
access-list Inbound permit icmp any any echo-reply
```

Notice that there is an object group already in use for CCIE-Rack. This may not seem necessary, as the same thing could be accomplished with the **range** keyword:

```
access-list Inbound line 3 permit tcp any host lab range 2033 2050
```

In fact, as you'll see shortly, the object group is converted to this line anyway. Some people argue that if an object group takes up more lines of configuration than the number of lines it is translated into, it shouldn't be used. I disagree. I like the fact that I can add a description to an object group. Additionally, I can easily add a service to the object group at a later time without having to change any access lists.

Here are the groups I've created based on the original access list. I've incorporated the services common to multiple servers into a group called *Webserver-svcs*. I've also created a group called *Webservers* that contains all of the web servers, another called *Webserver-svcs-udp* for UDP-based services like DNS, and one for ICMP packets called *ICMP-Types*. The ICMP-Types group is for return packets resulting from pings and traceroutes. The brackets in the description fields may look odd to you, but I like to add them to make the descriptions stand out:

```
object-group service CCIE-Rack tcp
  description [< For Terminal Server Reverse Telnet >]
  port-object range 2033 2050
object-group service Webserver-svcs tcp
  description [< Webserver TCP Services >]
  port-object eq www
  port-object eq ssh
  port-object eq domain
  port-object eq smtp
  port-object eq imap4
object-group service Webserver-svcs-udp udp
  description [< Webserver UDP Services >]
  port-object eq domain
object-group network Webservers
  description [< Webservers >]
  network-object host gto
  network-object host meg
object-group icmp-type ICMP-Types
  description [< Allowed ICMP Types >]
  icmp-object unreachable
  icmp-object time-exceeded
  icmp-object echo-reply
```

Now that I've organized all the services and servers into groups, it's time to rewrite the access list to use them:

```
access-list Inbound permit udp any object-group Webservers object-group Webserver-
svcs-udp
access-list Inbound permit tcp any object-group Webservers object-group Webserver-
svcs
access-list Inbound permit tcp any host lab eq telnet
access-list Inbound permit tcp any host lab object-group CCIE-Rack
```

```
access-list Inbound permit udp any host ASA-Outside eq 5060
access-list Inbound permit tcp any host lab eq 8080
access-list Inbound permit esp any any
access-list Inbound permit icmp any any object-group ICMP-Types
```

The access list has gone from 18 lines down to 8. This is only the visible configuration, remember. These lines will be expanded in the firewall's memory to the original 18 lines.

 The lines may not be sorted optimally, which can be an issue with complex configurations. As with most things, there are tradeoffs. For complex installations on Cisco PIX firewalls, make sure you enable Turbo ACLs (discussed in the following section).

Notice that groups do not necessarily mean less typing—in fact, the opposite is usually true. Even though this access list has shrunk from 18 to 8 lines, we had to type in more lines than we saved. The goal is to make the access list easier to read and maintain. It's up to you to determine whether the eventual benefits will justify the initial effort.

You can see the actual result of the configuration using the show access-list command. The output includes both the object-group configuration lines and the actual ACEs to which they translate. The object-group entries are shown in bold:

```
GAD-PIX#sho access-list

access-list cached ACL log flows: total 0, denied 0 (deny-flow-max 1024)
            alert-interval 300
access-list Inbound; 20 elements
access-list Inbound line 1 permit udp any object-group
Webservers object-group Webserver-svcs-udp
access-list Inbound line 1 permit udp any host gto eq domain (hitcnt=7265)
access-list Inbound line 1 permit udp any host meg eq domain (hitcnt=6943)
access-list Inbound line 2 permit tcp any object-group Webservers object-group
Webserver-svcs
access-list Inbound line 2 permit tcp any host gto eq www (hitcnt=21335)
access-list Inbound line 2 permit tcp any host gto eq ssh (hitcnt=4428)
access-list Inbound line 2 permit tcp any host gto eq domain (hitcnt=0)
access-list Inbound line 2 permit tcp any host gto eq smtp (hitcnt=1901)
access-list Inbound line 2 permit tcp any host gto eq imap4 (hitcnt=116)
access-list Inbound line 2 permit tcp any host meg eq www (hitcnt=23)
access-list Inbound line 2 permit tcp any host meg eq ssh (hitcnt=15)
access-list Inbound line 2 permit tcp any host meg eq domain (hitcnt=0)
access-list Inbound line 2 permit tcp any host meg eq smtp (hitcnt=1)
access-list Inbound line 2 permit tcp any host meg eq imap4 (hitcnt=0)
access-list Inbound line 3 permit tcp any host lab eq telnet (hitcnt=0)
access-list Inbound line 4 permit tcp any host lab object-group CCIE-Rack
access-list Inbound line 4 permit tcp any host lab range 2033 2050 (hitcnt=0)
access-list Inbound line 5 permit udp any host ASA-Outside eq 5060 (hitcnt=0)
access-list Inbound line 6 permit tcp any host lab eq 8080 (hitcnt=0)
access-list Inbound line 7 permit esp any any (hitcnt=26256)
access-list Inbound line 8 permit icmp any any object-group ICMP-Types
access-list Inbound line 8 permit icmp any any unreachable (hitcnt=359)
```

```
access-list Inbound line 8 permit icmp any any time-exceeded (hitcnt=14)
access-list Inbound line 8 permit icmp any any echo-reply (hitcnt=822)
```

Deleting ACLs

In the good old days, you could just issue the no `access-list` 101 command, and the entire 101 access list would be gone. On an ASA, that command doesn't do anything, because it wants you to enter a specific line to be deleted:

```
ASA-5540/GAD(config)# no access-list 101
ERROR: % Incomplete command
```

This is actually a good thing, as it will cut down on instances where you accidentally delete an entire access list when all you really wanted to do was delete one line. (Not that that's ever happened to me.) On an ASA, if you want to delete an entire access list, use the clear configure access-list *access-list-name* command:

```
ASA-5540/GAD(config)# clear configure access-list 101
```

Turbo ACLs

Normally, ACLs must be interpreted every time they are referenced. This can lead to significant processor usage, especially on devices with large ACLs.

One of the options for enhancing performance with large ACLs is to compile them. A compiled ACL is called a *Turbo ACL* (usually pronounced *turbo-ackle*). Compiling an ACL changes it to machine code, which no longer needs to be interpreted before processing. This can have a significant impact on performance.

PIX firewalls and Cisco routers support Turbo ACLs. On the PIX, the command access-list compiled tells the firewall to compile all access lists. Only Cisco routers in the 7100, 7200, 7500, and 12000 series (12.0(6)S and later) support Turbo ACLs. The IOS command to enable this feature is also access-list compiled. The latest versions of ASA code have Turbo ACLs enabled by default. This behavior cannot be negated.

When Turbo ACLs are enabled on a PIX, the output of show access-list is altered to indicate that the ACLs are compiled and show how much memory each ACL occupies. This output is not present on the newest versions of the ASAs:

```
PIX(config)#access-list comp
PIX(config)#show access-list
TurboACL statistics:
ACL                        State       Memory(KB)
----------------------- ----------- ----------
Inbound                    Operational 2          Shared memory usage: 2056 KB
access-list compiled
access-list cached ACL log flows: total 0, denied 0 (deny-flow-max 1024)
            alert-interval 300
access-list Inbound turbo-configured; 20 elements
access-list Inbound line 1 permit udp any object-group Webservers object-group
Webserver-svcs-udp
```

```
access-list Inbound line 1 permit udp any host gto eq domain (hitcnt=7611)
access-list Inbound line 1 permit udp any host meg eq domain (hitcnt=7244)
access-list Inbound line 2 permit tcp any object-group Webservers object-group
Webserver-svcs
access-list Inbound line 2 permit tcp any host gto eq www (hitcnt=22578)
access-list Inbound line 2 permit tcp any host gto eq ssh (hitcnt=4430)
[-- text removed --]
```

Allowing Outbound Traceroute and Ping

One of the more common frustrations with firewalls is the inability to ping and traceroute once the security rules are put in place. The idea that ICMP is dangerous is valid, but if you understand how ICMP behaves, you can allow only the types you need, and thus continue to enjoy the benefits of ping and traceroute.

Assuming that you're allowing all outbound traffic, you can apply packet filters that allow as inbound traffic only those reply packets that are the result of ping and traceroute commands. This will allow your tests to work when they're initiated from inside the network, while disallowing those same tests when they originate from outside the network. For these tools to work, you must allow the following ICMP packet types in from the outside:

ICMP unreachable
> There are many ICMP unreachable types, including network unreachable and host unreachable. Generally, allowing them all is acceptable, because they are response packets.

Time exceeded
> Time exceeded messages are sent back by traceroute at each hop of the path taken toward the intended destination.

Echo reply
> An echo reply is the response from a ping packet.

The packet filters are usually included at the end of whatever inbound access lists are already in place. They should generally be placed at the bottom of the ACL unless there is a large amount of ICMP traffic originating inside your network. Here are some examples of deploying these filters for Cisco routers and PIX firewalls:

IOS:
```
access-list 101 remark [< Allows PING and Traceroute >]
access-list 101 permit icmp any any unreachable
access-list 101 permit icmp any any time-exceeded
access-list 101 permit icmp any any echo-reply
!
interface Ethernet1
ip access-group 101 in
```

Or using named access lists:

```
ip access-list extended Allow-ICMP
 remark [< Allows PING and Traceroute >]
 permit icmp any any unreachable
 permit icmp any any time-exceeded
 permit icmp any any echo-reply
 !
interface GigabitEthernet1/0/1
 ip access-group Allow-ICMP in
```

Firewalls:

```
object-group icmp-type ICMP-Types
  description [< Allowed ICMP Types >]
  icmp-object unreachable
  icmp-object time-exceeded
  icmp-object echo-reply
 !
access-list Inbound permit icmp any any object-group ICMP-Types
 !
access-group Inbound in interface outside
```

Allowing MTU Path Discovery Packets

Maximum Transmission Unit (MTU) path discovery allows devices on remote networks to inform you of MTU limitations. To enable this, you must allow two more ICMP types: *source-quench* and *parameter-problem*. You can allow them on Cisco routers and PIX firewalls as follows:

Cisco routers:

```
access-list 101 remark [< Allows PING and Traceroute >]
access-list 101 permit icmp any any unreachable
access-list 101 permit icmp any any time-exceeded
access-list 101 permit icmp any any echo-reply
access-list 101 permit icmp any any parameter-problem
access-list 101 permit icmp any any source-quench
 !
interface Ethernet1
ip access-group 101 in
```

And with named access lists:

```
ip access-list extended Allow-ICMP
 remark [< Allows PING and Traceroute >]
 permit icmp any any unreachable
 permit icmp any any time-exceeded
 permit icmp any any echo-reply
 permit icmp any any parameter-problem
 permit icmp any any source-quench
 !
interface GigabitEthernet1/0/1
 ip access-group Allow-ICMP in
```

Firewalls:

```
object-group icmp-type ICMP-Types
  description [< Allowed ICMP Types >]
  icmp-object unreachable
  icmp-object time-exceeded
  icmp-object echo-reply
  icmp-object source-quench
  icmp-object parameter-problem
!
access-list Inbound permit icmp any any object-group ICMP-Types
!
access-group Inbound in interface outside
```

ACLs in Multilayer Switches

Multilayer switches, by nature of their design, allow for some security features not available on Layer-2 switches or routers.

The 3750 switch supports IP ACLs and Ethernet (MAC) ACLs. Access lists on a 3750 switch can be applied in the following ways:

Port ACLs
> Port ACLs are applied to Layer-2 interfaces on the switch. They cannot be applied to EtherChannels, SVIs, or any other virtual interfaces. Port ACLs can be applied to trunk interfaces, in which case they will filter every VLAN in the trunk. Standard IP, extended IP, and MAC ACLs can be assigned as port ACLs. Port ACLs can be applied only in the *inbound* direction.

Router ACLs
> Router ACLs are applied to Layer-3 interfaces on the switch. SVIs, Layer-3 physical interfaces (configured with `no switchport`, for example), and Layer-3 EtherChannels can have router ACLs applied to them. Standard IP and extended IP ACLs can be assigned as router ACLs, while MAC ACLs cannot. Router ACLs can be applied in both *inbound* and *outbound* directions.

VLAN maps
> VLAN maps are similar in design to route maps. They are assigned to VLANs, and can be configured to pass or drop packets based on a number of tests. VLAN maps control all traffic routed into, out of, or within a VLAN. They have no direction.

Configuring Port ACLs

Port ACLs are ACLs attached to a specific physical interface. Port ACLs can be used to deny a host within a VLAN access to any other host within the VLAN. They can also be used to limit access outside the VLAN.

Imagine that VLAN 100 has many hosts in it, including host A. Host A should not be able to communicate directly with any other host within the same VLAN; it should be able to communicate only with the default gateway, to communicate with the rest of the world. Assume that host A's IP address is 192.168.1.155/24; the default gateway's IP address is 192.168.1.1/24; and host A is connected to port G0/20 on the switch.

The first step in restricting host A's communications is to create the necessary ACL. You must allow access to the default gateway, then deny access to other hosts in the network, and, finally, permit access to the rest of the world. I'm going to continue using named access lists, though numbered access lists are still supported:

```
ip access-list extended Permit-Bob
 permit ip any host 192.168.1.1
 deny   ip any 192.168.1.0 0.0.0.255
 permit ip any any
```

Once you've created the ACL, you can apply it to the physical interface:

```
IOS-3750(config)#int g1/0/2
IOS-3750 (config-if)#switchport
IOS-3750 (config-if)#ip access-group Permit-Bob in
```

Notice that even though this is a Layer-2 switch port, a Layer-3 IP access list can be applied to it. The fact that the IP access list is applied to a switch port is what makes it a port ACL.

Port ACLs can also be MAC-based. Here's a small MAC access list that denies Apple-Talk packets while permitting everything else:

```
mac access-list extended No-Appletalk
 deny   any any appletalk
 permit any any
```

Assigning this access list to an interface makes it a port ACL:

```
IOS-3750 (config)#int g1/0/2
IOS-3750 (config-if)# mac access-group No-Appletalk in
```

MAC ACLs can be mixed with IP ACLs in a single interface. Here, you can see that the MAC access list and the IP access list are active on the interface:

```
IOS-3750# sho run int g1/0/2
interface GigabitEthernet1/0/2
 ip access-group Permit-Bob in
 mac access-group No-Appletalk in
end
```

Configuring Router ACLs

Router ACLs are probably what most people think of when they think of applying ACLs. Router ACLs are applied to Layer-3 interfaces. Older routers have only Layer-3 interfaces, so just about all older ACLs were router ACLs.

If you were to take the previous example and change the port from a Layer-2 interface to a Layer-3 interface, the ACL would become a router ACL:

```
IOS-3750(config-if)#int g1/0/2
IOS-3750(config-if)#no switchport
IOS-3750(config-if)#ip access-group Permit-Bob in
```

MAC access lists cannot be assigned as router ACLs.

When configuring router ACLs, you have the option to apply the ACLs outbound (though I'm not a big fan of outbound ACLs):

```
IOS-3750(config-if)#ip access-group Permit-Bob out
```

Remember that applying an ACL to any Layer-3 interface will make the ACL a router ACL. Be careful when applying port ACLs and router ACLs together:

```
2w3d: %FM-3-CONFLICT: Input router ACL Permit-Bob conflicts with port ACLs
```

This error message indicates that port ACLs and router ACLs are in place with over-lapping ranges (in this case, the same IP addresses). This message is generated because both ACLs will be active, but the port ACL will take precedence.

Having a port ACL in place while a router ACL is also in place can cause a good deal of confusion if you don't realize the port ACL is in place.

Configuring VLAN Maps

VLAN maps allow you to combine access lists in interesting ways. VLAN maps filter all traffic *within* a VLAN.

A port ACL filters only inbound packets on a single interface, and a router ACL filters packets only as they travel into or out of a Layer-3 interface. A VLAN map, on the other hand, filters every packet within a VLAN, regardless of the port type involved. For example, if you create a filter that prevents MAC address 1111.1111.1111 from talking to 2222.2222.2222 and apply it to an interface, moving the device to another interface will bypass the filter. But with a VLAN map, the filter will be applied no matter what interface is involved (assuming it was in the configured VLAN).

For this example, we'll create a filter that will disallow AppleTalk from VLAN 100. Here's the MAC access list:

```
IOS-3750(config)#mac access-list extended No-Appletalk
IOS-3750(config-ext-macl)#permit any any appletalk
```

Notice that we're permitting AppleTalk, though our goal is to deny it. This is due to the nature of VLAN maps, as you're about to see.

To deny AppleTalk within the VLAN, we need to build a VLAN map. VLAN maps have clauses, similar to route maps. The clauses are numbered, although unlike in a route map, we define the action within the clause, not in the clause's title.

First, we need to define the VLAN map, which we do with the `vlan access-map` command. This VLAN map will have two clauses. The first (10) matches the MAC access list No-Appletalk and drops any packets that match. This is why the access list needs to contain a `permit appletalk` instead of a `deny appletalk` line. The `permit` entry allows AppleTalk to be matched. The `action` statement in the VLAN map actually drops the packets:

```
vlan access-map Limit-V100 10
  action drop
  match mac address No-Appletalk
```

Next, we'll add another clause that forwards all remaining packets. Because there is no `match` statement in this clause, all packets are matched:

```
vlan access-map Limit-V100 20
  action forward
```

Here's the entire VLAN map:

```
vlan access-map Limit-V100 10
  action drop
  match mac address No-Appletalk
vlan access-map Limit-V100 20
  action forward
```

Now that we've built the VLAN map, we need to apply it to the VLAN. We do this the `vlan filter` global command:

```
IOS-3750(config)#vlan filter Limit-V100 vlan-list 100
```

 To apply a VLAN map to multiple VLANs, append each VLAN number to the end of the command.

You may be wondering, couldn't we just make a normal access list like the following one, and apply it to specific interfaces?

```
mac access-list extended No-Appletalk
  deny    any any appletalk
  permit any any
```

The answer is yes, but to do this, we'd have to figure out which interfaces might send AppleTalk packets, and hence, where to apply the list. Alternatively, we could apply it to all interfaces within the VLAN, but then we'd need to remember to apply it to any ports that are added to the VLAN in the future. Assigning the access list to the VLAN itself ensures that any AppleTalk packet that arrives in the VLAN, regardless of its source or destination, will be dropped.

To see which VLAN maps are assigned, use the `show vlan filter` command:

```
IOS-3750#sho vlan filter
VLAN Map Limit-V100 is filtering VLANs:
   100
```

Reflexive Access Lists

Reflexive access lists are dynamic filters that allow traffic based on the detection of traffic in the opposite direction. A simple example might be, "only allow Telnet inbound if I initiate Telnet outbound." When I first explain this to junior engineers, I often get a response similar to, "Doesn't it work that way anyway?" What confuses many people is the similarity of this feature to Port Address Translation (PAT). PAT only allows traffic inbound in response to outbound traffic originating on the network; this is due to PAT's nature, in which a translation must be created for the traffic to pass. Reflexive access lists are much more powerful, and can be applied for different reasons.

Without PAT, a filter denies traffic regardless of other traffic. Consider the network in Figure 25-3. There are two hosts, A and B, connected through a router. The router has no access lists installed. Requests from host A to host B are answered, as are requests from host B to host A.

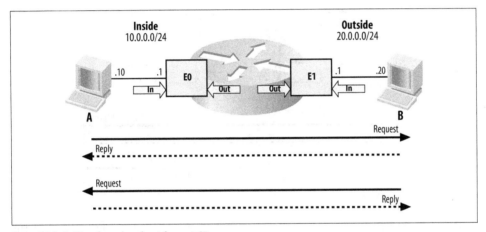

Figure 25-3. Simple network without ACLs

Say we want host A to be able to telnet to host B, but we don't want host B to be able to telnet to host A. If we apply a normal inbound access list to interface E1 on the router, we allow A to contact B, and prevent B from contacting A. Unfortunately, we also prevent B from replying to A. This limitation is illustrated in Figure 25-4.

This is too restrictive for our needs. While we've secured host A from host B's advances, we've also denied host A useful communications from host B. What we need is for the router to act more like a firewall: we need the router to deny requests from host B, but we want host B to be able to reply to host A's requests. Reflexive access lists solve this problem.

Reflexive access lists create ACLs on the fly to allow replies to requests. In this example, we'd like to permit traffic from B, but only if traffic from A is detected first. Should B initiate the traffic, we do not want to permit it. This concept is shown in Figure 25-5.

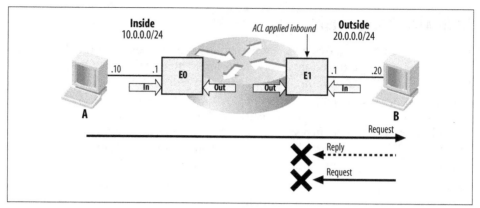

Figure 25-4. Simple access list applied inbound on E1

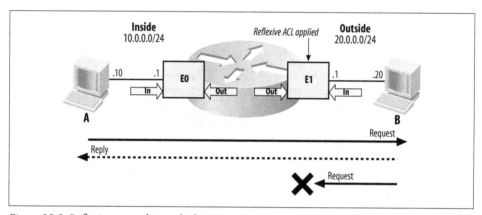

Figure 25-5. Reflexive access list applied to E1

Reflexive access lists create temporary `permit` statements that are reflections of the original statements. For example, if we permit Telnet outbound, a temporary `permit` statement will be created for Telnet inbound.

Reflexive access lists are very useful, but they do have some limitations:

- The temporary entry is always a `permit`, never a `deny`.
- The temporary entry is always the same protocol as the original (TCP, UDP, etc.).
- The temporary entry will have the opposite source and destination IP addresses from the originating traffic.
- The temporary entry will have the same port numbers as the originating traffic, though the source and destination will be reversed (ICMP, which does not use port numbers, will use type numbers).
- The temporary entry will be removed after the last packet is seen (usually a FIN or RST).

- The temporary entry will expire if no traffic is seen for a configurable amount of time (the default is five seconds).

You cannot create a reflexive access list that allows one protocol when another is detected. For example, you cannot allow HTTP inbound because a Telnet was initiated outbound. If you want to reflexively allow HTTP inbound, you must test for HTTP outbound.

Because the port numbers in the temporary entries are always the reverse of the port numbers from the original traffic, they are not suitable for protocols such as RPC that change source port numbers. Reflexive ACLs are also not suitable for protocols that create new streams, such as FTP.

FTP can still be used with reflexive access lists, provided *passive mode* is used.

Configuring Reflexive Access Lists

Reflexive access lists are a bit more complicated than regular access lists, because you must nest one ACL within another. Consider the need to test for two types of traffic: the original request and the resulting reply. An ACL must be created for each test. The ACL for the reply is created dynamically when the ACL for the original request is matched.

Cisco calls the way that reflexive access lists are configured *nesting*, though the configuration doesn't look like nested code to most programmers.

Continuing with the preceding example, let's create a reflexive access list for Telnet. We want host A to be able to telnet to host B, but we'll deny everything else. This scenario is overly restrictive for most real-world applications, but it'll help illustrate the functionality of reflexive access lists.

To configure reflexive access lists, we must create one ACL for outbound traffic and one for inbound traffic.

First, we'll create a named access list called TelnetOut:

```
ip access-list extended TelnetOut
  permit tcp host 10.0.0.10 host 20.0.0.20 eq telnet reflect GAD
  deny   ip any any
```

Reflexive access lists can only be created using named access lists.

This ACL is pretty straightforward, except for the addition of reflect GAD at the end of the permit line. This will be the name of the temporary access list created by the router when this permit entry is matched. The entry deny ip any any is not necessary, as all access lists include this by default, but I've included it here for clarity and to show the counters incrementing as traffic is denied later.

Next, we'll create a named access list called TelnetIn:

```
ip access-list extended TelnetIn
 evaluate GAD
 deny   ip any any
```

This access list has no permit statements, but it has the statement evaluate GAD. This line references the reflect line in the TelnetOut access list. GAD will be the name of the new access list created by the router.

To make these access lists take effect, we need to apply them to the router. We'll apply TelnetOut to interface E1 *outbound*, and TelnetIn to interface E1 *inbound*. Figure 25-6 illustrates.

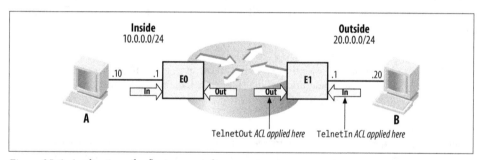

Figure 25-6. Application of reflexive access lists

Reflexive access lists are applied with the access-group interface command:

```
interface Ethernet1
 ip access-group TelnetIn in
 ip access-group TelnetOut out
```

The entire relevant configuration for the router is as follows:

```
interface Ethernet0
 ip address 10.0.0.1 255.255.255.0
!
interface Ethernet1
 ip address 20.0.0.1 255.255.255.0
 ip access-group TelnetIn in
```

```
   ip access-group TelnetOut out
 !
 ip access-list extended TelnetIn
  evaluate GAD
  deny   ip any any
 ip access-list extended TelnetOut
  permit tcp host 10.0.0.10 host 20.0.0.20 eq telnet reflect GAD
  deny   ip any any
```

Looking at the access lists with the `show access-list` command, we see them both exactly as we've configured them:

```
Router#sho access-list
Reflexive IP access list GAD
Extended IP access list TelnetIn
    evaluate GAD
    deny ip any any
Extended IP access list TelnetOut
    permit tcp host 10.0.0.10 host 20.0.0.20 eq telnet reflect GAD
    deny ip any any (155 matches)
```

Here, we can see that all non-Telnet traffic is being denied outbound. There really aren't any entries to permit anything inbound, but that will change when we trigger the reflexive access list.

After we initiate a Telnet request from host A to host B, the output changes. There is now an additional access list named GAD:

```
Router#sho access-list
Reflexive IP access list GAD
    permit tcp host 20.0.0.20 eq telnet host 10.0.0.10 eq 11002 (12 matches)
Extended IP access list TelnetIn
    evaluate GAD
    deny ip any any
Extended IP access list TelnetOut
    permit tcp host 10.0.0.10 host 20.0.0.20 eq telnet reflect GAD
    deny ip any any (155 matches)
```

This temporary access list has been created in response to outbound traffic matching the `permit` entry containing the `reflect GAD` statement. The destination port number is 11002; this was the source port number for the outbound Telnet request.

When the session has ended, or there is no activity matching the new access list, the reflexive access list is removed. You can configure the required inactivity period using the global `ip reflexive-list timeout seconds` command. This command affects all reflexive access lists on the router. The default timeout value is five seconds.

Authentication in Cisco Devices

Authentication refers to the process of verifying a user's identity. When a router challenges you for a login username and password, this is an example of authentication.

Authentication in Cisco devices is divided into two major types: normal and AAA (Authentication, Authorization, and Auditing).

Basic (Non-AAA) Authentication

Non-AAA authentication is the basic authentication capability built into a router or other network device's operating system. Non-AAA authentication does not require access to an external server. It is very simple to set up and maintain, but lacks flexibility and scalability. Using locally defined usernames as an example, each username needs to be configured locally in the router. Imagine a scenario where a single user might connect to any of a number of devices, such as at an ISP. The user configurations would have to be maintained across all devices, and the ISP might have tens of thousands of users. With each user needing a line of configuration in the router, the configuration for the router would be hundreds of pages long.

Normal authentication is good for small-scale authentication needs or as a backup to AAA.

Line Passwords

Lines are logical or physical interfaces on a router that are used for management of the router. The console and aux port on a router are lines, as are the logical VTY interfaces used for Telnet and SSH. Configuring a password on a line is a simple matter of adding it with the **password** command:

```
R1(config-line)#password Secret
```

VTY is an abbreviation for Virtual Teletype Terminal. In the olden days, teletype machines, which looked like huge typewriters, connected to mainframes using serial ports. When computers got more sophisticated and Telnet was developed, virtual interfaces were added as logical targets for Telnet. Using Telnet was described as using a virtual teletype.

Passwords are case-sensitive and may include spaces.

If a password is not set on the VTY lines, you will get an error when telneting to the device:

```
Password required, but none set
```

Passwords entered in clear text are shown in the configuration in clear text by default. To have IOS encrypt all passwords in the configuration, you must enable the password-encryption service with the **service password-encryption** command. Here's an example of passwords in the running configuration displayed in clear text:

```
R1#sho run | include password
 password Secret1
```

Here's how to configure the password-encryption service to encrypt all the passwords:

```
R1#conf t
Enter configuration commands, one per line. End with CNTL/Z.
R1(config)# service password-encryption
R1(config)# exit
```

And here's what the passwords look like in the configuration with the password-encryption service running:

```
R1#sho run | include password
 password 7 073C244F5C0C0D54
```

Do not assume encrypted passwords within IOS are totally secure. They can easily be cracked with tools freely available on the Internet.

If you would like to be able to telnet to your device without needing a password, you can disable the requirement with the no login command:

```
R1(config-line)#no login
```

This, of course, is a bad idea and should only be done in a lab environment.

The no login command is available only when aaa new-model is not enabled. Once aaa new-model has been enabled, the login command takes on a different meaning and syntax. This command is discussed in "Enabling AAA" on page 449.

NX-OS switches work a little differently when it comes to authentication. There are no passwords on VTYs the way there are on IOS devices. Instead, authentication is done either through local users or remotely.

Configuring Local Users

You can create users locally on your networking device. These usernames can then be used for authentication when users log into the device. This is useful when there is a small number of users or when using an external authentication server (discussed in "AAA Authentication" on page 449) is not practical. If you're using AAA authentication, this option is also useful as a backup: you can use the local users for authentication if the normal external authentication server becomes unavailable.

You create and manage users with the username command. Many options are available with this command; I'll focus on those that are useful for Telnet or SSH access to a network device.

The first step in creating a local user is to define the username. Here, I'll use the username GAD:

```
R1(config)#username GAD ?
  access-class          Restrict access by access-class
  autocommand           Automatically issue a command after the user logs in
  callback-dialstring   Callback dialstring
  callback-line         Associate a specific line with this callback
  callback-rotary       Associate a rotary group with this callback
  dnis                  Do not require password when obtained via DNIS
  nocallback-verify     Do not require authentication after callback
  noescape              Prevent the user from using an escape character
  nohangup              Do not disconnect after an automatic command
  nopassword            No password is required for the user to log in
  password              Specify the password for the user
  privilege             Set user privilege level
  secret                Specify the secret for the user
  user-maxlinks         Limit the user's number of inbound links
  view                  Set view name
  <cr>
```

Simply specifying the command username GAD will create a user named GAD with no password. To add a password, include the password keyword followed by the password:

```
R1(config)#username GAD password Secret1
```

Passwords are case-sensitive and can include spaces. Passwords are displayed in clear text in the configuration unless the password-encryption service is running. To include an encrypted password without using the password-encryption service, use the secret keyword instead of the password keyword:

```
R1(config)#username GAD secret Secret1
```

This command results in the following configuration entry:

```
username GAD secret 5 $1$uyU6$6iZp6GLI1WGE1hxGDfQxc/
```

Every command and user has an associated *privilege level*. The levels range from 0 to 15. The standard user EXEC mode is level 1. When you enter the command enable and authenticate with the enable or enable secret password, you change your level to *privileged EXEC mode*, which is level 15. If you'd like a user to be able to access privileged-level commands without entering the enable password, you can assign a higher privilege level to that user. In other words, configuring a user with a privilege level of 15 removes the need for that user to use the enable password to execute privileged commands:

```
R1(config)#username GAD privilege 15
```

When you enter separate commands for the same user (either on the same or separate command lines), as I've just done with the secret and privilege commands, the parser will combine the commands into a single configuration entry:

```
username GAD privilege 15 secret 5 $1$uyU6$6iZp6GLI1WGE1hxGDfQxc/
```

When this user logs into the router, she'll be greeted with the privileged # prompt instead of the normal exec prompt:

```
User Access Verification

Username: GAD
Password:
GAD-R1#
```

Another interesting feature of the username command is the ability to assign a command to run automatically when the user authenticates. Here, I've configured the show ip interface brief command to run upon authentication:

```
R1(config)#username GAD autocommand show ip interface brief
```

When this user logs in, she'll be shown the output from this command and then promptly disconnected:

```
User Access Verification

Username: GAD
Password:
Interface              IP-Address      OK? Method Status
Protocol
FastEthernet0/0        10.100.100.1    YES NVRAM  up                       up
FastEthernet0/1        unassigned      YES NVRAM  administratively down down
Serial0/0/0:0          unassigned      YES unset  down                     down
```

This may not seem like a useful feature until you consider the possibility that a first-line engineer may need to execute only one command. Why give him access to anything else?

Another possibility with the autocommand feature is to call a predefined menu of commands (configuring menus is outside the scope of this book):

```
R1(config)#username GAD autocommand menu root-menu
```

If you specify a command or menu that does not exist, the user will not be able to log in even with proper authentication.

You can disable the automatic disconnection after `autocommand` with the `nohangup` keyword:

```
R1(config)#username GAD nohangup autocommand menu root-menu
```

With NX-OS, you create local users with the `username` command, but you must also assign a role to each user. Before you can do that, and in fact, before you can even configure a Nexus switch, you must determine if you want to enable strong passwords.

When you first turn a Nexus switch on, or when you first connect to a newly created VDC, you will be greeted with the following dialog:

```
Daisy# switchto vdc Cozy

        ---- System Admin Account Setup ----

Do you want to enforce secure password standard (yes/no) [y]:
```

Enforcing secure password standards is a good idea, and it should be done whenever possible. It may even be required if you need to comply with standards such as PCI or SOX. It is sort of a pain because, much like Unix, it will force you to have 169 lowercase, uppercase, numeric, Greek, and Sumerian characters in your passwords. Actually, the password needs to be eight or more characters. OK, so I made up the part about Greek and Sumerian, too, but it sure feels like ancient languages are a requirement when you look at the strong password rules. According to Cisco's documentation, a strong password has the following characteristics:

- Is at least eight characters long
- Does not contain many consecutive characters (such as "abcd")
- Does not contain many repeating characters (such as "aaabbb")
- Does not contain dictionary words
- Does not contain proper names
- Contains both uppercase and lowercase characters
- Contains numbers

The same documentation goes on to list the following examples of strong passwords:

- If2CoM18
- 2004AsdfLkj30
- Cb1955S21

If you're like me, you'll spend a ridiculous amount of time coming up with a password that meets the requirements and is in any way memorable. Sometimes I think learning ancient Sumerian would be simpler. Still, if you work in a real environment with real security concerns—and who doesn't?—you'll need to employ strong passwords.

Since my examples were from a lab where the long arm of the PCI auditors could not reach, I opted for simple passwords.

```
Do you want to enforce secure password standard (yes/no) [y]: no

    Enter the password for "admin":
```

Feeling rebellious, I typed in admin as a password and went on with my work. Doing so results in the following command being added to the config:

```
username admin password 5 $1$uioc3i3ii$bO71x923gsUO9Ebu3/  role vdc-admin
```

User roles are an important feature in NX-OS. In this case, the admin user was added within a VDC. See Chapter 18 for more information on VDCs. The vdc-admin role means that this user has complete administrative rights, but only within this VDC. By default, there are four roles in a Nexus 7000:

network-admin
> Complete read and write access to the entire NX-OS device (only available in the default VDC).

network-operator
> Complete read access to the entire NX-OS device (only available in the default VDC).

vdc-admin
> Read and write access limited to a VDC.

vdc-operator
> Read access limited to a VDC.

You can create other roles to limit or add access as you see fit. See the Cisco documentation for more detail.

PPP Authentication

Authenticating a PPP connection is possible through one of two methods: Password Authentication Protocol (PAP) and Challenge Handshake Authentication Protocol (CHAP). PAP is the easier of the two to implement and understand, but it is of limited value because it transmits passwords in clear text. CHAP uses a more secure algorithm that does not include sending passwords. Both methods are outlined in RFC 1334. The RFC includes this warning about PAP:

> PAP is not a strong authentication method. Passwords are sent over the circuit "in the clear", and there is no protection from playback or repeated trial and error attacks. The peer is in control of the frequency and timing of the attempts.

> Any implementations which include a stronger authentication method (such as CHAP, described below) MUST offer to negotiate that method prior to PAP.

If a PPP authentication scheme is required, you must decide which scheme is right for you. Usually, CHAP is the right choice, due to its increased security, though PAP can be used when minimal security is desired or the possibility of capturing packets is at a minimum. To use either method, you must have a local user configured at least on the receiving (called) router, although, as you'll see, the requirements vary.

Configuring non-AAA authentication for PPP is covered here. To read about AAA PPP authentication using PAP and CHAP, see "Applying Method Lists" on page 456.

PAP

PAP can be configured for one-way or two-way authentication. One-way authentication indicates that only one side initiates a challenge. Two-way authentication indicates that both sides of the link authenticate each other.

One-way authentication. With one-way authentication, the calling router sends a username and password, which must match a username and password configured on the called router. The calling router must be configured as a `callin` router with the `ppp authen tication pap callin` command. The calling router must also be configured to send a username and password with the `ppp pap sent-username` command. Here are some example configurations. Configuration entries not specific to PPP authentication are not shown, for clarity:

Calling side:

```
interface BRI1/0
 encapsulation ppp
 ppp authentication pap callin
 ppp pap sent-username Bob password 0 ILikePie
```

Called side:

```
username Bob password 0 ILikePie
!
interface BRI1/0
 encapsulation ppp
 ppp authentication pap
```

 I thought about removing the ISDN references in this chapter. If you live in a major metropolitan area, chances are all of your ISDN has been replaced with broadband. The Cisco CCIE exam even removed it from the lab some time ago. Rest assured, though, that even in 2010, there are areas of the country that still do not have broadband available. I've worked on nationwide MPLS rollouts recently and we had to keep the aging ISDN head end infrastructure, because we had locations that had no access to DSL or cable Internet. While VPN is rapidly taking over the backup roles in most locations, ISDN is still out there.

Two-way authentication. With two-way authentication, the `callin` keyword is not necessary. Because the authentication is done in both directions, both routers must be configured with usernames/passwords and the `ppp pap sent-username` command. The end result is that both sides are configured the same way:

Calling side:

```
username Bob password 0 ILikePie
!
interface BRI1/0
 encapsulation ppp
 ppp authentication pap
 ppp pap sent-username Bob password 0 ILikePie
```

Called side:

```
username Bob password 0 ILikePie
!
interface BRI1/0
 encapsulation ppp
 ppp authentication pap
 ppp pap sent-username Bob password 0 ILikePie
```

Debugging PPP authentication. You debug PPP authentication with the `debug ppp authen` `tication` command. The results are usually quite specific and easy to understand. Here, the password being sent from the calling router is incorrect. The debug was run on the called router:

```
8w4d: BR1/0:1 PPP: Using dialer call direction
8w4d: BR1/0:1 PPP: Treating connection as a callin
8w4d: BR1/0:1 PAP: I AUTH-REQ id 4 len 18 from "Bob"
8w4d: BR1/0:1 PAP: Authenticating peer Bob
8w4d: BR1/0:1 PAP: O AUTH-NAK id 4 len 27 msg is "Authentication failure" Bad
password defined for username Bob
```

In the next example, two-way authentication has succeeded. Notice that additional requests have been made. First, the called router receives the authorization request (AUTH-REQ) from the calling router. The called router then sends an authorization acknowledgment (AUTH-ACK) and an AUTH-REQ of its own back to the calling router. The final line in bold shows the AUTH-ACK returned by the calling router, completing the two-way authentication. The I and O before the AUTH-ACK and AUTH-REQ entries indicate the direction of the message (*In* or *Out*):

```
00:00:41: %LINK-3-UPDOWN: Interface BRI1/0:1, changed state to up
00:00:41: BR1/0:1 PPP: Using dialer call direction
00:00:41: BR1/0:1 PPP: Treating connection as a callin
00:00:43: %ISDN-6-LAYER2UP: Layer 2 for Interface BR1/0, TEI 68 changed to up
00:00:45: BR1/0:1 AUTH: Started process 0 pid 62
00:00:45: BR1/0:1 PAP: I AUTH-REQ id 2 len 17 from "Bob"
00:00:45: BR1/0:1 PAP: Authenticating peer Bob
00:00:45: BR1/0:1 PAP: O AUTH-ACK id 2 len 5
00:00:45: BR1/0:1 PAP: O AUTH-REQ id 1 len 17 from "Bob"
00:00:45: BR1/0:1 PAP: I AUTH-ACK id 1 len 5
00:00:46: %LINEPROTO-5-UPDOWN: Line protocol on Interface BRI1/0:1, changed state
to up
00:00:47: %ISDN-6-CONNECT: Interface BRI1/0:1 is now connected to 7802000 Bob
```

CHAP

CHAP is more secure than PAP because it never sends passwords. Instead, it forms a hash value derived from the username and password, and sends that. The devices determine whether the hash values match in order to authenticate.

Figure 26-1 shows a simple two-router network. The Chicago router will call the New-York router. As with PAP, there are two ways to authenticate using CHAP: one-way and two-way.

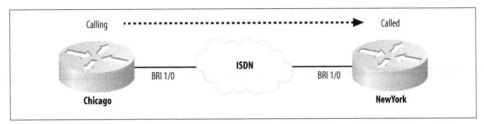

Figure 26-1. CHAP-authenticated ISDN call

CHAP can be a little harder to understand than PAP because of the way it operates. When Cisco routers authenticate using CHAP, by default, no username is needed on the calling router. Instead, the hostname of the router is used as the username. While people seem to grasp that concept easily enough, how passwords are handled is a little more complicated.

With PAP, one or more username/password pairs are configured on the called router. When the calling router attempts to authenticate, it must send a username and password that match a configured pair on the called router.

With CHAP, each router must have a username/password pair configured, but the username must be the hostname of the other router, and the passwords must be the same on *both* routers. Both the hostnames and the passwords are case-sensitive.

 Be careful when configuring passwords. A common mistake is to enter a space or control character after a password during configuration. It's hard to catch such an error, because everything will look normal. If you believe everything is configured correctly, but it's just not working, try removing the lines with the passwords and retyping them (using cut and paste usually doesn't solve the problem). While this can happen anytime passwords are being configured, I find it especially maddening when I'm using CHAP, because I'm constantly second-guessing my configuration.

One-way authentication. We'll begin with some examples of one-way authentication using CHAP. Notice that the username configured on each router matches the hostname of the other router. Notice also that the password is the same for both usernames. The password must be the same on both routers:

Calling side (Chicago):

```
Hostname Chicago
!
username NewYork
 password 0 Secret2
!
interface BRI1/0
 encapsulation ppp
 ppp authentication chap callin
```

Called side (NewYork):

```
Hostname NewYork
!
username Chicago
 password 0 Secret2
!
interface BRI1/0
 encapsulation ppp
 ppp authentication chap
```

Now, let's look at the debug output for a successful call using these configurations. The call was initiated from the Chicago router. If you look carefully, you'll see that the NewYork router is receiving a challenge from NewYork. The challenge entries in the debug output refer to the username, not the hostname. This can add to the confusion, as the username must match the hostname of the other router. Here's the debug output for both sides:

Calling side:

```
20:08:11: %LINK-3-UPDOWN: Interface BRI1/0:1, changed state to up
20:08:11: BR1/0:1 PPP: Using dialer call direction
20:08:11: BR1/0:1 PPP: Treating connection as a callout
20:08:11: BR1/0:1 CHAP: I CHALLENGE id 3 len 28 from "NewYork"
20:08:11: BR1/0:1 CHAP: O RESPONSE id 3 len 28 from "Chicago"
20:08:11: BR1/0:1 CHAP: I SUCCESS id 3 len 4
20:08:12: %LINEPROTO-5-UPDOWN: Line protocol on Interface BRI1/0:1, changed state
to up
20:08:17: %ISDN-6-CONNECT: Interface BRI1/0:1 is now connected to 7802000
```

Called side:

```
20:15:01: %LINK-3-UPDOWN: Interface BRI1/0:1, changed state to up
20:15:01: BR1/0:1 PPP: Using dialer call direction
20:15:01: BR1/0:1 PPP: Treating connection as a callin
20:15:02: BR1/0:1 CHAP: O CHALLENGE id 3 len 28 from "NewYork"
20:15:02: BR1/0:1 CHAP: I RESPONSE id 3 len 28 from "Chicago"
20:15:02: BR1/0:1 CHAP: O SUCCESS id 3 len 4
20:15:03: %LINEPROTO-5-UPDOWN: Line protocol on Interface BRI1/0:1, changed state
to up
20:15:07: %ISDN-6-CONNECT: Interface BRI1/0:1 is now connected to 7801000 Chicago
NewYork#
```

Two-way authentication. As with PAP, when you're configuring CHAP for two-way authentication, the difference is the removal of the `callin` keyword from the `ppp authentication chap` command on the calling router:

Calling side:

```
Hostname Chicago
!
username NewYork
 password 0 Secret2
!
interface BRI1/0
 encapsulation ppp
 ppp authentication chap
```

Called side:

```
Hostname NewYork
!
username Chicago
 password 0 Secret2
!
interface BRI1/0
 encapsulation ppp
 ppp authentication chap
```

Now, the output from `debug ppp authentication` is a bit more verbose, as authentication happens in both directions. I've included only the output for the called side here, for the sake of brevity:

```
20:01:59: %LINK-3-UPDOWN: Interface BRI1/0:1, changed state to up
20:01:59: BR1/0:1 PPP: Using dialer call direction
20:01:59: BR1/0:1 PPP: Treating connection as a callin
20:02:00: %ISDN-6-LAYER2UP: Layer 2 for Interface BR1/0, TEI 66 changed to up
20:02:00: BR1/0:1 CHAP: O CHALLENGE id 2 len 28 from "NewYork"
20:02:00: BR1/0:1 CHAP: I CHALLENGE id 2 len 28 from "Chicago"
20:02:00: BR1/0:1 CHAP: Waiting for peer to authenticate first
20:02:00: BR1/0:1 CHAP: I RESPONSE id 2 len 28 from "Chicago"
20:02:00: BR1/0:1 CHAP: O SUCCESS id 2 len 4
20:02:00: BR1/0:1 CHAP: Processing saved Challenge, id 2
20:02:00: BR1/0:1 CHAP: O RESPONSE id 2 len 28 from "NewYork"
20:02:00: BR1/0:1 CHAP: I SUCCESS id 2 len 4
20:02:01: %LINEPROTO-5-UPDOWN: Line protocol on Interface BRI1/0:1, changed state
to up
20:02:05: %ISDN-6-CONNECT: Interface BRI1/0:1 is now connected to 7801000 Chicago
```

Changing the sent hostname. Sometimes, the hostname of the calling router cannot be used for CHAP authentication. A common example is when you connect your router to an ISP. Figure 26-2 shows another simple two-router network: in this case, BobsRouter is connecting to a router named ISP. The service provider controlling the ISP router issues usernames and passwords to its clients. These usernames do not match the hostnames of the client's routers.

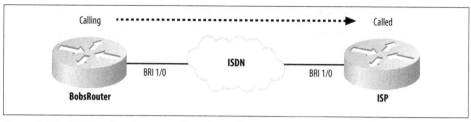

Figure 26-2. CHAP authentication with configured username

Bob, the client who is using BobsRouter, has been given the username Bob-01 and the password SuperSecret1. On the calling side, I've configured the additional command `ppp chap hostname`. This has the effect of using the name Bob-01 instead of the router's hostname for authentication. Notice that the username Bob-01 appears on the called side and that there is no reference on the called side to the hostname of the calling side:

Calling side:

```
Hostname BobsRouter
!
username ISP
 password 0 SuperSecret1
!
interface BRI1/0
 encapsulation ppp
 ppp authentication chap callin
 ppp chap hostname Bob-01
```

Called side:

```
Hostname ISP
!
username Bob-01
 password 0 SuperSecret1
!
interface BRI1/0
 encapsulation ppp
 ppp authentication chap
```

While this configuration works, chances are the only place you'd see it is on a certification exam. A far more logical approach is to configure the sent username and password in CHAP without having to configure a username that matches the hostname of the remote router:

Calling side:

```
Hostname BobsRouter
!
interface BRI1/0
 encapsulation ppp
 ppp authentication chap callin
 ppp chap hostname Bob-01
 ppp chap password 0 SuperSecret1
```

Called side:

```
Hostname ISP
!
username Bob-01
 password 0 SuperSecret1
!
interface BRI1/0
 encapsulation ppp
 ppp authentication chap
```

With this method, there is no confusion resulting from trying to match the hostnames and passwords in odd ways. Instead, you configure the username and password using the `ppp chap` interface commands on the calling side. The called side simply has the username and password configured to match. The hostnames, while included for completion, are not necessary in this example (though they are in all the previous CHAP examples).

Of all the non-AAA authentication methods available for PPP, this is the most secure and the easiest to understand.

AAA Authentication

Recall that AAA stands for Authentication, Authorization, and Accounting. *Authentication* is the process of verifying a user's identity to determine whether the user should be allowed access to a device. *Authorization* is the act of limiting or permitting access to certain features within the device once a user has been authenticated. *Accounting* is the recording of actions taken by the user once she has been authenticated and authorized. In this section, I will cover only authentication, as it is the most commonly used feature offered by AAA.

To use AAA authentication on an IOS switch or router, you must perform the following steps:

1. Enable AAA by entering the `aaa new-model` command.
2. Configure security server information, if you're using a security server. This step includes configuring TACACS+ and RADIUS information.
3. Create method lists by using the `aaa authentication` command.
4. Apply the method lists to interfaces or lines as needed.

In NX-OS, the commands are similar, but there is no `aaa new-model` command.

Enabling AAA

To use the AAA features discussed here, you'll need to issue the command `aaa new-model`:

```
Router(config)#aaa new-model
```

If you don't execute this command, the AAA commands discussed in this section will not be available. This step is not necessary in NX-OS.

 Be careful when configuring AAA for the first time. You can easily lock yourself out of the router by enabling AAA authentication without configuring any users.

Configuring Security Server Information

One of the benefits of using AAA is the ability to use an external server for authentication, authorization, and accounting. When an external server is used, all user information is stored externally to the networking device. Administration of user security is therefore centralized. This allows individual users to access many devices, while also allowing the administrator to limit the users' access.

RADIUS and TACACS+ are two protocols used for authentication and authorization applications. Each is used to authenticate users, though they can also be used for various other features (logging command usage, call detail records, and so on). Both are widely used, and at some point, you'll need to decide which one to choose. Here's a quick rundown:

RADIUS

> Livingston Enterprises (now Lucent Technologies) originally developed the Remote Authentication Dial-In User Service (RADIUS) for its PortMaster series of network access servers. These devices were widely used by ISPs in the days when 33.6 Kbps modems were the norm. RADIUS was later described in RFCs 2058 and 2059. It is now available in open source server applications. RADIUS includes authentication and authorization in the user profile. RADIUS usually uses UDP ports 1812 or 1645 for authentication, and ports 1813 or 1646 for accounting.

TACACS+

> The Terminal Access Controller Access-Control System (TACACS) was originally designed for remote authentication of Unix servers. TACACS+, a new Cisco-proprietary protocol that is incompatible with the original version, has since replaced TACACS. This updated version is widely used for authentication and authorization in networking devices. TACACS+ separates the authentication and authorization operations. It is defined in a Cisco RFC draft (*http://tools.ietf.org/html/draft-grant-tacacs-02*) and utilizes TCP port 49 by default.

Cisco generally recommends TACACS+ over RADIUS, though both are usually available for configuring authentication. One important consideration is that RADIUS does not allow users to limit the commands a user can execute. If you need this feature, choose TACACS+. For more information on the differences between TACACS+ and RADIUS, see Cisco's document ID 13838 (*http://www.cisco.com/en/US/tech/tk59/technologies_tech_note09186a0080094e99.shtml*).

Nexus switches seem to be more geared toward open standards. For example, in NX-OS, RADIUS is enabled by default while TACACS+ must be enabled with the `feature tacacs+` command.

To use a security server, you must configure *server groups*. Server groups are logical groups of servers that can be referenced with a single name. You can use default server groups or create your own custom groups.

Default RADIUS and TACACS+ server groups

TACACS+ servers are defined globally in a router with the `tacacs-server` command. You define where to find a TACACS+ server with the `host` keyword:

```
tacacs-server host 10.100.100.100
```

A hostname can be used, provided that you have configured DNS on the router. You can also list multiple servers, in which case they will be referenced in the order in which they appear:

```
tacacs-server host 10.100.100.100
tacacs-server host 10.100.100.101
```

The router will query the second server in the list only if the first server returns an error or is unavailable. A login failure is not considered an error.

Many installations require a secure key to be sent with the query. This key, which functions like a password for the server itself (as opposed to the user being authenticated), is configured through the `tacacs-server` command with the `key` keyword:

```
tacacs-server key Secret
```

The password will be stored in the configuration as plain text unless you have the password-encryption service enabled. With the password encrypted, the password line ends up looking like this:

```
tacacs-server key 7 01200307490E12
```

In NX-OS, all of these steps can be combined into one command. Here, I create both servers with one command each:

```
NX-7K-1-Cozy(config)# tacacs-server host 10.100.100.100 key Secret
NX-7K-1-Cozy(config)# tacacs-server host 10.100.100.101 key Secret
```

RADIUS servers are configured similarly. Most of the useful features are supplied in a single command. To accomplish the same sort of simple server configuration with a key, you can enter the following command:

```
radius-server host 10.100.200.200 key Secret
```

This will result in a configuration line that looks similar to this:

```
radius-server host 10.100.200.200 auth-port 1645 acct-port 1646 key Secret
```

Port 1645 is the default port for RADIUS and was added automatically by the router.

As with TACACS+, you can add multiple servers:

```
radius-server host 10.100.200.200 auth-port 1645 acct-port 1646 key Secret
radius-server host 10.100.200.201 auth-port 1645 acct-port 1646 key Secret2
```

Again, the second server will be accessed only if the first returns an error. Notice, however, that with RADIUS you can have a different key for each server. TACACS+ only allows you to specify a global key for all servers.

The commands for RADIUS servers are similar in NX-OS, though the order of keywords is shifted a bit:

```
NX-5K-1(config)# radius-server host 10.100.200.200 key secret auth-port 1645
acct-port 1646
NX-5K-1(config)# radius-server host 10.100.200.201 key secret2  auth-port 1645
acct-port 1646
```

Custom groups

Say you have two different sets of TACACS+ servers that you need to reference separately: two servers that you use for login authentication and two servers that you use for PPP authentication.

IOS and NX-OS both let you specify custom groups for either RADIUS or TACACS+ servers. Use the `aaa group server` command to create these groups. Add the keyword `tacacs+` or `radius`, followed by the name of the group you'd like to create. The commands are the same in IOS and NX-OS:

```
aaa group server tacacs+ Login-Servers
  server 10.100.1.100
  server 10.100.1.101

aaa group server radius PPP-Radius
  server 10.100.200.200 auth-port 1645 acct-port 1646
  server 10.100.200.201 auth-port 1645 acct-port 1646
```

Again, with RADIUS, the router adds the port numbers. The commands entered were simply:

```
R1(config)#aaa group server radius PPP-Radius
R1(config-sg-radius)# server 10.100.200.200
R1(config-sg-radius)# server 10.100.200.201
```

In IOS, if you have a TACACS+ server that requires key authentication, you can add the key to an individual server within a group by using the `server-private` command instead of the `server` command:

```
aaa group server tacacs+ Login-Servers
  server-private 10.100.1.72 key Secret
```

Creating Method Lists

A *method list* is a list of authentication methods to be used in order of preference. For example, you may want to first try TACACS+ and then, if that fails, use local user authentication. Once you've created a method list, you can configure an interface to call the method list for authentication.

A router can authenticate a user in a few different ways. They are:

Login
> Login authentication is the means whereby a user is challenged to access the router's CLI.

PPP
> PPP authentication provides authentication for Point-to-Point Protocol connectivity either on serial links or through something like modem connectivity.

ARAP
> AppleTalk Remote Access Protocol (ARAP) is a remote access protocol for AppleTalk users.

NASI
> NetWare Asynchronous Services Interface (NASI) is a remote access protocol for Novell Netware users.

In practice, you're likely to encounter only login and PPP authentication. With the advent of broadband Internet access in most homes and the adoption of VPN at most companies, modem connectivity is becoming a thing of the past in most metropolitan areas. I haven't seen ARAP or NASI in the field in years, so I'll only cover login and PPP authentication here.

IOS login authentication

When logging into an IOS-based network device, you can be challenged in a variety of ways. The default method is to be challenged to provide a password that's been entered in the configuration of the interface or line itself. For example, the following commands secure the console with a simple password:

```
line con 0
 password Secret1
```

This behavior is called *line authentication* when you are using AAA, and it is one of many methods available for authentication. The possible methods for login authentication are:

enable
> Use the configured enable password as the authentication password.

krb5
> Query a Kerberos 5 authentication server for authentication information.

`krb5-telnet`
> Use the Kerberos 5 Telnet authentication protocol when using Telnet to connect to the network device. If used, this method must be listed first.

`line`
> Use the configured `line` password as the authentication password.

`local`
> Use locally configured usernames and passwords (entered in the configuration of the device itself).

`local-case`
> Same as local, but the usernames are case-sensitive.

`none`
> This method essentially removes authentication. If `none` is the only method, access is granted without challenge.

`group radius`
> Query the list of RADIUS servers for authentication information.

`group tacacs+`
> Query the list of TACACS+ servers for authentication information.

Custom (group *group-name*)
> Query a custom group as defined in the local configuration.

A method list can contain multiple methods or just one. Method lists must be named. Here, I've specified a `login` method list called `GAD-Method`. The method being used is `local` users:

```
aaa authentication login GAD-Method local
```

If multiple methods are listed, they will be referenced in the order in which they appear. The second method will be referenced only if the first method fails; failure is not authentication failure, but rather, a failure to establish connectivity with that method.

Here, I've configured the `GAD-Method` method list to use TACACS+ first, followed by local users:

```
aaa authentication login GAD-Method group tacacs+ local
```

When using the server groups `tacacs+` and `radius`, you are referencing the globally configured TACACS+ and RADIUS servers. If you have defined a custom group of either type, you can reference the group name you created with the `aaa servers` command. For example, earlier we created a `Login-Servers` group. To reference this group in a method list, include the group name after the keyword `group`:

```
aaa authentication login default group Login-Servers
```

This example includes the `default` method, which, when implemented, is automatically applied to all interfaces.

If you're relying on external servers and you encounter problems, you can sometimes lock everyone out of the router. The none method allows anyone to access the router without authenticating. When the none method is included as the last method in a list, anyone will be able to access the router in the event that all other authentication methods fail:

```
aaa authentication login default group tacacs+ local none
```

Again, failure is defined here as failed communication with the server listed, not an incorrect password entry. Of course, including none can be dangerous, as it means that a malicious party can launch a denial-of-service attack on the authentication servers and thereby gain access to your devices (which is counterindicated by most network administrators). Instead, I prefer to use local-case as the last method in my method lists:

```
aaa authentication login default group tacacs+ local-case
```

I like to configure on all routers a standard username and password that will only be needed in the event of a server or network failure. I feel slightly better about using local-case than local, as it means I can include both uppercase and lowercase characters in the usernames and passwords. Be careful, though, as this practice is frowned upon in environments where credit card transactions occur. Payment Card Industry (PCI) compliance dictates many details about how user data is stored and accessed.

 You can use the same method list name for both PPP and login authentication, but be aware that creating a login method list doesn't automatically result in the creation of a ppp method list with the same name. If you want to have login and PPP method lists with the same names, you'll need to create them both:

```
aaa authentication login GAD-Login group GAD-Servers none
aaa authentication ppp GAD-Login group GAD-Servers none
```

NX-OS login authentication

NS-OS requires usernames. This behavior cannot be disabled. As such, there is no need to add the login command to VTY or CON interfaces. You also cannot assign a password to the console or VTYs as you can in IOS. You can, however, tell NX-OS to use RADIUS or TACACS+ for user authentication. The command is the same as the one we used in IOS:

```
NX-7K-1-Cozy(config)# aaa authentication login default group Login-Servers none
```

PPP authentication

PPP authentication is used when Point-to-Point Protocol connections are initiated into the router. These can include modem connections into a serial interface or connections of high-speed serial links such as T1s.

The possible methods for PPP authentication using AAA are:

`if-needed`
: If a user has already been authenticated on a TTY line, do not authenticate.

`krb5`
: Query a Kerberos 5 authentication server for authentication information (only for PAP).

`local`
: Use locally configured usernames and passwords (entered in the configuration of the device itself).

`local-case`
: Same as local, but the usernames are case-sensitive.

`none`
: This method essentially removes authentication. If none is the only method, there is no challenge.

`group radius`
: Query the list of RADIUS servers for authentication information.

`group tacacs+`
: Query the list of TACACS+ servers for authentication information

Custom (`group group-name`)
: Query a custom group as defined in the local configuration.

These methods are referenced in ppp method lists the same way methods are referenced in login method lists. An interesting addition to the list of methods is if-needed. This method instructs the router to authenticate the incoming connection only if the user has not already been authenticated on a VTY, console, or aux line. Here is a sample ppp method list:

```
aaa authentication ppp default group tacacs+ local-case
```

Applying Method Lists

Once you have created a method list, you need to apply it to the interface or line where you would like it to take effect. With login authentication, use the command login to apply an authentication method list. Here, I'm applying the GAD-Login method list created earlier to VTY lines 0–4. This will have the effect of challenging Telnet sessions to the router with whatever authentication methods exist in the GAD-Login method list:

```
line vty 0 4
 login authentication GAD-Login
```

To apply a PPP authentication method list to an interface, you must configure the interface with PPP encapsulation. The ppp authentication command is used to enable authentication. The authentication protocol must be specified along with the method list. Here, I have specified CHAP along with the method list GAD-Login:

```
interface Serial0/0/0:0
 no ip address
 encapsulation ppp
 ppp authentication chap GAD-Login
```

If you have not created a PPP method list, you will get an error, though the command will still be accepted:

```
R1(config-if)#ppp authentication pap GAD-Login
AAA: Warning, authentication list "GAD-Login" is not defined for PPP.
```

Using AAA with PAP or CHAP is much more scalable than using locally configured usernames and passwords.

## CHAPTER 27

Basic Firewall Theory

A firewall is the wall in a car that protects you from harm when the engine catches fire. At least, that's the definition that confused my mother when I told her I was writing this chapter. In networking, a firewall is a device that prevents certain types of traffic from entering or leaving your network. Usually, the danger comes from attackers attempting to gain access to your network from the Internet, but not always. Firewalls are often deployed when networks are connected to other entities that are not trusted, such as partner companies.

A firewall can be a standalone appliance, software running on a server or router, or a module integrated into a larger device, like a Cisco 6500 switch. These days, a firewall's functionality is often included in other devices, such as the ubiquitous cable-modem/router/firewall/wireless access point devices in many homes.

Modern firewalls can serve multiple functions, even when they're not part of combination devices. VPN services are often supported on firewalls. A firewall running as an application on a server may share the server with other functions such as DNS or mail, though generally, a firewall should restrict its activities to security-related tasks. The Cisco Adaptive Security Appliance (ASA) is a firewall that is bundled with other security features like VPN and IDS/IPS.

Best Practices

One of the things I tell my clients over and over is:

> Security is a balance between convenience and paranoia.

We all want security. If I told you that I could guarantee the security of your family, wouldn't you jump at the chance? But what if I told you that to achieve this goal, I needed to put steel plates over all the windows in your home, replace the garage door with a brick wall, and change the front door to one made of cast iron? You might reconsider—it wouldn't be very convenient, would it? Companies also often want a high level of security, but like you, they may not be willing to give up too many conveniences to achieve it.

A while ago, I was working as a consultant in Manhattan for a large firm that was having security problems. We gave them some options that we knew had worked for other organizations. These were the responses we received:

One-time password key fobs
> "We don't want that—the key fobs are a pain, and it takes too long to log in."

VPN
> "We like the idea, but can you make it so we don't have to enter any passwords?"

Putting the email server inside the firewall
> "Will we have to enter more than one password? Because if we do, forget it."

Password rotation
> "No way—we don't want to ever have to change our passwords!"

Needless to say, the meeting was a bit of a challenge. The clients wanted security, and they got very excited when we said we could offer them the same level of network security that the big banks used. But the minute they realized what was involved in implementing that level of security, they balked—they balked at the idea of any inconvenience.

More often than not, companies do come to an understanding that they need a certain level of security, even if some conveniences must be sacrificed for its sake. Sadly, for many companies, this happens only after their existing security has been compromised. Others may be forced into compliance by regulations like Sarbanes-Oxley and PCI.

If you find yourself designing a security solution, you should follow these best practices:

Simple is good
> This rule applies to all of networking, but it is especially relevant for security rules. When you are designing security rules and configuring firewalls, keep it simple. Make your rules easy to read and understand. Where applicable, use names instead of numbers. If your firewall has 60,000 rules in it, I'd be willing to bet you've got holes. And yes, there are plenty of firewalls out there with tens of thousands of rules.

Monitor the logs
> You must log your firewall status messages to a server, and you must look at these messages on a regular basis. If you have a firewall in place and you're not examining the logs, you are living with a false sense of security. Someone could be attacking your network right now and you'd have no idea. I've worked on sites that kept buying more Internet bandwidth, amazed at how much they needed. When I examined their firewall logs, I discovered that the main bandwidth consumers were warez sites that hackers had installed on their internal FTP servers. Because no one looked at the logs, no one knew there was a problem.

Deny everything; permit what you need

This is a very simple rule, but it's amazing how often it's ignored. As a best practice, this has got to be the one with the biggest benefit.

In practical terms, blocking all traffic in both directions is often viewed as too troublesome. This rule should always be followed to the letter on inbound firewalls—nothing should ever be allowed inbound unless there is a valid, documented business need for it. Restricting all outbound traffic except that which is needed is also the right thing to do, but it can be an administrative hassle. Here is a prime example of convenience outweighing security. On the plus side, if you implement this rule, you'll know that peer-to-peer file sharing services probably won't work, and you'll have a better handle on what's going on when users complain that their newly installed instant messenger clients don't work. The downside is that unless you have a documented security statement, you'll spend a lot of time arguing with people about what's allowed and what's not.

The default behavior of many firewalls, including the Cisco PIX and ASA, is to allow all outbound traffic. Restricting outbound traffic may be a good idea based on your environment and corporate culture, though I've found that most small and medium-size companies don't want the hassle. Additionally, many smaller companies don't have strict Internet usage policies, which can make enforcing outbound restrictions a challenge.

Everything that's not yours belongs outside the firewall

This is another simple rule that junior engineers often miss. Anything from another party that touches your network should be controlled by a firewall. Network links to other companies, including credit card verification services, should never be allowed without a firewall.

The corollary to this rule is that everything of yours should be inside the firewall (or in the DMZ, as described in the next section). The only devices that are regularly placed in such a way that the firewall cannot monitor them are VPN concentrators. VPN concentrators are often placed in parallel with firewalls. Everything else should be segregated with the firewall. Segregation can be accomplished with one or more DMZs.

 Firewalls get blamed for everything. It seems to be a law of corporate culture to blame the firewall the minute anything doesn't work. I believe there are two reasons for this. First, we naturally blame what we don't understand. Second, a firewall is designed to prevent traffic from flowing. When traffic isn't flowing, it makes sense to blame the firewall.

The DMZ

Firewalls often have what is commonly called a *DMZ*. DMZ stands for demilitarized zone, which of course has nothing to do with computing. This is a military/political term referring to a zone created between opposing forces in which no military activity is allowed. For example, a demilitarized zone was created between North and South Korea.

 Using military nomenclature is common in the computing world. From demilitarized zones to Trojan horses to network warriors, we seem to love to militarize what we do, if only in name.

In the network security realm, a DMZ is a network that is neither inside nor outside the firewall. The idea is that this third network can be accessed from inside (and probably outside) the firewall, but security rules will prohibit devices in the DMZ from connecting to devices on the inside. A DMZ is less secure than the inside network, but more secure than the outside network.

A common DMZ scenario is shown in Figure 27-1. The Internet is located on the outside interface. The users are on the inside interface. Any servers that need to be accessible from the Internet are located in the DMZ network.

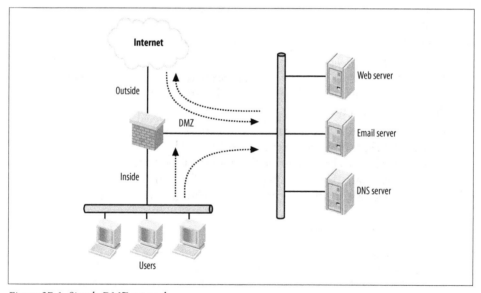

Figure 27-1. Simple DMZ network

In this network, the firewall should be configured as follows:

Inside network
  The inside network can initiate connections to any other network, but no other network can initiate connections to it.

Outside network

The outside network cannot initiate connections to the inside network. The outside network can initiate connections to the DMZ.

DMZ

The DMZ can initiate connections to the outside network, but not to the inside network. Any other network can initiate connections into the DMZ.

One of the main benefits of this type of design is isolation. Should the email server come under attack and become compromised, the attacker will not have access to the users on the inside network. However, in this design, the attacker *will* have access to the other servers in the DMZ because they're on the same physical network. (The servers can be further isolated with Cisco Ethernet switch features such as private VLANs, port ACLs, and VLAN maps; see Chapter 25 for more information.)

Servers in a DMZ should be locked down with security measures as if they were on the Internet. Rules on the firewall should be configured to allow services only as needed to the DMZ. For example:

Email server

POP, IMAP, and SMTP (TCP ports 110, 143, and 25) should be allowed. All other ports should not be permitted from the Internet.

Web server

HTTP and HTTPS (TCP ports 80 and 443) should be allowed. All other ports should be denied from the Internet.

DNS server

Only DNS (UDP port 53, and, possibly, TCP port 53) should be allowed from the Internet. All other ports should be denied.

Ideally, only the protocols needed to manage and maintain the servers should be allowed from the managing hosts inside to the DMZ.

Another DMZ Example

Another common DMZ implementation involves connectivity to a third party, such as a vendor or supplier. Figure 27-2 shows a simple network where a vendor is connected by a T1 to a router in the DMZ. Examples of vendors might include a credit card processing service or a supplier that allows your users to access its database. Some companies even outsource their email system to a third party, in which case the vendor's email server may be accessed through such a design.

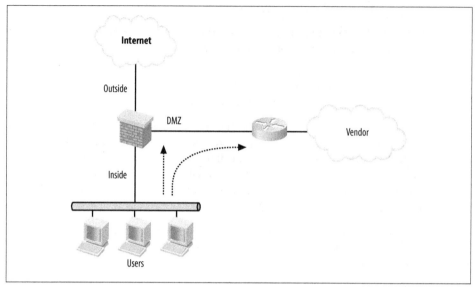

Figure 27-2. DMZ connecting to a vendor

In a network like this, the firewall should be configured as follows:

Inside network
> The inside network can initiate connections to any other network, but no other network can initiate connections to it.

Outside network
> The outside network cannot initiate connections to the inside network or to the DMZ. The inside network can initiate connections to the outside network, but the DMZ cannot.

DMZ
> The DMZ cannot initiate connections to any network. Only the inside network can initiate connections to the DMZ.

Multiple DMZ Example

The real world is not always as neat and orderly as my drawings would have you believe. The examples I've shown are valid, but larger companies have more complicated networks. Sometimes a single DMZ is not enough.

Figure 27-3 shows a network with multiple DMZs. The design is a combination of the first two examples. Outside is the Internet, and inside are the users. DMZ-1 is a connection to a vendor. DMZ-2 is where the Internet servers reside. The security rules are essentially the same as those outlined in the preceding section, but we must now also consider whether DMZ-1 should be allowed to initiate connections to DMZ-2 and vice versa. In this case, the answer is no.

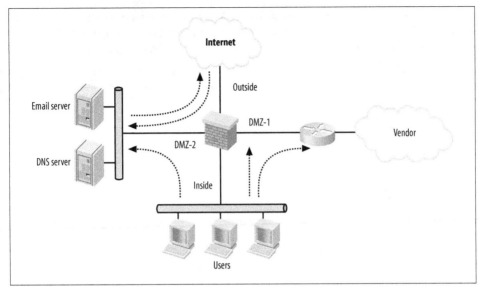

Figure 27-3. Multiple DMZs

The firewall should be configured as follows:

Inside network
> The inside network can initiate connections to any other network, but no other network can initiate connections to it.

Outside network
> The outside network cannot initiate connections to the inside network or to DMZ-1. The outside network can initiate connections to DMZ-2.

DMZ-1
> DMZ-1 cannot initiate connections to any other network. Only the inside network can initiate connections into DMZ-1.

DMZ-2
> DMZ-2 can initiate connections only to the outside network. The outside network and the inside network can initiate connections to DMZ-2.

Alternate Designs

The Internet is not always the outside interface of a firewall. Many companies have links to other companies (parent companies, sister companies, partner companies, etc.). In each case, even if the companies are related, separating the main company from the others with a firewall is an excellent practice to adopt.

Figure 27-4 shows a simplified layout where Your Company's Network is connected to three other external entities. Firewall A is protecting Your Company from the Internet, Firewall B is protecting Your Company from the parent company, and Firewall C is protecting Your Company from the sister company.

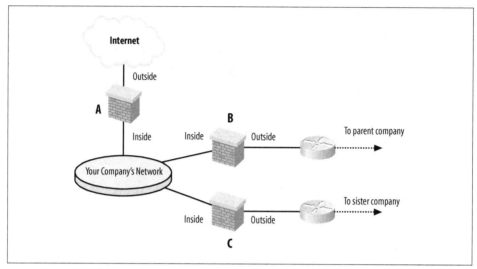

Figure 27-4. Multiple firewall example

Each firewall has an inside and an outside interface. While each of the firewalls' inside interfaces are connected to the same network, the outside interfaces are all connected to different networks.

Firewalls are also often used in multitiered architectures like those found in ecommerce websites. A common practice is to have firewalls not only at the point where the website connects to the Internet, but between the layers as well. Figure 27-5 shows such a network.

In a layered design like this, one firewall's inside network is the next firewall's outside network. There are four firewalls connected to the balancing layer. The top two, a failover pair, connect the balancing layer to the Internet layer. To these firewalls, the balancing layer is the inside network. The bottom two firewalls (another failover pair) connect the balancing layer to the web layer. To these firewalls, the balancing layer is the outside network.

Firewalls are another building block in your arsenal of networking devices. While there are some common design rules that should be followed, such as the ones I've outlined here, the needs of your business will ultimately dictate how you deploy your firewalls.

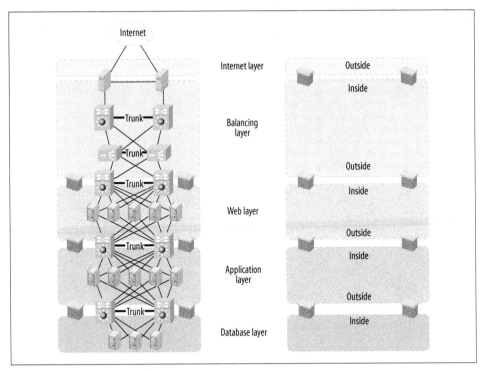

Figure 27-5. Ecommerce website

## CHAPTER 28

ASA Firewall Configuration

In this chapter, I will explain how to configure the most common features of an ASA firewall. Examples will be based on the ASA 5540, which uses the same commands as the entire ASA line. Most commands are the same on the PIX firewalls, but since they are no longer sold—with the exception of the Firewall Service Module (FWSM)—this chapter focuses on ASAs.

 There are slight differences among models. For example, the ASA 5505 base model cannot be run in failover or multicontext mode. The FWSM also operates differently in that it is a module and has no configurable physical interfaces.

ASA stands for Adaptive Security Appliance. This name indicates that these devices are capable of being a firewall, a VPN device, and an IPS/IDS device. In this chapter, I will concentrate on the basics of firewall services.

Configuring an ASA can be a bit confusing for people whose experience is with IOS-based devices. While there are similarities in the way the command-line interpreter works, there are some pretty interesting differences, too. One of my favorite features of the ASA and even the PIX firewalls is the fact that you can execute the show running-config command from within configuration mode. Recent versions of IOS allow similar functionality using the do command (do show run, for example) from within configuration mode, but using the command in the ASA is, in my opinion, more natural. NX-OS, the operating system for Cisco Nexus switches, implements this feature as well.

Around the time the ASAs were released, Cisco revamped the Adaptive Security Device Manager (ASDM) software used to control its PIX firewalls and ASA appliances. For the first time, this software became a viable tool for configuring and managing a Cisco firewall. While many of the examples in this chapter can also be accomplished with the ASDM, I tend to be an old-school command-line kind of guy. This chapter deals with configuring ASAs using the command line, and does not cover the ASDM. The ASDM is a pretty great tool, however, and I encourage you to explore its use on your own.

Contexts

Many ASAs can be divided into multiple contexts. Similar in principle to the way VMware allows multiple servers or workstations to reside on a single physical machine, multicontext mode allows multiple virtual firewalls within a single physical ASA. While VMware allows for multiple operating systems to run on a single machine, there is no such versatility allowed here. Multicontext mode allows multiple logical ASAs, and only ASAs, to appear within a single box. Each ASA appears as if it were a standalone unit, though there are some fairly severe tradeoffs to this. In multicontext mode, the following features are disabled:

- OSPF, RIP, and EIGRP; multicontext mode supports only static routes
- VPN
- Multicast routing (multicast bridging is supported)
- Threat detection
- QoS
- Phone proxy

As you can see, those are some pretty important features for a lot of installations. The inability to use VPN is a deal-breaker for many companies considering multicontext mode. If your needs tend toward regular firewalling, and you don't need any of the items just listed, multicontext mode can be a cool way to get your money's worth from an ASA. We'll talk about contexts in detail later in this chapter. For now, though, you need to know that the command prompt on a multicontext ASA, by default, is composed of `hostname/context-name#`. The ASA I use in my examples is named ASA-5540. Any commands issued from within a context use the context named GAD. For example, this is what config mode looks like from the system (default) context:

```
ASA-5540#
```

And this is what the command line looks like in the GAD context:

```
ASA-5540/GAD#
```

Interfaces and Security Levels

Each interface in an ASA firewall must have a physical name, a logical name, a security level, and an IP address. Interfaces may also be configured for features such as speed and duplex mode.

All model ASAs can be configured to run in *transparent* mode. In this mode, the ASA becomes a bridge and a *bump on the wire*, which is, in my opinion, about the dumbest description ever. Transparent mode is available so that you can drop your firewall into an existing network without renumbering any part of it. With only an IP address for management, a transparent firewall seems like the perfect solution.

I'm sure I'll get heat for this, but I recommend that you don't use transparent mode. Every installation I've ever seen where transparent mode ASAs or PIXes were involved has been a disaster. Why? Because the proper solution involved redesigning the network, and no one was willing to spend the time and/or money to do so. Transparent firewalls allow a solution to be shoe-horned into a network that wasn't designed for a firewall. Do yourself a favor and insist that the network be redesigned to support the traditional Layer-3 firewall model instead of using transparent mode.

On the ASA 5540, the standard physical interfaces are G0/0 through G0/3. An expansion card can be installed to add interfaces, which are numbered incrementally starting at G1/0. Each interface must be assigned a logical name. There are no default names for interfaces on an ASA, but *inside* and *outside* have special meaning.

Each interface must also have a security level assigned. By default, interfaces with higher security levels can send packets to interfaces with lower security levels, but interfaces with lower security levels cannot send packets to interfaces with higher security levels. An interface's security level is represented by an integer within the range 0–100.

The default security level for the inside interface is 100. The default security level for the outside interface is 0. On an ASA, when you assign the name outside or inside, it will assign the proper security level for you:

```
ASA-5540/GAD(config-if)# nameif outside
INFO: Security level for "outside" set to 0 by default.
```

If you add a third interface, its security level will typically be somewhere between these values. As of ASA/PIX version 7.x, you can have multiple interfaces with the same security level. Figure 28-1 shows a typical firewall with three interfaces: outside and inside interfaces, and a DMZ.

Given this design, by default, traffic may flow in the following ways:

- From inside to outside.
- From inside to the DMZ.
- From the DMZ to the outside, but not to the inside.
- Traffic from outside may not flow to any other interface.

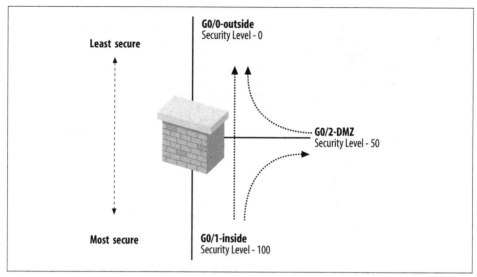

Figure 28-1. ASA interface security levels

 You can completely override the interface security level by using access lists, so don't fall into the trap of thinking these rules are set in stone.

To manually assign a priority to an interface, use the `security-level` interface command. For example, here I configure the inside interface:

```
ASA-5540/GAD(config)# int g0/0
ASA-5540/GAD(config-if)# nameif inside
ASA-5540/GAD(config-if)# security-level 100
```

And here I configure the outside interface:

```
ASA-5540/GAD(config)# int g0/1
ASA-5540/GAD(config-if)# nameif outside
ASA-5540/GAD(config-if)# security-level 0
```

These values are the defaults for an ASA firewall. To configure the third interface in Figure 28-1, use the following commands:

```
ASA-5540/GAD(config)# int g0/2
ASA-5540/GAD(config-if)# nameif DMZ
ASA-5540/GAD(config-if)# security-level 50
```

To configure the speeds and duplex modes of the interfaces, use the `interface` command:

```
ASA-5540(config)# int g0/0
ASA-5540(config-if)# speed 100
ASA-5540(config-if)# duplex full
```

In multicontext mode, interface characteristics can only be changed within the system context. See "Managing Contexts" on page 479 for more information.

To see the status of your interfaces, use the show interface command. The output of this command is similar to that produced in IOS, though the output changes depending on the context from which you enter the command. Since physical characteristics can only be changed from the system context, more information is provided there. From the system context:

```
ASA-5540# sho int g0/0
Interface GigabitEthernet0/0 "", is administratively down, line protocol is down
  Hardware is i82546GB rev03, BW 1000 Mbps, DLY 10 usec
        Full-Duplex, 100 Mbps
        Available for allocation to a context
        MAC address 0026.0b31.36d8, MTU not set
        IP address unassigned
        0 packets input, 0 bytes, 0 no buffer
        Received 0 broadcasts, 0 runts, 0 giants
        0 input errors, 0 CRC, 0 frame, 0 overrun, 0 ignored, 0 abort
        0 L2 decode drops
        0 packets output, 0 bytes, 0 underruns
        0 output errors, 0 collisions, 0 interface resets
        0 late collisions, 0 deferred
        0 input reset drops, 0 output reset drops
        input queue (curr/max packets): hardware (0/0) software (0/0)
        output queue (curr/max packets): hardware (0/0) software (0/0)
```

From within a regular context:

```
ASA-5540/GAD# sho int g0/0
Interface GigabitEthernet0/0 "inside", is down, line protocol is down
        MAC address 1200.0000.0700, MTU 1500
        IP address 10.10.10.1, subnet mask 255.255.255.0
   Traffic Statistics for "inside":
        0 packets input, 0 bytes
        0 packets output, 0 bytes
        0 packets dropped
```

Names

One of the more user-friendly features of the ASA and PIX OS is the ability to display IP addresses as names. To enable this feature, enter the names command in configuration mode:

```
ASA-5540/GAD(config)# names
```

With the names feature enabled, you can configure any IP address to be associated with a name. This is similar in principle to a basic form of DNS, but the names are local to the ASA or PIX being configured. Say that 10.10.10.10 is the IP address of a server called

FileServer. Using the name command, you can assign the name *FileServer* to the IP address within the ASA:

```
ASA-5540/GAD(config)# name 10.10.10.10 FileServer
```

You can then configure an access list like the following:

```
ASA-5540/GAD(config)# access-list Dingle permit tcp any host 10.10.10.10 eq www
```

 Access lists, including features specific to the ASA, are covered in detail in Chapter 25. The effects of using names like *Dingle* to identify your access lists have not been studied in depth. Use them at your own risk.

In the configuration, the IP address will be translated to the configured name:

```
ASA-5540/GAD# sho run | include Dingle
access-list Dingle extended permit tcp any host FileServer eq www
```

If you prefer to see the IP addresses, you can disable the names feature by negating the names command. The configuration will once again show the IP addresses:

```
ASA-5540/GAD(config)# no names
ASA-5540/GAD(config)# sho run | include Dingle
access-list Dingle extended permit tcp any host 10.10.10.10 eq www
```

 Even with names enabled, the output of the show interface command will always show the IP addresses.

If you need to see all the names configured on your ASA, use the show names command:

```
ASA-5540/GAD #sho names
name 10.10.10.1 ASA-Outside
name 10.10.10.10 FileServer
name 192.168.1.1 ASA-Inside
```

Thanks to the new capabilities in the OS, you can also use the sho run names command:

```
ASA-5540/GAD #sho run names
name 10.10.10.1 ASA-Outside
name 10.10.10.10 FileServer
name 192.168.1.1 ASA-Inside
```

The names feature is extremely helpful in that it makes ASA configurations easier to read. With very large configurations, the number of IP addresses can be staggering, and trying to remember them all is a practical impossibility.

Object Groups

Object groups allow a group of networks, IP addresses, protocols, or services to be referenced with a single name. This is extremely helpful when you're configuring complex access lists. Take the situation shown in Figure 28-2. There are three web servers, each of which offers the same three protocols: SMTP (TCP port 25), HTTP (TCP port 80), and HTTPS (TCP port 443).

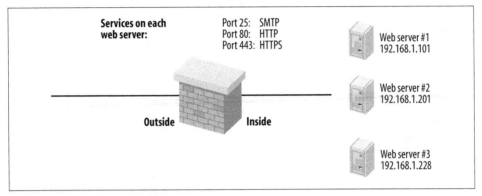

Figure 28-2. Complex access list scenario

 This example shows a collocated website. On a normal enterprise network, web servers should not reside on the inside network, but rather in a DMZ. Of course, "normal" is a very subjective word.

Because the IP addresses of the three servers are not in a range that can be addressed with a single subnet mask, each server must have its own access list entry. Additionally, there must be an entry for each protocol for each server.

As a result, you must configure nine access list entries to allow each of the three protocols to these three servers:

```
access-list In permit tcp any host 192.168.1.101 eq smtp
access-list In permit tcp any host 192.168.1.101 eq www
access-list In permit tcp any host 192.168.1.101 eq https
access-list In permit tcp any host 192.168.1.201 eq smtp
access-list In permit tcp any host 192.168.1.201 eq www
access-list In permit tcp any host 192.168.1.201 eq https
access-list In permit tcp any host 192.168.1.228 eq smtp
access-list In permit tcp any host 192.168.1.228 eq www
access-list In permit tcp any host 192.168.1.228 eq https
```

While this may not seem like a big deal, imagine if the firewall had six interfaces and supported 140 servers. I've seen Cisco firewalls that had access lists 17 printed pages long. Figuring out all the permutations of protocols and servers can be maddening. The potential complexity of the access lists has led many businesses to ignore Cisco when considering firewalls. With the `object-group` command, you can create a group of protocols, networks, ICMP types, or services that you can reference by a name:

```
ASA-5540/GAD(config)# object-group ?

configure mode commands/options:
  icmp-type  Specifies a group of ICMP types, such as echo
  network    Specifies a group of host or subnet IP addresses
  protocol   Specifies a group of protocols, such as TCP, etc
  service    Specifies a group of TCP/UDP ports/services
```

In the preceding example, each web server is using the same TCP ports. By assigning these common ports to a group, we can make the access list much smaller. Let's create an object group called *Webserver-svcs*. This will be a group of TCP services, which we'll define using `port-object` object group commands:

```
object-group service Webserver-svcs tcp
  description For Webservers
  port-object eq smtp
  port-object eq www
  port-object eq https
```

Now, instead of listing each service for each web server, we can simply reference the group for each web server. We do this by using the `object-group` keyword, followed by the group name:

```
access-list In permit tcp any host 192.168.1.101 object-group Webserver-svcs
access-list In permit tcp any host 192.168.1.201 object-group Webserver-svcs
access-list In permit tcp any host 192.168.1.228 object-group Webserver-svcs
```

This reduces the number of access list entries from nine to three, but we can do better. All of the IP addresses listed serve the same purpose—they are all web servers. Let's create another object group called *Webservers*. This time, the object group type will be network, and we'll use the `network-object` command to add objects to the group:

```
object-group network Webservers
  description Webservers
  network-object host 192.168.1.101
  network-object host 192.168.1.201
  network-object host 192.168.1.228
```

We can now simplify the access list even more:

```
access-list In permit tcp any object-group Webservers object-group Webserver-svcs
```

What started as a nine-line access list has been compressed to one line. When we execute the `show access-list` command, the object groups will be expanded, and the resulting access list will be visible:

```
ASA-5540/GAD(config)# show access-list Inbound
access-list Inboun; 9 elements
access-list In line 1 extended permit tcp any object-group Webservers object-group
Webserver-svcs 0x6484a1ba
  access-list In line 1 extended permit tcp any host 192.168.1.101 eq smtp
(hitcnt=0) 0x9ba9ede4
```

```
  access-list In line 1 extended permit tcp any host 192.168.1.101 eq www
(hitcnt=0) 0x34db9472
  access-list In line 1 extended permit tcp any host 192.168.1.101 eq https
(hitcnt=0) 0x821a0cfe
  access-list In line 1 extended permit tcp any host 192.168.1.201 eq smtp
(hitcnt=0) 0xb52bad46
  access-list In line 1 extended permit tcp any host 192.168.1.201 eq www
(hitcnt=0) 0x881944d5
  access-list In line 1 extended permit tcp any host 192.168.1.201 eq https
(hitcnt=0) 0x4c466f6a
  access-list In line 1 extended permit tcp any host 192.168.1.228 eq smtp
(hitcnt=0) 0x6c6c1ba9
  access-list In line 1 extended permit tcp any host 192.168.1.228 eq www
(hitcnt=0) 0xfca8e834
  access-list In line 1 extended permit tcp any host 192.168.1.228 eq https
(hitcnt=0) 0x7d7e2239
```

Notice that the line number for each entry is the same (line 1). This indicates that these entries are a result of the expansion of line 1, which in this example is the only line in the access list.

When an object group is in use, it cannot be deleted. The ASA will bark at us with the following error if we attempt to delete the object group:

```
ASA-5540/GAD(config-service)# no object-group service Webserver-svcs
Removing object-group (Webserver-svcs) not allowed;
object-group (Webserver-svcs), being used in access-list, would become empty
```

We must either remove the references to it in the offending access lists or remove the access lists altogether. Once we do so, the ASA will allow us to delete the object group:

```
ASA-5540/GAD(config)# clear configure access-list In
ASA-5540/GAD(config)# no object-group service Webserver-svcs
```

Inspects

Fixups were the features on a PIX firewall that inspected application protocols. They have been replaced with application inspections, or *inspects* for short. While fixups were much easier to configure, inspects follow a more IOS-like method of implementation in that they are embedded into a global service policy. It might look difficult, but it doesn't need to be.

Inspects are used to enable complex protocols, such as FTP, that have multiple streams. They are also used to make protocols more secure. For example, the SMTP inspect limits the commands that can be run through the ASA within the SMTP protocol.

To illustrate one of the common application inspections, I've connected through an ASA to a mail server using Telnet. This ASA is not running the SMTP fixup, which you should rarely see in the wild, as it is enabled by default. When I issue the SMTP command `EHLO someserver`, I get a list of information regarding the capabilities of the mail server:

```
[GAD@someserver GAD]$telnet mail.myserver.net 25
Trying 10.10.10.10...
Connected to mail.myserver.net.
Escape character is '^]'.
220 mail.myserver.net ESMTP Postfix
EHLO someserver
250-mail.myserver.net
250-PIPELINING
250-SIZE 10240000
250-ETRN
250 8BITMIME
```

This information is not necessary for the successful transfer of email messages, and could be useful to a hacker. For example, a hacker could try to pull email messages off the server using the ETRN deque command. The SMTP inspect intercepts and disables the ETRN command.

 ETRN is a very useful feature of SMTP that allows ISPs to queue mail for you should your email server become unavailable. If you need to use ETRN, you will have to disable the SMTP inspect on your firewall.

ASAs have most of the commonly used inspects enabled by default. Here, I'll enable the SMTP inspection, though normally you would not need to do this:

```
ASA-5540/GAD(config)# policy-map global_policy
ASA-5540/GAD(config-pmap)#  class inspection_default
ASA-5540/GAD(config-pmap-c)# inspect esmtp
```

Now the ASA will intercept and manage every SMTP request:

```
[GAD@someserver GAD]$telnet mail.myserver.net 25
Trying 10.10.10.10...
Connected to mail.myserver.net.
Escape character is '^]'.
220 ************************
EHLO someserver
502 Error: command not implemented
```

Look at the items in bold and compare the output to the previous example. Without the SMTP inspect enabled, the server responded to the Telnet request with the name of the mail server, the version of SMTP supported, and the mail transfer agent (MTA) software in use:

```
220 mail.myserver.net ESMTP Postfix.
```

With the SMTP inspect enabled, the firewall intercepts this reply and alters it to something useless:

```
220 ************************
```

This gives hackers much less to work with. Likewise, the inspect prevents the execution of the EHLO someserver command.

Different inspects are enabled by default on different versions of the ASA's OS. On version 8.0(4), the default configuration is:

```
policy-map global_policy
 class inspection_default
  inspect dns preset_dns_map
  inspect ftp
  inspect h323 h225
  inspect h323 ras
  inspect netbios
  inspect rsh
  inspect rtsp
  inspect skinny
  inspect esmtp
  inspect sqlnet
  inspect sunrpc
  inspect tftp
  inspect sip
  inspect xdmcp
  inspect http
```

Some of these inspects may not be needed and can be disabled, though they usually don't hurt anything when left active. To see which ones are active on your ASA, use the show service-policy global command:

```
ASA-5540/GAD# sho service-policy global

Global policy:
  Service-policy: global_policy
    Class-map: inspection_default
      Inspect: dns preset_dns_map, packet 0, drop 0, reset-drop 0
      Inspect: ftp, packet 0, drop 0, reset-drop 0
      Inspect: h323 h225 _default_h323_map, packet 0, drop 0, reset-drop 0
      Inspect: h323 ras _default_h323_map, packet 0, drop 0, reset-drop 0
      Inspect: netbios, packet 0, drop 0, reset-drop 0
      Inspect: rsh, packet 0, drop 0, reset-drop 0
      Inspect: rtsp, packet 0, drop 0, reset-drop 0
      Inspect: skinny , packet 0, drop 0, reset-drop 0
      Inspect: esmtp _default_esmtp_map, packet 0, drop 0, reset-drop 0
      Inspect: sqlnet, packet 0, drop 0, reset-drop 0
      Inspect: sunrpc, packet 0, drop 0, reset-drop 0
      Inspect: tftp, packet 0, drop 0, reset-drop 0
      Inspect: sip , packet 0, drop 0, reset-drop 0
      Inspect: xdmcp, packet 0, drop 0, reset-drop 0
      Inspect: http, packet 0, drop 0, reset-drop 0
```

Each inspect addresses the needs of a specific protocol. See the Cisco documentation for details.

Managing Contexts

Multicontext mode allows virtual firewalls to exist within a single ASA firewall or a pair of them. A failover pair of ASAs will support multicontext mode as well, with active/

active failover also being possible. Active/active failover is covered in "Failover" on page 490. Figure 28-3 shows a logical representation of multiple contexts residing within a single physical firewall.

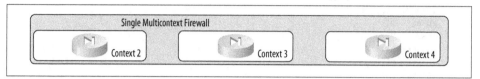

Figure 28-3. Multiple contexts within a physical ASA

Each context behaves as if it were a single standalone device, though there are ways that interfaces can be shared between contexts. Each context may have its own IP scheme, and networks can be replicated in multiple contexts without issue.

Most of the normal ASA features are available within each context, but there are some important features that are not. Though the ASA appliance is capable of many functions such as VPN, IDS, and the like, most of these additional features are disabled in multicontext mode. It bears repeating that multicontext mode disables the following features:

- Support for OSPF, RIP, and EIGRP
- VPN
- Multicast routing; multicast bridging is supported
- Threat detection
- QoS
- Phone proxy

That's a pretty significant list! For many, the inability to support VPN alone may make contexts unusable. The disabled QoS and phone proxy features may also be serious negatives when you're considering contexts. In a nutshell, if you need many firewalls with traditional PIX-like features, multicontext mode will serve you well. I have used them in ecommerce websites and in data center environments where each context supported a single customer. For these scenarios, contexts work quite well.

Context Types

There are three types of contexts in a multicontext ASA. They are the system context, the admin context, and what I call *regular* contexts or just *contexts*. Each of these contexts has features and limitations as shown in Figure 28-4:

System context
> The system context is where all contexts are created and managed. When you first log into the console of a multicontext ASA, you will find yourself in the system

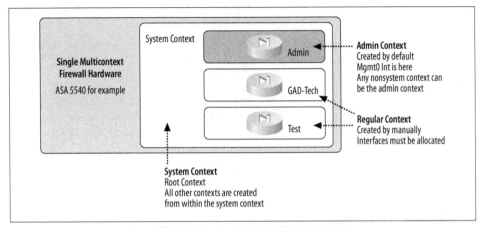

Figure 28-4. Context types within an ASA

context. The system context is where all failover is configured and managed. You can think of the system context as a sort of root context. The system context is not a usable virtual firewall like other contexts, since interface and security rules are not applied in the system context with the exception of failover interfaces.

With the ASA in multicontext mode, the speed and duplex on interfaces can be set *only* in the system context. This will likely drive you nuts the first time you use contexts; if you're like me, you'll quietly swear at Cisco for making a device that apparently can't support 10 Mb or 100 Mb devices, ignorant of the fact that the speed *can* be changed, just not in the context you're in.

The interfaces can only be changed in the system context because physical interfaces can be shared between contexts. It wouldn't do to have customer A changing the duplex on an interface being shared with customer B, now would it?

Admin context

The admin context behaves like any other nonsystem context; however, when administering the admin context, you can jump both to the system context and other contexts. There can be only one admin context, and it can be any context of your choosing. You perform tasks such as upgrading code through the admin context.

Context

A context is a virtual firewall, as previously outlined. This type of context is specifically not one of the other two types. When you're in a context, there may be no indications that you are in a virtual device except that some normally available configurations such as failover and interface speed/duplex commands don't exist. You may not be able to jump to other contexts unless you first arrived there from a system or admin context. Failover within the context (but not for other contexts) may be triggered from within the context, depending on the global failover configuration.

The Classifier

When there are multiple contexts sharing physical interfaces, there must be some way for the ASA to decide which context should receive a packet. This job is delegated to a process called the *classifier*.

The classifier is an important aspect of a multicontext ASA, and its operation and limitations must be understood. Failure to understand the classifier's operation will lead to heartache, depression, and perhaps most importantly, an ASA that won't work.

There are multiple ways in which contexts can be created, all of which have different limitations and configuration requirements due to how the classifier works.

No shared interfaces

The simplest design for a multicontext ASA is shown in Figure 28-5. In this figure, there are three contexts. Each context has a separate inside and outside interface. Each interface is physically allocated to only one context. In this design, each interface can be a VLAN-tagged subinterface, which is different than sharing an interface. When each context has its own interfaces, there is no interaction between contexts. It is truly as if each context were a standalone firewall.

This is the simplest of multicontext designs, and no special consideration needs to be given to how interfaces are addressed.

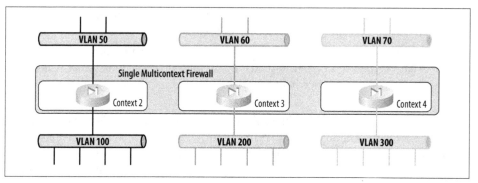

Figure 28-5. Multiple contexts with no shared interfaces

Another way to view such a design is shown in Figure 28-6. Again, no network or interface is shared between the contexts.

Shared outside interfaces

With multiple contexts, it is possible to share an interface between contexts, as shown in Figure 28-7. In this case, interface G0/0 is assigned to all three contexts. Here, each context has an IP address within the same network (hopefully), and they all have the same default gateway.

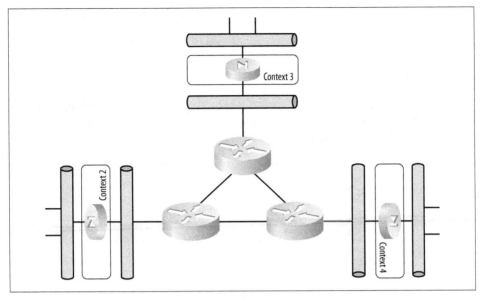

Figure 28-6. Another no-shared-interface multicontext scenario

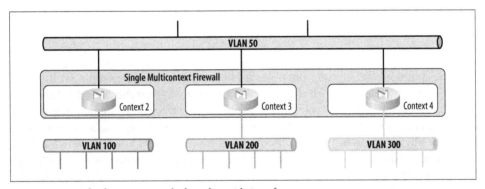

Figure 28-7. Multiple contexts with shared outside interface

A design like this might be popular in an ISP environment where multiple firewalls share a single outside public IP network on a single VLAN. This design is relatively simple for the classifier to understand, because the default gateway is usually on the outside interface. Packets with an unknown destination will be forwarded outbound to the default gateway, which will likely be the same on every context.

Inbound packets will be forwarded to the next-hop IP by the default gateway router, but each of these different IP addresses will (by default) have the same MAC address. The classifier will figure out to which context the packet should be sent based on the destination IP address. The destination IP address will either be a NAT address within a context or known within the routing table of a context.

A better way to configure this scenario is to enable unique MAC addresses per context. This will allow the outside router (default gateway) to forward directly to the proper context without the classifier being involved.

Shared inside interface

Another way that interfaces can be shared is shown in Figure 28-8. This is the opposite of the previous example (Figure 28-7). Here, though the outside interfaces are discrete, the inside interfaces all share an interface:

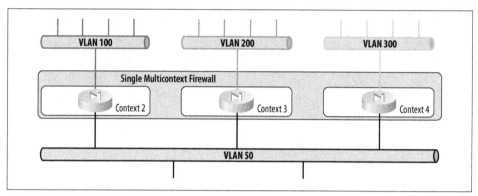

Figure 28-8. Multiple contexts sharing the inside interface

This design, while technically possible, is not recommended, especially on Internet-facing firewalls. The reason for this has to do with the way that the classifier deals with packets and how it switches them to the proper context. Since the default gateway for a firewall is usually found on the outside interface, the destination IP address in a packet might be any IP not found inside. The classifier has no way of knowing which default gateway should be chosen, since there are no IP routing entries on any context for the destination IP address, and no NAT entries to reference. In this case, the classifier may actually drop the packet. Unless you will be NATing outside addresses in a limited environment, sharing inside interfaces is not recommended.

Sharing inside and outside interfaces

It is theoretically possible to share interfaces on the inside and the outside of a multi-context ASA (Figure 28-9). This is not recommended, so don't do it. Simply put, it will drive the classifier, and likely you, quite mad.

Cascading contexts

Contexts can be *cascaded*. Cascaded contexts are configured to be in front of or behind one another. The preceding examples show interfaces being shared, but all the shared interfaces occur on the same side on each context. For example, we might share all of

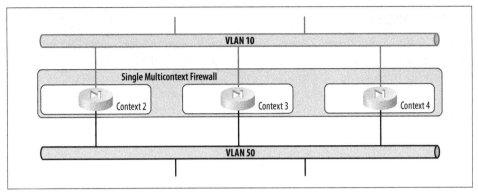

Figure 28-9. Multiple contexts sharing both outside and inside interfaces

the outside interfaces in an ISP scenario where the outside is a common public-IP segment.

You can cascade contexts by making the inside interface of one context shared with the outside context of another (Figure 28-10).

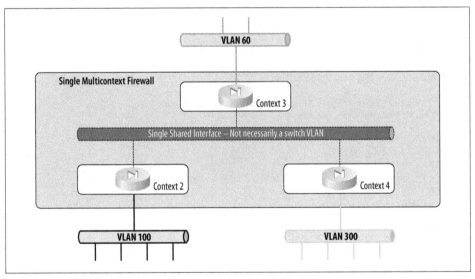

Figure 28-10. Cascaded contexts

This configuration might be useful where a single firewall controlled by the ISP needs to secure the network in addition to the security supplied by individual customers. Take care with this scenario, as you will likely need to replicate rules on each layer to allow traffic to flow.

Configuring Contexts

ASA firewalls that support contexts can operate in two modes: single and multiple. Single mode is a typical ASA appliance that supports all the features you've come to expect from an ASA. Multiple mode is what I like to call multicontext mode, where the ability to support multiple virtual firewalls is traded for all those cool features like routing and VPN. To see which mode your ASA is currently running, use the show mode command. Here you can see we're starting with our 5540 in single mode:

```
ASA-5540# sho mode
Security context mode: single
```

To start, we'll need to put the ASA into multicontext mode with the mode command. This is a high-impact command that changes the default behavior of the switch. The ASA will warn you of this when you initiate the command:

```
ASA-5540(config)# mode multiple
WARNING: This command will change the behavior of the device
WARNING: This command will initiate a Reboot
Proceed with change mode? [confirm]
```

Upon confirmation, we will be asked if we want to convert the system configuration. Once we commit, the ASA will reboot and initiate the process:

```
Convert the system configuration? [confirm]
!
The old running configuration file will be written to flash

The admin context configuration will be written to flash

The new running configuration file was written to flash
Security context mode: multiple

***
*** --- SHUTDOWN NOW ---
***
*** Message to all terminals:
***
***    change mode

Rebooting....
```

When the ASA reboots, it may report a pile of errors. If the ASA already had a configuration, many of those lines would likely fail, especially if any of them had to do with now-unsupported features such as VPN, QoS, or routing. Additionally, configuration having to do with interfaces may fail, since these interfaces have not been allocated to a context yet. A quick check with the show mode command will confirm that our ASA 5540 has been converted:

```
ASA-5540# sho mode
Security context mode: multiple
```

We now find ourselves in the system context. From here, we can manage all other contexts. Additionally, failover must be configured from the system context, as we'll see in the next section. Once the system has rebooted into multicontext mode, there will be one context preconfigured:

```
ASA-5540# sho context
Context Name      Class      Interfaces         URL
*admin            default    Management0/0      disk0:/admin.cfg

    Total active Security Contexts:
```

The admin context will have the following configuration associated with it:

```
admin-context admin
context admin
  allocate-interface Management0/0
  config-url disk0:/admin.cfg
```

Adding a new context is as easy as using the context command, though the context won't work right away:

```
ASA-5540(config)# context GAD-Tech
Creating context 'GAD-Tech'... Done. (4)
```

Notice that we're now in context configuration mode:

```
ASA-5540(config-ctx)#
```

Next, we can allocate some physical interfaces to the context:

```
ASA-5540(config-ctx)# allocate-interface g0/0
ASA-5540(config-ctx)# allocate-interface g0/1
```

We aren't limited to physical interfaces. We can allocate subinterfaces to contexts as well. Simply append a subinterface identifier like this:

```
ASA-5540(config-ctx)# allocate-interface g0/1.100
```

We still can't change to the context yet, and this gets me every single time:

```
ASA-5540# changeto context GAD-Tech
ERROR: Context hasn't been initialized with 'config-url'
```

We must manually configure a file where the configuration for our context will be saved:

```
ASA-5540(config)# context GAD-Tech
ASA-5540(config-ctx)#   config-url disk0:/gad-tech.cfg

INFO: Context GAD-Tech was created with URL disk0:/gad-tech.cfg
```

We can see the status of all the contexts from within the system context with the show context command. Here we can see our newly created context in addition to the default admin context:

```
ASA-5540# show context
Context Name      Class      Interfaces         URL
*admin            default    Management0/0      disk0:/admin.cfg
```

```
GAD-Tech          default    GigabitEthernet0/0,  disk0:/gad-tech.cfg
                             GigabitEthernet0/1
Test              default    GigabitEthernet0/0,  disk0:/test.cfg
                             GigabitEthernet0/2

Total active Security Contexts: 3
```

I added the *test* context after I added GAD-Tech to show that both of these contexts have interface G0/0 allocated to them. This is indicative of the shared interface scenario we talked about previously.

Now let's enter the GAD-Tech context. We do this with the changeto command.

 Some Nexus switches support Virtual Device Contexts (VDCs), which are similar in principle to the contexts we're dealing with here. Just to confuse us all, Cisco decided that the command to change between ASA contexts is switchto, while the command to change between Nexus VDCs is changeto. If you're working with me in a data center that has both, count on lots of profanity while I continuously use the wrong command on both platforms.

First we'll change to the GAD-Tech context:

```
ASA-5540# changeto context GAD-Tech
```

Notice that the prompt has changed from *hostname#* to *hostname/context#*. This behavior is configurable, but I like to leave it as-is because I find it useful. Next, from within the context, we can see that the output of the show context command is now limited to what can be seen from within the context:

```
ASA-5540/GAD-Tech# sho context
Context Name      Class      Interfaces           URL
   GAD-Tech       default    GigabitEthernet0/0,  disk0:/gad-tech.cfg
                             GigabitEthernet0/1
```

To change back to the system context, use the changeto system command:

```
ASA-5540/GAD-Tech# changeto system
ASA-5540#
```

 Once again, if you're used to Nexus VDCs, you might be frustrated in the ASA. The Nexus supports the command switchback, which sends you back from whence you came. The ASA has no *changeback* command.

If we exit the context without using the changeto system command, we will return to the system context, but we will no longer be in enable mode:

```
ASA-5540/GAD-Tech# exit

Logoff
```

```
Type help or '?' for a list of available commands.
ASA-5540>
```

Interfaces and Contexts

Once an interface has been allocated to a context, it appears within that context. For example, this ASA 5540 has four interfaces: G0/0–3. Here is the system context configuration for the GAD-Tech context, where I have allocated G0/0, G0/1.100 and G0/2 to the context:

```
ASA-5540# sho run context GAD-Tech
context GAD-Tech
  allocate-interface GigabitEthernet0/0
  allocate-interface GigabitEthernet0/1.100
  allocate-interface GigabitEthernet0/2
  config-url disk0:/gad-tech.cfg
```

From within the context, it appears as if only those interfaces exist:

```
ASA-5540/GAD-Tech# sho int
Interface GigabitEthernet0/0 "", is down, line protocol is down
        Available but not configured via nameif
Interface GigabitEthernet0/1.100 "", is down, line protocol is down
        Available but not configured via nameif
Interface GigabitEthernet0/2 "", is down, line protocol is down
        Available but not configured via nameif
```

We cannot change any physical characteristic for an interface from within any context except the system context. Of course, I forget that every time and stare at the screen like I just caught a glimpse of the Matrix for the first time (*whoa!*), but then I remember that I have to change to the system context to change speed and duplex. This may seem like a silly limitation, but think about the case where a single interface is shared between multiple contexts. We wouldn't want a customer in one context to be able to change the speed on the shared interface, thus bringing down all of the other contexts for which he doesn't have control.

Once you see the interfaces within a context, you can configure them with IP addresses, names, priorities, and most of the usual interface requirements.

Write Mem Behavior

When you issue the write memory command from within a context, it saves only that context's configuration.

Similarly, when you're in the system context, issuing the write mem command will save only the system context's configuration. There is no indication that we are only saving the system context, but this behavior is consistent within all contexts.

The `write mem` command saves only the context from which you issued the command.

```
ASA-5540(config)# wri mem
Building configuration...
Cryptochecksum: 60a2296d 904d7bb1 f2e9284a 5576c1dd

1023 bytes copied in 3.320 secs (341 bytes/sec)
[OK]
```

One of the benefits of being in the system context is that we can save the configurations of all the contexts at once using the `write mem all` command:

```
ASA-5540(config)# wri mem all
Building configuration...
Saving context :          system : (000/003 Contexts saved)
Cryptochecksum: 60a2296d 904d7bb1 f2e9284a 5576c1dd

1023 bytes copied in 3.320 secs (341 bytes/sec)
Saving context :           admin : (001/003 Contexts saved)
Cryptochecksum: f69086ec aa68219f d3ef18ff 391fe121

1780 bytes copied in 0.260 secs
Saving context :         GAD-Tech : (002/003 Contexts saved)
Cryptochecksum: 156bed5f 17788005 9fb9d182 231910ab

1503 bytes copied in 0.160 secs
Saving context :            Test : (003/003 Contexts saved)
Cryptochecksum: f39b8a45 e1b47f79 22f4b4e6 95b0cc8d

1499 bytes copied in 0.220 secs
[OK]
```

Failover

Most ASA appliances can be configured in high-availability pairs, provided that both ASAs in the pair have identical hardware specs. There are two ways to configure ASAs for failover: active/standby and active/active. In active/standby configuration, should the primary ASA fail, the secondary will take over. In an active/active standby configuration, both ASAs can forward traffic, but, as you'll see, that's not necessarily as exciting as it sounds.

To use this feature, the ASA must be licensed for it, though currently all models 5520 and higher come with the feature. To determine whether an ASA is capable of supporting failover, use the `show version` command:

```
ASA-5540# sho version | begin Licensed
Licensed features for this platform:
Maximum Physical Interfaces  : Unlimited
```

```
Maximum VLANs                         : 200
Inside Hosts                          : Unlimited
Failover                              : Active/Active
VPN-DES                               : Enabled
VPN-3DES-AES                          : Enabled
Security Contexts                     : 10
GTP/GPRS                              : Disabled
VPN Peers                             : 5000
WebVPN Peers                          : 2
AnyConnect for Mobile                 : Disabled
AnyConnect for Linksys phone          : Disabled
Advanced Endpoint Assessment          : Disabled
UC Proxy Sessions                     : 2
```

To be installed as a failover pair, each ASA must have the same software release installed, though minor differences are tolerated and will be indicated with a warning such as this:

```
************WARNING****WARNING****WARNING*******************************
    Mate version 8.0(3) is not identical with ours 8.0(4)
************WARNING****WARNING****WARNING*******************************
Beginning configuration replication: Sending to mate.
```

Each ASA in a failover pair must also have the exact same configuration. As a result, the hostname will be the same on both firewalls in the pair. If we attempt to configure the standby firewall, we will receive an error telling us that any changes we make will not be synchronized:

```
ASA-5540#conf t
**** WARNING ***
    Configuration Replication is NOT performed from Standby unit to Active unit.
    Configurations are no longer synchronized.
```

We won't actually be prevented from making the changes, though. I have stared stupidly at this message more times than I can count while making changes after working for 18 hours straight.

Failover Terminology

When in a failover pair, ASAs are referenced by specific names, depending on their roles:

Primary

   The primary ASA is the appliance on the *primary* end of the failover link. You configure the primary ASA manually using the `failover lan unit primary` command. The primary ASA is usually *active* when the pair is initialized. Once designated, it does not change. This is a physical designation.

Secondary

   The secondary ASA is the appliance on the *secondary* end of the failover link, and is not usually configured directly unless the primary ASA fails. The secondary ASA is usually the *standby* when the pair is initialized. Once designated, it does not change. This is a physical designation.

Active

An active ASA or context is one that is inspecting packets. The active ASA or context uses the system IP address configured for each interface. This is a logical designation; either the primary or the secondary ASA can be the active ASA or can contain active contexts.

In active/active failover mode, both the primary and secondary ASAs can contain active contexts.

Standby

A standby ASA or context is one that is not inspecting packets. It uses the failover IP address configured for each interface. Should the active ASA or context fail, the standby ASA or context will take over and become active. This is a logical designation; either the primary or the secondary ASA can be the standby ASA or contain standby contexts.

In active/active failover mode, both the primary and secondary ASA can contain standby contexts.

Stateful failover

When an active ASA or context fails and the standby ASA or context takes over, by default, all conversations that were active through the active side at the time of the failure are lost. To prevent these connections from being lost, you can use a dedicated Ethernet link between the active and standby ASAs to exchange the state of each conversation. With stateful failover configured, the standby ASA or context is constantly updated so that no connections are lost when a failover occurs.

Understanding Failover

The primary and secondary ASAs communicate over the configured failover interface. ASAs do not support a serial failover cable like PIX firewalls do.

Each ASA monitors the failover, power, and interface status of the other ASA. At regular intervals, each ASA sends a *hello* across the failover link and each active interface. If a hello is not received on an interface on either ASA for two consecutive intervals, the ASA puts that interface into *testing* mode. If the standby ASA does not receive a hello from the active ASA on the failover link for two consecutive intervals, the standby ASA initiates a failover.

The ASA platform is very flexible, so I won't cover all possible failover scenarios here. The underlying principles are the same for them all: if one ASA determines that the other is unavailable, it assumes that ASA has failed. In multicontext mode, the same idea applies, but failure can be contained within a single context (within certain limitations, as you'll see).

For failover to work, each ASA must be able to reach the other on each interface configured for failover. Usually, a pair of switches connects the firewalls. One switch connects to each ASA, and the switches are connected to each other, often with trunks. An example of such a design is shown in Figure 28-11. The link that connects the two ASA firewalls directly is the stateful failover link, which should not be switched, if possible.

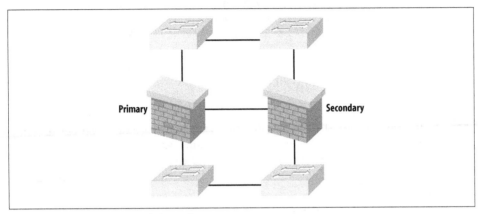

Figure 28-11. Common ASA failover design

Cisco recommends that the switch ports used to connect the ASA firewalls be set to spanning-tree portfast. With normal spanning tree timers, hellos will not be received during the initial tree states. This might cause an ASA to decide that the remote ASA is not responding and to initiate a failover.

 ASAs can be installed in *transparent mode* (the normal behavior is called *routed mode*). In transparent mode, the ASA acts as a bridge. When it's used in this manner, the spanning tree requirements are different. Consult the Cisco documentation for more information on transparent mode, or better yet, don't use it at all.

When a failover occurs, the standby ASA assumes the IP and MAC addresses of all interfaces configured for failover on the active ASA. This is transparent to the network. Here, you can see the different MAC addresses for int g0/0 before and after I pulled the failover link, causing a failover:

```
ASA-5540/GAD# sho int g0/0 | inc MAC
        MAC address 0200.0000.1300, MTU 1500
ASA-5540/GAD# Failover LAN Failed
ASA-5540/GAD# sho int g0/0 | inc MAC
        MAC address 1200.0000.0c00, MTU 1500
```

ASA failover works so well that device failures can go unnoticed. When you're using this feature, it is imperative that the appliances be managed in some way so that failures can be resolved. I have seen occasions where a primary ASA failed and the secondary ran for months until it, too, failed. When the secondary failed without another ASA to back it up, a complete outage occurred. If you're not monitoring your firewalls, your network is not as secure as you might think. Using SNMP with network management software such as CiscoWorks or OpenView will keep you apprised of any ASA failover events.

Configuring Failover—Active/Standby

Both ASAs in a failover pair must have the same major operating system version, or they will not synchronize their configurations. They really should be identical, or unpredictable results may occur. They must be the same models with the same hardware as well. Though failover may still work with minor code differences, having any differences in your ASAs is not recommended. The ASA will warn you if the code differs in your two ASAs:

```
************WARNING****WARNING****WARNING*******************************
  Mate version 8.0(4) is not identical with ours 8.0(3)
************WARNING****WARNING****WARNING*******************************
```

The first step in configuring failover is to enable the feature with the `failover` command:

```
ASA-5540(config)#failover
```

Each interface we wish to include (usually all of them) needs to have a failover IP address assigned to it. It's a good idea to assign pairs of IP addresses for firewalls when you're designing IP networks, even when installing a single ASA. For example, if the inside IP address on your firewall would normally be 192.168.1.1, reserve 192.168.1.2 as well. This way, if you expand your firewall to include another ASA for failover, the IP address for failover will already be allocated.

To illustrate failover configuration, let's build a pair of ASAs to support the network, shown in Figure 28-12. The failover link is connected through a switch or switches, and is not a crossover cable in this example.

The interface configuration for the primary ASA is as follows:

```
interface GigabitEthernet0/0
 nameif outside
 security-level 0
 ip address 10.0.0.1 255.255.255.0 standby 10.0.0.2
!
interface GigabitEthernet0/1
 nameif inside
 security-level 100
 ip address 192.168.1.1 255.255.255.0 standby 192.168.1.2
!
```

```
interface GigabitEthernet0/3
 description LAN/STATE Failover Interface!
```

The firewalls I'm using for these examples are ASA 5540s with four Gigabit Ethernet interfaces each. I'm using G0/0 and G0/1 in *outside* and *inside* roles, and I've assigned interface G0/3 as the stateful failover interface. The description for the failover interface will be added by the system.

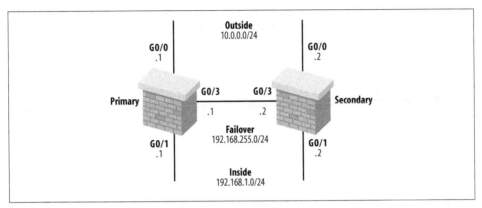

Figure 28-12. Sample ASA failover design

Each interface must be configured with a failover IP address to be used on the secondary ASA. These commands are entered on the primary ASA. The IP addresses following the **standby** keyword in the preceding output indicate the failover IP addresses for each interface. No IP address is assigned to the failover interface.

To configure the failover interface to be used for stateful failover, use the following commands on the primary ASA:

```
failover lan unit primary
failover lan interface Failover GigabitEthernet0/3
failover link Failover GigabitEthernet0/3
failover interface ip Failover 192.168.255.1 255.255.255.0 standby 192.168.255.2
```

The **failover lan interface** command makes G0/3 the failover interface. The **failover link** command makes the interface the stateful failover link. We are using the same interface for both needs, which is supported. You can split them if you want, and you can assign them to VLANs as well. Where possible, I like to dedicate an entire physical interface to failover.

To make the connection across a switched network, the failover interface must be configured on the secondary ASA as well. In this example, the following commands are needed:

```
failover lan unit secondary
failover lan interface Failover GigabitEthernet0/3
failover interface ip Failover 192.168.255.1 255.255.255.0 standby 192.168.255.2
```

Once failover is successfully configured, enable it with the `failover` command. If all is well, you should be rewarded with the following output:

```
ASA-5540#failover
ASA-5540#
Beginning configuration replication: Sending to mate.
End Configuration Replication to mate
```

 Interfaces that are not in use should always be placed in the `shutdown` state when employing ASA failover. Interfaces that are active but not cabled can trigger a failover, as the ASA will try unsuccessfully to contact the failover address if one was previously configured.

Monitoring Failover

The primary means of showing failover status is the `show failover` command:

```
ASA-5540# sho failover
Failover On
Failover unit Primary
Failover LAN Interface: Failover GigabitEthernet0/3 (up)
Unit Poll frequency 1 seconds, holdtime 15 seconds
Interface Poll frequency 5 seconds, holdtime 25 seconds
Interface Policy 1
Monitored Interfaces 2 of 250 maximum
Version: Ours 8.0(4), Mate 8.0(4)
Last Failover at: 14:07:24 UTC Aug 17 2010
        This host: Primary - Active
                Active time: 1313 (sec)
                slot 0: ASA5540 hw/sw rev (2.0/8.0(4)) status (Up Sys)
                    Interface outside (10.0.0.1): Link Down (Waiting)
                    Interface inside (192.168.1.1): Link Down (Waiting)
                slot 1: empty
        Other host: Secondary - Standby Ready
                Active time: 457 (sec)
                slot 0: ASA5540 hw/sw rev (2.0/8.0(4)) status (Up Sys)
                    Interface outside (10.0.0.2): Link Down (Waiting)
                    Interface inside (192.168.1.2): Link Down (Waiting)
                slot 1: empty

Stateful Failover Logical Update Statistics
        Link : Failover GigabitEthernet0/3 (up)
        Stateful Obj   xmit      xerr      rcv       rerr
        General        33        0         33        0
        sys cmd        33        0         33        0
        up time        0         0         0         0
        RPC services   0         0         0         0
        TCP conn       0         0         0         0
        UDP conn       0         0         0         0
        ARP tbl        0         0         0         0
        Xlate_Timeout  0         0         0         0
        VPN IKE upd    0         0         0         0
        VPN IPSEC upd  0         0         0         0
```

```
VPN CTCP upd     0          0          0          0
VPN SDI upd      0          0          0          0
VPN DHCP upd     0          0          0          0
SIP Session      0          0          0          0

Logical Update Queue Information
                 Cur        Max        Total
Recv Q:          0          17         33
Xmit Q:          0          1024       2780
```

This command shows you the state of both firewalls in the pair, as well as statistics for the stateful failover link. If this link is incrementing errors, you may lose connections during a failover.

Remember that with stateful failover active, you may experience a failover without knowing it. This command will show you if your primary ASA has failed. If the primary ASA is the standby ASA, the original primary has failed at some point:

```
ASA-5540# sho failover | inc host
        This host: Primary - Standby Ready
        Other host: Secondary - Active
```

If the active ASA fails, the standby ASA takes over. If the failed ASA comes back online, it does not automatically resume its role as the active ASA. Cisco's documentation states that there is "no reason to switch active and standby roles" in this circumstance. While I would have preferred a *preempt* ability similar to that used in HSRP, Cisco didn't invite me to write the failover code.

To force a standby ASA to become active, issue the `no failover active` command on the active ASA, or the `failover active` command on the standby ASA:

```
ASA-5540# failover active

        Switching to Active
```

Assuming a successful failover, the primary ASA should now be the active ASA once again.

Configuring Failover—Active/Active

When you're using active/standby failover with multiple contexts, all contexts are active on the active ASA. You can think of active/standby failover with multiple contexts like the setup shown in Figure 28-13.

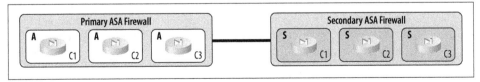

Figure 28-13. Active/standby failover with multiple contexts

When I first heard the term active/active, I got excited that Cisco had finally incorporated functionality similar to Checkpoint's clustering technology, where multiple physical firewalls can act as a single logical unit, thus distributing the load among them. I was disappointed to learn that this is not the case.

 As I was performing the final edits for this chapter, representatives at Cisco told me that Cisco is announcing true Checkpoint-esque active/active failover in an upcoming version of code. Unfortunately, it was not available for me to test before this book went to print.

The term active/active, while technically accurate, is a bit of a marketing term. Active/active mode on a multicontext ASA does not work the way a Checkpoint firewall cluster works. The ASAs are not a *cluster*, and they do not both forward packets for all contexts. When I hear a term like active/active, I expect all contexts to be active on both firewalls like the setup shown in Figure 28-14.

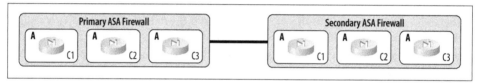

Figure 28-14. Active/active failover in my dreams

This is *not* how active/active mode works with ASAs. For an ASA to be configured in active/active mode, it must first be placed in multicontext mode. The reason for this is that some contexts can be active on one side and some can be active on the other side.

 You cannot configure a multicontext ASA to have all contexts active on both sides. In fact, you cannot configure an ASA to have *any* contexts active on both sides.

Active/active failover means that some contexts are active on the primary ASA, and some are active on the standby ASA. Think of it more like the setup shown in Figure 28-15.

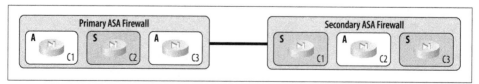

Figure 28-15. The reality of active/active failover

Be careful of this method of operation, as it carries with it some pretty severe caveats. For example, if you execute the command `write standby` on the primary ASA's system context (assuming the admin context is active on the primary side), contexts that are in the active state on the standby ASA will have all of their connections broken. Here is the Cisco documentation snippet for this limitation:

> If you enter the `write standby` command in the system execution space, the system configuration and the configurations for all of the security contexts on the adaptive security appliance [are] written to the peer unit. This includes configuration information for security contexts that are in the standby state. You must enter the command in the system execution space on the unit that has failover group 1 in the active state.
>
> **Note** If there are security contexts in the active state on the peer unit, the `write standby` command causes active connections through those contexts to be terminated. Use the `failover active` command on the unit providing the configuration to make sure all contexts are active on that unit before entering the `write standby` command.
>
> If you enter the `write standby` command in a security context, only the configuration for the security context is written to the peer unit. You must enter the command in the security context on the unit where the security context appears in the active state.

You should rarely, if ever, need to use the `write standby` command. The command should only be necessary if you've issued commands on the secondary ASA causing them to be out of sync. The firewalls will sync themselves under normal operation.

If, upon reading this, you're wondering "What's the point?" I'm with you. In addition to these limitations, active/active scenarios must be carefully managed so that the combined throughput of both firewalls does not exceed the capacity of one physical unit. If one unit were to fail, all traffic would traverse the other. If you've got more than half capacity running on both, you'll oversubscribe the single unit when failover occurs.

I don't recommend active/active scenarios using ASAs, because I'm not a fan of splitting traffic for the sake of keeping devices inline. Since no capacity is gained (when properly configured), and throughput does not increase, I rarely recommend active/active failover. That said, there could be situations where you put all your latency-sensitive traffic on one side and your heavy slow traffic on the other, but usually you'll end up recombining this traffic on the other side of the firewalls anyway. I do like having options, though.

If you're hell-bent on using active/active, here's how to go about it. Active/active mode is created by configuring contexts into one of two groups, which you do with the `failover group group#` command:

```
ASA-5540(config)# failover group ?

configure mode commands/options:
  <1-2>  group number
```

There can only be two groups—one for each physical ASA in the failover pair:

```
ASA-5540(config)# failover group 1
ASA-5540(config-fover-group)# ?
```

```
Failover User Group configuration mode:
  help                Help for user Failover Group configuration commands
  interface-policy    Set the policy for failover due to interface failures
  mac                 Specify the virtual mac address for a physical interface
  no                  Remove user failover group configuration
  polltime            Configure failover interface polling interval
  preempt             Allow preemption of lower priority active unit
  primary             Primary unit has higher priority
  replication         Configure the replication option
  secondary           Secondary unit has higher priority
```

The default behavior for a group is to be primary, so if you issue the primary command, it will not show up in the configuration. Call me crazy, but I like the primary group to be group 1 and the secondary group to be group 2:

```
ASA-5540(config)# failover group 1
ASA-5540(config-fover-group)# primary
ASA-5540(config-fover-group)# preempt
ASA-5540(config-fover-group)# exit

ASA-5540(config)# failover group 2
ASA-5540(config-fover-group)# secondary
ASA-5540(config-fover-group)# exit
```

Once the groups are created, configure the contexts so they fall into one of the two groups with the join-failover-group *group#* context command. In this case, any context configured into group 1 will be active on the primary ASA, and any context configured into group 2 will be active on the secondary ASA:

```
context GAD-Tech
  join-failover-group 1

context Test
  join-failover-group 2
```

You can show the status of failover for all contexts from the system context with the show failover command. Be careful with this command, because the output can be confusing. The group-specific information is in bold:

```
ASA-5540# sho failover
Failover On
Failover unit Primary
Failover LAN Interface: Failover GigabitEthernet0/3 (up)
Unit Poll frequency 1 seconds, holdtime 15 seconds
Interface Poll frequency 5 seconds, holdtime 25 seconds
Interface Policy 1
Monitored Interfaces 5 of 250 maximum
Version: Ours 8.0(4), Mate 8.0(4)
Group 1 last failover at: 07:33:09 UTC Jun 29 2010
Group 2 last failover at: 07:32:57 UTC Jun 29 2010

  This host:    Primary
  Group 1       State:        Active
                Active time:  92 (sec)
```

```
Group 2        State:        Standby Ready
               Active time:  0 (sec)

               slot 0: ASA5540 hw/sw rev (2.0/8.0(4)) status (Up Sys)
                 admin Interface management (192.168.1.1): No Link (Waiting)
                 GAD-Tech Interface outside (10.10.10.1): Link Down (Waiting)
                 GAD-Tech Interface inside (0.0.0.0): Link Down (Waiting)
                 Test Interface outside (10.10.10.21): Link Down (Waiting)
                 Test Interface inside (0.0.0.0): Link Down (Waiting)
               slot 1: empty

Other host:    Secondary
Group 1        State:        Standby Ready
               Active time:  2008 (sec)
Group 2        State:        Active
               Active time:  2101 (sec)

               slot 0: ASA5540 hw/sw rev (2.0/8.0(4)) status (Up Sys)
                 admin Interface management (0.0.0.0): No Link (Waiting)
                 GAD-Tech Interface outside (10.10.10.2): Link Down (Waiting)
                 GAD-Tech Interface inside (0.0.0.0): Link Down (Waiting)
                 Test Interface outside (10.10.10.20): Link Down (Waiting)
                 Test Interface inside (0.0.0.0): Link Down (Waiting)
               slot 1: empty

Stateful Failover Logical Update Statistics
        Link : Unconfigured.
```

Notice that even though interfaces may be allocated to contexts, their status is not shown within the group information in the show failover command output. Do not look at the interface section of the output to get a context's status. This makes sense if you think about it. In this case, interface G0/0 is allocated to both the GAD-Tech and Test contexts, yet GAD-Tech (group 1) is active on the primary ASA and Test (group 2) is active on the secondary ASA. The interfaces are not group-specific, but the contexts are.

NAT

Network Address Translation (NAT) is technically what Cisco refers to as translating one IP address to another. The majority of installations, including most home networks, translate many IP addresses to a single address. This is actually called *Port Address Translation* (PAT). PAT has also been called *NAT Overload* in IOS.

To complicate matters, in the ASA, NAT is used in a number of ways that may not seem obvious. For example, you may have to use a nat statement to allow packets from one interface to another, even though they both have public IP addresses and would normally require no translation.

NAT Commands

A few commands are used to configure the majority of NAT scenarios. Some, such as the nat command, have many options that aren't listed here. The subject of NAT on an ASA could fill a book itself. My goal is to keep it simple. If you need more information than what I've provided here, the Cisco command references are a good place to start. The commands you're most likely to need are:

nat

> The nat command is used when you're translating addresses from a more secure interface to a less secure one. For example, if you need to translate an address on the inside of your ASA to an address on the outside, use the nat command. Private IP addresses on the inside of an ASA are translated to one or more public IP addresses with the nat command. Technically, the addresses do not need to be private and public addresses, as described by RFC1918. The ASA documentation uses the terms "global" and "local" to describe addresses outside the ASA as opposed to those inside.

static

> The static command is used when you're translating addresses from a less secure interface to a more secure one. For example, if you have a server inside your ASA that needs to be accessed from outside, assign a public IP address to the private IP address of the server using the static command.

global

> The global command is used for PAT configurations where many addresses are translated to one address. It is also used to provide a pool of NAT addresses. This command is used in conjunction with the nat command.

NAT Examples

There are many possible NAT scenarios, some of which can become quite complicated. I will cover some of the more common scenarios here.

For these examples, I will be using 10.0.0.0 to represent a publicly routable IP network, and 192.168.1.0 as a private, unroutable network.

Simple PAT using the outside interface

One of the most common uses for a firewall is providing an office with protection from the Internet. Assuming all nodes inside the firewall require access to the Internet and no connections will be initiated inbound, a simple PAT configuration can be used.

Here, I've configured the outside interface to be used as the IP address for the global PAT. In other words, all packets that originate from the inside will be translated to the same IP address as the one used on the outside interface of the ASA:

```
global (outside) 1 interface
nat (inside) 1 0.0.0.0 0.0.0.0 0 0
```

All internal IP addresses will be translated, because the nat statement references 0.0.0.0, which means all addresses.

Simple PAT using a dedicated IP address

To accomplish PAT without using the interface's IP address, use the same configuration as the previous one, but specify the IP address used for the global PAT in the global command instead of the keyword interface:

```
global (outside) 1 10.0.0.5
nat (inside) 1 0.0.0.0 0.0.0.0 0 0
```

If you're playing along at home, you'll hopefully have realized that you must remove the previous NAT entries, or you'll receive a Duplicate NAT entry error upon entering this snippet of code. If you're not, read this note again until it makes sense.

Simple PAT with public servers on the inside

Small installations may have a server inside (not on a DMZ) that must be accessible from the public Internet. While this is usually not a good idea, it is nevertheless a distinct possibility that you'll need to configure such a solution. Smaller companies—and even home networks—often require such configurations because a DMZ is either impractical or impossible.

Here, I've designed a global PAT using the outside interface, with all addresses from the inside being translated. Additionally, I've created two static entries. The first forwards packets sent to the public IP address 10.0.0.10 to the private IP address 192.168.1.10. The second translates 10.0.0.11 to the private IP address 192.168.1.11:

```
global (outside) 1 interface
nat (inside) 1 0.0.0.0 0.0.0.0 0 0
static (inside,outside) 10.0.0.10 192.168.1.10 netmask 255.255.255.255 0 0
static (inside,outside) 10.0.0.11 192.168.1.11 netmask 255.255.255.255 0 0
```

static statements override the more generic nat statement, so these commands can be used together in this way without issue. Be wary when configuring static statements, however. The order of interfaces and networks can be confusing. If you look carefully at the preceding example, you'll see that the references are essentially:

```
(inside-int,outside-int) outside-net inside-net
```

Remember that these static statements are allowing connections from outside to come into these two IP addresses, which reside inside the secure network. This may sound dangerous, but because the outside interface has a security level of 0 and the inside interface has a security level of 100, traffic cannot flow from outside to inside unless it's permitted with an access list. In other words, you must now create an access list to allow the desired traffic to pass.

Port redirection

Port redirection is different from PAT. While PAT translates a pool of addresses to a single address by translating the ports within the packets being sent, port redirection does something else entirely.

Port redirection allows you to configure a static NAT where, though there is one IP address on the public side, there can be many IP addresses on the private side, each of which responds to a different port. PAT does not permit inbound connections. Port translation does.

Imagine we have only eight IP addresses on our public network, which are all in use:

    .0 - Network address
    .1 - ISP Router VIP (HSRP)
    .2 - ISP Router 1
    .3 - ISP Router 2
    .4 - Primary ASA
    .5 - Secondary ASA
    .6 - Web server public IP
    .7 - Broadcast address

While it might not seem realistic to have so much resilient equipment on such a small network, you might be surprised by what happens in the field. Many small-business networks are limited to eight addresses. In reality, many don't need any more than that.

In this example, we need to have only one static NAT configured—the web server. Here is the configuration relating to NAT:

```
global (outside) 1 interface
nat (inside) 1 0.0.0.0 0.0.0.0 0 0
static (inside,outside) 10.0.0.6 192.168.1.6 netmask 255.255.255.255 0 0
```

This configuration works fine, but what if we need another web server to be available on the Internet? Say a secure server has been built using HTTPS, which listens on TCP port 443. The problem is a lack of public IP addresses. Assuming that the original web server only listens on TCP port 80, we can solve the problem using port redirection.

Using capabilities introduced in release 6.x, we can specify that incoming traffic destined for the 10.0.0.6 IP address on TCP port 80 be translated to one IP address internally, while packets destined for the same IP address on TCP port 443 be sent to another IP address:

```
static (inside,outside) tcp 10.0.0.6 80 192.168.1.6 80 netmask 255.255.255.255
static (inside,outside) tcp 10.0.0.6 443 192.168.1.7 443 netmask 255.255.255.255
```

Normally, the `static` command includes only the outside and inside IP addresses, and all packets are sent between them. Including the port numbers makes the `static` statement more specific.

The result is that packets destined for 10.0.0.6 will be translated to different IP addresses internally, depending on their destination ports: a packet sent to 10.0.0.6:80 will be translated to 192.168.1.6:80, while a packet destined for 10.0.0.6:443 will be translated to 192.168.1.7:443. You can even change the port to something else if you like.

DMZ

Here is a very common scenario: a company has put an ASA in place for Internet security. Certain servers need to be accessed from the Internet. These servers will be in a DMZ. The outside interface connects to the Internet, the inside interface connects to the company LANs, and the DMZ contains the Internet-accessible servers. This network is shown in Figure 28-16.

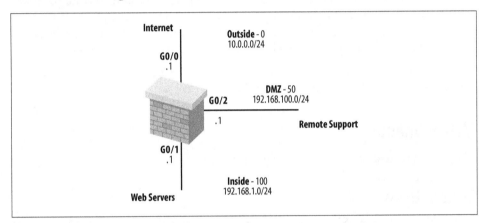

Figure 28-16. Firewall with DMZ

From a NAT point of view, we must remember that the security levels are important. The outside interface has a security level of 0, the inside interface has a level of 100, and the DMZ has a level of 50.

In this case, we want the servers in the DMZ to be accessible from outside. We also want hosts on the inside network to be able to access the DMZ servers, although the DMZ servers should not be able to access the inside network.

First, we need the `nat` and `global` statements for the inside network using the Internet:

```
global (outside) 1 interface
nat (inside) 1 192.168.1.0 255.255.255.0 0 0
```

Specifying a certain network, rather than using 0.0.0.0 as the address in the `nat` statement, ensures that only that network will be able to access the Internet. Should other networks that need Internet access be added internally, they will need to be added to the ASA with additional `nat (inside) 1` statements.

Now, we need to add the `static` statements so the servers on the DMZ can be accessed from the Internet:

```
static (DMZ,outside) 10.0.0.11 192.168.100.11 netmask 255.255.255.255
static (DMZ,outside) 10.0.0.12 192.168.100.12 netmask 255.255.255.255
static (DMZ,outside) 10.0.0.13 192.168.100.13 netmask 255.255.255.255
```

By default, the DMZ will not be able to access the inside network, because the DMZ has a lower security level than the inside network. In this case, we must use a `static` statement to allow the connections. However, it gets a little strange, because we don't need to translate the source network—we just need to allow the connection. As odd as it sounds, to accomplish this, we must statically NAT the inside network to itself:

```
static (inside,DMZ) 192.168.1.0 192.168.1.0 netmask 255.255.255.0
```

An ASA firewall must translate a higher-security interface for the network to be seen by a lower-security interface. Doing this can be confusing because it creates a "translation," even though nothing is being translated. The ASA must have a translation in place for the hosts on the inside network to be able to connect to the hosts on the DMZ. The IP addresses do not need to be changed, but the path needs to be built.

Once NAT is in place, all that's left to do is configure access lists to allow the required traffic from the DMZ to the inside network.

Miscellaneous

The following items are things that trip me up again and again in the field.

Remote Access

To be able to telnet or SSH to your ASA, we must specify the networks from which we will do so. You do this with the `telnet` and `ssh` commands:

```
ASA-5540(config)# telnet 192.168.1.0 255.255.255.0 inside
ASA-5540(config)# ssh 192.168.1.0 255.255.255.0 inside
```

Saving Configuration Changes

If you read the first edition of this book, you may remember that I complained of the PIX not accepting `wri` as an abbreviation for `write memory`. I'm happy to report that `wri` does work on the ASA platform. Of course, Cisco will tell you that you should use `copy run start`, but I'm a curmudgeonly old pain in the ass who dislikes change:

```
ASA-5540(config)# wri
Building configuration...
Cryptochecksum: 7401aa77 0584c65f 9ff42fa9 d5ed86ab
```

```
3191 bytes copied in 3.280 secs (1063 bytes/sec)
[OK]
```

The `copy running startup` command works, but it's ugly:

```
ASA-5540(config)# copy run startup-config

Source filename [running-config]?
Cryptochecksum: 7401aa77 0584c65f 9ff42fa9 d5ed86ab

3191 bytes copied in 3.280 secs (1063 bytes/sec)
```

When you're configuring the active ASA in a failover pair, each command should be sent to the standby PIX automatically after it's been submitted. And when you're saving changes on the active ASA, the `write memory` command should write the configuration to the standby ASA. To force a save to the standby PIX, use the `write standby` command:

```
ASA-5540#write standby
Building configuration...
[OK]
ASA-5540# Sync Started
.
Sync Completed
```

Notice that the preceding `Sync Started` entry is not a command, but rather the output of normal ASA logging when logging is enabled.

 You should not run `write standby` in active/active failover mode, as it will force all contexts to become active on the active ASA. See "Configuring Failover—Active/Active" on page 497 for details.

Logging

If you have a firewall in place, you should save and periodically review the logs it generates. When configured for logging, ASA firewalls create a great deal of information. Even on small networks, the logs can be substantial.

While logging to the ASA buffer may seem like a good idea, the logs can scroll by so fast that the buffer becomes all but unusable. If you log too much detail to the console, you can impact the firewall's performance. If you log to the monitor (your Telnet session), the logs will update so frequently that you'll end up turning them off so you can work.

I like to send all my ASA firewall logs to a syslog server. I generally use some flavor of Unix to do this, though, of course, you are free to use whatever you like. Two steps are required to enable logging: you must enable logging with the `logging on` command, and you must specify one or more logging destinations. When configuring logging destinations, you must also specify the level of logging for each destination. The levels are:

0 - System Unusable
1 - Take Immediate Action
2 - Critical Condition
3 - Error Message
4 - Warning Message
5 - Normal but significant condition
6 - Informational
7 - Debug Message

The useful logging information regarding traffic traversing the firewall is found in level 6. Here's a sample of level-6 logging:

```
302015: Built outbound UDP connection 3898824 for outside:11.1.1.1/123
(11.1.1.1/123) to inside:192.168.1.5/123 (10.1.1.5/334)
302013: Built inbound TCP connection 3898825 for outside:12.2.2.2/2737
(12.2.2.2/2737) to inside:192.168.1.21/80 (10.1.1.21/80)
302013: Built inbound TCP connection 3898826 for outside:13.3.3.3/49050
(13.3.3.3/49050) to inside:192.168.1.21/80 (10.1.1.21/80)
304001: 15.5.5.5 Accessed URL 10.1.1.21:/lab/index.html/
```

On a live network, this information will probably scroll by so fast that you won't be able to read it. Unfortunately, debug messages are a higher log level, so if you need to run debugs on the ASA, the output will be buried within these other log entries.

Here, I've enabled logging and set the console to receive level-5 logs, while all other logging destinations will receive level-7 logs:

```
logging on
logging console notifications
```

These commands apply only to the ASA itself. To send logs to a syslog host, you must configure a trap destination level, the syslog facility, and the host to receive the logs:

```
logging trap debugging
logging facility 22
logging host inside 192.168.1.200
```

On the syslog server, you then need to configure syslog to receive these alerts. Detailed syslog configuration is outside the scope of this book, so I'll just include the */etc/syslog.conf* entries from my Ubuntu server:

```
# Configuration for ASA logging
local6.debug                          /var/log/ASA
```

This will capture the ASA syslog entries and place them into the */var/log/ASA* file. Notice that the ASA is configured for `facility 22`, but the server is configured for `local6.debug`. The facilities are mapped as 16(LOCAL0)–23(LOCAL7). The default is 20(LOCAL4).

Once you've begun collecting syslog entries into a file, you can use the server to view and parse the logfile without affecting your CLI window. On Unix systems, you can use commands like `tail -f /var/log/ASA` to view the log in real time. You can also add

---

filters. For example, if you only want to see log entries containing the URL */lab/index.html/*, you can use the command `tail -f /var/log/ASA | grep '/lab/index.html/'`.

> For more information on logging, type `help logging` in ASA configuration mode. On a Unix system, you can learn more about syslog with the `man syslog` and `man syslogd` commands.

Troubleshooting

If you change an access list, change NAT, or do anything else that can alter which packets are allowed to flow through the firewall, you may not see the results until you execute the `clear xlate` command.

Xlate is short for translation. A translation is created for every conversation that is active on the ASA. To see which xlates are active on your ASA, use the `show xlate` command:

```
ASA-5540# show xlate
4 in use, 4 most used
Global 10.0.0.10 Local 192.168.1.10
Global 10.0.0.11 Local 192.168.1.11
PAT Global 10.0.0.6(80) Local 192.168.1.6(80)
PAT Global 10.0.0.6(443) Local 192.168.1.7(443)
```

The `PAT Global` entries are live connections from my PC to the Web. I had a download running through a web browser, plus a few web pages open. The last entry is a static translation resulting from the static configuration entered earlier.

To clear xlates, use the `clear xlate` command:

```
ASA-5540#clear xlate
```

> When you clear xlates, every session on the firewall will be broken and will need to be rebuilt. If your ASA is protecting an ecommerce website, transactions will be broken and customers may become unhappy. You should not clear xlates unless there is a valid reason.

While the `clear xlate` command runs with no fanfare on the ASA, every connection will be cleared. My IM client reset, and the download I had running aborted as a result of the xlates being cleared.

Another useful command for troubleshooting is `show conn`, which shows all of the active connections on the ASA:

```
ASA-5540#sho conn
8 in use, 199 most used
TCP out 10.233.161.147:80 in LAB-PC2:1151 idle 0:00:18 Bytes 6090 flags UIO
TCP out 10.46.109.49:1863 in LAB-SVR1:1736 idle 0:03:28 Bytes 7794 flags UIO
TCP out 10.188.8.176:5190 in LAB-PC2:4451 idle 0:00:52 Bytes 32827 flags UIO
```

```
TCP out 10.120.37.15:80 in LAB-PC:1789 idle 0:00:03 Bytes 19222477 flags UIO
TCP out 10.120.37.15:80 in LAB-PC:1802 idle 0:00:02 Bytes 20277173 flags UIO
TCP out 10.172.118.250:19093 in LAB-SVR2:80 idle 0:00:09 Bytes 11494 flags UIOB
TCP out 10.172.118.250:19075 in LAB-SVR2:80 idle 0:00:09 Bytes 219866 flags UIOB
UDP out 10.67.79.202:123 in RTR1:123 idle 0:00:32 flags -
```

This command shows the protocol, direction, source, and destination of each connection, as well as how long each connection has been idle and how many bytes have been sent. The flags are very useful, if you can remember them. You can view the entire list of flags along with a different format of the same data by appending the `detail` keyword to the command. This example was generated a few minutes later than the previous one:

```
ASA-5540# sho conn detail
4 in use, 4 most used
Flags: A - awaiting inside ACK to SYN, a - awaiting outside ACK to SYN,
       B - initial SYN from outside, C - CTIQBE media, D - DNS, d - dump,
       E - outside back connection, F - outside FIN, f - inside FIN,
       G - group, g - MGCP, H - H.323, h - H.225.0, I - inbound data,
       i - incomplete, J - GTP, j - GTP data, K - GTP t3-response
       k - Skinny media, M - SMTP data, m - SIP media, n - GUP
       O - outbound data, P - inside back connection, p - Phone-proxy TFTP connection,
       q - SQL*Net data, R - outside acknowledged FIN,
       R - UDP SUNRPC, r - inside acknowledged FIN, S - awaiting inside SYN,
       s - awaiting outside SYN, T - SIP, t - SIP transient, U - up,
       V - VPN orphan, W - WAAS,
       X - inspected by service module
TCP outside:10.46.109.49/1863 inside:LAB-PC2/1736 flags UIO
TCP outside:10.188.8.176/5190 inside:LAB-PC/4451 flags UIO
TCP outside:10.241.244.1/48849 inside:LAB-SVR1/80 flags UIOB
UDP outside:10.30.70.56/161 inside:RTR1/1031 flags -
```

## CHAPTER 29

Wireless

Wireless networking is a vast topic. From the basics of how it works to the vast and continuously evolving security concerns, there is no way I could address it all in a book designed to cover many topics. Add to that the complexity of how to design and implement a large-scale corporate roaming environment, and it was a challenge deciding what to include in this chapter. Whole books can be (and have been) written about wireless. I recommend O'Reilly's own *802.11 Wireless Networks: The Definitive Guide, Second Edition*, by Matthew Gast (*http://oreilly.com/catalog/9780596001834*) for a deeper discussion of this fascinating technology.

Wireless networks come in two flavors: *infrastructure* and *ad hoc*. In an infrastructure wireless LAN (WLAN), one or more wireless access points (WAPs) are used to gain access to the network. In this type of environment, all wireless communication is done through the WAPs, even communication between two wireless hosts on the WLAN. For a wireless client to use a WAP, it must first authenticate (if so configured) and then associate with the WAP. A client is only associated with one WAP at a time. If a client goes out of range of one WAP, then associates with another while maintaining its wireless configuration, the client is said to be roaming.

WAPs may be standalone autonomous devices, or they may be lightweight devices that are controlled by a wireless LAN controller. Wireless LAN controllers are common in large deployments, since they allow central control of a large number of WAPs.

An ad hoc wireless network is formed between two or more wireless endpoints. In this scenario, no WAP is involved and one node on the network may actually forward traffic destined for another node. Ham radio operators have been using a form of ad hoc wireless networking for decades, called *packet radio networks*. For the most part, enterprises do not use ad hoc networks.

Wireless Standards

If you've ever dealt with wireless networking, you know that there is a dizzying array of standards and protocols out there. If you take a look at the IEEE docs, you'll discover that there are even more wireless standards with names like 802.11k (radio resource measurement enhancements), 802.11y (3,650–3,700 MHz operation in the US), and many others. The ones in wide use today are the ones we're all aware of: 802.11a/b/g/n, described as follows:

802.11a

> Based on the 802.11-1997 standard, this standard operates in the 5 GHz range with a surprising (to me, at least) maximum net data rate of 54 Mbps, though with error correction and other overhead, the usable rate is 20 Mbps or lower. 802.11a has a relatively short range when compared with 802.11b.

802.11b

> 802.11b is the wireless that most of us became familiar with when wireless became popular around the year 2000. Since it has a better range than 802.11a and was aggressively marketed by vendors, this became the de facto wireless standard for many years. Even today, most wireless access points support 802.11b.

> 802.11b operates in the 2.4 GHz band, and as such suffers from interference from many household items such as cordless phones, baby monitors, and microwave ovens.

802.11g

> 802.11g also uses the 2.4 GHz band, but uses a robust transmission scheme called *Orthogonal Frequency-Division Multiplexing* (OFDM). OFDM is also used in 802.11a, but since 802.11g uses the 2.4GHz band, it has better range. 802.11g has a maximum rate of 54 Mbps, though with error correction and overhead, the average speed comes out to be about 22 Mbps.

> There can be problems with 802.11g, since it is backward compatible with 802.11a/b. When an 802.11b device operates with an 802.11g device, the 802.11g device may slow to 802.11b speeds.

802.11n

> The 802.11n standard was ratified in October 2009. Yet many vendors were selling 802.11n wireless devices before then. These vendors would take what was proposed and sell the devices with a big 802.11n sticker on the box. Why? Because a consortium of wireless vendors got together, called themselves the WiFi Alliance, and certified devices to be 802.11n-compliant based on the 2007 draft of the 802.11n proposal. The WiFi Alliance would test devices to ensure that they would interoperate properly, hopefully saving consumers from buying wireless devices from multiple vendors that wouldn't work together.

> 802.11 works within both the 2.4 GHz band and the 5 GHz band. 802.11n supports 40 MHz bandwidth, which is double that of 802.11a/b/g. 802.11n also supports something called multiinput multioutput (MIMO), which supports multiplexing multiple streams to multiple antennas. These features combine to make 802.11n capable of a theoretical maximum speed of 600 Mbps, though the average

consumer equipment will get nowhere near that for a variety of reasons, especially in congested signal environments.

 In my own house, I had a wireless access point that worked fine for me, but my wife complained that the connection was slow and that her sessions would drop. After a year or so, I decided to take a look and see what the problem was. Hey, I'm a busy guy. Anyway, everything seemed fine configuration-wise, and I wasn't having any problems.

I finally decided to further investigate when I bought her a new MacBook Pro that still exhibited the problem. No longer able to blame Windows or a cheap laptop, I did a wireless site survey of my house, only to discover that directly in the signal path between the wireless access point (WAP) and my wife's laptop sat, not only the microwave oven, but the cordless telephone base station as well. As soon as I moved the WAP to a different location in the house, her wireless problems ceased.

The lesson here is that placement of your WAP matters. Since I'd used the same WAP for years and carefully placed it wherever there was room on my desk, I not only limited her to an old standard, but managed to cause her the most problems possible given the interference sources in my house. In an enterprise environment, this problem would have been avoided by doing a proper wireless site survey.

Security

Security has always been a big concern with wireless. Even today, with wireless a mature technology, I can walk around any apartment complex with a laptop and probably get onto someone's insecure wireless network. I know people who haven't paid for Internet access in years because their neighbors don't secure their wireless, allowing anyone to steal their bandwidth. While theft of Internet bandwidth is a moral and security concern, the bigger worry should be that unfettered wireless access allows strangers into an insecure network. It's one thing to be able to surf the Net for free. It's something else entirely to have access to all the computers on someone else's network.

 Even wireless security isn't enough. I travel a lot and spend a lot of time in hotels. As soon as I authenticate and gain access to the wireless in the hotel, I see scores of computers advertising themselves and their file shares. People have provided easy access to personal photographs, medical and financial records, and even sensitive password lists. Do yourself a favor and turn off the file shares on your laptop when you travel. Rumor has it there are plenty of bored nerds out there with nothing better to do than see what you've got to share.

There are a few methods for securing a wireless network, which generally fall into two categories: authentication and encryption. Some of these methods include:

MAC ID filtering

MAC ID filtering is a valid authentication method for small networks or where someone can be dedicated to its upkeep. Simply put, the MAC address of the wireless host's network interface card (NIC) must be added to a list of approved MAC addresses. When the wireless node attempts to associate with the WAP, this list is referenced. If the MAC address is not on the list, the client will not be granted access to the wireless network. This is a rudimentary security measure that doesn't scale well, and is generally not used in larger enterprise networks.

WEP

WEP stands for Wired Equivalent Privacy, which is a form of encryption designed for wireless networks. As its name implies, this security was designed to make wireless as secure as using wire-based networks. Unfortunately, WEP is so insecure that commonly available tools can crack WEP in minutes. WEP is the simplest form of wireless security and is accomplished by the WAP and client each knowing a relatively small (40- or 128-bit) shared key. It should not be used in modern networks unless you're securing something that doesn't need security or you live in the woods and you're lazy. WEP uses a static key that is preprogrammed into the WAP and each client that needs to associate with it. This method of security is barely a step above simple clear-text passwords, due to a fundamental flaw in the WEP protocol. Though WEP-protected wireless networks are encrypted, anyone can download free tools that will crack the encryption in minutes, if not sooner.

 At my house, if someone were to try to steal my wireless, they would need to be inside my fence. Inside my fence, my wireless security consists of two 140-pound dogs with bad attitudes and little patience for intruders. Of course, that assumes you got past the sentries, claymores, tripwires, and snipers. And mimes. Watch out for the mimes.

EAP

The Extensible Authentication Protocol is a framework for authentication and a means to offer dynamic WEP keys to wireless devices. Since static WEP keys are easily discovered and cracked, changing them dynamically offers better security. EAP has many versions, including EAP-MD5, EAP-FAST, and EAP-TLS. It also has enhancements in the form of the Lightweight Extensible Authentication Protocol (LEAP) and the Protected Extensible Authentication Protocol (PEAP). Stronger types of EAP, such as EAP-TLS, are employed when you are using WPA2-Enterprise security.

TKIP

The Temporal Key Integrity Protocol is a group of algorithms designed to enhance WEP in a way that greatly improves key security. With WEP, a single key is used for all encryption. With TKIP, a different key is sent with each packet, making it much more difficult to break. Naturally, a flaw was discovered with TKIP, but it is still a far better option than simple WEP. TKIP should be used on devices that do not have the hardware to support AES-CCMP. TKIP is mandatory when you're using WPA.

AES-CCMP

AES-CCMP is the abbreviation for Advanced Encryption Standard-CCM (Counter Mode with Cipher Block Chaining Message Authentication Code) Protocol. Yeah, that's a mouthful, but don't worry about all those words. What you need to know is that this is the cipher method to choose if your hardware is capable of using it. Modern Wireless-N devices that have been certified by the WiFi Alliance must be capable of supporting AES-CCMP, as it is required when you're using WPA2.

WPA and WPA2

WPA stands for WiFi Protected Access. WPA is based on the IEEE standard 802.11i, and was designed to be a more robust solution to solve the inadequacies of WEP. WPA2 is an even stronger version of WPA, due to the inclusion of AES-CCMP. To use WPA and WPA2, you must include a cipher suite. For WPA, TKIP is required. For WPA2, AES-CCMP must be used. WPA2 is the preferred method of securing wireless networks in most cases. WPA should only be used on legacy hardware that is not capable of supporting AES-CCMP.

WPA can be installed in two flavors, called *personal,* which uses preshared keys (PSK) for local authentication, and *enterprise*, which uses 802.1x and an external authentication server such as RADIUS. You may see WPA2-Personal referred to as WPA2-PSK, WPA2-Enterperise referred to as WPA2-dot11x, and any number of other variations that should be pretty easy to understand.

So what should you use? Again, read up on the many forms of wireless security, design, and implementation found in books far more detailed than this one. For home use, WEP may be fine, but only if you have dogs and mimes trained in network security. For most small to medium-size implementations, WPA2-PSK is the best choice for balancing security and simplicity. For larger enterprises, complex WLANs employing wireless LAN controllers are the norm.

If you want to be painfully secure, allow your wireless network to have access to nothing but an authentication server and VPN device. Force two-factor authentication to the wireless network, and then force VPN with two-factor authentication to gain access to the network proper. This way, even if someone could gain access to the wireless network, she won't be able to see anything, since there are no resources available and all other transmissions are encoded with strong encryption. Chances are, no one will use the wireless because it's so complicated, but hey, security is a balance between convenience and paranoia. And yes, I worked at a site that required VPN over the WPA2-Enterprise wireless LAN.

Perhaps more important than the authentication methods used is the underlying network architecture built to support the wireless network. Guest VLANs, wireless VoIP VLANs, wireless LAN controllers, and the like are important facets of wireless networking that can have great impact on your security. Again, I recommend further reading in books dedicated to the topic, since I won't be going into it in that depth.

Configuring a WAP

Most people will configure an access point using a web browser, since many residential-class access points support only HTTP configuration. I'm a command-line kind of guy, so I'll show you how to configure a single Cisco 1231 WAP in an environment where only one WAP is required. Things get substantially more complicated when considerations such as roaming and wireless controllers come into play. In enterprise environments, it's common to use *lightweight access points* (LAPs) that are controlled entirely by wireless access controllers. Configuring a wireless network through a controller is a very different task than what I've outlined here. Again, I recommend a book dedicated to wireless networking for such detail.

> This configuration is very simple, and is designed to give you a basic understanding of what the IOS configuration in a simple WAP looks like. There are far better ways to configure wireless networks, including better security, the use of wireless VLANs, roaming, and so on. Please use your best judgment when designing wireless environments. Simple security such as WEP can pose serious security risks and should not be used in most corporate environments.

I'm configuring a single Cisco 1231 WAP for a small office that only has a few employees. They don't need multiple access points, and they have minimal security needs since their office is in a remote location protected by large dogs hungry for wireless-hacker meat. The first step is to enable bridging with the `bridge irb` command. I detest bridging in most environments, but for a WAP, it's just what we need. This will make all of the wireless nodes appear as if they are directly connected to the network:

```
Cisco-WAP(config)#bridge irb
```

Next, I'll configure a Service Set ID (SSID). My SSID will be called *Coolness*. The SSID is used to identify the wireless network to the client. Multiple SSIDs can exist on a single WAP, and they can even be tied to different VLANs. I will only be configuring one SSID:

```
Cisco-WAP(config)#dot11 ssid Coolness
Cisco-WAP(config-ssid)#authentication open
```

The authentication open command tells the WAP that no authentication is necessary to gain access to the wireless network. If we needed to have users authenticate to this WAP, we might use a shared key with the authentication shared command or even leap with the network eap command. Though WEP requires a shared key, which offers a rudimentary form of authentication, it is not strictly an authentication method.

 While open authentication sounds like a bad idea (and it is in the case of my single WAP), when you're using wireless LAN controllers, a guest VLAN would likely be set up with open access, and authentication would be performed by the controller. If you've ever stayed in a hotel where you were allowed to connect to the wireless LAN, and then presented with an authentication website, you've used this type of setup.

Now I need to configure a DHCP pool for the wireless clients to use. This pool will provide IP addresses to the clients when they connect, as well as DNS server and domain information. To make things interesting, I'm going to limit the range to the IP addresses 192.168.1.100 through 149. I wouldn't normally do this, because I prefer to allocate IP addresses on subnet boundaries, but this reflects some real installations I've seen. People tend not to think about subnet boundaries, after all. First, I need to exclude IP addresses from the range, specifically because I'm not using a range that fits within a subnet:

```
Cisco-WAP(config)#ip dhcp excluded-address 192.168.1.1 192.168.1.109
Cisco-WAP(config)#ip dhcp excluded-address 192.168.1.150 192.168.1.255
```

Now that I've created the exclusions, I can create the pool. Since this is a wireless device and there can be more than one SSID, the pool is assigned to the SSID. Here, I enter the ip dhcp pool SSID command and then issue the shown commands, all of which should be obvious to anyone who has worked with DHCP:

```
Cisco-WAP(config)#ip dhcp pool Coolness
Cisco-WAP(dhcp-config)#network 192.168.1.0 255.255.255.0
Cisco-WAP(dhcp-config)#default-router 192.168.1.1
Cisco-WAP(dhcp-config)#domain-name gad.net
Cisco-WAP(dhcp-config)#dns-server 192.168.1.200 192.168.1.205
Cisco-WAP(dhcp-config)#lease infinite
```

Now I'll configure the radio interface. This interface is named like any other, with the identifier *Dot11Radio*. Since there is only one on this device, the interface is *Dot11Radio0*:

```
Cisco-WAP(config)#interface Dot11Radio0
Cisco-WAP(config-if)#no ip address
```

Next, I'll configure WEP. This is the simplest possible security for a WAP. It's better than nothing, but in a modern commercial environment, I'd recommend using something a bit more robust. Here I used only a 40-bit WEP key to show a simple config. The actual command entered was encryption key 1 size 40bit 1234567890 transmit-key. The 10-digit string 1234567890 translates to exactly 40 bits. The encryption mode `wep mandatory` command makes it mandatory for all connections to be encrypted. The options are `mandatory` and `optional`. Don't ever use `optional` because, well, it shouldn't be optional. In fact, don't ever use 40-bit, either. If you must use WEP, use 128-bit. Better yet, use WPA2:

```
Cisco-WAP(config-if)#encryption key 1 size 40bit 7 9C3A6F2CBFBC transmit-key
Cisco-WAP(config-if)#encryption mode wep mandatory
```

To configure WPA-PSK instead, I can issue these commands. Notice that I'm using TKIP encryption on the interface:

```
Cisco-WAP(config)#dot11 ssid Coolness
Cisco-WAP(config-ssid)#authentication open
Cisco-WAP(config-ssid)#authentication key-management wpa
Cisco-WAP(config-ssid)#guest-mode
Cisco-WAP(config-ssid)#wpa-psk ascii 7 This-is-my-big-honking-insecure-passphrase
Cisco-WAP(config)#int dot11Radio 0
Cisco-WAP(config-if)#encryption mode ciphers tkip
```

To configure WPA2-PSK, I can issue the following commands. These commands are similar to the WPA configuration, except that I'm using AES encryption. Remember, AES encryption is only available on certain hardware, so if this doesn't work for you, make sure you have a WPA2-capable device:

```
Cisco-WAP(config)#dot11 ssid Coolness
Cisco-WAP(config-ssid)#authentication open
Cisco-WAP(config-ssid)#authentication key-management wpa
Cisco-WAP(config-ssid)#guest-mode
Cisco-WAP(config-ssid)#wpa-psk ascii 7 This-is-my-big-honking-insecure-passphrase
Cisco-WAP(config)#int dot11Radio 0
Cisco-WAP(config-if)#encryption mode ciphers aes-ccm
```

Next, I'll assign the SSID *Coolness* to this Dot11Radio interface:

```
Cisco-WAP(config-if)#ssid Coolness
```

If you've purchased your WAP used, or you have an older model, you may see a command like this in the configuration:

```
speed basic-1.0 basic-2.0 basic-5.5 6.0 9.0 basic-11.0 12.0 18.0 24.0 36.0 48.0 54.0
```

If this is configured incorrectly, the WAP may suffer from severely limited throughput. Luckily, you don't have to type any of that stuff to fix it. Instead, just use the command `speed default` to reset it:

```
Cisco-WAP(config-if)#speed default
```

I need to include the wireless interface into bridge group 1 and, as always, turn up the interface:

```
Cisco-WAP(config-if)#bridge-group 1
Cisco-WAP(config-if)#no shut
```

Next, I'll configure the Ethernet interface. Since this WAP is configured as a bridge, there are no IP addresses on the physical interfaces. Instead, the command `bridge-group 1` will include this interface in the bridge group that we will configure later:

```
Cisco-WAP(config)#int g0
Cisco-WAP(config-if)#no ip address
Cisco-WAP(config-if)#bridge-group 1
Cisco-WAP(config-if)#no shut
```

With the two physical interfaces configured, I now need to configure the Bridge Virtual Interface (BVI). This is where I put the IP address for the WAP:

```
Cisco-WAP(config-if)#interface BVI1
Cisco-WAP(config-if)#ip address 192.168.1.3 255.255.255.0
Cisco-WAP(config-if)#no shut
```

Since I've configured the WAP as a bridge, I need to assign a default gateway using the ip default-gateway command:

```
Cisco-WAP(config-if)#ip default-gateway 192.168.1.1
```

Now I need to allow IP through the bridge:

```
Cisco-WAP(config)#bridge 1 route ip
```

At this point, if I've done everything properly, I should have wireless clients associating. I can check this with the show dot11 associations command:

```
Cisco-WAP#sho dot11 associations

802.11 Client Stations on Dot11Radio0:

SSID [Coolness] :

MAC Address      IP address      Device     Name     Parent    State
001e.5275.6ee0   192.168.1.124   unknown    -        self      Assoc
7c6d.62a4.6aad   192.168.1.120   unknown    -        self      Assoc
```

After leaving this WAP up for a while and running some file transfers over it, I ran show interface on the radio interface. As you can see, it's pretty easy to overrun the wireless interface, especially with multiple heavy users. Wireless is great for convenience, but it's just not designed for serious performance:

```
Cisco-WAP#sho int dot11Radio 0
Dot11Radio0 is up, line protocol is up
  Hardware is 802.11G Radio, address is 0012.7f52.de80 (bia 0012.7f52.de80)
  MTU 1500 bytes, BW 54000 Kbit, DLY 1000 usec,
     reliability 255/255, txload 26/255, rxload 25/255
  Encapsulation ARPA, loopback not set
  ARP type: ARPA, ARP Timeout 04:00:00
  Last input 00:00:13, output 00:00:01, output hang never
  Last clearing of "show interface" counters 00:14:57
  Input queue: 0/75/15/0 (size/max/drops/flushes); Total output drops: 0
  Queueing strategy: fifo
  Output queue: 0/30 (size/max)
  5 minute input rate 5420000 bits/sec, 502 packets/sec
  5 minute output rate 5510000 bits/sec, 502 packets/sec
     377892 packets input, 523715591 bytes, 0 no buffer
     Received 38 broadcasts, 0 runts, 0 giants, 0 throttles
     0 input errors, 0 CRC, 0 frame, 0 overrun, 0 ignored
     0 input packets with dribble condition detected
```

```
378073 packets output, 532095123 bytes, 0 underruns
8 output errors, 0 collisions, 0 interface resets
0 babbles, 0 late collision, 0 deferred
0 lost carrier, 0 no carrier
0 output buffer failures, 0 output buffers swapped out
```

MAC Address Filtering

One of the simplest ways to lock down a WAP is by filtering which MAC addresses are
allowed to associate with it. The downside of this approach is the administrative overhead, since any new devices that will be using the wireless network must be manually
added to the list in the WAP. If you have multiple WAPs and are not using a wireless
controller, this method will require you to make these changes to each WAP. For a
small home or office, though, it's much simpler than building and maintaining a RA-
DIUS server. It is, however, a pretty weak system, since MAC addresses can be spoofed
and many wireless devices have their MAC addresses printed on them.

To create the access list, I went to all the wireless devices and collected their MAC
addresses. I now need to add them to an access list on the WAP. Standard MAC address
access lists use the range 700–799:

```
Cisco-WAP(config)#access-list ?
  <1-99>             IP standard access list
  <100-199>          IP extended access list
  <1100-1199>        Extended 48-bit MAC address access list
  <1300-1999>        IP standard access list (expanded range)
  <200-299>          Protocol type-code access list
  <2000-2699>        IP extended access list (expanded range)
  <700-799>          48-bit MAC address access list
  dynamic-extended   Extend the dynamic ACL absolute timer
```

Now I enter all my collected MAC addresses into access list 701:

```
Cisco-WAP(config)#access-list 701 permit 0025.0046.3f26 0000.0000.0000
Cisco-WAP(config)#access-list 701 permit 0014.a524.5b7a 0000.0000.0000
Cisco-WAP(config)#access-list 701 permit 001d.a231.6568 0000.0000.0000
Cisco-WAP(config)#access-list 701 permit 7c6d.62a4.6aad 0000.0000.0000
Cisco-WAP(config)#access-list 701 permit 001e.a98b.0018 0000.0000.0000
```

With the MAC address filter in place, I can apply it to the WAP with the dot11 asso
ciation mac-list *access-list* command. This will cause the dot11 radio interface to
reset, after which the MAC address filter will be enabled:

```
Cisco-WAP(config)#dot11 association mac-list 700
*Mar  1 01:51:19.543: %LINK-5-CHANGED: Interface Dot11Radio0, changed state to reset
*Mar  1 01:51:19.555: %LINK-3-UPDOWN: Interface Dot11Radio0, changed state to up
```

Troubleshooting

Here are some useful commands for troubleshooting a WAP. For me, the problems usually revolve around association. The command show dot11 associations is a great tool. If you have Cisco devices associated, it will even show you what they are:

```
Cisco-WAP#sho dot11 associations

802.11 Client Stations on Dot11Radio0:

SSID [Coolness] :

MAC Address     IP address      Device       Name             Parent    State
0014.a524.5b7a  192.168.1.129   ccx-client   hp-laptop        self      Assoc
001d.a231.6568  192.168.1.135   CP-7921      SEP001DA2316568  self      Assoc
001e.a98b.0018  192.168.1.120   unknown      -                self      Assoc
7c6d.62a4.6aad  192.168.1.110   unknown      -                self      Assoc
```

Keeping the monitor session active with the terminal monitor command is a must when troubleshooting association problems. This will ensure that console message are sent to your terminal session when you're using Telnet or SSH to connect to the WAP. Here is the console output that resulted from a wireless client losing power:

```
*Mar  1 00:56:54.671: %DOT11-6-DISASSOC: Interface Dot11Radio0, Deauthenticating
Station 0025.0046.3f26 Reason: Sending station has left the BSS
```

Here is the resulting console message after power was restored:

```
*Mar  1 00:58:25.607: %DOT11-6-ASSOC: Interface Dot11Radio0, Station
0025.0046.3f26 Associated KEY_MGMT[NONE]
```

These debug commands can be very helpful when you are troubleshooting wireless authentication:

```
debug dot11 aaa authenticator process
debug dot11 aaa authenticator state-machine
```

If WPA or WPA2 Enterprise is enabled and RADIUS is involved, debugging RADIUS can be handy as well:

```
debug radius authentication
```

The output of these debug commands can be pretty verbose. Cisco document ID#50843 (*http://www.cisco.com/en/US/products/hw/wireless/ps430/products_tech _note09186a008024aa4f.shtml*) contains examples of what to look for within the output of these commands.

CHAPTER 30

VoIP

Voice over IP (VoIP) has been the biggest thing to happen to network since IP itself. Maybe that's a stretch, but there's no denying the way VoIP has become a big deal for networking folks. So let's see what's involved, how it all works, and how to build a small phone system using a router, a switch, and some IP phones.

I'll be using Cisco gear for this chapter, just like all the others. Sure, there are other solutions out there, but chances are, if you're reading this book, you'll be at a Cisco shop or studying for a Cisco exam, so Cisco is what I'm using. If you're hell-bent on not using Cisco (and there are many execs who feel this way, especially when it comes to telephony), I recommend you check out the open source Asterisk project. Using SIP phones (read on to learn about SIP) and a Linux server, you can build a powerful phone system for little money. There's even an O'Reilly book to help you out: *Asterisk: The Future of Telephony, Second Edition*, by Jim Van Meggelen et al. (*http://oreilly.com/catalog/9780596009625/*).

VoIP is a huge topic, and there are entire books devoted to its use and configuration. As always, my goal here is to get you started, show you how it works, and provide a real-world example. This chapter will not explain everything there is to know about VoIP. It will show you how to make a small office run on Cisco VoIP using Call Manager Express and Cisco 79xx phones.

How VoIP Works

From a network standpoint, VoIP has two main functions: call control and the voice call itself. We'll cover call control in a minute, but first let's talk about the voice data stream.

Telephony is a means whereby an analog representation of a caller's voice is sent over wires to another phone, where it is heard. In the early days, this was all done with simple electricity. As telephony advanced, the analog signal was converted to digital for multiplexing on trunks such as T1 lines.

See Chapter 21 for more information on how T1s and multiplexing in telephony works.

When large companies started installing data networks, they discovered that maintaining (and paying for) a data network and a phone network was prohibitively expensive. Someone had the idea that a phone call could be digitized, packetized, and sent over a data network using IP. If they could converge two networks into one, the companies could significantly lower recurring costs. Yeah, the technology is cool and all, but the execs made VoIP mainstream because it allowed them to save money.

There is a problem, though, and that is call quality. Without getting too far into a very deep topic, suffice it to say that people were used to flawless quality when they picked up a phone and made a call. You may not realize it now, but phones used to sound *good*.

 Cell phones have significantly lowered our expectations for call quality. In the days before cell phones and VoIP, call quality was remarkably good, a fact upon which old-school telephony guys will happily expound when VoIP users complain.

To even approach the call quality of a traditional analog telephone, a digitized, packetized voice call must be sent quickly and reliably. Additionally, the packets must arrive in the order in which they were sent. Unfortunately, those requirements aren't all easily met with IP. For VoIP call packets to be sent quickly, UDP is used for speed, but UDP does not include any error checking, nor does it guarantee that packets arrive in order. To overcome these shortcomings, QoS is used to make sure that VoIP call packets are sent before any other packets and, once sent, are not dropped. To make things even more interesting, there must be a stream in each direction, since voice calls are full duplex.

 While Real-Time Protocol (RTP) does include timestamps and sequence numbers so that packet loss and packet order problems can be detected, it does not work to resolve these issues if they are discovered.

Communication between two endpoints is set up via *call control*. Call control is the means whereby a call, be it voice or video, is negotiated and established; it is initiated when you dial a phone number. Phone numbers mean something to switches in the cloud, and they are used to route your call. In IP telephony, the phone numbers are converted to endpoint IP addresses. The endpoints then negotiate and set up the two real-time data streams for the call itself.

In telephony terms, the control communication is called the *data channel*, while the RTP stream is called the *bearer channel*. We often use the term *bearer traffic* to describe the RTP stream.

The actual call is sent through RTP. To be accurate, RTP is also used for many types of media, including video. If you hear someone say *RTP stream*, he's talking about the actual voice or video traffic, not the call control.

From a network standpoint, try to remember this important nugget: call control should be prioritized at IP precedence 3, while the RTP stream should be prioritized at IP precedence 5. See Chapter 32 for an example.

Protocols

In the Cisco world, you will likely hear the term *H.323* thrown around. You may also hear *H.225*, *G.7.11*, *G.729*, *SIP*, and a host of other numbers and letters bandied about. These are all voice and video protocols used with IP telephony. Let's take a look at the more common ones:

H.323
> H.323 is an umbrella specification (technically a recommendation) from the International Telecommunications Union (ITU) that covers voice, video, and data transmission over IP. H.323 signaling is based on the ITU recommendation Q.931, which you may have seen in use on ISDN circuits. H.323 includes device descriptions for terminal, gatekeeper, gateway, and border elements, to name a few. H.323 is widely used in VoIP systems and video conferencing. H.323 was designed from a telephony point of view, and may seem complicated to those without a telephony background.

H.225
> H.225 is a call-control protocol used within the H.323 specification.

H.245
> H.245 is a protocol within the H.323 used for transmission of nontelephone signals such as encryption, flow control, and jitter management. It is also used for tunneling H225 and for DTMF (Dual-Tone Multifrequency) Relay.

SIP
> SIP (Session Initiation Protocol) is an IETF-defined call signaling protocol. SIP has gained great prominence in the past few years due to its open nature and, as a result, is the signaling protocol of choice for open source VoIP systems such as Asterisk. SIP is a very robust and configurable protocol. It is text-based, which, though easier to read and understand, can appear excessively wordy when compared with H323. In the 1990s, that might have been a problem with low-powered networking

equipment using slow-speed links, but in today's environment where power and speed are abundant, SIP is very popular. SIP was designed for the IP world, and may seem more familiar to those who don't have a telephony background.

Skinny Call Control Protocol (SCCP)

Skinny for short, SCCP is a Cisco-proprietary protocol used for signaling endpoints with Cisco's Unified Communications Manager (formerly Cisco Call Manager). SCCP is used by the Cisco IP phones in this chapter, the Cisco IP Communicator softphone, Analog Telephone Adapters (ATAs), and other Cisco telephony endpoints. This protocol is a matter of some consternation for engineers and executives alike. Executives don't like being forced into buying Cisco IP phones, often quoting the price compared with less expensive SIP phones. The benefit of SCCP is that it is simple to implement and is very lightweight, so it consumes few network resources. If you've got 5,000 IP phones registering with your Call Manager cluster, you'll want those registration messages to be short and sweet.

CODEC

CODEC stands for COder-DECoder. Although it is not itself a protocol, many of the protocols listed here are CODECs. CODECs describe how data or a signal is translated from one form to another. Common CODECs include MPEG, MP3 (a subset of MPEG), Dolby Digital surround sound, G.711, and G.729.

G.711

G.711 is a standard that outlines how to digitize an analog voice signal into digital. It is lossless, meaning that there is no degradation of call quality with its use. G. 711 is usually the best-sounding voice CODEC in common use, and it requires the least amount of DSP resources, because there is no compression. Unfortunately, great sound comes at a price, and G.711 consumes the most bandwidth (64 kbps per signal when sampled at 8 kHz). Since this is the same size as a traditional voice call, there is no economy of bandwidth, so it is rarely used on a converged network.

G.722

G.711 sounds good because it delivers the same sound quality as a traditional plain old telephone service (POTS) line. G.722 sounds even better because it delivers *better* sound quality than a POTS line. Commonly called *wide-band audio* because it samples at 16 kHz as opposed to 8 kHz for G.711, G.722 is supported on high-end phones like Cisco's 7575G. The downside of using this protocol is that it consumes more bandwidth than G.711. For this reason, it should be used only on local networks where bandwidth is plentiful.

G.729

G.729 is a CODEC that compresses a voice signal with an average of 8:1 compression. G.729 is very popular because it balances excellent voice quality with a significant reduction in network utilization. The downside is that G.729 requires more DSP resources. There are multiple versions of G.729—most notably, G.729a and G.729b. G.729a offers the same quality and compression, but uses an algorithm that requires fewer DSP resources. G.729b supports Voice Activity Detection

(VAD), a feature that lowers or eliminates network utilization during periods of silence.

Power over Ethernet (PoE)

You may not think of PoE as a protocol, but it is. In the Cisco world, there are generally two protocols in common use: Cisco prestandard PoE and standards-based 802.3af. Cisco was selling PoE devices before there was a standard, hence the prestandard moniker. Many modern Cisco switches support both protocols, but be careful if you are buying used gear. If you have an older Cisco switch and buy a non-Cisco phone, PoE may not work. Similarly, if you have a non-Cisco switch and buy certain Cisco phones, PoE won't work. For example, the Cisco 7960Gs discussed in this chapter support only Cisco prestandard PoE, while the 7971s I'm using support both protocols.

Telephony Terms

Since VoIP is telephony, there are some terms you're going to need to know. Some of these may seem confusing, but remember, they come from a 100-year-old industry that views us as the enemy at the gates, so be nice:

PBX

Private Branch Exchange. A PBX is essentially an office phone system.

ACD

Automatic Call Distributer. An ACD is the usually large, specialized phone system found in a call center. ACDs are designed to route calls to agents based on special scripts. They can also report call metrics such as average speed of answer, average call handle time, busy hour call volume, and so on.

ANI

Pronounced *Annie*, the Automatic Number Identifier (ANI) is the calling number. It also includes other information that doesn't matter to us in this chapter. ANI is similar to, but not the same as, the caller ID information you see when someone calls you. Even if caller ID is blocked, ANI is present.

DNIS

Pronounced *dee-niss*, the Dialed Number Identification Service (DNIS) is a code that usually references the number that the caller dialed. Call centers often reference DNIS to route calls.

Hairpin

Hairpinning a call (sometimes called tromboning) is the act of sending a call or message back from whence it came. Imagine two phones connected to a Call Manager Express (CME) system on the same interface. If one phone were to call another and the voice stream needed to traverse the router, the voice stream would go from phone A to the router, then back out the router's same interface to phone B; thus, this call would be hairpinned. This scenario is usually avoided, since the phones usually set up direct communication after call control is completed. While hairpinning is generally frowned upon in the IP networking world, I've seen it used in traditional telephony quite often.

FXO

Foreign Exchange Office. An FXO port connects the phone system to an outside line via the plain POTS. We'll connect our IP phone system to an outside POTS line later in this chapter. Think of FXO as a POTS line that connects to the *outside* or central *office* (hence the O in FXO).

FXS

Foreign Exchange Station. An FXS port is one to which a traditional analog phone is connected. FXS ports supply battery and dial tone, and generate ringing signals to the phone endpoint. If you have a POTS line in your house, the jack on the wall is an FXS port. Think of FXS as a POTS line for connecting a *station* (hence the S in FXS).

 If you're building an IP telephony lab that will connect to POTS lines and analog phones, you may be asking, "What type of ports do I need?" Phones need FXS ports. Outside POTS lines need FXO ports. You may also think of it this way: analog phones require voltage, and traditionally, the central office supplied that voltage. FXS ports supply voltage (S for supply), while FXO ports do not.

Softphone

An IP phone that exists only as software on another device. Softphones may exist on desktop or laptop computers, tablets, or even on smartphones.

Survivable Remote Site Telephony (SRST)

Imagine that you have a main office with 10 remote offices. Each remote office has 10 IP phones, all of which register and use the IP PBX in the main office. Should the main IP PBX become unavailable, all those branch phones will also become unavailable. By configuring a smaller-scale IP PBX at the branch, we can make each remote branch capable of surviving the failure. Thus, the remote site's telephony survives.

PLAR

PLAR stands for Private Line Automatic Ringdown. The common description for a PLAR line is the "bat phone." If Commissioner Gordon picks up the bat phone, the matching phone rings in the Batcave. No numbers need be dialed; if you need Batman, you need him *now*.

Cisco Telephony Terms

PVDM

PVDM stands for Packet Voice Digital Signal Processor. There are multiple versions—PVDM, PVDM2, and PVDM3, for example. PVDMs are Digital Signal

Processors (DSP). DSPs are specialized computers on a chip that convert signals from one format to another, compress or decompress a signal, or in some way alter or analyze a signal. They may convert from analog to digital or digital to analog like a DAC, but they may also convert from one CODEC to another. You may not need a PVDM if you're building the environment I've built in this chapter. Cisco IP phones have DSPs built into them, so they do the conversion from analog to digital and back again. If you're using a network for long-haul toll bypass (using the network instead of the phone company), you may need PVDMs to convert to a CODEC with more compression when sending the call across the cloud.

Cisco Unified Communications Manager

Formerly Cisco Call Manager (CCM), Cisco Unified Communications Manager (CUCM) is the Cisco IP equivalent of a PBX. It was likely renamed because it is capable of much more than just voice calls. CUCM is usually installed on one or more servers (possibly in a cluster) in a central location. There's a good chance you'll hear people call this product Call Manager regardless of what's actually installed.

Cisco Unified Communications Manager Express

Formerly Call Manager Express (CME), this product is a scaled-down version of CUCM that resides within a Cisco router. CUCM Express (CUCME) is also often used for SRST. CUCME is what we'll be using in this chapter. You'll notice that I use the term CME constantly even though I've got CUCME installed. I refuse to use the term CUCME when CME rolls off the tongue so well.

Cisco Unity

Unity is Cisco's Enterprise voicemail application, which encompasses Microsoft Exchange, Active Directory, and domain controllers. Cisco Unity is outside the scope of this book.

Cisco Unity Connection

Cisco Unity Connection is Cisco's new direction on voicemail; it decouples the entire Microsoft infrastructure used in Cisco Unity. Cisco Unity Connection is a Linux appliance running an Informix database that supports Unified and Integrated Messaging. In the latest versions, it also supports single-inbox for Exchange environments, where all of your messages, regardless of format (voice or text) are stored in the same inbox. This product is not covered in this book.

Cisco Unity Express

Cisco Unity Express (CUE) is a scaled-down version of Unity for use within Cisco voice-enabled routers. CUE resides on a small computer built into network modules or AIM daughter cards. These modules vary in capacity for use in different-size environments. While I will reference CUE in this chapter, its configuration will not be covered. We will, however, look at how to connect to a properly configured CUE from within CME, er, CUCME.

Common Issues with VoIP

When dealing with digitized voice, you'll encounter some common issues. These issues are not confined to VoIP, but you'll likely hear about them when working with other VoIP engineers. Let's take a look at them.

Latency

Latency is the amount of time it takes for packets to traverse the network. In VoIP, that translates roughly to ping times. The thing to remember is that the magic number for roundtrip VoIP is 300 ms. The ITU-T G.114 spec recommends no more than 150 ms latency one way for voice calls (hence 300 ms roundtrip). In reality, the average person will start to complain around 250 ms. Since I'm a control-freak pain in the ass with a low tolerance for latency, even 180 ms roundtrip latency annoys me.

 Ever notice when you're talking to someone, cell phone to cell phone, that you tend to both start talking at the same time? That's latency in real life. Consider a modern digital cell phone call: phone A converts your call to digital, compresses it, and then sends the signal to a local radio tower. That tower receives the call and sends it over one or more land-based networks (possibly between multiple carriers) to the tower nearest to phone B. That tower then transmits the signal phone B, which uncompresses the signal, converts it back to audio, and delivers it to the speaker. Each one of those steps adds latency. It all happens in "real time," but the latency is noticeable.

Latency usually has two distinct causes: propagational delay or computational delay. If you're sending your VoIP packets from the eastern United States to the Philippines, you'll need to haul those packets halfway around the world. Realistically, you cannot improve upon the speed in which bits traverse these links, so propagational delay is usually a fact of life, especially on undersea routes where there are few alternate paths.

 A land-based point-to-point link is often nothing of the sort at the physical layer. A link between New York and California may have many smaller hops within in it to take advantage of available capacity on existing intercity links. These added physical links are usually transparent to the subscriber, but can add latency in the form of added distance (and minor computational delay). I've seen examples where delay was cut almost in half after we convinced the provider to give us a more efficient route on the network.

Computational delay is a factor every time packets traverse a device that alters the packet. Routers, DSPs, cell phones, and PBXs all contribute to computational delay. Converting from G.711 to G.729 adds compression, which introduces even more computational delay. The way to resolve computational delay is to remove hardware from the path, lower compression complexity, add faster hardware, and so on. Latency presents itself as delayed audio or perceived echo. See Chapter 20 for more information on latency.

Packet loss

Packet loss in a VoIP call is bad news and must be resolved, or you'll be faced with a mob of angry users wielding torches and pitchforks. The main weapon in the battle against packet loss is QoS. If you're still losing packets with QoS properly configured and tuned, you need more bandwidth or you may have bad hardware.

 Remember, there is no QoS on the Internet! Sure, Internet-based VoIP is cheap, but one of the things you give up is quality. Telephony circuits deliver a certain amount of quality that is simply not available when you use Internet-based VoIP. We can approach that level of quality when using private networks and QoS, but the moment your packet leaves your network and enters the great Internet cloud, it is at the mercy of (potentially) many providers, routers, and links, all of which may be seriously oversubscribed.

Loss of far less than 1% of packets will cause significantly degraded audio quality on a VoIP call. Packet loss is usually a symptom of oversubscribed links, improperly configured (or missing) QoS, or bad hardware. Packet loss is usually described by users as *choppy calls*, though if the loss is significant, calls might be dropped altogether. Packet loss can also cause mechanical-sounding audio or other user complaints.

Jitter

Jitter has to do with timely delivery of packets. If your packets are being delivered in order, but the first five are bunched together while the next five are separated by huge FTP packets (or worse—jumbo frames), the receiving end will have trouble decoding the signal into recognizable audio. The technical term for this problem is *packet-to-packet delay variation*.

Since this can be a microsecond issue, most modern VoIP devices incorporate something called a *jitter buffer* to lessen its effects. Jitter buffers hold the incoming packets for a short time until they can be processed properly. This removes the delivery delay problem, but introduces new latency, since the packets sit in a buffer for a short time before being decoded. If jitter is extreme, the jitter buffer can usually be enlarged, but this often results in latency that exceeds the average user's annoyance threshold.

Jitter is the gremlin of the VoIP world. If you've got jitter, it can be tough to find the culprit, though improperly configured (or missing) QoS is a common cause.

Small-Office VoIP Example

In a Cisco VoIP environment, there will be endpoints (phones), a PBX (UCM, Call Manager, or the express versions of these products), and probably voicemail (Cisco Unity). In this chapter, we'll be building the design shown in Figure 30-1. This IP phone system is designed for the needs of the office of a small but successful consulting company. Any similarities to companies or persons either living or dead are purely coincidental.

> There are almost limitless ways in which an IP phone system can be configured. In this chapter, I will show you one way of doing things, but you can likely accomplish the same goal using different methods. As long as the client's needs are met and there are no vulnerabilities or shortcomings, the way that works is the right way. While there are certainly best practices, when it comes to topics like dial plans, dial peers, and features required, every installation is different.

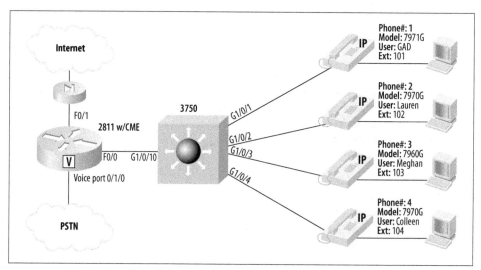

Figure 30-1. Small-office Cisco CME VoIP deployment

I'm going to build a small-office IP telephony solution using a Cisco 2811 router. Within the router, I have UCM Express, a Cisco Unity Express AIM card (AIM-CUE), and a four-port FXO card to connect to the POTS lines. There is also a PVDM2-48 for CO-DEC conversion, but it is not needed for the design shown here. For phones, I am using a Cisco 7971G, two Cisco 7970Gs, and a Cisco 7960G. The phones connect to the network via a Cisco 3750 PoE switch.

If you're building a VoIP solution in your lab, the phones don't matter much, but if you're designing one for a customer, the phones are everything. Remember, the user experiences the phone system through the phone. If the phone sucks, the system sucks as far as the customer is concerned. Little things like a backlit display and backlit line buttons make a huge difference when it comes to end-user experience. I got my 7960G phones cheap because a company was pulling them all in favor of the newer 7961Gs. The company spent thousands of dollars on new phones because it could not deal with the fact that the line buttons did not light up when the line was in use.

A common scenario for this sort of environment is to include a Cisco switch module in the router. The configuration is, for all intents, identical to the one shown in Figure 30-1 and would be drawn the same way, since the switch module connects via an internal gigabit interface in the router and behaves as if it were a standalone 3750.

VLANs

The first thing we need to do is plan our VLAN environment. Though you can put your phone traffic on the same VLAN as your data traffic, I don't recommend it. The standard VoIP designs from Cisco indicate that the phone traffic should be isolated to a voice VLAN. The VLAN layout is shown in Figure 30-2.

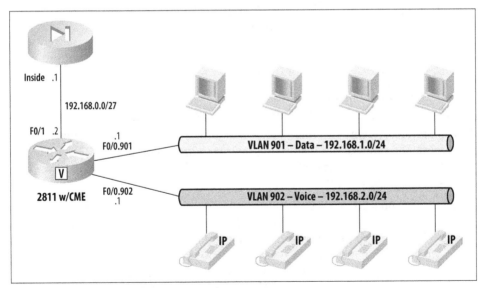

Figure 30-2. VLAN layout for VoIP network

Since our network is pretty simple, we'll create two VLANs on our switch, one for voice and one for data:

```
SW-3750(config-vlan)#vlan 901
SW-3750(config-vlan)#name Data
SW-3750(config-vlan)#vlan 902
SW-3750(config-vlan)#name Voice
```

To get the router talking to the switch, we'll need to configure a trunk between them. First the switch:

```
SW-3750(config)#interface GigabitEthernet1/0/10
SW-3750(config-if)# description [ R1-PBX F0/0 ]
SW-3750(config-if)# switchport trunk encapsulation dot1q
SW-3750(config-if)# switchport trunk allowed vlan 901,902
SW-3750(config-if)# switchport mode trunk
SW-3750(config-if)# speed 100
SW-3750(config-if)# duplex full
SW-3750(config-if)# no shut
```

Now we'll configure the router. To make it talk to the switch over a trunk, we'll need to configure one Ethernet subinterface for each VLAN. First the physical interface:

```
R1-PBX(config)#interface FastEthernet0/0
R1-PBX(config-if)# description [ Trunk to 3750 ]
R1-PBX(config-if)# no ip address
R1-PBX(config-if)# duplex full
R1-PBX(config-if)# speed 100
```

Next, we'll configure the subinterface for VLAN 901, the data VLAN:

```
R1-PBX(config-if)#interface FastEthernet0/0.901
R1-PBX(config-subif)# description [ Data ]
R1-PBX(config-subif)# encapsulation dot1Q 901
R1-PBX(config-subif)# ip address 192.168.1.1 255.255.255.0
```

Finally, we'll configure the subinterface for the voice VLAN:

```
R1-PBX(config-subif)#interface FastEthernet0/0.902
R1-PBX(config-subif)# description [ Voice ]
R1-PBX(config-subif)# encapsulation dot1Q 902
R1-PBX(config-subif)# ip address 192.168.2.1 255.255.255.0
```

None of this may seem to have anything to do with VoIP, and while that may be true, it's important to understand that we're trunking to the router and using Ethernet subinterfaces to do so. Alternatively, I could have made VLAN 901 the native VLAN and only configured the voice VLAN as a dot1q subinterface.

You may have noticed that the VLAN design shows the phones in one VLAN and the workstations in another, yet the physical drawing shows the PCs connecting to the phones. The key thing to understand here is that the Cisco phones I'm using have two-port switches built into them. They will connect to the switch with a trunk containing both VLANs. The PCs will connect to the phone on the other port. The phone will grant access to the PC on the data VLAN, while the phones will communicate on the voice VLAN. The phone ports are illustrated in Figure 30-3. This behavior is configurable in all sorts of interesting ways, but we'll stick with the standard.

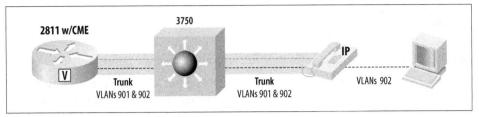

Figure 30-3. Cisco IP phone and workstation connectivity

Switch Ports

Since the phones will connect to the switch via trunks, let's configure the interfaces on the 3750 that will have phones attached. I've reserved interfaces 1–9 on the switch for phones. Using the `interface range` command, we'll configure them all at once:

```
SW-3750(config)#int range g1/0/1 - 9
SW-3750(config-if-range)# description [ IP-Phone ]
SW-3750(config-if-range)# switchport trunk encapsulation dot1q
SW-3750(config-if-range)# switchport trunk native vlan 901
SW-3750(config-if-range)# switchport mode trunk
SW-3750(config-if-range)# switchport nonegotiate
SW-3750(config-if-range)# switchport voice vlan 902
SW-3750(config-if-range)# spanning-tree portfast
```

Additionally, every port that has a Cisco IP phone should have QoS configured such that the switch will trust marked packets originating from the phone. We do this with the `auto qos` interface command. There are a few options as shown below. Choose the proper one based on the device connected:

```
SW-3750(config-if-range)#auto qos voip ?
  cisco-phone       Trust the QoS marking of Cisco IP Phone
  cisco-softphone   Trust the QoS marking of Cisco IP SoftPhone
  trust             Trust the DSCP/CoS marking
```

Since I'm using all Cisco IP phones, I'll use the `cisco-phone` option:

```
SW-3750(config-if-range)#auto qos voip cisco-phone
```

If you enter this command after you've already connected your phones, you'll get output similar to this:

```
1w3d: %SWITCH_QOS_TB-5-TRUST_DEVICE_DETECTED: cisco-phone detected on port Gi1/0/1,
port's configured trust state is now operational.
```

Don't be surprised if you see a full page of `mls qos` commands the next time you view your running config. On my switch, it added 45 or so ugly commands right at the top of the config so that you have to page by them to see anything else. See Chapter 19 for an example. Enabling AutoQoS also polluted the configuration of each phone interface with the following additions:

```
srr-queue bandwidth share 10 10 60 20
srr-queue bandwidth shape  10  0  0  0
queue-set 2
```

```
mls qos trust device cisco-phone
mls qos trust cos
auto qos voip cisco-phone
```

Sure, it's ugly, but when it comes to VoIP, QoS should not be ignored.

As far as the 3750 is concerned, we're pretty much done. The only thing left would be to configure a VLAN and interfaces for the outside network between the router and the firewall. Since that's not strictly VoIP-related, I'll leave you to your own devices.

QoS on the CME Router

We should apply some QoS to the router interfaces, so let's make it as simple as possible. I'll configure classes for voice control and the voice RTP stream. Everything else can fend for itself. For a more detailed QoS example, see Chapter 32. This QoS scheme assumes that the phones will mark their packets appropriately. Since we're using Cisco phones, this is a safe assumption. First, we'll set up the class-maps to identify and classify traffic:

```
R1-PBX(config)#class-map match-any Voice-Calls
R1-PBX(config-cmap)#description [---[ RTP Calls ]---]
R1-PBX(config-cmap)#match ip dscp ef
R1-PBX(config-cmap)#match ip precedence 5
R1-PBX(config-cmap)#class-map match-any Voice-Control
R1-PBX(config-cmap)#description [---[ Call Control ]---]
R1-PBX(config-cmap)#match ip dscp af31
R1-PBX(config-cmap)#match ip precedence 3
```

Yeah, the match lines in each class are generally superfluous, but I just can't help myself. I've done it this way forever, and old habits die hard. We now need to create a policy-map for our class maps. This policy map allows for four concurrent G.711 calls with generous space for call control:

```
R1-PBX(config-cmap)#policy-map Ethernet-QoS
R1-PBX(config-pmap)#description [---[ Apply Treatment for Classes ]---]
R1-PBX(config-pmap)#class Voice-Calls
R1-PBX(config-pmap-c)#priority 256 64
R1-PBX(config-pmap-c)#class Voice-Control
R1-PBX(config-pmap-c)#bandwidth 128
R1-PBX(config-pmap-c)#class class-default
R1-PBX(config-pmap-c)#fair-queue
```

If you have multiple VLANs attached to your interfaces, you cannot apply the policy map to a subinterface. Instead, you need to traffic-shape the interface and then apply the service-policy under the class-default class of that policy. Here, I've applied traffic shaping to 50 Mbps outbound (the speed of the Internet link, in this case) and applied the WAN-edge service policy:

```
R1-PBX(config)#policy-map SubInt-QoS
R1-PBX(config-pmap)#class class-default
R1-PBX(config-pmap-c)#shape average 50000000
R1-PBX(config-pmap-c)#service-policy Ethernet-QoS
```

Now, I'll apply my policy map to my Ethernet interfaces:

```
R1-PBX(config-if)#int f0/0
R1-PBX(config-if)#service-policy output Ethernet-QoS
R1-PBX(config-if)#int f0/1
R1-PBX(config-if)#service-policy output Ethernet-QoS
```

If you have subinterfaces, you can apply the SubInt-QoS policy to the subinterfaces:

```
R1-PBX(config-if)#int f0/0.902
R1-PBX(config-subif)#service-policy output SubInt-QoS
```

You cannot apply service policies in the same direction on both the physical interface and the subinterfaces beneath it. The router will complain if you try:

```
R1-PBX(config-if)#service-policy output Ethernet-QoS
Attaching service policy to main and sub-interface in the same direction
concurrently is not allowed
```

DHCP for Phones

Moving on to the router, the first thing we need to do is configure a DHCP scope for our phones. Remember, the phones will all reside in VLAN 902 and have an IP address in the 192.168.2.0/24 space. To keep the phones from grabbing the IP addresses of the routers and other critical systems, let's keep the DHCP scope within the .129–.222 range:

```
ip dhcp excluded-address 192.168.2.1 192.168.2.128
ip dhcp excluded-address 192.168.2.223 192.168.2.255
!
ip dhcp pool Phones
   network 192.168.2.0 255.255.255.0
   option 150 ip 192.168.2.1
   default-router 192.168.2.1
   dns-server 192.168.1.200 192.168.1.205
```

The command option 150 ip 192.168.2.1 allows the IP phones to learn the address for the TFTP server. The phones need somewhere from which they can retrieve firmware and configuration files. We'll be configuring our 2811 router to be the TFTP server, so I've specified the voice VLAN's IP address on the router to be the TFTP server address. We could also use option 66, which would allow us to specify a DNS-resolvable name.

TFTP Service

When a Cisco IP phone boots, it talks to the switch via CDP to determine things like how much power it requires (if we're using PoE), which VLANs it should use, and so on. It then requests an IP address, a TFTP server, and, once connected, some information from the TFTP server.

To ensure compatibility, we can load the desired firmware files on the router and tell the phone to load them when it connects. This guarantees that all phones are running the right code, which minimizes problems. The code is based on phone model. Thus, you'll need the firmware files for each type of phone in your network for the revision of CME or UCME in use. In my case, I need the firmware files for a Cisco 7970G and a 7960G. These files are included with the CME package.

 If you're building a home lab and buying your switches used, you will likely have many phones with different versions of code loaded. This will probably work fine, but you'll be better off learning how to get the files and installing them. Cisco recently made that difficult for people without a valid contract. If you have some Cisco phones but can't get the firmware files to complete this step, don't sweat it. The phones will probably still work, though I have seen firmware discrepancy issues.

The files are not always obvious-looking. For example, the firmware I'm using for the 7960Gs is named *P00308010200*. There are also multiple files involved for each model. Once you get the files onto the router, you need to configure the TFTP server to serve them. Here, I've added the files for my 7960Gs and 7970Gs:

```
tftp-server flash:apps70.9-1-1TH1-16.sbn
tftp-server flash:cnu70.9-1-1TH1-16.sbn
tftp-server flash:cvm70sccp.9-1-1TH1-16.sbn
tftp-server flash:dsp70.9-1-1TH1-16.sbn
tftp-server flash:jar70sccp.9-1-1TH1-16.sbn
tftp-server flash:SCCP70.9-1-1SR1S.loads
tftp-server flash:term70.default.loads
tftp-server flash:term71.default.loads
tftp-server flash:OS79XX.TXT
tftp-server flash:P00308010200.loads
tftp-server flash:P00308010200.bin
tftp-server flash:P00308010200.sbn
tftp-server flash:P00308010200.sb2
```

 If you download the CME/UCME package from Cisco Connection On-line (CCO), you'll get all the firmware files as well as a script for adding all the TFTP server statements. For a production environment, this is the way to go; should any supported Cisco phone be added, you won't have to chase down the firmware files. It fills the `flash:` drive and configuration with a lot of unneeded entries, but it will save you time in the future.

Make sure all the files are there. You'll see in a bit how the phone knows which ones to read.

Telephony Service

CME is configured with the `telephony-service` command. There are two ways to configure it—manually or with a setup script:

```
R1-PBX(config)#telephony-service ?
  setup  Start setup for Cisco Call Manager Express. Please refer to
         www.cisco.com/univercd/cc/td/doc/product/access/ip_ph/ip_ks/index.htm
         for full documentation.
  <cr>
```

If you're in a lab environment, I encourage you to run the setup script at least once. This might be of limited use in the real world, but it's a good idea to get a feel for what it will configure. Since I'm a command-line geek, I'm going in full bore and configuring it the hard way.

Within the telephony service configuration, we will specify the firmware the phones should load. First, we'll tell CME to create the phone configuration files automatically from the firmware and config. We do this with the create cnf-files command:

```
R1-PBX(config)#telephony-service
R1-PBX(config-telephony)#create cnf-files
Creating CNF files
```

Now we specify which firmware files should be loaded for each model phone in our environment:

```
R1-PBX(config-telephony)# load 7960-7940 P00308000900
Updating CNF files
CNF files updating complete

R1-PBX(config-telephony)# load 7970 SCCP70.9-1-1SR1S
Updating CNF files
CNF files update complete
```

The "Updating CNF files" message appears as a result of the create cnf-files command we ran earlier. If we hadn't run that first, nothing would happen when we issued the load command. The order isn't important. If we were to run the load command first, the config files would be generated when we ran the create cnf-files command. You can always rerun the command to regenerate the config files if you wish:

```
R1-PBX(config-telephony)#create cnf-files
Creating CNF files
```

Next, we're going to put some limits in our system. I'm going to limit the number of phones to 16 and the number of dial numbers to 128:

```
R1-PBX(config-telephony)#max-ephones 16
R1-PBX(config-telephony)#max-dn 128
```

Why limit the number of phones? If you have a very static environment, limiting the number of phones will prevent rogue phones from registering. Believe it or not, this can be a real problem. If you try to lower this number later, you will be treated to this message:

```
R1-PBX(config-telephony)#max-ephones 8
Please remove ephone 9 to 16 by re-configuring or reloading the system!!
```

Setting the max-dn value can help you rein in your dial plan. Both settings default to zero.

Next, we'll configure the phone system so that it uses the IP address of the voice VLAN on this router (int f0/0.902):

```
R1-PBX(config-telephony)# ip source-address 192.168.2.1 port 2000
CNF files updating complete
```

Since this information is critical to the phones' operation, the config files are automatically updated, again because of the `create cnf-files` command entered earlier.

Now we'll configure the system message. This message will appear on every registered phone. Generally, this is the company name, but it can be anything that you or the client want it to be:

```
R1-PBX(config-telephony)#system message GAD Technology
```

We need to set the time zone for the phone system. The phone system defaults to universal time as learned from the router, so, regardless of the router's time zone setting, you will need to configure the time zone here. You must choose the number of the time zone from the included list:

```
R1-PBX(config-telephony)#time-zone ?
  <1-53>  select timezone name used by IP phones (offset in minutes)
  1 Dateline Standard Time -720
  2 Samoa Standard Time -660
  3 Hawaiian Standard Time -600
  4 Alaskan Standard/Daylight Time -540
  5 Pacific Standard/Daylight Time -480
  6 Mountain Standard/Daylight Time -420
  7 US Mountain Standard Time -420
  8 Central Standard/Daylight Time -360
  9 Mexico Standard/Daylight Time -360
  10 Canada Central Standard Time -360
  11 SA Pacific Standard Time -300
  12 Eastern Standard/Daylight Time -300
  13 US Eastern Standard Time -300
```

I'm in the US Eastern time zone, so I must use 13:

```
R1-PBX(config-telephony)#time-zone 13
```

 Make sure your router has a valid NTP source or three (see Chapter 38 for more information). Time is very important to a phone system, since it's displayed on every phone and is used in reporting. You might be surprised at how many people use their phones as a clock.

This router has an AIM-CUE card that supplies voicemail using CUE. The configuration of CUE is outside the scope of this book, but we must configure the PBX with the extension to dial to reach the voicemail system. I've configured CUE to answer to extension 222:

```
R1-PBX(config-telephony)#voicemail 222
```

Since this is a PBX, when you pick up a handset, you get a PBX dial tone. To dial a number outside the PBX's dial plan, you must select a number that will get you an outside line. Traditionally, this number has been 9, but many offices prefer 8 to avoid confusion when people need to dial 911. I prefer 9, so that's what I'm going to use. We'll see how to prevent 911 dial confusion later in this chapter:

```
R1-PBX(config-telephony)#secondary-dialtone 9
```

Finally, we must configure how the system handles transfers, which occur when you forward a call from one extension to another. There are four transfer types supported in CME: *blind*, *full-blind*, *full-consult*, and *local-consult*. These can be distilled down to two major types: blind and consult.

Blind transfer

Imagine that you've answered a call, but it's for Frank Doodleputz in Accounting. You need to get the call to Frank, but you dislike talking to him, since he talks continuously about his adventures playing tuba with his polka band. If you forward the call to Frank's extension but don't call him to warn him about it, that's a blind transfer. You may also hear this referred to as an *unannounced*, *unattended*, or *cold* transfer.

Consult transfer

Imagine that you've answered a call, but it's for Barbie Browneyes in Marketing. You've been looking for an excuse to talk to her for months, and here is your chance. You forward the call to her extension, she answers the phone, and you exchange pleasantries. After listening to her angelic voice for a bit, you tell her that you have a call for her. When you hang up, the original call is transferred to her extension. You've introduced the caller to her with your soothing baritone, practically guaranteeing another conversation with Barbie the next time you meet. You may also hear this referred to as an *announced*, *attended*, or *warm* transfer.

In our telephony configuration, we have the following options:

```
R1-PBX(config-telephony)#transfer-system ?
  blind          Perform blind call transfers (without consultation) with single
                 phone line using Cisco proprietary method
  full-blind     Perform call transfers without consultation using H.450.2 or
                 SIP REFER standard methods
  full-consult   Perform H.450.2/SIP call transfers with consultation using
                 second phone line if available, fallback to full-blind if second
                 line unavailable. This is the recommended mode for most systems.
                 See also 'supplementary-service' commands under 'voice service
                 voip' and dial-peer.
  local-consult  Perform call transfers with local consultation using second
                 phone line if available, fallback to blind for non-local
                 consultation/transfer target. Uses Cisco proprietary method.
```

I tend to like the full-consult method because it behaves the way that most users expect it to. Yeah, sometimes you have to talk to the Doodleputzes of the world, but it's worth it in the long run when you have to forward a call to Barbie:

```
R1-PBX(config-telephony)#transfer-system full-consult
```

Dial Plan

Dial plans can be simple, or they can be ridiculously complicated. Try to keep yours as simple and as logical as possible. This example will be very simple, since I have only four phones. Each user will have an extension, numbered from 101 upward. Since there are only four people in the company, I will assign line 111 to be the outside line. This will also be the general mailbox for callers who don't know who they want to speak to.

If you have multiple locations, you'll need to come up with a more complicated plan that makes sense. Just remember to account for growth; however many offices you have now, you may increase this number by at least one order of magnitude over time. If you've got 10, count on 100. If you've got 130, count on 1,000. Why? Because it's easier to get users used to long numbers now than it is to change the dial plan in the future. I'd go so far as to say that it's easier to get everyone in a company to convert from Windows to Mac than it is to have them learn a new dial plan. People don't like change, especially when it comes to their phone system.

Logical dial plans make your dial peers simpler. They also make your numbering scheme easier to understand. If you've got 100 branches with five users in each branch, consider six-digit extensions like BBBXXX, where B equals the branch number and X equals the extension number. Thus extension 501002 would be extension 2 in branch 501. Users within branch 501 could just dial 2, but users in other branches would need to dial 501002.

The five users in my company and their extensions are shown here:

GAD	101
Lauren	102
Meghan	103
Colleen	104
General	111

There are no hard and fast rules here, but try to make it scalable. My solution here is fine for a small company that will never grow, but what happens when I get an 11th user? Suddenly I'll have users who have extension numbers higher than the general mailbox. The users won't care, but it can cause headaches when we need to create dial peers.

Voice Ports

This router has a POTS line connected to it. The POTS lines are connected into a four-port FXO card in HWIC slot number 1. I'm going to configure only one of them for now:

```
R1-PBX(config)#voice-port 0/1/0
R1-PBX(config-voiceport)#connection plar 111
R1-PBX(config-voiceport)#caller-id enable
```

The `caller-id` command should be obvious. It allows caller ID information to be sent to the phones. The `connection plar` command forwards incoming calls to extension 111. Notice that I haven't specified the line's phone number anywhere. It's not needed, but to keep things clear, we can label the port with a description:

```
R1-PBX(config-voiceport)#description 555-123-4567
```

Chances are, in a corporate environment, you're more likely to have a PRI T1 installed. Small offices, like the one used in this chapter's examples, don't have the need for 24 lines, so they may still use POTS lines.

Configuring Phones

There are two major steps to configuring the buttons on your phones. There are many things that Cisco IP phones can do, but at a minimum, users will need to be able to pick up a line and make a call. The lines on a phone are tied to the phone's buttons. Phones have a lot of buttons, but the buttons on the right side of the Cisco phone's display (*line keys* in Cisco parlance) are the ones to which I am referring. Generally, these buttons are assigned to a phone extension, which is an *ephone-DN* in our configuration. In our example, I'll be assigning the owner of the phone's line to the first button and configure buttons for the other three users below it. Finally, I'll add another button for the general line. The buttons are shown in Figure 30-4. Notice the system message (GAD Technology) shown on the bottom left of the screen.

The lines need to be configured first. For each line, we need a configuration entry called an `ephone-dn`. The `ephone-dn` serves multiple purposes; first, it defines an extension on the system, and second, it provides a reference for us to use when configuring the phone buttons. Let's see how that works.

Ephone-DN

Since I'm the king boss, I get the first extension. To define it, I'll create the first ephone-dn:

```
R1-PBX(config)#ephone-dn 1 dual-line
R1-PBX(config-ephone-dn)#
```

The `dual-line` keyword enables this line to make or receive a call while already on a call. Generally, I make all lines dual-line capable.

The next step is to define the line number for the ephone-DN. This is the extension number that the user will be assigned. That's not always the case, as you'll see, but for this line, it's true. Since I'm the king boss and get the first extension, my line number is 101:

```
R1-PBX(config-ephone-dn)#number 101
```

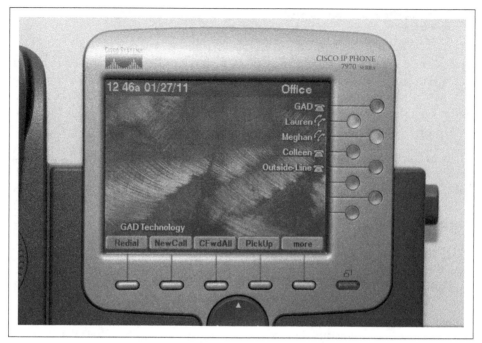

Figure 30-4. Cisco 7970 phone; the line key buttons are on the right

You can assign multiple numbers to a line using the secondary keyword as follows:

```
R1-PBX(config-ephone-dn)#number 101 secondary 9735554333
```

We won't use the secondary feature, though, so we're just going to stick with `number 101` for now.

There are multiple ways in which we can describe this line: label, description, and name. The label will be what appears next to the button on your phones. The description is the DN Qualified Display Name, which appears on the top of the phone when assigned to the first button. The name is the DN username that appears on other phones receiving calls from this number. In Figure 30-4, you can see that the first button is labeled as GAD. Here's how we make that happen:

```
R1-PBX(config-ephone-dn)#label GAD
```

Looking again at Figure 30-4, notice that the top of the display says *Office*. This is displaying the DN Qualified Display Name for the first configured line. We configure this with the `description` command:

```
R1-PBX(config-ephone-dn)#description Office
```

I've configured voicemail to answer extension 222, so now I'll configure this line to forward to voicemail. There are two important times that voicemail should be automatically invoked: when the line is busy and when the line is not answered. Both are configured with the `call-forward` command:

```
R1-PBX(config-ephone-dn)# call-forward busy 222
R1-PBX(config-ephone-dn)# call-forward noan 222 timeout 10
```

The number after the `timeout` keyword is the number of seconds that the system will wait until forwarding an unanswered call. This doesn't have to be to voicemail—we can just as easily forward to another user's extension if we want to.

I've configured the remaining lines in a similar fashion. Here's the configuration for all four user lines:

```
ephone-dn  1  dual-line
 number 101
 label GAD
 description Office
 name Office
 call-forward busy 222
 call-forward noan 222 timeout 10
!
ephone-dn  2  dual-line
 number 102
 label Lauren
 description Lauren
 name Lauren
 call-forward busy 222
 call-forward noan 222 timeout 10
!
ephone-dn  3  dual-line
 number 103
 label Meghan
 description Meghan
 name Meghan
 call-forward busy 222
 call-forward noan 222 timeout 10
!
ephone-dn  4  dual-line
 number 104
 label Colleen
 description Colleen
 name Colleen
 call-forward busy 222
 call-forward noan 222 timeout 10
```

Next, I'm going to assign an ephone-DN for what I'll call the general line. In this environment, there is only a single outside phone line. I'll be configuring this line on every phone so that when a call comes in, every phone will ring and the button will light.

 As I've already said, IP telephony is an almost limitless topic. This may not be the way you would design your system. Since every installation is different, I encourage you to discover more about VoIP to learn how to configure different solutions.

I'm assigning the line number 111 for this purpose. As you'll see in a minute, it's important to keep this within my dialing plan:

```
ephone-dn 10 dual-line
  number 111
  label Outside-Line
  name Outside Line
  call-forward busy 222
  call-forward noan 222 timeout 15
```

 I learned the hard way that even when I had only one outside POTS line feeding the system, I still had to configure the extension as a dual line. Without dual line configured on this line, when someone on the system calls voicemail from this extension, the extension becomes busy, even though the outside line is not in use. In this case, incoming calls will get forwarded to voicemail with a `call-forward busy` configured, or get a fast busy without. With dual line configured, should a call come in while the line is busy with a call to voicemail, the phone in use will beep and display the caller ID of the incoming call.

Paging

Here's a nice feature that's simple to install. We'll create a special dial number that, when dialed, will open a line on every phone configured to receive the call. The call will open a line, enable the speaker, and allow the caller to address the group. Multiple groups can be configured, though here I'll just configure one that will page every phone.

All we need to do is create an ephone-DN, but we need to incorporate the special `paging ip` command. This command allows us to configure a multicast address and port that will be used for paging. Here, I'll configure the system for paging when the number 555 is dialed:

```
R1-PBX(config)#ephone-dn 20
R1-PBX(config-ephone-dn)#number 555
R1-PBX(config-ephone-dn)#description Page All Phones
R1-PBX(config-ephone-dn)#paging ip 239.1.1.10 port 2000
```

You'll see in the next section how to configure the phones to listen for this paging group.

Ephone

Now that we have our extensions and incoming line configured, we need to configure the phones themselves. We do this with the `ephone` command. As with the `ephone-dn` command, we need to specify an ephone descriptor—a description helps to keep all the phones straight:

```
R1-PBX(config)#ephone 1
R1-PBX(config-ephone)#description GAD
```

Phones are referenced by their MAC addresses, which can be found on a sticker on the bottom of Cisco IP phones. Feel free to use your networking skills to learn the MAC address through other means:

```
R1-PBX(config-ephone)#mac-address 0019.AA96.D096
```

To make this phone part of the paging group we created earlier, we'll use the paging-dn command, followed by the DN numbered we created:

```
R1-PBX(config-ephone)#paging-dn 20
```

By configuring the phone type, the system will know which firmware files to serve it when it registers:

```
R1-PBX(config-ephone)#type 7971
```

Now it's time to configure the phone's buttons. In its simplest form, you specify the button number and pair it with an ephone-DN. Thus, 1:1 will attach the extension configured in ephone-DN 1 to button number 1 on the phone. The buttons are numbered from the top down. The phone model you're using will dictate how many buttons you can configure. Since I'm configuring a 7971G phone, I have eight buttons, of which I'll be using five.

Buttons can be configured in a number of interesting ways. Here's the system's output from the button help command:

```
R1-PBX(config-ephone)#button ?
  LINE  button-index:dn-index pairs example 1:2 2:5
Configuration line:button with separator feature options:
: normal phone lines
        example    button 1:2 2:5
s silent ring, ringer muted, call waiting beep muted
        example    button 1s2 2s5
b silent ring, ringer muted, call waiting beep not muted
        example    button 1b2 2b5
f feature ring
        example    button 1f2 2f5
        see also 'no dnd feature-ring'
m monitor line, silent ring, call waiting display suppressed
        example    button 1m2 2m5
        see also 'transfer-system full-consult dss'
w watch line (BLF), watch the phone offhook status via the phone's primary ephone-dn
        example    button 1w2 2w5
o overlay lines, combine multiple lines per physical button
        example    button 1o2,3,4,5
c overlay call-waiting, combine multiple lines per physical button
        example    button 1c2,3,4,5
        see also  'huntstop channel' for ephone-dn dual-line
x expansion/overflow, define additional expansion lines that are
        used when the primary line for an overlay button is
        occupied by an active call
        Expansion works with 'button o' and not with 'button c'
        example    button 4o21,22,23,24,25
                   button 5x4
                   button 6x4
```

```
Different separator options may be used for each button
     example    button 1:2 2s5 3b7 4f9 5m22 6w10
```

Not all options are available on all versions of CME. This output is from CME v8.0. Though it may seem daunting, the help display explains most of the options pretty well. I'm only going to use two of them, normal and monitor. Normal lines behave as you'd expect—when a call comes into this line, the phone will ring and the button will light up (assuming the phone has button lights).

Where it gets interesting is when you have the same extension configured on two phones. When both phones have simple buttons configured, the line rings on both phones. If the phones have lighted buttons like the 7970s do, the light blinks amber when the line rings. If the other phone has the line seized, the button glows red.

When the button is configured as a monitor button, the line does not ring when a call comes in. The button glows red as soon as the other phone goes off-hook on the line. The display screen will also react as appropriate for other events. For example, if there is a voicemail message waiting for the extension, an envelope will appear on the display next to the line's button on each phone. Here's an example. Extension 101 is my line. When someone calls that extension, my phone will ring, but the other phones (set to monitor this extension) will not. They will display an indication that my line is ringing, though.

I'm going to configure the main line on each phone as a standard button. I'll then monitor the other lines and add a final button for the general line and mailbox. Here's how I'll assign the buttons on my phone:

```
R1-PBX(config-ephone)#button  1:1 2m2 3m3 4m4 5:10
```

This will configure the phone buttons as shown in Figure 30-4.

The system will not allow you to assign the same DN to two buttons. Here I try to assign DN 3 to buttons 1 and 4:

```
R1-PBX(config-ephone)#button 1:3 4m3
duplicate dn [3] assignment: button 4, 3
  only button 1:3 accepted
```

Following this scheme, here are the configurations for the four phones in our small office:

Phone 1

```
ephone  1
 description GAD
 mac-address 0019.AA96.D096
 paging-dn 20
 type 7971
 button  1:1 2m2 3m3 4m4 5:10
```

Phone 2

```
ephone  2
 description Lauren
 mac-address 001D.4595.7FE5
 paging-dn 20
 type 7970
 button  1:2 2m1 3m3 4m4 5:10
```

Phone 3

```
ephone  3
 description Meghan
 mac-address 0012.4362.C4D2
 paging-dn 20
 type 7960
 button  1:3 2m1 3m2 4m4 5:10
```

Phone 4

```
ephone  4
 description Colleen
 mac-address 000D.BC50.FC2C
 paging-dn 20
 type 7960
 button  1:4 2m1 3m2 4m3 5:10
```

Each phone will ring for its primary assigned extension, and will also ring for incoming calls on the POTS line (button 5, linked to ephone-DN 10).

PTT

If you've got Cisco wireless IP phones such as the Cisco 7921G, you can configure the Push To Talk (PTT) button to initiate paging. Remember that we've got a paging-DN already set up. Here it is for review:

```
ephone-dn  20
 number 555 no-reg primary
 description Page All Phones
 paging ip 239.1.1.10 port 2000
```

Paging works with this configuration, but only when 555 is dialed. To get PTT working on the 7921G, we'll need to assign a button to a new DN, which will then reference the paging DN. It's a bit convoluted, but I didn't write the code, so you can't blame me.

First, we need to create another ephone-DN that references the paging-DN. This DN will use the intercom command, which in our case means, "When 556 is dialed, dial 555":

```
R1-PBX(config)#ephone-dn  21
R1-PBX(config-ephone-dn)# number 556
R1-PBX(config-ephone-dn)# name IP-Paging
R1-PBX(config-ephone-dn)# intercom 555 label "PTT Paging"
```

To make the button work on the Cisco 7921G, we need to use XML to configure the phone's PTT feature. We do this with the `service phone thumbButton1` command in the `telephony-services` section. Here I'm basically telling the phone, "When I push the PTT button, dial the DN assigned to button 6":

```
R1-PBX(config)#telephony-service
R1-PBX(config-telephony)#service phone thumbButton1 PTTH6
```

This method configures the phone so that the PTT button is assigned to button 6. If you have multiple 7921G phones and you do not want this behavior on all of them, see the Cisco documentation for alternative methods.

Finally, you'll need to assign button 6 (referenced in the preceding code as PTTH6) to ephone-DN 21:

```
R1-PBX(config)#ephone 2
R1-PBX(config-ephone)#button 6:21
```

Message waiting lamps

Though we're not configuring voicemail in this chapter, it's installed, so we need to configure the phones to interact with the AIM-CUE. One of the must-have features of voicemail is called MWI, short for Message Waiting Indicator.

MWI works with ephone-DNs. Unity Express dials a configured number appended with the extension to enable the message lamp. It then dials another configured number, again appending the extension in order to turn the message lamp off. I've configured CUE to dial 8000 to enable the lamps and 8001 to disable the lamps. We'll talk more about pattern matching in "Dial Peers" on page 551, but for now, understand that a period in a number string means *match any number*:

```
R1-PBX(config)#ephone-dn 40
R1-PBX(config-ephone-dn)#number 8000...
R1-PBX(config-ephone-dn)#mwi on
```

And here's the matching ephone-DN needed to turn the lamps off:

```
R1-PBX(config)#ephone-dn 41
R1-PBX(config-ephone-dn)#number 8001...
R1-PBX(config-ephone-dn)#mwi off
```

One of the fun ways to test this is to actually dial the number. Go to a phone, pick up the handset, and dial 8000xxx, where xxx is the extension of your phone. The light should come on. Dial 8001xxx, and it will turn back off.

 I absolutely don't recommend dialing your friend's MWI-on code at work, thus making him think he has a message when he has none. The confusion and frustration he will experience after days of his light mysteriously going on when there are no messages waiting is not funny at all. Seriously—don't do that.

This, by the way, is why I didn't number the extension for the outside line as the full 10-digit phone number. If I had, MWI would have required more complex dial peers or possibly variable-length dial peers.

Dial Peers

Dial peers seem to confuse a lot of people when they first encounter them. Logical thought is required to make them elegantly simple, which consumes time that a lot of engineers don't think they have. I've seen some horrendously complicated dial peers, numbering in the hundreds, that, after careful thought, we consolidated into fewer than 10. Think of dial peers like static routes—the more you can aggregate them, the happier you'll be.

Dial peers are another VoIP feature that's almost infinitely configurable. There are many ways to accomplish the same goal, so if you don't like the ones I've listed here, or can think of a better way to write them, by all means, give it a try.

There are many types of dial peers you can use, based on their intended purpose:

```
R1-PBX(config)#dial-peer ?
  cor         Class of Restriction
  data        Data type
  hunt        Define the dial peer hunting choice
  inbound     Define the inbound options
  outbound    Define the outbound options
  search      Define dial peer search service
  terminator  Define the address terminate character
  voice       Voice type
```

The only ones we're interested in here are voice dial peers. There are multiple types of voice dial peers, some of which aren't used much anymore. The type of dial peer you choose depends on where you're sending the call:

```
R1-PBX(config)#dial-peer voice 10 ?
  mmoip  Multi Media Over IP
  pots   Telephony
  voatm  Voice over ATM
  vofr   Voice over Frame Relay
  voip   Voice over IP
```

The two we are concerned with in this chapter are POTS and VoIP, so let's take a look at each.

POTS

POTS dial peers are used for referencing POTS lines. Clever, huh? In our small-office phone system, we've got only one POTS line, so we need to configure some POTS dial peers to send our calls there. Since we're only going to send a call to the POTS line if someone first dials 9, let's start with the simplest possible dial peer:

```
R1-PBX(config)#dial-peer voice 1 pots
R1-PBX(config-dial-peer)# destination-pattern 9T
R1-PBX(config-dial-peer)# port 0/1/0
```

The destination-pattern says, "Match the number 9, and then continue to capture digits until the timeout value expires." Imagine picking up a phone and dialing to order 400 copies of *Network Warrior*, Second Edition, to give as gifts. As you dial, you forget the last four digits of the phone number and hold the phone while you quickly look it up. The phone system will only wait for you so long before it gives up and delivers a reorder tone (fast-busy) to you. The reason the system waits is because of a configuration such as this combined with the *interdigit timer*. The interdigit timer tells the system how long to wait after each digit is dialed. The T tells the dial peer that the dialed number can be of any length.

In this example, the timeout value is configurable on the voice port:

```
R1-PBX(config)#voice-port 0/1/0
R1-PBX(config-voiceport)#timeouts interdigit ?
  <0-120>  seconds
```

Really, we could just leave this dial peer, and all outbound calls would work. The problem is that after any number is dialed, the user will have to wait for the interdigit time (default of 10 seconds on CME) to expire before the system initiates the call. I don't wait more than 2 seconds for a website to load. Do you think I'm going to wait 10 seconds for the phone system to initiate my call? Not a chance. That's why we configure more specific dial peers—to pacify short-tempered whiners like me.

Let's start with a dial peer that will match on 9+10-digit phone numbers:

```
R1-PBX(config)#dial-peer voice 100 pots
R1-PBX(config-dial-peer)# destination-pattern 9[2-9].........
R1-PBX(config-dial-peer)# port 0/1/0
R1-PBX(config-dial-peer)# forward-digits 10
```

There are two things to look at here. First, the destination-pattern of 9[2-9]......... (there are nine dots). The pattern means, "Someone dialed 9, then a number inclusive of 2 through 9, then nine other digits." Why 2–9? US-based area codes never start with the number 1. The forward-digits 10 command tells the router to send only the 10 rightmost digits, thus discarding the leading 9.

Apologies are in order to all my international readers. The dizzying array of phone number patterns throughout the world makes it unrealistic to cover them all. Since I've concentrated on US-based telephony, here are some things to know about US-based telephony:

- The format of US phone numbers is 1+NPA–NXX–Subscriber-Number.
- Phone numbers are traditionally shown as (NPA) NXX–9999, where 9999 is the subscriber number.
- 1 is often used as a "trunk code" to initiate a long-distance call (11-digit dialing).
- 1 is also the ITU country calling code for the US.
- NPAs (area codes) are three digits that start with [2–9].
- NXXs (CO exchange codes) are three digits that start with [2–9].
- 0 is used to dial the operator or to initiate operator-assisted calls.

Here's a POTS dial-peer pattern for people who dial a 9+1+10-digit number:

```
R1-PBX(config)#dial-peer voice 110 pots
R1-PBX(config-dial-peer)# destination-pattern 91..........
R1-PBX(config-dial-peer)# port 0/1/0
R1-PBX(config-dial-peer)# forward-digits 11
```

What about 911? We'll need a dial peer or two for that. Here's one that covers people dialing 9+911:

```
R1-PBX(config)#dial-peer voice 120 pots
R1-PBX(config-dial-peer)# destination-pattern 9911
R1-PBX(config-dial-peer)# port 0/1/0
R1-PBX(config-dial-peer)# forward-digits 3
```

And another for someone who panics and only dials 911:

```
R1-PBX(config)#dial-peer voice 130 pots
R1-PBX(config-dial-peer)# destination-pattern 911
R1-PBX(config-dial-peer)# port 0/1/0
R1-PBX(config-dial-peer)# forward-digits all
```

VoIP

VoIP dial peers, as you might imagine, are used when the call will be sent to an IP address or some similar destination. The destination should specifically not be an ATM or Frame Relay interface, since there are dial peers for that purpose.

The simplest form of dial peer sends the call to an IP address. We'll use one here for our voicemail system. Here, I've simplified it to its core functionality:

```
dial-peer voice 2 voip
 destination-pattern 222
 session target ipv4:192.168.1.11
 codec g711ulaw
```

If a call is destined for the number 222, send it to the IP address 192.168.1.11 and use the G.711 CODEC. There are a bunch of permutations we can and will use when we get to the "SIP" section, but in a nutshell, this is what a VoIP dial peer does.

Dial-peer pattern matching

Dial peers are processed according to strict rules, the details of which can be read elsewhere, but we need to cover some basics.

 The definitive guide for dial-peer matching in IOS is titled "Understanding Inbound and Outbound Dial Peers Matching on IOS Platforms." This document can be found on Cisco's website (*http://www .cisco.com/en/US/tech/tk652/tk90/technologies_tech _note09186a008010fed1.shtml*).

Outbound dial peers. *Outbound* refers to calls that are exiting the device being configured. The basic rule for outgoing dial peers is *the longest explicit match wins.* Let's say we have two dial peers that look like this:

```
dial-peer voice 3 voip
 destination-pattern 222...
 session target ipv4:10.10.10.10
!
dial-peer voice 4 voip
 destination-pattern 2222..
 session target ipv4:20.20.20.20
```

If you were to dial 222111, dial peer 3 would match. If you were to dial 2222111, dial peer 4 would match, even though the number also matches the pattern in dial peer 3.

Be careful, though, because when it comes to nonexplicit matching, the shortest will win. Let's look at another example:

```
dial-peer voice 10 voip
 destination-pattern 2..
 session target ipv4:10.10.10.10
!
dial-peer voice 20 voip
 destination-pattern 2......
 session target ipv4:20.20.20.20
```

With these two dial peers, if I dial 2111111, it will match dial peer 10, even though you may perceive dial peer 20 to be a better match.

Inbound dial peers. Inbound dial peers are evaluated in the following order:

1. Called number with `incoming called-number` command
2. Calling number with `answer-address` command
3. Calling number with `destination-pattern` command
4. Voice port configuration

5. Default dial peer 0

My examples in this chapter are very simple, so I've stuck with `destination-pattern`, since all my incoming calls will be automatically sent to a single extension as a result of the `plar 111` command on the voice port.

SIP

SIP has become a very popular protocol for a lot of reasons, not the least of which is the fact that it's an open standard. Many providers are now offering SIP trunks that allow businesses to serve their primary phone services over their existing Internet links.

SIP devices are called user agents. A user agent can be a user agent client, a user agent server, or both. As you might expect, an IP phone will generally be a user agent client. Our CME PBX will also be a client, since we'll need to register with a server at the provider's network to make outbound calls. If we were using SIP phones, then it could be a user agent server as well. There are four types of servers you'll likely encounter:

Proxy server
> Also commonly called a SIP proxy, a proxy server sends requests on a client's behalf if the client doesn't know the address of the recipient in advance. A SIP proxy is sort of like a computerized phone operator.

Redirect server
> Redirect servers send message back to the user agent if the recipient has been moved or deleted.

Registrar
> Phones (*user agent clients* in SIP-speak) have to register, and the registrar's job is to process these registrations. On Cisco IP PBXs, skinny phones register with their MAC addresses. SIP clients register with their IP addresses.

Location server
> When a registrar processes a registration, the locations of the clients are stored in a location server.

Usually, all these server types are combined into a single server for ease of connection by end users. Unless you're building SIP systems, you'll probably see only a SIP proxy, or if you need to enter multiple SIP server designations (as we will), they will likely all be the same server address.

SIP call setup is pretty straightforward at a high level. SIP messages may include the following:

REGISTER
> Register a client's location to the server.

INVITE
> When you dial a phone, it sends a SIP INVITE.

ACK

Acknowledge a SIP message.

CANCEL

Cancel an INVITE before the call has been established. This is like hanging up the phone while the far end is ringing.

INFO

Used for signaling during a call.

OPTIONS

Ask SIP server for information about its capabilities.

BYE

Terminate a connection. When you hang up a SIP phone, it sends a BYE message.

Figure 30-5 shows how two small offices might connect if each had Cisco CME and SIP trunks provided by different SIP providers. Each phone will register using SCCP to the local CME-enabled router. Each router's CME will register as a SIP client to its provider's SIP servers.

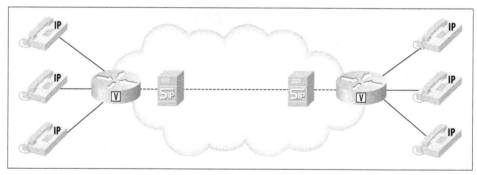

Figure 30-5. Two offices with CME and SIP trunks

The beauty of most SIP providers is that they often provide complete PBX functionality, negating the need for a CME (or any other) IP PBX at the site. This also negates the need for people like us, which is why so many companies are pursuing this model. A non-CME SIP environment is shown in Figure 30-6.

In this case, the phones register directly with the SIP provider's SIP proxy. Since there are no CMEs involved, SCCP is no longer used.

If you're building or experimenting with a SIP-only solution using Cisco IP phones, you may have to load SIP-based firmware on them. Check Cisco's website to see how to accomplish this. Many newer Cisco phones are SIP-based, so check carefully if you're buying used.

In this case, all PBX functionality—from extension provisioning to voicemail and beyond—is handled by the provider in the cloud. Configuration is generally done by

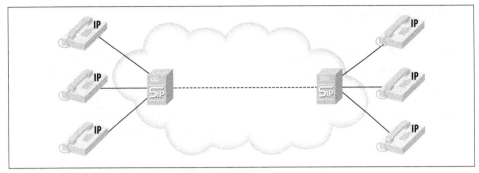

Figure 30-6. Two offices using SIP phones without CME

minimally trained users through the provider's web page. If you have Vonage or Magic Jack or something similar, you are using this model. Many executives love this idea, as evidenced by the many SIP providers that have entered the game in the past few years. I've seen companies with over 100 employees use this type of service successfully.

For our example, I'm going to build a SIP trunk into the cloud for our CME system. We'll get a SIP trunk or two from a SIP provider and configure the system to use these trunks for incoming and outgoing calls. The network will resemble what's shown in Figure 30-7.

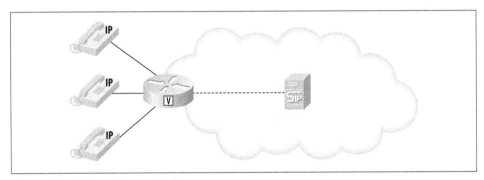

Figure 30-7. SIP trunk for outside lines

The first thing to do is get the information regarding the trunks from the SIP provider, who will likely provide you with a phone number for inward dialing, a username, and a password. The username and password may also be called an *authname* and *key*. For our two SIP trunks, we've been given the following information:

SIP Proxy information
   SIP-Proxy: sbc.sip-provider.com

Trunk1
   Number: 9735554222
   Authname: 557333333

Key: 123456789
Trunk2
Number: 9735554333
Authname: 608222222
Key: 123456789

This information will allow us to authenticate to the SIP proxy in order to register our trunks for incoming calls, and to authenticate when making outgoing calls.

 Ten different SIP providers may have 10 different methods for connectivity. While the underlying principles and protocols are the same, don't fall into the trap of thinking that what you see here will work as-is on any SIP trunk. By following this example, though, you should be able to determine what you might need to change to make your system work with your provider.

There are a few sections of the SIP configuration that we need to address. First is the `voice service voip` section:

```
voice service voip
 allow-connections h323 to h323
 allow-connections h323 to sip
 allow-connections sip to h323
 allow-connections sip to sip
 no supplementary-service sip moved-temporarily
 no supplementary-service sip refer
```

 If you're building an actual system from this chapter, now that we're working on SIP, make sure to shut down your voice port and POTS dial peers so that they don't interfere with what we're doing here.

The first few commands should be pretty obvious. The last two commands disable the SIP 302 *moved temporarily* message to make call forwarding work better on a CME system. The last command addresses the CME, sending a SIP REFER message when calls are transferred on CME. Since most SIP providers don't support the SIP REFER message, this forces the CME to hairpin the call instead.

We need to do three things to make our SIP trunks work at a basic level: tell CME where the SIP proxy is located, authenticate outbound calls, and register our numbers so that the SIP provider knows where to send calls destined for us. We perform all of these actions within the `sip-ua` configuration mode. First we'll define the SIP proxy:

```
R1-PBX(config)#sip-ua
R1-PBX(config-sip-ua)#registrar dns:sbc.sip-provider.com expires 3600
R1-PBX(config-sip-ua)#sip-server dns:sbc.sip-provider.com
```

Notice that the SIP servers are referenced as DNS hostnames. You can reference them as IPv4, IPv6, or DNS names. If you enter an incorrectly formed address, you will be treated to this most excellent of error messages:

```
R1-PBX(config-sip-ua)#registrar gad
Malformed SIP Registrar address. Valid formats are:
        ^((dns:.*)|(ipv4:[0-9]?[0-9]?[0-9]?\.[0-9]?[0-9]?[0-9]?\.[0-9]?[0-9]
?[0-9]?\.[0-9]?[0-9]?[0-9]?(:[0-9]+)?)|(ipv6:\[([0-9A-Fa-f.:])+\](:[0-9]+)?))$
```

Not so scary if you're used to regular expressions, but a tad overwhelming if you're not. If you're using DNS names in your config, you'll need to at least configure your router to know where to get DNS resolved:

```
R1-PBX(config)#ip name-server 192.168.1.200
R1-PBX(config)#ip name-server 192.168.1.205
```

If, like me, you've disabled DNS lookups on all your routers so you don't have to watch your typing mistakes try to resolve in DNS, you're going to need to turn that functionality back on for DNS to work:

```
R1-PBX(config)#ip domain-lookup
```

The following command puts the name from the `registrar` command into SIP *diversion headers* used in call forwarding. Normally, CME will use the domain from the router itself:

```
R1-PBX(config-sip-ua)# host-registrar
```

Next, we'll configure the authentication outbound:

```
R1-PBX(config-sip-ua)# authentication username 608222222 password 123456789
```

Notice that I'm not referencing my telephone numbers anywhere. That threw me when I first started with SIP on CME. That may be different with different providers, too. For example, providers may use your assigned telephone number as your username.

Next, we'll configure the credentials to allow our CME to register with our provider:

```
R1-PBX(config-sip-ua)# credentials username 608222222 password 123456789 realm
voip.sip-provider.com
```

Here's where things get complicated. I have two SIP trunks, and I'll need to register them both if I want people to be able to call into both numbers. Here's what happens when I register the second trunk:

```
R1-PBX(config-sip-ua)#$ credentials username 557333333 password 123456789 realm
voip.sip-provider.com
```

No errors whatsoever!

Here's the rub. It only works great with multiple trunks like this on IOS 15.0(1)XA5 or later, which means I'm on CME 8.0. During my testing, I had to upgrade my router four times to get certain features pertaining to SIP to work right. I started this project on CME 3.3, and everything worked fine. By the time I was done with multiple SIP trunks, I had gone from CME version 3.3 to 4.0 to 7.1 to 8.0, where it finally all worked. The main driver for this was having dual SIP trunks actively registered to the same provider. That's likely not a requirement for many people, since, depending on your service, you may be able to send and receive multiple calls at once on a single SIP trunk (unless you need multiple inbound numbers). A more likely scenario is to have two SIP trunks from different providers for diversity and/or redundancy.

If these trunks were from different providers, we'd have multiple realms configured.

One of the benefits of running on CME 8.0 and later is the ability to include the number keyword in the credentials command. The problem I discovered with my provider was that if I actually included the phone number, the trunks wouldn't register properly. I needed to add the username into the number field to make it work:

```
R1-PBX(config-sip-ua)# credentials number 608222222 username 608222222 password
123456789 realm voip.sip-provider.com
R1-PBX(config-sip-ua)# credentials number 557333333 username 557333333 password
7 123456789 realm voip.sip-provider.com
```

Again, different providers may deal with this differently, so you might have to play around to determine what works best for your situation.

To see if your credentials worked, use the show sip-ua register status command:

```
R1-PBX#sho sip-ua register status
Line            peer            expires(sec)  registered   P-Associated-URI
============    ============    ============  ===========  ================
101             20001           1857          yes
102             20002           1857          yes
103             20003           1857          yes
104             20004           1857          yes
557333333       -1              2340          yes
608222222       -1              2145          yes
```

The way I've designed this system, the SIP trunks will be used only for communication outside the office. Thus, the phones do not need to register with the SIP provider. By default, they will try and, depending on how your SIP provider is configured and the type of service you've bought, they may very well succeed. I don't want that to happen, so I'm going to prevent it by telling each ephone-DN *not* to register with SIP. To prevent your extensions from registering to your SIP provider, use the no-reg keyword on your ephone-dn number statements. This affects only the SIP connectivity. The normal SCCP phone registration will work just fine:

```
R1-PBX(config-ephone-dn)#ephone-dn 1 dual-line
R1-PBX(config-ephone-dn)#number 101 no-reg
```

If you've decided to actually apply your SIP telephone number to an extension, you can exclude only the extension from registering. I've opted not to do this for the reasons concerning MWI addressed previously. If you want to try this, configure such a scenario like this:

```
R1-PBX(config-ephone-dn)#ephone-dn 1 dual-line
R1-PBX(config-ephone-dn)#number 101 secondary 9735554333 no-reg primary
```

After repeating this for each of our four internal extensions, the SIP registration status looks much cleaner:

```
R1-PBX#sho sip-ua register stat
Line            peer            expires(sec)  registered   P-Associated-URI
=============   =============   ============  ===========  =================
557333333       -1              2000          yes
608222222       -1              1805          yes
```

Some timers and retry counters that work for me are included next. These all relate to SIP messages and should be fairly obvious based on the command syntax.

 If you look online for SIP trunking to CME examples, you'll see various versions of these timer values. It may seem odd to have to retry all these SIP messages, but it's not just about packets being lost. I've often seen SIP invites come back "unauthorized," only to have the retry accepted without incident.

```
R1-PBX(config-sip-ua)# retry invite 2
R1-PBX(config-sip-ua)# retry response 3
R1-PBX(config-sip-ua)# retry bye 2
R1-PBX(config-sip-ua)# retry cancel 2
R1-PBX(config-sip-ua)# retry register 10
R1-PBX(config-sip-ua)# timers connect 100
R1-PBX(config-sip-ua)# timers register 250
```

SIP and NAT

SIP doesn't always play well with NAT. Since the SIP messages contain the IP address of the device originating the messages, it's common for them to include private IP addresses, which the receiving device likely won't be able to route properly.

On Cisco CME, enter the following commands to make SIP work with NAT:

```
R1-PBX(config)#sip-ua
R1-PBX(config-sip-ua)# nat symmetric role active
R1-PBX(config-sip-ua)# nat symmetric check-media-src
R1-PBX(config-sip-ua)# connection-reuse
```

The connection-reuse sip-ua command is hidden in every version of IOS I've used (up to and including version 15.0(1)XA5).

Here's the entire sip-ua configuration section for reference:

```
sip-ua
 credentials number 608222222 username 608222222 password 7 023510541B4B3B294D5A48
realm voip.sip-provider.com
 credentials number 557333333 username 557333333 password 7 023510541B4B3B294D5A48
realm voip.sip-provider.com
 authentication username 608222222 password 7 023510541B4B3B294D5A48
 nat symmetric role active
 nat symmetric check-media-src
 no remote-party-id
 no redirection
 retry invite 2
 retry response 3
 retry bye 2
 retry cancel 2
 retry register 10
 timers connect 100
 timers register 250
 registrar dns:sbc.sip-provider.com expires 3600
 sip-server dns:sbc.sip-provider.com
 connection-reuse
 host-registrar
```

Now that our SIP trunks are configured, we need to configure the router to accept and send calls. We will need to create two VoIP dial peers. First, we need to do some prep work. I'd like all my calls to use the G.711 CODEC, because I'm a sucker for good sound quality. If that's not allowed, I'll allow G.729r8 to be used. I need to configure a voice class with my preferences. I'll then reference this class in my dial peer:

```
R1-PBX(config-dial-peer)#voice class codec 1
R1-PBX(config-class)# codec preference 1 g711ulaw
R1-PBX(config-class)# codec preference 2 g729r8
```

Now I can build my incoming SIP dial peer:

```
R1-PBX(config)#dial-peer voice 89 voip
R1-PBX(config-dial-peer)# description [ Incoming SIP Call ]
```

We need to tell the dial peer that SIP is the protocol in use and that calls matching should be sent to the SIP server, which was configured in the sip-ua section earlier. This may seem odd, since the call is incoming, but the SIP server on the router will know how to transcode the call to H323 so it can be sent to our Cisco phones:

```
R1-PBX(config-dial-peer)# session protocol sipv2
R1-PBX(config-dial-peer)# session target sip-server
```

This next line matches any incoming call:

```
R1-PBX(config-dial-peer)# incoming called-number .%
```

This may or may not work for you. In my case, it looked great and everything was fine until I started working with voicemail and MWIs. Since the AIM-CUE uses SIP to send MWI commands, these messages were matched by the SIP dial peer, making all the phones ring anytime a message lamp status was changed. I fixed this by making the called-number command match any number longer than the MWI-configured dial peer's match. My MWI dial peer is 800[12]..., so this statement matches anything longer than 7 digits. Since all incoming calls from my SIP provider have full 10-digit numbers, this works perfectly:

```
R1-PBX(config-dial-peer)# incoming called-number .......+
```

Here's where we reference the voice class that we just configured so we can support G.711 and G.729:

```
R1-PBX(config-dial-peer)# voice-class codec 1
```

This command helps translate DTMF tones to *named telephone events*. On compressed calls (such as when G.729 is used), DTMF tones can become distorted. This command translates DTMF tones into text-based numbers used in SIP packets:

```
R1-PBX(config-dial-peer)# dtmf-relay rtp-nte
```

Voice activity detection (VAD) is also sometimes called *silence suppression*. With VAD enabled, perceived silence causes the router to stop sending voice packets. While this saves a lot of bandwidth, the resulting pure silence often causes people to think that the call has died. This can be prevented by injecting synthetic *comfort noise* on the far end to simulate normal background noise. I generally prefer to avoid VAD altogether unless I have a dramatic need for it:

```
R1-PBX(config-dial-peer)# no vad
```

With our incoming dial peer configured, theoretically we should now be able to receive calls. In actuality, though, we cannot. Though our SIP trunks are properly registered, any calls to our numbers results in a "number not available" message from our provider. This is maddening if you're new to the whole SIP experience, so let me save you some heartache. Here's the output from debug ccsip messages showing the failed call (see "Troubleshooting" on page 567 for more information):

```
Feb  3 19:07:35.084: //-1/xxxxxxxxxxxx/SIP/Msg/ccsipDisplayMsg:
Sent:
SIP/2.0 404 Not Found
Via: SIP/2.0/UDP 208.73.146.95:5060;branch=z9hG4bK6gmsg8300gk1vmsmj4g0.1
From: "DONAHUE GARY    " <sip:+19735551212@192.168.101.113:5060>;tag=gK0a3f2f72
To: <sip:9735554333@192.168.101.100:5060>;tag=3DF80A8-23C0
Date: Thu, 03 Feb 2011 19:07:35 GMT
Call-ID: pcst129676005500836719310@192.168.201.113
CSeq: 1 INVITE
Allow-Events: telephone-event
Server: Cisco-SIPGateway/IOS-12.x
Reason: Q.850;cause=1
Content-Length: 0
```

Clearly, the SIP trunk is registered and the SIP INVITE made it to our router, but the provider still tells callers that our number is unavailable. The problem is that we have no ephone-DNs configured with the phone number. If we added the following ephone-DN and applied it to a phone button, the calls would ring on that phone:

```
ephone-dn 22  dual-line
 number 9735554333 no-reg primary
 label SIP-Line-1
 name SIP-Line-1
```

I didn't want to do this, for a couple of reasons. First, since this is a small office with only a few extensions, I'd prefer to have all the phones show only extension numbers and not the actual outside phone number. Second, since the phone number doesn't match my rudimentary dial plan (all my extensions are 1xx), if I create a generic voice mailbox for the outside line, the message indicator lights won't work.

 Again, there are almost limitless ways to accomplish this. You may prefer to have a button with your actual phone number attached. That's fine, and I encourage you to play around with such a config. Also, if we used the secondary number example shown previously, the SIP calls would have rung on that configured extension.

Instead of adding a new ephone-DN for the SIP trunks, I've created a new extension for each:

```
ephone-dn 32  dual-line
 number 132 no-reg primary
 label SIP-4332
 call-forward busy 222
 call-forward noan 222 timeout 15
!
ephone-dn 33  dual-line
 number 133 no-reg primary
 label SIP-4333
 call-forward busy 222
 call-forward noan 222 timeout 15
```

But when the SIP INVITE comes in, it is looking for 9735554333 or 9735554222. How do I get the call sent to my new ephone-DNs? The answer lies in a feature called *voice translations*.

With voice translations, I can translate any incoming or outgoing number in just about any way I want. Translation rules work like regular expressions. Here, I tell rule 1 within translation-rule 11 to replace any number with 133:

```
R1-PBX(config)#voice translation-rule 11
R1-PBX(cfg-translation-rule)# rule 1 /.*/ /133/
```

Once the rule is created, we need to assign it to a voice translation-profile and name it:

```
R1-PBX(config)#voice translation-profile SIP-Inbound
R1-PBX(cfg-translation-profile)# translate called 11
```

Once that's done, we can assign our translation-profile to the incoming dial peer:

```
R1-PBX(config)#dial-peer voice 89 voip
R1-PBX(config-dial-peer)# translation-profile incoming SIP-Inbound
```

Remember when I said I'd broken MWI SIP dial peer? This translation is one of the reasons why. When the AIM-CUE dialed 8000101 to enable the MWI on my phone, it used SIP. The number matched the dial peer (.%) and was then translated to 133 because of this rule, which caused all the phones to ring.

Now when I get an incoming call, it's routed to the phones that have ephone-DN 33 assigned to them. Here's the same call as before, but with the incoming translation applied:

```
Feb  3 19:29:03.668: //-1/xxxxxxxxxxxx/SIP/Msg/ccsipDisplayMsg:
Sent:
SIP/2.0 100 Trying
Via: SIP/2.0/UDP 208.73.146.95:5060;branch=z9hG4bK8v1qso00903gmpgqi501.1
From: "DONAHUE GARY   " <sip:+19735551212@192.168.101.112:5060>;tag=gK025eb403
To: <sip:9735554333@192.168.101.100:5060>
Date: Thu, 03 Feb 2011 19:29:03 GMT
Call-ID: pcst12967613435153831028210@192.168.201.112
CSeq: 1 INVITE
Allow-Events: telephone-event
Server: Cisco-SIPGateway/IOS-12.x
Content-Length: 0


Feb  3 19:29:03.672: //-1/xxxxxxxxxxxx/SIP/Msg/ccsipDisplayMsg:
Sent:
SIP/2.0 180 Ringing
Via: SIP/2.0/UDP 208.73.146.95:5060;branch=z9hG4bK8v1qso00903gmpgqi501.1
From: "DONAHUE GARY   " <sip:+19735551212@192.168.101.112:5060>;tag=gK025eb403
To: <sip:9735554333@192.168.101.100:5060>;tag=3F32A10-2138
Date: Thu, 03 Feb 2011 19:29:03 GMT
Call-ID: pcst12967613435153831028210@192.168.201.112
CSeq: 1 INVITE
Allow: INVITE, OPTIONS, BYE, CANCEL, ACK, PRACK, UPDATE, REFER, SUBSCRIBE, NOTIFY,
INFO, REGISTER
Allow-Events: telephone-event
Remote-Party-ID: <sip:133@192.168.0.3>;party=called;screen=no;privacy=off
Contact: <sip:608222222@192.168.0.3:5060>
Server: Cisco-SIPGateway/IOS-12.x
Content-Length: 0
```

 This output can vary significantly from version to version. When I was using CME v4, the To: <sip:9735554333... actually changed to <sip: 133... after the translation was applied.

Now that we've got calls coming in, let's set up our outgoing dial peers. With your newfound experience, you probably realize that we'll likely have to do translations outbound, too. In my case, if I dial from any extension, the SIP messages will include those extensions in the SIP INVITE and I'll get a "not authorized" message from the provider, because my extensions are not registered. I'll need to create a translation rule that replaces anything that could appear as a source calling number and replace it with my username for one of my SIP trunks:

```
R1-PBX(config)#voice translation-rule 1
R1-PBX(cfg-translation-rule)# rule 1 /^.*/ /608222222/
```

Another problem involves the fact that I've configured the system to require users to dial 9 before calling an external number. Since any call that even makes it to the SIP trunk will have required the caller to dial 9, we'll need to strip those leading 9s from outgoing calls:

```
R1-PBX(config)#voice translation-rule 2
R1-PBX(cfg-translation-rule)# rule 1 /^9/ //
```

Next, we'll need to create a new translation profile that includes these two rules:

```
R1-PBX(config)#voice translation-profile SIP-Outbound
R1-PBX(cfg-translation-profile)# translate calling 1
R1-PBX(cfg-translation-profile)# translate called 2
```

Now that we've got our translations in order, we can create the dial peer. You could create the dial peer before you made the translation, but it just wouldn't work. The commands are all the same as the incoming peer with the exception that we're configuring a destination-pattern this time. This destination pattern matches any 11-digit dialed number that starts with a 9:

```
R1-PBX(config)#dial-peer voice 90 voip
R1-PBX(config-dial-peer)# translation-profile outgoing SIP-Outbound
R1-PBX(config-dial-peer)# destination-pattern 9..........
R1-PBX(config-dial-peer)# session protocol sipv2
R1-PBX(config-dial-peer)# session target sip-server
R1-PBX(config-dial-peer)# dtmf-relay rtp-nte
R1-PBX(config-dial-peer)# codec g711ulaw
R1-PBX(config-dial-peer)# no vad
```

This works well for dialing friends and family, but one thing we need to consider is people dialing 911 for emergencies. There are a couple of ways to deal with this, depending on whether your provider supplies E-911 service. Ours does, so all we need to do is provide a dial plan that will accept 911 as a destination pattern, since the one we just created does not. The first dial peer addresses people who dial 911 in a panic without remembering that they need to dial 9 first:

```
R1-PBX(config)#dial-peer voice 91 voip
R1-PBX(config-dial-peer)# translation-profile outgoing SIP-Outbound
R1-PBX(config-dial-peer)# destination-pattern 911
R1-PBX(config-dial-peer)# session protocol sipv2
R1-PBX(config-dial-peer)# session target sip-server
R1-PBX(config-dial-peer)# dtmf-relay rtp-nte
R1-PBX(config-dial-peer)# codec g711ulaw
R1-PBX(config-dial-peer)# no vad
```

We need another to match in the case that someone *does* remember to dial 9 first. Everything is the same except for the dial peer identifier and the destination pattern, so to save space, I'll show only the destination pattern:

```
R1-PBX(config-dial-peer)# destination-pattern 9911
```

Here's a destination pattern that allows 411 and 911 (as well as 211, 311, 511, 611, 711, and 811):

```
R1-PBX(config-dial-peer)# destination-pattern 9[2-9]11
```

And another that allows for international calls (from the US):

```
R1-PBX(config-dial-peer)# destination-pattern 9011T
```

At this point, our system is capable of sending and receiving calls over the SIP trunk. If someone calls either number provided to us, extension 133 will ring. If a user dials any properly formed phone number, it will forward out the SIP trunk. Users can call extension-to-extension with ease, and voicemail works all around.

Troubleshooting

Troubleshooting VoIP and SIP on CME is pretty straightforward, but as with any feature on Cisco equipment, you need to know the magic commands that show the useful bits of information.

Phone Registration

When phones register properly, they will generate console messages, which you can see through Telnet or SSH if you've issued the terminal monitor command. Here are the console messages that resulted when I turned on my softphone:

```
Feb  3 01:44:52.667: %IPPHONE-6-UNREGISTER_NORMAL: ephone-10:SEP001C42D1565D
IP:192.168.10.1 Socket:7 DeviceType:Phone has unregistered normally.
Feb  3 01:45:32.264: %IPPHONE-6-REG_ALARM: 25: Name=SEP001C42D1565D Load= 7.0.5.0
Last=Initialized
Feb  3 01:45:32.268: %IPPHONE-6-REGISTER: ephone-10:SEP001C42D1565D IP:10.211.55.11
Socket:8 DeviceType:Phone has registered.
```

Here's the message that resulted when I stopped the program without properly shutting it down (similar to unplugging an IP phone):

```
Feb  3 02:08:03.692: %IPPHONE-6-UNREGISTER_ABNORMAL: ephone-10:SEP001C42D1565D
IP:192.168.10.1 Socket:7 DeviceType:Phone has unregistered abnormally.
```

To see if your ephones are properly registered, use the show ephone command. Here, you can see that the first two configured ephones are not registered, but the third phone has registered properly. You can see which buttons are configured, which numbers are assigned to those buttons, and in what way:

```
R1-PBX#sho ephone

ephone-1[0] Mac:0019.AA96.D096 TCP socket:[-1] activeLine:0 whisperLine:0 UNREGISTERED
mediaActive:0 whisper_mediaActive:0 startMedia:0 offhook:0 ringing:0 reset:0
reset_sent:0 paging 0 debug:0 caps:0
IP:0.0.0.0* 0 Unknown 0  keepalive 0 max_line 0 available_line 0
```

```
          paging-dn 20
          Preferred Codec: g711ulaw
          Lpcor Type: none

          ephone-2[1] Mac:001D.4595.7FE5 TCP socket:[-1] activeLine:0 whisperLine:0 UNREGISTERED
          mediaActive:0 whisper_mediaActive:0 startMedia:0 offhook:0 ringing:0 reset:0
          reset_sent:0 paging 0 debug:0 caps:0
          IP:0.0.0.0* 0 Unknown 0  keepalive 0 max_line 0 available_line 0
          paging-dn 20
          Preferred Codec: g711ulaw
          Lpcor Type: none

          ephone-3[2] Mac:0012.4362.C4D2 TCP socket:[2] activeLine:0 whisperLine:0 REGISTERED
          in SCCP ver 11/9 max_streams=0
          mediaActive:0 whisper_mediaActive:0 startMedia:0 offhook:0 ringing:0 reset:0
          reset_sent:0 paging 0 debug:0 caps:8
          IP:192.168.2.131 * 49916 Telecaster 7960  keepalive 87 max_line 6 available_line 6
          button 1: cw:1 ccw:(0 0)
            dn 3  number 103 CH1    IDLE          CH2    IDLE          shared with monitor-ring
          button 2: cw:1 ccw:(0 0)
            dn 1  number 101 CH1    DOWN          CH2    DOWN          monitor-ring shared
          button 3: cw:1 ccw:(0 0)
            dn 2  number 102 CH1    IDLE          CH2    IDLE          monitor-ring shared
          button 4: cw:1 ccw:(0 0)
            dn 4  number 104 CH1    IDLE          CH2    IDLE          monitor-ring shared
          button 6: cw:1 ccw:(0 0)
            dn 10 number 111 CH1    IDLE          CH2    IDLE          shared
          paging-dn 20
          Preferred Codec: g711ulaw
          Lpcor Type: none
```

TFTP

Watching what TFTP is up to can help you see what your phones are doing when they register. Enable TFTP debug with the debug tftp events command:

```
R1-PBX#debug tftp events
TFTP Event debugging is on
```

Now I'll reboot my softphone and see what it does:

```
R1-PBX(config-ephone)#restart
restarting 001C.42D1.565D
Feb  3 01:34:30.291: %IPPHONE-6-UNREGISTER_NORMAL: ephone-10:SEP001C42D1565D
IP:192.168.10.1 Socket:6 DeviceType:Phone has unregistered normally.
Feb  3 01:34:30.335: TFTP: Looking for CTLSEP001C42D1565D.tlv
Feb  3 01:34:30.451: TFTP: Looking for CTLSEP001C42D1565D.tlv
Feb  3 01:34:30.615: TFTP: Looking for CTLSEP001C42D1565D.tlv
Feb  3 01:34:30.795: TFTP: Looking for SEP001C42D1565D.cnf.xml
Feb  3 01:34:30.951: TFTP: Looking for CTLSEP001C42D1565D.tlv
Feb  3 01:34:31.143: TFTP: Looking for XMLDefault.cnf.xml
Feb  3 01:34:31.643: TFTP: Opened system:/its/vrf1/XMLDefault.cnf.xml, fd 10,
size 3088 for process 210
Feb  3 01:34:32.451: TFTP: Finished system:/its/vrf1/XMLDefault.cnf.xml,
time 00:00:00 for process 210
```

It's also a great tool to use when you add ringtones or desktop images for color phones. When you first choose the option on a 7970 to change your desktop image, the phone will request the *List.xml* file from the proper directory. Here, we can see that in action:

```
Feb  3 01:37:56.976: TFTP: Looking for Desktops/320x212x12/List.xml
Feb  3 01:37:56.980: TFTP: Opened flash:Desktops/320x212x12/List.xml, fd 10,
size 1116 for process 210
Feb  3 01:37:57.400: TFTP: Finished flash:Desktops/320x212x12/List.xml, time
00:00:00 for process 210
```

Dial Peer

On older versions of IOS, the command to debug your dial peers was debug dial peer. That's changed to debug voip dialpeer all on modern versions:

```
R1-PBX#debug dialpeer
This CLI command is now 'debug voip dialpeer all'
R1-PBX#debug voip dialpeer all
voip dialpeer all debugging is on
```

You can also debug more specific dialpeer events:

```
R1-PBX#debug voip dialpeer ?
  all       Enable all debugs
  default   Enable default debugs
  detail    detail debug
  error     major call and software errors debug
  function  function debug
  inout     inout debug
  <cr>
```

This debug delivers some verbose output that looks like this:

```
Feb  3 21:08:20.935: //-1/xxxxxxxxxxxx/DPM/dpMatchPeersCore:
   Calling Number=608222222, Called Number=608222222, Peer Info
Type=DIALPEER_INFO_SPEECH
Feb  3 21:08:20.939: //-1/xxxxxxxxxxxx/DPM/dpMatchPeersCore:
   Match Rule=DP_MATCH_DEST; Called Number=608222222
Feb  3 21:08:20.939: //-1/xxxxxxxxxxxx/DPM/dpMatchPeersCore:
   No Outgoing Dial-peer Is Matched; Result=NO_MATCH(-1)
Feb  3 21:08:20.939: //-1/xxxxxxxxxxxx/DPM/dpMatchSafModulePlugin:
   dialstring=608222222, saf_enabled=1, saf_dndb_lookup=1, dp_result=-1
Feb  3 21:08:20.939: //-1/xxxxxxxxxxxx/DPM/dpMatchPeersMoreArg:
   Result=NO_MATCH(-1)
Feb  3 21:08:20.939: //-1/xxxxxxxxxxxx/DPM/dpAssociateIncomingPeerCore:
   Calling Number=+19735551212, Called Number=, Voice-Interface=0x0,
   Timeout=TRUE, Peer Encap Type=ENCAP_VOIP, Peer Search Type=PEER_TYPE_VOICE,
   Peer Info Type=DIALPEER_INFO_SPEECH
```

By using the show dialplan number *number-string* command, you can see how and if your dial peers are matching. This command doesn't actually dial anything, but just reports on which dial peers have matched your number string. The output can be extensive, but it's easy to find the relevant information. Here's an example from when our system was configured to use POTS dial peers:

```
R1-PBX#sho dialplan number 92111111111
Macro Exp.: 92111111111

VoiceEncapPeer100
        peer type = voice, system default peer = FALSE, information type = voice,
        description = `',
        tag = 100, destination-pattern = `9[2-9].........',
        voice reg type = 0, corresponding tag = 0,
        allow watch = FALSE
        answer-address = `', preference=0,
        CLID Restriction = None
        CLID Network Number = `'
[--output truncated--]
```

Here's the same command run with only the VoIP dial peers enabled:

```
R1-PBX#sho dialplan number 92111111111
Macro Exp.: 92111111111

VoiceOverIpPeer90
        peer type = voice, system default peer = FALSE, information type = voice,
        description = `',
        tag = 90, destination-pattern = `9..........',
        voice reg type = 0, corresponding tag = 0,
        allow watch = FALSE
        answer-address = `', preference=0,
        CLID Restriction = None
        CLID Network Number = `'
```

SIP

To see if your SIP endpoints are registered, use the show sip-ua register status command. Since we're using SIP only for our trunks and we've used the no-reg keyword on our ephone-DNs, that's all we see. If we were using SIP phones, we'd see those numbers registered here as well:

```
R1-PBX#sho sip-ua reg status
Line           peer            expires(sec)  registered  P-Associated-URI
============   =============   ============  ==========  =================
557333333      -1              2175          yes
608222222      -1              2172          yes
```

To see all the messages that SIP sends and receives, use the debug ccsip messages command. This is a fabulous tool that will show you every bit of SIP communication from phone and trunk registrations to INVITES, CANCELs, BYEs, and all their associated responses. If you've got a problem with your SIP trunks, this is the command that will show you exactly what's going on:

```
R1-PBX#debug ccsip messages
SIP Call messages tracing is enabled
```

To give you an idea of how verbose SIP can be, here's the output from me dialing a phone number from my softphone, then hanging up before there's an answer:

```
*Feb  3 01:17:07.740: //-1/xxxxxxxxxxxx/SIP/Msg/ccsipDisplayMsg:
Sent:
INVITE sip:9735554471@sbc.sip-provider.com:5060 SIP/2.0
Via: SIP/2.0/UDP 192.168.0.3:5060;branch=z9hG4bKB1761
From: <sip:9735551212@sbc.sip-provider.com>;tag=383B4-0
To: <sip:9735554471@sbc.sip-provider.com>
Date: Thu, 03 Feb 2011 01:17:07 GMT
Call-ID: 26F3EF99-2E6A11E0-800D80A2-733EA81A@192.168.0.3
Supported: 100rel,timer,resource-priority,replaces,sdp-anat
Min-SE:  1800
Cisco-Guid: 0563478376-0778703328-2148040866-1933486106
User-Agent: Cisco-SIPGateway/IOS-12.x
Allow: INVITE, OPTIONS, BYE, CANCEL, ACK, PRACK, UPDATE, REFER, SUBSCRIBE, NOTIFY,
INFO, REGISTER
CSeq: 102 INVITE
Max-Forwards: 70
Timestamp: 1296695827
Contact: <sip:9735551212@192.168.0.3:5060>
Expires: 180
Allow-Events: telephone-event
Proxy-Authorization: Digest username="9735551212",realm="voip.sip-provider.com",
uri="sip:9735554471@sbc.sip-provider.com:5060",
response="48fab7d8750961aa91e43f11879ddd4f",nonce="9967d6506474325b254afb6d6bc1baf4",
algorithm=md5
Content-Type: application/sdp
Content-Disposition: session;handling=required
Content-Length: 264

v=0
o=CiscoSystemsSIP-GW-UserAgent 8383 1800 IN IP4 192.168.0.3
s=SIP Call
c=IN IP4 192.168.0.3
t=0 0
m=audio 18674 RTP/AVP 0 101
c=IN IP4 192.168.0.3
a=rtpmap:0 PCMU/8000
a=rtpmap:101 telephone-event/8000
a=fmtp:101 0-16
a=ptime:20
a=direction:active

*Feb  3 01:17:07.844: //-1/xxxxxxxxxxxx/SIP/Msg/ccsipDisplayMsg:
Received:
SIP/2.0 100 Trying
Via: SIP/2.0/UDP 192.168.0.3:5060;branch=z9hG4bKB1761
From: <sip:9735551212@sbc.sip-provider.com>;tag=383B4-0
To: <sip:9735554471@sbc.sip-provider.com>
Call-ID: 26F3EF99-2E6A11E0-800D80A2-733EA81A@192.168.0.3
CSeq: 102 INVITE
Timestamp: 1296695827

*Feb  3 01:17:11.004: //-1/xxxxxxxxxxxx/SIP/Msg/ccsipDisplayMsg:
Sent:
CANCEL sip:9735551212@sbc.sip-provider.com:5060 SIP/2.0
Via: SIP/2.0/UDP 192.168.0.3:5060;branch=z9hG4bKB1761
```

```
From: <sip:9735551212@sbc.sip-provider.com>;tag=383B4-0
To: <sip:9735551212@sbc.sip-provider.com>
Date: Thu, 03 Feb 2011 01:17:07 GMT
Call-ID: 26F3EF99-2E6A11E0-800D80A2-733EA81A@192.168.0.3
CSeq: 102 CANCEL
Max-Forwards: 70
Timestamp: 1296695831
Reason: Q.850;cause=16
Content-Length: 0


*Feb  3 01:17:11.112: //-1/xxxxxxxxxxxx/SIP/Msg/ccsipDisplayMsg:
Received:
SIP/2.0 200 OK
Via: SIP/2.0/UDP 192.168.0.3:5060;branch=z9hG4bKB1761
From: <sip:9735551212@sbc.sip-provider.com>;tag=383B4-0
To: <sip:9735551212@sbc.sip-provider.com>;tag=aprq1smnhp0-l46jaq00000c6
Call-ID: 26F3EF99-2E6A11E0-800D80A2-733EA81A@192.168.0.3
CSeq: 102 CANCEL
Timestamp: 1296695831


*Feb  3 01:17:11.136: //-1/xxxxxxxxxxxx/SIP/Msg/ccsipDisplayMsg:
Received:
SIP/2.0 487 Request Terminated
Via: SIP/2.0/UDP 192.168.0.3:5060;branch=z9hG4bKB1761
From: <sip:9735551212@sbc.sip-provider.com>;tag=383B4-0
To: <sip:9735551212@sbc.sip-provider.com>;tag=131481110
Call-ID: 26F3EF99-2E6A11E0-800D80A2-733EA81A@192.168.0.3
CSeq: 102 INVITE
Timestamp: 1296695827
Contact: <sip:9735551212@208.73.146.95:5060;transport=udp>
Content-Length: 0
User-Agent: Cisco-SIPGateway/IOS-12.x


*Feb  3 01:17:11.144: //-1/xxxxxxxxxxxx/SIP/Msg/ccsipDisplayMsg:
Sent:
ACK sip:9735551212@sbc.sip-provider.com:5060 SIP/2.0
Via: SIP/2.0/UDP 192.168.0.3:5060;branch=z9hG4bKB1761
From: <sip:9735551212@sbc.sip-provider.com>;tag=383B4-0
To: <sip:9735551212@sbc.sip-provider.com>;tag=131481110
Date: Thu, 03 Feb 2011 01:17:07 GMT
Call-ID: 26F3EF99-2E6A11E0-800D80A2-733EA81A@192.168.0.3
Max-Forwards: 70
CSeq: 102 ACK
Allow-Events: telephone-event
Content-Length: 0
```

## CHAPTER 31

Introduction to QoS

Quality of service (QoS) is deployed to prevent data from saturating a link to the point that other data cannot gain access to it. Remember, WAN links are serial links, which means that bits go in one end and come out the other end in the same order. Regardless of whether the link is a 1.5 Mbps T1 or a 155 Mbps OC3, the bits go in one at a time, and they come out one at a time.

QoS allows certain types of traffic to be given a higher priority than other traffic. Once traffic is classified, traffic with the highest priority can be sent first, while lower-priority traffic is queued. The fundamental purpose of QoS is to determine which traffic should be given priority access to the link.

Figure 31-1 shows two buildings connected by a single T1. Building B has a T1 connection to the Internet. There are servers and roughly 100 users in each building. The servers replicate their contents to each other throughout the day. The users in each building have IP phones, and interbuilding communication is common. Users in both buildings are allowed to use the Internet.

The only path out of the network in Building A is the T1 to Building B. What happens when every user in that building decides to use that single link at once? The link is only 1.5 Mbps, and each user may have a 100 Mbps (or even 1 Gbps) Ethernet connection to the network.

> A good designer should never have built a network with these limitations, and the admin (if one exists) should not have let the problem get so severe. Still, the real world is filled with networks like this just waiting for someone to fix them. Many smaller companies don't have dedicated network administrators on staff, so problems like this can and do occur.

Let's say, for example, that 30 of the 100 users start to download the free demo of *GAD's Rockin' Guitar Solos, Volume VIII*. Let's also say that 20 of the users decide to surf the O'Reilly website. Another 20 need to download the latest service packs from

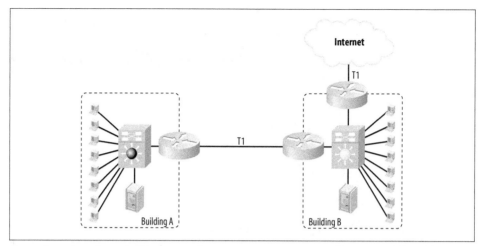

Figure 31-1. Simple two-building network

their favorite operating system vendors, and the remaining 30 want to use their VoIP phones.

The problem is that the T1 isn't "big" enough for the amount of traffic that's about to be created. Imagine you had a hose with a funnel on top, as shown in Figure 31-2. The hose is capable of allowing one liter per minute to flow through it. As long as you only pour one liter of water every minute into the funnel, you'll be fine.

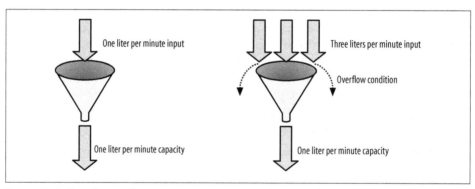

Figure 31-2. Overflow condition

Now, imagine you decide to get a little crazy and pour three liters into the funnel in one minute's time. The hose will only allow one liter per minute to flow out the bottom of the funnel. So what happens to the other two liters? They will first fill the funnel, then pour over the top of the funnel all over the floor, literally creating an *overflow* condition.

Our T1 is similar, but instead of water, we've got packets, which have the property of being discrete logical objects as opposed to being a fluid. A T1 can handle roughly

1,500,000 bits per second. When the rate of bits being sent to the T1 exceeds this rate, the T1 interface on the router buffers as many of the packets as possible (like the funnel does with the water), and then, when the buffer gets full, it overflows. Instead of spilling water all over the floor, the interface drops packets. At this point, data goes into the proverbial "bit bucket." Sadly, that's just a fun term. There's no bucket—when packets are dropped, they are gone forever.

Water is just water, but some types of packets may be more important than other types of packets. Packets are categorized in different ways: UDP, TCP, FTP, HTTP, and VoIP, to name a few. Not only can different packets have different priorities, but in many instances, they can be time-sensitive as well. Some protocols require that packets arrive in order. Other protocols may be sensitive to packet loss. Let's take a look at some of these protocols and see how they differ:

TCP

>   TCP includes algorithms that alert the sending station of lost or damaged packets so they can be resent. Because of this, TCP-based applications are generally not sensitive to lost packets; in addition, they tend to be less time-sensitive than UDP-based applications.

UDP

>   UDP does not do any error checking and does not report on lost packets. Because of this, UDP-based applications may be sensitive to packet loss.

HTTP

>   HTTP is TCP-based. Generally, HTTP applications are not time-sensitive. When you're viewing a web page, having to wait longer for an image to load due to a dropped packet is not usually a problem.

FTP

>   FTP is TCP-based. FTP is not a real-time protocol, nor is it time-sensitive. If packets are dropped while you're downloading a file, it's usually not a problem to wait the extra time for the packets to be resent.

Telnet and SSH

>   Telnet and SSH are both TCP-based. While they may appear to be real time, they're not. When packets are resent, the problem manifests as slow responses while you're typing. This may be annoying, but no damage is done when packets are dropped and resent.

VoIP

>   VoIP is UDP-based for the Real-Time Protocol (RTP) voice stream and TCP-based for the call-control stream. VoIP requires extreme reliability and speed, and cannot tolerate packets being delivered out of order. The use of UDP may seem odd, since UDP is not generally used for reliable packet delivery. VoIP uses UDP to avoid the processing and bandwidth overheads involved in TCP. The speed gained from using UDP is significant. Reliability issues can be resolved with QoS; in fact, VoIP is one of the main reasons that companies deploy QoS.

Assuming a FIFO (first in, first out) interface for this example, packets may be sent out of a serial interface in a noncontiguous fashion. In Figure 31-3, there are three types of packets being delivered: HTTP, FTP, and voice. Voice information, in particular, is very sensitive to packets being delivered out of order. It is also very sensitive to packets being lost. Remember, voice traffic is UDP-based, and there is no reliable transport mechanism, so if the buffer overflows and a voice packet is dropped, it's gone forever. This will result in choppy voice calls, irritated users, and executives yelling at you.

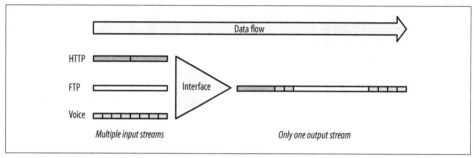

Figure 31-3. Packets through a serial interface

QoS can alleviate (if not, perhaps, solve) these problems. QoS can be daunting, as it has a lot of facets. If you decide at some point to pursue the CCIE, you'll need to know them all in detail, and you'll need to know how to abuse them in all sorts of odd ways. Most of those test-specific games don't have any basis in the real world, though. For our purposes, we will stick to more common scenarios.

In the real world, QoS is often used for a couple of reasons. Either there's some sort of streaming media (like voice or video) that requires low latency and timely delivery, or you've got an oversubscribed link and the powers that be want to make it work better so they don't have to buy a more expensive one. Perhaps the new circuit has been ordered, but due to facility problems, it won't be delivered for 120 days. QoS is the answer to help make the existing link a little more useful until the bigger link is delivered.

QoS can also be used for some more interesting applications. For example, you can configure your network so that Telnet and SSH have priority over all other traffic. When a virus hits and you need to telnet to your routers, the Telnet and/or SSH traffic will always get through (assuming you've rate-limited the CPUs on said routers). Or, if you're eager to please the boss, you can prioritize his traffic above everyone else's (except, of course, your own) so he'll have a better online experience. While these examples may seem far-fetched, I've been asked to do just these sorts of things for customers. In many cases, the Operations department needs better network access than the rest of the company. And once an executive learns about QoS, he may demand that he get "better" treatment on the network. I wouldn't recommend this, but I've seen it happen.

In a nutshell, any traffic that can be identified can be prioritized. Deciding whether the traffic should be prioritized (and, if so, in what order) is your job, and it can be an interesting one, to say the least.

Types of QoS

The term QoS is used to describe any of the myriad functions used to limit how much bandwidth may be used, guarantee how much bandwidth may be used, or prioritize certain traffic over other traffic. Technically, QoS is only one of a broader range of protocols and ideas. The same term can refer to CoS (class of service), QoS, queuing, marking, policing, or even traffic shaping.

For example, on Cisco routers, any serial link under 2 Mbps has weighted fair queuing (WFQ) enabled. To quote the Cisco documentation:

> WFQ is one of Cisco's premier queuing techniques. It is a flow-based queuing algorithm that does two things simultaneously: it schedules interactive traffic to the front of the queue to reduce response time, and it fairly shares the remaining bandwidth between high bandwidth flows.

Sounds like QoS to me! It is, and it's probably already in use on your network. Turning off WFQ on a saturated link can have a dramatic impact.

Some forms of QoS are very simple to implement, and affect only the interfaces on which they are configured. Other types can be installed on a single interface or deployed from end to end on an enterprise network. VoIP is probably the biggest reason a large-scale QoS deployment might be considered.

Consider Figure 31-4, which shows a simple two-building network with VoIP phones. There are PCs and IP phones in both buildings. With a simple installation, all resources share the network equally, but this is a problem in a VoIP world, because voice packets must be delivered in a timely fashion, in order, and should not be dropped. Because the VoIP voice stream is UDP-based, reliable transport for these packets is not guaranteed like it is in TCP. VoIP packets must compete for bandwidth with other traffic when other protocols are in use.

Let's assume that a VoIP call is active between Buildings A and B, and everything is working fine. Now, let's say a PC in Building A pulls a large file from the server in Building B using FTP. Suddenly, the voice call gets choppy. If you've got luck like mine, the call will be from the CEO to the payroll company about your raise—which will now be canceled because the voice quality was so bad.

At any rate, let's look at the problem and see if we can come up with some solutions by discussing the way QoS works and how different types of QoS might be deployed.

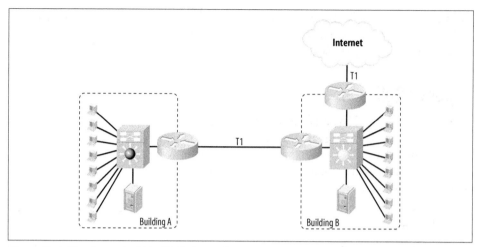

Figure 31-4. Simple two-building VoIP network

QoS Mechanics

QoS is usually deployed by first marking packets, then policing the packets, and, finally, scheduling the packets. *Marking* refers to deciding what priority a packet should be and labeling it accordingly. For example, a voice RTP stream would have the highest priority. *Policing* refers to the actions the router takes based on how the packets are marked. For example, we might specify that any packet marked with the highest priority should be guaranteed 10 percent of the overall link's available bandwidth. *Scheduling* refers to the interface actually serving the packets in the order determined by how the marked packets are policed. In other words, in the case of high-priority voice RTP packets, we will deliver them first and then deliver all other packets according to their priorities (if applicable).

All of these steps can be carried out on the same device or on separate devices. For example, Cisco IP phones can automatically set their voice RTP packets to a high priority. This means you don't have to test for that packet type on the router. Marking on a router adds processing load, so if it can be offloaded to a device that can do it natively, that's generally a good idea.

Priorities

Every IP packet has a field in it called the type of service (TOS) field. This eight-bit field is split up into a couple of sections that can be a little confusing. The beauty of the design is buried in its logic, so hang in there while I explain.

Two primary types of IP prioritization are used at Layer 3: *IP precedence* and *differential services* (diffserv).

IP precedence goes way back to the early days of the Internet. Diffserv is much newer. The values for diffserv are called *differential service code point* (DSCP) values.

The TOS field is illustrated in Figure 31-5.

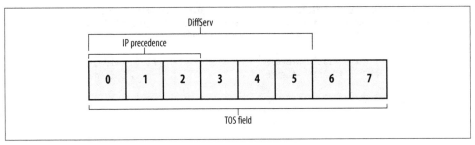

Figure 31-5. The IP TOS field

The field is eight bits long, with the first three bits used for IP precedence. The IP precedence values are called *service mappings*, and are defined in RFC 795 as follows:

```
Network Working Group                                    J. Postel
Request for Comments:  795                                    ISI
                                                  September 1981

                        SERVICE MAPPINGS
                        ----------------

This memo describes the relationship between the Internet Protocol (IP) [1]
Type of Service and the service parameters of specific networks.

The IP Type of Service has the following fields:

    Bits 0-2:  Precedence.
    Bit   3:  0 = Normal Delay,      1 = Low Delay.
    Bits  4:  0 = Normal Throughput, 1 = High Throughput.
    Bits  5:  0 = Normal Relibility, 1 = High Relibility.
    Bit 6-7:  Reserved for Future Use.

      0     1     2     3     4     5     6     7
   +-----+-----+-----+-----+-----+-----+-----+-----+
   |                 |     |     |     |     |     |
   |   PRECEDENCE    |  D  |  T  |  R  |  0  |  0  |
   |                 |     |     |     |     |     |
   +-----+-----+-----+-----+-----+-----+-----+-----+

    111 - Network Control
    110 - Internetwork Control
    101 - CRITIC/ECP
    100 - Flash Override
    011 - Flash
    010 - Immediate
    001 - Priority
    000 - Routine
```

The early Internet (this RFC was written in 1981) was pretty simple by today's standards, and three bits of IP precedence were fine. But eventually, the issue of scalability became apparent as users began to want more than eight levels of distinction in their priorities. So, along came RFC 2474, which redefined the TOS field:

3. Differentiated Services Field Definition

A replacement header field, called the DS field, is defined, which is intended to supersede the existing definitions of the IPv4 TOS octet [RFC791] and the IPv6 Traffic Class octet [IPv6].

Six bits of the DS field are used as a codepoint (DSCP) to select the PHB a packet experiences at each node. A two-bit currently unused (CU) field is reserved and its definition and interpretation are outside the scope of this document. The value of the CU bits are ignored by differentiated services-compliant nodes when determining the per-hop behavior to apply to a received packet.

The DS field structure is presented below:

```
  0   1   2   3   4   5   6   7
+---+---+---+---+---+---+---+---+
|          DSCP         |  CU   |
+---+---+---+---+---+---+---+---+

  DSCP: differentiated services codepoint
  CU:   currently unused
```

Here's where the beauty of the design comes into play. Let's assume our TOS field contains the bits 10100000. The TOS field is always eight bits (an octet). If we look at it using the rules of IP precedence, only the first three bits are significant, giving us a value of 5. If we look at it using the rules of diffserv, however, the first six bits are significant, giving us a value of 40. And if we look at the entire field, with all eight bits being significant, we get a value of 160. The relationship between IP precedence, diffserv, and the TOS field is shown in Figure 31-6.

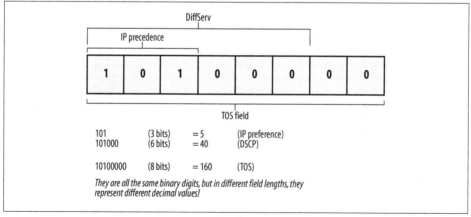

Figure 31-6. Different decimal values depending on the number of significant bits in the TOS field

Knowing that a value of 160 in the TOS field equals an IP precedence of 5 can be valuable when you're looking at packet captures. Because the field is known only as TOS to IP, the packet-capture tool will usually report the TOS value.

CoS is a Layer-2 form of QoS. CoS works under the same principles as IP precedence in that there are only eight values determined within a three-bit field. The difference is that these bits are in the 802.1P frame header, not the IP header. CoS values are Ethernet-specific, so they will be lost if frames are forwarded out of Ethernet networks. The good news is that because they map so perfectly to IP precedence values, rules can be created to read CoS values and translate them to IP precedence values.

In Cisco catalyst switches, there can be multiple queues for each Ethernet interface. CoS values can be mapped to these queues, allowing for prioritization. Ethernet priorities can be different from WAN-link priorities, though in practice, they're usually mapped one to one.

Table 31-1 shows how CoS, IP precedence, and DSCP values are related. If you take a look at IP precedence 5, you'll see that it is the same as a DSCP value of between 40 and 47. The decimal value 40 is 101000 in binary. The decimal value 47 is 101111 in binary. However, 48 is 110000 in binary—the first three bits change from 101 to 110, thus changing the IP precedence significant bits in the TOS field from 5 to 6.

Table 31-1. Priority levels of different QoS types

CoS	IP precedence	DSCP	Name
0	0	0–7	Routing (Best Effort)
1	1	8–15	Priority
2	2	16–23	Immediate
3	3	24–31	Flash
4	4	32–39	Flash-Override
5	5	40–47	Critical
6	6	48–55	Internet
7	7	56–63	Network

Because the IP precedence values and the DSCP values are so closely related, they can usually be interchanged. For example, if you're running a diffserv environment that uses DSCP values, but you have IP phones that will mark packets using only IP precedence values, you're still OK, because a diffserv value of 40 is the same bitwise as an IP precedence value of 5.

Flavors of QoS

The following are the most commonly seen forms of QoS. If you're working with a VoIP network, you'll probably see CBWFQ on your routers and CoS on your switches:

WFQ

WFQ is the default queuing mechanism on 2 Mbps and slower serial links. For most implementations, the default configuration works fine. WFQ can be configured very specifically, but it usually isn't configured at all. When VoIP is involved, low-latency queuing is typically used in place of WFQ.

Class-based weighted fair queuing

Class-based weighted fair queuing (CBWFQ) allows you to configure classes of traffic and assign them to priorities and queues. CBWFQ is the basis for low-latency queuing.

Priority queuing

Priority queuing works just how it sounds: queues are created, and each class of packet is assigned to an appropriate queue based on priorities you design.

Custom queuing

Custom queuing is one of those features that you probably won't see much. You'll see it on Cisco exams, and you may see it on networks that had specific problems to be solved where voice was not a concern at the time of the resolution. That's not to say that custom queuing is not suitable for voice, but again, low-latency queuing is the QoS method of choice for voice-enabled networks.

Low-latency queuing

Low-latency queuing (LLQ) is class-based WFQ with a *strict priority queue*—one in which hardware is used to send packets that need to be sent with the lowest latency possible. This is especially useful for voice and video, where any latency or delay causes problems. LLQ is the preferred method of QoS for voice networks, and is the QoS method I focus on in this book.

Traffic shaping

Traffic shaping is slightly different from other forms of queuing. Traffic shaping monitors traffic, and when a configured threshold is met, packets are queued until a point where we want them to be sent. Traffic shaping can be employed for better utilization of bandwidth or to properly pace packets for a smaller remote link. The benefits are a smoother use of bandwidth (Figure 31-7) and the fact that packets are buffered and not just dropped. The downside is that traffic shaping requires memory to function, because it buffers packets. Also, if the configured buffer overflows, packets will be discarded.

In the first edition of this book, I commented that traffic shaping is not used for voice and is not often seen in modern networks. I have since proven myself wrong. I love when I'm proven wrong, especially when I prove it myself. In fact, traffic shaping became such a big deal to one of my clients that I decided to add a section on it.

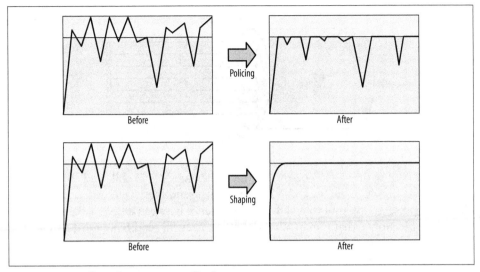

Figure 31-7. Traffic policing versus traffic shaping

Traffic-shaping theory

I was working in a large retail environment where we had 300+ retail stores all connecting back to the main office. We were upgrading from Frame Relay service (as low as 256k) to MPLS (full T1) at all sites. The main office upgraded from a DS3 (45 Mbps) to OC3 (155 Mbps). We were also preparing the network for VoIP.

We quickly ran into a problem when the MPLS cloud appeared to be dropping packets. It was, but not because of any fault of the provider. The problem was with the speed of the links on each end. We also discovered that the client had been having the same problem on its Frame Relay network for years. The client just figured that the links were so slow that painful performance was to be expected. When I did some packet analysis, I discovered that the protocols in use weren't using even half of the available link. Why, then, were they reporting bad performance?

The problem most people encounter when trying to grasp the concept of traffic shaping is a misunderstanding of how serial links work. Let's talk T1 versus DS3 for a bit. A DS3 is not a *bigger* pipe, as so many of us like to say. It is, instead, a *faster* link. We constantly reinforce the misconception that a DS3 is bigger than a T1, because we say things like, "A DS3 contains 28 T1s." That's true, but many people, especially executives, believe that the image in Figure 31-8 is representative of the difference, when it is not. This is further exacerbated by the constant misuse of the word *bandwidth*. Yes, I do this myself throughout the book. Why? Because I'm a creature of habit and for over 25 years we've all said that we need more bandwidth, when what we need is more *throughput*. If I tell an exec we need more throughput than the T1 can deliver, he'll ask me to explain. If I say we need more bandwidth, he'll ask me how much it will cost, and I'll get out of his office that much faster.

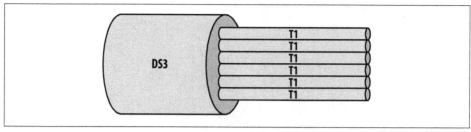

Figure 31-8. Faster links are not bigger links

Multiple T1s fit within a DS3 because of multiplexing. A DS3 still sends bits one at a time, as does an OC3 and an OC192. Faster links send bits, well, faster. Figure 31-9 shows a representation (not to scale) of the difference between a DS3, a T1, and a 256k fractional T1. Notice that they're all serial links. They all send bits one at a time. The DS3 just sends them faster.

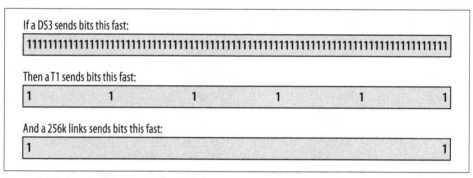

Figure 31-9. Speed of bits over different links

The problem in this case had to do with the fact that the branches could only receive bits at 256 *thousand* bits per second, while the main office was sending them at 45 *million* bits per second. The cloud was so efficient that it delivered the bits at 45 Mbps right up until the provider end of the branch's 256 Kbps link, where the buffers would then become overrun (Figure 31-10).

Figure 31-10. Speed difference between two links

The key here was buffers. The device at the provider end of the branch's fractional T1 link would buffer the packets, but the main office was sending bits so fast that the provider's router sending bits to the branch couldn't buffer all of them (Figure 31-11).

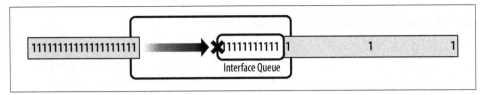

Figure 31-11. Too many bits in buffer—bits get dropped

This is not a link oversubscription issue. Utilization rarely exceeded 50 percent, yet packet loss was severe. This buffer problem was something we called *microbursting*, since the issue started and stopped so quickly that the bandwidth reports never showed it. This problem is also not limited to Frame Relay. It can occur anytime there is a large discrepancy in the speed of the links connecting two sites. This usually happens in multipoint or mesh topologies such as Frame Relay or MPLS, where there are one or more hub locations on the network that the rest of the network must access. As you'll see in the next chapter, it was easy to fix in a Frame Relay environment because of the virtual circuits used in the design.

Luckily, there was a way to solve our problem: traffic shaping. With traffic shaping, we used the main office router to queue the bits being sent to each branch. We then sent those bits out at a speed that the far end could accept. We did this by inserting the bits into the DS3's data stream at a predetermined interval, closely matching the speed at which the far end could receive them (Figure 31-12).

As soon as we implemented this solution, there was an immediate and dramatic improvement in the user experience at the branch, and we hadn't even upgraded the links yet. I love when that happens.

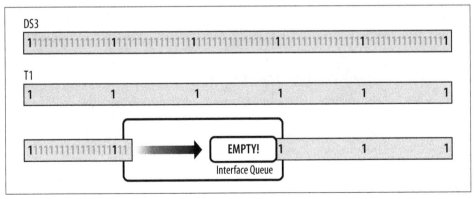

Figure 31-12. Traffic shaping slows down the bits

Traffic shaping can be pretty tough to understand and implement, but once you grasp it, you'll see how it can solve this type of problem. I know you're excited to see how it works, but be patient. I'll go into the configuration details in the next chapter.

Common QoS Misconceptions

There are some fairly wide-ranging misconceptions about what QoS can do. QoS is pretty complex, and a lot of people just skim the documentation and make assumptions based on what they've read. Still others read only executive summaries, or worse, extrapolate from information they've heard from other misinformed people.

QoS is a very useful technology, but it is not a miracle. It cannot make a T1 perform like a DS3, and it cannot completely prevent packets from being dropped. What QoS can do for you depends on your network and your requirements. If you have a DS3's worth of bandwidth requirements, no amount of queuing or reservation will make a T1 good enough. In this section, we'll examine a few common misconceptions.

QoS "Carves Up" a Link into Smaller Logical Links

I can't tell you how many times I've heard this in meetings and technical discussions regarding QoS. While the analogy is useful in certain circumstances, it is a dangerous one because the perception is that each "chunk" of the link cannot be used for other traffic. This is simply not true. The important thing to remember here is that while scheduling of packets always takes place, the limits set are really only enforced during congestion.

Using low-latency queuing as an example, let's think about the process. Packets come into the interface and are scheduled according to your configuration. Say you've used the following allocations for the link:

- Voice: 10 percent
- Voice control: 10 percent
- FTP: 10 percent
- Email: 10 percent
- Telnet/SSH: 10 percent
- Remainder (default queue): remaining 50 percent

It is very tempting to assume that the link is now divided into six pieces, with half evenly divided among voice, voice control, FTP, email, and Telnet/SSH, and the other half devoted to everything else. I think the reason this is such a common misconception is because it's a very simple view and, as such, is very easy to understand.

In reality, if email is the only traffic riding over the link, it will use up 100 percent of the link. The same is true for any type of traffic. When there is no congestion, any protocol can use any amount of available bandwidth (there I go again) it needs. Say a single user decides to download a massive file using HTTP. If there is no other data traversing the link, that download may saturate the link.

Now, say someone else starts a similar download using FTP. Because FTP is guaranteed 10 percent of the link, the scheduler will forward the FTP packets before it will forward the HTTP packets. Because the FTP queue will be serviced before the default queue, the FTP download will impact the HTTP download. Without getting too deep into how the scheduler works, it's worth pondering the following issue: in this scenario, with no other traffic, will FTP get better service or will HTTP get better service? FTP is only guaranteed 10 percent of the link. That means that HTTP can take up the remainder, right? Wouldn't that mean that HTTP would get better service than FTP?

The truth lies in the way the scheduler works. Because FTP is configured as a priority over HTTP (which falls into the default queue), the scheduler will service FTP packets before HTTP packets. The difference will probably not be obvious to the users, though, *unless there is congestion*. This is an important distinction. The scheduler will service FTP first, which means there will be a higher probability that HTTP packets will be dropped. Packets are dropped only when there is congestion, however, so both protocols will seem to operate normally until the link is saturated.

To summarize, if there is congestion, QoS helps determine which packets should be serviced and which packets can be dropped. In the case of the FTP versus HTTP example, since FTP is configured as a priority and HTTP is not, if there is congestion, HTTP packets will probably be dropped. Without congestion, FTP packets will be sent first, but the HTTP packets will, at worst, be queued for a short time before being sent.

QoS Limits Bandwidth

Let's get semantic. QoS does not *limit* bandwidth, it *guarantees* it, which is not the same thing. That is to say, if you have a 1.5 Mbps T1 and you want to run 1 Mbps of FTP across it, a configuration that guarantees 10 percent of the link for FTP will not limit FTP to only 10 percent.

Again, with no congestion, any protocol can use up as much bandwidth as it likes, provided no other configured protocol needs its share. If I configure 20 protocols on a DS3 and each one needs 1 Mbps, any one of those protocols can use all the bandwidth it wants, provided that (are you sick of me saying this yet?) there is no congestion on the link.

QoS Resolves a Need for More Bandwidth

As I've said earlier, if you need a DS3, QoS will not make your T1 "just as good." If you have an oversubscribed link, the best QoS can do is to prioritize which packets should be sent first, which also means it's determining which packets can be dropped! That's right—not only does QoS help some protocols, but it makes others worse. Remember the distinction, though: *only during congestion*.

If you have a T1 and you're trying to shove 20 Mbps through it, it doesn't matter how you prioritize and queue your packets, you're going to drop a lot of them.

Of course, QoS not resolving a need for bandwidth is the corollary to "throwing more bandwidth at the problem will not always fix it." Knowing the difference is what makes you, the engineer, valuable to management. If you have a T1 link and you're dropping 50 percent of your packets, assuming there are no physical layer problems, you probably need more bandwidth.

If you're running VoIP over a T1 and the calls are choppy, adding more bandwidth may not solve your problem, because the problem probably isn't simply a matter of bandwidth. The key here again is congestion. If you've got choppy calls and your links aren't congested, you need QoS to prioritize those voice packets so they get delivered first.

QoS Prevents Packets from Being Dropped

If you've got a problem with excessive packet drops, QoS will likely not solve it. What QoS will do for you is help you get the important packets through so that only the less important packets get dropped.

Traffic shaping *can* prevent packets from being dropped (assuming certain buffers are not similarly saturated), though this gets complicated, as you'll see. Additionally, traffic shaping only buffers packets to a point, so if you're oversubscribing your link all day long, traffic shaping won't help you.

QoS Will Make You More Attractive to the Opposite Sex

Sad to say, I'm afraid this isn't true either, though in theory, it is possible that your dream date could be reading this very book right now!

## CHAPTER 32

Designing QoS

Designing a QoS scheme can be a relatively simple task or a very large project. The scale of the solution depends on the complexity of your network and the needs of your business. As a general rule, I like to plan everything I do with an end-state design in mind. Even if I'm implementing a QoS scheme for a company that currently doesn't have VoIP, I'll design one that assumes VoIP is coming in the future.

In this chapter, I'll walk you through designing a QoS scheme for a network that will require VoIP. Designing QoS is a two-part process: first, you must determine the requirements for the system, and then you have to configure the routers. We'll use low-latency queuing (LLQ), which is the recommended solution according to Cisco. I will also outline two traffic-shaping scenarios and show the steps necessary to implement them.

LLQ Scenario

The first part of the QoS design process will require some investigative work on your part. You should interview all the business groups that use the network and determine which protocols are important to them. Assume from the onset that every group will tell you that its protocols are the most important and should get the lion's share of the bandwidth. You will need to assimilate all of this data and make some decisions about how to allocate the bandwidth. With the help of good management, you should be able to come up with a list of requirements from which you can work.

Protocols

Compile a list of the protocols in use on your network. Tools to help you with this task include packet-capture applications such as Ethereal, netflow switching on Cisco routers, and Network Analysis Modules in 6500 switches. Take careful notes. Also, bear in mind that companies like to change the default ports for popular protocols. You might have web traffic on ports 80, 443, and 8080, for example.

Record who is using each protocol and how the protocols behave. Some protocols can be tricky. For example, RTP is used for the voice stream of Cisco VoIP. If you assume that all RTP packets should get top priority to ensure voice quality, there may be unintended consequences. Other applications, such as streaming video, may also use RTP. If you design a QoS scheme that prioritizes RTP at the highest level without any further granularity, video conferencing could cause quality problems in voice calls. If you know that video conferencing is only done from the executive boardroom, however, you can prioritize that traffic accordingly to avoid problems.

Priorities

Determining priorities can be tough. Politics may well play a part in this step, so be prepared to play the game.

There are certain best practices for QoS. For example:

- You shouldn't use IP precedence 6 and 7, as they are reserved for *internetwork control* and *network control*.
- Voice RTP packets should always be marked IP precedence 5 (DSCP: EF).
- All voice control packets should be marked IP precedence 3 (DSCP: AF31).
- All data traffic should be marked with lower priorities than voice RTP and control packets.

You may have noticed that if you follow these best practices, you'll be running pretty short of IP precedence levels. Of the original eight, only levels 0, 1, 2, and 4 remain. IP precedence 4 should be used for critical applications that are not quite as critical as voice, such as video conferencing. IP precedence 0 (essentially, no priority) is used for "best effort" traffic, which leaves only levels 1 and 2. As you can see, IP precedence doesn't scale well. It's generally best to use diffserv where possible.

Don't forget about yourself. When the links get congested and you need to troubleshoot a router problem on the other side of your network, you don't want to have your Telnet or SSH traffic being dropped in favor of an FTP download. Because SSH and Telnet don't require much bandwidth, the impact of giving them a high priority is small, but the return during a crisis is enormous.

By now, you should be compiling an ordered list of how you want to prioritize your protocols. The best-effort line should always be at the bottom. This will end up being your default queue. It's also a good idea to keep an entry labeled "to be determined," which serves as a placeholder for normal traffic. Assuming you keep the highest priorities on top, the list might look something like this:

- Voice RTP
- Voice control
- Telnet/SSH (multiple protocols can share the same priority and queue)

- ---to be determined---
- Everything else (default—best effort)

In general, you should resist the urge to put HTTP traffic in any queue other than the default. HTTP traffic is not typically mission-critical. However, in some environments —for instance, call-center agents using a web-based application on a remote server— it is important to prioritize HTTP. We'll use this as an example and assume that all traffic to or from the server (10.10.100.100) on port 80 should be prioritized. The list should now look like this:

- Voice RTP
- Voice control
- Telnet/SSH
- HTTP to/from 10.10.100.100
- ---to be determined---
- Everything else (default—best effort)

Notice I've kept Telnet/SSH above the call-center traffic. Remember, we're keeping that as our ace in the hole for when there's an outage.

Our next consideration is email, which can eat up a lot of bandwidth on a network. In many older (and still used) Microsoft Exchange environments, personal email folders are stored in files called postoffice (.pst) files. You may have users on one end of a link with their .pst files stored on a file server in a remote office. I've run into problems where the execs had 1 GB .pst files that were opened across the WAN. What's more, all the users who were configured this way came in around the same time and requested their huge .pst files at the same time every morning, bringing the network to a crawl. Still, the executives insisted that email should be prioritized, so in the spirit of giving executives what they want, we'll put it just above the default queue in our scheme:

- Voice RTP
- Voice control
- Telnet/SSH
- HTTP to/from 10.10.100.100
- ---to be determined---
- Email (SMTP, POP, IMAP, Exchange)
- Everything else (default—best effort)

In my experience, email problems can usually be attributed to poorly enforced (or even nonexistent) acceptable use policies. For example, one user sending an email message with a 20 MB attachment to everyone in the company can have a significant impact on the network.

Removing the placeholder, we now have the following final list of protocols, in descending order of priority:

- Voice RTP
- Voice control
- Telnet/SSH
- HTTP to/from 10.10.100.100
- Email (SMTP, POP, IMAP, Exchange)
- Everything else (default—best effort)

This list is a good representation of some real-world environments I've seen, and implementing it will illustrate how to mark different types of traffic in different ways.

Determine Bandwidth Requirements

To illustrate how to determine the bandwidth requirements for the various protocols, we'll use the sample network from the previous chapter, shown here in Figure 32-1.

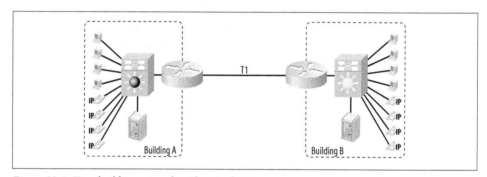

Figure 32-1. Two-building network with a single T1

Low-latency queuing is the preferred QoS method for VoIP. When using this method, you create a single high-priority queue for data streams that cannot suffer dropped packets (voice, video, etc.), and the remaining data is queued according to a hierarchy of priorities.

The priority queue may be assigned a percentage of the available bandwidth (15 percent, for example), or a finite amount of bandwidth (300 Kbps, for example). The priority queue should not consume more than three-quarters of the available bandwidth. In fact, the Cisco IOS prevents you from allocating more than 75 percent to the priority queue, though this value can be altered with the max-reserved-bandwidth interface command:

```
Config-if# max-reserved-bandwidth 80
```

WAN links should never be built with more than 75 percent planned utilization. You should always leave 25 percent for overhead, routing protocols, administration, etc. Because of the way the scheduler works, if you assign an unusually large value to the priority queue, none of the other queues will ever get serviced. This will result in apparent outages, because only the priority queue's traffic will get through.

We're going to assign voice RTP to the strict priority queue. For our purposes, let's say we'll need to allocate space for four G.729a CODEC VoIP calls (50 packets per second) at any given time. Some quick research shows that each call should take no more than 37 Kbps. Four calls at 37 Kbps equals 148 Kbps, which is the amount we'll assign to the priority queue:

> Voice RTP—priority queue—148 Kbps

Call control requires very minimal bandwidth. Some Cisco documentation states that 150 bps (plus overhead) per phone should be guaranteed for call control. For four calls, that's only 600 bps. Other documentation states that 2–5 percent of overall link bandwidth should be allocated for call control. For a T1, that's about 30–77 Kbps. Let's take the middle ground and say we need 30 Kbps for call control:

> Voice control—30 Kbps

We're only prioritizing Telnet and SSH for emergencies, so these don't need a lot of bandwidth. Allocating 64 Kbps should be more than enough, and this amount won't impact other protocols:

> Telnet/SSH—64 Kbps

HTTP to and from 10.10.100.100 is a critical app on our network, so we'll give it a sizable chunk of bandwidth. Let's say during our discovery process, HTTP traffic hovered at around 300 Kbps. We'll plan for growth, and allocate 384 Kbps:

> HTTP to/from 10.10.100.100—384 Kbps

Email is prioritized only to appease the executives, so we'll allocate it a small amount of bandwidth: 128 Kbps. This should give it enough bandwidth to function while still leaving plenty for other applications:

> Email (SMTP, POP, IMAP, Exchange)—128 Kbps

The default queue will be allocated the remaining amount of bandwidth after the other queues are considered. Assuming a T1 at 1544 Kbps and the queues we've decided upon, we get the following results: 1,544 – (148 + 30 + 64 + 384 + 128) = 754 Kbps. So, the final element will be:

> Everything else (default—best effort)—remainder (754k)

Our final list looks like this:

- Voice RTP—priority queue—148 Kbps

- Voice control—30 Kbps
- Telnet/SSH—64 Kbps
- HTTP to/from 10.10.100.100—384 Kbps
- Email (SMTP, POP, IMAP, Exchange)—128 Kbps
- Everything else (default—best effort)—remainder (754 Kbps)

Configuring the Routers

We've done all of our discovery and planning. Now it's time to get to the meat of the exercise: configuring the routers. For this implementation, we're going to configure QoS on the edge routers that connect the T1 to the individual buildings. We will do marking, classification, and policing on the same device, but remember that these steps can be separated onto discrete devices as needed. VoIP phones will usually mark their packets, so we'll assume that they're doing so on our network.

To configure LLQ, we need to configure three things: class maps, policy maps, and service policies.

Class Maps

We need to identify which packets should be marked. To do this, we will create *class maps*, which will match specific types of traffic. There are a wide variety of matching possibilities for class maps—they can match specific IP precedence values, DSCP values, or even ACLs. The only function class maps accomplish is matching.

The following class map, called Voice-Calls, matches either DSCP EF (express forwarding) or IP precedence 5:

```
class-map match-any Voice-Calls
   description [---[ Actual Calls (Set on IP Phones and Dial-Peers) ]---]
   match ip dscp ef
   match ip precedence 5
```

This is technically unnecessary, however, because (as discussed in Chapter 31) the two are synonymous. Let's change it so it's easier to read:

```
class-map match-any Voice-Calls
   description [---[ Actual Calls (Set on IP Phones and Dial-Peers) ]---]
   match ip precedence 5
```

We could just as easily have used DSCP EF, but this is a simple configuration, so we'll stick with IP precedence.

We now need to create class maps for the other items in our list. Next is call control:

```
class-map match-any Voice-Control
   description [---[ Call Control (Set on CallManager and IP Phones) ]---]
   match ip precedence 3
```

Call Manager, the voice gateways, and the IP phones are all capable of setting the precedence values for us, so we'll take advantage of that and assume that all voice call-control traffic has been marked with an IP precedence of 3.

The next item in our list is Telnet and SSH. In this example, we'll match the protocols by name in the class map:

```
class-map match-any Telnet-Traffic
  description [---[ Telnet & SSH ]---]
  match protocol telnet
  match protocol ssh
```

For HTTP, however, we need to include more than just the protocol name. We can't simply say `match protocol http`, because then we'd match HTTP traffic from any source to any destination. Our requirements indicate that we need a way to match HTTP (only port 80) traffic either sourced from or destined for 10.10.100.100. Access lists to the rescue:

```
class-map match-any HTTP-Call-Center
  description [---[ Call Center HTTP ]--]
  match access-group 121
```

Now we need to create an ACL to match our `access-group` statement:

```
access-list 121 remark [---[ Call Center HTTP ]---]
access-list 121 permit tcp any 10.10.100.100 0.0.0.0 eq www
access-list 121 permit tcp any eq www 10.10.100.100 0.0.0.0
```

ACLs allow for a great deal of flexibility when used in class maps. For example, we could:

- Create a time-based ACL (different QoS for different times of the day!).
- Create an IP-based ACL (certain IP addresses get priority).
- Give a group minus one person priority (put a single deny on top, then a permit for the group).
- Create a dynamic ACL. ("If I'm using SSH, don't prioritize Bob's SSH packets.")

You can use pretty much anything you can dream up, but be careful—the more complex your rules are, the harder they are to manage and maintain.

For the email item on our list, we can again use protocol names. Because email involves many protocols, we'll list them all. The router is even smart enough to reference "exchange" as a traffic type:

```
class-map match-any Mail-Traffic
  description [---[ Any Mail Traffic (Set on WAN Router) ]---]
  match protocol smtp
  match protocol pop3
  match protocol imap
  match protocol exchange
```

Policy Maps

Now that we have our class maps defined, we need to create the policy maps. While class maps determine *which* packets get policed, the policy map determines *how* they get policed. This step is actually pretty easy if you've done all your planning up front like we have.

Because we're only concerned with one T1, we only need to make one policy map. Let's call it WAN-Link:

```
policy-map WAN-Link
 description [---[ Apply Treatment for Classes ]---]
```

You've probably noticed that I use a lot of descriptions. I think descrip tion statements are the single best thing to ever happen to Cisco IOS. As I've said, simple is good, and well-documented code is always a plus. Anytime you have the option of adding a comment to your configuration, I highly encourage you to do so.

A policy map is simply a list of all your class maps with commands for each. First, we'll create the policy map, and an entry for the Voice-Calls class:

```
policy-map WAN-Link
 description [---[ Apply Treatment for Classes ]---]
 class Voice-Calls
  priority 148
```

Using the priority command within the class map tells the router to assign this class to the strict priority queue. The number after the command is the amount of bandwidth to allocate to the priority queue. In this case, we're allocating 148 Kbps to the priority queue. There are additional subcommands that I encourage you to learn about, but for the present example, this is all we need.

Some newer versions of IOS allow you to allocate based on a percentage of the entire link. To do this, use a command like priority percent 10 (this will allocate 10 percent of the circuit's total bandwidth to the priority queue).

Now that we've configured the priority queue, let's configure the rest of the queues. We no longer need to use the priority command. From this point on, we'll allocate bandwidth using the bandwidth command in each class. This set of commands allocates 30 Kbps of the link's total bandwidth to the Voice-Control class:

```
class Voice-Control
 bandwidth 30
```

On newer versions of IOS, you can specify a percentage of the remaining bandwidth to allocate to each nonpriority queue. For example, if you applied 10 percent to the priority queue and wanted to apply 5 percent of the remaining bandwidth (that is, the bandwidth left after the first 10 percent is used) to the Voice-Control class, you can use the following commands instead:

```
class Voice-Control
  bandwidth remaining percent 5
```

Each remaining class will be configured the same way, including the appropriate bandwidth assignments:

```
class Telnet-Traffic
  bandwidth 64
class HTTP-Call-Center
  bandwidth 384
class Mail-Traffic
  bandwidth 128
```

Finally, we need to configure the default queue. To ensure that weighted fair queuing is applied to the remainder of the traffic, we must reference the class-default class in our policy map:

```
class class-default
  fair-queue
```

class-default is a reserved name; you cannot create this class, but you should configure it in your policy maps.

Service Policies

service-policy is the command that applies your class maps and policy maps to an interface. Because we're looking to improve performance on the WAN link, we'll apply our service-policy statement to the T1 interfaces on the WAN routers:

```
int S0/0
  service-policy output WAN-Link
```

Service policies are applied on the output side of an interface. Remember that we're trying to affect how packets are sent onto a link. Received packets have already traversed the link, so there's nothing we can do about them on the receive side.

Be warned that when you change the service policy on an interface, you clear the interface so it can apply the new queuing mechanism. For IP data traffic, this is not usually a problem, but it may disconnect or, at the very least, cause audible gaps in voice calls.

Once you apply the service policy, all of your policies are in effect.

Our final configuration is as follows:

```
class-map match-any Mail-Traffic
  description [---[ Any Mail Traffic (Set on WAN Router) ]---]
  match protocol smtp
  match protocol pop3
  match protocol imap
  match protocol exchange
!
policy-map WAN-Link
  description [---[ Apply Treatment for Classes ]---]
  class Voice-Calls
   priority 148
  class Voice-Control
   bandwidth 30
  class Telnet-Traffic
   bandwidth 64
  class HTTP-Call-Center
   bandwidth 384
  class Mail-Traffic
   bandwidth 128
  class class-default
   fair-queue
!
int S0/0
 service-policy output WAN-Edge
```

Traffic-Shaping Scenarios

There are two scenarios where I've found traffic shaping advantageous. The first involved an Ethernet handoff with a higher-speed transport such as an OC3, and the second involved Frame Relay with a large number of nodes. Let's start with the former.

Scenario 1: Ethernet Handoff

Telco providers now offer Ethernet handoffs from traditional circuits. This can have the significant advantage of reducing cost for the end customer. Take, for example, an OC3 circuit. To terminate an OC3, you'll need a router that can support an OC3 card. These routers and the requisite cards are a bit more expensive than your run-of-the-mill remote office routers. If you can get that same OC3 circuit, converted by telco into a Gigabit Ethernet connection, you could plug that link directly into one of your existing switches.

There are some downsides to this that may not be immediately apparent. The first is QoS. If you require LLQ on your link, you may not be able to provision it on a switch in the way I've shown. Remember, switches are designed for LANs, so they generally employ CoS, not QoS. As such, many switches will simply not accept the commands I've shown previously in this chapter, and you won't be able to apply your QoS scheme in this way. If this is a requirement, plan accordingly up front.

I've made this mistake so you won't have to. We were planning a nationwide rollout of MPLS and ordered Ethernet handoffs with the assumption that we could just plug into existing switches. When we went to apply our QoS commands, they simply would not work. A quick call to Cisco confirmed that I was an idiot and that if I wanted to run these commands, I'd need a router. The interface didn't matter. We ended up buying a router and applying the QoS commands to the Ethernet interface. The problem was that I had to go to the CIO and report that my assumed cost savings were impossible and that we now needed routers. CIOs love to be told that the networking team needs more money.

Once we had the right equipment, we still had another issue that we hadn't thought about, and it was, once again, a speed discrepancy problem.

Providers often provide an Ethernet handoff by putting a device on your premises that has OC3 (in this case) on one side and Gigabit Ethernet on the other. The issue is that you'll be sending packets to this device at one *billion* bits per second, while the OC3 can only send them at 155 *million* bits per second. As with the Frame Relay scenario outlined in the Chapter 31, the OC3 interface will only queue so many packets before it drops them, and with an oversubscription rate of 10:1.5, it will probably drop a lot of packets.

The solution was to traffic-shape the data coming out of the Gigabit Ethernet link on our side, thus slowing down the relevant data stream so the OC3 could receive (and then send) it.

The first step is to create a policy map. This is a very simple policy map, since there are no other CoS or QoS statements involved. There are a lot of options and a lot of ways to make a mess of this, but all we really need to do is tell the interface that we're going to shape average with the desired rate, applied to the default class:

```
policy-map Provider-Outbound
  description [--[ For 150M Ethernet Handoff ]--]
 class class-default
  shape average 150000000
```

If you want to add other CoS commands, you must place them after the shape aver age command. If you place them before, the CoS will be applied before traffic shaping occurs, and you'll end up dropping your prioritized packets when the 155 Mbps buffer gets overrun with 1 Gbps packets. Luckily, policy maps can cascade, so we can apply them beneath the class-default class. I actually did something similar in Chapter 30 when I applied QoS to a subinterface:

```
policy-map Provider-Outbound
  description [--[ For 150M Ethernet Handoff ]--]
 class class-default
  shape average 150000000
  service-policy Police-CoS
```

Of course, you would need to have a *Police-CoS* policy map in place. Such a solution would apply if you had an Ethernet handoff to an MPLS cloud with QoS levels in place. Let's take that a step further and look at what the CoS policy map might look like. Remember, though, this has nothing to do with traffic shaping, but it is part of a real-world solution. Here, I have a simple policy map adhering to the levels of service given by the provider. In this case, the levels are:

- Priority queue: 60 percent
- Secondary queue: 20 percent
- Tertiary queue: 10 percent
- Best effort: remaining 10 percent

This code outlines the policy and class maps necessary to accomplish those stats:

```
class-map match-any CoS1
 match  dscp ef
class-map match-any CoS2
 match  dscp af31
 match  dscp af32
class-map match-any CoS3
 match  dscp af21
 match  dscp af22
!
policy-map Police-CoS
 class CoS1
  set dscp ef
  priority percent 60
 class CoS2
  bandwidth remaining percent 60
 class CoS3
  bandwidth remaining percent 30
 class class-default
  fair-queue
```

Now you just need to apply this policy map to the interface with the `service-policy` command:

```
interface GigabitEthernet0/0
 description *** Provider MPLS Ethernet 150M ***
 bandwidth 150000
 ip address 10.10.10.1 255.255.255.252
 duplex auto
 speed auto
 media-type sfp
 no negotiation auto
 service-policy output Provider-Outbound
```

With all this code in place, we're now traffic shaping, so let's take a look at the output using the `show policy-map interface int-name` command:

```
Router# sho policy-map interface g0/0
 GigabitEthernet0/0
```

```
Service-policy output: Provider-Outbound

    Class-map: class-default (match-any)
      2989747764 packets, 2763665319444 bytes
      5 minute offered rate 83672000 bps, drop rate 0 bps
    Match: any
    Traffic Shaping
         Target/Average  Byte   Sustain   Excess    Interval  Increment
         Rate            Limit  bits/int  bits/int  (ms)      (bytes)
      150000000/150000000 937500 3750000  3750000   25        468750

      Adapt  Queue   Packets    Bytes       Packets  Bytes    Shaping
      Active Depth                          Delayed  Delayed  Active
      -      0       2989747911 2001535028  217      144908   no
[--continued--]
```

This paragraph of output shows the statistics for our traffic-shaping parameters. We can see that the five-minute average is about 83 Mbps and we have dropped zero bits. In most of the places I've worked, dropping zero bits is a good thing. Notice that the output reports Shaping Active: no. Don't worry about this too much. It only reports the status for the millisecond in which you pressed Return. If you execute the command again, it will likely report yes. The Bytes Delayed output indicates that traffic shaping is working. These are the bytes that traffic shaping has saved from buffer-overflow death.

The remainder of the output shows the results of our post-traffic-shaping CoS policy maps:

```
Service-policy : Police-CoS

        Class-map: CoS1 (match-any)
          292144914 packets, 21611629756 bytes
          5 minute offered rate 1189000 bps, drop rate 0 bps
          Match:  dscp ef (46)
            292144912 packets, 21611629608 bytes
            5 minute rate 1189000 bps
          QoS Set
            dscp ef
              Packets marked 292144916
          Queueing
            Strict Priority
            Output Queue: Conversation 264
            Bandwidth 60 (%)
            Bandwidth 90000 (kbps) Burst 2250000 (Bytes)
            (pkts matched/bytes matched) 48/3552
            (total drops/bytes drops) 0/0

        Class-map: CoS2 (match-any)
          17228250 packets, 6205496922 bytes
          5 minute offered rate 264000 bps, drop rate 0 bps
          Match:  dscp af31 (26)
            17228250 packets, 6205496922 bytes
            5 minute rate 264000 bps
          Match:  dscp af32 (28)
```

```
            0 packets, 0 bytes
            5 minute rate 0 bps
         Queueing
            Output Queue: Conversation 265
            Bandwidth remaining 60 (%)Max Threshold 64 (packets)
            (pkts matched/bytes matched) 3/214
      (depth/total drops/no-buffer drops) 0/0/0

      Class-map: CoS3 (match-any)
         2189761162 packets, 2514045625716 bytes
         5 minute offered rate 71825000 bps, drop rate 0 bps
         Match:  dscp af21 (18)
            44743755 packets, 28337090377 bytes
            5 minute rate 835000 bps
         Match:  dscp af22 (20)
            2145017432 packets, 2485708545019 bytes
            5 minute rate 70984000 bps
         Queueing
            Output Queue: Conversation 266
            Bandwidth remaining 30 (%)Max Threshold 64 (packets)
            (pkts matched/bytes matched) 121/120844
      (depth/total drops/no-buffer drops) 0/12/0

      Class-map: class-default (match-any)
         490613498 packets, 221802649874 bytes
         5 minute offered rate 10374000 bps, drop rate 0 bps
         Match: any
         Queueing
            Flow Based Fair Queueing
            Maximum Number of Hashed Queues 256
      (total queued/total drops/no-buffer drops) 0/0/0
```

Remember that there are practically infinite ways to configure QoS, and this solution may not work for you. In my experience, though, this type of QoS application has served me well.

Scenario 2: Frame Relay Speed Mismatch

Now let's take a look at how we solved the Frame Relay speed mismatch problem from Chapter 31. Figure 32-2 shows the network in question.

This solution works because the Frame Relay network incorporates private virtual circuits (PVCs) between each branch and the main office. Thus, logically, the network looks like Figure 32-3.

This is an important distinction, because we're going to use the subinterfaces created for each branch to apply our traffic shaping.

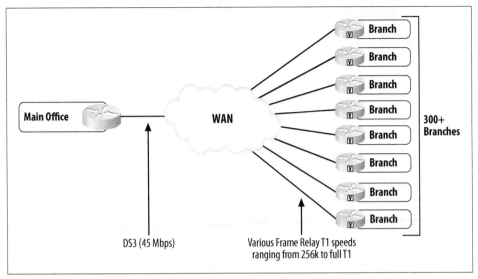

Figure 32-2. Frame Relay mismatched speeds

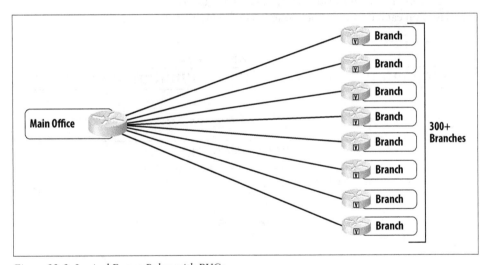

Figure 32-3. Logical Frame Relay with PVCs

 Because MPLS does not have a logical segregation of links at the head end (the main office, in this case) like Frame Relay does, this solution would not be directly applicable. Still, I believe this is extremely valuable information to learn, and you never know when a scenario will present itself that can be solved in such a way.

Traffic-shaping terminology

The following terms pop up in the context of traffic-shaping math. This can be pretty painful when you first start to deal with it, but for our uses, it will be pretty simple, so hang in there:

CIR
>Committed information rate in bits per second

B_c
>Committed *burst size* in bits (*not* bps!)
>
>Usually B_c = CIR * T_c (assuming 2× burst)

T_c
>The amount of time it takes to send B_c
>
>Usually T_c = B_c / CIR (assuming 2× burst)

B_e
>Excess burst in bits (*not* bps!) (not normally required)

To configure traffic shaping, we need to slow down the bits being sent to each branch (Figure 32-4). To accomplish this, we need to figure out how fast the DS3 is sending bits based on each branch's connection speed. Hang on, kids, here comes some math.

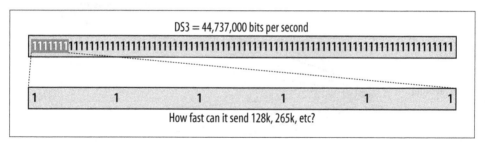

Figure 32-4. DS3 speed versus 128k

A DS3 sends data at 44,736,000 bits per second. Therefore, 128,000 bits (as in 128 Kbps) will be sent over a DS3 in .0029 seconds or 2.9 milliseconds (128,000 / 44,736,000 = 0.0028612). Let's apply this information to a sample link. For a 256 Kbps link with a 2× burst (512 Kbps), the values for traffic shaping will be as follows, assuming the DS3 head-end link in our network:

CIR: 256000

B_c: 1465 (256000 * .0057)

T_c: .0057

B_e: Not required

I've gone ahead and done the math for all speeds T1 and under, for a DS3 head end incorporating common burst speeds. The values are given in Table 32-1.

Table 32-1. Traffic-shaping values for common T1 speeds

CIR	Burst	Port	T_c	B_c
128k	128k (2x)	256k	.0029 sec [2.9 ms]	366
256k	256k (2x)	512k	.0057 sec [5.7 ms]	1465
384k	384k (2x)	768k	.0086 sec [8.6 ms]	3296
512k	512k (2x)	1024k	.0114 sec [11.4 ms]	5860
640k	640k (2x)	1280k	.0143 sec [14.3 ms]	9156
768k	768k (2x)	1536k	.0172 sec [17.2 ms]	13185
896k	640k	1536k	.0200 sec [20.0 ms]	9156
1024k	512k	1536k	.0229 sec [22.9 ms]	5860
1152k	384k	1536k	.0258 sec [25.8 ms]	3296
1280k	256k	1536k	.0286 sec [28.6 ms]	1465
1408k	128k	1536k	.0315 sec [31.5 ms]	366
1536k	0k	1536k	.0343 sec [34.3 ms]	0

You got all that? Good, because as much as you need to understand it, we don't need any of it for this exercise. Luckily, our requirements are simple. The router assumes a 2× burst, so you don't need to configure a burst if that's what you've got in place. Here are the policy maps for four different speed links, all with 2× bursts (128 Kbps, 256 Kbps, 384 Kbps and 512 Kbps). In a nutshell, we create a policy map for each speed we'll encounter, and then tell the default class (class-default) on each subinterface what speed to shape to using the **shape peak** *bps* command:

```
policy-map Frame-128
  description [--[ For 128k CIR - 256k burst  ]--]
 class class-default
  shape peak 128000

policy-map Frame-256
  description [--[ For 256k CIR - 512k burst ]--]
 class class-default
  shape peak 256000

policy-map Frame-384
  description [--[ For 384k CIR - 768k burst  ]--]
 class class-default
  shape peak 384000

policy-map Frame-512
  description [--[ For 512k CIR - 1024k burst ]--]
 class class-default
  shape peak 512000
```

As stated previously, for this to work, you must have a subinterface for each branch's PVC. This adds a lot to the router's configuration, but as the saying goes, that's life.

In the Ethernet handoff example, I used shape average, and here I'm using shape peak. The reason for the difference is that I'm configuring for Frame Relay now, which allows for bursting speeds. Where bursting is possible, use the peak option. Otherwise, use average.

To apply this, use the service-policy command on the subinterfaces. Here's a sample of Branch 100's subinterface:

```
interface Serial0/0.100 point-to-point
 description [< Branch 100 >]
 bandwidth 256
 ip address 10.10.20.1 255.255.255.252
 frame-relay interface-dlci 100
 service-policy output Frame-128
end
```

Observant readers will have noticed that I specified the bandwidth to be 256 Kbps, but applied the 128 Kbps policy map to the interface. This is due to the nature of Frame Relay bursting. For the graphs and stats to look right, the bandwidth needs to be the burst size. Traffic shaping is configured based on the CIR, though, and the CIR of this link is 128 Kbps.

You can view the traffic-shaping status with the show policy-map interface *interface-name* command:

```
Main-Office-Router#sho policy-map interface s0/0.100

 Serial0/0.100

  Service-policy output: Frame-128

    Class-map: class-default (match-any)
      1147178 packets, 583516684 bytes
      5 minute offered rate 23000 bps, drop rate 0 bps
      Match: any
      Traffic Shaping
           Target/Average   Byte   Sustain   Excess    Interval  Increment
              Rate          Limit  bits/int  bits/int  (ms)      (bytes)
           256000/128000    1984   7936      7936      62        1984

       Adapt  Queue    Packets  Bytes          Packets  Bytes      Shaping
       Active Depth                            Delayed  Delayed    Active
       -      0        1146896  583184180      411456   434751961  no
```

Again, don't worry if it says Shaping Active = no. It's only showing whether shaping is active during the millisecond you press Return. It changes off/on constantly. The important facts are that packets have been delayed and the drop rate is 0 bps. You can also see from this output that even though we only configured the CIR of 128 Kbps, it has assumed a burst of 2×, as shown by the Target/Average Rate.

## CHAPTER 33

The Congested Network

A congested network is one where there's too much data and not enough bandwidth to support it. QoS can help with a congested network, but it cannot cure the root problem. The only ways to cure congestion on a network are to add more bandwidth or reduce the amount of data trying to flow over it. That being said, let's look at a congested network and see how we might ease the pain using QoS.

Determining Whether the Network Is Congested

How do you know if your network is congested? Let's look at our favorite two-building company again (Figure 33-1).

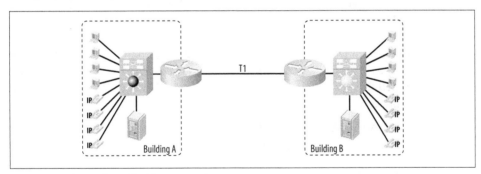

Figure 33-1. Typical two-building network

Users at each building have been complaining that access to the other building is slow. So, let's take a look at the interfaces on one of the routers that connects the T1 between buildings. Here's the output from the show interface command for the serial interface on Building B's router:

```
Bldg-B-Rtr#sho int s0/0
Serial0/0 is up, line protocol is up
  Hardware is PowerQUICC Serial
  Description: <[ T1 WAN Link ]> ❶
```

```
Internet address is 10.10.10.2/30
MTU 1500 bytes, BW 1544 Kbit, DLY 20000 usec, ❷
    reliability 255/255, txload 42/255, rxload 249/255 ❸
Encapsulation PPP, loopback not set
Keepalive set (10 sec)
LCP Open
Open: IPCP, CDPCP
Last input 00:00:00, output 00:00:00, output hang never
Last clearing of "show interface" counters 3w4d
Queueing strategy: fifo
Output queue 0/40, 548941 drops; input queue 0/75, 3717 drops
5 minute input rate 1509000 bits/sec, 258 packets/sec ❹
5 minute output rate 259000 bits/sec, 241 packets/sec ❺
    287554125 packets input, 3659652949 bytes, 0 no buffer
    Received 0 broadcasts, 0 runts, 0 giants, 0 throttles
    819 input errors, 559 CRC, 227 frame, 0 overrun, 0 ignored, 33 abort
    282883104 packets output, 3613739796 bytes, 0 underruns
    0 output errors, 0 collisions, 1 interface resets
    0 output buffer failures, 0 output buffers swapped out
    0 carrier transitions
    DCD=up  DSR=up  DTR=up  RTS=up  CTS=up
```

Looking at this information, you should notice some things right away. First, this is a T1, and second, the bandwidth is 1,544 Kbps (see ❶ and ❷).

Remember that the bandwidth given when you use show interface is not necessarily representative of the true bandwidth of the link. While this value is correct by default, it can be changed with the bandwidth interface command. This field is used for calculations in EIGRP and other protocols, which is why it can be altered.

Looking further down (❹), you can see that the five-minute input rate is 1,509,000 bps at 258 packets per second (pps). That's 1,509 Kbps used on a 1,544 Kbps link. You might be tempted to say, "Hey, the link's got 33 Kbps left!" However, remember that this is a five-minute *average*.

Perhaps an easier way to get a sense of the utilization is on ❸, which shows:

```
reliability 255/255, txload 42/255, rxload 249/255
```

Looking at these numbers, you can see that the transmit load (txload) is only 42 out of 255, but the receive load (rxload) is 249 out of 255. If you use some simple math (249/255 * 100), you can see that the link is 97.65 percent utilized.

Ever wonder why the rxload and txload numbers are based on 255 and not 100? The decimal number 100 in hex is 64. If we need to burn two hex digits in the router's memory, why not use them to their fullest? The largest number we can represent with two hex digits is FF, which is 255. By using 255 instead of 100, we get more than twice the granularity in our measurements.

The link is saturated, but only in one direction: while rxload is 249/255, txload is only 42/255. To view this as bandwidth used, look at ❹ and ❺. They show we're receiving 1,509 Kbps, but transmitting only 259 Kbps. Remember that T1s are full duplex. What happens in one direction, for the most part, does not affect what happens in the other direction.

> T1s, like most telecom links, are full duplex. They are rated at 1.54 Mbps and can transmit this speed in both directions simultaneously.

An even easier way to see whether your links are saturated is to deploy a tool such as the Multi Router Traffic Grapher (MRTG), which gives you a quick graphical representation of the traffic on your links.

Figure 33-2 shows an MRTG graph for this link. Each number along the bottom of the graph represents an hour of the day. The small triangle on the righthand edge of the graph indicates the current time (i.e., the time the graph was created—in this case, 12:12 p.m.). The vertical line at 0 on the graph indicates midnight. Starting at around 9:30 or 10:00 a.m., and continuing until the current time, the link became completely saturated in one direction. This coincides nicely with what we're seeing on the router.

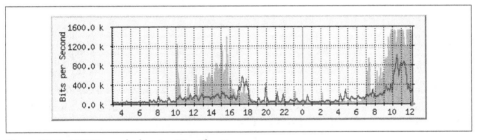

Figure 33-2. MRTG graph showing T1 utilization

OK, so the link is saturated. So what? We're getting our money's worth, right? If that's the case, why are users complaining of slowdowns? Let's look deeper. The first thing you should always look for is problems at the physical layer. Look for errors in the show interface output. The bold lines toward the bottom of the output do indeed indicate some errors:

```
    819 input errors, 559 CRC, 227 frame, 0 overrun, 0 ignored, 33 abort
        0 output errors, 0 collisions, 1 interface resets
```

These two lines show input errors, CRC errors, framing errors, abort errors, and an interface reset. Hmm. Not so good. Let's not get excited just yet, though. The first thing you should do when you see errors—especially when they're relatively small in number, as in this case—is to wait a few minutes and do a show interface again. Here are the relevant results after executing the same command 10 minutes later:

```
819 input errors, 559 CRC, 227 frame, 0 overrun, 0 ignored, 33 abort
    0 output errors, 0 collisions, 1 interface resets
```

As you can see, they're identical; none of the counters are incrementing. This indicates to me that there was probably a problem in the past that led someone to pull out the T1 cable and quickly reset it. Or it could be that the telecom provider had a blip on the line. Either way, it's not worth worrying about right now. Once we've established that the counters are not incrementing, we should clear them so we don't waste time chasing ghosts the next time we're in the router. We don't want to do that yet, though—we still need the data.

The next thing we need to look at is the health of the input and output queues. The previous show interface output includes the following:

```
Queueing strategy: fifo
  Output queue 0/40, 548941 drops; input queue 0/75, 3717 drops
```

The first thing you should notice is that the *queueing strategy* is FIFO (first in, first out). Links 2 Mbps and below should be using weighted fair queuing (WFQ), so there's something to investigate. Looking further, you'll see that there have been 548,941 drops on the output queue and 3,717 drops on the input queue. This means that since the last time the counters were cleared (now you know why we didn't clear them), we've dropped 548,941 packets while transmitting.

Line 13 shows how long it's been since the counters were cleared:

```
Last clearing of "show interface" counters 3w4d
```

Line 22 shows how many packets we've sent:

```
282883104 packets output, 3613739796 bytes, 0 underruns
```

So, in three weeks and four days, we've transmitted 282,883,104 packets and dropped 548,941. Some simple math shows that this is only 1/10th of one percent of all the packets. So, why do we have a problem?

OK, I'll admit it, I led you down the wrong path, but I did it to give you some real-world experience. Let's think for a moment here. These numbers look good to me. Sure, we're saturated, but we're not dropping all that many packets, are we? Why, then, are we getting complaints?

The answer is a deceptively simple one: we're looking at the wrong side of the link. Take another look at ❹ and ❺:

```
5 minute input rate 1509000 bits/sec, 258 packets/sec
5 minute output rate 259000 bits/sec, 241 packets/sec
```

The input is almost maxed, not the output! When we drop packets due to congestion, we drop them on the outbound journey. Remember the funnel example from Chapter 31? We're looking at the bottom of the hose here. The only packets that can come out of it are the ones that made it through the funnel! We'll never see the ones that were dropped on the other side from this point of view.

So, let's take a look at the other side of the link with the same show interface command:

```
Bldg-A-Rtr#sho int s0/0
Serial0/0 is up, line protocol is up
  Hardware is PowerQUICC Serial
  Description: [-- T1 WAN Link --]
  Internet address is 10.10.10.1/30
  MTU 1500 bytes, BW 1544 Kbit, DLY 20000 usec,
      reliability 255/255, txload 250/255, rxload 47/255
  Encapsulation PPP, loopback not set
  Keepalive set (10 sec)
  LCP Open
  Open: IPCP, CDPCP
  Last input 00:00:00, output 00:00:00, output hang never
  Last clearing of "show interface" counters 3w4d
  Input queue: 0/75/0 (size/max/drops); Total output drops: 152195125
  Queueing strategy: weighted fair
  Output queue: 63/1000/64/152195113 (size/max total/threshold/drops)
      Conversations  7/223/256 (active/max active/max total)
      Reserved Conversations 0/0 (allocated/max allocated)
  5 minute input rate 261000 bits/sec, 238 packets/sec
  5 minute output rate 1511000 bits/sec, 249 packets/sec
      282883104 packets input, 3613739796 bytes, 0 no buffer
      Received 0 broadcasts, 0 runts, 0 giants, 0 throttles
      872 input errors, 472 CRC, 357 frame, 0 overrun, 0 ignored, 12 abort
      1326931662 packets output, 2869922208 bytes, 0 underruns
      0 output errors, 0 collisions, 1 interface resets
      0 output buffer failures, 0 output buffers swapped out
      0 carrier transitions
      DCD=up  DSR=up  DTR=up  RTS=up  CTS=up
```

A quick look at the load stats shows us that we're looking at the right side now:

```
      reliability 255/255, txload 250/255, rxload 47/255
```

The errors look about the same, and are not of concern:

```
      Received 0 broadcasts, 0 runts, 0 giants, 0 throttles
      872 input errors, 472 CRC, 357 frame, 0 overrun, 0 ignored, 12 abort
```

Now, let's look at the queues:

```
  Input queue: 0/75/0 (size/max/drops); Total output drops: 152195125
  Queueing strategy: weighted fair
  Output queue: 63/1000/64/152195113 (size/max total/threshold/drops)
      Conversations  7/223/256 (active/max active/max total)
      Reserved Conversations 0/0 (allocated/max allocated)
```

The first thing that pops out at me is that this end of the link is running with WFQ enabled (as it should be). Remember that the other side was FIFO. They don't need to match, but there's probably no reason for the other side to be FIFO.

And wow! 152,195,113 packets dropped on the output queue! If we divide that into the total number of packets (152,195,113 / 1,326,931,662 * 100), we get 11.47 percent of all packets dropped. I'd say we've found our problem. This link is so saturated that more than 1 out of every 10 packets is being discarded. It's no wonder users are complaining!

A total of 11.47 percent might not seem like a lot of dropped packets, but remember that VoIP cannot stand to have packets dropped. Even 1 percent would be a problem for VoIP. And for protocols that can recover lost packets, the result is a perceived slowdown. So, what should your dropped-packet counters look like? In a perfect world, they should be zero. More practically, they should not increment as you watch them, and they should be as close as possible to 0 percent of your total packets sent. If you're dropping even 1 percent of your packets over a serial link, you've got a congestion problem.

Now that we know what the problem is, we need to monitor the link over time. We want to ensure that all those packets weren't dropped in the last 10 minutes (though that's unlikely given the high numbers). It is probably safe to make some assumptions, though. If you've configured MRTG to monitor usage for you, the historical information it provides can help, and the pretty graphs make explaining things to the executives a whole lot easier.

Figure 33-3 shows that the link is saturated pretty much all day long. The problem starts roughly when the users come into work and ends roughly when they all go home. See how the graph peaks and then runs flat up near 1,600 Kbps all day, every day? This link is oversubscribed.

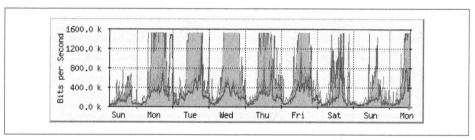

Figure 33-3. One week's historical MRTG graph for our link

Resolving the Problem

So, what do we do? Can QoS save the day? Well, yes and no. QoS is, in fact, already running on the link (WFQ), but it's making certain assumptions as to which traffic should be prioritized. WFQ is also only running in one direction (luckily, the direction in which we need it to be running, which is the direction that most of the data is flowing).

We've already talked about what QoS cannot do. One of the big things that it cannot do is resolve a need for more bandwidth. This link is clearly in need of a larger pipe, because we're dropping more than 10 percent of all packets sent from Building A to

Building B. In this case, the only ways to prevent these packets from being dropped is to install a faster link between the buildings or stop sending so much data.

What we *can* use QoS to do is determine more specifically which packets should and should not be dropped. (See Chapters 31 and 32 for more information on designing a QoS scheme.)

Let's clear those counters now, so that the next time we look we'll have some fresh data:

```
Bldg-A-Rtr#clear counters s0/0
Clear "show interface" counters on this interface [confirm]
```

And on the other side as well:

```
Bldg-B-Rtr#clear counters s0/0
Clear "show interface" counters on this interface [confirm]
```

If you think you need a faster link, you will need to collect some real data to support your case. When you approach management with your concerns, having information similar to what I've shown you in this chapter will help justify the expense of more bandwidth. SNMP network monitoring is one of the most useful tools you can deploy on your network. You don't need fancy systems like CiscoWorks or OpenView, though if you can afford those tools, they are worth having. Free tools such as the MRTG are very powerful and useful, especially for justifying larger links.

## CHAPTER 34

The Converged Network

In this chapter, you'll see a converged network in action. While the network will be very simple, the principles shown will scale to networks and links of almost any size.

Figure 34-1 shows the network we'll use for the examples in this chapter. R1 and R2 each have two Ethernet networks attached: one with an IP phone and one with a personal computer. The routers are connected with a T1 that terminates into S0/1 on each.

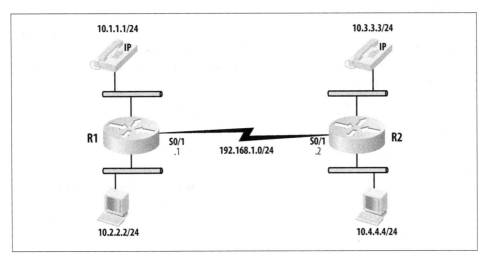

Figure 34-1. Simple converged network

Configuration

The interface we'll be concentrating on is S0/1 on R1. Here is the configuration:

```
interface Serial0/1
 ip address 192.168.1.1 255.255.255.0
 service-policy output WAN
```

The service-policy statement maps the policy map named *WAN* to the interface. Here is the configuration for the policy map:

```
policy-map WAN
  class Voice-RTP
    priority 128
  class Voice-Control
   bandwidth percent 5
  class HTTP
   bandwidth percent 10
  class class-default
   fair-queue
```

The policy map references four classes: Voice-RTP, Voice-Control, HTTP, and the special class class-default. Remember that class-default is a special class name used when you're building the default class. The default class is where packets not matching any other class are queued. The queues are designed as follows:

Voice-RTP

Packets in this class will be put into the strict priority queue. The queue will be sized for 128 Kbps. This is roughly the size of two 64 Kbps G711-encoded VoIP calls. Packets with an IP precedence of 5 will be put into this queue. This is defined in the Voice-RTP class map.

Voice-Control

The voice control for the VoIP class should not consume much bandwidth. I have guaranteed 5 percent of the link's total bandwidth to this class. Packets marked with an IP precedence of 3 will be put into this queue. This is defined in the Voice-Control class map.

HTTP

I have guaranteed this class 10 percent of the link's total bandwidth. Any traffic with a destination port of 80 will match this class, as referenced by the HTTP class map and access list 101.

class-default

This queue is where packets that don't match any other queue will end up. The only definition for the queue is that these packets will be *fair-queued*. They will be treated as they would be on a regular T1 serial link, but only after the other queues have been processed.

The configuration for the class maps is as follows. class-default is a default class in IOS that requires no configuration:

```
class-map match-any HTTP
  match access-group 101
class-map match-any Voice-RTP
  match ip precedence 5
class-map match-all Voice-Control
  match ip precedence 3
```

The HTTP class references access list 101 for matching packets. The access list checks for the presence of HTTP packets:

```
access-list 101 permit tcp any any eq www
access-list 101 permit tcp any any eq 443
```

I could have used the statement match protocol http in the class map instead of calling an access list. However, this would have matched only port 80. Using an access list allows the flexibility of adding HTTPS (port 443) or HTTP running on nonstandard ports such as 8080.

Monitoring QoS

You monitor queues primarily through a couple of simple commands. The output of these commands contains a lot of information, so I'll explain what you need to look for. First, run the show interface command:

```
R1#sho int s0/1
Serial0/1 is up, line protocol is up
  Hardware is PQUICC with Fractional T1 CSU/DSU
  Internet address is 192.168.1.1/24
  MTU 1500 bytes, BW 1544 Kbit, DLY 20000 usec,
     reliability 255/255, txload 21/255, rxload 22/255
  Encapsulation HDLC, loopback not set
  Keepalive set (10 sec)
  Last input 00:00:00, output 00:00:00, output hang never
  Last clearing of "show interface" counters 5d04h
  Input queue: 2/75/0/0 (size/max/drops/flushes); Total output drops: 0
  Queueing strategy: weighted fair
  Output queue: 0/1000/64/0 (size/max total/threshold/drops)
     Conversations  0/4/256 (active/max active/max total)
     Reserved Conversations 2/2 (allocated/max allocated)
     Available Bandwidth 1030 kilobits/sec
  5 minute input rate 134000 bits/sec, 53 packets/sec
  5 minute output rate 131000 bits/sec, 53 packets/sec
     22874566 packets input, 2838065420 bytes, 0 no buffer
     Received 52348 broadcasts, 0 runts, 0 giants, 0 throttles
     0 input errors, 0 CRC, 0 frame, 0 overrun, 0 ignored, 0 abort
     22964396 packets output, 2678320888 bytes, 0 underruns
     0 output errors, 0 collisions, 0 interface resets
     0 output buffer failures, 0 output buffers swapped out
     0 carrier transitions
     DCD=up  DSR=up  DTR=up  RTS=up  CTS=up
```

The output indicates that the queuing strategy is *weighted fair*. We're using low-latency queuing (LLQ), so why does show interface tell us something different? LLQ is technically class-based weighted fair queuing (CBWFQ) with a strict priority queue. Because CBWFQ is a type of weighted fair queuing, the router simply reports the queuing strategy as *weighted fair*.

Notice that show interface does not show the individual queues that we specified in the policy map. To show their statuses, we need to use the show policy-map interface

interface# command. This command produces a lot of output, and the more queues you have configured, the longer the output will be:

```
R1#sho policy-map interface s0/1
 Serial0/1

  Service-policy output: WAN

    Class-map: Voice-RTP (match-any)
      19211963 packets, 3918472220 bytes
      5 minute offered rate 81000 bps, drop rate 0 bps
      Match: ip precedence 5
        19211963 packets, 3918472220 bytes
        5 minute rate 81000 bps
      Queueing
        Strict Priority
        Output Queue: Conversation 264
        Bandwidth 128 (kbps) Burst 3200 (Bytes)
        (pkts matched/bytes matched) 19211963/3918472220
        (total drops/bytes drops) 0/0

    Class-map: Voice-Control (match-all)
      793462 packets, 161097064 bytes
      5 minute offered rate 0 bps, drop rate 0 bps
      Match: ip precedence 3
      Queueing
        Output Queue: Conversation 265
        Bandwidth 5 (%) Max Threshold 64 (packets)
        (pkts matched/bytes matched) 793462/161097064
        (depth/total drops/no-buffer drops) 0/0/0

    Class-map: HTTP (match-any)
      717928 packets, 42537234 bytes
      5 minute offered rate 0 bps, drop rate 0 bps
      Match: access-group 101
        717928 packets, 42537234 bytes
        5 minute rate 0 bps
      Queueing
        Output Queue: Conversation 266
        Bandwidth 10 (%) Max Threshold 64 (packets)
        (pkts matched/bytes matched) 717934/42537620
        (depth/total drops/no-buffer drops) 0/0/0

    Class-map: class-default (match-any)
      2243454 packets, 2851898036 bytes
      5 minute offered rate 52000 bps, drop rate 0 bps
      Match: any
      Queueing
        Flow Based Fair Queueing
        Maximum Number of Hashed Queues 256
        (total queued/total drops/no-buffer drops) 0/0/0
```

Each queue is shown in detail with slightly different information reported. The strict priority queue is used in the class map Voice-RTP. Here is the output for that queue:

```
Class-map: Voice-RTP (match-any)
   19211963 packets, 3918472220 bytes
   5 minute offered rate 81000 bps, drop rate 0 bps
   Match: ip precedence 5
      19211963 packets, 3918472220 bytes
      5 minute rate 81000 bps
   Queueing
      Strict Priority
      Output Queue: Conversation 264
      Bandwidth 128 (kbps) Burst 3200 (Bytes)
      (pkts matched/bytes matched) 19211963/3918472220
      (total drops/bytes drops) 0/0
```

The interesting tidbits are in bold. The first bold line shows the *5 minute offered rate* followed by the *drop rate*. The drop rate should always be zero, especially in the priority queue. If you're dropping packets, your queue is too small. The five-minute offered rate lets us know how much of the queue is being used. This information is also shown later in the output as the *5 minute rate*.

Under the Queuing paragraph, we can see that this map is using the strict priority queue. Beneath that is a report of the queue size. Lastly, the number of packets and bytes dropped is reported. This should always be 0/0. If your traffic spikes beyond your planned levels, however, you may start to drop packets. When you're dealing with voice calls in the strict priority queue, dropped packets result in distorted or choppy voice quality and unhappy users.

The information for the next queue is a little different. Because this is not the strict priority queue, the queue is described as we've designed it:

```
Class-map: Voice-Control (match-all)
   793462 packets, 161097064 bytes
   5 minute offered rate 0 bps, drop rate 0 bps
   Match: ip precedence 3
   Queueing
      Output Queue: Conversation 265
      Bandwidth 5 (%) Max Threshold 64 (packets)
      (pkts matched/bytes matched) 793462/161097064
      (depth/total drops/no-buffer drops) 0/0/0
```

In this example, the five-minute offered rate is zero. This is call control, and packets should only hit this queue when calls are set up or torn down. If no calls have been started or completed in the last five minutes, this rate could be valid.

Further down, we can see that 5 percent of the bandwidth has been allocated for this queue. The last line again shows that no packets have been dropped for this queue. The *depth* is the number of packets currently in the queue. On busy links, this number may show fluctuating values. As long as there are no drops, you're in good shape.

Skipping down to the last queue, we get yet another view:

```
Class-map: class-default (match-any)
   2243454 packets, 2851898036 bytes
   5 minute offered rate 52000 bps, drop rate 0 bps
```

```
Match: any
Queueing
  Flow Based Fair Queueing
  Maximum Number of Hashed Queues 256
  (total queued/total drops/no-buffer drops) 0/0/0
```

The first line in bold should be closely monitored. If all your other queues are behaving properly, this line will show you how much bandwidth has been needed for the default queue. It also shows you the drop rate, which should be zero. If there is one queue where it's permissible to drop packets, it's this one. This is the queue where all your noncritical traffic goes. If you need to drop packets due to congestion, it should be the noncritical traffic that suffers, not the important stuff like voice calls.

Troubleshooting a Converged Network

Dropping packets within specific queues can be hard to diagnose. After you've worked with a converged network for a while, though, you will get a feel for how the queues should behave. While every network is different, here are some common symptoms to look out for.

Incorrect Queue Configuration

When all the queues are configured correctly, none of them should drop packets when the link is congestion-free. When congestion occurs, packets should be dropped from the least important queue first. The least important queue is the class-default queue, which contains all nonprioritized packets.

Here, I have routed excessive traffic across our sample network's T1 link. While most of the queues are busy, only the class-default queue is showing dropped packets:

```
R1#sho policy-map interface s0/1
 Serial0/1

  Service-policy output: WAN

    Class-map: Voice-RTP (match-any)
      11091627 packets, 2262021588 bytes
      5 minute offered rate 324000 bps, drop rate 0 bps
      Match: ip precedence 5
        11091627 packets, 2262021588 bytes
        5 minute rate 324000 bps
      Queueing
        Strict Priority
        Output Queue: Conversation 264
        Bandwidth 500 (kbps) Burst 12500 (Bytes)
        (pkts matched/bytes matched) 11091627/2262021588
        (total drops/bytes drops) 0/0

    Class-map: Voice-Control (match-all)
      7312459 packets, 1477128588 bytes
```

```
      5 minute offered rate 255000 bps, drop rate 0 bps
    Match: ip precedence 3
    Queueing
      Output Queue: Conversation 265
      Bandwidth 5 (%) Max Threshold 64 (packets)
      (pkts matched/bytes matched) 7312784/1477194238
      (depth/total drops/no-buffer drops) 0/0/0

  Class-map: HTTP (match-any)
    79255 packets, 4690398 bytes
    5 minute offered rate 1000 bps, drop rate 0 bps
    Match: access-group 101
      79255 packets, 4690398 bytes
      5 minute rate 1000 bps
    Queueing
      Output Queue: Conversation 266
      Bandwidth 10 (%) Max Threshold 64 (packets)
      (pkts matched/bytes matched) 78903/4669112
      (depth/total drops/no-buffer drops) 0/0/0

  Class-map: class-default (match-any)
    23750755 packets, 2030244008 bytes
    5 minute offered rate 887000 bps, drop rate 4000 bps
    Match: any
    Queueing
      Flow Based Fair Queueing
      Maximum Number of Hashed Queues 256
      (total queued/total drops/no-buffer drops) 12/16501/0
```

If users are complaining at this point, there are a few things to consider:

- The link may be saturated, in which case it should be replaced with a larger link.

- Some traffic in the class-default queue may need to be prioritized above this queue.

- One or more of the queues may not be configured appropriately. Look at the HTTP queue. While it's performing well, the five-minute offered rate is only 1,000 bps. The queue has been allocated 10 percent of the link. If we make this queue's allocation smaller, the default queue might stop dropping packets. Actually, given the amount of traffic on the link, in this case, that is unlikely. The five-minute offered rate in the class-default queue is 887,000 bps. That's almost two-thirds of a T1 in and of itself!

Priority Queue Too Small

The rate for the Voice-RTP queue seems stable at about 80 Kbps. For fun, I'll lower the size of the priority queue to 64 Kbps:

```
R1#conf t
R1(config)# policy-map WAN
R1(config-pmap)# class Voice-RTP
R1(config-pmap-c)# priority 64
```

Now, let's take another look at the queues using the `show policy-map interface` *inter face#* command:

```
R1#sho policy-map interface s0/1
 Serial0/1

  Service-policy output: WAN

    Class-map: Voice-RTP (match-any)
      19682025 packets, 4014346028 bytes
      5 minute offered rate 79000 bps, drop rate 17000 bps
      Match: ip precedence 5
        19682025 packets, 4014346028 bytes
        5 minute rate 79000 bps
      Queueing
        Strict Priority
        Output Queue: Conversation 264
        Bandwidth 64 (kbps) Burst 1600 (Bytes)
        (pkts matched/bytes matched) 19682025/4014346028
        (total drops/bytes drops) 1538/313752
```

Look at the drop statistics. The first line in bold shows a drop rate of 17,000 bps. This is a severe problem indicating that the queue is too small. This line is telling us that the queue offered up 79,000 bps, but had to drop 17,000 bps. To prevent packets from being dropped, the queue should be set to a minimum of 79,000 + 17,000 = 90,000 bps. If you see anything other than zero in the drop rate section of this output, you've got a problem.

The last line of output shows the total drops and bytes dropped. This is a counter, so it will display an incrementing total until the interface is reset or the counters are cleared. To illustrate this point, I let the router run with the priority queue set too small for an hour, then set the bandwidth value back to 128 Kbps. I waited five minutes to let the counters settle, then executed the command again:

```
R1#sho policy-map interface  s0/1
 Serial0/1

  Service-policy output: WAN

    Class-map: Voice-RTP (match-any)
      20049682 packets, 4089333416 bytes
      5 minute offered rate 79000 bps, drop rate 0 bps
      Match: ip precedence 5
        20049682 packets, 4089333416 bytes
        5 minute rate 79000 bps
      Queueing
        Strict Priority
        Output Queue: Conversation 264
        Bandwidth 128 (kbps) Burst 3200 (Bytes)
        (pkts matched/bytes matched) 20049682/4089333416
        (total drops/bytes drops) 78648/16044192
```

The drop rate in the first bold line is now zero, as it should be. However, the last line still shows some very high numbers. If I were to see something like this on a normally healthy link, I would suspect that one of two things had happened:

- Someone altered the configuration like I just did, but did not clear the counters after resolving the issue.
- There was a surge of traffic in this queue that exceeded the queue's configured size.

In either case, you should try to determine what's happened. If there was a surge of traffic in the priority queue, it's possible that either there were more active phone calls than you anticipated or the active calls were not using the proper CODEC. Even worse, packets might be getting marked as IP precedence 5 when they shouldn't be.

 If the priority queue is saturated, even if additional capacity is available, packets will still be dropped from the priority queue. The priority queue differs from the other queues in that it will not use the remaining available bandwidth on the link for overflow. When this queue is too small, packets will be dropped.

Priority Queue Too Large

When the priority queue is too large, it can affect network performance. However, this problem can be very difficult to diagnose. Here, the priority queue has been set to 256 Kbps, but the traffic hitting the queue is only about 80 Kbps:

```
Class-map: Voice-RTP (match-any)
  3150111 packets, 642496644 bytes
  5 minute offered rate 81000 bps, drop rate 0 bps
  Match: ip precedence 5
    3150111 packets, 642496644 bytes
    5 minute rate 81000 bps
  Queueing
    Strict Priority
    Output Queue: Conversation 264
    Bandwidth 256 (kbps) Burst 6400 (Bytes)
    (pkts matched/bytes matched) 3150111/642496644
    (total drops/bytes drops) 0/0
```

This queue looks healthy, and it is, for all practical purposes. The problem is far subtler than can be determined from the numbers.

The queues are serviced by something called the *scheduler*. The scheduler serves each queue according to its size and its position in the configuration. The priority queue is always serviced first. Only when the priority queue is empty will other queues be serviced.

I have seen problems on large links such as DS3s when the priority queue is set to a very high level. For example, setting the priority queue near 75 percent of the total link speed causes the queues beneath the priority queue to be starved. In other words, the scheduler spends so much time servicing the priority queue that, even if there is little traffic, the other queues never get serviced. This results in packets being dropped in the lower queues, even if there is plenty of capacity to serve them all. Try to keep the priority queue near the level of the expected traffic peaks.

Nonpriority Queue Too Small

Our example is using a T1, and the Voice-Control queue is set to use 5 percent of the link. Five percent of 1.544 Mbps is about 77 Kbps. Here, I've increased the call-control traffic to exceed the queue size. I'm now pushing 90 Kbps through this queue:

```
Class-map: Voice-Control (match-all)
  213781 packets, 40614182 bytes
  5 minute offered rate 90000 bps, drop rate 0 bps
  Match: ip precedence 3
  Queueing
    Output Queue: Conversation 265
    Bandwidth 5 (%) Max Threshold 64 (packets)
    (pkts matched/bytes matched) 213900/40638220
    (depth/total drops/no-buffer drops) 3/0/0
```

Notice that the queue is not dropping packets, even though it is now too small. This behavior is quite different from what we saw in the priority queue. When saturated, the priority queue will drop packets, even if there is additional bandwidth available on the link. Other queues do not drop packets unless the entire link is saturated. The 3/0/0 in the last line shows the queue depth, total drops, and no-buffer drops values. The queue depth indicates that there are three packets queued, but that's a rarity, even with the link now running at more than 50 percent utilization:

```
R1#sho int s0/1 | include minute
  5 minute input rate 883000 bits/sec, 830 packets/sec
  5 minute output rate 897000 bits/sec, 846 packets/sec
```

Even when I increase the traffic so this queue is running at over triple capacity, *as long as the link is not saturated*, no packets are dropped:

```
Class-map: Voice-Control (match-all)
  281655 packets, 54324322 bytes
  5 minute offered rate 237000 bps, drop rate 0 bps
  Match: ip precedence 3
  Queueing
    Output Queue: Conversation 265
    Bandwidth 5 (%) Max Threshold 64 (packets)
    (pkts matched/bytes matched) 281936/54381084
    (depth/total drops/no-buffer drops) 0/0/0
```

With a saturated link, the queue will drop packets when full.

Nonpriority Queue Too Large

As with the priority queue, when a nonpriority queue is too large, the problem will not be obvious. The scheduler may spend too much time servicing the queue unnecessarily, which can result in drops in lower-priority queues, but only after servicing the strict priority queue. Here, the HTTP queue is configured for 40 percent of the link's total speed. With the link being a T1, this translates to more than 600 Kbps. However, the queue is only showing 1 Kbps being offered:

```
Class-map: HTTP (match-any)
   79255 packets, 4690398 bytes
   5 minute offered rate 1000 bps, drop rate 0 bps
   Match: access-group 101
      79255 packets, 4690398 bytes
      5 minute rate 1000 bps
   Queueing
      Output Queue: Conversation 266
      Bandwidth 40 (%) Max Threshold 64 (packets)
      (pkts matched/bytes matched) 78903/4669112
      (depth/total drops/no-buffer drops) 0/0/0

Class-map: class-default (match-any)
   23750755 packets, 2030244008 bytes
   5 minute offered rate 887000 bps, drop rate 4000 bps
   Match: any
   Queueing
      Flow Based Fair Queueing
      Maximum Number of Hashed Queues 256
      (total queued/total drops/no-buffer drops) 12/16501/0
```

Notice that the default queue is dropping packets at a rate of 4,000 bps.

As soon as I change the HTTP queue to be allowed only 5 percent instead of 40 percent, the router almost completely stops dropping packets in the class-default queue:

```
Class-map: HTTP (match-any)
   86935 packets, 5150618 bytes
   5 minute offered rate 1000 bps, drop rate 0 bps
   Match: access-group 101
      86935 packets, 5150618 bytes
      5 minute rate 1000 bps
   Queueing
      Output Queue: Conversation 266
      Bandwidth 5 (%) Max Threshold 64 (packets)
      (pkts matched/bytes matched) 86204/5106232
      (depth/total drops/no-buffer drops) 0/0/0
Class-map: class-default (match-any)
   26519010 packets, 2404610690 bytes
   5 minute offered rate 849000 bps, drop rate 0 bps
   Match: any
   Queueing
      Flow Based Fair Queueing
      Maximum Number of Hashed Queues 256
      (total queued/total drops/no-buffer drops) 0/32252/0
```

The trick here is that the configuration of one queue directly affected the behavior of another queue—specifically, the one beneath it. In this case, there was nothing I could have done to the class-default queue to increase its performance; the changes had to be made to the queue above it.

Default Queue Too Small

The size of the class-default queue is not directly configurable. If the queue is too small, either the link is too small or the other queues are too large. In either case, you'll end up dropping packets in the class-default queue.

Default Queue Too Large

I would argue that the default queue cannot be too large. If you have a large class-default queue, you have ample capacity and life should be good—for now, anyway!

## CHAPTER 35

Designing Networks

There are hundreds of books out there that will tell you how to build a three-tier corporate network. This is not one of them. Instead, I'm going to show you what you need to do *before* you build your network. Then I'll show you some real-world examples of network designs.

This is not the sort of technical information you learn from getting certified. This is information that will help you do your job better. For the most part, this chapter is written with the assumption that you'll be designing a network from scratch. While that's not often the case, the information contained herein is applicable to any network project.

Documentation

Documentation is the bane of many an engineer's existence. I'm not entirely sure why this is the case, but an engineer who likes to write documentation seems to be a rarity. Writing is hard work (try writing a book!), but the payoffs are enormous.

Some engineers seem to believe that if they hoard information, they become irreplaceable. Trust me on this one—you and I are replaceable. In fact, I've made a living by coming in to document networks when "irreplaceable" engineers were fired.

Well-written documentation saves time and money. If someone can fix your network by reading your documentation, you've done a good job. If no one but you can fix your network, you're not doing a good job.

Whenever possible, even on small networks, you should document every detail of your network. Just because a network is small enough for you to memorize every IP address doesn't mean it should not be documented. Start with your home network. My home network has better documentation than many company networks, but to be fair, it's likely more complicated than many company networks as well. I take great pride in my documentation, and samples of my work have landed me jobs. Given two equally skilled engineers, I'll hire the one with better documentation skills every time.

Requirements Documents

One of the things you should do at the start of any project, regardless of your perception of available time, is write a requirements document. This document should include all the requirements for the project as you understand them, as well as all assumptions being made. Even if the requirement is simply "design a new corporate network," write that down, and include all the assumptions that you'll be making to accomplish that goal.

When you've finished your requirements document, send it to everyone who's involved. This list should include your boss, at an absolute minimum. Depending on the corporate culture, you may also wish to include project managers, the VP responsible for funding the project (the sponsor), and anyone else involved in the process. Your boss may wish to forward this document to the other parties instead of having you send it to them directly. Either way, you need to publish something that dictates what you will be designing and why.

Writing a requirements document is one of the best things you can do to protect yourself later on when the project scope changes.

 The scope will change. I can't think of a single project that I've worked on where it didn't. Scope change is a fact of life with projects.

For example, if you order a T1 for Internet connectivity, and the VP later gives you grief because he doesn't think it's enough bandwidth, you should be able to point to the requirements document that you published at the beginning of the project (which hopefully backs up your decision). This takes the heat off of you, because you sent out a document describing the needs being met by your design. If he didn't know about the T1, he didn't read the document.

A requirements document does not need to be large or complicated—in fact, the simpler the document is, the better chance it has of being understood. All points should be made as simply as possible (especially assumptions). Here's an example requirements document:

Requirement:

- The network must support 300 users.

Assumptions:

- Each user will have one workstation.
- Each workstation will have only one Ethernet interface.
- All interfaces will be cabled for 1 Gbps Ethernet.
- The network does not need to support 1 Gbps for all users at the same time.

- Each user will have one phone supporting one phone line.
- All phones will be non-IP phones.
- VoIP will not be run on the network for the foreseeable future.
- Each user will equal one cube or office.
- Each cube or office will have two data jacks and one phone jack.
- All cabling runs will terminate into the computer room (home runs).

When a VP says, "We need a network to support 300 users," he doesn't always understand the implications of this simple statement. Your job is partially to make sure that the other people involved have all the information they need to understand what's happening, and partially to cover your own butt should someone fail to understand what you're doing. If you publish all your assumptions, the VP should be able to read your document and pose any questions he may have. Perhaps there's a plan in the works to move the phone system to VoIP in the next year, and you need to be advised to order equipment that will support that vision.

I've seen many projects fail because no requirements document was written. I've also witnessed (and been party to) many heated arguments about what was said months ago but not put into writing.

Just because people say they understand something, don't assume they do—especially if they are not "technical" people. I once designed an elaborate Internet failover mechanism for a company. When the DS3s were being delivered (after a 60-day lead time), the VP who had signed the order for them started screaming at me because he didn't understand why we needed them. I'd never realized that he didn't understand the design. I had assumed we were all on the same page, but because I had not written a requirements document, there was literally no page for us to be on.

Port Layout Spreadsheets

After the requirements are documented and approved, the design phase can begin. The first step I take when designing any network is to compile a list of all the devices that will be accessing the network. In the case of LANs, here are some things to think about:

- How many users will the network need to support?
- How many servers will the network need to support?
- How many printers will be attached to the network, and what will their locations be?
- What are the applications running on the network? How will users interact with these applications (HTTP, client software, terminals, Citrix)?
- What type of security do you need?
- Is high availability desired and/or affordable?
- What percentage of growth should you assume?

- Do all interfaces need to be gigabit?
- Do you need 10-gigabit?
- Will the network need to support VoIP?
- Will you be supporting one physical location or many (including multiple floors in a single building)?

Your goal is to come up with a target number of each interface type for each location. Once you have these numbers in mind, you can decide what sort of equipment you need to order. Gigabit Ethernet switches come in multiples of 48 at the highest port densities currently available. To determine how many 48-port switches or modules you need, divide the total number of gigabit interfaces required by 48. For example, if you need 340 gigabit interfaces in one location, you'll need 340 / 48 = 7.08 (in other words, eight modules).

 When figuring out how many ports you need, don't forget servers that offer high availability. Many servers today will allow multiple Ethernet interfaces to be connected to one of two switches in a failover pair. Talk with your systems people and find out what they're doing so you don't come up short.

You should also plan for a certain amount of growth. A good rule of thumb for capacity planning is to plan for a minimum of 15 percent growth: 340 * 1.15 = 391. Divide this number by 48 to see how many modules you'll need if you want to allow for growth: 391 / 48 = 8.15. This means you'll need nine modules, which will provide a total of 432 ports. Nine is an odd number, which means one switch will have more modules than the other. This may or may not matter in your environment, but I like to have each side match exactly. It's always better to have too many ports, rather than too few, as long as the budget allows it. Rounding out the modules to 5 on each chassis brings you to 10 modules, totaling 480 ports.

Now you have 480 ports available and a present requirement for 340. This allows for a growth factor of almost 30 percent. Chances are you've missed something (I always do), so having room for more than 15 percent growth is not a bad thing. In cases like this, I make sure to reserve extra ports for expansion purposes. They always come in handy later.

Another requirement that engineers often forget is interswitch trunks. Switches in failover pairs need to be connected to each other, usually with multigigabit links. If you're using Firewall Services Modules, they should have dedicated trunks. ACE modules should also have their own trunks, as should RSPAN, if you'll be using it. If you assume a 2 Gbps EtherChannel for each of these trunks, you've just allocated 16 ports (8 on each side).

I've worked on high-bandwidth networks where each of these trunks required 4 Gbps EtherChannels. A design like this would require 32 ports (16 on each side). That's almost an entire 48-port module just for interswitch communication!

If you need 10-gigabit, remember that these ports can be expensive, and unless you're using Nexus switches, port density can be a problem. Watch out for 10 Gb needs. Modern blade server enclosures will burn two 10 Gb ports, so depending on your environment, they can get used up quickly.

Once you've determined how many ports you'll require, map out the devices you'll need and figure out which devices will serve which purposes. Here, I've decided that 6509-V-E switches will be used in the core, and 2921 routers will be used for Internet and backend connectivity to the corporate website, located in a collocation facility. Figure 35-1 shows my spreadsheet for this information.

Name	Device	Function	Location	Slots	Interfaces			
					T1	DS3	1G	10G
Core-1	6509-E	Core switch/router	Rack #2	9	0	0	240	0
Core-2	6509-E	Core switch/router	Rack #3	9	0	0	240	0
Internet	2811	Internet router	Rack #2	1	2	0	2	0
HQ-Colo	2811	Colo connection router	Rack #3	1	2	0	2	0

Figure 35-1. Sample equipment list

When you've decided what equipment you'll be using, you should break down each device so that you know exactly what hardware to order. This step will help you immensely throughout the process of designing and building the network. When you get the equipment, you can expand the spreadsheet to include the actual serial numbers of each part. Figure 35-2 shows a sample spreadsheet for planning one of the 6509s I've chosen. Notice that I've included not only the modules, but the extra memory as well. Don't worry about extreme detail—your sales rep will flesh this list out with all sorts of ancillary items when she runs it through the Cisco configuration builder.

Name	Device	Function	Slots	Interfaces 10/100/1G	GBIC	SF-GBIC	10G
Core-1	**WS-C6509-VE**	Core Switch/Router	9	240	0	4	12
Slot1	WS-X6748-GE-TX	48 Port 10/100/1000 FE Blade		48			
Slot2	WS-X6748-GE-TX	48 Port 10/100/1000 FE Blade		48			
Slot3	WS-X6748-GE-TX	48 Port 10/100/1000 FE Blade		48			
Slot4	WS-X6748-GE-TX	48 Port 10/100/1000 FE Blade		48			
Slot5	VS-S720-10G-3C	Supervisor - 720 10G		2		2	2
Slot6	VS-S720-10G-3C=	Supervisor - 720 10G		2		2	2
Slot7	WS-SVC-FWM-1-K9=	Firewall Switch Module					
Slot8	WS-X6708-10GE	8-port 10G Module					8
Slot9	WS-X6748-GE-TX	48 Port 10/100/1000 FE Blade		48			
MSFC Mem	MEM-MSFC2-512MB	MSFC - 512M DRAM					
Sup Mem	MEM-S2-512MB	Sup - 512M DRAM					
Flash Mem	MEM-C6K-CPTFL256M	1G Compact Flash Upgrade					
Fan Tray	WS-C6509-E-FAN	Fan Tray					
PS #1	WS-CAC-3000W-US	6000W Power Supply					
PS #2	WS-CAC-3000W-US/2	6000W Power Supply					

Figure 35-2. Core switch hardware detail

Once you have the hardware figured out, it's often up to management to get the equipment ordered. You'll probably need to help with the ordering process by providing lists of part numbers and quantities. Once the order is submitted, you may have to wait several weeks for the equipment to arrive.

Now you need to map every interface on every device. This may sound excessive to some, but planning where every device will connect will save you aggravation later. Having a plan like this can also let you hand off the work of connecting the devices to someone else. This step lets you work on a large chunk of the final documentation before the equipment arrives.

I create a spreadsheet for every device and, sometimes, for every module in a device. It doesn't need to be anything elaborate. A simple list of the ports, the devices connected, and maybe the IP or VLAN to be configured (such as the list in Figure 35-3) suffices.

Physical	VLAN/Trunk/IP	Device	Remote Interface
1/1	VLAN 10	Internet Router	F0/0
1/2		Reserved	
1/3			
1/4			
1/5	VLAN 777	Core-2 FWSM Failover link-1	G1/5
1/6	VLAN 777	Core-2 FWSM Failover link-2	G1/6

Figure 35-3. Sample port assignments

If you have planned your network to this level, when the equipment arrives, all you have to do is install it in the racks and cable together the devices according to the plan.

IP and VLAN Spreadsheets

Along with the physical planning of equipment and port allocation, you'll need to plan the IP network and VLAN layouts. I like to make pretty detailed spreadsheets of this information, just as I did for the physical devices, modules, and ports.

In Figure 35-4, I've allocated my IP networks. I'm allocating a /23 network for each VLAN and reserving the /23 beyond each allocation for future expansion.

Network	Mask	VLAN	Description
10.1.0.0			
10.1.1.0			
10.1.2.0			
10.1.3.0			
10.1.4.0			
10.1.5.0			
10.1.6.0			
10.1.7.0			
10.1.8.0	255.255.254.0	VLAN 10	Internet DMZ
10.1.9.0			
10.1.10.0			*reserved for expansion*
10.1.11.0			*reserved for expansion*
10.1.12.0	255.255.254.0	VLAN 100	VLAN 100
10.1.13.0			
10.1.14.0			*reserved for expansion*
10.1.15.0			*reserved for expansion*

Figure 35-4. IP network layout sheet

I created a spreadsheet for each IP network I'll be using and populated it with specific information regarding every device on the network. This is an excellent exercise that will force you to once again think about every device you'll be connecting. Figure 35-5 shows a sample IP address layout spreadsheet.

Once you have all this information documented, building the configurations should be a snap. As an added bonus, the spreadsheets are excellent documents for the network. They can be printed and put in binders or simply stored somewhere for easy access.

Once the network is built, I suggest printing out a copy of all the documentation you've made. This way, when something changes, you have documented evidence of the condition of the network at the time of its implementation.

Navigation: Master IP spreadsheet

IP address	Subnet mask	VLAN	Description
10.1.32.0			HQ Networks
10.1.32.1	255.255.254.0	VLAN 130	Default Gateway (HSRP VIP)
10.1.32.2	255.255.254.0	VLAN 130	Core-1 VLAN 130 IP
10.1.32.3	255.255.254.0	VLAN 130	Core-2 VLAN 130 IP
10.1.32.4	255.255.254.0	VLAN 130	*Reserved*
10.1.32.5	255.255.254.0	VLAN 130	*Reserved*
10.1.32.6	255.255.254.0	VLAN 130	*Reserved*
10.1.32.7	255.255.254.0	VLAN 130	*Reserved*
10.1.32.8	255.255.254.0	VLAN 130	Color Printer in Charlie's office
10.1.32.9	255.255.254.0	VLAN 130	Color Printer in Lucy's office
10.1.32.10	255.255.254.0	VLAN 130	Color Copier #1
10.1.32.11	255.255.254.0	VLAN 130	Color Copier #2

Figure 35-5. IP address layout sheet

Bay Face Layouts

If you're unfamiliar with the term, *bay face layouts* are diagrams showing how each rack will be built, including every detail. I've also heard the term *rack elevations* used for the same purpose. For me, the biggest benefit of bay face layouts is that once I've created them, I can have someone else install the equipment, if need be. I can turn over all the boxes and a copy of the bay face layouts and say, "Make it look like this." A bay face layout example is shown in Figure 35-6.

There are three things that many engineers forget when designing or planning rack space: power, cabling, and patch panels. All of these items take up space in your racks.

Getting your rack space requirements wrong can be a costly mistake, especially if you're renting collocation space. Bay face layouts are an excellent sanity check to ensure that you have enough racks to support all the equipment you've bought.

Power and Cooling Requirements

This is a good time to work out your power requirements. Most vendors list the power consumption of their equipment on their web pages. Simply find out what kind of power the devices require (AC/DC, voltage, and amperage) and the connectors needed, and add up the requirements for each rack. Talk with the person responsible for the environment where your racks are located, and make sure that it can support the equipment you're putting into your racks.

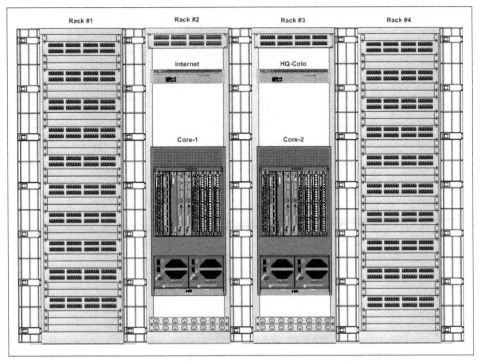

Figure 35-6. Bay face layout

Just because you can fit forty 1 RU servers in a rack doesn't mean you can power them! The default AC power installed in a rack in a collocation facility is often two 20-amp AC power strips. If your 1 RU servers each draw 2 amps and have two power supplies, you can only install 10 in each rack. If you want to add more, you'll need to order extra power, which costs more money. You will also consume more cooling, which may also cost you more money.

Don't forget cooling requirements, either. Along with power specifications, vendors will list the British Thermal Unit (BTU) values for their devices. The person responsible for the environment where the equipment will be installed will also need to know this information. Even though you can physically install two 6509s in a rack, the required air conditioning systems to keep them cool may not be in place.

To find power and heat values for 6500 switches, search Cisco's site for "6500 power and heat numbers." Because the power draw and heat output vary depending on the modules installed, you must figure out this information for each installation. The numbers for the 6509-V-E specified earlier are shown in Figure 35-7. You should compile a similar spreadsheet for every device you will be installing.

| Name | Device | Function | Environment | |
			Watts	BTU/Hr
Core-1	**WS-C6509-V-E**	9-Slot front-back airflow 6500 switch chassis		
Slot1	WS-X6748-GE-TX	48 Port 10/100/1000 FE Blade	367.50	1,255.01
Slot2	WS-X6748-GE-TX	48 Port 10/100/1000 FE Blade	367.50	1,255.01
Slot3	WS-X6748-GE-TX	48 Port 10/100/1000 FE Blade	367.50	1,255.01
Slot4	WS-X6748-GE-TX	48 Port 10/100/1000 FE Blade	367.50	1,255.01
Slot5	VS-S720-10G-3C	VSS Supervisor - 720 Fabric Enabled	422.63	1,443.26
Slot6	VS-S720-10G-3C	VSS Supervisor - 720 Fabric Enabled	422.63	1,443.26
Slot7	WS-SVC-FWM-1-K9	FWSM	214.73	733.29
Slot8	WS-X6708-10G-3C	8-port 10G Ethernet Module	555.45	1,896.86
Slot9	WS-X6748-GE-TX	48 Port 10/100/1000 FE Blade	367.50	1,255.01
MSFC Mem Upgrade	MEM-MSFC2-512MB	MSFC - 512M DRAM		
Sup Mem Upgrade	MEM-S2-512MB	Sup - 512M DRAM		
Flash Mem Upgrade	MEM-C6K-CPTFL512M	512M Compact Flash Upgrade	302.00	1,031.00
Fan Tray	WS-C6509-V-E-FAN	Fan Tray		
Cable Management	WS-C6509-V-E-CM	Cable Management for 6509 V-E Chassis		
PS #1	WS-CAC-3000W-US	6000W Power Supply		
PS #2	WS-CAC-3000W-US/2	6000W Power Supply		
		Totals	3,754.94	12,822.72

Figure 35-7. Power and BTU values for a 6509-V-E

Remember that there will be limits on how many devices can be placed in a rack. In the first edition of this book, I showed how you may not be able to fit more than ten to twelve 1 RU servers in a rack due to power and cooling limitations. In the time since the first edition was published, virtualization and blade servers have both caught on in a big way. This has led many enterprises to adopt them, which has radically changed the way we build racks.

Where we used to try to cram as many servers as possible into a rack, we now try to cram as many virtual servers as possible into as many blades as possible, all within a single blade enclosure. This has a drastic effect on the way we design racks, mostly because of the massive power and cooling requirements these blade servers have. Many times, we can only fit one blade chassis in a rack because of power and cooling limitations. These enclosures often only consume a quarter to a third of the rack, leaving a significant amount of unused physical space. These blade enclosures also commonly require 10 Gb uplinks due to the high number of virtual servers contained within.

Tips for Network Diagrams

Engineers seem to like to make their documents so complicated that even they have trouble reading them. Here are some tips to help you produce documentation that will get you noticed:

Keep it simple

Take a look at any of the drawings in this book. Each is designed to convey a single idea. The more you try to include in a drawing, the harder it will be to understand.

Separate physical and logical ideas

Physical connectivity is very important, but try to keep it separate from VLANs, routing, and other logical subjects. I like to make two drawings: one for the physical ports and another with the VLANs and IP addresses. With the use of SVIs, this becomes even more important.

Don't cross lines

Every time you cross a line in a drawing, the drawing gets harder to read. Sometimes it's unavoidable, but try to keep crossed lines to a minimum.

Orient your straight lines

If you put together a drawing in which the straight lines are slightly off the horizontal or vertical, it will look like the etchings of a serial killer. When you take the time to orient all the lines, the difference is dramatic. Similarly, lines drawn at an angle should all be at the same angle where possible.

Delineate when you can

If there are two locations in your drawing, separate them somehow. Put each one in a rectangle (many people rounded rectangles). Using colors or even shades of gray can help as well.

Line up your icons

If you have a row of icons in your drawing, take the time to line them all up along a single axis.

Naming Conventions for Devices

Hostnames should be constructed so that anyone with a rudimentary knowledge of the network can determine the devices' functions. However, there seems to be a tendency among IT people to give their devices the most incomprehensible names possible. For example, here's a real hostname from my time in the field (I've changed the company name and details to protect the guilty): gadnslax1mai750901. What the heck does that mean? Is it relevant? Can I tell what the system is from the hostname? More importantly, can you?

In a training session for the network containing these wacky hostnames, one of the students asked what the hostnames meant. No one could answer without looking up the document describing the hostname layout. Hostnames should not require research! Here's the breakdown of the offending name:

gadnslax1mai750901

gad - The name of the company (GAD Technology)

ns - Network services

lax - Los Angeles

1 - It's the first, um, thing in Los Angeles

mai - Main Street

7509 - The device is a Cisco 7509

01 - It's the first 7509 in this location

The purpose of a hostname is to identify a device. Hostnames should be easy to remember. When a hostname is harder to remember than an IP address, using one is counterproductive.

When a hostname is coupled with a domain name to make a *fully qualified domain name* (FQDN), the resulting string should be obvious and simple. sw1.gad.net (*http:// sw1.gad.net*) is a simple and obvious FQDN that describes the first switch in the *gad* network provider domain.

I like hostnames that describe one thing—the function of the device. *WAN-Router* is an excellent hostname. For companies that have multiple locations, adding the location to the hostname (e.g., *LAX-WAN-Router*) is useful. Equipment is usually deployed in pairs, in which case it's also a good idea to number the device (e.g., *LAX-WAN-Router-1*). In my opinion, though, that name is too long. The fact that the device is a router is irrelevant to its function; *LAX-WAN-1* will suffice. If you want to use DNS hierarchies, *wan-1.lax.domain.com* works nicely as well.

Every company has unique needs. If you work at an ISP, you may have devices at the premises of many customers. In this case, including the customer name is beneficial (e.g., *GAD-WAN-1*). You should resist the urge to document your network with the hostname. You don't need to include the serial number of the device in the hostname, either (yes, I've really seen this). Of course, everyone has their own opinions on hostnames, but my advice is to keep them as simple as possible. That being said, *Lauren* is not a good name for a router either. It's a pretty name, but it doesn't give any indication of the router's function!

Once I have my hostnames figured out, I prepend interface names to the hostnames for DNS. For example, Serial 0/0/0:1 on *LAX-WAN-1* would have the DNS hostname of *s0-0-0-1-lax-wan-1* (because DNS can only use hyphens, I replace each slash and colon with a hyphen). This makes traceroutes very readable, because each node and IP interface within the node is clearly labeled:

```
[gad]$traceroute switch9.mydomain.com
traceroute to switch9.mydomain.com (10.10.10.10), 30 hops max, 40 byte packets
1  s0-0.router1.mydomain.com 9.854 ms  10.978 ms  11.368 ms
2  f0-1.switch2.mydomain.com 2.340 ms  1.475 ms  1.138 ms
3  g0-0-12.switch9.mydomain.com 1.844 ms  1.430 ms  1.833 ms
```

Network Designs

I can't tell you how you should design your network. I can, however, show you some of the more common corporate and ecommerce network designs out there and explain why I've chosen to focus on these designs.

Corporate Networks

Most networks are designed along the lines of the classic *three-tier model*. The three-tier model has *core*, *distribution*, and *access* levels. These levels are clearly delineated and served by different devices. Traditionally, routing was the slowest, most expensive process. For these reasons, routing was done in the core. All the other levels were usually switched.

With the advent of inexpensive Layer-3 switching, the three-tiered model is now often collapsed for corporate networks. We'll look at the traditional model as it might be used today, as well as a couple of collapsed-core models.

Three-tiered architecture

The three-tiered architecture that is most commonly seen in textbooks is still widely used in the industry. Physical separation of the three levels usually occurs when there is a physical need to do so. An excellent example is a college or business campus: there might be core switches (possibly in a central location), distribution switches in each building, and access switches close to the users in each building. The specifics depend on the physical layout of the campus. Figure 35-8 shows a textbook three-tiered corporate network.

At the bottom of the drawing, users, printers, IP phones, and wireless access points (APs) are connected to the access-layer switches. The access-layer switches are connected to the distribution-layer switches in the middle row. The distribution switches connect to the top two switches, which are the core of the network. The Internet and the server farm are both connected to the core in this example.

Collapsed core—no distribution

Collapsed-core networks are very common. I work a lot in Manhattan, where skyscrapers are the norm. Office space in skyscrapers is usually allocated on a floor-by-floor basis. Wiring is usually run from points on the floor to a central location on the same floor. Floors are usually interconnected with conduits that run between floors. When a company occupies multiple floors, the wiring of each floor lends itself to a collapsed-core design, because there are limited wiring possibilities between floors.

Because the amount of space on each floor is limited, there is typically little need for more than two physical network layers. With the core switches on one floor and access switches on the remaining floors, the access switches can act as distribution-layer

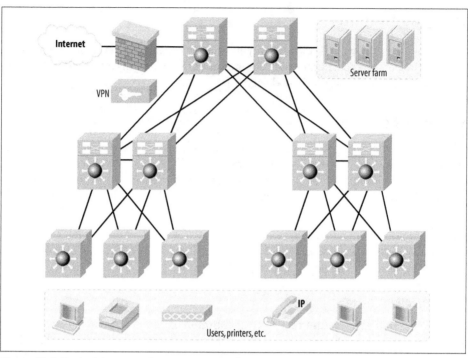

Figure 35-8. Typical three-tiered corporate network

switches as well. Port density is usually not an issue, as each floor does not occupy much physical space. From a logical standpoint, the distribution layer may be collapsed into the core as well. You may not even need a logical distribution layer at all. Again, each environment is different.

Server Farms—Where Do They Belong?

Do servers belong near the users that they serve, or in a farm near the core? Where servers belong in your network depends on how your network is designed, and often on the type of server in question. Some servers should be in the core. Centrally locating email servers, for instance, makes sense. Other servers should be closer to the users they serve. For example, in a campus network, it would not make sense to put accounting servers in the core if the entire Accounting department is located in one building. Then again, there may not be space in each building for servers.

A lot depends on the layout of your network, too. Many companies these days are building completely flat networks, with the core/distribution/access model being completely collapsed into a single pair of large switches, such as Cisco 6509s. In this case, everything is connected to the same switches, making the argument moot.

Another scenario I've seen that lends itself to this type of design is the segmented building. One project I worked on involved redesigning the network for a major stadium. The stadium was divided into four segments, each of which had its own infrastructure room (closet). The users' cables were run to these closets, and the closets were linked together with fiber.

Figure 35-9 shows an example of a collapsed-core network without a distribution layer.

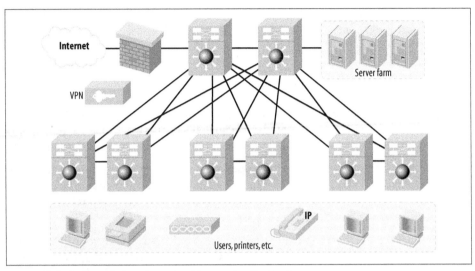

Figure 35-9. Collapsed-core network without a distribution layer

Collapsed core—no distribution or access

A very popular design in companies that are contained within a single building is the collapsed network, where there are only core switches. A company with hundreds of employees that are all in a single location can often manage to have its computer room central to the environment. As long as the Ethernet runs can remain within the distance limitations of the cabling in use, all runs can be home runs back to the core switches. A pair of high-density, high-availability switches like Cisco 6509s can support hundreds of users. Such a network design is shown in Figure 35-10.

Configuration concerns

I'm not going to go through the detailed steps of configuring a corporate network here. Instead, I'll point out some elements you should consider when designing such a network, and try to point you in the right direction. I will be using a collapsed-core model with no distribution layer as an example. You can use Figure 35-9 as a reference.

Trunks. Trunks may be necessary anywhere switches are interconnected. The obvious points are between the two core switches and the links connecting the access switches to the core. And don't forget the links between each pair of access switches.

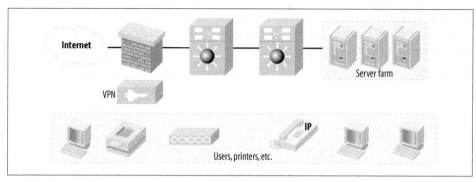

Figure 35-10. Collapsed-core network consisting of only one layer

You may choose to design your network such that the links between switches are IP links, not trunks. This is perfectly valid, and can make the network easier to understand for many people. If you do choose a Layer-3 network design, you will need fewer trunks.

EtherChannels. I like to link my switches together with a minimum of two connections bound together by an EtherChannel. This provides a bit of resiliency and increases the bandwidth between the switches. Depending on your network, you may want to increase the size of the bundles to three, four, or even more.

You may have servers that require EtherChannels as well. Check with your server group to see if this feature is required and, if so, how it should be configured. Check Chapter 18 for details on Virtual Port Channels (vPCs) that can span multiple devices using Nexus switches. Similarly, the 6500 VSS system can support Multichassis Etherchannel (MEC).

If your core switches will have modules such as FWSMs that require dedicated links between failover pairs, you may need to design EtherChannels for these as well. For more information on EtherChannels, refer to Chapter 7.

Spanning tree. Determine which ports will be user or server ports, and configure them for `spanning-tree portfast`. Configure one of the core switches to be the spanning tree root bridge, and the other core switch to be the secondary root bridge. See Chapter 8 for additional details.

VTP. I'm not a big fan of Virtual Trunking Protocol (VTP), especially for small networks, but even if you don't use it, you'll need to configure a VTP domain name. Trunk negotiation requires the VTP domain to be set properly. See Chapters 5 and 6 for more details.

VLANs. How many VLANs will you need? Make sure you plan them all out ahead of time. Here's a list I came up with just by looking at Figure 35-9:

- Internet
- Internet inside
- Server farm

- User VLANs

Planning ahead of time will save you from having to make last-minute decisions and wasting time.

Ecommerce Websites

An ecommerce website is one on which goods are sold and money is exchanged, and thus it involves some concerns that don't exist with simple websites. The biggest challenge is security. If you throw together a Linux server and host a simple website on it, you only have to worry about security for the web server. With an ecommerce website, you will probably have multiple web servers. Each of those web servers will probably need to access a database, which should not be accessible from the Internet. In fact, the database shouldn't even be directly accessible from the web servers! Instead, there should be a layer of servers that process requests to the database on the web servers' behalf. This layer of servers is called the *application layer*. Now you have to worry about security for web servers, application servers, and database servers. Some or all of these servers may need to be load balanced, and all of them will need to be managed. Management can be an interesting challenge because, as I've said, database servers should not be accessible from the Internet.

The database servers will contain customer information and possibly credit card data. This information must be protected. Keeping the servers away from the Internet is one of the best ways to accomplish the required protection.

The standard design for an ecommerce website is composed of three tiers. The first tier contains the web servers, which are reachable from the Internet. This is called the Internet layer. The second tier contains the application servers, which cannot usually be reached from the Internet. These servers can talk to the web servers above them and the database servers beneath them. The lowest layer is the database layer, which can be accessed only from the application layer.

 There are many ways to design an ecommerce website. The network design will be determined, in large part, by the software in use and the developer's methods. I've worked on ecommerce websites that had only two layers and others with four. Sometimes, developers will insist on a single layer. If the application simply does not support multiple layers, forcing the issue will only waste time. Still, when dealing with servers that store credit card data, make sure your design adheres to Payment Card Industry (PCI) standards for security.

The Internet layer is the least secure layer, because it is accessible from the Internet. Even though this layer is protected by a firewall, the general population has access to services residing in this layer. The most secure layer is the database layer. The only way to access the database layer is through the application servers. These servers will have special applications residing on them that can process and possibly cache database information for the web servers.

The three-tier ecommerce architecture is shown in Figure 35-11. The Internet layer contains the most servers. The number of servers generally decreases in the lower layers, though this is not a universal truth. For example, the database layer may be composed of an Oracle cluster, which could use many smaller servers.

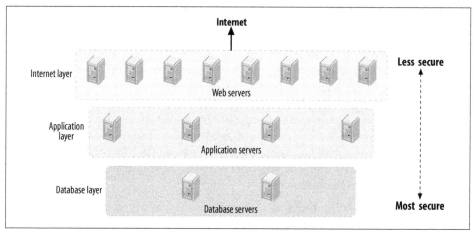

Figure 35-11. Typical three-tier ecommerce website

The servers at each level connect with servers in the adjacent level or levels. For example, application servers have interfaces in the database layer and the Internet layer. All servers must have multiple interfaces. In the case of high-availability networks, the servers may need four interfaces: two for the level above (one in each switch) and two for the level below.

There are two generally accepted methods for accomplishing this layering. I'll call them *bridging* and *routing*. In the bridging method, the lower interfaces of the upper layer are connected to the same VLAN as the upper interfaces of the layer beneath them. Figure 35-12 shows an example of a bridged ecommerce design. The advantages of this design include simplicity and speed. There are only three VLANs, and there are no routers or firewalls separating the layers. The disadvantage is decreased security, as there are no devices separating the servers on one layer from the servers on the next.

The servers in a bridged design need to talk to the networks directly connected to them. The web servers are the only servers that require a default gateway in this design.

The more secure alternative to the bridged design is the routed design. Routing between the layers allows firewalls to be placed between them. Figure 35-13 shows a typical routed three-tier ecommerce design.

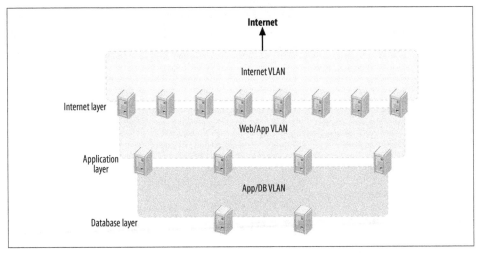

Figure 35-12. Bridged three-tier ecommerce design

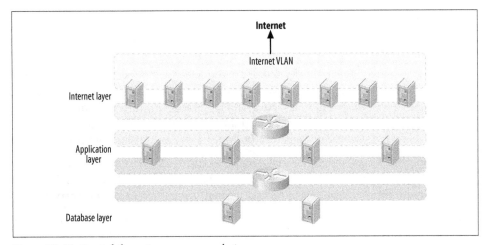

Figure 35-13. Routed three-tier ecommerce design

The routed design is more complicated because there are almost twice as many VLANs, each of which must have an SVI or router interface associated with it. Because there are physical or logical routers separating the VLANs, the servers on each level must have default gateways or route statements configured. The benefit of a routed design is security. Because all traffic must pass through a router, the router can be a firewall.

The problem with both of these designs is that there is no easy way to manage the servers remotely. If you have easy access to the servers, having a Keyboard Video Monitor (KVM) switch in each rack can solve this problem. However, ecommerce websites are typically hosted in separate collocation facilities. In this case, remote management capabilities are vital.

Remote management is often accomplished with another VLAN that connects to every server and network device at the site. This management VLAN then connects to a router or firewall that allows connectivity to the main site. Figure 35-14 shows such a design.

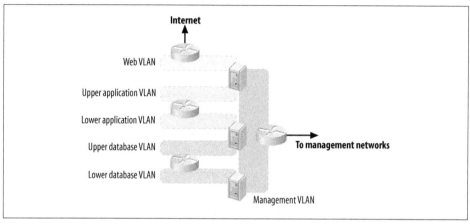

Figure 35-14. Ecommerce management network

You've gone through great pains to make sure the servers are secure. You've separated all of the servers into layers and prohibited the web servers from communicating with the database servers. Now you've added another VLAN that connects them all together. If you're thinking that this looks like a bad idea, you're right. The benefits of a management network do outweigh the risks, but only if you design the network properly.

Management networks should be very secure. Features like port security and private VLANs can help keep the network secure. No server should be allowed to talk to any other server on this network, with the exception of backup and telemetry servers.

The problem with all these VLANs is that they are usually combined with a high-availability network design. For every VLAN a server must connect to, it must use two Ethernet interfaces: one for each switch in the high-availability pair. While this may not sound like a big deal, with only three VLANs for the average server, that's six Ethernet interfaces in use. Figure 35-15 shows a typical server connected to three VLANs on two switches.

When designing a network like this, make sure you work closely with your systems people. There are a lot of things to think about. Here's a short list:

- Every interface will need an IP address.
- In some server high-availability solutions, you'll need a third IP address for each VLAN. For example, IP multipathing requires a virtual IP address on each VLAN in addition to one for each physical interface.
- Every IP address you assign may need a DNS entry (including virtual IP addresses).

- Which interface is primary?
- Does the server need a default gateway? If so, where does it go? Can the server support multiple defaults? How will this work? Web servers need a default gateway that points to the Internet. This will require your management VLAN to have specific routes on the servers.
- How many physical network cards do you need in a server to support six Ethernet interfaces? Make sure you have enough. Extra interfaces are even better.
- Will the servers have both interfaces active in each VLAN, or just one? Some server high-availability solutions require the switches to be configured a certain way, while others require different configurations. Work this out in a lab before you build your network.
- Will your servers support remote Ethernet consoles? Will you need a dedicated network for this traffic?

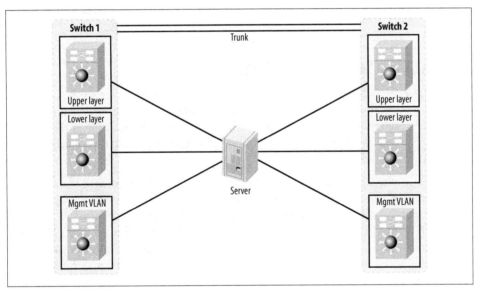

Figure 35-15. Ethernet interfaces in use on a server

When you're figuring out your IP scheme, it's a good idea to make the last octet (or octets) the same for every interface on each server. In other words, if your upper network is 10.1.10.0/24 and your lower network is 10.1.20.0/24, make the last octet match for the server on each network. Thus, the upper IP address would be 10.1.10.10, and the lower IP address would be 10.1.20.10. Remember that you must assign an IP address for each interface, so make the last octet match for each switch. Figure 35-16 shows how such an IP scheme might work.

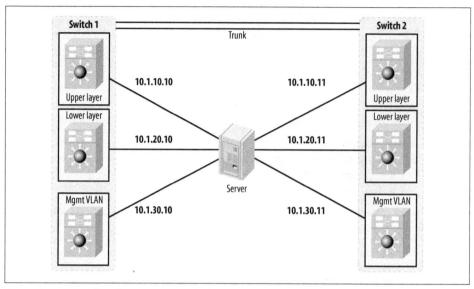

Figure 35-16. Matching last octet on multiple VLANs and switches

Modern Virtual Server Environments

Many data centers have migrated away from the rack-mount server scenario in favor of blade servers that reside in a chassis. These chassis-based servers usually allow aggregation of networking links into multiple 10 Gb links. This may lower the number of ports required for your network, though you'll need to provision properly with 10 Gb–capable network devices.

Additionally, virtual servers have become very popular. Combined with blade servers, the IP requirements can be staggering. With physical network interfaces replaced by virtual devices (within virtual servers), it's very tempting for server admins to just add another NIC to a server where they might not with traditional hardware. When designing for these new server architectures, remember that they will likely need 10 Gb ports, usually configured as trunks. To get the most from your links, consider multichassis link aggregation such as VSS or Nexus vPC. Watch your QoS, too, as some blade server chassis "carve up" bandwidth without using QoS.

Small Networks

Many small companies don't need elaborate three-tiered networks. Maybe they have only one office, or even three, but the offices are small and the networks are simple. Even some larger companies do not have elaborate networks. No matter the size or complexity of the network, every aspect of it should be thoroughly documented.

## CHAPTER 36

IP Design

When a network or group of networks is designed well, the payoff can be substantial. The payoff, however, is in hours *not* spent, which can be very hard to quantify. Believe me, though—designing IP space the right way the first time can save literally thousands of work hours over the lifetime of the network.

IP address allocation is rarely done properly, and many unlucky network administrators end up inheriting a mess of IP networks that's just been thrown together over time. In many cases, small networks are built with no vision of where the companies might end up, resulting in massive undertakings when the IP networks need to be changed. And even the best of IP address schemes can be rent asunder by a merger or acquisition.

Think about how long it takes to put an IP address, subnet mask, and default gateway on a server. Not long at all when you're installing the server. Now think about what is involved when the IP address, subnet mask, or default gateway needs to be changed. The server must be taken offline, which usually involves a change control. In many environments, the change needs to happen during a change-control window, which may involve you coming into the office or data center at 2:00 a.m. Now imagine that your company has 100, 200, or 1,000 servers. Don't forget that DNS and/or WINS and Active Directory will need to be updated, too.

IP network design is not a glamorous project. It is not something that the CTO will pat you on the back for in a meeting. IP network design is not something that many people will appreciate at all, until it is explained to them. Still, careful planning and design are required to create an IP schema that will allow growth for years to come.

Public Versus Private IP Space

If you've taken any certification exams, you should be familiar with the idea of public versus private IP space. In a nutshell, there are a select number of IP networks that should not be routed on the public Internet. These networks are described in RFC 1918 ("Address Allocation for Private Internets") as follows:

3. Private Address Space

The Internet Assigned Numbers Authority (IANA) has reserved the following three blocks of the IP address space for private internets:

10.0.0.0 – 10.255.255.255 (10/8 prefix)

172.16.0.0 – 172.31.255.255 (172.16/12 prefix)

192.168.0.0 - 192.168.255.255 (192.168/16 prefix)

A quick note about these ranges is in order. First, the 172.16.0.0 network is not just the /16 range, and it is not the 172.0.0.0/8 range. The range allocated for 172.16.0.0 is a /12. The IP range included in this private range is 172.16.0.0–172.31.255.255. The ranges 172.0.0.0–172.15.255.255 and 172.32.0.0–172.255.255.255 are not composed of private addresses and should not be used as such. This is a common mistake in the real world.

Other ranges are also reserved and should not be used. A now-common example is the use of the 169.254.0.0/16 network when DHCP requests go unanswered. RFC 3330 (Special-Use IPv4 Addresses) describes these networks. The entry for 169.254.0.0 is as follows:

169.254.0.0/16 - This is the "link local" block. It is allocated for communication between hosts on a single link. Hosts obtain these addresses by auto-configuration, such as when a DHCP server may not be found.

Over the years, I have encountered more than one company whose entire scheme was based on the network 128.0.0.0 because it was easy to decipher in binary (10000000.00000000.00000000.00000000). This is a dangerous practice. Again, RFC 3330 provides the details:

128.0.0.0/16 - This block, corresponding to the numerically lowest of the former Class B addresses, was initially and is still reserved by the IANA. Given the present classless nature of the IP address space, the basis for the reservation no longer applies and addresses in this block are subject to future allocation to a Regional Internet Registry for assignment in the normal manner.

Similarly, you should never use the 127.0.0.0/8 network when designing IP networks. Though many people are familiar with the fact that 127.0.0.1 is a local loopback address, many are unaware that the entire network is reserved. RFC 3330 explains:

127.0.0.0/8 - This block is assigned for use as the Internet host loopback address. A datagram sent by a higher level protocol to an address anywhere within this block should loop back inside the host. This is ordinarily implemented using only 127.0.0.1/32 for loopback, but no addresses within this block should ever appear on any network anywhere [RFC1700, page 5].

Many companies design their IP networks with a complete disregard for the rules, often using IP ranges that correspond to addresses, building numbers, or branch numbers. The risks of such designs have to do with connectivity and the rules of routing. If a host on the improperly numbered network 15.1.1.1/24 tries to get to a web page on a server with the same IP network and mask, the rules of routing will indicate that they are on the same network, so the packet will never be forwarded to the default gateway. Some would argue that a firewall with NAT is the solution for poor IP design, but because the host will never forward the packets to the default gateway, they will never be NATed.

Additionally, when companies form partnerships with other companies, they often link their networks together. A smart company will not link with a company that violates the IP rules, as it, too, will be affected, since it will inherit routes to the improperly used IP spaces.

Remember, if there is a route in the routing table for a destination network, the default gateway is not involved. Should a valid public network be misused internally, your users will never be able to get to any services on that valid public network.

Figure 36-1 shows an example of an improperly used public IP network. In this example, the world's most interesting web page has a legitimate IP address of 25.25.25.40 with a subnet mask of 255.255.255.0. Bob, in Company A, has an improperly used IP address of 25.0.0.15 with a subnet mask of 255.0.0.0. What is important to understand in this example is that even though the subnet masks are different, no one in either Company A or Company B can get to the world's most interesting web page.

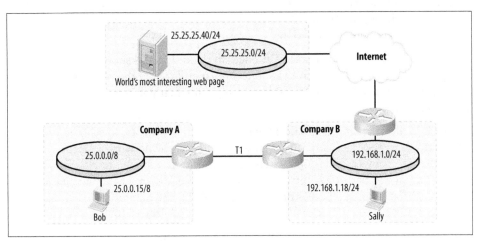

Figure 36-1. Invalid use of a public IP network

Bob cannot get to the world's most interesting web page because, as far as the routers are concerned, he is on the same IP network as the destination. The IP stack on his machine will assume that because the destination is on the same network, it does not need to forward the packets to the default gateway. In this case, Bob's computer will either send the packets to a local device (should one exist with the same IP address as the world's most interesting web page), or fail to resolve the IP address to a local MAC address. Either way, Bob will never be able to see the world's most interesting web page.

Assuming Company B would like its employees or servers to be able to get to Company A's devices (why else would there be a link?), the router connecting Company B to the Internet must have a route to Company A's network—in this case, 25.0.0.0 255.0.0.0. Because the default route will only be used if there are no matching routes in the routing table and because, in this case, there is a matching route in the routing table, the packets destined for the world's most interesting web page will be forwarded to Company A. Therefore, Sally will not be able to access the world's most interesting web page either.

VLSM

Variable Length Subnet Masking (VLSM) is the best thing to happen to IP networking since subnet masks. In a nutshell, according to what we'll call *classful subnetting rules*, if a network is divided into subnets, each subnet within the classful network must be the same size. Figure 36-2 shows the ways in which a Class C network can be divided. Under the traditional classful rules, these are the only divisions possible. The reason for this is the binary nature of the subnet mask.

When IP was developed, there were more IP addresses available than anyone could have possibly wanted—or so we all thought! But as the world progressed, we quickly discovered that we were running out of IP address space at an alarming rate. Some bright minds determined that if the rules of subnetting could be altered a bit, we could give ourselves some breathing room. The result was VLSM.

VLSM states that when a network is subnetted, the individual subnets do *not* need be of equal size. The caveat is that the subnets must still follow the rules of binary; that is, they must exist where they would normally fall when you're subnetting using the traditional rules.

Figure 36-3 shows examples of a normally subnetted network, a proper VLSM network, and an invalid VLSM network. In the invalid example, the network 192.168.1.200/28 is not permitted by the rules of subnetting. Remember, a subnet must exist where it would normally fit had you subnetted the entire network with that subnet mask. If you were to configure an IP address of 192.168.1.200/28, the network address would be 192.168.1.192 and the broadcast address would be 192.168.1.207.

The benefits of VLSM should be apparent. In the old days, we used to have to put aside entire classful networks just for /30 subnets (once a /30 subnet was allocated within a classful network, the entire network had to be allocated with the same subnet mask). Often, 80 percent of the network was wasted because it had to be allocated as /30 subnets, when only 10 or so /30 subnets were needed. With VLSM, you can use 25 percent of a network for /30 subnets, another 25 percent for /27 subnets, and so on. Needless to say, VLSM has had a serious impact on the allocation of IP space, both on the Internet and in private networks.

Figure 36-2. *Classful subnets of a /24 network*

/24	/25	/26	/27	/28	/29	/30
192.168.1.0/24	192.168.1.0/25	192.168.1.0/26	192.168.1.0/27	192.168.1.0/28	192.168.1.0/29	192.168.1.0/30
						192.168.1.4/30
					192.168.1.8/29	192.168.1.8/30
						192.168.1.12/30
				192.168.1.16/28	192.168.1.16/29	192.168.1.16/30
						192.168.1.20/30
					192.168.1.24/29	192.168.1.24/30
						192.168.1.28/30
			192.168.1.32/27	192.168.1.32/28	192.168.1.32/29	192.168.1.32/30
						192.168.1.36/30
					192.168.1.40/29	192.168.1.40/30
						192.168.1.44/30
				192.168.1.48/28	192.168.1.48/29	192.168.1.48/30
						192.168.1.52/30
					192.168.1.56/29	192.168.1.56/30
						192.168.1.60/30
		192.168.1.64/26	192.168.1.64/27	192.168.1.64/28	192.168.1.64/29	192.168.1.64/30
						192.168.1.68/30
					192.168.1.72/29	192.168.1.72/30
						192.168.1.76/30
				192.168.1.80/28	192.168.1.80/29	192.168.1.80/30
						192.168.1.84/30
					192.168.1.88/29	192.168.1.88/30
						192.168.1.92/30
			192.168.1.96/27	192.168.1.96/28	192.168.1.96/29	192.168.1.96/30
						192.168.1.100/30
					192.168.1.104/29	192.168.1.104/30
						192.168.1.108/30
				192.168.1.112/28	192.168.1.112/29	192.168.1.112/30
						192.168.1.116/30
					192.168.1.120/29	192.168.1.120/30
						192.168.1.124/30
	192.168.1.128/25	192.168.1.128/26	192.168.1.128/27	192.168.1.128/28	192.168.1.128/29	192.168.1.128/30
						192.168.1.132/30
					192.168.1.136/29	192.168.1.136/30
						192.168.1.140/30
				192.168.1.144/28	192.168.1.144/29	192.168.1.144/30
						192.168.1.148/30
					192.168.1.152/29	192.168.1.152/30
						192.168.1.156/30
			192.168.1.160/27	192.168.1.160/28	192.168.1.160/29	192.168.1.160/30
						192.168.1.164/30
					192.168.1.168/29	192.168.1.168/30
						192.168.1.172/30
				192.168.1.176/28	192.168.1.176/29	192.168.1.176/30
						192.168.1.180/30
					192.168.1.184/29	192.168.1.184/30
						192.168.1.188/30
		192.168.1.192/26	192.168.1.192/27	192.168.1.192/28	192.168.1.192/29	192.168.1.192/30
						192.168.1.196/30
					192.168.1.200/29	192.168.1.200/30
						192.168.1.204/30
				192.168.1.208/28	192.168.1.208/29	192.168.1.208/30
						192.168.1.212/30
					192.168.1.216/29	192.168.1.216/30
						192.168.1.220/30
			192.168.1.224/27	192.168.1.224/28	192.168.1.224/29	192.168.1.224/30
						192.168.1.228/30
					192.168.1.232/29	192.168.1.232/30
						192.168.1.236/30
				192.168.1.240/28	192.168.1.240/29	192.168.1.240/30
						192.168.1.244/30
					192.168.1.248/29	192.168.1.248/30
						192.168.1.252/30

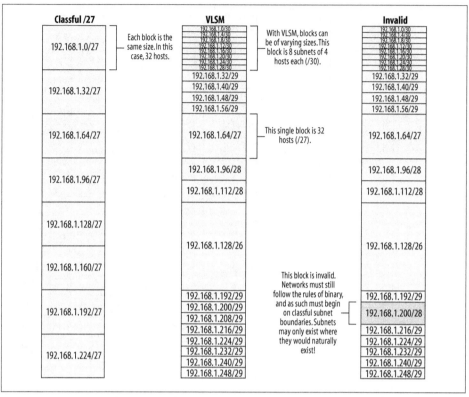

Figure 36-3. Correct and incorrect subnets using VLSM

CIDR

If you deal with large numbers of IP networks, like ISPs do, *Classless Internet Domain Routing* (CIDR) is a most useful tool. While VLSM has had a dramatic impact on IP space allocation within corporate networks, CIDR has had an equally impressive impact on public Internet networks allocated to ISPs.

CIDR is sort of the inverse of VLSM: whereas VLSM prescribes rules for subdividing networks, CIDR prescribes rules for referencing groups of networks with a single route statement.

Aggregating routes may seem like a solution looking for a problem if you've only ever dealt with small or medium-size corporate networks, but, rest assured, it provides a real benefit. Usually, small or medium-size companies use one of the private IP networks described by RFC 1918. If a company uses the entire 10.0.0.0/8 network and subdivides it to maximize efficiency, each of these subdivisions is technically a subnet. While VLSM deals with subnets, CIDR deals with groups of *major* or *classful* networks.

Figure 36-4 shows how a single route statement can reference 16 Class C networks. The route is called an *aggregate* route or a *summary* route.

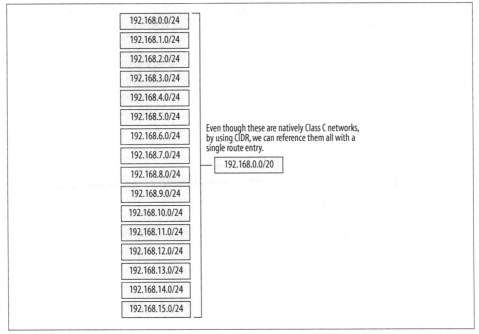

Figure 36-4. CIDR route aggregation

On Internet-attached routers with *full tables*, the routing tables may contain hundreds of thousands of routes. Anyone can see them at any time by connecting to one of many publicly available route servers. To illustrate this point, here's a sample of the number of routes the AT&T IP Services Route Monitor shows as of this writing:

```
route-server>sho ip bgp summary
BGP router identifier 12.0.1.28, local AS number 65000
BGP table version is 75630579, main routing table version 75630579
324578 network entries using 39273938 bytes of memory
5975892 path entries using 310746384 bytes of memory
362530/55439 BGP path/bestpath attribute entries using 50754200 bytes of memory
76457 BGP AS-PATH entries using 1996260 bytes of memory
156 BGP community entries using 3744 bytes of memory
0 BGP route-map cache entries using 0 bytes of memory
0 BGP filter-list cache entries using 0 bytes of memory
BGP using 402774526 total bytes of memory
Dampening enabled. 1280 history paths, 1747 dampened paths
BGP activity 1828537/1503956 prefixes, 50259731/44283836 paths, scan interval 60 secs
```

When I wrote the first edition of this book, there were 182,347 network entries on this route server. Roughly four years later, there are 324,578. It is reasonable to assume that any router connected to the Internet that is receiving full tables will contain a similar number of network entries. Notice the fourth line:

```
324578 network entries using 39273938 bytes of memory
```

Those entries are taking up 39,273,938 bytes of memory in the router versus only 18,417,047 bytes four years ago. More importantly, anytime a change is made to the paths to any of these networks, the entire world of BGP-connected routers must be notified.

CIDR comes into play on the Internet because it helps to make these massive tables smaller. It also helps smaller networks (and, more importantly, their administrators) by making local routing tables smaller. Smaller routing tables are more logical, easier to understand, and much simpler to troubleshoot during outages.

Allocating IP Network Space

One of the problems I've seen repeatedly over the years is improper allocation of IP network space. Whether the trouble is the use of public IP addresses that are not rightfully owned or just a designer's lack of understanding of the benefits of proper IP allocation, a poorly designed IP network can cause daily headaches and increased troubleshooting time. And because a poorly designed IP scheme can take months to rectify, the problem usually gets worse over time because no one wants to take on the task of renumbering the entire network.

There are some simple rules that can help when you're designing a network using IP address space. Here is the first one:

> When allocating IP address space, endeavor to allocate a block that can be referenced with a single access list entry.

Following this simple rule will make everything from server allocations to global network design much simpler.

Assume for a minute that you've been asked to create a network for a new server farm. The powers that be insist there will only ever be 30 servers in the farm. You, being the bright admin, ask what kind of servers they will be. The response is that they will all be Oracle servers.

The average admin might be quick to say that a /27 (255.255.255.224) network is in order, as it provides 32 host addresses. Two of these are used for network and broadcast addresses, however, leaving no room for growth. This leads us to our next rule:

> Always allocate more IP address space than is originally requested.

If your boss requests 30 IP addresses, give her a block of 64; if she requests 60, give her 128. While this may seem wasteful on the surface, you are always better off with excess IP addresses within a subnet. You must learn to balance the need for growth with the overall availability of addresses. Allocating 256 addresses when only 30 are requested is usually foolish given normal growth patterns. Allowing for 30 percent growth is a good rule of thumb. Rounding up until you get to binary boundaries (16, 32, 64, etc.) makes this rule pretty easy to implement.

To make things even more interesting, let's say there is already a server farm in your network. The IP network for the server farm is 10.100.100.0/24. There are already 10 servers in place, as well as a router port that connects the network to the rest of the company. Assume the IP addresses in use are 1–11 (people like to allocate numbers in order).

When asked for 30 more IP addresses, why not just provide the addresses 12–42? You could do this, and everyone would be fat, dumb, and happy. But here's where you can be smarter than the average admin. Instead of allocating a random list of IP addresses based on the last number used, allocate a block that agrees with our first rule: *when allocating IP address space, endeavor to allocate a block that can be referenced with a single access list entry*. If you allocate the range of 32–63, not only have you allocated enough IP addresses, but you can reference the range like this:

```
Access-list 101 permit ip any 10.100.100.32 255.255.255.224 eq web
```

But what about our second rule? *Always allocate more IP address space than is originally requested*. Because 30 IP addresses were requested, you should think ahead and allocate 64. This changes things a bit, because according to the rules of subnetting, you can't allocate 64 contiguous IP addresses starting at 32. Looking back at Figure 36-3, you can see that you'll need to start at a multiple of 64. So, allocate 64–127:

```
Access-list 101 permit ip any 10.100.100.64 255.255.255.192 eq web
```

Still only one ACL entry!

Now you can create security rules based on logical groups of devices where none previously existed. By comparison if you'd used 12–42, you would have needed the following lines to achieve the same thing as the single line above:

```
Access-list 101 permit ip and 10.100.100.12 255.255.255.252 eq web
Access-list 101 permit ip and 10.100.100.16 255.255.255.248 eq web
Access-list 101 permit ip and 10.100.100.32 255.255.255.250 eq web
Access-list 101 permit ip and 10.100.100.40 255.255.255.254 eq web
Access-list 101 permit ip and 10.100.100.42 255.255.255.255 eq web
```

You've allocated twice the requested number of IP addresses, and you can address them using one-fifth the number of ACL entries.

When you allocate groups of similar servers into what I like to call *subnettable ranges*, another benefit comes to light. When servers are grouped like this, you can remove them from the network and place them on their own physical networks without changing the IP scheme. This takes some planning, but when it pays off, it pays off in a big way.

Figure 36-5 shows how this idea might be applied. Even though the network in place is 10.100.100.0/24, if you apply your servers within logical groups of IP addresses corresponding to subnet boundaries, later on you can actually subnet the network without changing the IP addresses of any servers. You'll only need to change the subnet masks and default gateways.

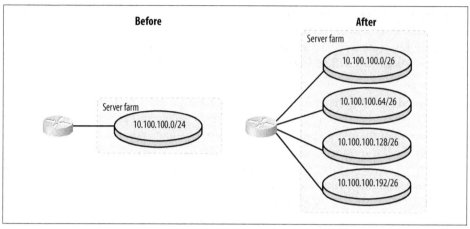

Figure 36-5. Subnetting an existing range

This kind of thing happens more often than you might think. Perhaps the boss will decide that all of the Oracle servers should be on their own physical network for security reasons. No problem! Because you were smart enough to allocate their IP space along subnet boundaries, the entire range can easily be pulled out and moved to another interface. All the IP addresses will stay the same; only the subnet masks will change.

The catch (isn't there always a catch?) is that you must be vigilant! If even one IP address is allocated in violation of these rules, you will have to renumber something to move a section of the existing network.

Allocating IP Subnets

When allocating IP subnets within a network, take care to allocate them in a logical fashion. You should strive for two goals:

- Allow for the largest possible remaining addressable space (i.e., the largest subnets possible in the remaining space).
- Allow as many subnets as possible to be expanded into the surrounding available space.

As you will see, achieving both of these goals is a balancing act.

I've encountered three methods for allocating IP subnets. I'll call these methods *sequential*, *divide by half*, and *reverse binary*.

Sequential

Most people's first inclination seems to be to allocate IP addresses and IP subnets in numerical order. That is, they allocate the first numerical subnet, then the next, and so on. If such a person were subnetting the 192.168.100.0/24 network into /30 subnets, she would likely allocate them in this order: 0, 4, 8, 12, etc. Sequential allocation of subnets in a network is what most admins seem naturally prone to do. It works, it's easy to understand, and it's pretty easy to tell where the next available network will be.

Of the three methods I'll discuss here, this is the least desirable and the most often deployed. There are some serious problems with this method. First, there is no room for expansion in any of the subnets, except for possibly the last one used. If the subnet 192.168.100.16 grows and now needs 18 addresses instead of 16, the entire subnet must be renumbered to a larger subnet space elsewhere. Second, this method does not allocate addresses in a manner that allows for the largest available block to be concurrent and addressable. Another problem is future availability of subnets. Remember, with VLSM, you are not limited to having every subnet be the same size. If you plan carefully, you can use your given space very efficiently.

Figure 36-6 shows how we might sequentially allocate a series of /28 subnets within the 192.168.1.0/24 network. Each time we need another /28 subnet, we allocate the next one available. I've broken out the subnets to show the largest possible network space remaining after each allocation.

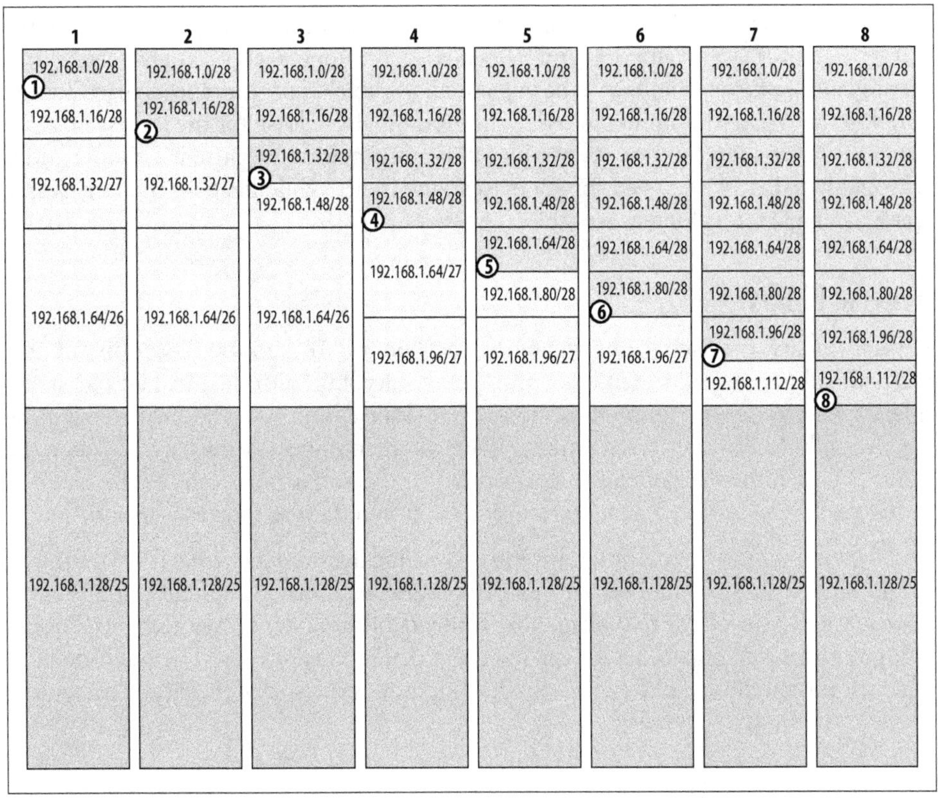

1	2	3	4	5	6	7	8
192.168.1.0/28 ①	192.168.1.0/28	192.168.1.0/28	192.168.1.0/28	192.168.1.0/28	192.168.1.0/28	192.168.1.0/28	192.168.1.0/28
192.168.1.16/28	192.168.1.16/28 ②	192.168.1.16/28	192.168.1.16/28	192.168.1.16/28	192.168.1.16/28	192.168.1.16/28	192.168.1.16/28
192.168.1.32/27	192.168.1.32/27	192.168.1.32/28 ③	192.168.1.32/28	192.168.1.32/28	192.168.1.32/28	192.168.1.32/28	192.168.1.32/28
		192.168.1.48/28	192.168.1.48/28 ④	192.168.1.48/28	192.168.1.48/28	192.168.1.48/28	192.168.1.48/28
			192.168.1.64/27	192.168.1.64/28 ⑤	192.168.1.64/28	192.168.1.64/28	192.168.1.64/28
				192.168.1.80/28	192.168.1.80/28 ⑥	192.168.1.80/28	192.168.1.80/28
192.168.1.64/26	192.168.1.64/26	192.168.1.64/26	192.168.1.96/27	192.168.1.96/27	192.168.1.96/27	192.168.1.96/28 ⑦	192.168.1.96/28
						192.168.1.112/28	192.168.1.112/28 ⑧
192.168.1.128/25	192.168.1.128/25	192.168.1.128/25	192.168.1.128/25	192.168.1.128/25	192.168.1.128/25	192.168.1.128/25	192.168.1.128/25

Figure 36-6. Sequential IP subnet allocation

In the first edition of this book, I stated that the broadcast network was unusable. Old habits die hard, especially for old nerds like me. It still pains me to use the last network when designing networks, but that's more an indication that I've been doing this for far too long than anything else. Cisco documentation (*http://www.cisco.com/en/US/ tech/tk648/tk361/technologies_tech_note09186a0080093f18.shtml*) states:

> On the issue of using subnet zero and the all-ones subnet, RFC 1878 states, "This practice (of excluding all-zeros and all-ones subnets) is obsolete. Modern software will be able to utilize all definable networks." Today, the use of subnet zero and the all-ones subnet is generally accepted and most vendors support their use. However, on certain networks, particularly the ones using legacy software, the use of subnet zero and the all-ones subnet can lead to problems.

Divide by Half

This method prescribes that every time a new network is allocated, the smallest available chunk of addresses is divided by half. The idea here is to maintain the largest possible block of addressable space. To that end, we allocate the middle subnet first, thus leaving the large /25 block available.

Figure 36-7 shows the divide-by-half method in action. In this example, I've taken the same 192.168.1.0/24 network and allocated /28 subnets accordingly. Using this method allows for each subnet to be expanded, as there is space after each used subnet equal to the size of the subnet in use. This method also allows for the largest possible subnet to be available at any given time. I like this method because it's simple and it reasonably balances the need for subnet expandability while keeping the largest free space available for as long as possible.

Reverse Binary

Reverse binary is Cisco's recommended method for IP subnet allocation. In this method, subnets are allocated by counting in binary, but with the most and least significant bits reversed. Figure 36-8 shows how reverse binary works. By reversing the significant bit order, we create a mirror image of the numbers in binary (shown on the right). These numbers happen to correspond to the subnets that should be used, in order, regardless of size. The pattern may be continued for as long as is useful.

By allocating subnets in this order, we end up spacing the subnets so that no two subnets are adjacent unless the subnets are of varying sizes (a distinct possibility using VLSM). This method also offers the reasonable tradeoff of allowing the largest possible remaining addressable space while offering the expandability desired. The real difference between this method and the divide-by-half method is the size of the largest remaining block in the source IP network.

1	2	3	4	5	6	7	8
192.168.1.0/25	192.168.1.0/25	192.168.1.0/25	192.168.1.0/25	192.168.1.0/26	192.168.1.0/26	192.168.1.0/27	192.168.1.0/28 ⑧
							192.168.1.16/28
						192.168.1.32/28 ⑦	192.168.1.32/28
						192.168.1.48/28	192.168.1.48/28
				192.168.1.64/28 ⑤	192.168.1.64/28	192.168.1.64/28	192.168.1.64/28
				192.168.1.80/28	192.168.1.80/28	192.168.1.80/28	192.168.1.80/28
				192.168.1.96/27	192.168.1.96/28 ⑥	192.168.1.96/28	192.168.1.96/28
					192.168.1.112/28	192.168.1.112/28	192.168.1.112/28
192.168.1.128/28 ①	192.168.1.128/28	192.168.1.128/28	192.168.1.128/28	192.168.1.128/28	192.168.1.128/28	192.168.1.128/28	192.168.1.128/28
192.168.1.144/28	192.168.1.144/28	192.168.1.144/28	192.168.1.144/28	192.168.1.144/28	192.168.1.144/28	192.168.1.144/28	192.168.1.144/28
192.168.1.160/27	192.168.1.160/27	192.168.1.160/28 ③	192.168.1.160/28	192.168.1.160/28	192.168.1.160/28	192.168.1.160/28	192.168.1.160/28
		192.168.1.176/28	192.168.1.176/28	192.168.1.176/28	192.168.1.176/28	192.168.1.176/28	192.168.1.176/28
192.168.1.192/26	192.168.1.192/28 ②	192.168.1.192/28	192.168.1.192/28	192.168.1.192/28	192.168.1.192/28	192.168.1.192/28	192.168.1.192/28
	192.168.1.208/28	192.168.1.208/28	192.168.1.208/28	192.168.1.208/28	192.168.1.208/28	192.168.1.208/28	192.168.1.208/28
	192.168.1.224/27	192.168.1.224/27	192.168.1.224/28 ④	192.168.1.224/28	192.168.1.224/28	192.168.1.224/28	192.168.1.224/28
			192.168.1.240/28	192.168.1.240/28	192.168.1.240/28	192.168.1.240/28	192.168.1.240/28

Figure 36-7. Divide-by-half IP subnet allocation

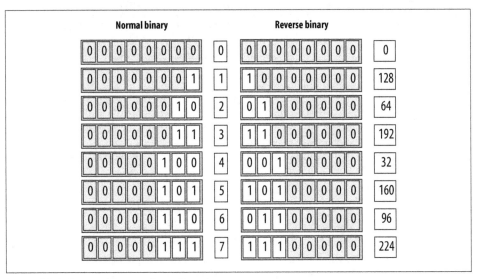

Figure 36-8. Reverse binary subnet allocation

The exception to these rules for me is the allocation of /30 networks. Because these networks are generally used for point-to-point links, and as such will never expand, I usually allocate an entire /24 network (or more, depending on the overall need) just for /30 subnets.

The results of using the reverse binary method to divide our 192.168.1.0/24 network are shown in Figure 36-9. Each allocated network can be expanded with no IP address changes. A reasonable balance is achieved, with large pools of available addresses remaining after each allocation. The differences between the reverse binary and divide-by-half methods all but disappear by the eighth subnet allocation, where, in our example, each subnet has an equally sized subnet adjacent to it.

1	2	3	4	5	6	7	8
192.168.1.0/25	192.168.1.0/26	192.168.1.0/26	192.168.1.0/27	192.168.1.0/27	192.168.1.0/27	192.168.1.0/27	192.168.1.0/28 (8)
							192.168.1.16/28
			192.168.1.32/28 (4)	192.168.1.32/28	192.168.1.32/28	192.168.1.32/28	192.168.1.32/28
			192.168.1.48/28	192.168.1.48/28	192.168.1.48/28	192.168.1.48/28	192.168.1.48/28
	192.168.1.64/28 (2)	192.168.1.64/28	192.168.1.64/28	192.168.1.64/28	192.168.1.64/28	192.168.1.64/28	192.168.1.64/28
	192.168.1.80/28	192.168.1.80/28	192.168.1.80/28	192.168.1.80/28	192.168.1.80/28	192.168.1.80/28	192.168.1.80/28
	192.168.1.96/27	192.168.1.96/27	192.168.1.96/27	192.168.1.96/27	192.168.1.96/28 (6)	192.168.1.96/28	192.168.1.96/28
					192.168.1.112/28	192.168.1.112/28	192.168.1.112/28
192.168.1.128/28 (1)	192.168.1.128/28	192.168.1.128/28	192.168.1.128/28	192.168.1.128/28	192.168.1.128/28	192.168.1.128/28	192.168.1.128/28
192.168.1.144/28	192.168.1.144/28	192.168.1.144/28	192.168.1.144/28	192.168.1.144/28	192.168.1.144/28	192.168.1.144/28	192.168.1.144/28
192.168.1.160/27	192.168.1.160/27	192.168.1.160/27	192.168.1.160/27	192.168.1.160/28 (5)	192.168.1.160/28	192.168.1.160/28	192.168.1.160/28
				192.168.1.176/28	192.168.1.176/28	192.168.1.176/28	192.168.1.176/28
192.168.1.192/26	192.168.1.192/26	192.168.1.192/28 (3)	192.168.1.192/28	192.168.1.192/28	192.168.1.192/28	192.168.1.192/28	192.168.1.192/28
		192.168.1.208/28	192.168.1.208/28	192.168.1.208/28	192.168.1.208/28	192.168.1.208/28	192.168.1.208/28
		192.168.1.224/27	192.168.1.224/27	192.168.1.224/27	192.168.1.244/27	192.168.1.224/28 (7)	192.168.1.224/28
						192.168.1.240/28	192.168.1.240/28

Figure 36-9. Reverse binary IP subnet allocation

The reverse binary method of IP subnet allocation is the most logical choice mathematically, but it can be the hardest to understand. Maintain proper documentation at all times to avoid confusion, regardless of the method you use.

IP Subnetting Made Easy

IP subnetting seems to trip up quite a few people in the networking world. I've known experienced consultants who have worked in the industry for 15 years and still resort to subnet calculators.

IP subnetting can be a daunting subject for those who are not familiar with it. The principles of subnetting are based on binary (and some mathematical) principles such as eXclusive-OR (XOR), which, for many people, are foreign concepts or aspects of college courses long since forgotten.

There are really only two times when your average networking people need to know how subnet math truly works: when they study for their first networking certification (the CCNA) and when they study for their last (the CCIE). In fact, I don't really think you need the math for the CCNA coursework, although Cisco makes you learn it. The CCIE exam does make you do bizarre things with subnet masks that require a full understanding of the math behind the topic. However, these things are rarely, if ever, seen in the real world, and are not a topic for this book.

If you want to be able to do IP subnetting in your head, there are a couple of things you will need to understand. First, Cisco, along with every other major manufacturer out there, wants you to learn subnetting its way. Why? So its tests are harder to pass and so everyone who's certified speaks the same language.

Cisco, in particular, seems to want people to think in a way that makes it harder to figure out what's really going on. As an example, in Cisco parlance, a native Class C network with a subnet mask of 255.255.255.224 is said to consist of 6 networks with 30 hosts in each network.

Call me pedantic, but that's incorrect. The subnet mask actually results in 8 networks with 32 hosts each. Cisco's point is that, using classful networking rules, there are only 6 *available* networks, with 30 *available* hosts in each network. While this is a valid concept, I believe it causes confusion, especially given our previous discussion showing how the all-zero and all-ones networks are usable.

The reason Cisco's method causes confusion is simple: there is no easy way to prove the answer. Using the method I will outline here, however, you will always have an easy way to prove your answer. In this case, 8 * 32 = 256.

Everything having to do with subnet masks has something to do with the number 256. In fact, this will be our first rule:

> Every result will either produce 256 or be divisible by 256.

Looking at a subnet mask, the maximum value for an octet is 255. Remember, though, that the values start with 0, so 255 is really the 256th number possible. This is a very important concept, because everything else is predicated on it.

The second rule astounds many people. In fact, it astounded me when I discovered it while writing my own subnet calculator program:

> Only nine values are possible for any octet in a subnet mask. They are: 0, 128, 192, 224, 240, 248, 252, 254, and 255.

Subnet masks are, by their nature, inclusive. That is to say, you can only add or subtract bits from the mask in bit order, and they must be added from left to right—you cannot skip a bit in a subnet mask. Figure 36-10 shows bits validly and invalidly used, with their resulting decimal octets.

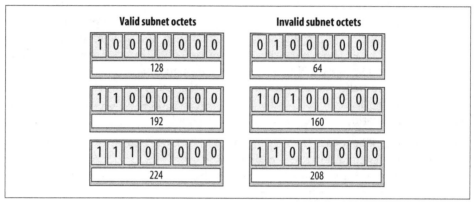

Figure 36-10. Valid and invalid subnet octets

 The CCIE exam requires knowledge of manipulating subnet masks in unnatural ways, but you should never see this in the real world. While it is possible to use subnet masks in nonobvious ways, you should never do it outside a lab environment.

Because there are only eight bits in an octet, if you limit yourself to only allowing bits to be added or subtracted, there can only be a finite number of values represented in binary. Those values are shown in Figure 36-11.

Notice the column titled Ratio. This is something you won't see in the manufacturers' texts, which is a shame, because I believe it is the very essence of subnet masks in the real world.

In Figure 36-12, I've laid out the ratios as they apply to any octet in any position in the subnet mask. You don't need to memorize any of this, as it will all become clear shortly. Notice the patterns at work here. The ratio you will learn to use for a Class C network works for any class network. Simply by moving the ratio to the proper position in the subnet mask, you can figure out what the octet should be.

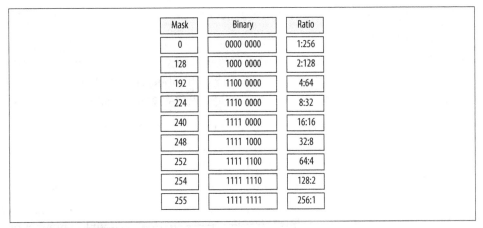

Mask	Binary	Ratio
0	0000 0000	1:256
128	1000 0000	2:128
192	1100 0000	4:64
224	1110 0000	8:32
240	1111 0000	16:16
248	1111 1000	32:8
252	1111 1100	64:4
254	1111 1110	128:2
255	1111 1111	256:1

Figure 36-11. Possible subnet octet values

Mask	First octet		Second octet		Third octet		Fourth octet	
0	1	256 * 256 * 256 * 256	256 * 1	256 * 256 * 256	256 * 256 * 1	256 * 256	256 * 256 * 256 * 1	256
128	2	128 * 256 * 256 * 256	256 * 2	128 * 256 * 256	256 * 256 * 2	128 * 256	256 * 256 * 256 * 2	128
192	4	64 * 256 * 256 * 256	256 * 4	64 * 256 * 256	256 * 256 * 4	64 * 256	256 * 256 * 256 * 4	64
224	8	32 * 256 * 256 * 256	256 * 8	32 * 256 * 256	256 * 256 * 8	32 * 256	256 * 256 * 256 * 8	32
240	16	16 * 256 * 256 * 256	256 * 16	16 * 256 * 256	256 * 256 * 16	16 * 256	256 * 256 * 256 * 16	16
248	32	8 * 256 * 256 * 256	256 * 32	8 * 256 * 256	256 * 256 * 32	8 * 256	256 * 256 * 256 * 32	8
252	64	4 * 256 * 256 * 256	256 * 64	4 * 256 * 256	256 * 256 * 64	4 * 256	256 * 256 * 256 * 64	4
254	128	2 * 256 * 256 * 256	256 * 128	2 * 256 * 256	256 * 256 * 128	2 * 256	256 * 256 * 256 * 128	2
255	256	1 * 256 * 256 * 256	256 * 256	1 * 256 * 256	256 * 256 * 256	1 * 256	256 * 256 * 256 * 256	1

Figure 36-12. Subnet octet ratios

Using the Class C network 192.168.1.0 255.255.255.0 as an example, if you apply a subnet mask of 255.255.255.224, the result is 8 subnets with 32 hosts in each. Look at Figure 36-11, and you'll see that the ratio for the subnet octet 224 is 8:32.

The ratios happen to correlate with the number of subnets and hosts per subnet in a native class C network. If you look at the other columns, you'll notice that the ratio is the same, but it is in a different position in the equation.

Let's look at a single example. Figure 36-13 shows the ratios for the subnet octet of 224.

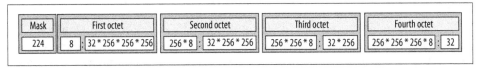

Mask	First octet		Second octet		Third octet		Fourth octet	
224	8	32 * 256 * 256 * 256	256 * 8	32 * 256 * 256	256 * 256 * 8	32 * 256	256 * 256 * 256 * 8	32

Figure 36-13. Ratios for 224

In practice, here's what the Figure 36-13 is saying, using the network 10.0.0.0:

- 10.0.0.0 224.0.0.0 = 8 subnets of 536,870,912 (32 * 256 * 256 * 256) hosts
- 10.0.0.0 255.224.0.0 = 2,048 (256 * 8) subnets of 2,097,156 (32 * 256 * 256) hosts
- 10.0.0.0 255.255.224.0 = 524,288 (256 * 256 * 8) subnets of 8,192 (32 * 256) hosts
- 10.0.0.0 255.255.255.224 = 134,217,728 (256 * 256 * 256 * 8) subnets of 32 hosts

Notice that in each case, the ratio of 8:32 appears somewhere in the equation.

That's all well and good, but it still looks like a lot of icky math to me, so let's make it even simpler. This leads us to our third rule:

When you know these rules, all you need to be able to do is double or halve numbers.

Subnet masks, like all things computer-related, are based on binary. Because binary is based on powers of two, all you really need to be able to do is to double a number or cut it in half.

Memorize the nine possible values for subnet masks (two are easy—0 and 255), and write them down on a sheet of paper (as shown in Figure 36-14). Once you have those down, you've successfully done all the memorization you need.

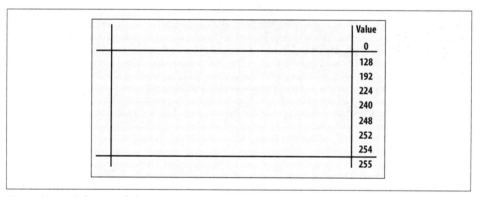

Figure 36-14. Subnet worksheet step #1

You'll fill in the rest of the sheet by using the simplest math possible: halving and doubling. Write the numbers 1:256 next to the 0 at the top. This is easy to remember. How many natural networks are there in a Class C? 1. How many hosts are there in a Class C? 256. Remember that everything regarding subnets comes back to the number 256.

Now, take the number to the left of the colon, and double it (1 * 2 = 2), and take the number to the right of the colon, and cut it in half (256 / 2 = 128). Repeat this process until you get to the bottom of the sheet. You've just figured out the network:host ratios for a native Class C network! Your paper should look like the example in Figure 36-15.

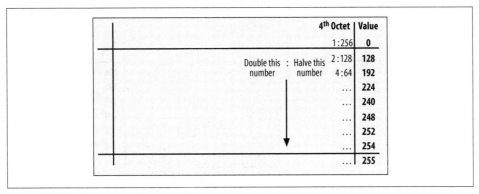

4th Octet	Value
1:256	0
2:128	128
4:64	192
...	224
...	240
...	248
...	252
...	254
...	255

Double this number : Halve this number

Figure 36-15. Subnet worksheet step #2

This trick is so simple that when I take mentally exhausting exams like the CCIE lab, I actually write out a sheet like this so I don't have to think at all during the lab. Now that you have all the ratios, you're set for working on a Class C network—but what about other networks? Well, you have two choices: always carry this book with you (which certainly would appeal to me) or apply some simple logic to what you've already learned.

As an example, let's use the private network 172.16.0.0 255.255.0.0, which is /16. People often get confused when working with ranges other than /24 because these ranges aren't usually seen in small companies. In practice, when you're using this method, there is no difference. We'll divide the network into eight pieces. Using your subnet worksheet, which octet value has an 8 on the left of the colon? Replace the leftmost zero in the native subnet mask with this number, and you have your answer: the subnet mask you need is 255.255.224.0. It's that simple.

Now let's try a more complex problem, like one you might see on an exam. With a network of 172.16.0.0 255.255.0.0, what subnet mask would you need to allow a network with 1,200 hosts in it? Here's the easy way to figure this one out. A /24 network has 256 hosts in it. Double this number until you get a number larger than 1,200:

$$256 \times 2 = 512$$
$$512 \times 2 = 1{,}024$$
$$1{,}024 \times 2 = 2{,}048$$

Let's fill in the sheet some more. Draw a line under the top entry and another above the bottom entry, as shown in Figure 36-16. The entries between the lines are subnet octet values that fall between classful boundaries. This third column of numbers in Figure 36-16 indicates a further binary progression.

These numbers relate to the number of hosts in a subnet. You can keep the progression going as long as you need. When you get to the top of the sheet, start a new column to the left. These values will be the number of hosts for your second and first octets.

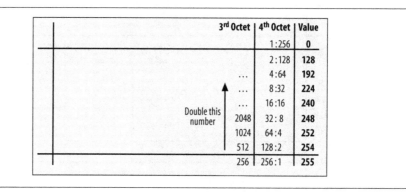

	3rd Octet	4th Octet	Value
		1:256	0
		2:128	128
	...	4:64	192
	...	8:32	224
	...	16:16	240
Double this number	2048	32:8	248
	1024	64:4	252
	512	128:2	254
	256	256:1	255

Figure 36-16. Subnet worksheet step #3

Looking at this worksheet reveals that the required subnet mask is 255.255.248.0. The network 172.16.0.0 with a subnet mask of 255.255.248.0 will result in 32 subnets with 2,048 hosts in each. To validate the math, perform this equation: 8 * 256 = 2,048.

Beware of a trick question you may see on tests. When using this method, you must remember that the first and last subnet may not be used given classical subnetting rules, and the first and last host may not be used. Therefore, if you encounter the question, "What would the subnet mask be for a network that required 1,024 hosts to be on the network?" the answer would not be 252, as it might appear, because two of those hosts are unusable (network and broadcast). If you require 1,024 hosts to be live devices on the network, you must have a network capable of supporting 2,048 hosts. This is one of the limitations of using a binary system.

Similarly, if you need 8 usable hosts on the network, you must provide 16 host addresses, not 8.

Figure 36-17 shows the same information as that presented in the preceding worksheet, but in a different format. Some people respond better to seeing this information in a horizontal rather than a vertical format. I like this model, because it is laid out the same way the bits are laid out in a subnet mask. Use whichever format works for you. There are no tests in this book.

Remember, a proper subnet mask can have only one of nine values in any single octet. If you start with a value of 1 on the bottom left and a value of 256 on the top right, then double those numbers under each subsequent value, you can quickly figure out what your subnet mask needs to be based on how many hosts or subnets it needs to have.

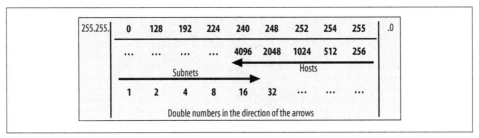

255.255.	0	128	192	224	240	248	252	254	255	.0
	...	...	...	...	4096	2048	1024	512	256	
			Subnets				Hosts			
	1	2	4	8	16	32	...	...	...	

Double numbers in the direction of the arrows

Figure 36-17. Horizontal format of the subnet worksheet

Once you have memorized the nine subnet octet values (remember, two are easy!) and can double and halve the rest in your head, you'll find that the numbers become obvious. You'll see all of these numbers over and over if you're around computers for any length of time. They're all powers of two, and when you start to recognize the patterns I've outlined for you, calculating any subnet mask will be only a matter of doing some quick, very simple math in your head.

## CHAPTER 37

IPv6

You've no doubt heard the news stating that we will run out of IP addresses in the next half hour or so. Forgive my glibness, but I've been hearing this for 10 years or more.

 As I was editing this edition for publication, the Number Resource Organization (NRO) reported that as of February 3, 2011, the free pool of IPv4 address space has been depleted. You can read all about it here: *http://www.nro.net/news/ipv4-free-pool-depleted.*

There are a finite number of IP addresses, and they were horribly mismanaged when the Internet was young. Network Address Translation (NAT), Classless Internet Domain Routing (CIDR), and Variable Length Subnet Masks (VLSM) changed all that, and we got some breathing room. That was about 10 years ago, and the news is once again reporting that we're about to run out of IP addresses. While everyone panics, I try to remind nervous CEOs that this is only an issue with publicly routable IP addresses. Still, given that there are a finite number of these addresses, we'll hit the wall sooner or later.

IPv4 (the currently well-known standard) uses 32-bit addresses. This translates to 4,294,967,296 (4.2×10^9) IP addresses, though large blocks of them are considered either reserved or unroutable. For example, 16 million of them are contained within the 10.0.0.0/8 private address space. Let's say, for the sake of argument, that there are four billion public IP addresses. Are we really running out of them? Where have they gone?

If you're not familiar with scientific notation, allow me to explain it, since I use it a lot in this chapter. Scientific notation allows us to represent ridiculously large numbers in an easy-to-read format. Simply put, take any number, and then move the decimal until the number is a single digit with one decimal. The number of places you moved the decimal point is a power of 10. The number 1,000 would be written 1.0×10^3. Another way to think of it (though technically inaccurate) is "one with three zeros." Here are some other examples to help you wrap your head around scientific notation. As you can see, scientific notation is easier to read and process in print than listing a pile of zeros:

$1.0 \times 10^6 = 1,000,000$ (one million)

$1.0 \times 10^9 = 1,000,000,000$ (one billion)

$1.0 \times 10^{12} = 1,000,000,000,000$ (one trillion)

$1.0 \times 10^{15} = 1,000,000,000,000,000$ (one quadrillion)

For more information on the naming of large numbers, check out the nerd-friendly Wikipedia entry titled "Names of Large Numbers" at the following URL: *http://en.wikipedia.org/wiki/Names_of_large_numbers*.

I have eight IP addresses, though I only rent them from my provider. My mother uses one. The average person might consume one if he has a cable or DSL Internet connection. Companies that connect directly to the Internet might have 256, though they probably don't use them all. There are many developing countries coming online that are consuming large quantities of IP addresses. Heck, there are almost seven billion people on Earth today. There aren't enough IP addresses for everyone, even if I give up my eight, and I'm not about to.

To resolve this situation, The Internet Engineering Task Force (IETF) came up with the next version of IP, called IPv6.

Why not IPv5, you ask? The version is identified in the version field of the IP packet. Version 4 is naturally used for IPv4, but version 5 was already allocated for something called the Internet Stream Protocol (ST, ST+, and ST2), so the IETF had to use the next best thing. If you're interested in learning more about the Internet Stream Protocol, check out RFC 1819.

IPv6 was originally published in 1998 within RFC 2460 and, as of this writing, has been updated with RFCs 5095, 5722, and 5871. There are many other RFCs that cover IPv6 or how other protocols have been modified to work with IPv6. Per RFC 2460, the changes from IPv4 fall primarily into the following categories:

Expanded addressing capabilities

IPv6 increases the IP address size from 32 bits to 128 bits to support more levels of addressing hierarchy, a much greater number of addressable nodes, and simpler autoconfiguration of addresses. The scalability of multicast routing has been improved by the addition of a "scope" field to multicast addresses. And a new type of address, called an *anycast address*, has been defined to send a packet to any one of a group of nodes.

Header format simplification

Some IPv4 header fields have been dropped or made optional to reduce the common-case processing cost of packet handling and to limit the bandwidth cost of the IPv6 header.

Improved support for extensions and options

Changes in the way IP header options are encoded allow for more efficient forwarding, less stringent limits on the length of options, and greater flexibility for introducing new options in the future.

Flow labeling capability

A new capability has been added to enable the labeling of packets belonging to particular traffic flows for which the sender requests special handling, such as nondefault quality of service or real-time service.

Authentication and privacy capabilities

Extensions to support authentication, data integrity, and (optional) data confidentiality have been specified for IPv6.

IPv6 includes some significant changes to the headers at the IP layer. I suggest reading the RFCs to see what those changes are. Instead of boring you with packet diagrams, I'm going to focus on what you should know to get started with IPv6 and how you configure IPv6 on a router.

Addressing

IPv6 addresses are a bit more complicated than IPv4 addresses. To start with, where IPv4 uses only 32-bit addresses, IPv6 uses 128-bit addresses. That equates to $3.40292367 \times 10^{38}$ addresses. That's roughly 2^{95} IP addresses for every person on Earth in 2011. In other words, that's a lot. For you number geeks out there, 3.40×10^{38} is 340 undecillion (*http://en.wikipedia.org/wiki/Undecillion*).

Really, though, the address scheme was designed to support efficient route aggregation. Subnets in IPv6 are supposed to contain 2^{64} addresses. To put that number in perspective, consider that all the IP addresses in the IPv4 universe would consume $1/64^{th}$ of the address space available in just one IPv6 subnet. Like I said, there are a lot of addresses in the IPv6 space.

IPv6 addresses don't use decimals like IPv4, and that is the first hurdle many people struggle with using IPv6. IPv6 addresses are composed of groups of four-digit hexadecimal numbers separated by colons. Luckily, leading zeros can be eliminated within each set of colons. For example:

AA76:0000:0000:0000:0012:A322:FE33:2267

may be represented as:

AA76:0:0:0:12:A322:FE33:2267

These two addresses are identical. Only their written representation has changed. Additionally, any consecutive number of zeros can be replaced by a double colon. Thus:

AA76:0000:0000:0000:0012:A322:FE33:2267

may also be written as:

AA76::12:A322:FE33:2267

To summarize, the following three addresses are identical:

AA76:0000:0000:0000:0012:A322:FE33:2267
AA76:0:0:0:12:A322:FE33:2267
AA76::12:A322:FE33:2267

If you're wondering why hexadecimal is used, let's compare the preceding address to its decimal counterpart:

HEX: AA76:0000:0000:0000:0012:A322:FE33:2267
DEC: 170.118.0.0.0.0.0.0.0.18.163.34.254.51.34.103

Even with all those zeros and two-digit octets, the address is still longer in decimal. This should give you an idea of just how many more addresses there are, though, since each octet means 256 times more addresses, and there are 12 more octets than you see in IPv4 addresses.

In environments where IPv4 interoperates with IPv6, IPv4 addresses can be written in IPv6 notation. You do this by setting the first 80 bits to 0 and the next 16 bits to 1, with the final bits being those of the IPv4 address. Even better, most implementations will allow you to reference the IPv4 portion of the address in dotted decimal notation. For example, the IPv6 address format for the IPv4 address of 10.20.30.40 would be:

0000:0000:0000:0000:0000:0000:ffff:10.20.30.40

or:

0:0:0:0:0:0:ffff:10.20.30.40

or:

::ffff:10.20.30.40.

See? Easy as pie. OK, so it's not a very tasty pie, but at least there is a logic that can be studied and understood. Change is hard, but soon enough, we will have no choice. There are already job postings requiring IPv6, so knowing this stuff makes you more marketable to employers, and that's never a bad thing.

Subnet Masks

Masking IPv6 addresses is similar to IPv4 in that we use prefix lengths. The lengths just seem odd because the addresses are so long. Seeing a /64 address in IPv4 would be nonsensical, but you'll see it a lot in IPv6.

Where IPv6 differs is the way that addresses are with regard to considering network masks. With IPv4 and CIDR, there are no classes, so almost any number of bits can be used in the network mask. With IPv6, there are more defined rules:

Network address range
> The first 48 bits of IPv6 addresses are reserved for Internet routing:
>
> > ffff:ffff:ffff:0000:0000:0000:0000:0000

Subnetting range
> The 16 bits from bit number 49 to bit number 54 are for defining subnets:
>
> > 0000:0000:0000:ffff:0000:0000:0000:0000

Device range
> The last 64 bits are for device addresses:
>
> > 0000:0000:0000:0000:ffff:ffff:ffff:ffff

You can use a portion of the device address to further refine a subnet, but it is not recommended. You'll see why in a bit.

Address Types

Like IPv4, certain addresses are special and are identified by their high-order bits. These address types are identified in RFC 4291 (section 2.4) and are given in Table 37-1.

Table 37-1. IPv6 address types

Address type	Binary prefix	IPv6 notation	Section
Unspecified	00...0 (128 bits)	::/128	2.5.2
Loopback	00...1 (128 bits)	::1/128	2.5.3
Multicast	11111111	FF00::/8	2.7
Link-local unicast	1111111010	FE80::/10	2.5.6
Global unicast	(everything else)		

Unspecified address
> An unspecified address is an address of all zeros. Packets with an unspecified destination will be dropped by routers. The source address may be unspecified by devices that have yet to learn their address.

Loopback address

The loopback address in IPv6 is 0:0:0:0:0:0:0:1 or ::1/128. This is analogous to 127.0.0.1 in IPv4.

 Be careful of your subnet masks. /32 in IPv4 indicates an all-ones mask or a specific host address. /32 in IPv6 means something entirely different, namely a very large-scale aggregate Internet route. Host routes in IPv6 are /128, not /32.

Multicast

Multicast is a bit different in IPv6, though the basic principle is the same. The first thing you should notice is that there is no concept of a broadcast in IPv6. If you want to send a packet to all nodes, you should use the *link-local all nodes* multicast address of ff02::1.

Global unicast

Global unicast addresses are what you might call "normal" addresses, and will be assigned to interfaces on your devices. Global unicast addresses must be 64 bits in length except when they start with 000, as listed in Table 37-1.

Link-local unicast

Link-local unicast addresses are described in RFC 2373 (section 2.5.8) as follows:

Link-Local addresses are designed to be used for addressing on a single link for purposes such as automatic address configuration, neighbor discovery, or when no routers are present.

Routers must not forward any packets with Link-Local source or destination addresses to other links.

So what does that all mean? If you've ever booted a Windows machine and it couldn't find its DHCP server, you've probably seen it use a 169.254.x.x address. This range (169.254.1.0–169.254.254.255) is a link-local address block in IPv4. You can't route this block over the Internet

IPv6 link-local addresses reside in the network fe80::/10. IPv6 requires operating systems to assign a link-local address to every interface automatically. The format for this address is the routing prefix combined with the MAC address. The MAC address has had an ff:fe jammed in the middle, and there's a 02 at the beginning. Why? The ff:fe converts the MAC address into the Extended Unique Identifier 64 (EUI-64) format. The 02 is actually the result of flipping the seventh bit in the first octet of the MAC address. This bit is the *locally administered* bit, indicating that the OS has altered the address. Here's a snippet from a Linux machine. All I did was configure an IPv4 address, yet there's an IPv6 link-local address already there. As you can see, the end of the address matches the MAC address, altered as I've described:

```
[gad@cozy ~]$ ifconfig eth0
eth0      Link encap:Ethernet  HWaddr 00:02:55:b7:da:9d
```

```
inet addr:192.168.1.200  Bcast:192.168.1.255  Mask:255.255.255.0
inet6 addr: fe80::202:55ff:feb7:da9d/64 Scope:Link
UP BROADCAST RUNNING MULTICAST  MTU:1500  Metric:1
RX packets:193321787 errors:0 dropped:0 overruns:0 frame:0
TX packets:196670319 errors:0 dropped:0 overruns:0 carrier:0
collisions:0 txqueuelen:1000
RX bytes:3569684877 (3.3 GB)  TX bytes:3127898656 (2.9 GB)
Interrupt:16
```

Here is a similar result from a Cisco router. First the MAC address from the interface:

```
R1#sho int f0/0 | inc Hardware
   Hardware is MV96340 Ethernet, address is 0012.43b9.2c70 (bia 0012.43b9.2c70)
```

And here is the automatically configured link-local address:

```
R1#sho ipv6 interface f0/0 | inc link-local
   IPv6 is enabled, link-local address is FE80::212:43FF:FEB9:2C70
```

In the link-local address, you can see the same leading 2 resulting from the flipped bit, and the *FF:FE* in the middle of the MAC address.

Subnetting

Because the first 48 bits are reserved for Internet routing, you will likely never have to deal with masks larger than /48 unless you work with Internet routing tables and aggregation. Since the next 8 bits are reserved for subnetting, you will have access to 65,535 subnets with over 18 quintillion devices per subnet for each /48 allocated.

Now that's cool and all, but do I need to allocate 18 quintillion addresses for each point-to-point link? Need is not really the right word. You don't *need* to, but you really *should*. There are a couple of good reasons why.

First off, we've grown so accustomed to trying to limit IP address usage that using only the bare minimum has become second nature. Why use 256 IP address on a point-to-point link when you only need 4? This thinking has saved us in the past, and habits, especially good ones, are hard to break. The fact remains that there are so many IPv6 addresses that we won't hit the wall for a long, long time. How long? Long after Skynet and the terminators destroy human civilization as we know it.

There are protocols that require IPv6 addresses to be 64-bits, Stateless Address Autoconfiguration being the most commonly quoted. That means your subnet mask should never be smaller than /64. In fact, all IPv6 networks in common use should have a 64-bit mask. ARIN (American Registry for Internet Numbers) will allocate IPv6 networks as follows, according to *http://www.arin.net/policy/nrpm.html#six54*:

> End-users are assigned an end site assignment from their LIR or ISP. The exact size of the assignment is a local decision for the LIR or ISP to make, using a minimum value of a /64 (when only one subnet is anticipated for the end site) up to the normal maximum of /48, except in cases of extra large end sites where a larger assignment can be justified.

The following guidelines may be useful (but they are only guidelines):

/64 when it is known that one and only one subnet is needed

/56 for small sites, those expected to need only a few subnets over the next 5 years.

/48 for larger sites

While it is technically possible to use a VLSM-type paradigm with IPv6, you shouldn't. Instead, use /64 everywhere. Besides, even if you don't, your link-local address on that interface will be /64 anyway. For reference, a /48 would give you 2×10^{16} (20,000,000,000,000,000) /64 subnets. I think you can spare a couple for your serial links.

Imagine—every IPv6 subnet on your network will have a /64 prefix. No more trying to figure out how many hosts exist within a subnet. Each one has 18 quintillion. In other words, for all practical purposes, it no longer matters.

The IETF recommends that all IPv6 networks be /64, even for point-to-point links. Further, it recommends that every home network be allocated a /48. You can read for yourself in RFC 3177. Here's a snippet:

In particular, we recommend:

- Home network subscribers, connecting through on-demand or always-on connections should receive a /48.
- Small and large enterprises should receive a /48.
- Very large subscribers could receive a /47 or slightly shorter prefix, or multiple /48's.
- Mobile networks, such as vehicles or mobile phones with an additional network interface (such as bluetooth or 802.11b) should receive a static /64 prefix to allow the connection of multiple devices through one subnet.
- A single PC, with no additional need to subnet, dialing-up from a hotel room may receive its /128 IPv6 address for a PPP style connection as part of a /64 prefix.

Read that carefully. The IETF is recommending that every car and cell phone receive a /64! That's a reflection of the staggering number of IPv6 addresses that are available. Suddenly, my state-of-the-art smartphone seems woefully inadequate with its paltry single IPv4 address.

NAT

NAT was one of the great inventions that gave us breathing room when we thought we were running out of IPv4 addresses. How do we use NAT with IPv6?

We don't.

IPv6 does not support NAT. There are so many addresses that we simply don't need it. There is, however, an argument that hiding your real IP addresses behind a different IP address is good for security. The counterargument is that this is not really security as much as *perceived* security through obscurity. There have been many talks about including it into the IPv6 specs, but as of now, nothing has been solidified.

There are features called NAT-PT and NAPT-PT that allow you to translate IPv6 to IPv4 addresses (NAPT-PT allows port translation as well), but these are designed as migration tools to help you get off of IPv4.

Before NAT existed, everyone got publicly routable IP addresses. IPv6 simply returns us to where we started. Will NAT be included in IPv6? Maybe. I much prefer the idea of a world without NAT, though.

Simple Router Configuration

Here, I have two routers connected through a switch. R1 has an IPv4 address of 10.0.0.1/24 on f0/0, and R6 has an IPv4 address of 10.0.0.6/24 on f0/0. To establish an IPv6 link-local address on these interfaces, I've done absolutely nothing other than enabling the interfaces (there is an IPv4 address applied, but it doesn't affect this testing):

```
R1(config)#int f0/0
R1(config-if)#ipv6 address autoconfig
```

Running the show interface command on the revision of code I'm using gives no indication of an IPv6 address:

```
R1#sho int f0/0
FastEthernet0/0 is up, line protocol is up
  Hardware is MV96340 Ethernet, address is 0012.43b9.2c70 (bia 0012.43b9.2c70)
  Internet address is 10.0.0.1/24
  MTU 1500 bytes, BW 100000 Kbit, DLY 100 usec,
     reliability 255/255, txload 1/255, rxload 1/255
  Encapsulation ARPA, loopback not set
  Keepalive set (10 sec)
  Full-duplex, 100Mb/s, 100BaseTX/FX
  ARP type: ARPA, ARP Timeout 04:00:00
  Last input 00:00:00, output 00:00:03, output hang never
  Last clearing of "show interface" counters never
  Input queue: 0/75/0/0 (size/max/drops/flushes); Total output drops: 0
  Queueing strategy: fifo
  Output queue: 0/40 (size/max)
  5 minute input rate 3000 bits/sec, 0 packets/sec
  5 minute output rate 0 bits/sec, 0 packets/sec
     3403 packets input, 1970499 bytes
     Received 3393 broadcasts, 0 runts, 0 giants, 0 throttles
     0 input errors, 0 CRC, 0 frame, 0 overrun, 0 ignored
     0 watchdog
     0 input packets with dribble condition detected
     755 packets output, 77707 bytes, 0 underruns
     0 output errors, 0 collisions, 1 interface resets
     0 babbles, 0 late collision, 0 deferred
     0 lost carrier, 0 no carrier
     0 output buffer failures, 0 output buffers swapped out
```

To see the automatically configured link-local address, I need to use the show ipv6 interface *interface-name* command:

```
R1#sho ipv6 int f0/0
FastEthernet0/0 is up, line protocol is up
  IPv6 is enabled, link-local address is FE80::212:43FF:FEB9:2C70
  No global unicast address is configured
  Joined group address(es):
    FF02::1
    FF02::2
    FF02::1:FFB9:2C70
  MTU is 1500 bytes
  ICMP error messages limited to one every 100 milliseconds
  ICMP redirects are enabled
  ND DAD is enabled, number of DAD attempts: 1
  ND reachable time is 30000 milliseconds
```

Here is the IPv6 link-local address from R6:

```
R6#sho ipv6 interface f0/0 | inc link-local
  IPv6 is enabled, link-local address is FE80::214:6AFF:FEA2:D438
```

What does any network guy do when configuring two devices on a network? Ping them, of course. Let's ping R6 from R1. To ping using IPv6, we still use the ping command, but we need to add the ipv6 keyword:

```
R1#ping ipv6 FE80::214:6AFF:FEA2:D438
Output Interface: f0/0
% Invalid interface. Use full interface name without spaces (e.g. Serial0/1)
```

That's annoying, but we do what we must:

```
Output Interface: fastethernet0/0
Type escape sequence to abort.
Sending 5, 100-byte ICMP Echos to FE80::214:6AFF:FEA2:D438, timeout is 2 seconds:
Packet sent with a source address of FE80::212:43FF:FEB9:2C70
!!!!!
Success rate is 100 percent (5/5), round-trip min/avg/max = 0/0/4 ms
```

Ping works just like you'd expect it to, though we had to include the source interface and spell it out. Why? Because the network for this IP address is the same on every interface—remember, it's a link-local address, so the router will not forward it between interfaces. The real difference is the terribly long IPv6 addresses. We all like to rattle off IP addresses like we're some sort of savant. I'd venture a guess that for most of us, IPv6 will have us firmly believing in proper DNS usage.

This is all well and good, but link-local addresses are dropped by routers, since those addresses are designed to be used only on the network on which they reside. What's the point of having a router if you can't forward packets from one interface to another?

To forward packets, by definition, each interface on the router needs to be in a different network. In my opinion, this is where IPv6 can become a network admin's dream.

IPv6 allows you to address interfaces without assigning a host address. Since we can create an address by translating the MAC address into a EUI-64 format, we can quickly connect devices just by telling them what network we're on. An example of this is shown in Figure 37-1.

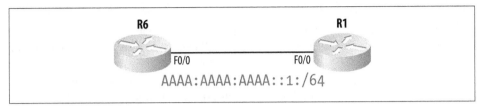

R6 **R1**

F0/0   F0/0

AAAA:AAAA:AAAA::1:/64

Figure 37-1. Simple IPv6 network with two routers

Here on R1, we've already got a link-local address, but as we've covered, that's almost useless for real-world networking. With the `ipv6 address` *address/mask* `eui-64` interface command, I'll assign a network address to the F0/0 interface. Let's say that I've been allocated the `AAAA:AAAA:AAAA::/48` address block. I'll start by using the `:1:` subnet:

```
R1(config-if)#ipv6 address AAAA:AAAA:AAAA:1::/64 eui-64
```

 This is fine in a lab environment, but remember that in the real world, you should have a properly allocated /64 prefix given to you by your provider, ARIN, or some other authority.

Now the interface will have a network address of `aaaa:aaaa:aaaa:1::/64`, and the host address will be the EUI-64 address resolved from the interface's MAC address. The `:1:` represents the subnet I've allocated from the /48 range `aaaa:aaaa:aaaa`. We can see this with the `show ipv6 interface` *interface-name* command:

```
R1#sho ipv6 int f0/0
FastEthernet0/0 is up, line protocol is up
  IPv6 is enabled, link-local address is FE80::212:43FF:FEB9:2C70
  Global unicast address(es):
    AAAA:AAAA:AAAA:1:212:43FF:FEB9:2C70, subnet is AAAA:AAAA:AAAA:1::/64 [EUI]
  Joined group address(es):
    FF02::1
    FF02::2
    FF02::1:FF00:0
    FF02::1:FFB9:2C70
  MTU is 1500 bytes
  ICMP error messages limited to one every 100 milliseconds
  ICMP redirects are enabled
  ND DAD is enabled, number of DAD attempts: 1
  ND reachable time is 30000 milliseconds
  ND advertised reachable time is 0 milliseconds
  ND advertised retransmit interval is 0 milliseconds
  ND router advertisements are sent every 200 seconds
  ND router advertisements live for 1800 seconds
  Hosts use stateless autoconfig for addresses.
```

The interface now has a link-local address of FE80::212:43FF:FEB9:2C70, so defined because of the FE80::2 prefix, and a global unicast address of AAAA:AAAA:AAAA:1:212:43FF:FEB9:2C70. The last 14 hex digits are the same on both addresses, because they both reflect the MAC address of the interface (with the added FF:FE in the middle).

Let's think about this for a minute. Imagine if all devices on the network had been configured this way. If we wanted to renumber, all we would need to change would be the network address. We no longer need to allocate IP addresses, no one needs to maintain a continuously out-of-date spreadsheet, and no one will have any idea what the address of any host is. Wait, that last one doesn't sound like a benefit. I believe that it is, though.

All the control freaks out there (like me) who like to make your router the first or last IP address on your network are out of luck now. Whatever shall we do? We will do what we should have been doing all along—using DNS to name our addresses. If the adoption of IPv6 does nothing but force everyone to properly use DNS, I will consider it a success.

OK, so you're too much of a control freak and you simply must manually configure your devices. Of course, you can. Here I'll assign the host address of 1 to the interface:

```
R1(config-if)#ipv6 address aaaa:aaaa:aaaa:1::1/64
```

Let's take a look:

```
R1#sho ipv6 interface f0/0
FastEthernet0/0 is up, line protocol is up
  IPv6 is enabled, link-local address is FE80::212:43FF:FEB9:2C70
  Global unicast address(es):
    AAAA:AAAA:AAAA:1::1, subnet is AAAA:AAAA:AAAA:1::/64 [ANY]
    AAAA:AAAA:AAAA:1:212:43FF:FEB9:2C70, subnet is AAAA:AAAA:AAAA:1::/64 [EUI]
  [--output truncated--]
```

Wait a minute—why is the EUI address still there? Because this isn't IPv4. You can have multiple addresses on an interface, and you do not need the **secondary** keyword to do so. Be careful of this. If you want to remove the other address, you'll need to do it manually:

```
R1(config)#int f0/0
R1(config-if)#no ipv6 address AAAA:AAAA:AAAA:1::/64 eui-64
```

Now we've got our single IPv6 address that we've obsessively configured as ::1:

```
R1#sho ipv6 interface f0/0
FastEthernet0/0 is up, line protocol is up
  IPv6 is enabled, link-local address is FE80::212:43FF:FEB9:2C70
  Global unicast address(es):
    AAAA:AAAA:AAAA:1::1, subnet is AAAA:AAAA:AAAA:1::/64 [ANY]
  [--output truncated--]
```

Remember how I've got R1 linked to R6? I configured R6's f0/0 interface with the **ipv6 address autoconfig** interface command. When I look at it, I see that something fascinating has happened. First, let's look at the interface configuration to show that I'm not nuts (like that's enough proof):

```
interface FastEthernet0/0
 ip address 10.0.0.6 255.255.255.0
 duplex auto
 speed auto
 ipv6 address autoconfig
```

And here's the output of the show ipv6 interface *interface-name* command:

```
R6#sho ipv6 int f0/0
FastEthernet0/0 is up, line protocol is up
  IPv6 is enabled, link-local address is FE80::214:6AFF:FEA2:D438
  Global unicast address(es):
    AAAA:AAAA:AAAA:1:214:6AFF:FEA2:D438, subnet is AAAA:AAAA:AAAA:1::/64 [PRE]
      valid lifetime 2591981 preferred lifetime 604781
  Joined group address(es):
    FF02::1
    FF02::2
    FF02::1:FFA2:D438
  MTU is 1500 bytes
  ICMP error messages limited to one every 100 milliseconds
  ICMP redirects are enabled
  ND DAD is enabled, number of DAD attempts: 1
  ND reachable time is 30000 milliseconds
  Default router is FE80::212:43FF:FEB9:2C70 on FastEthernet0/0
```

Not only does this router have a link-local address, but it also has a global unicast address and a default router configured. Where did it get all this information? It learned it from R1.

Routers send out something called *router advertisements* in IPv6. These advertisements are sent in response to router solicitation messages. Though it's not strictly analogous, you can think of this a bit like DHCP. R6 learned that the prefix on this network is AAAA:AAAA:AAAA:1::/64, and since it's configured for autoconfig, it applied its EUI-64 host address to the prefix and configured an IPv6 address by itself.

Let's assign an IPv6 address that's easier to read for our lab testing. I'll apply the host address of ::6 to the f0/0 interface on R6. Remember, this is in prefix AAAA:AAAA:AAAA:: with a subnet of :1:

```
R6(config)#int f0/0
R6(config-if)#ipv6 address aaaa:aaaa:aaaa:1::6/64
```

A quick ping is in order to make sure we're configured properly. I'll ping the ::1 address on R1:

```
R6#ping ipv6 aaaa:aaaa:aaaa:1::1

Type escape sequence to abort.
Sending 5, 100-byte ICMP Echos to AAAA:AAAA:AAAA:1::1, timeout is 2 seconds:
!!!!!
Success rate is 100 percent (5/5), round-trip min/avg/max = 0/157/788 ms
```

Success! Notice how we didn't have to specify an interface this time? That's because we've assigned a non-link-local network to the interface. Now let's make our little network a tad more interesting. I'll add a third router, R4, hanging off of F0/1 on R1. It will look like Figure 37-2.

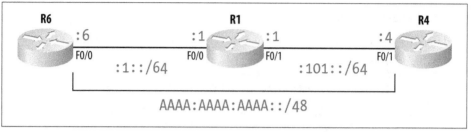

Figure 37-2. A three-router IPV6 network

First, the f0/1 interface on R1. This is the same prefix, but with a subnet of :101:

```
interface FastEthernet0/1
 ipv6 address AAAA:AAAA:AAAA:101::1/64
```

And now, on R4, I'll add the host address of ::4 on the same prefix and subnet:

```
R4(config)#int f0/1
R4(config-if)#ipv6 address aaaa:aaaa:aaaa:101::4/64
```

Another quick ping, and we're in business:

```
R4#ping ipv6 aaaa:aaaa:aaaa:101::1

Type escape sequence to abort.
Sending 5, 100-byte ICMP Echos to AAAA:AAAA:AAAA:101::1, timeout is 2 seconds:
!!!!!
Success rate is 100 percent (5/5), round-trip min/avg/max = 0/146/728 ms
```

But we can't ping the other subnet's router interface on R1:

```
R4#ping ipv6 aaaa:aaaa:aaaa:1::1

Type escape sequence to abort.
Sending 5, 100-byte ICMP Echos to AAAA:AAAA:AAAA:1::1, timeout is 2 seconds:
.....
Success rate is 0 percent (0/5)
```

Why not? Shouldn't R1 forward packets for connected interfaces? Not by default in IPv6. With IPv6 on a Cisco device, you must enable IPv6 unicast-forwarding:

```
R1(config)#ipv6 unicast-routing
```

Once I've done this, I can ping through the R1 router to its other interface:

```
R4#ping ipv6 aaaa:aaaa:aaaa:1::1

Type escape sequence to abort.
Sending 5, 100-byte ICMP Echos to AAAA:AAAA:AAAA:1::1, timeout is 2 seconds:
```

```
!!!!!
Success rate is 100 percent (5/5), round-trip min/avg/max = 0/0/4 ms
```

But check this out—I can also ping the f0/0 interface on R6:

```
R4#ping ipv6 aaaa:aaaa:aaaa:1::6

Type escape sequence to abort.
Sending 5, 100-byte ICMP Echos to AAAA:AAAA:AAAA:1::6, timeout is 2 seconds:
!!!!!
Success rate is 100 percent (5/5), round-trip min/avg/max = 0/0/4 ms
```

There is no routing configured on R1. R1 will route locally connected interfaces by default, but we haven't configured any default gateways or static routes on either R6 or R4. What gives?

Remember those router advertisements I talked about earlier? They advertised R1 as a router, and IPv6 used that information. If we look at show ipv6 interface f0/1 on R4 before and after I added the ipv6 unicast-routing command on R1, we see an interesting difference:

Before:

```
R4#sho ipv6 int f0/1
FastEthernet0/1 is up, line protocol is up
  IPv6 is enabled, link-local address is FE80::212:80FF:FE31:E259
  Global unicast address(es):
    AAAA:AAAA:AAAA:101::4, subnet is AAAA:AAAA:AAAA:101::/64
  Joined group address(es):
    FF02::1
    FF02::2
    FF02::1:FF00:4
    FF02::1:FF31:E259
  MTU is 1500 bytes
  ICMP error messages limited to one every 100 milliseconds
  ICMP redirects are enabled
  ND DAD is enabled, number of DAD attempts: 1
  ND reachable time is 30000 milliseconds
```

After:

```
R4#sho ipv6 int f0/1
FastEthernet0/1 is up, line protocol is up
  IPv6 is enabled, link-local address is FE80::212:80FF:FE31:E259
  Global unicast address(es):
    AAAA:AAAA:AAAA:101::4, subnet is AAAA:AAAA:AAAA:101::/64
  Joined group address(es):
    FF02::1
    FF02::2
    FF02::1:FF00:4
    FF02::1:FF31:E259
  MTU is 1500 bytes
  ICMP error messages limited to one every 100 milliseconds
  ICMP redirects are enabled
  ND DAD is enabled, number of DAD attempts: 1
```

```
 ND reachable time is 30000 milliseconds
 Default router is FE80::212:43FF:FEB9:2C71 on FastEthernet0/1
```

The interface now shows a default router with the EUI-64 IPv6 address of R1's F0/1 interface. Want to bet there's a similar default router shown on the f0/0 interface of R6? Let's take a look:

```
R6#sho ipv6 int f0/0
FastEthernet0/0 is up, line protocol is up
  IPv6 is enabled, link-local address is FE80::214:6AFF:FEA2:D438
  Global unicast address(es):
    AAAA:AAAA:AAAA:1::6, subnet is AAAA:AAAA:AAAA:1::/64
    AAAA:AAAA:AAAA:1:214:6AFF:FEA2:D438, subnet is AAAA:AAAA:AAAA:1::/64 [PRE]
      valid lifetime 2591990 preferred lifetime 604790
  Joined group address(es):
    FF02::1
    FF02::2
    FF02::1:FF00:6
    FF02::1:FFA2:D438
  MTU is 1500 bytes
  ICMP error messages limited to one every 100 milliseconds
  ICMP redirects are enabled
  ND DAD is enabled, number of DAD attempts: 1
  ND reachable time is 30000 milliseconds
  Default router is FE80::212:43FF:FEB9:2C70 on FastEthernet0/0
```

Pretty cool, huh? Maybe, and maybe not. In my experience, letting routers build their own networks is a dangerous proposition. When every network can talk to every other network, developers start using paths that shouldn't exist. Then when you later lock them down, applications break and you're the bad guy. Even worse, tests like the CCIE lab exam will take advantage of this autoconfiguration and if you're not sure what's happening, you'll fail the lab. So the natural question for me is, how do we disable this behavior?

You can suppress the router advertisements on an interface basis with the `ipv6 nd-suppress-ra` interface command:

```
R1(config-if)#int f0/0
R1(config-if)#ipv6 nd suppress-ra
R1(config-if)#int f0/1
R1(config-if)#ipv6 nd suppress-ra
```

Once I do this, the other routers will not receive these advertisements or learn the default router, and the dynamic network will break.

Now for a final step, let's add traditional routes and a default gateway on R6 and R4:

First, I'll add a static route on R6 to allow access to the :101: subnet:

```
R6(config)#ipv6 route aaaa:aaaa:aaaa:101::/64 aaaa:aaaa:aaaa:1::1
```

On R4, I'll add a default gateway instead. With IPv6, default routes are a little different than they are in IPv4, mostly due to the way addresses are written. While you might be tempted to write 0:0:0:0::0/0 to match any route, that will make you look like an IPv6 newbie (though it works):

```
R4(config)#ipv6 route 0:0:0:0::/0 aaaa:aaaa:aaaa:101::1
```

The supercool-IPv6-guy way to reference the 0/0 route in IPv6 is with ::/0:

```
R4(config)#ipv6 route ::/0 aaaa:aaaa:aaaa:101::1
```

We can look at our routes with the show ipv6 route command. Here are the outputs from all three routers:

R6:

```
R6#sho ipv6 route
IPv6 Routing Table - 6 entries
Codes: C - Connected, L - Local, S - Static, R - RIP, B - BGP
       U - Per-user Static route
       I1 - ISIS L1, I2 - ISIS L2, IA - ISIS interarea, IS - ISIS summary
       O - OSPF intra, OI - OSPF inter, OE1 - OSPF ext 1, OE2 - OSPF ext 2
       ON1 - OSPF NSSA ext 1, ON2 - OSPF NSSA ext 2
C   AAAA:AAAA:AAAA:1::/64 [0/0]
     via ::, FastEthernet0/0
L   AAAA:AAAA:AAAA:1::6/128 [0/0]
     via ::, FastEthernet0/0
L   AAAA:AAAA:AAAA:1:214:6AFF:FEA2:D438/128 [0/0]
     via ::, FastEthernet0/0
S   AAAA:AAAA:AAAA:101::/64 [1/0]
     via AAAA:AAAA:AAAA:1::1
L   FE80::/10 [0/0]
     via ::, Null0
L   FF00::/8 [0/0]
     via ::, Null0
```

R1:

```
R1#sho ipv6 route
IPv6 Routing Table - 8 entries
Codes: C - Connected, L - Local, S - Static, R - RIP, B - BGP
       U - Per-user Static route
       I1 - ISIS L1, I2 - ISIS L2, IA - ISIS interarea, IS - ISIS summary
       O - OSPF intra, OI - OSPF inter, OE1 - OSPF ext 1, OE2 - OSPF ext 2
       ON1 - OSPF NSSA ext 1, ON2 - OSPF NSSA ext 2
C   AAAA:AAAA:AAAA:1::/64 [0/0]
     via ::, FastEthernet0/0
L   AAAA:AAAA:AAAA:1::1/128 [0/0]
     via ::, FastEthernet0/0
L   AAAA:AAAA:AAAA:1::2/128 [0/0]
     via ::, FastEthernet0/0
L   AAAA:AAAA:AAAA:1:212:43FF:FEB9:2C70/128 [0/0]
     via ::, FastEthernet0/0
C   AAAA:AAAA:AAAA:101::/64 [0/0]
     via ::, FastEthernet0/1
L   AAAA:AAAA:AAAA:101::1/128 [0/0]
     via ::, FastEthernet0/1
L   FE80::/10 [0/0]
     via ::, Null0
```

```
L    FF00::/8 [0/0]
       via ::, Null0
```

R4:

```
R4#sho ipv6 route
IPv6 Routing Table - 5 entries
Codes: C - Connected, L - Local, S - Static, R - RIP, B - BGP
       U - Per-user Static route
       I1 - ISIS L1, I2 - ISIS L2, IA - ISIS interarea, IS - ISIS summary
       O - OSPF intra, OI - OSPF inter, OE1 - OSPF ext 1, OE2 - OSPF ext 2
       ON1 - OSPF NSSA ext 1, ON2 - OSPF NSSA ext 2
S    ::/0 [1/0]
       via AAAA:AAAA:AAAA:101::1
C    AAAA:AAAA:AAAA:101::/64 [0/0]
       via ::, FastEthernet0/1
L    AAAA:AAAA:AAAA:101::4/128 [0/0]
       via ::, FastEthernet0/1
L    FE80::/10 [0/0]
       via ::, Null0
L    FF00::/8 [0/0]
       via ::, Null0
```

R6 has its static route, R1 has the routes directly connected, and R4 has a default pointing to R1. It all works like a charm:

```
R4#ping ipv6 aaaa:aaaa:aaaa:1::6

Type escape sequence to abort.
Sending 5, 100-byte ICMP Echos to AAAA:AAAA:AAAA:1::6, timeout is 2 seconds:
!!!!!
Success rate is 100 percent (5/5), round-trip min/avg/max = 0/1/4 ms
```

There is a lot more to IPv6 than the stuff I've included here, but hopefully this chapter will help to dispel some of the trepidation many people have about what's coming in the future. IPv6 is not that difficult, really. Sure, the addresses are huge, but once you spend some time with it, you'll learn how to see the addresses as network and host addresses.

## CHAPTER 38

Network Time Protocol

The Network Time Protocol (NTP) is an Internet protocol used for synchronizing a device's clock with a reference source across a network. When accurate time is required on your networking equipment or computers, you should use NTP—in other words, you should always use it.

NTP was originally defined in RFC 958. The last documented version is version 3, which is defined in RFC 1305. To learn more about NTP, check out its home page: *http://www.ntp.org*.

The interesting stuff relating to how NTP really works is found in RFC 1129, which is available only in PostScript or PDF format. If you get excited when you see the type of math shown in Figure 38-1, RFC 1129 is for you.

$$e_{i+1} = \frac{d_i}{K_g} \frac{q^{n_i} - 1}{q - 1} + \frac{1}{K_f} \sum_{j=1}^{i} \frac{n_j d_j}{a_{j-1} u_{j-1}} .$$

Figure 38-1. Actual math from RFC 1129

If, like most people I know, you can't be bothered with the math and just want to know what you need to do to make NTP work for you, read on.

What Is Accurate Time?

How do we measure time? How long is a second? Who defined how long a second is, and why does it matter? These are questions most people don't think about. Most of us take time for granted.

Every electronic device you own, from your personal computer to your television, relies on time being accurate to a certain degree. The power in your home oscillates at

60 cycles per second (60 Hz). 1080p high-definition televisions update their screens at 60 (or 120, 240, or even 480) frames per second. Modems, T1s, DS3s, and all other data services send information at a set number of bits per second. When two pieces of equipment communicate, they must agree on the length of a second.

For a long time, a second was defined as 1/86,400 of a *sidereal day* (24 hours * 60 minutes * 60 seconds = 86,400 seconds). A sidereal day is the time it takes for Earth to spin once (360 degrees) on its axis. Astronomers will tell you that a sidereal day is the amount of time it takes for a star in the sky to transit the meridian twice. A *solar day* is shorter than a sidereal day by four minutes, which is why we have leap years: the calendar has to reset itself due to the accumulation of these four-minute errors each day. Thus, 1 sidereal second = 1.00278 solar seconds. A solar second is defined with the same formula (1/86,400 of a solar day) but uses the sun as the reference point in the sky instead of a distant star. Because Earth rotates around the sun, the position of the sun in the sky changes every day.

As you can see, agreeing on the length of a second is not as straightforward as you might think. Currently, the definition of one second is accepted to be the duration of 9,192,631,770 periods of the radiation corresponding to the transition between the two hyperfine levels of the ground state of the cesium 133 atom. That clears things up, doesn't it? This definition refers to the reference used by atomic clocks. Atomic clocks are the most accurate clocks available to the public. They are considered to be the reference by which all other clocks should be set.

If we consider atomic clocks to be the gold standard by which other clocks should be measured, we can also categorize other clocks by how accurate they are compared to the atomic clock standard.

In NTP, each clock exists inside a *stratum*. An actual atomic clock is a stratum-zero time source. A device that serves NTP requests and is directly connected to the atomic clock is considered to be at stratum one. If you set up an NTP server that learns time from a stratum-one NTP server, your server will become a stratum-two server, and so on down the line. Strata in NTP reference how many levels of clocks the device is removed from the actual time source. A clock operating in stratum 16 is considered to be unsynchronized.

Strata are defined differently in NTP than they are in telecommunications systems. In telecom, stratum levels reference the holdover performance of an oscillator if synchronization is lost. If an oscillator is accurate to $1.0 * 10^{11}$, it is considered to be stratum one. Stratum-two oscillators are accurate to $1.6 * 10^{8}$. In other words, the level of accuracy is not tied to the distance from the source clock, as it is with NTP.

NTP Design

NTP is often not designed, but rather implemented, in the simplest possible way. Many people mistakenly believe all they need to do is configure a single NTP source, and their time problems will be solved. This idea is perpetuated because it usually works. But what would happen to your network if the original time source stopped responding or became inaccurate?

I learned about NTP the hard way when I configured a single time source for the core switches on a large network. I thought I was being clever by having all the other devices on the network get accurate time from my core switches. This meant that only the core switches needed to take up Internet bandwidth with NTP requests, instead of potentially hundreds of other devices.

One day, the time source stopped responding to our requests, but we never knew about the problem. The core switches (6509s) were still acting as NTP servers, so everyone appeared to have accurate time. In this case, the devices were all close in time to one another, but not to the real time (Coordinated Universal Time, or UTC). Still, the difference between UTC and the time being reported was minor—perhaps a minute different over the course of a few months.

 Lesson #1: Always have more than one time source. Not only will NTP failover to another source in the event of a failure, but it will choose the most accurate one available. Configure a minimum of three NTP servers for core devices.

At some point, we needed to reboot the core switches for some maintenance. The next day was a disaster. Somehow, every device in the network—including all servers and workstations—had decided that it was a day earlier than it actually was.

 Lesson #2: Some Cisco devices have a clock and a calendar. The clock keeps time for the current running session. When the device reboots without an NTP source, it will learn its time from the calendar. Always configure devices that contain calendars to update the calendars automatically from NTP.

When the core switches rebooted, they loaded time from their internal calendars and used that time to set their clocks. Because I hadn't configured the calendars, they defaulted to the wrong date and time. When NTP initialized, it would have fixed the time had it been able to establish connectivity with an accurate clock. However, it couldn't. Because every device in the company derived its time from the core switches, they all lost a day. This became a problem when programs that duplicated data to backup servers determined that the last save was invalid, as the last save's date was in the future.

The company ended up losing an entire day's worth of transactions because of my inability to correctly deploy NTP. That was not a good day.

The problem boiled down to my belief that I only needed to configure a single NTP server. I assumed that all time would be accurate from that point on because I had configured the network devices to learn accurate time from a third party.

When designing NTP for a network, I still like to limit the number of devices that will make inquiries from the Internet. Usually, I make the two core switches the NTP servers for the entire network. I configure these two switches (assuming a high-availability pair) to receive time from a minimum of three Internet time servers. The switches also act as *NTP peers*. An NTP peer is considered to be an equal in a stratum. This allows each switch to learn time from the other as an additional source.

I then configure all other networking devices to receive their time from the core switches. Assuming the Internet time servers are all operating at stratum one, the core switches should operate at stratum two. The rest of the switches in the network operate at stratum three. This hierarchy is shown in Figure 38-2.

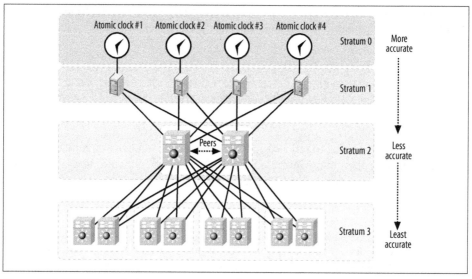

Figure 38-2. NTP hierarchy in a corporate network

 Older versions of Windows such as Windows 2000 server do not support NTP. Instead, they support Simple NTP (SNTP). Because of this limitation, you cannot use Cisco devices as NTP servers for these older Windows machines without adding a true NTP client to them. This is rarely a problem anymore, but watch out for old versions of any operating system that doesn't play well with NTP.

To find publicly available Internet time servers, search the Web for "public NTP servers." Some servers require registration, while others are freely available to the public.

Configuring NTP

NTP is a client/server application. Devices participating in NTP are either NTP servers, which provide time to other devices, or NTP clients, which request time from NTP servers. Servers are also clients and can be peered with each other as well. Configuring an IOS or NX-OS device as an NTP client is the simpler of the two models, so we'll start there.

NTP Client

To configure an IOS or NX-OS device to request accurate time from an NTP server, use the `ntp server` command. You can list as many NTP servers as you need, each on a separate line. Here, I've listed seven publicly available NTP servers. Using so many will help illustrate how NTP behaves.

 On Nexus switches with multiple VDCs, only the default VDC may have NTP configured.

```
ntp server 132.163.4.102
ntp server 193.67.79.202
ntp server 152.1.58.124
ntp server 128.118.46.3
ntp server 129.6.15.29
ntp server 64.236.96.53
ntp server 208.184.49.9
```

Once you've configured the NTP servers, you should begin receiving accurate time signals (assuming you can reach them).

To see the status of the NTP servers in IOS, use the command `show ntp associa tions`. In this chapter, I'll use the IP-PBX system I built in Chapter 30. This is a 2811 router running IOS version 15.0(1)M4:

```
R1-PBX#sho ntp associations

  address          ref clock       st   when   poll reach delay   offset    disp
 ~127.127.1.1      .LOCL.           7      7     16    37  0.000    0.000  437.71
 ~128.118.46.3     .INIT.          16      -     64     0  0.000    0.000  15937.
 ~208.184.49.9     .INIT.          16      -     64     0  0.000    0.000  15937.
+~129.6.15.29      .ACTS.           1     63     64    36 23.087   -4.829  939.32
*~64.236.96.53     .ACTS.           1      8     64    37 18.705   -4.804  438.60
+~193.67.79.202    .PPS.            1      2     64    37 109.59   -5.209  439.79
 ~132.163.4.102    .ACTS.           1     56     64    17 118.13   15.596  938.89
 ~192.168.1.250    64.236.96.53     2     32     64    37  2.802   -2.104  439.79
```

```
~152.1.58.124    .INIT.        16      -     64    0 0.000   0.000 15937.
* sys.peer, # selected, + candidate, - outlyer, x falseticker, ~ configured
```

A lot of information is presented, but you only need to know what some of it means. The address is, obviously, the server you configured. To the left of the address are one or more symbols indicating the status of the server. The key for these symbols appears in the last line of the output; Table 38-1 provides more detailed explanations. The line beginning with an asterisk indicates the NTP server with which the router has synced its time. Notice how some of the entries have a stratum of 16 with a delay and offset of 0.000? These are dead NTP servers. You'll likely find many dead NTP servers if you look for them online. In fact, I took this list from the first edition of this book. Back in 2007, all of these IP addresses were live NTP servers.

 Make sure you check your configurations every year or so to make sure your configured NTP servers are still active.

Table 38-1. NTP association characters

Character	Description
*	Synchronized to this peer
#	Almost synchronized to this peer
+	Peer selected for possible synchronization
−	Peer is a candidate for selection
~	Peer is statically configured

The next column indicates the reference clock used for the listed server. This can be useful, but is usually only informative. For example, the first entry shows a reference clock of ACTS (Automated Computer Time Service). ACTS is a dial-up service from the National Institute of Standards and Technology (NIST). The second server shows a reference of GPS, indicating that it is receiving time from Global Positioning System satellites, which contain atomic clocks.

The third column shows the stratum of the server listed. Servers that show stratum 16 are unavailable and are not providing time.

To see whether your clock is synchronized, use the show ntp status command in IOS. This command will show you the status of NTP, including the stratum within which it is operating:

```
R1-PBX#sho ntp stat
Clock is synchronized, stratum 2, reference is 64.236.96.53
nominal freq is 250.0000 Hz, actual freq is 249.9924 Hz, precision is 2**24
reference time is D117CE2C.7FAFBB96 (14:57:32.498 EST Tue Mar 1 2011)
clock offset is -4.8047 msec, root delay is 18.70 msec
root dispersion is 444.19 msec, peer dispersion is 438.60 msec
```

```
loopfilter state is 'CTRL' (Normal Controlled Loop), drift is 0.000030117 s/s
system poll interval is 64, last update was 3 sec ago.
```

If your clock is not synchronized, the show ntp status command will explain the reasons why. In this example, I've removed all the NTP servers so that there is no reference clock. Notice that the stratum is now 16:

```
R1-PBX#sho ntp status
Clock is unsynchronized, stratum 16, no reference clock
nominal freq is 250.0000 Hz, actual freq is 249.9924 Hz, precision is 2**24
reference time is D117CB70.76B05259 (14:45:52.463 EST Tue Mar 1 2011)
clock offset is 0.0000 msec, root delay is 0.00 msec
root dispersion is 0.42 msec, peer dispersion is 0.00 msec
loopfilter state is 'CTRL' (Normal Controlled Loop), drift is 0.000030140 s/s
system poll interval is 64, last update was 376 sec ago.
```

Another way to show that NTP is driving the system clock is with the show clock detail command:

```
R1-PBX#sho clock detail
15:02:07.371 EST Tue Mar 1 2011
Time source is NTP
Summer time starts 02:00:00 EST Sun Mar 13 2011
Summer time ends 02:00:00 EDT Sun Nov 6 2011
```

Sadly, my sophomoric side can no longer giggle at the abbreviated command show ntp ass, since the show ntp association command doesn't exist in NX-OS. In NX-OS, to show the status of NTP servers, use the show ntp peers command. Here, I have configured the same servers on a Nexus 7000:

```
NX-7K-1(config)# sho ntp peers
--------------------------------------------------
 Peer IP Address              Serv/Peer
--------------------------------------------------
 132.163.4.102               Server (configured)
 193.67.79.202               Server (configured)
 152.1.58.124                Server (configured)
 128.118.46.3                Server (configured)
 129.6.15.29                 Server (configured)
 64.236.96.53                Server (configured)
 208.184.49.9                Server (configured)
```

The show ntp peer-status command will show more information regarding NTP peers. My output shows no connections, because Nexus 7000s were in a lab environment and I had no Internet access:

```
NX-7K-1(config)# sho ntp peer-status
Total peers : 4
* - selected for sync, + - peer mode(active),
- - peer mode(passive), = - polled in client mode
    remote            local            st  poll  reach delay   vrf
-------------------------------------------------------------------------
+132.163.4.102        0.0.0.0          16  16     0    0.00000 default
=193.67.79.202        0.0.0.0          16  64     0    0.00000 default
=152.1.58.124         0.0.0.0          16  64     0    0.00000 default
```

=128.118.46.3	0.0.0.0	16	64	0	0.00000 default
=129.6.15.29	0.0.0.0	16	64	0	0.00000 default
=64.236.96.53	0.0.0.0	16	64	0	0.00000 default
=208.184.49.9	0.0.0.0	16	64	0	0.00000 default

NTP Server

To configure an IOS device to be an NTP server, enter the command ntp master:

```
6509(config)#ntp master
```

 When you're configuring an IOS device as an NTP server, it can take five minutes or more for the clock to become synchronized. You cannot force this process.

On a device that has a calendar, you also need to enter the ntp update-calender command:

```
6509(config)#ntp update-calendar
```

To configure another device within the same stratum as an NTP peer, use the ntp peer *ip-address* command:

```
6509(config)#ntp peer 10.10.10.1
```

This will allow another device in the same stratum to share time with this device.

## CHAPTER 39

Failures

Outright failures can often be detected easily; when a router fails completely, there are usually some pretty obvious symptoms. When a WAN Interface Card (WIC) starts mangling packets, the problem can be a little harder to diagnose. In this chapter, I'll cover some examples of what can cause failures and discuss how to troubleshoot them effectively.

Human Error

Human error can be one of the hardest problems to track, and, once discovered, may be almost impossible to prove. Getting people to own up to mistakes they've made can be a troublesome task—especially if the person responsible is you!

Once, I was working on a global network, administering changes to the access lists that allowed or denied SNMP traffic to the routers themselves. We'd just added a new network management server and we needed to add its address to all the routers so they could be monitored and managed from the central office.

Instead of properly writing the configurations ahead of time, testing them in a lab, and then deploying the proven changes during a change-control window, I decided that because I was so smart, I would apply the changes on the fly. The changes were minuscule—just one line—so what could go wrong?

Naturally, I bungled something in one of the routers and ended up removing an active ACL on the inbound interface. The router was the sole means of entry into the entire continent of Australia for this company. Because nothing simple ever happens to me, the disaster struck on a Friday night (Australia time) on a holiday weekend. No one could be reached onsite until the following Tuesday. For three days, the global financial institution was unable to access any of its servers in Australia due to (my) human error. I like to chalk up events like this to "experience."

A neat way to prevent this sort of disaster is with the `reload` command. With this command, you can make a router reboot in a set amount of time. Because the configuration that caused the router to become unavailable will not have been saved, having the router reboot automatically will bring the router back to life.

To reboot the router in 15 minutes, issue the `reload in` command, as shown here:

```
TS-1#reload in 15
Reload scheduled in 15 minutes
Proceed with reload? [confirm]
```

Alternatively, you can specify a time at which to reload the router with the `reload at` command:

```
TS-1#reload at 12:05 July 10
Reload scheduled for 12:05:00 UTC Mon Jul 10 2006 (in 566 hours and 33 minutes)
Proceed with reload? [confirm]
```

Be warned that if you've already started to make your changes, the router will prompt you to save them before you reload.

Remember to cancel the reboot when you've successfully made your change! To cancel an impending scheduled reload, execute the `reload cancel` command:

```
TS-1#reload cancel
TS-1#

***
*** --- SHUTDOWN ABORTED ---
***
```

Multiple Component Failure

Many networks are designed to avoid single points of failure. What usually brings these networks down is multiple component failure. Multiple component failure can be triggered by a root cause such as dirty or unreliable power, or it can just be a fluke. One device can also sometimes cause failures in other devices.

Many enterprise networks employ Cisco PIX or ASA firewalls in redundant pairs. This is a reliable and proven way to ensure that your firewall isn't a single point of failure. If the standby firewall fails and nobody knows about it, the remaining firewall is a single point of failure. The problem is that many people install these failover pairs and then don't monitor them in any way. I once had a client whose secondary firewall had been offline for months. When the primary failed, the entire network went offline and the executives started screaming. Since no one had been checking the firewalls, everyone assumed that all was well. Nothing sells network management tools like a previously unknown failure causing a system-wide outage. Some of the biggest outages I've witnessed have been a result of an offline secondary system failing to back up a primary when it failed.

Sometimes, multiple devices fail for reasons known only to them. In one installation, I saw a dual-supervisor 6509 have a compound failure in which the primary supervisor failed, but the primary MSFC stayed active. Because the MSFC is tied physically to the supervisor to get connectivity to the networks in the switch, the entire location went down, even though the secondary supervisor was up and had failed over properly. The MSFC that was still active on the failed supervisor had no networks to route. Problems like this don't normally happen when you're using newer versions of IOS, but then, I would have told you at the time that what we were seeing was not possible, either.

Disaster Chains

Modern commercial aircraft are some of the most amazingly redundant systems on Earth. When one device fails, another device takes over. When two systems fail, a third can take over with a reduced capacity, and so on. Commercial airplanes even have multiple pilots! Still, these testaments to fail-safe engineering can and do crash. When they do, the crash is usually discovered to have been caused by a series of events. These events, all relatively innocuous in and of themselves, spell disaster when strung together. Such a chain of events is called an *accident chain*.

Massively redundant networks can suffer from accident chains, too. Considering the impact such compound networking failures can have on a business (not to mention one's paycheck), I like to use the term *disaster chains* to describe them.

Imagine a network with two Cisco 6509 switches in the core. An outage is planned to upgrade one, then the other. Because they're in a redundant pair, one can be brought down without bringing down the network. The first switch is brought down without incident. But, as I'm working, I manage to get my foot tangled in the power cord of the other 6509, and pull it out of the power supply. Of course, the 6509 AC power supplies allow the power cables to be secured with clamps, but the last engineer to work on the switches forgot to retighten the clamps. Each 6509 has two power supplies, which are connected to different circuits, so pulling one power cord should not be an issue. However, the engineer who forgot to retighten the clamps decided that the cables would look neater if he wire-tied them together. When I tripped over the cable, it was really both cables bound together, which means I ended up unplugging all the power from the 6509 that was supporting the network. The result: complete network failure.

To recap, the following combination of events caused the outage:

- I was born completely without grace or coordination.
- The last engineer to work on the system tied the power cords together and left them out where I could trip on them.
- The last engineer did not tighten the AC power cord clamps to the power supplies.
- I shut down one 6509.
- I tripped over the cords to the remaining 6509.

Any one of these events in isolation would not have caused an outage. In fact, any two would probably not have caused an outage. If the power cords had been left unclamped, but the cables were not tied together, my big clown-size feet would probably have only pulled one cable, leaving the switch with one active power supply.

Disaster chains can take some digging to uncover. In the case of me tripping over the power cord, the exec who was grilling me asked, "How could this happen?" Having an answer to a question like this can save your job, especially when the answer appears to be as simple as you being a klutz.

No Failover Testing

I once worked with a team designing a large ecommerce website infrastructure. When I say large, I mean eight Cisco 6509 switches serving more than 200 physical servers (most with multiple virtual machines), providing upward of a gigabit per second of content. Timelines were tight, and everyone was stressed. In all the compression of timelines that occurred during the life of the project, one of the key phases eliminated was failure testing.

After the site went live, a device failed. The site was designed to withstand any single point of failure, yet the site stopped functioning properly. It turned out the failover device had been misconfigured in a way that only presented a problem when the active device failed. Because the failure caused a loss of connectivity to the site, we had no way of getting to the failed equipment, except to drive to the collocation facility. This failure, which should not have been possible, resulted in a two-hour outage while someone drove to the facility with a console cable.

Had failover testing been done, the problem would have been found during testing, and the outage would have been avoided. The design was correct, but its implementation was not. Always insist on failure testing in high-availability environments. Failure testing should be done on a regular basis and included in normal maintenance at scheduled intervals. Believing that your network is redundant is not the same as proving it.

Troubleshooting

Entire books have been written on troubleshooting techniques. I've seen people who are natural troubleshooters and people who aren't. Some people can seem to smell the source of a complex problem, while others can't figure out what's wrong even when *they* are the cause of the problem.

The most interesting problems are usually the ones that cause the most damage. These are the problems that can make or break your career. I've been in the middle of website failures where downtime means zero income for the company for the duration of the outage. I've worked through failures in banking networks, where each minute of outage costs millions of dollars in lost trades. The best resolutions were the ones that happened quickly and weren't necessitated by my mistakes. The ones that were my fault were identified as such as quickly as possible. People make mistakes. When people try to hide their mistakes so they won't be identified as the causes of outages, the outages often last longer than they would have if the people troubleshooting had been properly informed.

Regardless of the problem or the situation, there are some things to remember when you're troubleshooting an outage. Here's my short list.

Remain Calm

I once worked with a former Marine sergeant. He had been in combat and had lived though months of rehabilitation after a gunshot wound to his shoulder. He was now working for me as a senior network engineer supporting a global network that included more than 10,000 nodes.

One day, we were in the middle of an outage that had the vice presidents standing over his shoulder while he worked to isolate and resolve the issue. He was getting more stressed by the minute, and I could see that it was hampering his ability to troubleshoot effectively. As his boss, the first thing I did was to usher away the executives with the promise that I would give them updates every 10 minutes. The second thing I did was to write on his whiteboard, "Relax—no one is shooting at you." He smiled at me and became visibly more relaxed. We had the problem isolated and resolved in time for the next executive update.

Network outages usually do not put lives at risk. In extreme cases, they may put your job at risk, but you'll still be able to go home and hug your kids, your spouse, your dog, or your Xbox, if that's what makes you happy.

The more stressed you allow yourself to become, the longer the outage will last.

Log Your Actions

When you're troubleshooting an outage, every time you do something, write it down and record the time. Eventually, you'll need to document what happened in a post-mortem report. Keeping a log of your actions will prove invaluable later. It will also serve as a way for you to keep track of what you've already done so you don't waste time repeating steps that were ineffectual.

Find Out What Changed

Outages do not happen without cause. Even if there has not been an obvious device failure, if everything has been working and now it's not, something has changed. In some environments, people will confess, and in others, they won't. Either way, the first question you should ask is, "What changed?" If something changed just before the outage, there is a good chance the change is related to the outage. Figure out if you can reverse the change, but make sure you know before you act what the impact of your reversal will be.

Outages can be caused by seemingly unrelated changes. When I used to work with mainframes, I witnessed some pretty strange outage scenarios. One customer complained that his mainframe was crashing every night between midnight and 1:00 a.m. There were no obvious causes for the crashes, but they happened every weeknight, and had only started about a month earlier. While the customer was very helpful and understanding, backups were not completing because of the crashes, and this was causing problems. Finally, we sent someone out to the site to literally sit with the system for a week to see what was going on.

The person we sent to babysit the system noticed a police officer parked in the company's parking lot every weeknight at around midnight. When the officer left the parking lot, he called the dispatcher on his radio. As soon as the officer pushed the button on his radio microphone, the system crashed.

We determined that the system administrator had disconnected a group of terminals from the mainframe about a month prior to our visit. He had removed the terminals, but had left the serial cables connected to the mainframe. These cables were acting as antennas. When the police officer keyed up his radio, the serial cables received the signal, and the resulting electrical impulses entering the mainframe caused it to crash.

If you can't figure out the cause of a problem or outage, look for any changes, no matter how inconsequential they may seem.

Check the Physical Layer First!

My boss taught me this rule when I worked at an ISP. He used to teach troubleshooting to telecom field engineers for one of the RBOCs. The idea here is that most failures are caused by physical faults. Cabling or hardware should be suspected first and, between the two, look at the cabling first. Once you plant this idea in your mind, you'll be amazed how often it's borne out. To this day, I can hear him barking, "Physical layer first!" at me during outages.

Assume Nothing; Prove Everything

When you assume something, it will return to bite you. As soon as you hear someone (including yourself) say, "It can't be that because...," set out to prove that statement true or false. During outages, there seems to be a tendency for engineers to convince themselves that something must be true because they think it is. Don't assume anything is true unless you've proven it.

Isolate the Problem

Problems are often represented by multiple symptoms. Problems are also sometimes caused by other problems. For example, you may think you have a complex routing problem because packets are flowing in a way you think is wrong. However, the problem might be caused by an interface failure. You could spend hours trying to figure out a routing problem in a complex network, while the root cause is a simple interface outage. Try to isolate problems to root causes. Though compound failures can and do happen, single failures are far more common. Rule things out systematically and logically, and you should eventually discover the root cause.

Don't Look for Zebras

I once had a doctor who told me, "If you hear thundering hooves, don't assume they're zebras." This statement is similar to Occam's Razor, which is usually paraphrased as, "With all things being equal, the simplest answer is usually the correct answer." Just because I was getting a lot of headaches didn't mean I had a brain tumor.

The same principle can be applied to any problem you're trying to solve. If you're seeing packets that have bits transposed, it's probably not due to aliens altering your data in an effort to destroy the world. I'd check the cabling first. NORAD won't take my calls anymore, anyway.

Do a Physical Audit

If you've been going round and round in circles and nothing is making sense, do a physical audit. Chances are that assumptions are being made, and an audit will disprove those assumptions. Sometimes, the documentation is outdated or simply wrong. When in doubt, redraw the networking diagrams from scratch. Using a whiteboard or a legal pad is fine for this exercise. You're not looking for beautiful documents, but rather, factual data. In the mainframe example I described earlier, a physical audit would have solved the problem, because we had standing orders to remove unterminated serial cables.

I once got involved in a network problem after another team had worked on it for more than a week. The network was deceptively simple: the nodes involved included two T1s, four routers, and two servers. A team of people could not find the problem, no matter what they tried. When I got involved, I looked over their notes and instructed them to do a complete audit of the network, down to every device, interface, and IP address. I also instructed the team to test connectivity from every node to every other node in the network. Within an hour, I was informed that they had discovered the problem. A T1 WIC had gone bad and was deforming packets. The problem did not become obvious until they'd run through the process of auditing the network in detail. By testing connectivity between all points in the simple network, they soon discovered the root cause.

Escalate

If you can't figure out what's wrong, escalate to someone else. Usually, your boss will want you to escalate to Cisco if the network is the problem (and Cisco is your vendor). If you have an internal department you can call first, by all means, do that. If you feel the problem is beyond you, don't waste any time—call for reinforcements. Sometimes getting the right people on the phone can take time. I've been in environments where we had standing orders to open a TAC case the moment the problem was discovered, regardless of whether or not we thought we could fix it. If we could fix it, we just cancelled the call. If we could not, we were already well on our way to getting the right person on the phone.

Troubleshooting in a Team Environment

When there is a team of people troubleshooting the same problem, someone needs to be the leader. I could write an entire book on this subject alone. If you find yourself troubleshooting as part of a team, work only on the piece of the puzzle you've been assigned. If you try to fix someone else's piece, you're wasting your time as well as his.

If someone else is trying to solve a problem, standing over his shoulder and yelling out ideas will not help. If you're sure of the answer, but no one is listening, find a way to prove your solution, and push to be heard.

The Janitor Principle

The Janitor Principle states that explaining your problem to someone who doesn't understand it will cause you to make connections you've previously missed. This is an amazingly powerful tool. To explain a complex problem to someone who doesn't understand it, you need to reduce the problem to its simplest elements. This action forces you to think about your problem from a different viewpoint. Looking at a problem differently is often all it takes to find a solution.

## CHAPTER 40

GAD's Maxims

Over the years I've been in the industry, it has become apparent to me that there are certain driving forces in the IT universe. These forces are evident in just about all aspects of life, but their application is never more evident than it is in IT.

In every situation where an engineer does not get to do what she wants to do—or worse, in her eyes, to do what she believes is right—these forces come into play. I believe that if more people understood them, there would be less conflict between engineers and their superiors.

My initials are GAD, and people often call me by that acronym. It is with the utmost humility that I present to you GAD's Maxims.

Maxim #1

The driving forces of network design are summarized here:

- Politics
- Money
- The right way to do it

 GAD's Maxim #1: Network designs are based on politics, money, and the right way to do it—in that order.

Figure 40-1 shows it all in a nutshell. The idea is simple, really. Engineers want to "do it the right way," which is usually considered best practice. To do whatever it is "the right way," money will be required. To get money, someone will have to be adept at politics. To put it another way, if you want to do it the right way, you need money, and the only way to get money is through politics. I can hear your voices in my head as you read this, groaning, "I hate politics." The truth is, you don't hate politics—you hate *dirty* politics. There is a distinct difference between the two.

Let's take a closer look at the three elements and how they're interrelated.

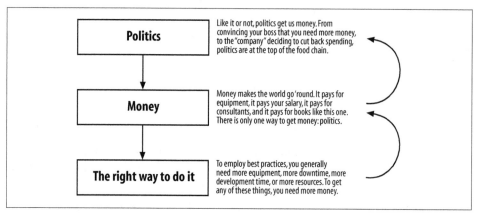

Figure 40-1. GAD's three rules of network design

Politics

Politics isn't just about the president stumping for votes or the vice president hiring his brother rather than the best person for the job. Politics is, among other things, *intrigue or maneuvering within a political unit or group to gain control or power*. A group, like it or not, is two or more people. Every conversation you have with another person is political in some form. Every time you say hello to someone, your attitude and your demeanor help shape that person's opinion of you. This is politics. If you have the best idea the world has ever seen and you go in to tell it to your boss so she can get the funding for you, how supportive do you think she'll be if only yesterday you called her a pencil-necked knucklehead? Would she be acting politically if she turned you down? Maybe you were being political when you assaulted her with badly formed insults.

My point is that anytime there are two people in a room, politics comes into play. If you have a reputation for being difficult, that reputation will be considered (whether consciously or not) whenever you ask for something. Conversely, if you have a reputation for being levelheaded and easy to work with, that can work in your favor.

Now that you understand that politics are not always bad, let's look at the realities of how politics may affect you. I've already stated that without politics, there will not be money, but what does that really mean? Here's an example.

A midsize company is considering a new network, and the vice president of technology, who was a developer for his whole working life until getting into management, is in charge of the project. As the lead engineer, you propose a completely fault-tolerant design consisting of $2 million worth of equipment, which will require six months of work to implement. The plan is perfect. You know every detail of the hardware and how it will all work. It will be a masterpiece.

The VP takes a look at your proposal and says simply, "It's too expensive, and it will take too long. The budget is only $1 million for equipment and consulting."

You feel as though the wind has been knocked out of you. Your first response is probably something along the lines of, "But this is what we need," or "But we can't do it for less than this!"

This is politics. The VP may have the power to get the additional funding. In fact, that's usually what VPs are best at. If you can explain to the vice president all of the benefits of the design and why you feel the $2 million in hardware alone will be well spent, he may listen. Better yet, if you can explain how the company will get a return on its investment in only six months because of your design, you've got a fighting chance!

If instead you sulk and whine about how the company is mismanaged and only cares about money, and how the VP doesn't understand the technology, he will likely think you don't understand reality and are incapable of working within real constraints. You may both be wrong, but either way, you won't get your funding. This happens every day all around the world.

Here's a news flash: if you're going to present ideas to VPs and expect to gain their respect and backing, you need to learn to play on their field. Like it or not, they have the money, the power, and the influence. If you don't know what ROI is or how to talk about depreciation of equipment, don't expect VPs to give you more money.

Money

Money is what we all want. As I've already said, you need to understand politics to get the money you want or need. There is no way around it. If you're getting money and you're not involved in the politics, someone must be rooting for you behind the scenes.

If there is not enough money, chances are you will not be able to do what you want (i.e., do it "the right way").

The Right Way to Do It

This is the goal engineers pursue. "It" is whatever they happen to be working on at the time. Engineers know what "the right way" is, and they are often frustrated because they're "not allowed" to do "it" the right way.

If you're not willing to play the game, my advice here is, "Get over it." You simply cannot do anything "the right way" without money, and you will not get the money you need without politics.

If your company is short on cash, you're out of luck. If your company is in the middle of political turmoil that is preventing you from getting money or approval, you are out of luck. If you want to change things, learn politics. It's that simple.

 Some of the best advice I ever received on the subject of politics came from the book *How to Win Friends and Influence People*, by Dale Carnegie (Simon & Schuster). I recommend this book for anyone who's ever been frustrated by human interaction in any form.

Maxim #2

Many years ago, I was a manager at a large company. The network was in trouble: there were constant failures due to a poor existing design, as well as political issues galore. I had a group of very smart engineers working for me, and they all had ideas about how to make things better. The engineers all believed their changes should be implemented, solely because they thought their ideas were sound (some were, others weren't). My problem was how to get the engineers to understand that they could not simply make any changes they wished.

In an effort to get the engineers to understand that not all changes are good changes, and to encourage them to think about the implications of the changes they were proposing, I came up with three rules for them to follow. The rules were simple—each only a word. For me to consider a change, it had to follow one of the three rules. The rules were:

- Simplify
- Standardize
- Stabilize

 GAD's Maxim #2: The only valid reasons to change a properly sized production network are simplification, standardization, and stabilization.

If the proposed change did not accomplish one of the three stated goals, I would not even consider the change request. At first, the engineers were constantly frustrated. They wanted to effect change, but they were not being allowed to do what they thought was needed. Over the course of about a month, however, they started to catch on. Within six months, we had so greatly improved the network that it was no longer the source of any problems. With a stable network came stable services and very proud engineers.

Long-term thinking is the only way to accomplish stability in an unstable environment. Enforcing these three simple rules transformed the network from a point of ridicule for upper management to a source of pride.

Here's a closer look at the three rules.

Simplify

This one is pretty straightforward. To comply with this rule, a proposed change must simplify the network or its operation in some way. Examples might include removing equipment or replacing a complex IP scheme with one that's easier to understand or maintain. Perhaps the change will cause all of the routers to have the same revision of code. Anything that makes the operation or troubleshooting of the network less complex saves time and money. Simple is good. If you can easily explain how a change will enhance the simplicity of the network, chances are the change is a valid one.

Standardize

Standardization can also make networks more cost-effective and easier to maintain. If you have 200 routers and they're all the same model, you will know what to expect from each router when you connect to it. While that may not be realistic, having a standard device for every function and standard ways to deploy services *is* realistic. You can make all of your edge routers, the core switches in every building, and so on, the same type. If you deploy NTP, it should be deployed the same way everywhere.

Standardization allows for spares to be more readily available, and it allows for devices to be swapped in from less critical places in an emergency.

Stabilize

How to enhance stability is not always obvious. Perhaps the revision of IOS code that has been standardized on all the VoIP gateways has been reported to have an issue that might affect your environment. That code should no longer be considered stable and should be updated. Likewise, if there is a piece of hardware that has caused problems in the past, it should be replaced. These sorts of changes are valid and will increase the network's stability.

Maxim #3

There are a finite number of reasons why a company will fund changes to an existing network. The reasons are surprisingly simple and fairly obvious:

- Lower costs
- Increase performance or capacity

- Increase reliability

Unless you can prove that your idea will meet one of these goals, chances are you will be denied the funds you need.

 GAD's Maxim #3: Companies only spend money on IT projects that lower costs, increase performance or capacity, or increase reliability.

Let's explore the three goals.

Lower Costs

I once worked for a large telecom company that had DS3s crisscrossing the globe. The network was perfection in terms of design. Every node had multiple network entry points, latency was acceptable, resiliency was excellent, and downtime was extremely rare. The network was as close to perfect as we could make it, and my team and I were very proud of the work we had done.

One day, word got to me that the network needed to be changed. More specifically, I was told we needed to cut $1 million from the budget. The choices were telecom or personnel. Welcome to the world of business—I was told to either destroy my perfect network or choose who should be let go.

My team and I went to work, and we managed to redesign a network with a $12 million annual cost into one that was almost as good, but cost only $10 million annually. We were never as proud of this network, because it involved a lot of compromises that we didn't believe in, but the company saw this as a victory.

The point of this story is that the changes we made did not benefit the company in terms of resiliency or performance. Instead, the changes were approved because they saved the company money. In the company's eyes *good enough* was better than *perfect* because it saved $2 million a year.

If you have an idea for a network change, one of the best ways to get it approved is to show how it can save money—especially recurring expenses, such as telecom costs, maintenance contract costs, and consulting fees.

While my example was one of a forced change rather than a desired change, the point is that cost is a high priority for a business. If you have an idea that will save the company money, chances are management will listen. From most managers' point of view, all engineers want to do is spend money. Producing an idea that will actually save money will make you stand out from the crowd.

Remember that there are different types of costs that a business must deal with. Examples of these costs are:

Equipment costs

Hardware, cabling, and the like are examples of equipment costs. If you can replace three routers in a planned design with two, you've reduced equipment costs.

Recurring costs

Maintenance contract costs and telecom costs such as T1 bills, telephone bills, and the like are all recurring costs. Cutting recurring costs can have a dramatic impact on a company's bottom line.

Human resource costs

Your salary is a cost for the company. If there are 10 people in your department making $100,000 each, and you design a change that costs $200,000 but lowers your staffing needs by 2 people, after less than a year, the company will have made a return on its investment.

Engineers are not often aware of what it costs to keep them. For example, did you know that the taxes taken out of your salary are only a portion of those required by the government? If you have a salary of $100,000/year, the company might pay as much as $25,000 a year in taxes above and beyond what you pay. Suddenly, you're costing the company $125,000 a year. And let's not forget other things we all take for granted, such as 401k contributions and healthcare. Those two alone could total another $25,000 a year. Now you're costing the company $150,000 a year. Do you get a bonus? Add that to the total. And let's not forget that it costs money for you to have a cube or office (rent). The company also has to pay to cool and heat the air you breathe (facilities), and for you to have a computer, a telephone, and probably a cellular phone. When all is said and done, you may easily cost the company twice what you consider to be your annual salary.

Consulting costs

Consulting costs are often reported differently from HR costs (this is why sometimes salaried employees are let go and consultants are brought in to do the same work for the same or more pay). If you can redesign a network that currently is supported by three consultants so it only needs one, you've lowered consulting costs.

Increase Performance or Capacity

Increasing performance is rarely a bad thing. The exception might be improving performance where no increase is necessary. Remote branches with 10 users probably don't need ASA 5580 firewalls capable of a gigabit of throughput.

On the other hand, devices that are near their limits will soon become problems if normal growth continues. Telecom links that are running in excess of 70 percent utilization should be upgraded. Routers, switches, and firewalls that are regularly running at more than 50 percent CPU utilization should be considered for replacement with larger devices.

VoIP is an excellent example of how performance bottlenecks can be serious. If your gateways can only support 50 concurrent calls, and you suddenly become busy due to growth and start dropping customer service calls, you can bet that the money will be found to upgrade those gateways so they can support more calls.

The smarter engineers will watch the network and spot trends. If you can quantify a trend that will translate into a required upgrade in the next budgetary cycle, you will be very well received, because the change can be planned for and budgeted for ahead of time. Remember, managers don't like surprises. Try to spot these opportunities before there's a problem. Telling your boss the network should be improved after an outage has occurred will not make you a hero.

Increase Reliability

Chassis-based switches are more reliable than 1 RU access switches. Why? Because they usually have dual power supplies and can often support dual processors. Reliability is an important consideration in any network design. Reliable components such as chassis-based switches are usually more expensive than their less reliable counterparts, though, so smaller companies usually do not employ them.

As smaller companies grow into midsize and larger companies, however, they often discover that unplanned outages cost them more money than they would have spent on more reliable equipment. At this point, they start to spend money in an effort to increase reliability.

Another example of increasing reliability is replacing a single ASA firewall with an active/standby pair.

Reliability can be an easy sell if your company has experienced an outage due to a single point of failure or if your management has experience with such a failure. Sure, there are those managers who understand that single points of failure are bad, but those who have lived through an outage caused by lack of foresight are generally more receptive to spending money to avoid having such an experience again.

While citing any one of the previous reasons will make your change more desirable, combining the first (lower cost) with one of the others will make your idea as close to a sure thing as possible. If you can come up with an idea that combines all three, you will be lifted upon the shoulders of management and paraded through the halls like a conquering hero.

If, on the other hand, you know what needs to be done to increase performance or reliability, but you don't let anyone else know, when the failures happen, they will likely be viewed as your fault. Most engineers know what needs to be done to ensure a healthy network. Using these tips, you should be able to convince your boss that the changes are worth implementing.

## CHAPTER 41

Avoiding Frustration

I've been working in the computer and networking industries for more than 25 years, and in that time I've witnessed people getting frustrated about the same things again and again. I've learned a lot in that time, and the lessons haven't always come easily. My aim in this chapter is to try to help you avoid some of the frustrations you're likely to encounter in the course of your work, and thereby make your job more enjoyable.

Why Everything Is Messed Up

I can't tell you how often I've heard this question: "Why is everything so messed up?" Of course, the language is often more colorful than that, but decorum prohibits me from including examples here. Suffice it to say that the phrase "messed up" is often replaced with something more satisfying when used in moments of frustration and anger.

The situation is a common one. A company has grown to the point where it needs a reliable network. Management decides, for whatever reason, that the in-house staff is not able to get the network where it needs to be, so they call in consultants. That's when I usually arrive and am greeted by the aforementioned question. Sometimes it comes from employees at the company, and sometimes it's posed by the junior consultants working with me.

The answer to the question is usually based in a set of simple truths.

 Truth #1: Companies that start small and experience intense growth often end up with complicated networks that cannot scale to the new demands placed upon them.

Small companies that grow to be large companies often do so at a fast pace. Companies that are quick to solve problems are often the ones that do well in today's economy. When these companies are small, they hire computer professionals with server experience. Networking professionals are not usually required at smaller companies, and the server people do a great job of keeping the place running.

As the small companies grow, the networks grow with them. The skilled server engineers, who are experts at server scalability and design, may not be experts at network scalability and design. This often leads to networks being pieced together to solve immediate problems, rather than being planned carefully and built with an end-state design in mind. This in no way should be held against the server engineers. They have risen to the occasion and performed miracles above and beyond the call of duty. The problem usually lies in the fact that they are server engineers, not network engineers. Remember that small companies don't tend to require network engineers at first. Many find it hard to accept that they need them as they grow larger.

Truth #2: Networks are often pieced together instead of designed.

Networks are often viewed as nothing more than a means to get the workstations talking to the servers and the Internet. Especially in smaller environments, the network takes a backseat to server and workstation issues. This is related to Truth #1, but is more a case of management not understanding the value of the network. I've seen managers say things like, "Just put a server in that remote location with a VPN." To them, the meaning of VPN is "magic stuff that replaces a real network."

Network infrastructure is often viewed in the same category as buildings, chairs, and such. That is to say, the network is not perceived to be a competitive advantage, but rather a necessity that consumes capital. Because it's not a profit center, why waste money on it? That is the perception a lot of management has regarding networking equipment and staffing. This attitude is usually prevalent in smaller, nontechnical companies, though it is certainly found elsewhere as well. As the network is often an afterthought, training is usually not a high priority, either. And people who have devoted their careers to servers are likely to choose further server training over network training.

Truth #3: Network design is not high on upper management's list of priorities.

The upper management of many small and midsize companies often doesn't understand the impact a poorly built network can have. While news of the latest viruses and server security holes is plastered on the front pages of CNN and the *New York Times*, the networks usually chug along without any fanfare. When the networks fail, these managers usually wake up, at which point it's too late and major changes must be made. Again, this is when the consultants show up.

I have spent weeks designing elegant IP schemes for large companies. The scheme for one client was so impressive it could be described only as magnificent. It was a masterpiece. The scalability was measured in decades, and the flexibility was unheard of. It was so impressive that only the two of us who designed it understand it to this day. As far as I know, it is still in place. The principle of the design, like gravity (if I may be so bold), did not need to be understood to be implemented.

The moral here is that we spent weeks on the scheme, which cost the client quite a bit in billable hours. The benefits were not obvious and the time spent was questioned. The benefits were not obvious because they were intangible. Measuring the amount of time that will be saved by never needing to renumber servers is impossible. How much future time and effort will be saved because servers of similar types can be referenced by a single access list entry? What about locations? Countries? We designed the scheme so that every component of the network could be aggregated into a larger chunk. We designed it so that entire locations could be moved and only the second octet would change. But all of the time saved was *potential*. You cannot bank potential time saved. This makes IP scheme design a hard sell to management. But for the employees who work with the network on a daily basis, a great IP scheme can make life substantially easier.

 Truth #4: Engineers are not always adept at communicating needs to management.

Management's view of the network is typically based on a combination of personal experience and input from the engineers. If the engineers are not skilled at communicating with their managers, the managers' perceptions are affected accordingly. This really complements all the other issues I've listed. If an engineer knows what needs to be fixed but can't get his manager to understand the need, the manager won't secure the funding for the resolution.

I once went to a customer's site to investigate client/server problems. The customer was an advertising agency that used very large images, and there were complaints that it was taking too long for the 80 MB graphics files to move from the server to the workstations (this was in the late 1990s, when 80 MB graphics files were unheard of). The problem was a result of having too many devices on a network that was based on hubs. I recommended the replacement of at least the central hub with a switch. But back then, switches were expensive, and only the largest of companies could afford to make such a change.

The management refused to replace anything on the network and insisted that I look further into the servers. They felt that something had to be wrong with the servers, because that was what they understood. They had no idea how networks operated and that there were limits to how much traffic they could handle.

I gave the management a small lesson on networking and explained why they were having problems. I offered them a guarantee that if the introduction of a switch did not resolve their problems, we would take the switch back at no cost. The switch did solve their immediate problems, and I made a regular customer into a loyal customer.

Small companies like that one focus on what they're good at. In this case, the client was good at advertising. They didn't care about computers or networks, but they understood computers because they used them on a daily basis. They had no daily interaction with the networking equipment; it just worked, until it started to become a problem.

 Truth #5: Sometimes, the problem is simply that no one knows or even cares that there are problems.

People in advertising should not need to learn how a switch works. The network is there simply to facilitate the work they need to do.

How to Sell Your Ideas to Management

You've got a great idea that you believe will change something for the better. Maybe it's the network, or maybe it's the way the company hires and interviews people, but you know it's worth doing. The problem is that you can't get anyone in management to listen to you. In your mind, they're all idiots. In their minds, you're wasting their time. Who's right? You both are.

Good managers want to know what you're thinking and will listen to you. If your idea does not have merit, they will give you meaningful feedback and help you refine it. Other managers worry only about rocking the boat and will not entertain any notion that upsets the status quo. If your manager is of the second type, you can either work to convince him that change is good (at least, as it pertains to your idea) or bypass him altogether. In the latter case, my advice is to ask permission, or at least inform your boss, if you plan to go over his head. No one likes to be blindsided. If you sneak around, you'll only make an enemy.

Engineers are full of great ideas. Making things better is what we're built to do. However, when it comes to engineers, there seems to be an inverse relationship between great ideas and great communication skills. This is what gets us into trouble.

While sitting in a meeting, I once got everyone's attention by announcing that the entire network was about to fail. We were paying out millions in penalties for service-level agreements that we were not meeting. The room was tense, and I had just raised the tension with my statement. The focus was on me, and I was ready to make my move. I explained to the long table of executives how their failure to make the right decisions had caused the mess we were in. I pointed out specific individuals and made it clear how they were to blame. I was on a roll, and I let it all out. I was their superhero, and I could save their world. That was my message, delivered from on high as the mighty engineer-god, and woe betide anyone who dared not listen.

My view of the world was absolute. Certain people had been shortsighted, and thus cheap, which had caused failures, which in turn had created angry customers. I could fix it all if they'd just shut up and let me do what they'd hired me to do.

Does any of this sound familiar?

I had trouble understanding why my recommendations weren't taken as gospel and why the executives didn't throw themselves at my feet and lavish me with gifts (I like Ferraris). It wasn't until I'd finished my rant that one of the executives pulled me aside and explained that I had not only made a complete fool of myself, but also destroyed any credibility I might have had with every person in the room.

I've learned a lot since then. Hopefully, I can help others learn from my mistakes. What did I do wrong? *Everything*. First and foremost, I did not speak with respect. Forget about respecting people because of their positions. I don't believe in that. I mean respecting people because they are human beings. If anyone ever talked to me the way I talked to that roomful of executives, I'd get up and walk out. Yet somehow I felt justified in speaking to them like I was their father. I also got emotional. I looked down on the whole group and then started ranting. That will never get you where you want to go in the business world.

So, how do you talk to management? How do you translate your internal engineer's rage into useful business-speak that will get the results you want? Here are some tips:

Document your idea
> If your idea is sound, your boss will want you to give him something that he can show his boss. This should be a short document outlining your idea, along with the benefits of its implementation. It should begin with an executive summary containing a minimum of technical jargon, followed by a few pages of concise technical explanations relating the details. Include timelines and budgets—even estimates are better than nothing. If you don't know how to do these things, enlist the help of someone who does. Alternatively, a nice PowerPoint slide deck will probably work equally well. Why not do both?

Be grammatically correct
> When producing documentation, make sure that everything you write is grammatically correct. Make sure you use a spellchecker on your documents and proofread them *at least* twice. Have someone else proofread them as well, and then proofread them again yourself. You'll be amazed at how many mistakes you'll find on even the third reading.

I've had the pleasure of working with some very smart people. I've worked with CCIEs, PhDs, teachers, doctors, lawyers, scientists, and many other people with far more education than I have. I am constantly amazed by the unreadable documentation produced by people of all ranks. If you want to be taken seriously, make sure your documentation is grammatically sound and looks professional.

Take emotion out of the equation

Any emotion involved in the delivery of your message will be held against you. The only possible exception to this rule is passion. Feeling passionate about your ideas is a good thing. Keep an eye on your passion, though, as it can easily turn into anger or frustration.

If you're like me, you feel passionate about the things you believe in. For an engineer, it's very easy to believe in an idea or concept. We all know that following certain best practices can make our lives easier, but I've seen engineers lose their cool because a VP approved only one DNS server instead of two. A calm engineer should be able to discuss the benefits and drawbacks of redundant DNS servers, and perhaps convince the VP to change his mind. An emotional engineer will simply be ignored. As soon as you inject emotion into your presentation, you will lose credibility.

I like to argue. I don't mean that I like to scream at my wife while she hurls cooking utensils at me. I like to argue in the strict definition of the term. I like to debate a proposition with an opponent whose premise differs from mine. If I'm arguing with you and I can get you to become emotional, I've practically won. Why? Because when emotion swells, reason abates. The more emotional you become, the less reasonable you will be.

If you become emotional while presenting an idea, everyone around you will know you're not being rational. Irrational people are, at best, ignored. Passionate people are revered, though, so where do you draw the line? Being excited about your idea is a good thing. Being belligerent when faced with a counterpoint is not.

Be polite

Above all, be polite. If you are anything less than polite, it's probably because you've allowed yourself to get emotional. Regardless of the reason, a failure to be polite is a failure to be respectful. If you don't treat others with respect, chances are others will not treat you with respect, either. Politeness is a form of respect you should practice with everyone, but if you fail to practice it with your superiors, especially when presenting a new idea, you probably won't get the results you desire.

Be succinct

Managers don't have a lot of free time, and any time they devote to you and your ideas should be used thoughtfully. They'll be looking for a summary of your idea and the benefits it offers. Once they're interested, you will be able to go into detail, but you have to start with the sales pitch. If your idea is valid, you will have plenty of time to expound on the details later.

Understand the shortcomings of your ideas

No ideas are perfect. If you don't know the possible arguments against your idea, someone else will produce them. Chances are they'll assault you with them during your presentation. A professional knows the limitations and shortcomings of his ideas and has answers prepared when questioned about them.

This point is so frequently missed that you can often make a big impact with executives just by addressing their questions before they have a chance to ask them.

Accept "no" as an answer

Don't whine or complain if the answer is "no." This would be unprofessional and would further discourage management from considering your ideas in the future. Sometimes there is not enough funding or the timing is not right. Sometimes the answer will be "no" for reasons that cannot be told. Regardless of the reasons, accepting defeat gracefully will add credence to your next request. It is perfectly permissible to ask why your idea was rejected, but don't press the point.

Escalate

Sometimes when you propose an idea to your manager, you get the brush-off. Maybe your boss doesn't like you or he has a preconceived notion that your idea will fail. Regardless of the reasons, you may still feel that the idea should be heard and want the opportunity to present it. In this case, the proper thing to do is to ask permission from your direct manager to propose the idea to his boss. You may be surprised at the response—he may be happy to be able to palm you off on a superior. If he says "no," you may be suffering under a boss who doesn't want to rock the boat. Going around your boss to talk to his boss is not politically smart, but if you believe strongly in your idea and feel that he is squelching it, this may be the only available path.

No surprises

Do not spring the fact in a meeting that the network will fail in 18 minutes. Tell your boss ahead of time. In fact, tell your boss, and let him tell the group in the meeting. If there is one sure way to make enemies in the business world, it's to blindside people in front of their peers.

What is it that managers, directors, VPs, and officers of the company need to know? More often than not, it's how much you need to spend, how long your idea will take to implement, and your justification for the expense. If you need to spend money that wasn't budgeted, you'd better have a good explanation, because if you don't, you won't get a dime.

Vice presidents don't want to hear that you can't do your job because you don't have a Nexus 7018 switch next to your desk. They want to know how to keep their bosses (often the stockholders) happy, what you're doing to make their lives easier, and that you're not just being difficult.

I once had a boss whose rule for the engineers was, "If it's cool, you can't have it." His reasoning (which was usually dead-on) was that if we thought it was "cool," it didn't have a real business purpose. Sadly, I still use that rule for myself to this day.

Usually, when I ask engineers why they need the new things they've asked for, the answer is either emotional or technical. Upper management won't care if a new $400,000 pair of routers makes you happy, no matter what problems they solve. However, if you can explain how the $400,000 investment will make the network more resilient and thus save the company from paying any more penalties, you'll have a captive audience.

So, what is it that your boss wants to hear? Consider these questions:

- How will your idea save money? Examples include:

  Capital expenditure (Capex)
    It will replace multiple other pieces that need to be replaced anyway.

  Operating expenditure (Opex)
    It will reduce circuit costs or personnel costs.

  Return on investment (ROI)
    Spending the money now will produce a return on investment over the next X months.

- How will your idea increase revenues?
- How will your idea increase profits?
- How will your idea make the department (and thus your boss) look good?

If you can answer several of these questions effectively, your presentation will build momentum quickly.

When to Upgrade and Why

Upgrading your routers and switches is not a fun job, but it's got to be done at some point. Some people like to be on the bleeding edge of technology and run the latest versions of software and operating systems. For networking equipment, that's not such a good idea, for a variety of reasons that I'll cover here.

It may seem obvious to you that if a new feature is announced, you should upgrade immediately to get it. But this is rarely how things work in the real world. The only time that happens is in small networks without change control and with no restrictions or penalties relating to downtime.

Upgrading should not be done lightly. The code that runs your switch or router is just software, and software can have bugs, including security vulnerabilities. While the major vendors do a good job of version control and beta testing, there are plenty of bugs listed on any vendor's site to prove my point.

What about upgrading something like memory? Easy enough, right? It might be as simple as swapping out a DRAM SIMM or even just adding a new one, but you can never rule out complications.

The Dangers of Upgrading

Here are some reasons to be wary about upgrading:

Introduction of new bugs

Upgrading might resolve the bug that's causing you grief, but the new code revision might have another bug you didn't know about. The best way to prevent this is through due diligence. Cisco can help you cross-reference bug lists and determine which code release you should be running on your equipment. If you have a problem after getting Cisco's OK, at least you can present your boss with an email message from Cisco recommending the change. Beats saying, "Wow, I should have checked into that!"

Hardware problems

Upgrading a network device is not necessarily hard work, but it does involve rebooting the device in most cases. Rebooting is (hopefully) something that does not happen often, and there's always room for error and unforeseen disasters.

I once observed a simple upgrade of memory for a major ecommerce website that went horribly wrong. A new SIMM was swapped with an old SIMM in a 6506 chassis switch. The change-control request was approved, and the operation began. Total estimated downtime: 15 minutes. Change-control window (the time allotted for us to do the work): four hours. Actual downtime: *seven hours*. Apparently, a small chunk of dust landed in the memory socket when we pulled out the old SIMM. When the new SIMM was installed, the dust bunny got mashed into the socket, preventing the SIMM from contacting all the pins. Reseating the chip didn't resolve the problem. Backing out the change didn't solve the problem either, because the old chip used the same socket. The moral: any hardware change should be considered a major change and should not be undertaken lightly.

Human error

If people are involved, problems are more likely. Human error, whether it's due to simple typos, fatigue, carelessness, or clumsiness, causes more failures than just about anything else. Once I sweated through three hours of a four-hour change control. The time to back out all changes was coming, and nothing was working. We were installing a new T1 link, which was not a complicated task, but it wasn't going right. The problem turned out to be human error. My instructions clearly stated that the T1 was to be in the port marked 4 in a panel with eight ports. What the documents didn't say was that there were two panels marked the same way, and I was in the wrong panel. I managed to bring down the entire operation's phone system, and for three hours, the company took no calls. This is called "a learning experience." My hope is that you will learn from mine, but most people need to learn these lessons on their own.

Change of default behavior in software

Over the years, Cisco has decided (rightfully) that certain commands should be the default behavior of Cisco routers—for example, `ip subnet-zero` and `ip class less`. If you designed your network without these features turned on and somehow relied on the fact that they were turned off, you'll be in for a surprise if you upgrade and find that some of your networks are now not functioning.

Valid Reasons to Upgrade

The following are legitimate reasons to upgrade:

To resolve a problem

If you have a router that crashes every time you type the `show arp` command, chances are you've got a bug that can be fixed by upgrading that router. Determining whether you truly have a bug should be a job for tech support, but bug listings are available online and can be searched by anyone with Internet access.

Software or hardware is end-of-life

Vendors stop supporting products. If your software or hardware is end-of-life, it won't be supported anymore, and if you have any problems, you will not be able to get them resolved. Unsupported hardware is a risk to the ongoing operation of your network and should be upgraded.

A new feature is needed

Notice I didn't say, "A new feature is wanted." Sometimes a new feature is a necessity. I once worked on a large network with DS3s crossing the globe. We had almost 40 of them. When one bounced a few times within a few minutes, it wreaked havoc with our VoIP environment. This network supported upward of 300 calls per second, so bouncing links was a severe problem. The answer was IP route dampening, which was in a cutting-edge version of the code (this was EIGRP, not BGP, so route dampening was not inherent in the protocol). Normally, I would never advocate using a cutting-edge release, but in this case, the feature was so necessary to the continued successful operation of the network that we decided to go ahead. Luckily, the feature solved our problems without adding any new ones.

A technology change

If you had a T1 and now you have a DS3, you probably need to add a DS3 interface card to support the DS3.

To increase performance

Sometimes, companies simply outgrow their hardware. I've seen websites go from PIX 515s to 520s to 525s to Firewall Services Modules for no other reason than that they were exceeding the aggregate bandwidth the devices could handle.

To increase simplicity

I'm a big fan of integrated CSU/DSU WICs. If you have T1s that are still using CSU/DSUs with V.35 cables, you can eliminate connection points and separate devices by integrating the CSU/DSU into the router. This is a single example, but many similar situations exist.

To increase reliability

If you have one firewall, adding a second firewall so they act as a failover pair increases the reliability of the network. High availability is a good thing and should be implemented whenever your budget allows.

To lower costs

If you can prove that upgrading some hardware or software will lower costs, upgrading is a viable option. An example is collapsing a router and a switch into a single 3750 multilayer switch. When you combine the two devices, you only need to have a maintenance contract on one, which might lower yearly maintenance costs.

Why Change Control Is Your Friend

If you've been working in a small company that's grown into a larger company or if you've moved from a smaller to a larger company, you've probably run into change control. *Change control* is the means whereby a company limits the changes that are made to the network (or anything, for that matter) until they are understood and scheduled. If you want to upgrade a router with change control active, you need to submit a request. The request then needs to be approved, at which point the change might be scheduled. In some companies, a single person approves or denies change requests. In other companies, committees review every request. I've seen companies where the change-control committee meets only on, say, Tuesdays. If your change is denied, you have to wait until the next Tuesday for an alternative change to be considered.

Scheduling changes is one of those things that seems to make engineers a bit nutty. Why should you have to wait for a team of people who don't understand what you're doing to tell you it's OK to do it? Why waste time if you know you can fix a problem with a single command that won't hurt anything? To engineers, change control can seem like a waste of time and energy that does nothing but interfere with their ability to get work done.

Over the years, I've held many positions, ranging from junior engineer to director of a large consulting company to head of my own business. During those years, I've learned a few things about how businesses operate and how engineers think. Running a business while also being an engineer has given me a unique insight into both worlds.

Change control is important for any company for the simple reason that failures cost money. Take a large ecommerce website, for example. If an engineer makes a change that causes the site to become unavailable, the company loses income until it's fixed. What's more, the company's reputation may be affected when users try to make purchases online only to find the site unavailable. Most users probably won't wait more than 10 seconds for a page to load if they can get the same information or products elsewhere. Imagine the impact of having a site offline for hours because of a simple mistake!

Change control aims to prevent these types of outages, through careful planning and acceptance methods. Achieving availability metrics such as the coveted five-nines (99.999 percent uptime) is simply not possible without change control.

Human error is probably the number one cause of outages today. Change control minimizes human error in a number of ways. Embracing change control will also make you a better engineer who is better able to communicate with management. Let's take a look at some of the benefits:

Change control teaches forethought

A good change-control program will insist that you lay out, in detail, every step of the work you would like to do, including every command you will enter into any device you will touch. Doing this is an excellent way to think through what you will be doing. It is also an excellent way to understand how a router/switch/firewall works, because you need to think through how your changes will affect everything else.

Change control improves documentation skills

Change-control programs generally involve documentation of your proposed changes before you complete them. Many engineers dislike documentation and avoid it at all costs. The best way to get over something like this is to do it regularly. A team of people, ranging from engineers to managers and directors, will probably review your change-control documentation. If it's not concise and clearly written, you'll end up having to answer a lot of questions and probably rewrite it anyway.

Change control improves communication skills

Change control usually includes a review process, where your proposed change is evaluated, commented upon, and then approved or refused. You must be able to communicate your technical ideas to people who may not have a technical background. Failure to accomplish this may result in a denial of your change request.

Change control helps you find mistakes before they occur

Change control is designed so that any mistakes in the thought process or configuration process can be discovered before they are made. Usually, it only takes a couple of instances of someone else finding your mistakes before you learn to be more careful.

The biggest advantage of change control is that it can help you look good. If you make some change on the fly, and it causes hours or days of downtime and possibly lost revenue, what do you suppose the upper echelon of your company will think of you? Do you think you'll be the first on their list for promotion or a raise? Probably not.

Now, think how management will view you if you have a reputation for always following change-control procedures, always presenting well-documented change-control requests, and always performing successful change controls.

Change control is about protecting the company's interests. Like it or not, the company's interests are more important to the company than your disinclination to follow change-control processes. The long and short of all this is that you should learn to love change control. If you accept it as a learning experience and understand that all successful large-scale businesses employ some version of change control, you'll be happier in the long run.

How Not to Be a Computer Jerk

The computer industry is known for attracting a certain type of individual: the archetypal "computer guy" who thinks he's smarter than everyone around him and talks to people like they're idiots because they don't know what the fuser does in a laser printer. To be fair, most people in the industry are not like this—and not all of the ones who are this way are guys!

What is it that makes these people the way they are, and why are they attracted to the computer industry? While I don't have any studies to back me up, I have made some observations over the years, both of myself and of others. Yes, I'll admit I was one of these annoying people in a past life, and I'll share with you how I recovered to become a successful professional.

There are a couple of things that contribute to the *computer jerk* phenomenon. Some of them are self-induced, and some are environmental. Some computer jerks are actually nurtured (usually unconsciously) by peers and leaders, though people in these positions often have the power to turn them around. After you examine these traits and influences, my hope is that you'll be able to help someone you know—or perhaps even yourself—to become a more balanced, useful computer person rather than a computer jerk.

In my opinion, the primary influences fall into three principal categories.

Behavioral

Everything we do is based on habit, including our patterns of interaction. If you're used to dealing with people a certain way, you will tend to stick to these patterns. However, that's not to say these habits cannot be broken. We deal with different types of people in different ways. For example, we typically treat women differently from men, and we treat people in positions of power differently from our peers. While many people will argue that they treat everyone the same, the simple truth is that they do not. The very fact that you have friends indicates that you somehow treat them differently from others.

One of the ways computer jerks operate is through constant attempts to let other people know how smart they are. These people are usually very intelligent, but for some reason, they seem to need to prove it to everyone around them. Unfortunately, they go about it the wrong way.

There are two ways to look smarter than other people:

Be smarter than the people around you
> Knowledge is different from intelligence. Knowing a lot of things is not the same as being able to troubleshoot a problem. Memorizing a book on anatomy is not the same as being a surgeon. People who are naturally smarter than the people around them—and who don't need to flaunt it—are widely known to be smart people. The people who are the smartest are often the most humble, for they have nothing to prove.

Make the people around you look stupid
> This is the way the computer jerk likes to operate. He believes that if he makes everyone around him look stupid, those people will see how smart he is. Sadly, what the computer jerk misses is the fact that all of those people will come to dislike the person who made them look stupid. If computer jerks could stop doing this, many things would change in their lives.

Everyone you meet is good at something. I learned this the hard way all those years ago. Remember that there will always be someone smarter than you, and there will always be someone better than you.

The smartest person in a computer department often suffers from what I call *alpha-geek syndrome*. Alpha-geeks need everyone around them to know that they are the smartest and the best. But often, these people are only the "best" within their small circles, and have no real view into their ranks within the wider world of professional IT consulting. When a consultant is brought in or a new person with a wide breadth of skills is hired, the alpha-geek will try very hard to discredit this person in the hopes of retaining his alpha-geek status. When faced with a confident, intelligent adversary, however, the alpha-geek will usually fail to discredit the interloper and end up looking foolish.

Another problem that computer people often have is delivery. Remember that you're not the smartest person on Earth and that everyone should be treated with respect, and you'll go far. People don't need to be told the mistakes they've made (particularly in front of an audience), and they don't need to be told what they've done wrong.

Tell people that *you've* done something wrong, and list the reasons why, and they'll respect you for it.

Tell people that *they've* done something wrong, and list the reasons why, and they'll think you're obnoxious.

Sharing knowledge is good; withholding it is bad. People seem to think that they should never share what they know because they'll lose their jobs. This could not be further from the truth, unless you're working for a despot. Teams work better together, and respect is formed when information is shared. Troubleshooting is more efficient when more than one person knows how something works. Think about who you admire in the computer industry. Chances are you admire those people because they've taught you something.

Finally, if you know something is catastrophically wrong with a project, don't wait until a meeting to blindside everyone with it. This tactic is a hallmark of the computer jerk. Bringing up bad news in a meeting adds shock value to his statement and ensures that everyone will listen to him. What's more, the computer jerk believes that doing this shows everyone how smart he really is. Managers, in particular, don't like surprises, especially during meetings. The proper way to deal with the delivery of bad news is to quietly inform your manager so she can spread the word. Then the *problem* can be dealt with in the meeting, instead of the reactions to the announcement.

Environmental

I believe that computer jerks are the way they are because they are allowed and, in some cases, encouraged to be this way. One of the key influencing factors is lack of self-esteem. People want to be liked, or even better, respected. The problem with computer jerks is that they think the way to gain respect is to show people how smart they are.

I used to work in a company that reinforced the alpha-geek personality in someone who exhibited the archetypal alpha-geek tendencies. The problem was that this guy *was* good—he just wasn't as good as he'd made everyone believe. This led to no end of bad designs and problems that the management teams supported, directly fueling the personality traits that were causing the problems in the first place.

When I sat with this person and explained that his ideas were valuable—but needed some tweaking to be better—he was interested. When I sat with him and explained that his personality was holding him back, he was also interested. Within weeks of me working with him, he changed for the better. With leadership and mentoring, I was able to break the environmental reinforcements.

Leadership and Mentoring

In my experience, people who behave like computer jerks can be changed. Usually, the instrument of change is someone who they respect and who has authority over them. In my case, I was working in a chemical manufacturing plant and thought I was the king of the world. I ran the minicomputer, managed all the PCs, and even managed the network, which at the time was a Santa Clara Systems version 1.1 network with 10Base-2 coax cabling throughout the plant (for those of you who don't know Santa Clara Systems, they merged with a company named Novell in 1986).

On one of the days when I was feeling particularly smug, I managed to offend my boss by speaking to him in a condescending tone when he needed help with something. This was a man I liked quite a bit and admired a great deal, and from whom I had learned a lot. Still, at the age of 22, I thought I was smarter than he was.

My boss called me into his office and calmly asked me what I knew about toluol, methyl methacrylate, and the dispersion process. When I said that I didn't know anything, he proceeded to explain to me that he knew quite a bit about all of these things and then asked me why someone like me, who was probably a third of his age, would think that I had the right to speak to him the way I had. He was right, and I knew it. I was being a jerk.

The point of this story is that he took the time to tell me I was being a jerk, and did it in such a way that I listened. The fact that I respected him already helped a great deal, but the fact that someone pulled me aside and explained to me that I was out of line made all the difference in the world.

I believe that most of the people out there who habitually tread on others in an effort to prove how smart they are simply need a lesson from a leader or mentor to help them understand how they should change.

Index

Symbols

802.xx standards (see standards beginning with IEEE)

A

AAA authentication
  applying method lists, 456
  creating method lists, 453–456
  defined, 449
  enabling, 449
  security server information, 450–452
aaa authentication command, 449
aaa group server command, 452
aaa new-model command, 449
aaa servers command, 454
ABR (area border router), 138
access control entries (ACEs), 415
access control lists (see access lists)
access lists
  applying, 417
  creating, 595
  deleting, 418, 424
  designing, 415–426
  functionality, 197, 415
  GRE and, 178
  grouping, 421–423
  most-used on top, 419–421
  MTU path discovery packets, 426
  in multilayer switches, 427–430
  named versus numbered, 415
  naming, 418
  object groups and, 475
  outbound traceroute and ping, 425
  reflexive, 431–435
  top-down processing, 419
  Turbo ACLs, 423, 424
  wildcard masks, 416
access-group command, 418, 434
access-list compiled command, 424
accounting, defined, 449
ACD (Automatic Call Distributor), 342, 527
ACE (Application Control Engine) modules, 15, 246
ACEs (access control entries), 415
ACLs (see access lists)
active ASA, 492
Active Virtual Forwarder (AVF), 190
Active Virtual Gateway (AVG), 190
ACTS (Automated Computer Time Service), 694
ad hoc wireless networks, 511
Adaptive Security Appliances (see ASAs)
Adaptive Security Device Manager (ASDM), 469
add/drop CSU/DSU, 342
Address Resolution Protocol (see ARP)
adjacency table, 215
admin context, 481
administrative distance
  defined, 107, 122
  routing protocol table, 107, 125
administrator tag, 161
Advanced Encryption Standard-CCM Protocol (AES-CCMP), 515
advertisement requests, 52
AES-CCMP (Advanced Encryption Standard-CCM Protocol), 515
aggregate route (see summary route)
AIS (alarm indication signal), 366

We'd like to hear your suggestions for improving our indexes. Send email to *index@oreilly.com*.

Digital Signal Processors (DSPs), 529
digital signals
    defined, 343
    DS hierarchy, 346
disabled state, 91
disaster chains, 699
distance-vector protocols, 124
distributed Cisco Express Forwarding (dCEF),
        235
diversion headers, 559
divide-by-half method (subnet allocation), 660
DLCI (data link control identifier), 388, 401
DMZ (demilitarized zone), 461, 505
DNIS (Dialed Number Identification Service),
        527
do command, 277, 469
documentation
    bay face layouts, 634
    IP and VLAN spreadsheets, 633
    need for, 627
    network diagrams, 636
    port layout spreadsheets, 629–633
    power and cooling requirements, 634
    requirements documents, 628
    selling ideas to management, 719
dotted decimal notation, 674
DR (designated router), 138
DS3 (Digital Signal 3)
    about, 375
    configuring, 379–384
    framing, 375
    line coding, 379
DSCP (differential service code point), 579
DSPs (Digital Signal Processors), 529
DTE (data terminal equipment), 394, 395
DTMF (Dual-Tone Multifrequency) Relay,
        525
DTP (Dynamic Trunking Protocol), 40
Dual-Tone Multifrequency (DTMF) Relay,
        525
duplex command, 23
duplex modes
    autonegotiation failure and, 21
    configuring parameter, 23
    defined, 19
    duplex mismatch problem, 100
    Ethernet support levels, 20
dynamic secure MAC addresses, 329
Dynamic Trunking Protocol (DTP), 40

E

E-carrier hierarchy, 346
EAP (Extensible Authentication Protocol), 514
ecommerce websites, 643–647
EGP (Exterior Gateway Protocol), 107, 126
egrep command (NX-OS), 278
EHLO command (SMTP), 477
802.xx standards (see standards beginning with
        IEEE)
EIGRP (Enhanced Interior Gateway Routing
        Protocol)
    administrative distance, 107, 126
    communication considerations, 120
    functionality, 133–137
    redistributing into, 152–154
    routing tables and, 106
eigrp log-neighbor-changes command, 136
enable method, 453
encapsulation frame-relay command, 396
encapsulation frame-relay ietf command, 396
encoding
    defined, 357
    T1, 357–359
encryption key command, 517
encryption mode wep mandatory command,
        517
encryption, wireless networks and, 514
end command (NX-OS), 278
Enhanced Interior Gateway Routing Protocol
        (see EIGRP)
EOBC (Ethernet Out-of-Band Channel), 234
ephone command, 546–550
ephone-dn command, 543–546, 560
errdisable recovery cause psecure-violation
        command, 331
Errored Second counter, 363
ESF (Extended Super Frame), 360
EtherChannel
    configuring, 68–75
    cross-stack, 75
    FEX considerations, 290
    flex links and, 324
    functionality, 63
    load balancing, 64–68
    managing, 68–75
    Multichassis EtherChannel, 75
    network design considerations, 642
    protocols supported, 68
    virtual Port-Channel, 75–80, 297

administrative distance, 107, 126
bandwidth-based metrics, 124
communication considerations, 121
functionality, 137–143
redistributing into, 154–156
routing tables and, 106
out-of-band signaling, 357, 359
out-of-frame (OOF), 362
overclocking, 377
oversubscription, 393

P

PA-A3-T3 module, 381
Pacific Bell, 351
packet loss, 531, 575
Packet Voice Digital Signal Processor (PVDM), 528
packet-to-packet delay variation, 531
packets
  address types and, 675
  defined, 10
  malformed, 217
  marking, 578
  MPLS support, 409
  MTU path discovery, 426
  multicast, 120
  policing, 578
  protocols and, 524, 575
  QoS misconceptions, 588
  RIP considerations, 152
  route maps and, 198
  routing, 207, 208
  scheduling, 578
  switching, 207, 208
  TOS field, 578–581
  VLANs and, 25
paging feature, 546
paging-dn command, 547
PAgP (Port Aggregation Control Protocol), 68, 260
PAP (Password Authentication Protocol), 442, 443–444
partial mesh networks, 391
passive-interface command, 132, 133
passthru mode (FEX), 290
Password Authentication Protocol (PAP), 442, 443–444
password command, 437
passwords, 437

(see also authentication)
  best practices, 460
  line, 437–439
  VTP, 57
PAT (Port Address Translation)
  interface examples, 502–504
  NAT Overload and, 501
  port redirection and, 504
  reflexive access lists and, 431
pattern matching, dial peers, 554
payload loopback, 367
Payment Card Industry (PCI), 643
PBX (private branch exchange), 350, 527
PCI (Payment Card Industry), 643
PEAP (Protected Extensible Authentication Protocol), 514
peer keepalive links, 76, 296
Per-VLAN Spanning Tree (PVST), 91
performance monitoring
  about, 362
  bipolar violation, 362
  CRC6, 363
  Errored Second counter, 363
  Extreme Errored Seconds counter, 363
  loss of signal, 362
  out-of-frame, 362
permanent virtual circuit (PVC), 387, 401, 403–407
permit clause (route maps), 199
PFC (policy feature card), 238
phase-locked loop (PLL), 371
phone configuration
  ephone command, 546–550
  ephone-dn command, 543–546
  message waiting lamps, 550
  paging feature, 546
  process overview, 543
phone registration, 567
physical audits, 703
physical layer first rule, 702
ping tool, 425, 680
pinning, defined, 293
PIX firewalls
  ASDM software, 469
  displaying IP addresses as names, 473–474
  fixups feature, 477
  grouping, 421–423
  most-used on top example, 420–421
  transparent mode, 470

About the Author

Gary A. Donahue is a working consultant who has been in the computer industry for 27 years. Gary has worked as a programmer, mainframe administrator, Technical Assistance Center engineer, network administrator, network architect, and consultant. Gary has worked as the Director of Network Infrastructure for a national consulting company and is the president of his own New Jersey consulting company, GAD Technologies.

Colophon

The animal on the cover of *Network Warrior* is a German boarhound. More commonly known as the Great Dane, the German boarhound is an imposing yet elegant and affectionate dog that usually weighs between 100 and 130 pounds and measures between 28 and 32 inches in height. German boarhounds range in color from brindle to light grayish brown to harlequin and have a lifespan of 7 to 10 years.

A bit of controversy surrounds the German boarhound's background, with some claiming the dog originates from Denmark, and others, Germany. However, over time, breeders in Germany have made the dog what it is today.

The name German boarhound comes from the breed's ability in its hunting years to pull boars, wolves, and stags to the ground. The kings of Denmark and England often thought of the hound as holy, and at one time it was said that boarhounds lived in every castle in Germany.

Paintings of the German boarhound can be found on the walls of Egyptian tombs. In *Beowulf*, the boarhound makes an appearance as the hunting dog Dene. During the Middle Ages, the dogs were buried alongside their owners, as they were thought to be spirit guides to the afterlife. But their spirit selves were not always welcomed—the dog was sometimes thought of as a hellhound, called Black Shuck, a wraith-like black dog that was most likely the inspiration for Sir Arthur Conan Doyle's third Sherlock Holmes novel, *The Hound of the Baskervilles*.

The cover image is from *Lydekker's Library of Natural History*. The cover font is Adobe ITC Garamond. The text font is Linotype Birka; the heading font is Adobe Myriad Condensed; and the code font is LucasFont's TheSansMonoCondensed.

Related Titles from O'Reilly

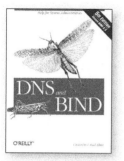
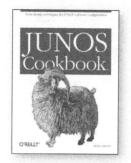

Networking

802.11 Wireless Networks: The Definitive Guide, *2nd Edition*

Asterisk: The Future of Telephony, *2nd Edition*

Cisco IOS Cookbook, *2nd Edition*

Cisco IOS Access Lists

Cisco IOS in a Nutshell, *2nd Edition*

DNS & BIND Cookbook

DNS and BIND, *5th Edition*

Essential SNMP, *2nd Edition*

Exchange Server Cookbook

IP Routing

IPv6 Essentials, *2nd Edition*

IPv6 Network Administration

JUNOS Cookbook

JUNOS Enterprise Routing

LDAP System Administration

Managing NFS and NIS, *2nd Edition*

Network Troubleshooting Tools

Network Warrior

RADIUS

ScreenOS Cookbook

sendmail, *4th Edition*

sendmail Cookbook

SpamAssassin

Switching to VoIP

TCP/IP Network Administration, *3rd Edition*

Time Management for System Administrators

Using Samba, *3rd Edition*

Using SANs and NAS

VoIP Hacks

Windows Server 2003 Network Administration

Wireless Hacks, *2nd Edition*

Zero Configuration Networking: The Definitive Guide

Our books are available at most retail and online bookstores.
To order direct: 1-800-998-9938 • *order@oreilly.com* • *www.oreilly.com*
Online editions of most O'Reilly titles are available by subscription at *safari.oreilly.com*

O'REILLY®

There's much more where this came from.

Experience books, videos, live online training courses, and more from O'Reilly and our 200+ partners—all in one place.

Learn more at oreilly.com/online-learning

CPSIA information can be obtained
at www.ICGtesting.com
Printed in the USA
LVHW101545190620
658570LV00006B/166